Advances in Mathematics Education

Series Editors
Gabriele Kaiser, University of Hamburg, Hamburg, Germany
Bharath Sriraman, University of Montana, Missoula, MT, USA

International Editorial Board
Ubiratan d'Ambrosio (São Paulo, Brazil)
Jinfa Cai (Newark, NJ, USA)
Helen Forgasz (Melbourne, VIC, Australia)
Jeremy Kilpatrick (Athens, GA, USA)
Christine Knipping (Bremen, Germany)
Oh Nam Kwon (Seoul, Republic of Korea)

More information about this series at http://www.springer.com/series/8392

Luc Trouche • Ghislaine Gueudet • Birgit Pepin
Editors

The 'Resource' Approach to Mathematics Education

Editors
Luc Trouche
Institut Français de l'Education
Ecole Normale Supérieure de Lyon
Lyon, France

Ghislaine Gueudet
CREAD, ESPE Bretagne
Université de Bretagne Occidentale
RENNES, France

Birgit Pepin
Eindhoven School of Education- ESoE
Eindhoven University of Technology- TU/e
Eindhoven, The Netherlands

ISSN 1869-4918 ISSN 1869-4926 (electronic)
Advances in Mathematics Education
ISBN 978-3-030-20395-5 ISBN 978-3-030-20393-1 (eBook)
https://doi.org/10.1007/978-3-030-20393-1

© Springer Nature Switzerland AG 2019
Open Access Chapter 7 is licensed under the terms of the Creative Commons Attribution 4.0 International License (http://creativecommons.org/licenses/by/4.0/). For further details see licence information in the chapter.
This work is subject to copyright. All rights are reserved by the Publisher, whether the whole or part of the material is concerned, specifically the rights of translation, reprinting, reuse of illustrations, recitation, broadcasting, reproduction on microfilms or in any other physical way, and transmission or information storage and retrieval, electronic adaptation, computer software, or by similar or dissimilar methodology now known or hereafter developed.
The use of general descriptive names, registered names, trademarks, service marks, etc. in this publication does not imply, even in the absence of a specific statement, that such names are exempt from the relevant protective laws and regulations and therefore free for general use.
The publisher, the authors, and the editors are safe to assume that the advice and information in this book are believed to be true and accurate at the date of publication. Neither the publisher nor the authors or the editors give a warranty, express or implied, with respect to the material contained herein or for any errors or omissions that may have been made. The publisher remains neutral with regard to jurisdictional claims in published maps and institutional affiliations.

This Springer imprint is published by the registered company Springer Nature Switzerland AG.
The registered company address is: Gewerbestrasse 11, 6330 Cham, Switzerland

Foreword

In the past two decades we have witnessed an enormous growth of interest in and development of the relationship between teachers and the resources they use. The Re(s)sources 2018 conference that was organized to give collective and cumulative voice to this work, to identify progress and forge a research agenda that lies up ahead, thus comes as no surprise. What is significant about this volume is that it is not simply a record of the conference. The collection of chapters in this book take a step beyond the conference. The invited talks, invited plenary panel as area for debate (represented in Chaps. 1, 2, 3, 4, 5, 6 and 7), the working groups where the substantive interaction and discussion among participants took place within the conference (represented in Chaps. 8, 9, 10 and 11), and the deep reflection on the documentational approach to didactics (DAD), on its "missing resources" and then a suggested research program going forward (Chap. 12) have been coordinated into a substantial work resulting in a significant contribution to the field at this juncture.

So, what then is this accumulation and its sources? The impetus for the interest in and development of the field of teachers' activity with resources converges into three spheres of influence. First is the spread of reform initiatives in mathematics education and the introduction of new curriculum texts of various kinds. With this came the rapid appreciation that teachers interpret texts. Implementation of reform with curriculum texts is thus a complex phenomenon and a challenge for research. Second is the increase in digital resources. There is now, indeed, an explosion of information available to teachers. Here too there is a need to understand the selection and integration of such resources in teachers' practice. Linked to both, yet separate is the third influence: the field of teacher development wherein teachers interact with and produce related resources – what in key chapters in this book is called their documentation – and research on this interaction. These three themes are identified and described in a similar way in the introduction to this volume, and elaborated through the various chapters. Each of these themes articulates a problem of practice in mathematics education, and all are related to some form of change impacting on or being impacted by teachers' work. A fourth thread lies in a number of chapters

v

that give serious attention to the evolution of various aspects of the field, and so a capturing of change and its processes.

There is a great deal of rich and reflective writing in this book, providing readers with insights into progress in the field and ways of moving the field forward. I note just a few examples. There is deep reflection through the chapters, and then comprehensively in Chapter 1, on the variety of concepts and constructs that have come to frame the domain, with debate on which might be considered "solid," with others needing to be more firmly established through research. The notion of a "pivotal" resource, for example, is argued as "solid," with some suggesting that "resource system" requires further work. There is discussion on resource as process and/or product and arguments for a focus on both if teachers' activity with resources is to be fully described and understood. There is an interesting reflection on the importance of teachers' planning with resources, and how this occurs in different ways in China and Japan where teachers' collective work not only has a long history, but has also taken place inside and outside of the school. A more recent and, in my view, critical focus of attention has been on the resource itself, and a concern with the quality of its mathematical and/or pedagogical affordances. In other words, a resource is not a benign "object" with which teachers interact. It itself shapes teachers' work and its effects. The editors together with all authors have produced a text worth reading!

My own interest in resources has a resonant yet different location in a problem of practice, going back some two decades to my work researching a professional development program with mathematics, science, and English language teachers in South Africa (see Adler & Reed, 2002). This was a program in the early post-apartheid context and so also concerned with change. More specifically, it was a formalized upgrading program, making available both knowledge and material resources for teaching these key subjects to teachers in urban and rural school contexts. I was challenged by teachers' constant refrain "we have no resources." At face value, this was completely understandable. Their conditions of work were structured by varying levels of poverty, and hence limited material and infrastructural resources. At the same time, while teachers lamented their "lack" I was struck by what they did do with the little that was available. Other "resources" became visible in that they were impacting teachers' work. Time, for example, and how it is demarcated, structures formal schooling, yet the affordances and constraints of how time is punctuated and used was seemingly taken for granted. Was time, then, not a "cultural" resource, a function of the particular socio-economic school context, and the context of schooling? How teachers interacted with colleagues in their schools and in the project was an obvious social resource. In South Africa's multilingual context, language is a critical resource, here both in terms of which languages are used and valued, and then how these languages are used. There was also a range of physical and material resources in the classroom (number of desks, state of the chalkboard and available chalk, and curriculum materials like textbooks, new and old, to name a few). Curriculum resources also ranged from the more physical, like a geometric peg board, to the more ideational, like a designed task and worksheet. In addition to the consideration of what might be a resource in teaching, it was also apparent in our observations of teaching that the insertion of new curriculum resources did not equate their productive use. A need emerged for a broader conceptualization of resources in and for teaching, and in two ways. Firstly it was important to expand a conceptualization of resources beyond the physical and material to include social and cultural resources. Secondly, and there is now wide appreciation of this, it became apparent that while an important question in contexts of poverty must be on what and whether resources are available, a critical question is how what is available is used. And hence the emphasis on resource, not only as a noun but also a verb, and thus the refocusing on the teacher-working-with-resources.

Looking back and having had the privilege of reading the chapters in this volume, I have been reflecting on the question of what makes something a resource? Using the notion of variation in some of my current work, the answer to this question must include a reflection, then, on what is not a resource? My earlier view described above was that a resource lay in its use, and use included all that was available in the cultural, social, and physical/material domains. I extended my earlier work to include teachers' knowledge as a resource in and for teaching, studying domains of knowledge teachers drew on in their practice, distinguishing between, for example, principled mathematical knowledge, procedural knowledge, everyday and practical knowledge. So what then is not a resource? As the field has grown so have the distinctions and deliberations around boundaries of what is/is not a "resource," with arguments against knowledge being considered a resource, for example, and thus the earlier conceptualization too wide. And as with other fields, boundaries are broken and re-figured as a shared language is refined and "solidified."

The book itself creates a boundary around the notion of resources in terms of what is and is not reflected on, and a comprehensive overview of chapters is provided in the introductory chapter. Coming from a multilingual context, I was struck by an apparent absence of reflection on language as a resource or concern across many chapters. For those working in multilingual contexts in particular, language is a critical resource, and a substantial focus of attention in research on language and mathematics education – a large research domain in itself. Here "language as a resource" is a discursive move against "language as a problem" and so an orientation to learners in multilingual classrooms being not what they "lack" in relation to the language of instruction, but to the range of linguistic resources they bring and use (e.g., Setati Phakeng, 2012; Planas, 2018; Barwell, 2018). How is teachers' documentation related to the language used and the way it is used, by teachers, learners, and in texts? Does this matter? As intimated, I refer here not only to the language (i.e., French, English, Japanese) in which teacher-resource interaction occurs, but also to the way in which language is used, and hence discursive acts in mathematics teaching and learning activity. Chapter 12 confronts this issue, engaging with some ways in which issues of language use (in both senses) can and should frame research up ahead.

Less conspicuous in its absence, but also worth thinking further about, is how the notion of resources has entered research on identity. Nazir and Cooks (2009) talk of practice-linked identity resources, and distinguish ideational, material, and relational resources. Together with a colleague we have explored teachers' learning and identity formation through a study of the practice-linked identity resources made available in a professional development program, and teachers "take-up" (use) of these in their talk and in their practice (Ntow and Adler, 2019). We suggest that the notion of ideational resources is particularly productive in studying take-up from professional development in that much of what is offered in professional development is ideational, carried either in mediated activity or texts. There is perhaps overlap here with the call for more reflection on the affordances of a resource and concern with the quality of teachers' interaction with resources.

In raising language and identity resources, I point to how widely the notion of resource has come to be used in our field. And hence, again, the question, what then is not a resource? In the introductory chapters, the editors point to the intention of the book, and so the boundary it creates, "not to circumscribe" but to rather push towards operational invariants, and regularities of practice that take the field forward in a rigorous way. There is deep appreciation of the dialectic at play as the book pulls together diverse elements of an emerging field, it simultaneously becomes part of this emergence. It is a substantial contribution!

University of the Witwatersrand   Jill Adler
Johannesburg, South Africa   jill.adler@wits.ac.za

References

Adler, J., & Reed, Y. (2002). *Challenges of teacher development: An investigation of take-up in South Africa*. Pretoria, South Africa: Van Schaik.

Barwell, R. (2018). From language as a resource to sources of meaning in multilingual mathematics classrooms. *Journal of Mathematical Behavior 50*. doi: 10.1016/j.jmathb.2018.02.007

Ntow, F., & Adler, J. (2019 online first). Identity resources and mathematics teaching identity: an exploratory study. *ZDM – Mathematics Education*. https://doi.org/10.1007/s11858-019-01025-z

Planas, N. (2018). Language as resource: A key notion for understanding the complexity of mathematics learning. *Educational Studies in Mathematics 98*(3), 215–229.

Setati Phakeng, M. (2012). Mathematics in multilingual classrooms in South Africa: from understanding the problem to exploring possible solutions. In B. Herbel-Eisenmann, J. Choppin, & D. Wagner (Eds.), *Equity in Discourse for Mathematics Education: Theories, Practices and Policies* (pp. 125–145). Switzerland: Springer.

Contents

1 Introduction 1
Ghislaine Gueudet, Birgit Pepin, and Luc Trouche

Part I Framing the Field of Research

**2 Studying Teachers' Documentation Work:
Emergence of a Theoretical Approach** 17
Ghislaine Gueudet

**3 The Construct of 'Resource System' as an Analytic
Tool in Understanding the Work of Teaching** 43
Kenneth Ruthven

**4 How Did Mathematics Masters Work Four Thousand Years Ago?
Curricula and Progressions in Mesopotamia** 61
Christine Proust

**5 Reflecting on a Theoretical Approach from a Networking
Perspective: The Case of the Documentational
Approach to Didactics** 89
Michèle Artigue

Part II A Comparative Perspective

**6 Mathematics Teachers as Curriculum Designers:
An International Perspective to Develop a Deeper
Understanding of the Concept** 121
Birgit Pepin, Michèle Artigue, Verônica Gitirana,
Takeshi Miyakawa, Kenneth Ruthven, and Binyan Xu

x   Contents

7 Teachers' Collective Work Inside and Outside School as an Essential Source of Mathematics Teachers' Documentation Work: Experiences from Japan and China 145
Takeshi Miyakawa and Binyan Xu

8 Teachers' Use of Mathematics Resources: A Look Across Cultural Boundaries 173
Janine T. Remillard

Part III New Resources Needed, Perspectives for Further Research

9 Teachers' Resource Systems: Their Constitution, Structure and Evolution 197
Jana Trgalová, Moustapha Sokhna, Cibelle Assis, Mohammad Dames Alturkmani, Elisângela Espindola, Rim Hammoud, and Karima Sayah

10 Analyzing Teachers' Work with Resources: Methodological Issues 257
Catherine Loisy, Hussein Sabra, Scott A. Courtney, Katiane Rocha, Dubravka Glasnović Gracin, Gilles Aldon, Mathias Front, Marie-Line Gardes, Eugenia Taranto, Ferdinando Arzarello, and Ornella Robutti

11 Documentation Work, Design Capacity, and Teachers' Expertise in Designing Instruction 323
Sebastian Rezat, Carole Le Hénaff, Jana Visnovska, Ok-Kyeong Kim, Laurence Leroyer, Hussein Sabra, Suzane El Hage, and Chongyang Wang

12 Transitions Toward Digital Resources: Change, Invariance, and Orchestration 389
Paul Drijvers, Verônica Gitirana, John Monaghan, Samet Okumus, Sylvaine Besnier, Cerenus Pfeiffer, Christian Mercat, Amanda Thomas, Danilo Christo, Franck Bellemain, Eleonora Faggiano, José Orozco-Santiago, Mdutshekelwa Ndlovu, Marianne van Dijke-Droogers, Rogério da Silva Ignácio, Osama Swidan, Pedro Lealdino Filho, Rafael Marinho de Albuquerque, Said Hadjerrouit, Tuğçe Kozaklı Ülger, Anders Støle Fidje, Elisabete Cunha, Freddy Yesid Villamizar Araque, Gael Nongni, Sonia Igliori, Elena Naftaliev, Giorgos Psycharis, Tiphaine Carton, Charlotte Krog Skott, Jorge Gaona, Rosilângela Lucena, José Vieira do Nascimento Júnior, Ricardo Tibúrcio, and Anderson Rodrigues

Contents

Part IV Conclusions

13 Evidencing Missing Resources of the Documentational Approach to Didactics. Toward Ten Programs of Research/Development for Enriching This Approach 447
Luc Trouche

14 Afterword: Reflections on the Documentational Approach to Didactics 491
Jeffrey Choppin

References 503

Index 543

Editors and Contributors

About the Editors

- **Luc Trouche** is Emeritus Professor of mathematics education at the French Institute of Education, École normale supérieure de Lyon (France). He began his career in studying ICT integration in mathematics education, introducing the notion of orchestration to model the management of available artefacts. His current research, in the frame of the documentational approach to didactics, focuses on mathematics teachers interacting with resources, with a special interest for teachers' collective work, in various contexts (mainly China and France). For further information, see https://ens-lyon.academia.edu/enslyonacademiaedu
- **Ghislaine Gueudet** has been, since 2009, a Full Professor in Mathematics Didactics at the University of Brest and a Member of the CREAD (Center for Research on Education, Learning, and Didactics). Her research concerns the use of resources, including digital resources for the learning and teaching of mathematics from preschool to university and in teacher education. She contributes since 2006 to the development of the documentational approach of didactics. For more details, see http://cread.espe-bretagne.fr/membres/ggueudet.
- **Birgit Pepin** is Professor of mathematics/STEM education at Eindhoven School of Education of Eindhoven University of Technology, the Netherlands, since 2015. Educated to master's degree in Germany and as a Mathematics Teacher at Oxford University, she worked as a Mathematics Teacher in England, before conducting her PhD study on mathematics teachers' pedagogic practices in England, France, and Germany. This led to her research into mathematics textbooks and their use in different European countries. During her time at Manchester University, and later in Trondheim (Norway) as Professor of Mathematics Education, she conducted research into transition in higher education mathematics, subsequently enlarged to teacher/student use of mathematics resources. She also further developed her previous research on curriculum materials, to include digital (curriculum) resources, and advanced the notions of *teacher design* and *design capacity*. For further information, see

https://www.tue.nl/en/our-university/departments/eindhoven-school-of-education/about-esoe/staff/detail/ep/e/d/ep-uid/20143164/.

Contributors

Foreword

- **Jill Adler** holds the SARChI Mathematics Education Chair at the University of the Witwatersrand, which focuses on research and development in secondary mathematics education, and is the 2017–2020 President of the International Commission on Mathematical Instruction (ICMI). She is the Recipient of numerous awards, the most significant of which are the 2012 Academy of Science of South Africa (ASSAf) Gold Medal for Science in the Service of Society and the 2015 Freudenthal Award.

Chapter 1 – Ghislaine Gueudet, Birgit Pepin, and Luc Trouche

- (See editors)

Part I

Chapter 2 – Ghislaine Gueudet

- (See editors)

Chapter 3 – Kenneth Ruthven

- Kenneth Ruthven is Emeritus Professor of education at the University of Cambridge in England and Guest Professor in mathematics education at Karlstad University in Sweden and at the University of Agder in Norway. His research examines curriculum, pedagogy, and assessment, especially in mathematics, and particularly in the light of technological change. He is an Advisory Editor of the international journals *Educational Studies in Mathematics* and *Research in Mathematics Education*, and a Fellow of the Academy of Social Sciences. For further information, see http://www.educ.cam.ac.uk/people/staff/ruthven/.

Chapter 4 – Christine Proust

- Christine Proust is a Historian of mathematics and ancient sciences. She is *Directrice de Recherche* (Senior Researcher) at the SPHERE Lab (CNRS and University Paris Diderot). Her researches focus on the history and historiography of mathematics in the ancient Near East, with a special interest for institutional contexts, textuality, and philology of numbers and quantities. She studied the organization of mathematical curriculum in Nippur's scribal schools during the Old Babylonian period (early second millennium BCE) and the mathematical practices in high administrations during the earliest periods (fourth and third millennium BCE) and in priestly milieus during the late periods (fourth to first-century BCE).

Chapter 5 – Michèle Artigue

- Michèle Artigue, after a doctorate in Mathematical Logics, progressively entered the field of mathematics education. In this field, her fields of interest have been diverse, from the teaching and learning of Calculus and Analysis and the integration of computer technologies to the networking of theoretical frames and comparative research. She is currently Emeritus Professor at the University Paris Diderot – Paris 7. She has had and still has many editorial and scientific responsibilities at national and international level. Especially, she has been Vice President and then President of the ICMI (International Commission on Mathematical Instruction). In 2013, she was awarded the Felix Klein Medal by the ICMI for her lifelong research achievement, and, in 2015, the Luis Santaló Medal by the IACME (Inter-American Committee on *Mathematics Education)* for her support to the development of Mathematics Education in Latin America.

Part II

Chapter 6 – Birgit Pepin, Michèle Artigue, Verônica Gitirana, Takeshi Miyakawa, Kenneth Ruthven, and Binyan Xu

- Birgit Pepin (see editors)
- Michèle Artigue (see Chap. 5)
- Verônica Gitirana is Associate Professor at the Federal University of Pernambuco of Brazil. Her research interests are digital resources for teaching mathematics and teacher education (pre- and in-service), especially related to theories such as instrumental orchestration and instrumental meta-orchestration, teacher documentation, and teaching activity.
- Takeshi Miyakawa (see Chap. 7)
- Kenneth Ruthven (see Chap. 3)
- Binyan Xu (see Chap. 7)

Chapter 7 – Takeshi Miyakawa and Binyan Xu

- Takeshi Miyakawa earned his doctorate in didactics of mathematics from the Université Joseph Fourier at Grenoble, France, in 2005. He spent several years as a Postdoctoral Fellow in Japan (Tsukuba) and in the United States (Michigan), before serving as an Associate Professor of mathematics education at Joetsu University of Education in Japan. His research interest is twofold: teaching and learning of proof, which have been his research topic since his doctoral studies, and mathematics teacher knowledge and teacher learning occurring in teachers' collective work such as lesson studies in Japan. His research often adopts the international comparative perspective, in order to elucidate cultural aspects of mathematics education. He recently moved to Tokyo and started working as a Full Professor at Waseda University.
- Binyan Xu received her PhD in mathematics education at the University of Osnabrueck in Germany. Currently, she is Professor of mathematics education at the East China Normal University. Her research interests focus on the assessment of students' mathematics core competences and the design of mathematics projects to improve students' engagement in mathematics activities in the classroom. She is a Key Member for the development of mathematics standards in Shanghai. Presently, she is the Co-chair of Local Organizing Committee of the 14th International Congress on Mathematics Education (ICME 14) in 2020 in Shanghai. Since 2017, she is the EC Member of the International Commission of Mathematical Instruction.

Chapter 8 – Janine T. Remillard

- Janine Remillard is a Professor of mathematics education at the University of Pennsylvania Graduate School of Education, where she serves as the Faculty Director of Teacher Education and the Director of the Collaboratory for Teacher Education. Her research interests include teachers' interactions with mathematics curriculum resources, teacher development for urban classrooms, and locally relevant mathematics instruction. Since 1999, she has received funding from the National Science Foundation to support research and development projects on teacher learning, mathematics curriculum use, and formative assessment. She is Coeditor of the volume *Mathematics Teachers at Work: Connecting Curriculum Materials and Classroom Instruction*. She is active in the mathematics education community in the United States and internationally, including serving as Chair of the US National Commission on Mathematics Instruction, a commission of the National Academy of Sciences. She is also involved in international, cross-cultural research on teachers' use of mathematics curriculum resources.

Part III

Chapter 9 – Cibelle Assis, Moustapha Sokhna, and Jana Trgalová,

with Mohammad Dames Alturkmani, Elisângela Espindola, Rim Hammoud, and Karima Sayah

- Cibelle Assis received her bachelor's and master's degrees in mathematics (2002 and 2004, respectively), her PhD in mathematics education (2010) by the postgraduation program in education in UFPE-Brazil in the line of didactics of specific contents (distance education), and her postgraduate diploma in mathematics education (2016-2018) with internships in the Ifé, from ENS/Lyon, France, from the UFPB, Brazil. She is Professor of the Department of Exact Sciences (DCX) of the CCAE of the UFPB/Campus IV and Professor of the postgraduate program in teaching of sciences and mathematics of the State University of Paraíba (UEPB). Her experiences are in the area of mathematics education and use of technologies in the subjects of methodologies of teaching, teaching-learning, and teacher training. She works in the research groups GEPEM of the UFPB and LEMATEC of the UFPE. She is currently developing research in the area of mathematics didactics and its developments in the perspective of the documentational approach to didactics.
- Moustapha Sokhna has a PhD in mathematics and mathematics education. He is Assessor of the education sciences and Technology Faculty at the Cheikh Anta Diop University in Dakar (Senegal) where he coordinates training and research activities. He is also Director of the doctoral program in mathematics education at the Mathematics and Computer Science Doctoral School. His research interest focuses on the design and use of resources by mathematics teachers.
- Jana Trgalová is Associate Professor at Claude Bernard University in Lyon, France. She obtained her master's degrees in mathematics from Comenius University (Bratislava, Slovakia) and in mathematics education from Joseph Fourier University (Grenoble France) and her PhD in mathematics education from the same university. She is involved in primary and secondary mathematics teacher education. Her research focus on digital technology and resources for mathematics education and their design, appropriation, use, and evaluation. She was involved in several national and international research projects. She is active in the international research community in the field of technology in mathematics education: she was Member of the International Program Committee of the 5th ERME Topic Conference Mathematics Education in the Digital Age (MEDA) in 2018, co-chaired the 13th International Conference on Technology in Mathematics Teaching (ICTMT13) in 2017, and led the technology group at the Congress of the European Research in Mathematics Education (CERME) in 2011, 2013, and 2015.
- Mohammad Dames Alturkmani obtained his PhD in educational sciences and didactics of physics and chemistry at École Normale Supérieure (ENS) in Lyon in 2015. He has studied the relationships that teachers build with the disciplines

they teach through their interactions with resources, by introducing four concepts: disciplinary affinity, didactic affinity, structuring mother resource, and oriented daughter resource. Then, he worked in two programs as a Postdoctoral Fellow at ENS in Lyon: ANR ReVEA (living resources for teaching and learning, 2014–2018) and PREMaTT (thinking the resources of teaching mathematics in a time of transitions, 2017–2019) of the Carnot Institute of Education. In the first project, he led the production chain of situations and web documents of analysis related to the documentation work of the teachers in the AnA.doc platform. In the second project, he is interested in the process of resource design and collaborative work between teachers and researchers to renew the teaching of mathematics in cycles three and four.

- Elisângela Espindola is Professor at the Federal Rural University of Pernambuco in Brazil. She is Member of the postgraduate program in teaching mathematics and science. She received her PhD in education sciences in 2014 from both Claude Bernard University in Lyon, France, and Federal University of Pernambuco in Recife, Brazil. Her research interest is in mathematics teachers' professional practices and decision-taking.

- Rim Hammoud is Professor at the Faculty of Education, Lebanese University, where she is currently coordinating the research and professional masters in didactics of chemistry and didactics of physics. Specialized in didactics of sciences (in particular of chemistry), she contributed through her thesis to the development of the documentational approach of didactics as much on the theoretical level as on the methodological one. She is also responsible for a project on collaborative research in partnership with the French Institute of Education, IFE, Lyon. In this project that brings together researchers from the Faculty of Education (Lebanese University) and education professionals from six Lebanese schools, she will deepen, through the use of the documentational approach, the study of the collective work of teachers from several disciplines considered around the design and implementation of resources that synergize these disciplines.

- Karima Sayah received her PhD degree in science education and mathematics education in 2018 from Claude Bernard University in Lyon, France. Her field of research focuses on the mathematics teacher's resource systems: approaching both their structure and evolution in order to follow their professional development. As a Director of an Arabic institution, she is involved in teacher training with French (online) resources to integrate them into their context. The second topic of her field of research focuses on mathematical laboratories and the experimental teaching of this subject. She follows the teaching of mathematics from kindergarten where she also gives an important place to the training of teachers from this level to primary level.

Editors and Contributors

Chapter 10 – Catherine Loisy, Hussein Sabra, and Scott Courtney,

with Gilles Aldon, Fernando Arzarello, Mathias Front, Marie-Lines Gardes, Dubravka Glasnović Gracin, Ornella Robutti, Katiane Rocha, and Eugenia Taranto

- Catherine Loisy is Senior Lecturer in psychology and science of education at the French Institute of Education (IFÉ) associated to the École Normale Supérieure (ENS) in Lyon. Her research theme mainly focuses on the professional development of teachers in the digital age. She studies how interactions supported by digital devices contribute to learning and development, especially for higher education teachers. In order to study the development trajectories of professionals, she works on the elaboration of a methodology based on Vygotsky's approach, which considers development as an appropriation of historical-social artifacts. She also questions the effects of the introduction of digital technologies on pedagogy in higher education. She has conducted several national studies supported by the General Directorate of Higher Education and Professional Integration of the Ministry of Higher Education, Research, and Innovation in France. She is a National Expert on the issue of teachers' digital competences.
- Hussein Sabra is Assistant Professor in mathematics education at the University of Reims Champagne-Ardenne. He received his PhD from the University of Lyon I – Claude Bernard (PhD Supervisor of Luc Trouche). His research interest concerns the documentational work of mathematics teachers. He develops methodological tools to consider the issue of interactions of teachers with resources. He is also interested in analyzing resources and their use by mathematics teachers. He particularly focuses his research on the individual and collective processes of design resources. While his initial research was focused at the secondary level, he is currently interested in higher education, particularly the relation between teaching and research activities through the lens of interaction with resources and resources for teaching mathematics to nonspecialists (science, technology, and engineering).
- Scott Courtney is a Mathematics Education Associate Professor in the School of Teaching, Learning, and Curriculum Studies at Kent State University in the United States. He has directed multiple state-funded mathematics and science partnership projects. His research interests include teachers' conceptions of mathematics and statistics in grades 6–14, instructional engagements propitious for student development of intended ideas and ways of thinking, and teachers' conceptions and ways of thinking that support or constrain their capacity to transform their cognitions with cognitive structures that are more conceptually oriented. His current activities include the following: a project focused on mathematical literacy as a means to confront non-factual thinking and flawed reasoning and to support decision-making, the development of synchronous online workshops and courses for mathematics teachers, and the formation of cross-district mathematics teacher collectives throughout the state of Ohio (in the United States).

- Gilles Aldon is a Retired Teacher from the French Institute of Education (IFE). His main research focus is dedicated to the use of technology in mathematics teaching and learning, more particularly, on issues involving modifications of teaching and learning mathematics in a digital era, the contribution of technology in the experimental dimension of mathematics and in the processes of problem solving, and the role of technology in formative assessment. As part of the EducTice team, where he has worked since 2011, he participated in research to examine design-based research methodology in collaborative research. In particular, this research combined the intentions, often diverse, of different communities working together on a particular object so that each actor benefited from the collaborative work by combining both the impact to the theoretical field (with academic results) and the practical dimension (with professional development).
- Ferdinando Arzarello is Professor Emeritus of Mathematics at Turin University and Past President of ERME (European Society for Research in Mathematics Education) and of the ICMI (International Commission on Mathematical Instruction). His main research interests are related to the teaching of mathematics, in particular the teaching of algebra, geometry, and analysis; the curriculum; the study of teaching/learning processes in mathematics, with particular reference to the use of different systems of semiotic representation by teachers and students; and the use of new technologies in mathematics teaching. He has worked at different international projects, involving scholars and researchers from various parts of the world. He authored more than 150 scientific publications, mostly in international journals and monographs, and has been invited to give lectures at various universities and at major scientific conferences in Europe, America (North, Central, South), Africa, Asia, and Oceania. He directs a group of didactic research in Turin, which was attended by university professors, doctoral students, and teachers at pre-university levels.
- Mathias Front is a Mathematics Teacher Educator at the École Supérieure de Professorat et l'Éducation de l'Académie de Lyon. He is Doctor in didactics of mathematics and conducts his research in the S2HEP (Sciences, Society, Historicity, Education, and Practices) laboratory of Lyon University. His work focuses on the emergence and evolution of mathematical objects in research situations. He is interested in object-subject relations in situations where the experimental dimension of mathematics is strongly present and allows the student to construct mathematical objects in a process of going back and forth between the exploration of the problem and the theoretical elaborations that make possible to explain it. He uses the resources provided by history and the epistemology of mathematics to rethink didactical situations. In charge of the training of teacher trainees in mathematics, he is also interested in new ways of helping along these trainee teachers.
- Marie-Line Gardes is Associate Professor in didactics of mathematics at the University of Lyon. She is involved in training pre-elementary, elementary, and secondary school teachers in math education. Her research is conducted at the Institute of Science Cognitive and mainly focused on learning by problem-solving

and the relationships between math education and cognitive science. She conducts epistemological and didactical studies of the research process undertaken by researchers and students involved in problem-solving. She developed a tool to analyze different research processes and the complexity of the type of reasoning implemented in a math research activity. She also questions the design and use of specific resources for teachers in order to teach through problem-solving. Her research also focuses on the relationship between education and cognitive science. She studies the contribution of cognitive sciences for education and conducts impact studies articulating methodologies in cognitive sciences and didactics of mathematics.

- Dubravka Glasnović Gracin is Assistant Professor of mathematics education at the Faculty of Teacher Education, University of Zagreb, Croatia. Her research interests are analysis of curriculum resources and their use by teachers and students. She is particularly interested in textbook analysis, with the emphasis on the study of different frameworks for analyses of textbook tasks. Her interest in the textbook use by students and teachers refers to the social and institutional reasons why the textbooks are used or not used, including the interactive interplay of textbooks with other resources. She has participated in several national projects related to students' STEM beliefs, STEM gifted students, and developing mathematics picture books.

- Ornella Robutti is Associate Professor in mathematics education in the Department of Mathematics of the University of Torino. Her fields of research are the following: the teaching and learning cognitive processes in mathematics with the support of technologies, the professional role of mathematics teachers as individuals and in communities, and the meanings of mathematical objects and their construction. She is Author of articles and book chapters in her research fields and present as Team Leader/Lecturer/Participant in many international congresses (PME, CERME, CIEAEM, CADGME, ICME). In Italy, she is Member of CIIM Commission (http://www.umi-ciim.it/) in UMI (Italian Mathematical Union); is the Person in Charge of the GeoGebra Institute of Torino, the project of teachers' professional development Piano Lauree Scientifiche in Piedmont; the project Liceo Matematico; and the national congress DIFIMA; and has been Member of scientific committees of national programs with technologies: m@t.abel, PON-m@t.abel.

- Katiane Rocha completed her undergraduate and master's degrees at the Federal University of Mato grosso do Sul (UFMS, Brazil). She started her PhD study in 2015 under the supervision of Luc Trouche at the French Institute of Education in École Normale de Supérieure de Lyon (France), funded by the National Council for Scientific and Technological Development (CNPq, Brazil). She investigates experiences and trajectories developed by teachers through their interactions with resources throughout their career.

- Eugenia Taranto obtained her doctorate in pure and applied mathematics at the University of Turin and the Polytechnic University of Turin, Italy. She is currently in a postdoctoral position at the University of Catania, Italy. Her research fields include MOOCs (massive open online courses), teacher education with the use of technologies, methodologies and resources for e-learning, and teaching/learning mathematics.

Chapter 11 – Sebastian Rezat, Carole Le Hénaff, and Jana Visnovska,

with Suzane El Hage, Ok-Kyeong Kim, Laurence Leroyer, Hussein Sabra, and Chongyang Wang

Sebastian Rezat is a Full Professor of mathematics education at the Institute of Mathematics at Paderborn University (Germany). In his research, he investigates the use of traditional and digital mathematics textbooks at primary and secondary level. He is particularly interested in students' interactions with (digital) textbooks and the interplay between students' and teachers' use of it. In collaboration with Rudolf Sträßer, he has developed the socio-didactical tetrahedron as a model for understanding the context of the use of artifacts and resources. Currently, he is the Chair of the International Programme Committee (IPC) of the Third International Conference on Mathematics Textbook Research and Development (ICMT3), to be held in the Germany, 2019.

Carole Le Hénaff is Associate Professor in science education at the University of Western Brittany since 2016. She is a Researcher in didactics of foreign languages and cultures at the Center for Research on Education, Learning, and Didactics (CREAD), ESPE de Bretagne, France.

Jana Visnovska is Lecturer in mathematics education at the University of Queensland, Australia. Her research interests focus on the means of supporting mathematics teachers that empower them in providing all students with opportunities to learn meaningful mathematics. To this end, she explores features of teachers' resources, forms of professional development, and institutional conditions required to support the learning and instructional interactions of teachers in transition. She contributes to instructional design research in area of *fractions as measures* and collaborates on international research and development projects that take place in under-resourced classrooms in Mexico, South Africa, and Slovakia. She is a Coeditor of the last 4 yearly volume on *Journal for Research in Mathematics Education* in Australasia (2012–2015) and a Coauthor of a mathematical story and activity book on fractions as measures (https://www.ru.ac.za/sanc/teacherdevelopment/miclegr4-7/), and her most recent article is being published in *Mathematical Thinking and Learning*.

Suzane El Hage is Associate Professor in science education at the University of Reims Champagne-Ardenne since 2014. She is a Researcher in didactics of sciences at the Center for Studies and Researches on Employment and Professionalization (CEREP).

Ok-Kyeong Kim is Professor of mathematics education at Western Michigan University, USA. She has taught elementary school in South Korea and preservice teachers in elementary and middle school levels in the United States. She has conducted research on teaching and learning of mathematics in elementary and middle school classrooms. She has also investigated developing and using mathematical thinking and reasoning in school and nonschool settings. Her current research centers on the role of teacher and curriculum resources in mathematics instruction and the relationship among teacher, curriculum, and instruction that supports students' learning of mathematics. She is particularly interested in teacher knowledge and capacity needed for using curricular resources productively to teach mathematics and curricular support for mathematics teaching and learning. Currently, she is designing and examining systematic ways that support preservice and in-service teachers to develop their knowledge and capacity to use curricular resources productively.

Laurence Leroyer is Lecturer in educational sciences at the higher school of teaching profession and of education, University of Caen, France. In 2011, her PhD focused on "primary school teachers' relationships to teaching materials in preparation for work in mathematics." Since her PhD, she investigates the documentation work in mathematics of primary school teachers in initial training and also of primary school teachers that teach pupils with special educational needs. She is also interested in the documentation work of teacher trainers. She seeks to understand how the characteristics of teachers or trainers (relationship to mathematics, to teaching or training, to learning and learners, etc.) influence the documentational genesis and, consequently, the design of learning or training supports.

Hussein Sabra (see Chap. 10)

Chongyang Wang is PhD Candidate of East China Normal University (ECNU) and ENS de Lyon in the context of a teaching and research project (JORISS) involving the two universities. The China Scholarship Council (CSC) funds her study in France from 2015 to 2019. Supervised by Binyan Xu (ECNU) and Luc Trouche (ENS de Lyon), her current research interest focuses on teaching resources and teacher professional development in mathematics education. Born in Hebei Province in China, she graduated in mathematics education in ECNU with a Master of Science in Education in 2014 and a Bachelor of Science in Technology Education in Jiangnan University in 2012. Her PhD defense has been held in April 2019.

Chapter 12 – Paul Drijvers, Verônica Gitirana, John Monaghan, and Samet Okumus

with Franck Bellemain, Sylvaine Besnier, Tiphaine Carton, Danilo Christo, Elisabete Cunha, Eleonora Faggiano, Anders Støle Fidje, Pedro Lealdino Filho, Jorge Gaona, Said Hadjerrouit, Sonia Igliori, Rogério Ignácio, Rosilângela Lucena, Rafael Marinho de Albuquerque, Christian Mercat, Elena Naftaliev, Mdutshekelwa Ndlovu, Gael Nongni, José Orozco, Cerenus Pfeiffer, Giorgos Psycharis, Anderson Rodrigues, Charlotte Krog Skott, Osama Swidan, Ricardo Tibúrcio, Amanda Thomas, Tuğçe Kozaklı Ülger, Marianne van Dijke-Droogers, José Vieira do Nascimento Júnior, and Freddy Yesid Villamizar Araque

Paul Drijvers is Full Professor of mathematics education at the Freudenthal Institute Faculty of Science, Utrecht University. His research interests include the role of ICT in mathematics education, the teaching and learning of algebra, and teachers' professional development. He also works as a Professor in mathematics education at HU University of Applied Sciences Utrecht.

Verônica Gitirana (see Chap. 6)

John Monaghan is Emeritus Professor at the University of Leeds and Professor at the University of Agder. His research mainly addresses the didactics of mathematics at the 14–21-year-old student level using sociocultural approaches.

Samet Okumus is Assistant Professor of mathematics education at Recep Tayyip Erdoğan University. He conducts research on teacher practice, especially in geometry instruction. Also, he conducts research in 6–12 mathematics education in the context of geometry teaching and learning.

Franck Bellemain is Associate Professor at the Centro de Artes e Comunicações, Universidade Federal de Pernambuco, Recife, Brazil. He is a Member of the Technologic and Mathematics Education Postgraduate Program.

Sylvaine Besnier works at the Center for Research on Education, Learning, and Didactic (CREAD) at the University of Rennes 2, Brittany, France. She received her PHD in educational sciences and now focuses on the preschool teachers' professional development regarding their use of resources, especially digital resources.

Tiphaine Carton is a PhD Student at Paris 8 University (CEMTI-ACME laboratory), France. She studies teachers' representations which are modelized in the platform webpedago.com.

Danilo dos Santos Christo works as a Lecturer in Higher Education at the Pontifícia Universidade Católica de São Paulo (PUC/SP), Brazil. He is currently a PhD Student in mathematics education at PUC/SP.

Elisabete Cunha works at the Instituto Politécnico de Viana do Castelo, ARC4DigiT, Portugal. She has a PhD in information and communication on digital platforms. One of her interests is graphical and tangible programming in the development of geometric and transversal competences.

Eleonora Faggiano is Assistant Professor at the University of Bari Aldo Moro, Italy. Her interests concern the use of technology in mathematics education.

Anders S. Fidje is a PhD Student at the University of Agder in Norway. His research is related to teachers using student-produced videos in mathematics teaching.

Pedro Lealdino Filho works as Consultant in Brazil. He received his PhD in mathematics education and information technology from the Université Claude Bernard, Lyon. His research focuses on the creative mathematics thinking.

Jorge Gaona has a PhD in didactics of mathematics from the Université Paris Diderot and currently works at the School of Pedagogy in Mathematics, Universidad Academia Humanismo Cristiano, Chile.

Said Hadjerrouit works at the University of Agder, Kristiansand, Norway. He is a Professor of mathematics education. His research focuses on digital resources, and he has more than 150 publications in international journals.

Sonia Igliori works as Professor at the Pontifícia Universidade Católica de São Paulo (PUC-SP), Brazil. She has a PhD in mathematics and postdoctorate in mathematics education. Her research interest is mathematics education of higher education.

Rogério da Silva Ignacio currently teaches at the Colégio de Aplicação, Universidade Federal de Pernambuco, Brazil. His research interest is the use of new technologies in teaching.

Rosilângela Lucena works at the Universidade Federal de Pernambuco, Brazil. She received her PhD in Technologic and Mathematics Education, and she had doctoral stays at the IFÉ/ENS de Lyon. Her research focus is instrumental orchestration for teacher education.

Rafael Marinho de Albuquerque is a Master's student in Technological and Mathematics Education at the Universidade Federal de Pernambuco, Brazil. He is currently interested in studying the design and use of digital mathematics textbooks.

Christian Mercat is Director of the Institute for Research on Math Education at the Université Claude Bernard Lyon 1 in Lyon, France. His main focus is technology in mathematics education, in particular creativity and STEAM.

Elena Naftaliev is a Lecturer in the Department of Mathematics at the Achva Academic College, Israel. She is the Director of "Alfa" – the project for the preparation of teachers for high school mathematics.

Mdutshekelwa Ndlovu works at the University of Johannesburg, South Africa. He is Associate Professor of mathematics education in the Department of Science and Technology Education, Faculty of Education, Auckland Park Kingsway Campus.

Gael Nongni works at the Université Laval, Canada, after finishing his PhD in 2019. His research interests are in teacher education and the teaching and learning of statistics.

Jose Orozco-Santiago is currently doing his PhD at the Mathematics Education Department, Cinvestav-IPN, Centre for Research and Advanced Studies, Mexico. He is investigating teaching linear algebra and the interaction between technology, mathematics, and education through instrumental genesis and instrumental orchestration.

Cerenus Pfeiffer works at the Centre for Pedagogy, Stellenbosch University, South Africa, as Mathematics Facilitator for the Teacher Professional Learning component. His PhD research involves GeoGebra-focused learning environments.

Giorgos Psycharis works as Assistant Professor of Mathematics Education in the Department of Mathematics, National and Kapodistrian University of Athens, Greece.

Anderson Douglas Pereira Rodrigues works at the Universidade Federal de Pernambuco (UFPE), Brazil. In 2015, he received a Master in Technology and Mathematics Education and started his doctorate in the same area, investigating a software development for magnitudes.

Charlotte Krog Skott works at the University College Copenhagen, Denmark. Her research areas include the design of learning activities with digital resources, professional development of mathematics teachers, and lesson study in the Danish context.

Osama Swidan works as Assistant Professor in the Department for Science and Technology Education, Ben-Gurion University of the Negev, Beer Shiva, Israel. He does research in designing professional development programs for teachers' use of innovative digital tools.

Amanda Thomas works as an Assistant Professor at the College of Education and Human Sciences, University of Nebraska, Lincoln. In 2013, she received her PhD in Mathematics Education at the University of Missouri-Columbia.

Ricardo Tiburcio works at the Universidade Federal de Pernambuco (UFPE), Brazil. He received his Doctorate Student in Technological and Mathematics Education and also works as a Teacher at a state school. Currently, he investigates digital technologies in the teaching of mathematics in face and distance modalities.

Tuğçe Kozaklı Ülger works as a PhD Student and Research Assistant at the Bursa Uludağ University, Turkey. His research interests include the development of mathematical competencies and the use of technology in mathematical education.

Marianne Van Dijke-Droogers works at Utrecht University, the Netherlands. Since 1996, she has been working as a Teacher in primary, secondary, and higher education. In 2016, she started a PhD research in statistical education at Utrecht University.

José Vieira do Nascimento Júnior works at the Universidade Estadual de Feira de Santana, Bahia, Brazil. He received his PhD in physical chemistry. His research interests are anthropological theory of didactics, theory of didactic situations, and instrumental genesis.

Freddy Yesid Villamizar Araque works at the Center for Research and Advanced Studies of IPN, México. He has a DSc in mathematics education, and his research involves the design of didactic activities mediated with the use of digital technologies.

Part IV

Chapter 13 – Luc Trouche

- See editors

Chapter 14 – Jeffrey Choppin

- Jeffrey Choppin research focuses on teachers' use and understanding of curriculum resources, including teacher learning from the use of innovative materials and on the mediating effect of curriculum materials on the implementation of the official curriculum. His current research project focuses on how a three-part online professional development for rural teachers can support their efforts to engage in robust classroom discourse focused on student thinking. His work has appeared in *Journal of Mathematics Teacher Education, Mathematical Thinking and Learning, ZDM Mathematics Education, Action in Teacher Education, Journal of Educational Policy, Journal for Research in Mathematics Education Research*, and *Curriculum Inquiry*, in addition to serving on editorial boards for *Mathematical Thinking and Learning* and *Elementary School Journal*.

Chapter 1
Introduction

The 'Resource' Approach to Mathematics Education. Situating an Emerging Field of Research

Ghislaine Gueudet, Birgit Pepin, and Luc Trouche

Abstract This book presents the emergence of a new field of research in mathematics education, which can be described as the study of *The 'Resource' Approach to Mathematics Education* (RAME). In this introductory chapter, we first present how and why this book is inserted within the *Advances in Mathematics Education* book series. Second, we attempt to characterize the RAME research field and to situate it in the landscape of mathematics education research. The Documentational Approach to Didactics (DAD) plays a particular role in this field; we discuss its links with other theoretical approaches in the third section. Fourth, we evoke the 'Re(s)sources 2018 conference', which took place in Lyon in May 2018 and has been a central source for this book. Fifth, we present the content of the book, and finally some perspectives for further research.

Keywords Curriculum material · Documentational Approach to Didactics · Educational technologies · Resource approach to mathematics education · Resource system · Resources · Teacher collective work · Teacher design capacity · Teacher professional development

The project of this book is to report on the emergence of a new field of research in mathematics education, which can be described as the study of *The 'Resource'*

G. Gueudet (✉)
CREAD, ESPE de Bretagne, University of Brest, Brest, France
e-mail: ghislaine.gueudet@espe-bretagne.fr

B. Pepin
Eindhoven University of Technology, Eindhoven, The Netherlands

L. Trouche
ENS de Lyon, Lyon, France

© Springer Nature Switzerland AG 2019
L. Trouche et al. (eds.), *The 'Resource' Approach to Mathematics Education*,
Advances in Mathematics Education,
https://doi.org/10.1007/978-3-030-20393-1_1

Approach to Mathematics Education (RAME in what follows), and to present to the reader a particular view on this field.

In this introduction, we first present how and why this book is inserted within the *Advances in Mathematics Education* book series. Second, we attempt to characterize the RAME research field and to situate it in the landscape of mathematics education research. The Documentational Approach to Didactics (DAD) plays a particular role in this field; we discuss its links with other theoretical approaches in the third section. Fourth, we evoke the 'Re(s)sources 2018 Conference', which took place in Lyon in May 2018 and has been a central source for this book. Fifth, we present the content of the book and finally some perspectives for further research.

1.1 A Book in the *Advances in Mathematics Education* Series

The insertion of this book in the *Advances in Mathematics Education* series is coherent from different points of view. Firstly, this book is linked with and complements several titles of the series. Teaching resources include curriculum materials (textbooks in particular), which are the subject of the book entitled *Mathematics Curriculum in School Education* (Li and Lappan 2014). Such resources also include technology, studied in the book *Mathematics and Technology*, presenting the work done within the International Commission for the Study and Improvement of Mathematics Teaching (CIEAEM,[1] Aldon et al. 2017). Moreover, some important aspects of this book are also linked with other titles of the series, for example, concerning the networking of theories (Bikner-Ahsbahs et al. 2014) or concerning lesson studies (Huang et al. 2019). Secondly and most importantly, the project of the series is to continue the tradition of the international journal *ZDM Mathematics Education* and to extend the already published themed issues of ZDM. The present book can be considered as an extension of the ZDM special issue entitled *Re-Sourcing Teacher Work and Interaction: New Perspectives on Resource Design, Use and Teacher Collaboration* (Pepin et al. 2013). When this special issue was published, the theme was relatively new, and there have been significant developments since. One of these evolutions has been the development and availability of an increasing amount of digital (curriculum) resources and the associated issues of quality and design; this has led to another ZDM special issue: *Digital curricula in mathematics education* (Pepin et al. 2017b). Complementing these ZDM special issues, this book presents the most recent developments of the research on 'Resources in Mathematics Teachers' Professional Activity' as potential advances in mathematics education and describes their insertion in a historical process.

---

[1] http://www.cieaem.org/

1 Introduction

1.2 The 'Resource' Approach to Mathematics Education: A New Research Field in Mathematics Education

The interactions between teachers (or students) and different kinds of resources have been studied for several decades in different domains of research in mathematics education. Here we claim that a new process has started, in terms of re-conceptualization of the field. Researchers from different domains have recognized common elements in their studies linked with teachers interactions with resources, regardless of the theoretical frame retained. The Re(s)sources 2018 International Conference evidenced this fact (see Sect. 1.4 below), as does the Thematic Working Group 22 of the CERME 10 conference (created at CERME10 in 2017) entitled 'Curriculum resources and task design in mathematics education' (Pepin et al. 2017c).

We can cite in particular the three following domains:

- Domain 1. Educational technologies and their use by teachers in class (with the instrumental approach, see, e.g. Guin et al. 2005) and the integration of instructional technology into teachers' resource system (Ruthven 2009).
- Domain 2. Curriculum materials (in particular textbooks), their features, design and use by teachers (e.g. Remillard 2005).
- Domain 3. Teachers' professional development and the notion of teachers' resources (Adler 2000). This included teachers' collective work (fostering professional growth).

How can we delineate the RAME emerging field? An important common point of interest has been text resources actually used or potentially useable by teachers. Below, we review the three domains evoked above to investigate how they articulate with the emerging field of RAME.

Concerning the first domain, Pepin et al. (2017b) introduced a distinction between digital curriculum resources and educational technologies:

> It is the attention to sequencing—of grade-, or age-level learning topics, or of content associated with a particular course of study (e.g. algebra)—so as to cover (all or part of) a curriculum specification, which differentiates Digital Curriculum Resources from other types of digital instructional tools or educational software programs. ... Of course, Digital Curriculum Resources make use of these other types of tool and software: indeed, what differentiates them from pre-digital curriculum programs is that they are made accessible on electronic devices and that they often incorporate the dynamic features of digital technologies. (p. 647)

Educational technologies are specific resources for the teachers, often associated with digital curriculum resources. Hence, the research on the purposive use/integration of educational technologies by teachers for enhanced student learning belongs to the RAME field. Moreover, all research linked to the instrumental approach also belongs to this field, since an artefact can be considered as a resource.

Concerning curriculum materials (domain 2), the research on its use by teachers squarely fits and belongs to the field. This encompasses studies within textbook research considering the interactions between teachers and textbooks and also studies about digital curriculum resources as defined above, for example, studies about the e-textbook (Pepin et al. 2016). It also comprises studies about educative resources (e.g. Pepin 2018). The recently introduced field called 'Curriculum ergonomics' (Choppin et al. 2018), which focuses on the interactions between curriculum design and curriculum use, also widely intersects the field we portray here.

Concerning teacher professional development (domain 3), one part of the research field is now interested in teachers' (or teacher educators') resources, as curriculum resources are an important and 'natural' constituent of teachers' work. With a growing market of digital resources (e.g. on the web, offered by publishers) and widespread digitization in schools, the importance of (curriculum) resources and their influence on teachers' work and professional development have increased. Many teacher education/professionalization courses offer resources on platforms or organize teachers' collective work of different kinds always involving resources. It seems more and more frequent to consider that the interactions between the teachers, following teacher education courses, and the resources they use are important and that they can enlighten evolutions in teachers' knowledge and practices.

Researchers who join this new field may consider that analyzing the interactions (actual or potential) between teachers and resources can be informative, even if it is not the central focus of their research.

1.3 The Documentational Approach to Didactics in the Theoretical Landscape of This Field

The three fields mentioned above were also the origin of the DAD (Gueudet and Trouche 2009), in the sense that it appeared that a theoretical frame was needed that would theorize RAME. DAD plays a specific role in it, since it has been developed with the objective of studying the central issues of the field. In Chap. 5, Artigue discusses in detail theoretical connections of DAD with other theories; here we shortly recall some central theoretical links.

Several theories have played a central role in the development of DAD, and some of their notions are linked to notions within DAD. The instrumental approach (including the concept of schemes, Vergnaud 1998 and the notion of instrumental orchestration, Guin et al. 2005), the Structuring Features of the Classroom Practice (SFCP, in particular the notion of resource system, Ruthven 2009), the teacher-curriculum material interactions (Remillard 2005) and the concept of resource for the teacher's practice (Adler 2000) intervened in this development. DAD is strongly linked with these theories, and these theories are indeed used side by side with DAD.

Another kind of theoretical links is the combination of DAD with more general theories that complement it, or offer a general frame where DAD can intervene to focus on specific aspects. The Anthropological Theory of the Didactics (ATD, Chevallard 2006) is used for situating/framing the work of the teacher (including his/her documentation work) in an institution, shaping the mathematical knowledge taught. The Cultural-Historical Activity Theory (CHAT, Engeström 2001) permits to consider that the teacher works within a complete activity system. Besides DAD,

1 Introduction

ATD and CHAT have been already associated for analyzing teachers' interaction with resources (Trouche et al. 2019). The Communities of Practice Theory (CoP, Wenger 1998) provides also tools to study teachers' collective documentation work. Different theories about *teacher knowledge* (e.g. Mathematical Knowledge for Teaching, Ball et al. 2008) and *beliefs* have also been associated with DAD in selected research works (e.g. Shaaban et al. 2015).

The chapters of this book acknowledge these theoretical connections. In particular in the chapters of Part III, while DAD appears as a central framework, all the theories cited above are also mentioned and used in case studies. Moreover, other theories also intervene; their use and their links with DAD are questioned according to the theme of each chapter. For example, Chap. 9 (about resource systems) uses the structure of the *milieu* (Margolinas 2004), within the Theory of Didactical Situations (Brousseau 1997), to investigate the structure of these systems; Chap. 10 (about methodology) investigates how theory and methodology can be linked and in this respect compares DAD and Vygotsky's (1978) sociocultural theory; Chap. 11 (about documentation work) studies how different theoretical frameworks enlighten this work, adding in particular the socio-didactical tetrahedron (Rezat and Sträßer 2012) to theories cited above; and Chap. 12 (about technology) uses frameworks focusing on technology (e.g. Technological Pedagogical Content Knowledge, TPACK; Mishra and Koehler 2006). These are only some examples of the rich set of theories mentioned in Part III.

In fact, new theoretical links involving DAD appear in many chapters of this book. These links might lead to the introduction of new concepts within DAD; or they might remain theoretical complements outside of DAD. A central example concerns the issue of 'teachers as designers' and the need to gain a better understanding of this issue, in particular through the concept of teachers design capacity (Pepin et al. 2017a, see also Chaps. 6 and 11). Chapter 5 of this book evokes some possibilities for investigating the links between DAD and these other theories. A systematic investigation of these links is a perspective for future research, and one of the research programs evoked in Chap. 13.

1.4 The Re(s)sources 2018 Conference

The Re(s)sources 2018 Conference took place in Lyon, France (28–30 May 2018). The name *Re(s)sources* was chosen as a wink to the Adler's (2000) definition of a resource as something *re-sourcing* teacher's work and also to the word *Ressources* (with two s's), French translation of the English resource. The title of the conference announced as objective: 'Understanding teachers' work through their interactions with resources for teaching'. It gathered 130 participants from 30 countries. The interventions of the participants evidenced a variety of research concerning the topic of the conference:

- This research is clearly international and spread across all the continents.
- All the research specialties evoked in the previous section were represented.

- The research works presented concerned all school levels from kindergarten to university and teacher education.
- Most participants were mathematics education specialists; nevertheless, researchers in science education and language education were also present. This is one of the evolutions evidenced in this book: the study of the interactions between teachers and resources is clearly not limited to mathematics. Considering other disciplines can lead to theoretical propositions and to a larger view on teaching and learning in interacting with resources.

The conference was prepared through a website (https://resources-2018.sciencesconf.org/), still available, hosted by the French Ministry of Research and Higher Education. The proceedings, published online before the conference (Gitirana et al. 2018), give access to the presentation of its major events (lectures, panel, working groups, young researcher workshop) and to the whole set of accepted contributions (80 papers and 7 posters). The videos of the plenary events (opening and closing ceremonies, lectures and panel) are also available online.[2]

The sources of this book are the seven plenary lectures, the plenary panel and the four working groups, chosen by the scientific committee to tackle issues appearing as especially delicate in the present state of research. The corresponding texts have been proposed by the lecturers, the panelists and selected contributors to the working groups. Subsequently, the chapters have undergone a process of internal cross reading and reviewing. The book could then be considered as a follow-up of the conference. The lectures and the panel are included in Parts I and II and to the conclusion section of this book. The working groups contributed to the four chapters of Part III.

The discussions in the Re(s)sources 2018 Conference led to new ideas of possible theoretical connections and to reflections on the methods used. Moreover, it also provided an idea of the diversity of empirical research in the field and of the interest in its outcomes. The young researchers' workshop, following the conference, was also a good place for discussing new issues, in three directions:

- The role of *didactic metadata* for sequencing, describing and sharing learning activities, a critical reflection for supporting teachers as curriculum designers (Cooper et al. 2018).
- The role of *web documents*, integrating a variety of mediational means (videos, sounds and various Internet links), a critical reflection for supporting teacher-collective documentation work (Bellemain et al. 2018).
- The interest of analyzing the *naming systems* developed by teachers when interacting with resources, for better understanding their resource systems, a critical reflection for taking into account the cultural and historical constraints of their documentation work (Wang et al. To be published).

---

[2] https://www.canalu.tv/producteurs/ecole_normale_superieure_de_lyon/colloques_seminaires_et_workshop/conference_re_s_sources_2018

1 Introduction

In the book, there is no specific section dedicated to this workshop, but one could find traces of the corresponding issues in the conference proceedings and in the last section of the book: the young researcher workshop acted as an incubator of new programs of research (see Chap. 13).

1.5 Presentation of the Content of This Book

We briefly present here the content of the four sections of the book.

Part I frames the field of research in two main directions: a historical direction and a theoretical one; its four chapters are based on four plenary conferences at the Re(s)sources 2018 International Conference.

We first present here these chapters according to the historical aspects they consider (hence the presentation does not follow the order of the chapters in the book). Chapter 4 (Proust) is a contribution coming from the history of mathematics and of mathematics education, concerning the work of teachers in the scribal schools of Mesopotamia in the mid-fourth millennium before the Common Era. The teaching resources permit to evidence several didactical structures, corresponding to different perspectives on mathematics education. This history of mathematics perspective is also important in Chap. 3 (Ruthven), deepening the understanding of the concept of resource system. Indeed, this chapter draws on two historical examples of resource systems, Euclid's *Elements* and Durell's *A New Geometry*, discussing their specific features and differences. Chapter 2 (Gueudet) also develops a historical perspective, but on a much shorter time scale: it focuses indeed on the history of DAD. It presents the main evolutions of the questions studied, of the theories and of the methodologies used during the brief history (2007–2018) of DAD. These evolutions (and thus the historical dimension) are also studied in Chap. 5 (Artigue), with a lens of theoretical networking.

The theoretical aspect is presented in Chap. 2, in particular with the presentations of the main theoretical sources of DAD. In Chap. 3, one of these sources is especially discussed: the Structuring Features of the Teacher's Practices (including the resource system). But the main chapter, in terms of reflection on theoretical connections, is Chap. 5, which considers DAD with the tools recently developed by the Networking Theories Group, in particular the concept of research praxeology (Artigue et al. 2011). Research praxeologies are composed of two blocks. The praxis block is made of research tasks and research techniques or methods used in order to solve these tasks, while the logos block is made of the technological discourse used to describe, explain and justify research methods and of the theories themselves. Artigue (this volume) evidences that the emergence of DAD can be interpreted as a continuous and coherent progression of research praxeologies, whose core characteristics stabilized rapidly. In this chapter, Artigue describes the increasing diversity of theoretical connections between DAD and other theoretical approaches and constructs, established by both the founders of this approach and its users. Artigue also observes the difficulty of reaching advanced forms of networking resulting from the distance between research praxeologies and the importance of collaborative work to overcome these limitations.

Part II contains three chapters illustrating international research on different aspects of the field of 'The 'Resource' Approach to Mathematics Education'. Chap. 6 evolved from the panel discussion at the 'Re(s)sources 2018' Conference. In this chapter, the authors (Pepin, Artigue, Gitirana, Miyakawa, Ruthven and Xu) report on an investigation of the notion of 'teachers as curriculum designers' from (a) the literature and (b) six international perspectives, with the intention to develop a deeper understanding of the concept and to provide an international perspective and illustrations of the different facets of teacher design. Based on a literature/document analysis, and a case study approach (analyzing the six countries' cases), different modes of teacher design were found: from teacher **d**esign activities at micro level (e.g. lesson preparation alone or in small groups), over those at meso level (e.g. **D/d**esigning in collectives of colleagues for the purpose of use by others), to **D**esign at macro level (e.g. involvement in the design of national frameworks designed in professional design teams for the use of many others). More generally, the authors claim that the often casually used term of 'teacher design' had different meanings in different contexts and that teacher design activities might be for different purposes and for different expected end results. Here a major distinction was whether the design was more oriented towards the process (e.g. in the Japanese case) or the product (e.g. in the English case). In addition, it was argued that distinguishing between the different modes of design and the desired outcomes of those design activities/modes of design (be they process or product oriented) has important implications for teacher education and professionalism.

Chapter 7 reports on an analysis of one Japanese and one Chinese case in terms of teacher collaborative work inside and outside school. In their detailed descriptions of the rich cases, they show how different institutional frameworks at different levels (ranging from school to national level) provide teachers with opportunities to work collaboratively and in groups (e.g. Teaching Research Groups in China; Lesson Study in Japan). In terms of teacher professional development, China and Japan appear to adopt a form of practice-based professional development, including the design and evaluation of particular innovative pedagogic practices, where the term 'research' is used for inquiry into practical problems of teaching. Interestingly, in both countries, the textbook seems to occupy a prominent place among teachers' resources, and the study of textbooks is an essential part of teachers' work. Moreover, the teacher communities in both countries are equipped with the publication infrastructure of professional journals or books that allow for the teachers to disseminate their work and hence to help to 're-source' other teachers.

In Chap. 8, Remillard reflects on her encounters with the growing body of research on mathematics teachers' use of resources, focusing on the documentational approach and its impact on her own research. First, she describes her early encounters with the documentational genesis framework in 2008, which had strong resonance with her own work at the time, and introduced her to new language, frameworks and colleagues from a different cultural context. Second, she details two subsequent research projects undertaken by her: one in USA and the other involving four different contexts: Finland, Flanders (Belgium), Sweden and USA. She explains that these projects have allowed her to refine and deploy the participatory perspective (Remillard 2005) in relation to the documentational approach and have contributed to her understanding of teachers' interactions with mathematics curriculum resources. Third, she offers four propositions for research on teachers' interactions with curriculum resources: three linked to the theoretical perspectives of the documentational framework and one connected to findings from her own research.

In Part III, the four chapters come from the discussions occurring during and after the conference in the frame of the four working groups at the Re(s)sources 2018 Conference. They keep the traces of ongoing discussions, each of them standing somewhere between two extreme formats: a collection of interrelated contributions vs. an organized synthesis evidencing different necessary perspectives of research.

Chapter 9, coordinated by Trgalová, Sokhna and Assis, is dedicated to *Teachers' resource systems, their structure, their evolution and their mapping*. Several theoretical attempts have been made along the years within DAD for elucidating the notion of resource system, and none of them is completely satisfactory. This chapter proposes a double entry:

- From the resources themselves: What are the available resources (for a given subject matter or didactical goal or school level)? How can these resources be mapped to learning and/or teaching objectives?
- From the teacher's work: How do teachers constitute their resource systems? How do teachers structure their resource systems? How do teachers' resource systems evolve?

Chapter 10, coordinated by Loisy, Sabra and Courtney, is dedicated to *Methodological issues for analyzing teachers' work with resources*. The complexity of following/'measuring' the interactions between teachers and resources has been acknowledged in DAD from its beginning. This chapter is based on two main assumptions: the dialectical relationship between theoretical and methodological choices and the intertwined processes of teachers' work with resources and professional development, opening new avenues for research and methodological developments. These assumptions guide the presentation of different cases, offering a view on different data collection and data analysis tools and giving means for understanding their affordances and constraints.

Chapter 11, coordinated by Rezat, Le Henaff and Visnovska, is dedicated to *Documentation work, design capacity and teachers' expertise in designing instruction*. Studying the link between design capacity and DAD is one of the most recent evolutions in terms of theoretical connections and one of the most promising perspectives (see also Chap. 6). This chapter discusses four different conceptualizations of teachers' knowledge and skills in interacting with resources and their aims and illustrates them with case studies in which such conceptualizations are used. It questions then 'the affordances, constraints, and blind spots of these frameworks, and indicate how they overlap and complement each other'.

The final chapter of this section, Chap. 12, coordinated by Drijvers, Gitirana, Monaghan and Okumus, is dedicated to *Transitions towards digital resources: change, invariance and orchestration*. It focuses on what is/remains specific about technology within all the different kinds of mathematics teachers' resources, through five central sections on instrumental genesis, instrumental orchestration, the documentational approach to didactics, digital resources and teacher education and the design of learning environments with the use of digital resources. These five sections are situated in different theoretical approaches, and the opening section addresses issues in 'theoretical networking'. The chapter offers a broad view on people interacting with digital resources in the field of mathematics education: people could be teachers, as well as students or teacher educators, considered individually or collectively; a large range of digital resources and applications are considered and the interactions consist in using, adapting or designing resources. The chapter offers both a retrospective view on past research and a prospective view on further research.

Finally, Part IV is composed of two chapters. Chap. 13 proposes an insider view, starting from determining some essential resources missing of DAD to proposing 10 programs of research/development for developing DAD. It could be considered as a follow-up of Chap. 2, where Gueudet situates the current state of DAD in looking back to its origin. In Chap. 13, Trouche proposes a possible future of this approach in analyzing its current state. He proposes to determine the missing resources of DAD in questioning current and past PhD students who have anchored their research in DAD. What did/do they learn in using DAD as a main theoretical resource; to which extent did/do they estimate that they have enriched DAD by their own work? Which are, according to them, the still missing resources of DAD? Which of these resources should be developed by DAD from itself and/or in a theoretical co-working with other theoretical framework? From this inquiry, Trouche proposes ten perspectives of research, aiming to develop some theoretical blind points of DAD, or to develop some methodological tools, or to deepen the cultural/social aspects of DAD in questioning the naming systems used by teachers when interacting with resources. This chapter echoes actually different perspectives of research already present, as promising germs, in previous chapters. Chapter 14 proposes an outsider view, under the form of a afterword. Its author, Choppin, defines himself as a 'friendly outsider', standing in the field of curriculum ergonomics (see Sect. 1.2), which, according to us, belongs to RAME. Choppin explores the contributions of DAD to mathematics education, its strength as a holistic approach to teachers' work and its connecting power to other theories, as well as its potential limitations and issues. Finally, he acts as a broker, questioning the connections between DAD and curriculum ergonomics.

1.6 Outcomes and Perspectives

This book brings together international research on RAME. As such, it both presents this new emerging field (as mentioned at the beginning of this introduction) and contributes to its emergence. In this introductory text, we have attempted to outline this emergence from a 'contributory' point of view, describing in particular the contribution of previous research to this process; more generally, we have also outlined the situation of RAME seen from a mathematics education point of view.

The content of the book provides the reader with a detailed and precise account of RAME research in 2018. The present editors have previously edited the book entitled *From Textbooks to 'Lived' Resources: Mathematics Curriculum Materials and Teacher Documentation* (Gueudet et al. 2012), which also concerned RAME – at the time RAME was not a clearly distinguished field of research. Comparing the present book with the previous one leads to observe many evolutions. Here we emphasize evolutions concerning theoretical issues and evolutions concerning the scope of the research presented.

The chapters of the present book evidence, from different points of view, that if DAD is a central theoretical framework for the study of teachers' activity with resources, many other theories contribute and have contributed to it. Comparing and contrasting the contribution of each theory, studying how and for which purposes they can be combined, is a major issue for present and future research. These chapters also evidence how large the scope of RAME is from preschool to university teachers, from novice teachers to 'experts'; it even goes further than what is captured by *The 'Resource' Approach to Mathematics Education*. For example, some research also considers mathematics teacher educators' activities or science teachers' activities. Moreover, these studies are conducted in different countries all over the world corresponding to very different educational contexts. This variety allows in particular conducting comparative studies (see, e.g. Chap. 6 in this book). We consider the development of such comparative studies (not only between different countries but also, e.g. between different school subjects) as a major perspective for RAME empirical research.

In this introduction, we do not give a detailed account of the perspectives for future research; the reader will find ten prospective research programs in Chap. 13. Many ongoing national (in different countries) or international research projects belong to or at least concern RAME. As examples, we point to the Brazilian project *The documentation systems of teachers who teach mathematics in rural schools*[3] (Lima 2018) or to the various projects presented in the chapters of this book.

Many international conferences, involving most of the authors of this book, include working groups on RAME: e.g. TWG22 'Curricular Resources and Task Design in Mathematics Education' at CERME11 (Congress of the European Society

---

[3] *O sistema de documentação de professores que ensinam matemáticas em escolas do campo*, project of the Federal University of Pernambuc (2019–2021), led by Iranete Lima.

for Research in Mathematics Education)[4] and TSG41 'Research and development on textbooks and resources for learning and teaching mathematics' at ICME14 (International Congress on Mathematical Education[5]). Some topical conferences are directly linked to RAME, like ICMT (International Conference on Mathematics Textbook Research and Development[6]).

The rich field of RAME is developing rapidly; the evolutions of the available resources and of different aspects of teachers' work might lead to evolutions of new research questions and results that we cannot yet anticipate. This book presents a particular view on research within this field at the end of 2018; we hope that it will open the path for many further works.

We acknowledge all the authors of the book, particularly the coordinators of chapters, for their contributions and their participation to the editing process. And we particularly thank Jill Adler for the foreword.

References

Adler, J. (2000). Conceptualising resources as a theme for teacher education. *Journal of Mathematics Teacher Education, 3*, 205–224.

Aldon, G., Hitt, F., Bazzini, L., & Gellert, U. (Eds.). (2017). *Mathematics and Technology: A C.I.E.A.E.M. Sourcebook*. New York: Springer International Publishing.

Artigue, M., Bosch, M., & Gascón, J. (2011). La TAD face au problème de l'interaction entre cadres théoriques en didactique des mathématiques. In M. Bosch, J. Gascón, A. Ruiz Olarría, M. Artaud, A. Bronner, Y. Chevallard, G. Cirade, C. Ladage, & M. Larguier (Eds.), *Un panorama de la TAD. Actes du troisième congrès de la TAD* (pp. 33–56). Barcelona: Centre de Recerca Matemàtica.

Ball, D. L., Thames, M., & Phelps, G. (2008). Content knowledge for teaching: What makes it special? *Journal of Teacher Education, 59*(5), 389–407.

Bellemain, F., Rodrigues, A., & Rodrigues, A. (2018). LEMATEC Studium: a support resource for teaching mathematics. In V. Gitirana, T. Miyakawa, M. Rafalska, S. Soury-Lavergne, & L. Trouche (Eds.), *Proceedings of the Re(s)sources 2018 International Conference* (pp. 255–258). Lyon: ENS de Lyon. Retrieved on November 8th, 2018 at https://hal.archives-ouvertes.fr/hal-01764563.

Bikner-Ahsbahs, A., Prediger, S., & Networking Theories Group (Eds). (2014). *Networking of theories as a research practice in mathematics education*. New York: Springer International Publishing.

Brousseau, G. (1997). In N. Balacheff, M. Cooper, R. Sutherland, & V. Warfield (Eds.), *Theory of didactical situations in mathematics*. Dordrecht: Kluwer Academic Publisher.

---

[4] CERME 11 has been held in Utrecht (Netherlands) in February 2019. TWG 22 (Thematic Working Group) is chaired by Birgit Pepin: https://cerme11.org/wp-content/uploads/2018/04/TWG_22_cfp.pdf

[5] ICME 14 will be held in July 2020 in Shanghai (China). TSG 41 (Topic Study Group) is chaired by Sebastian Rezat and Jana Visnovska: http://www.icme14.org/static/en/news/37.html?v=1546405283868

[6] ICMT 3, chaired by Sebastian Rezat, will be held in Paderborn (Germany) in September 2019: https://tagung.math.uni-paderborn.de/event/1/

1 Introduction

Chevallard, Y. (2006). Steps towards a new epistemology in mathematics education. In M. Bosch (Ed.), *Proceedings of the fourth congress of the European society for research in mathematics education* (pp. 21–30). Barcelona: FUNDEMI-1QS.

Choppin, J., Roth McDuffie, A., Drake, C., & Davis, J. (2018). Curriculum ergonomics: conceptualizing the interactions between curriculum design and use. *International Journal of Educational Research, 92*, 75–85. Retrieved on February 21st at https://doi.org/10.1016/j.ijer.2018.09.015.

Cooper, J., Olsher, S., & Yerushalmy, M. (2018). Reflecting on didactic metadata of learning sequences. In V. Gitirana, T. Miyakawa, M. Rafalska, S. Soury-Lavergne, & L. Trouche (Eds.), *Proceedings of the Re(s)sources 2018 international conference* (pp. 191–194). Lyon: ENS de Lyon. Retrieved on November 8th 2018 at https://hal.archives-ouvertes.fr/hal-01764563.

Engeström, Y. (2001). Expansive learning at work: Toward an activity theoretical reconceptualization. *Journal of Education, 14*(1), 133–156.

Gitirana, V., Miyakawa, T., Rafalska, M., Soury-Lavergne, S., & Trouche, L. (2018). *Proceedings of the Re(s)sources 2018 international conference*. Lyon: ENS de Lyon. Retrieved on November 8th, 2018 at https://hal.archives-ouvertes.fr/hal-01764563.

Gueudet, G., & Trouche, L. (2009). Towards new documentation systems for mathematics teachers? *Educational Studies in Mathematics, 71*(3), 199–218.

Gueudet, G., Pepin, B., & Trouche, L. (Eds.). (2012). *From textbooks to 'lived' resources: mathematics curriculum materials and teacher documentation*. New York: Springer.

Guin, D., Ruthven, K., & Trouche, L. (Eds.). (2005). *The didactical challenge of symbolic calculators: Turning a computational device into a mathematical instrument*. New York: Springer.

Huang, R., Takahashi, A., & da Ponte, J. P. (Eds.) (2019). Theory and practice of lesson studies. New York: Springer International Publishing.

Li, Y., & Lappan, G. (Eds.). (2014). *Mathematics curriculum in school education*. New York: Springer International Publishing.

Lima, I. (2018). The textbook for field public schools in Brazil -PNLD field. In V. Gitirana, T. Miyakawa, M. Rafalska, S. Soury-Lavergne, & L. Trouche (Eds.), *Proceedings of the Re(s) sources 2018 international conference* (pp. 129–131). Lyon: ENS de Lyon. Retrieved on November 8th, 2018 at https://hal.archives-ouvertes.fr/hal-01764563.

Margolinas, C. (2004). *Points de vue de l'élève et du professeur. Essai de développement de la théorie des situations didactiques. HDR*. Marseille: Université Aix-Marseille. https://tel.archives-ouvertes.fr/tel-00429580v2/document.

Mishra, P., & Koehler, M. J. (2006). Technological pedagogical content knowledge: A framework for teacher knowledge. *Teachers College Record, 108*(6), 1017–1054.

Pepin, B. (2018). Enhancing teacher learning with curriculum resources. In L. Fan, L. Trouche, C. Qi, S. Rezat, & J. Visnovska (Eds.), *Research on mathematics textbooks and teachers' resources: Advances and issues, ICME 13 Monograph* (pp. 359–374). Cham: Springer.

Pepin, B., Gueudet, G., & Trouche, L. (Eds.). (2013). Resourcing teacher work and interaction: New perspectives on resources design, use, and teacher collaboration. *ZDM -Mathematics Education, special issue*, (7), 45.

Pepin, B., Gueudet, G., Yerushalmy, M., Trouche, L., & Chazan, D. (2016). E-Textbooks in/for teaching and learning mathematics: A disruptive and potentially transformative educational technology. In L. English & D. Kirshner (Eds.), *Handbook of international research in mathematics education* (pp. 636–661). New York: Taylor & Francis.

Pepin, B., Gueudet, G., & Trouche, L. (2017a). Refining teacher design capacity: Mathematics teachers' interactions with digital curriculum resources. *ZDM – Mathematics Education, 49*(5), 799–812.

Pepin, B., Choppin, J., Ruthven, K., & Sinclair, N. (2017b). Digital curriculum resources in mathematics education: Foundations for change. *ZDM - Mathematics Education, 49*(5), 645–661.

Pepin, B., Delaney, S., Rezat, S., & Stylianides, A. J. (2017c). Introduction to the papers of TWG22: Curricular resources and task design in mathematics education. In T. Dooley & G. Gueudet (Eds.), *Proceedings of the tenth congress of the European mathematical society for research in mathematics education* (pp. 3615–3618). Dublin: DCU Institute of Education and ERME.

Remillard, J. T. (2005). Examining key concepts in research on teachers' use of mathematics curricula. *Review of Educational Research, 75*(2), 211–246.

Rezat, S., & Sträßer, R. (2012). From the didactical triangle to the socio-didactical tetrahedron: artifacts as fundamental constituents of the didactical situation. *ZDM – Mathematics Education, 44*(5), 641–651.

Ruthven, K. (2009). Towards a naturalistic conceptualisation of technology integration in classroom practice: The example of school mathematics. *Education & Didactique, 3*(1), 131–149.

Shaaban, E., Khalil, I., & Trouche, L. (2015). Interactions between digital resources and biology teachers' conceptions about genetic determinism: A case study of two Lebanese teachers. *International Journal of Science and Research, 4*(10), 1190–1200.

Trouche, L., Gitirana, V., Miyakawa, T., Pepin, B., & Wang, C. (2019). Studying mathematics teachers interactions with curriculum materials through different lenses: towards a deeper understanding of the processes at stake. *International Journal of Educational Research, 93*, 53–67. Retrieved on February 21st at https://doi.org/10.1016/j.ijer.2018.09.002.

Vergnaud, G. (1998). Toward a cognitive theory of practice. In A. Sierpinska & J. Kilpatrick (Eds.), *Mathematics education as a research domain: a search for identity* (pp. 227–241). Dordrecht: Kluwer Academic Publisher.

Vygotski, L. (1978). *Mind in society.* Cambridge, MA: Harvard University Press.

Wang, C., Salinas, U., & Trouche, L. (To be published). From teachers' naming systems of resources to teachers' resource systems: Contrasting a Chinese and a Mexican case. In U. T. Jankvist, M. van den Heuvel- Panhuizen, & M. Veldhuis (Eds.), *Proceedings of the Eleventh Congress of the European Society for Research in Mathematics Education.* Utrecht: Freudenthal Group & Freudenthal Institute, Utrecht University and ERME.

Wenger, E. (1998). *Communities of practice. Learning, meaning, identity.* New York: Cambridge University Press.

Part I
Framing the Field of Research

Chapter 2
Studying Teachers' Documentation Work: Emergence of a Theoretical Approach

Ghislaine Gueudet

Abstract The documentational approach to didactics is a young theory – it was less than 10 years old in 2018. In this chapter I look back at the process of development of this approach. I recall the initial context, motivating the elaboration of a specific frame for studying teachers' documentation work. Several kinds of evolutions are emphasized: theoretical, methodological, but also evolutions of the questions studied in the research works referring to the documentational approach. I conclude by evidencing the main evolutions so far and evoking some perspectives.

Keywords Documentational approach to didactics · Reflective investigation method · Resource system · Teachers' resources

2.1 Introduction

This text proposes the analysis of a historical process: the development of the documentational approach to didactics (DAD in what follows). I do not claim to present a scientific analysis: I have been actively involved in this process; what I describe here is my own view on it. I consider in particular that this short history (from 2007 to 2018) can be divided into four important periods, and this chapter is organized according to these successive periods. The first period corresponds to the initial proposition of the theoretical approach; Sect. 2.1 presents the sources used for this theoretical construction and this early version of the approach. In Sect. 2.2, I present the second period (2008–2010), which has seen the development of methods and the investigation of secondary school mathematics teachers' documentation work. Then

---

This chapter originates from a lecture given to the Re(s)sources 2018 International Conference. Video in English, with French subtitles at http://video.ens-lyon.fr/ife/2018/2018-05-28_003_Ressources2018_Ghislaine_Gueudet_v1.fra.mp4

G. Gueudet (✉)
CREAD, ESPE de Bretagne, University of Brest, Brest, France
e-mail: ghislaine.gueudet@espe-bretagne.fr

© Springer Nature Switzerland AG 2019
L. Trouche et al. (eds.), *The 'Resource' Approach to Mathematics Education*,
Advances in Mathematics Education,
https://doi.org/10.1007/978-3-030-20393-1_2

the 2011–2013 period (Sect. 2.3) marked the enlargement of the scope of the approach, in different directions. In Sect. 2.4, I present works done since 2014 and discuss the major ongoing evolutions. Naturally these dates must not be considered as very precise borders between different periods: the work in the projects and the corresponding publications can be separated from several years; the development of DAD was a continuous process. Nevertheless this somehow artificial splitting in periods is helpful to evidence the main steps of this short history.

2.2 Origins and First Theoretical Propositions (2007 and Before)

The development of DAD took place in a context of generalized availability of online resources for teachers and students. The first version of the theory has been presented at the French Mathematics Didactic Summer School (an event taking place every 2 years) in 2007 by Ghislaine Gueudet and Luc Trouche (Gueudet and Trouche 2009a, Fig. 2.1).

The work in the Mathematics Didactic Summer School is organized according to themes, each theme proposing courses and associated tutorials. In the 14th Summer School, we were co-responsible for a theme entitled "Mathematical situations and teachers' documents" and decided to give in it a course about teachers' work in this evolving context. This decision has been driven by our previous work in related fields (Sect. 2.2.1). We had from the beginning the aim to propose theoretical constructs, and we drew for this objective on diverse sources (Sect. 2.2.2). We also

Fig. 2.1 A teacher at work. An illustration by Serge Cecconi (Cecconi 2007), used in Gueudet and Trouche (2009a, p. 109)

2 Studying Teachers' Documentation Work: Emergence of a Theoretical Approach

collected some data on teachers' work; all this led to an early version of DAD (Sect. 2.2.3).

2.2.1 Previous Works by Luc Trouche and Ghislaine Gueudet

Our previous works related to the development of DAD mainly concerned educational technologies.

Luc Trouche has been one of the early contributors of the introduction of the instrumental approach in mathematics education research. While his first works mainly concerned the use of the calculator by students (Guin et al. 2005), he also introduced the notion of instrumental orchestration (Trouche 2004), which contributed to a shift of the focus with a new attention to the use of technologies by teachers. Another dimension of Luc Trouche's work that has been strongly influential was his interest for teachers' collective work, strongly linked with the SFODEM project (Guin and Trouche 2005). The SFODEM (2000–2006) was a project of in-service teacher training, mainly at distance, aiming to support the integration of ICT in the teachers' practices by a rich offer of resources on a platform. Studying the SFODEM's case led to raise the issue of the collective design of resources. Finally, Luc Trouche also contributed to a collective book entitled *Technological Environments and Digital Resources for Learning* (*Environnements informatisés et ressources numériques pour l'apprentissage*; the book published in French has not been translated). This book initiated a coordination between several research fields: mathematics education, computer science and cognitive ergonomics, but also what is called in France "document engineering", which played a determining role as we will see below.

On my side, after several years of research (including my PhD) on the teaching and learning of linear algebra at university, I started around 2000 to work on learning processes with online exercises. This led me to use the instrumental approach (see, e.g. Cazes et al. 2007) and to develop an interest for all the kinds of online resources for the teaching and learning of mathematics. The focus of my research went beyond university to include all school levels, and shifted to teachers' work, considering online exercises as resources for teachers. Following a work by Haspekian (2014), I considered with my colleague Laetitia Bueno-Ravel teachers' instrumental geneses (Bueno-Ravel and Gueudet 2007), and we tried to build connections between these instrumental geneses and the structuring features of the classroom practice framework as introduced by Kenneth Ruthven, in particular in his plenary at the CERME5 conference (Ruthven 2007).

In a context where the Internet became a major tool in teachers' work, extending these previous works by the collective construction of a relevant frame to study the consequences of the ongoing evolutions was natural. For this aim we drew on a variety of theoretical sources, presented in the next section.

2.2.2 Theoretical Sources

The first theoretical source for DAD was naturally the instrumental approach (Rabardel 1995). The instrumental approach distinguishes between an artefact, product of the human activity, designed for a goal-directed human activity, and an instrument developed by a subject using the artefact. The instrument is a mixed entity, comprising the artefact and a scheme of use (Vergnaud 1998) of this artefact. A scheme of use is a stable organization of the activity, for a given class of activity situations: a set of situations corresponding to the same aim of the activity. The scheme comprises several components: the aim of the activity; rules of action, rules of control and rules for taking information; operational invariants; and possibilities of inferences. The operational invariants are of two kinds: theorems-in-action and concepts-in-action. A theorem-in-action is a proposition considered as true by the subject; a concept-in-action is a concept considered as relevant. The development of an instrument is called an instrumental genesis. The process has two strongly interrelated components: instrumentation (the features of the artefact shape the schemes developed by the subject) and instrumentalization (the subject modifies the artefact according to his/her existing schemes).

Along these first concepts, which directly inspired DAD, other aspects of the instrumental approach nurtured our first theoretical constructs. I mentioned above the instrumental orchestration (Trouche 2004), leading to a focus on the teacher. Another important idea was the "double instrumental genesis" (Haspekian 2014). This concept has been introduced by Haspekian to emphasize the fact that a teacher working with a software develops two instruments: a personal instrument, when he/she learns the functionalities of the software (e.g. how a spreadsheet works), and a professional instrument, developed for teaching objectives (e.g. how to use a spreadsheet to support the learning of Algebra by Grade 9 students). Other concepts came more directly from the work of Rabardel and his team. The activity families are sets of classes of situations with the same kind of aim. The subjects develop instrument systems (Rabardel and Bourmaud 2005), structured according to the activity families. Hence we have used these families in our attempts to identify, from the beginning, the structure of the document systems; we discuss it below (§ 12.1.4). We also referred to the principle of design-in-use and design-for-use (Folcher 2005): the artefacts are designed for a given, initial use; but their design continues during their use. Researchers working within the instrumental approach have used this statement as a principle, guiding an efficient design: the users must be associated with the design from the beginning.

The second source came from the research field of document management, which was extensively represented in a book coordinated by Luc Trouche and colleagues (Baron et al. 2007). In this field the consequences of the use of digital resources was at that time a major issue. Researchers of this field introduced a distinction between resource and document. "The notion of resource is used as resource to design documents…. The document bears an intention depending of the context of use" (Crozat 2007, p.260). This distinction is linked with the study of digital resources. Pédauque (2006, 2007) stressed that with the digital means, each reading was not only associated with re-interpreting, but even possibly led to re-writing, hence producing something different from the initial resources. For Pédauque, a document is "a contract between humans" (Pédauque 2006 p.12). The intentions, in the documents, can be interpreted as possible aims and hence as components of schemes.

Another important source was the theory of communities of practice (Wenger 1998) which was inspired from the beginning of the work on teacher collaboration within DAD. A community of practice in a group is characterized by a shared objective, a shared commitment and a shared repertoire. This repertoire can be considered as a set of resources shared by the members of the community. Moreover, Wenger emphasizes the dialectical link between participation (in the common practice) and reification (design of new resources in the repertoire). A community of practice always designs resources, whatever its common project is. This link between the collective practice (or activity) and the resources used and produced by this activity coincided with some of the observations made about collective work in the case of the SFODEM (Guin and Trouche 2005).

While our sources, except for Wenger, were mostly French, an international opening came from the work of Ruthven, presented as a plenary conference at the CERME5 congress in 2005 (Ruthven 2007). The frame of the structuring features of the classroom practice (SFCP), presented at this conference, comprised five components: working environment, resource system, activity format, curriculum script and time economy. Several of these features appeared as linked with the instrumental approach: the idea of resource system, connected with instrument systems, but also the curriculum script. This concept was indeed defined by Ruthven as "a loosely ordered model of relevant goals and actions which serves to guide [the teacher's] teaching of the topic" (Ruthven 2007, p.61). In this definition, the goal suggests a possible connection with schemes. The curriculum script could be interpreted as a set of schemes developed by the teacher. The interested reader can find in Chap. 3 of this book a presentation of the SFCP frame, its origins, its evolutions and its links with DAD, in particular concerning the concept of resource system.

Along these concepts, the CERME5 plenary by Ruthven also played another central role in the early stage of DAD. In this plenary indeed, Ruthven referred to the development of new conceptualizations of how teachers use curriculum material and in particular to the work of Janine Remillard (2005). The field of research on curriculum material was not known in France at that time; it became very influential in the development of DAD. The perspective developed by Remillard was indeed very close from the instrumental approach, considering that teachers shape and are shaped by the curriculum material they use. It confirmed for us the relevance of an extension of the instrumental approach (as it was used in mathematics education research), to encompass not only educational technologies but also all the kinds of resources used by the teachers.

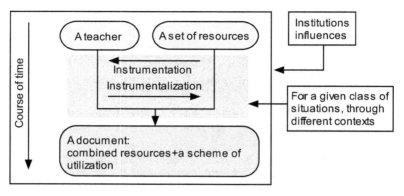

Fig. 2.2 A documentational genesis

2.2.3 The Early Version of DAD

In the summer school course on DAD, where the first version of the theory was presented, finally a single question was studied, corresponding to the aim of theoretical development:

"Which concepts are needed to analyse the activity and professional development of secondary school mathematics teachers?"

Along the theoretical work, drawing on the sources presented above, we also used empirical data. We met nine secondary school teachers for interviews at their homes where their documentation work took place. We asked them about their documentation work, about its evolutions (during the last 10 years) and its expected evolutions (during the next 10 years). This methodology was clearly limited and in particular did not include observations in class. Nevertheless the empirical data usefully complemented the theoretical work.

We presented in Gueudet and Trouche (2009a) a first version of DAD. It already introduced the notions of documentation work, resources, documents (defined as a set of recombined resources and a scheme of use of these resources) and documentational genesis (defined as the process of development of a document, Fig. 2.2).

The methods we used only allowed us to formulate hypotheses on possible schemes (since we only relied on teachers' declarations). For example, Benoîte declared that with her Grade 6 class, she started every course by 10 min of mental calculation. She used these slides that she found online on the Sésamath[1] website. We considered that Benoîte developed a document, with the aim to "practice mental calculation". This document comprised the original resources (slides), modified by Benoîte who introduced her own calculations; a rule of action: "I start every course with ten minutes of mental calculation using a slideshow" and operational invariants. "Mental calculation" is a concept-in-action; "the Grade 6 students need to practice every day mental calculation" is a theorem-in-action.

---

[1] http://www.sesamath.net/

The course considered individual documentation work, but also documentation work in communities of practice, drawing, for example, on the case of the SFODEM mentioned above (Guin and Trouche 2005). It also introduced document systems, defined as "the system of all documents developed by the teacher", structured by the situation classes (sets of situations with the same aim of the activity) and activity families (sets of situation classes with the same type of aim). The resource systems were at that time defined as the "resource part" of the document systems.

We made in this course some first attempts to investigate the structure of document systems. We suggested that teachers' work was organized according to three activity families:

1. Design and organize the teaching.
2. Participate in the school's organization.
3. Reflect on his/her practice.

We also formulated a hypothesis, concerning the existence of "pivotal documents", defined as documents that:

- Have a central place in the document system.
- Contribute to articulate other documents.
- Play a privileged role on the time axis, concentrate the memory of previous resources and intervene for the integration of new resources.

Moreover, we hypothesized that one of these pivotal documents was central, articulating the other documents and playing a role of integration and memory of new resources. We called it "le recueil" in French, which can be translated in English as "the compendium".

As we will see in the next sections, these first attempts to investigate the structure of the document systems were not satisfactory. They have been followed by other propositions, and the issue of the structure of document system and resource system remains unresolved.

2.3   Theoretical and Methodological Developments (2008–2010)

From 2008 to 2010, starting from the first version, we deepened the work on DAD (Gueudet and Trouche 2008, Gueudet and Trouche 2009b, Gueudet and Trouche 2010). Probably the most important evolutions concerned the methods, with the introduction of the reflective investigation method (Sect. 2.3.2), but the sources and the theory also evolved.

2.3.1 Evolutions of the Sources

At the very beginning of 2008, we found out the work by Jill Adler (2000) and her proposed conceptualization of resources for teachers. It became, and remained, a major source for DAD. Jill Adler proposes indeed to focus on resources-in-use. According to her, "it is possible to think about resource as the verb re-source, to source again or differently" (Adler 2000, p. 207). This perspective invites to consider material, but also sociocultural and human resources. This definition of resource was especially relevant to DAD. Indeed, instead of focusing on some digital artefacts (the instrumental approach would be enough for this), our aim was to consider all the resources intervening in the teacher's activity. Hence the definition proposed by Adler became the definition of resource retained by DAD, with some modifications/differences. We did not indeed consider human resources as such. While networks and collective works are central in DAD, we do not consider humans themselves as resources. The resource is for us a discussion with a colleague, in presence or by e-mail, a student's production or even a puzzled expression on the face of a student.

Gueudet and Trouche (2010) had a collective book in French which accounts for all these sources. It starts with a translation in French of Adler's (2000) paper on resources. It also contains a chapter by Ruthven (2010) and by Remillard (2010) (translations in French of original papers). The French sources are also present; in particular the field of document management is represented by a chapter by Bachimont (2010): *Digital Medium for Knowledge: Between Materialization and Interpretation.* Moreover this book intended to gather a variety of works from the French community of mathematics education research, directly addressing the issue of teachers' resources (e.g. Margolinas and Wozniak 2010) or relevant to it (e.g. Chevallard and Cirade 2010 and Sensevy 2010).

One direction of our theoretical work at that time was also to better situate DAD within the landscape of French theories in mathematics education (these links are summarized in Gueudet and Trouche 2008; see also Chap. 5 by Artigue in this volume). The Anthropological Theory of the Didactics (ATD, Chevallard 2006) has been presented from the beginning as a reference used by DAD: the work of the teacher is indeed situated within institutions, which clearly influence the available resources and their use. In Gueudet and Trouche (2008), we developed it further by using the concept of didactical moments to refine the structure of the documents systems (see Sect. 2.3.3 below). The link with the theory of didactical situations (Brousseau 1998) has been explained in Gueudet and Trouche (2008) by saying that the set of all the resources available for the teacher can be considered as the *milieu* of the teacher. Moreover, DAD is linked with the Joint Action Theory in Didactics (JATD, Sensevy 2012), since it considers the students' productions and utterances as central resources for the teacher, acknowledging a joint action of the teacher and the students in class but also out of class. For example JATD has extensively studied the design of lessons by groups associating teachers and researchers and has evidenced that students' productions can be essential resources in this design process

2 Studying Teachers' Documentation Work: Emergence of a Theoretical Approach

(Sensevy 2012). The same processes could be studied by DAD – but the focus would be on the documents developed by teachers, producing different research results.

2.3.2 Evolution of the Methods: Introducing the Reflective Investigation

The interviews used in the early stages of development of the approach were clearly not sufficient to obtain results in terms of documentational geneses. The elements of schemes are not all conscious; hence, the declarations of the teachers have to be confronted with the observation of their actual activity. These statements led us to the development of a specific method, which we called *the reflective investigation method*. The data collection with this method follows four principles:

– The teacher is actively involved in the collection of resources in a reflective stance.
– The activity of the teacher is observed in class and out of class.
– The resources used and produced by the teacher are collected.
– The follow-up is organized over a "long" period of time, in order to observe stabilities and evolutions.

These principles can lead to different kinds of data collection. Figure 2.3 presents one example (extracted from Gueudet et al. 2012a, p. 29).

In this case, the follow-up was organized during 3 weeks – with the intention to follow the same chapter the following year. The researcher first encountered the teacher to present the data collection organization. A first visit was organized at the teacher's home. Indeed at that stage the work still only concerned the secondary school teachers in France, who prepare their courses at home. During this visit, the teacher is interviewed about his/her resources in general and about a specific chapter

First encounter:	First visit:	Second visit:	Classroom observation	Third visit:
- presentation of the methodology, its spirit and its tools	- about the resources in general; - about the chapter followed.	- about the lesson observed.		- About the lesson observed; - Complements about the chapter and resources.
Tools:	Tools:	Tools:	Tools:	Tools:
- Schedule; - Questionnaire; - Logbook.	- Interview guidelines; - SRRS	- Interview guidelines	- Observation guidelines	- Interview guidelines; - SRRS; - Collection of resources
Week 1		Week 2		Week 3
Filling the logbook				

Fig. 2.3 Data collection following the reflective investigation principles

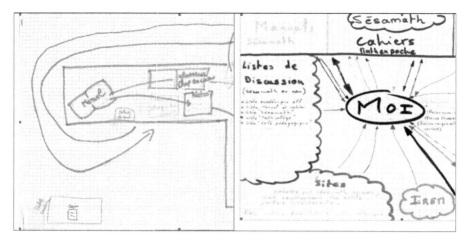

Fig. 2.4 Examples of schematic representations of the resource system by two lower secondary school mathematics teachers. On the left, Corinne; on the right, Pierre

and a lesson in this chapter. The lesson in class was observed and video-recorded and then discussed during a new interview. Two specific data collection tools were used during this follow-up. Firstly, the teacher noted in a logbook all his/her activity, the resources he/she used, with whom he/she worked, etc. Secondly, the teacher was asked to produce a schematic representation of his/her resource system (SRRS, see Fig. 2.4). This representation was progressively produced during the 3 weeks.

The reflective investigation method can also take other forms, as long as it follows the four principles presented above; we will discuss some of its evolutions in Part III. It is naturally associated with case studies. For a single teacher, or group of teachers, it provides an important quantity of data. The different kinds of data have to be confronted and discussed with the teacher. In particular, the classroom observations and the resources used and produced are confronted with the teachers' declarations, in order to infer operational invariants. Indeed the operational invariants are propositions considered as true (theorems-in-action) or concepts considered as relevant (concepts-in-action) which guide the teacher activity. This link between the convictions expressed by the teachers and their actual activity is thus central.

2.3.3 Evolutions of the Theory

Using the reflective investigation method, during this period, our aim was to study the documentation work of teachers, hence to answer questions like:

- Which are the documents developed by secondary school mathematics teachers along their professional activity?

2 Studying Teachers' Documentation Work: Emergence of a Theoretical Approach 27

- How do the schemes of use of resources evolve; which are the operational invariants in such schemes?
- Which are the consequences for the documents developed by mathematics teachers of the generalized availability of digital resources?
- How are the resources systems and the document systems of an individual teacher structured?
- How does the resources system of a community evolve, along individual and collective contributions?

While our central aim was to use DAD in order to understand the transactions between teachers and resources, and their consequences in terms of professional development, studying these questions also led us to further theoretical attempts.

Concerning the structure of the documentation system, we were still trying to elucidate the relevant activity families for the teacher. Instead of three families (see Sect. 2.2.3 above), we suggested that the teachers' activity was structured by nine activity families:

1. Reflecting on his/her practice.
2. Planning.
3. Preparing and setting up introductory activities.
4. Preparing and setting up syntheses.
5. Preparing and setting up drill and practice.
6. Preparing and setting up assessment.
7. Manage the class and follow the students.
8. Participate to the school life.
9. Participate to collective work out of class.

The activity families numbered from 3 to 7 came from the work of Chevallard (2002) who introduced the notion of didactic moments. These nine activity families were coherent with our case studies. Nevertheless, they have not been used since by other authors or even by ourselves in recent works.

We also replaced the notion of "pivotal document", proposing to use instead "pivotal resources", defined as resources engaged in several activity families. Indeed, it appeared clearly in our case studies that a given resource could be used by the teachers for different aims, corresponding to different activity families. In particular the textbook was used by several teachers for "preparing and setting up introductory activities" and for "preparing and setting up drill and practice", sometimes also for "planning". This resource led to the development of a different document for each different aim. Indeed a single document cannot correspond to several activity families, since an activity family is defined by an aim, and this aim is one of the components of the scheme, hence of the document. Thus the concept of "pivotal resource" is more relevant; it has been used in several works after its introduction.

Another aspect to be retained from this period is that some authors very early appropriated the terms of the documentational approach and introduced personal theoretical constructs. In particular, Sánchez (2010) introduced the concept of "documentational orchestration" as a natural extension of instrumental orchestra-tion, for the study of teacher education programs.

2.4 Extension of the Scope and New Contributions (2011–2013)

The determining collaboration with Birgit Pepin started in 2011; once again thanks to Kenneth Ruthven who introduced us to Birgit Pepin and to her work on text-books. We first worked together on the book *Lived Resources* (Gueudet et al. 2012a). Far from being a translation of the French book "Ressources vives" (Gueudet and Trouche 2010), this work constituted a determining step in the insertion of DAD within a landscape of international works. While 12 of the 18 chapters in the French book were written by French authors, the book in English comprised only 5 chapters from French authors (for a total of 17 chapters). New authors have been involved, coming from various countries from Europe (Germany, Norway, the Netherlands) and outside Europe (Canada, Mexico, Australia, USA). Soon after this book, we edited together a special issue of ZDM entitled "Resourcing Teacher Work and Interaction: New Perspectives on Resources Design, Use, and Teacher Collaboration" (Pepin et al. 2013), associating again new authors. More generally, this 2011–2013 period was a period of extension: of the international links, but also of the issues studied with the approach, of the school levels considered and even of the disciplines, with the first works using the approach outside of mathematics (in chemistry, with the PhD of Hammoud 2012).

2.4.1 New Issues Studied and Extension of the Scope

2.4.1.1 From the Study of Teacher Education Programs to Perspectives on Collective Design

An important issue studied during this period concerned professional development programs for in-service teachers (it was already present in the work of other researchers, like Sánchez 2010, but new in our work). The ministry of education in France opened indeed at that time a national platform called "Pairform@nce". This platform offered "training paths", which are structured sets of resources for the organization of blended teacher education courses. The ministry wanted researchers to be associated with this innovative project: for designing training paths and for assessing their use by teacher educators and by trainees.

Fig. 2.5 First page of the training path "Using online exercises to individualize teaching"

This context opened for us different new research directions. The first one concerned the kind of teacher in-service education programs likely to lead to evolutions in the teachers' practice. DAD suggested that collective documentation work was likely to contribute to professional development. This guided our choices for the training paths and for the associated teacher education programs (Fig. 2.5).

Studying these teacher education programs permitted to confirm the relevance of this hypothesis. We observed indeed a rich collective documentation work by teams of trainees, and changes in their classroom practices, linked with the professional development aims of the training path (Gueudet and Trouche 2011). A second direction was the study of the documentation work of teacher educators. Indeed the training paths can be considered as resources for the teacher educators who decided to use it for setting up their own training. We organized an experiment where two teams of "training path" designers became teacher educators using the path designed by another team. We observed this way documentational geneses of the teacher educators (Gueudet et al. 2012b). We also incorporated the improvements suggested by the users in a new version of the training paths. Beyond teacher education issues, this work led us to a new and more general research direction: the design of curriculum resources, in particular collective design. According to DAD, this design is linked with the documentation work and its outcomes. It is a continuous process, incorporating the contribution of users (e.g. teachers or teacher educators) in "living resources". First developments of this perspective on design can be found, for example, in Pepin et al. (2013); it is still central in our present work (see Chaps. 6 and 13 for more details about teacher design).

2.4.1.2 Documentation Work at Kindergarten and Primary School

The design of curriculum resources became also central in another research project, called "TREMA-1" for Technologies and Resources in Mathematics at primary school. In this project primary school teachers, teacher educators and researchers worked together to study the use of technologies at primary school and at the same time to design teaching resources. The research question guiding the beginning of the project was "Which are the factors shaping the integration or non-integration of technologies by primary school teachers in their mathematics teaching practices?" We studied this question in terms of integration of technologies in the resource system of the primary school teachers (Poisard et al. 2011) and documents developed by the teachers incorporating technologies. Following the reflective investigation methodology, we identified documents developed by the teachers and in particular operational invariants. Some new operational invariants were developed; the already existing operational invariants played a central role for the integration of a new resource. The compatibility with other resources already present in the teacher's resources system was also an important factor. These results guided a further stage of the work within this project: the design of curriculum resources supporting the integration of technologies by primary school teachers. This work on design issues was only initiated at this stage; in fact it is still a major issue in 2018 as I will discuss it in the next sections.

I want to emphasize here another aspect of this project: it led us indeed to investigate for the first time the documentation work of primary school teachers. We observed important differences, compared with secondary school mathematics teachers. In France the primary school teachers mostly work in the schools, while the secondary school teachers prepare their lessons at home. Hence the resources are present in the classroom. The kind of resources used is also different: manipulatives are very important resources (in particular at kindergarten; see e.g. Besnier (2016)). Moreover primary school teachers in France teach all the subjects: mathematics, but also French, science, sports, arts, etc. It means that their document system and resource system concern all these subjects, which makes even more complex the issue of the document system structure. We considered that these teachers develop a subsystem of documents for their teaching of mathematics. Nevertheless some resources are clearly used for different subjects, for example, to make syntheses at the end of a work in groups (much more frequent at primary school). Hence the structure of the resources system, in the case of primary school teachers, is especially complex.

2.4.1.3 Documentation Work at University

This period also marked the beginning of works concerning the documentation work of university teachers (Gueudet 2013). Here the complexity does not come from the teaching of several subjects, but from the links between teaching and research. Interviews with lecturers evidenced that they developed documents not only for their teaching activity but also for their research activity. This suggests a new development of the approach: it can be used for different aims of the professional activity.

Lecturers have a document system for teaching and a document system for research. The links between both systems are complex. Moreover we observed that, in a context where lecturers do not receive any teacher education (for most countries), the participation in communities engaged in a collective documentation work plays a central role for professional development. For this reason, the teaching practices at university are probably even more stable than the practices at secondary school, for example. At secondary school, changes in the curriculum and in teaching approaches can be supported by in-service or preservice teacher education. At university, beginning teachers, in an instrumentation movement, develop operational invariants influenced by the resources they use. These resources have been designed by their colleagues in previous years. Aligning with these resources, the beginning teachers contribute to the stability of the teaching practices (and even sometimes to the stability of the curriculum, while changes in the secondary school curriculum would require modifications). These issues require specific investigations, which are still ongoing now.

2.4.2 Evolution of the Methods and Contribution of the First PhDs

During this period, the reflective investigation method was complemented in several ways.

The first way was the introduction of what is called since "the documentation valise" (Fig. 2.6). While the metaphor of the valise was chosen at the beginning to evoke the resources gathered by the teacher for a journey, the content of the valise

▼ 📁 Vera, France, statistics, grade 8, 2013
    📄 0. Valise description.doc
▶ 📁 1. Methodology
▶ 📁 2. Context description
▶ 📁 3. Teacher background
▶ 📁 4. Teacher's general resources
▶ 📁 5. Teacher's resources related to the lesson
▶ 📁 6. Videos of the lesson cycle
▶ 📁 7. Students resources related to the lesson
▶ 📁 8. Associated research

Fig. 2.6 Example of a documentation valise, the case of Vera. (http://educmath.ens-lyon.fr/Educmath/recherche/approche_documentaire/documentation-valise/documentation-valise-1)

goes far beyond such resources. It is more a valise for the researcher, gathering all the data of a teacher's case study. This new organization of the data was linked with the intention of sharing data with other researchers. Indeed the data collection with the reflective investigation method is a long process. Gathering many cases is an important aim, to observe regularities across cases and to allow comparisons (e.g. international comparisons). This can only be achieved by researchers working together and sharing their data. This project had new developments and produced important results in recent years (see Chap. 13 by Luc Trouche).

Other methodological developments have been proposed in the two first PhDs defended using the documentational approach: Aldon (2011) and Sabra (2011). Aldon studied communities of teachers and researchers designing resources to support the integration of technologies by secondary school mathematics teachers. He introduced the notion of "incident", defined as an unplanned event. He used it as a methodological tool: indeed when such an incident happened in class (linked in his study with the use of technology), the teacher had to draw on his/her professional knowledge to react on the spot (this could be connected with the aspect of instrumental orchestrations described by Drijvers et al. (2010) as on-the-spot decisions, part of the didactical performance). The circumstance made the knowledge more visible.

Sabra also used the notion of documentational incident. His work addressed especially collective documentation work, in the context of the French association Sésamath whose members produce free online resources, including e-textbooks. For this purpose Sabra introduced new methodological tools, in particular a collective logbook for the community of textbook authors. Comparing the collective logbook and the individual logbooks can reveal tensions in the collective work or at least differences in the interpretations of the teachers. This work by Sabra has been the source for many future works concerning the documentation work in communities of practice. Indeed Sésamath remains a unique case in France and probably at an international level: a community of teachers that produced digital resources, including e-textbooks and a complete virtual learning environment (LaboMEP) covering the whole secondary school curriculum and widely used by teachers. While the documentation work of teachers using Sésamath resources has been researched with DAD from the beginning, the work by Sabra was the first one studying the design processes in communities of Sésamath authors.

These two early PhDs contributed to the development of methods for the identification of documents developed by teachers, individually or collectively.

2.5 Recent Works (2014 and After)

I will only mention here some recent works using the documentational approach and evoke related evolutions of the theory. A more complete account can be found in Chap. 13. I focus on the evolutions brought by a French national project: REVEA. I firstly present the REVEA project and then describe methodological developments and theoretical evolutions resulting from works linked with this project.

2.5.1 Living Resources for Teaching and Learning (REVEA): A National Project in France

"Living resources for teaching and learning" was a national project in France (financed by the National Research Agency, ANR) involving five different research teams and piloted by Eric Bruillard. It took place between April 2014 and March 2018. The aim of this project was to investigate the documentation work of secondary school teachers and its consequences for four subjects: English, mathematics, science and technology. The use of digital resources and its consequences received a specific attention.

The comparison of different subjects within the project evidenced that, even if the development of documents is an individual process, there are some regularities across teachers of the same subject. These regularities can naturally concern the kind of resources used: English teachers use more videos than mathematics teachers; in mathematics the textbook is central, but not in technology, etc. But other kinds of regularities exist: the alignment, or not, with the official curriculum and the more or less important involvement in collective work, for example. Concerning the use of digital resources, according to the subject-specific software can be more or less used. Nevertheless all the teachers followed in the project declare that they spend more time (now, compared with 5 years before) searching for online resources. In the different secondary schools followed in the project, we observed the use of digital means to share resources with colleagues. Nevertheless this use does not seem to be stable yet: sometimes a group of colleagues only uses e-mail, sometimes they share a folder in the school virtual learning environment (or another institutional platform) and sometimes they use Google Drive, etc. We even observed in some groups of colleagues working together that some members of the group were not aware of the existence of a shared folder.

The REVEA project also examined the collective work of groups of teachers working out of schools with an objective of resources design. Drawing on the work of Sabra concerning the Sésamath association (2011), it studied the "life" of communities of practice designing resources, including three different communities concerning mathematics. Studying these communities led in particular to observe specific features of their resource systems. These systems comprised indeed meta-resources: resources whose aim is to support the design in the community. They also included pivotal resources, which articulate different other resources designed with different aims (Trouche et al. 2018a). More details on the theoretical and methodological developments linked with collective documentation work can be found in Chap. 13.

The REVEA project also evidenced the need to combine studies of the documentation work at different scales: from processes developing on several years and concerning groups of teachers to evolutions of schemes of a single teacher, during a few weeks. We will illustrate this reflection on macro-scale/micro-scale studies in the next sections, concerning, respectively, methodology and theory.

2.5.2 Methodological Developments

The REVEA project also opened opportunities for several methodological developments. We present here two of them, chosen to illustrate the different time scales that the documentational approach has to take into account.

Investigating schemes and, in particular, operational invariants (Vergnaud 1998) is a complex issue. As coined by Vergnaud, only a minor part of operational invariants corresponds to explicit knowledge. Some of them are not conscious. Thus, it is impossible to reach them only by asking the teacher: "Why did you act this way?". Most of the time the answer to this question is not accessible to the teacher.

For this reason, after gathering all the data mentioned above with the reflective investigation method, the researcher(s) builds from them a "documents table" (Table 2.1; see, e.g. Gruson et al. (2018)). This table comprises elements of the document: the goal of the activity, the resources used, the rules of action and potentially corresponding operational invariants. The goal and operational invariants are inferred from the declarations of the teacher in the interviews. The resources used and the rules of action are observed in the activity.

This table is then submitted to the teacher who complements or corrects if necessary. The "documents tables" are efficient methodological tools to support the identification of the documents developed by the teachers. For example, using Table 2.1, we can claim that Valeria has developed a document, for the aim: "prepare and implement the stabilization of previous knowledge" (at least with her Grade 10 students). The document comprises online exercises chosen on LaboMEP (a virtual learning environment designed by the Sésamath association), rules of action (e.g. "Before starting a new chapter, I assess the students previous knowledge with online exercises"; "I propose online exercises for the students who do not master the

Table 2.1 Example of a "documents table" in the case of Valeria (Gruson et al. 2018)

Goal of the activity: Prepare and implement	Resources used	Rules of action	Operational invariants
Stabilization of previous knowledge	"LaboMEP" (online exercises)	Valeria chooses exercises in LaboMEP to test whether the students master previous knowledge and to supplement if necessary	"Some of the grade 10 students need to practice on grade 9 knowledge"

2 Studying Teachers' Documentation Work: Emergence of a Theoretical Approach

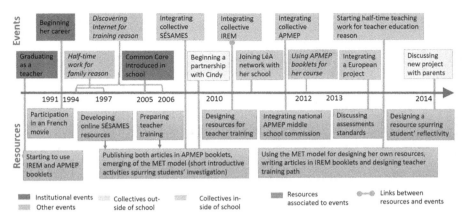

Fig. 2.7 Example of reflective mapping of documentational trajectory. (Rocha 2018)

previous knowledge") and an operational invariant (e.g. "Some of the Grade 10 students need to practice on Grade 9 knowledge").

At a completely different time scale, Rocha (2018) introduces the notion of "documentational experience" (defined as the accumulation of documentation work along the years) and "documentational trajectory" (defined as the set of collective and individual events that took place along this experience). It led her to propose a new methodological tool: Reflective Mapping of Documentational Trajectory (RMDT). It is a new kind of representation produced by the teacher during a reflective interview, concerning his/her experience since the beginning of his/her career (Fig. 2.7).

It permits to identify crucial events, important collaborations, etc., still influential in the teacher's work, even many years after their end.

2.5.3 E-Textbooks and Theoretical Evolutions

The REVEA project concerned all kinds of teachers' resources. For mathematics teachers, it confirmed the importance of textbooks in their resources systems. In France, secondary school teachers use between four and eight different textbooks to search for "introductory activities", to build the organization of the mathematical content over the year (their "yearly progression"). One of them is the classroom textbook, shared with the students. It is mainly used to give exercises: homework or work in class. Nowadays, a pdf version of each textbook is provided to the teacher with the textbook on paper. The teachers use this pdf version for projection in class: even if a student has forgotten his/her textbook, he/she can read the text of the exercise. Moreover, some publishers developed e-textbooks: private publishers and the Sésamath association (studied by Sabra in his PhD, 2011). The e-textbooks from private publishers are still quite expensive, hence not much used. The Sésamath

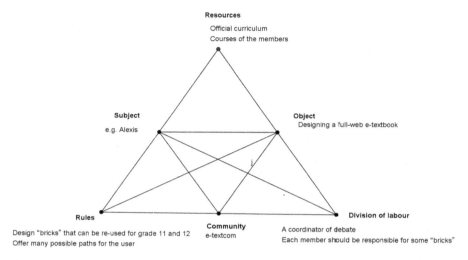

Fig. 2.8 The activity system of an author of the Sésamath e-textbook

e-textbook is free, associated with a complete environment called LaboMEP, and used by many teachers.

Within the REVEA project, we worked on e-textbooks, in particular the Sésamath e-textbook. It led us to propose specific theoretical constructions and articulations.

Firstly we investigated the design of the Sésamath e-textbook. It involved a community of practice of authors, coordinators and developers. We consider this design as a collective documentation work. Its development during several years led us to use the Cultural-Historical Activity Theory (CHAT, Engeström 2001) and to combine it with DAD. In Gueudet and Lebaud (2016), we proposed to associate two scales, to investigate the activity of the e-textbook designers (Fig. 2.8).

The macro-scale considers the evolution of the different components of the activity system, resulting from tensions between different aspects of this system. The micro-scale refers to DAD and studies the development of documents by some of the community members. We focus on documents concerning particular mathematical topics; for this reason we refer to this aspect as "micro".

After this study of the design of the Sésamath e-textbook, we worked more generally on the features of e-textbooks (including the Sésamath e-textbook). It led us to introduce the concept of "connectivity" (drawing in particular on "connectivism" (Siemens 2005)). An e-textbook is a structured set of resources; many possibilities for building links exist within such a textbook and with its environment. We defined connectivity (in Gueudet et al. 2018) as "connecting potential [of an e-textbook] for a given user (student or teacher) both practically as well as cognitively". We distinguished again a macro- and a micro-level for the analysis of an e-textbook connectivity:

- The macro-level takes into account the potential connections "outside" of the e-textbook (connections with other online resources, but also connections with the user's resources system).
- The micro-level considers connections within the textbook, for a given mathematical theme (connections between representations, between different aspects of a given concepts, etc.).

We designed an analysis grid for e-textbooks using these two categories. We argued that this grid was helpful to characterize different kinds of e-textbooks.

Linking DAD and the study of particular resources can seem surprising: DAD is originally devoted to the study of the teacher's work. The criteria we used for defining the connectivity of e-textbooks incorporate the DAD perspective for the macro-level. Indeed, this macro-level includes the possibilities of connections between the e-textbook and the user's resource system (e.g. possibility for the user to download extracts of the book). Thus it takes into account the potential of the e-textbook for the documentation work of the user.

Naturally the period starting in 2014 has seen many other research works referring to DAD that also contributed to the evolution of the questions, methods and theory: the reader of this book has many opportunities to observe it in other chapters.

2.6 Conclusions: Towards Solid Findings in DAD?

In this chapter I have tried to synthesize the short history of the documentational approach. I did not present a literature review; I have not taken a scientific stance; I have only described my point of view on this history. The previous sections evidence many evolutions: in the theory, in the methods, in the questions studied and in the scope of the approach. In this conclusion I present what I consider to be the most striking evolutions and perspectives (for a more complete discussion on perspectives, see Chap. 13).

Firstly, I will look at the theoretical evolutions through the lens of "solid findings". The concept of solid findings in mathematics education has been introduced by the European Mathematical Society educational committee in 2011 (EMS 2011) and defined as findings that (EMS 2011, p. 46):

1. "Result from trustworthy, disciplined inquiry, thus being sound and convincing in shedding light on the question(s) they set out to answer;
2. Are generally recognized as important contributions that have significantly influenced and/or may significantly influence the research field;
3. Can be applied to circumstances and/or domains beyond those involved in this particular research;
4. Can be summarized in a brief and comprehensible way to an interested but critical audience of non-specialists (especially mathematicians and mathematics teachers)".

I will mainly use criteria 2 and 3 and consider as solid the concepts that have been used since by other colleagues and that have been applied to other contexts (meaning here, not only applied to secondary school mathematics teachers).

The notions of resources, documentation work (individual or collective), documentational genesis and document seem now to be "solid concepts", since they are used by a large international community of researchers, in mathematics education and beyond. Moreover, people using these concepts share the same definitions.

While the notions of *resource system* and *documents system* are also used by several researchers (in particular, asking teachers to draw a SRRS relies on the assumption of a shared meaning for the term resource system, at least in this context), I argue that these concepts cannot yet be considered as solid. Concerning resource systems, a new definition has been introduced recently: "We call the set formed by all the resources used by the teacher his/her *resource system*" (Trouche et al. 2018b). With this perspective, the resource system can be considered independently of the document system. The consequences of the change of perspective still need to be investigated. Chapter 3 of this book contributes to this investigation, by identifying different possible meanings of the concept of resource system. Concerning document systems, I have described several attempts to approach their structure: first with three activity families (Gueudet and Trouche 2009a) and then with nine such families (Gueudet and Trouche 2010). These two propositions have never been used by other authors afterwards. This is directly linked with the complexity of the issue of resource system and document system structure. Only the concept of "pivotal resource", as resource used for several activity families, seems to start becoming more stable and shared, while "pivotal document" has disappeared from recent papers.

More generally, in recent publications referring to DAD, I observe that the concept of "resource" appears much more frequently than the concept of "document" (the conference in 2018 was entitled "Re(s)sources 2018", which is probably also significant about this matter). This can be linked with the methodological complexity for the identification of schemes. This evolution should not obscure two important issues. The move towards a focus on resources should not be limited to material resources, easier to observe. Evidencing that resources are not only material is a major contribution of DAD, coming from the work of Adler (2000). Moreover another major contribution from DAD is to offer theoretical tools to link teachers' use of resources with their professional growth. The already existing schemes and operational invariants of a teacher shape his or her use of resources. The work with resources leads to the development of new schemes. Thus it is essential to continue to investigate documents (which means not only resources but also schemes).

The theoretical evolutions also concern theoretical connections, whose development appeared in this chapter. The original connections with the instrumental approach (Rabardel 1995), with the communities of practice (Wenger 1998), with ATD (Chevallard 2006), etc., naturally remain. New connections have been developed; I have presented here connections with activity theory (Engeström 2001); other links are central in recent works, for example, with teacher design capacity (Pepin et al. 2017; see also Chap. 6 of this book) or curriculum ergonomics (Choppin et al. 2018). Chapter 5 of this book provides a frame to study this theoretical networking and opens the path for a reflection on these theoretical links, which is also a promising direction for future research.

Concerning the methods, in the recent evolutions I retain the apparent need to take into account a combination of different scales. These scales can concern the mathematical content (from a precise theme to a whole year for a given class) or the periods of time (from a few weeks to the whole career of the teachers). Some studies have also started to use quantitative methods, about the use of particular resources, for example (e.g. see Gueudet and Lebaud (2016) about the choice and use of the textbook). Combining quantitative methods with case studies could also bring new results about teachers' documentation work and its evolution.

Concerning the scope of DAD, I consider that its expansion is one of the most striking evolutions during these last years. While we started by a work limited to experienced secondary school mathematics teachers, DAD is now used from kindergarten to university and in-service teacher education and for several subjects: chemistry, physics, biology and language education. Researchers still investigate the documentational geneses of experienced teachers, but also of preservice and novice teachers, of teacher educators and recently even of students (at university; see Gueudet and Pepin 2018). The proceedings of the Re(s)sources 2018 conference (Gitirana et al. 2018) and Chaps. 9, 10, 11 and 12 (Part III of this book) provide abundant evidence of this expansion.

Maintaining and extending collectively the reflection initiated in this chapter (and in the other chapters of Part I) could be useful in this context of expansion. It could contribute to a coherent development of the manifold research works and to the production of more solid findings concerning teachers' documentation work.

References

Adler, J. (2000). Conceptualising resources as a theme for teacher education. *Journal of Mathematics Teacher Education, 3*, 205–224.

Aldon, G., (2011). *Interactions didactiques dans la classe de mathématiques en environnement numérique: construction et mise à l'épreuve d'un cadre d'analyse exploitant la notion d'incident.* PhD. Lyon, France: Université Lyon 1, https://tel.archives-ouvertes.fr/tel-00679121v2/document

Bachimont, B. (2010). Le numérique comme support de la connaissance: entre matérialisation et interprétation. In G. Gueudet & L. Trouche (Eds.), *Ressources vives. Le travail documentaire des professeurs en mathématiques* (pp. 75–90). Rennes/Lyon: Presses Universitaires de Rennes et INRP.

Baron, M., Guin, D., & Trouche, L. (dir.) (2007). *Environnements informatisés et ressources numériques pour l'apprentissage: conception et usages, regards croisés.* Paris: Hermès.

Besnier, S. (2016). Usages de ressources technologiques pour l'enseignement du nombre à l'école maternelle et développement professionnel des professeurs, *Adjectif.net.* Retreived on February 2019 at http://www.adjectif.net/spip/spip.php?article415

Brousseau, G. (1998). *Théorie des situations didactiques.* Grenoble: La pensée sauvage.

Bueno-Ravel, L., & Gueudet, G. (2007). Online resources in mathematics: Teachers' genesis of use. In D. Pitta-Pantazi & G. Philippou (Eds.), *Proceedings of the fifth congress of the European*

Society for Research in mathematics education (pp. 1369–1378). University of Cyprus and ERME: Larnaca.

Cazes, C., Gueudet, G., Hersant, M., & Vandebrouck, F. (2007). Using e-exercise bases in mathematics: Case studies at university. *International Journal of Computers for Mathematical Learning, 11*(3), 327–350.

Cecconi, S. (2007). *Site personnel du dessinateur Serge Cecconi* (IREM de Grenoble) http://perso. orange.fr/serge.cecconi/cariboost2/index.html.

Chevallard, Y. (2002). Ecologie et régulation. In J.-L. Dorier, M. Artaud, M. Artigue, R. Berthelot, & R. Floris (dir.), *Actes de la XIème Ecole d'été de didactique des mathématiques, Corps* (pp. 41–56). Grenoble: La Pensée Sauvage.

Chevallard, Y. (2006). Steps towards a new epistemology in mathematics education. In M. Bosch (Ed.), *Proceedings of the fourth congress of the European society for research in mathematics education* (pp. 21–30). Barcelona: FUNDEMI-1QS and ERME.

Chevallard, Y., & Cirade, G. (2010). Les ressources manquantes comme problème professionnel. In G. Gueudet & L. Trouche (Eds.), *Ressources vives. Le travail documentaire des professeurs en mathématiques* (pp. 41–56). Rennes/Lyon, Presses Universitaires de Rennes et INRP.

Choppin, J., Roth McDuffie, A., Drake, C., & Davis, J. (2018). Curriculum ergonomics: Conceptualizing the interactions between curriculum design and use. *International Journal of Educational Research, 92*, 75–85. Retrieved on February 2019 at https://doi.org/10.1016/j. ijer.2018.09.015.

Crozat, S. (2007). Bonnes pratiques pour l'exploitation multi-usages de contenus pédagogiques: la raison du calcul est toujours la meilleure. In M. Baron, D. Guin, & L. Trouche (dir.), *Environnements informatisés et ressources numériques pour l'apprentissage: conception et usages, regards croisés* (pp. 255–286). Paris: Hermès.

Drijvers, P., Doorman, M., Boon, P., Reed, H., & Gravemeijer, K. (2010). The teacher and the tool: Instrumental orchestrations in the technology-rich mathematics classroom. *Educational Studies in Mathematics, 75*(2), 213–234.

Education Committee of the EMS. (2011). "Solid findings" in mathematics education. *Newsletter of the European Mathematical Society, 81*, 46–48.

Engeström, Y. (2001). Expansive learning at work: Toward an activity theoretical reconceptualization. *Journal of Education, 14*(1), 133–156.

Folcher, V. (2005). De la conception pour l'usage au développement de ressources pour l'activité. In P. Rabardel, & P. Pastré (dir.) *Modèles du sujet pour la conception* (pp. 189–210). Toulouse: Octarès.

Gitirana, V., Miyakawa, T., Rafalska, M., Soury-Lavergne, S., & Trouche, L. (2018). *Proceedings of the Re(s)sources 2018 International Conference*. Lyon: ENS de Lyon, retrieved on November 8th 2018 at https://hal.archives-ouvertes.fr/hal-01764563.

Gruson, B., Gueudet, G., Le Hénaff, C., & Lebaud, M.-P. (2018). Investigating teachers' work with digital resources. A comparison between the teaching of mathematics and English. *Revue Suisse des Sciences de l'Education, 40*(2), 485–501.

Gueudet, G. (2013). Digital resources and mathematics teacher development at university. In B. Ubuz, Ç. Haser, & M. A. Mariotti (Eds.), *Proceedings of the eighth congress of the European Society for Research in mathematics education* (pp. 2336–2345). Ankara: Middle East Technical University and ERME.

Gueudet, G., & Lebaud, M.-P. (2016). Comment les enseignants de mathématiques choisissent les manuels ? Étude sur le cas des manuels de seconde, édition 2014. *Repères IREM, 102*, 85–97.

Gueudet, G., & Pepin, B. (2018). Didactic contract at university: A focus on resources and their use. *International Journal of Research in Undergraduate Mathematics Education, 4*(1), 56–73.

Gueudet, G., & Trouche, L. (2008). Du travail documentaire des enseignants: Genèses, collectifs, communautés. *Le cas des mathématiques. Education & Didactique, 2*(3), 7–33.

Gueudet, G., & Trouche, L. (2009a). Vers de nouveaux systèmes documentaires des professeurs de mathématiques ? In I. Bloch & F. Conne (Eds.), *Nouvelles perspectives en didactique des*

2 Studying Teachers' Documentation Work: Emergence of a Theoretical Approach

mathématiques. Cours de la XIVe école d'été de didactique des mathématiques (pp. 109–133). Grenoble: La pensée sauvage.

Gueudet, G., & Trouche, L. (2009b). Towards new documentation systems for teachers. *Educational Studies in Mathematics, 71*(3), 199–218.

Gueudet, G., & Trouche, L. (Eds.). (2010). *Ressources vives. Le travail documentaire des professeurs en mathématiques*. Rennes/Lyon: Presses Universitaires de Rennes/INRP.

Gueudet, G., & Trouche, L. (2011). Mathematics teacher education advanced methods: An example in dynamic geometry. *ZDM – Mathematics Education, 43*(3), 399–411.

Gueudet, G., Pepin, B., & Trouche, L. (Eds.). (2012a). *From textbooks to 'lived' resources: Mathematics curriculum materials and teacher documentation*. New York: Springer.

Gueudet, G., Sacristan, A. I., Soury-Lavergne, S., & Trouche, L. (2012b). Online paths in mathematics teacher training: New resources and new skills for teacher educators. *ZDM – Mathematics Education, 44*(6), 717–731.

Gueudet, G., Pepin, B., Sabra, H., Restrepo, A., & Trouche, L. (2018). E-textbooks and connectivity: Proposing an analytical framework. *International Journal for Science and Mathematics Education, 16*(3), 539–558.

Guin, D., & Trouche, L. (2005). Distance training, a key mode to support teachers in the integration of ICT? In M. Bosch (Ed.), *Proceedings of the fourth European conference on research on mathematics education* (pp. 1020–1029). Barcelona: FUNDEMI IQS—Universitat Ramon Llull and ERME.

Guin, D., Ruthven, K., & Trouche, L. (Eds.). (2005). *The didactical challenge of symbolic calculators: Turning a computational device into a mathematical instrument*. New York: Springer.

Hammoud, R. (2012). *Le travail collectif des professeurs en chimie comme levier pour la mise en oeuvre de démarches d'investigation et le développement des connaissances professionnelles. Contribution au développement de l'approche documentaire du didactique*. PhD. Lyon, France: Université Lyon 1, https://tel.archives-ouvertes.fr/tel-00762964/document

Haspekian, M. (2014). Teachers' instrumental geneses when integrating spreadsheet software. In A. Clark-Wilson, O. Robutti, & N. Sinclair (Eds.), *The mathematics teacher in the digital era* (pp. 241–275). New York: Springer.

Margolinas, C., & Wozniak, F. (2010). Rôle de la documentation scolaire dans la situation du professeur: le cas de l'enseignement des mathématiques à l'école élémentaire. In G. Gueudet & L. Trouche (Eds.), *Ressources vives. Le travail documentaire des professeurs en mathématiques* (pp. 223–251). Rennes/Lyon: Presses Universitaires de Rennes et INRP.

Pédauque, R. T. (coll.) (2006). *Le document à la lumière du numérique*. Caen: C & F éditions.

Pédauque, R. T. (coll.) (2007). La redocumentarisation du monde. Toulouse: Cépaduès éditions.

Pepin, B., Gueudet, G., & Trouche, L. (Eds.). (2013). Resourcing teacher work and interaction: New perspectives on resources design, use, and teacher collaboration. *ZDM – Mathematics Education, special issue*, (7), 45.

Pepin, B., Gueudet, G., & Trouche, L. (2017). Refining teacher design capacity: Mathematics teachers' interactions with digital curriculum resources. *ZDM – Mathematics Education, 49*(5), 799–812.

Poisard, C., Bueno-Ravel, L., & Gueudet, G. (2011). Comprendre l'intégration de ressources technologiques en mathématiques par des professeurs des écoles. *Recherches en didactique des mathématiques, 31*(2), 151–189.

Rabardel, P. (1995). *Les hommes et les technologies, approche cognitive des instruments contemporains*. Paris: Armand Colin.

Rabardel, P., & Bourmaud, G. (2005). Instruments et systèmes d'instruments, in P. Rabardel, P. Pastré (dir.), *Modèles du sujet pour la conception. Dialectiques activités développement* (pp. 211–229). Toulouse: Octarès.

Remillard, J. T. (2005). Examining key concepts in research on teachers' use of mathematics curricula. *Review of Educational Research, 75*(2), 211–246.

Remillard, J. T. (2010). Modes d'engagements: comprendre les transactions des professeurs avec les ressources curriculaires en mathématiques. In G. Gueudet & L. Trouche (Eds.), *Ressources vives. Le travail documentaire des professeurs en mathématiques* (pp. 201–216). Rennes/Lyon: Presses Universitaires de Rennes et INRP.

Rocha, K. (2018). Uses of online resources and documentational trajectories: The case of Sésamath. In L. Fan, L. Trouche, S. Rezat, C. Qi, & J. Visnovska (Eds.), *Research on mathematics textbooks and teachers' resources: Advances and issues* (ICME 13 Monograph) (pp. 235–258). Cham: Springer.

Ruthven, K. (2007). Teachers, technologies and the structures of schooling, In D. Pitta-Pantazi, & G. Philippou), Proceedings of the fifth congress of the European society for research in mathematics education (pp. 52–67). Larnaca: University of Cyprus and ERME.

Ruthven, K. (2010). Constituer les outils et les supports numériques en ressources pour la classe. In G. Gueudet & L. Trouche (Eds.), *Ressources vives. Le travail documentaire des professeurs en mathématiques* (pp. 183–200). Rennes/Lyon: Presses Universitaires de Rennes et INRP.

Sabra, H. (2011). *Contribution à l'étude du travail documentaire des enseignants de mathématiques: les incidents comme révélateurs des rapports entre documentations individuelle et communautaire*. PhD. Lyon, France: Université Lyon 1, https://tel.archives-ouvertes.fr/tel-00768508/document

Sánchez, M. (2010). Orquestación documentacional: herramienta para la estructuración y el análisis del trabajo documentacional colectivo en linea. *Recherches en didactique des mathématiques, 30*(3), 367–397.

Sensevy, G. (2010). Formes de l'intention didactique, collectifs et travail documentaire. In G. Gueudet & L. Trouche (Eds.), *Ressources vives. Le travail documentaire des professeurs en mathématiques* (pp. 147–163). Rennes/Lyon: Presses Universitaires de Rennes et INRP.

Sensevy, G. (2012). Patterns of didactic intentions, thought collective and documentation work. In G. Gueudet, B. Pepin, & L. Trouche (Eds.), *From textbooks to 'Lived' resources: Mathematics curriculum materials and teacher documentation* (pp. 43–57). New York: Springer.

Siemens, G. (2005). *Connectivism: a learning theory for the digital age*. Retrieved July 2016 from http://www.elearnspace.org/Articles/connectivism.htm

Trouche, L. (2004). Managing the complexity of human/machine interactions in computerized learning environments: Guiding students' command process through instrumental orchestrations. *International Journal of Computers for Mathematical Learning, 9*, 281–307.

Trouche, L., Trgalová, J., Loisy, C., & Alturkmani, M. (2018a). *Ressources vivantes pour l'apprentissage. Rapport scientifique des composantes IFE et S2HEP*. https://hal.archives-ouvertes.fr/hal-01743212v2

Trouche, L., Gueudet, G., & Pepin, B. (2018b). The documentational approach to didactics. In S. Lerman (Ed.), *Encyclopedia of mathematics education*. New York: Springer.

Vergnaud, G. (1998). Towards a cognitive theory of practice. In A. Sierpinska & J. Kilpatrick (Eds.), *Mathematics education as a research domain: A search for identity* (pp. 227–241). Dordrecht: Kluwer Academic Publisher.

Wenger, E. (1998). *Communities of practice. Learning, meaning, identity*. New York: Cambridge University Press.

Chapter 3
The Construct of 'Resource System' as an Analytic Tool in Understanding the Work of Teaching

Kenneth Ruthven

Abstract This chapter examines professionally situated notions of 'resource system' relevant to the work of teaching, giving specific attention to mathematics teaching. Two historically significant exemplars are examined in the form of Euclid's *Elements* as a systematic logical organisation of resources and Durell's *A New Geometry* as a systematic didactical organisation of resources. Noting a subsequent shift towards the use of multi-sourced collections of resources, the chapter examines how teachers create organised systems, considering the evolving notions of 'resource system' in two contemporary theoretical frames: structuring features of classroom practice (Ruthven K, Education & Didactique 3:131–149, 2009) and the documentational approach (Gueudet G, Trouche L, Educational Studies in Mathematics 71:199–218, 2009). Different perspectives situate 'resource system' in contrasting ways: as adhering to a particular type of agent (teacher, student, designer) or as intervening between such agents; as relating to a specific educational entity (especially the classroom, the course or the lesson) or as ranging across and beyond these. Professionals and researchers have clearly found each of these variations useful for some purpose: an implication is that we could benefit from an expanded notion of 'resource system' which acknowledges all these dimensions and encourages users of the term to take more explicit account of them.

Keywords Documentational approach to didactics · Durell's *A New Geometry* · Euclid's *Elements* · Mathematics teaching · Resource system · Structuring features of classroom practice

---

This chapter originates from a lecture given to the Re(s)sources 2018 International Conference. Video in English, with French subtitles at http://video.ens-lyon.fr/ife/2018/2018-05-28_002_Ressources2018_Kenneth_Ruthven_v1.fra.mp4

K. Ruthven (✉)
University of Cambridge, Cambridge, UK
e-mail: kr18@cam.ac.uk

© Springer Nature Switzerland AG 2019
L. Trouche et al. (eds.), *The 'Resource' Approach to Mathematics Education*,
Advances in Mathematics Education,
https://doi.org/10.1007/978-3-030-20393-1_3

3.1 Notions of 'Resource' and 'System'

When researchers use notions of 'resource' and 'system' – and join them together to form 'resource system' – they appeal to ideas already established in ordinary language and in the professional discourse of teaching. In due course this chapter will consider particular notions that educational researchers have developed in recent years. First, however, it is important to examine the everyday and professional usages of these terms, in which – by virtue of such choice of words – researchers ground their own specialised meanings.

In established everyday usage, a resource is an asset – typically monetary, material or human – capable of providing some form of support. In the field of education (as the Oxford English Dictionary records), a specialised usage of 'resource' developed during the 1960s, referring specifically to curriculum-related materials intended to support learning or teaching activity. This specialised usage remains predominant in the professional field, and it provides the focus for this chapter. Nevertheless, in theorising the notion within the research field, there has been some reversion towards the more general usage in recognising a much wider range of human and cultural – as well as material – assets as resources for teaching and learning about a topic (Adler 2000), as this chapter will acknowledge where appropriate.

The professionally specific usage of 'resources' to refer to curriculum-related materials arose in response to technological changes – notably increasing provision of audio-visual and reprographic facilities – which broadened the range of media in which such materials could be created and facilitated their local production and reproduction. Indeed the institutionalisation of this trend was marked by a key educational site being renamed: as its functionality was reconceived, the traditional library became the modern 'resource centre' (Beswick 1974). This space now accommodated resources in a more diverse range of media – notably audio-visual materials as well as printed texts. Moreover, it catered for an expanded pedagogical repertoire. In particular, by allowing a user to select from – and make copies of – a varied stock of 'curricular', 'learning' or 'teaching' resources, it made possible forms of 'resource-based' learning and teaching involving more active curriculum design by teachers and more independent study by pupils (Graystone 1978). Over recent years, the advance of computer-based information and communication technologies has produced a further shift towards accessing such resources online in digital form, with the role of web portals and Internet repositories growing correspondingly (Recker et al. 2004; de los Arcos et al. 2016).

The central idea of a 'system' is one of organisation: the term may refer to some structure resulting from multiple entities being organised to form a functioning whole or to some scheme or method which provides a basis for such organisation. Within the professional field, two corresponding notions of 'resource system' have developed. One usage – expanding the traditional notion of textbook – refers to a systematic curriculum scheme created through combining diverse resources to form a comprehensive programme (Gillespie and Humphreys 1970). Another usage –

3 The Construct of 'Resource System' as an Analytic Tool 45

expanding the traditional notion of library – refers to organising and cataloguing a resource repository systematically so as to make its contents readily searchable and usable (Zhao et al. 1996).

This chapter will make reference to both of these notions of 'resource system'. Nowadays, indeed, the distinction between the two has become blurred. In particular, there is a growing tendency to regard any text as just one source amongst many, providing a collection of smaller resource units to be raided and combined with others. But this is to disregard the systematic way in which a text seeks to organise these many resource units to provide a coherent whole. To illustrate this point, I will examine two illuminating historical exemplars of the text as resource system *avant la lettre*.

3.2 Euclid's *Elements* as a Systematic Logical Organisation of Resources

In the history of teaching and learning mathematics, one resource towers above all others in terms of its longevity and influence. The *Elements* of Euclid was created around 300 BCE and was subsequently annotated and adapted by others in more than a thousand editions. In one form or another, the *Elements* was widely studied until the early years of the twentieth century. Euclid's achievement was to combine and adapt mathematical sources already available to produce what was taken to be a comprehensive and coherent text providing a logically systematic exposition of a core of classical mathematics. Thanks to the remarkable Library of Alexandria, Euclid was able to draw on disparate mathematical texts from across the ancient world in compiling the *Elements*: texts created variously by Pythagoras, Hippocrates, Eudoxus, Theaetetus – father and son – and many others (Rouse Ball 1908). The result provides a prime example of Hilbert's nostrum that the importance of a great book is determined 'by the number of previous publications it makes superfluous to read' (Brock 1975).

Nevertheless, there is a sense in which there are as many *Elements* as there are editions. Not only, in the early days, did copyists introduce inadvertent changes, but – much more significantly – later translators and editors created *Elements* which accorded variously with their conception of rigorous argument, their favoured didactical approach or their image of Greek mathematics (Barrow-Green 2006; Chemla 2012). Amongst other things, they selected from different source editions, reorganised the sequencing of material, filled out perceived gaps in argument, modified the presentation of figures and introduced new diagrammatic conventions. Thus, what is taken as constituting the *Elements* has been shaped not just by Euclid's original selection and organisation of resources but by a continuing process of interpretation and adaptation.

However, despite this ongoing recreation of the *Elements*, it is possible to pick out some key features generally regarded as forming its core. The overarching organising principle of the *Elements* is one of logical deduction. From a base of 'definitions' of geometrical entities and of axioms taken to be self-evident – either in the form of 'postulates' about geometrical entities or of 'common notions' about magnitudes – the *Elements* derives a succession of 'propositions'. These propositions are numbered in sequence and organised thematically into 'books', providing a global structure for the text. Equally, the *Elements* employs a consistent local structure to present each proposition (Heath 1908, following Proclus). First, an 'enunciation' states what situation is given and what new result is sought. If required, a 'setting-out' then provides a labelled figure exemplifying the given situation; a 'definition' or 'specification' relates that figure to the enunciation; and finally a 'construction' or 'mechanism' elaborates the figure to support reasoning to produce the desired result. A step-by-step deductive 'proof' follows, in which the warrant for each step is indicated by indexing the relevant definition, postulate, common notion or prior proposition. Finally, a 'conclusion' relates the demonstration back to the original enunciation. This provides the standard template through which the *Elements* presents its propositions.

Thus, as a text for study, the *Elements* provides a means of gaining access not just to the substantive mathematical content of the disparate sources that Euclid drew from but to the logical method that he employed to organise these sources systematically, enabling him to present their content in a consistent and coherent manner. Over time, then, the *Elements* came to fulfil an important sociocognitive function as a canonical text, providing a shared framework – both of substantive knowledge and argumentative forms – supporting and shaping the diffusion and development of mathematical knowledge. In particular, the *Elements* found favour within an approach to liberal education based on familiarising students with the classical models of thought displayed in 'great books'. Indeed, the *Elements* was studied less for its content than for the habits of mind that such study was thought to inculcate. Induction into the Euclidean system through (what I cannot resist calling) exposure to the *Elements* was intended to teach students to reason in an abstract realm removed from sensory perception (Howsam et al. 2007).

Yet actual practice could be very different, so that study of the *Elements* often became associated with a reductive mnemonic pedagogy. For example, in England at the start of the twentieth century, we can find the reformer Perry criticising the requirement – in order to gain a pass degree at Oxford University – to memorise two books of Euclid, even down to the lettering of figures, with no original exercises being required (Cajori 1910). As reformers gained the upper hand, then, the 'great book' gave way to the 'school book'; the *Elements* was replaced by texts written specifically to introduce school pupils to geometry: textbooks which gave a place to practical experimentation and took a less restrictive approach to modes of reasoning – in line with the didactical precepts of the reform movement.

3.3 Durell's *A New Geometry* as a Systematic Didactical Organisation of Resources

To characterise the 'school books' which took the educational place of Euclid's 'great book', I will use the example of Durell's *A New Geometry for Schools*. This text was first published in 1939, and – according to my 1945 copy – reprinted no less than once and often twice in each of the following years. Indeed, C. V. Durell[1] has been described by Quadling – in his review of English mathematics textbooks of the twentieth century – as 'the most prolific author of the century' so that his 'name was for many pupils almost synonymous with mathematics' (Quadling 1996, p. 121).

Durell published his first geometry textbook in 1909, and others had followed before he embarked on writing *A New Geometry*. In his preface, Durell acknowledges what we might now describe as a process of documentational genesis:

> It is now almost fourteen years since the author's Elementary Geometry was published and, in writing this entirely new book, he has taken the opportunity to recast his treatment of the subject in the light of experience gained, and the suggestions received since Elementary Geometry appeared. He has been able also, as will be seen later, to make use of the Second Report of the Mathematical Association on the Teaching of Geometry. (Durell 1939, pp. iv)

This testifies, then, to a range of prior resources – both personal and institutional, both human and material and encountered as much as teacher as textbook author – on which Durell drew in developing the approach taken by the new text.

Durell's approach was aligned with the contemporary reform movement, and particularly the recommendations of the Mathematical Association report, as the book's subtitle – Stage A and Stage B – signals. Thus *A New Geometry* opens with a (Stage A) section in which more practical, experimental methods are employed with the intention of building geometrical intuition and developing informal geometrical reasoning. The following (Stage B) sections proceed to a more expository and deductive approach. Durell sets out the systematic didactical organisation around which this main part of the book is designed:

> The plan adopted throughout is to develop each group of geometrical facts by the following successive stages:
>
> (i) Examples for oral discussion.... This oral work gives the pupil a clear understanding of the relevant facts, familiarises him with the arguments which will be used later in the formal proofs of theorems, and trains him in methods for solving riders....
>
> (ii) An exercise of numerical examples. This gives practice in applying the facts deduced from oral discussion and ensures a firm grasp of these facts.
>
> (iii) Formal proofs of the corresponding theorems. The preliminary work makes it possible to deal with these proofs rapidly. Practice in writing out theorems is essential for

---

[1] Initials of forenames included to distinguish C.V. Durell from his American contemporary author of mathematics textbooks, F. Durell.

examination purposes, but it will often be found sufficient to confine this to the key-theorem of each group, regarding the others as simple riders.

(iv) An exercise of riders. The early examples in each exercise are direct and very simple applications of the properties of the group. Some assistance is supplied for the harder examples.... (Durell 1939, pp. v-vi).

This didactically inspired organisational scheme, then, provides for the systematic sequencing of activity within each topical unit of the text into four stages: each stage is linked to particular types of learning goal and a corresponding form of classroom activity. Consistent use of this scheme throughout the main part of the textbook accustoms teacher and pupils to conceiving and conducting their activity in terms of these stages, enabling them to focus on the mathematical tasks and learning goals in play. Stages (i) and (ii) provide a more informal introduction to the topic under consideration followed by simple reinforcement of key points. Stage (iii) provides a degree of continuity with the logical approach of the *Elements*, but is more selective in its attention to formal proofs and employs a simplified local template. Grouping geometrical facts so as to organise them conceptually around a key theorem incorporates a powerful learning principle. Equally this focus on a key theorem (rather than on a complete cluster) produces a balance, over the course of stages (iii) and (iv), between experience of formal proof and of solving riders.

The core of *A New Geometry* is the sequence of topic-specific resource units forming the chapters of the book, each employing the standard staged organisation outlined above. This core corresponds to the first sense of resource system noted earlier: that of a systematic curricular sequence of resource units forming a coherent programme. Equally, *A New Geometry* recognises the need for certain auxiliary resources beyond this core curricular sequence. For example, it includes a lengthy early chapter introducing students to the geometrical instruments that practical, experimental methods call into play and covering the main usages of this tool system in constructing and measuring geometrical figures. Likewise, the book makes provision not just for the exposition of new material but for periodic review – marked by the inclusion of revision exercises. To support this review function, the text provides a systematic organisation and cataloguing of its contents so as to be readily searchable. As well as the table of contents at the beginning and the index at the end, there are appendices summarising, respectively, the constructions and the theorems covered by the book and indicating where they are treated more fully in the main body of the text. Such a text, then, is designed with the creation of a comprehensive resource system in mind: one meeting the various needs of teachers and pupils over the course as a whole. It is this explicit and systematic didactical organisation which makes Durell's text identifiably a textbook.

3.4 From Multi-Sourced Collections of Resources to Organised Systems

As resource-based approaches to teaching and learning have become increasingly influential, there has been a shift away from the traditional model of a single course text. In his review of a century of mathematics textbooks, Quadling reported that:

> whilst the majority of teachers still felt the need for the security of a course textbook, by the 1970s an alternative style of mathematics teaching was emerging. Declaring that 'there is no right textbook for my needs', some teachers chose to equip their classrooms with small numbers of copies of several books, and to supplement these with self-produced materials. (Quadling 1996, p. 125)

As Quadling noted:

> This new concept of the textbook, as a guidebook rather than a package tour, needed the support of a well thought out curriculum for pupils to retain a sense of purpose and achievement. Not surprisingly, it was most effective when implemented collaboratively in a group of schools with advisory support, such as the SMILE programme of individualised learning which originated in the Inner London Education Authority. (Quadling 1996, p. 125)

A key feature of early resource-based initiatives such as SMILE (Gibbons 1975; Povey 2014) was the development of a curriculum map into which carefully chosen (or specially devised) resources from different sources could be inserted. In the case of SMILE, this curriculum map came to be paralleled by a graded assessment system, GAIM, based on criteria describing specific cognitively based strategies representing significant steps in mathematical development (Brown 1989). Here, then, was a resource system which combined a curricular model of domains of mathematical knowledge with a cognitive model of progression in mathematical thinking.

Nowadays, the ready availability of digital resources online, combined with their provisionality, facilitates the curation and adaptation of resources by teachers, but the same issue of coherence remains (Pepin et al. 2017). A modern equivalent to the integrated SMILE/GAIM map of curriculum and assessment is the Math-Mapper digital learning system (Confrey et al. 2017). Indeed, the choice to designate Math-Mapper as a 'digital learning system' rather than as an 'e-textbook' reflects a concern to organise the system around learning trajectories intended to reflect progression in student thinking. The intention of this subject-specific learning 'shell' is to guide the learning efforts of students (and teacher support for these efforts) by first setting appropriate learning targets (according to the recognised learning trajectories), then identifying corresponding learning opportunities (through digital curriculum resources mapped to those targets) and eventually (through the assessment functionality of the system) providing diagnostic feedback on the success of these efforts and analysing progress so as to inform the next cycle.

Nevertheless, initiatives such as SMILE developed into comprehensive curriculum programmes – comprising a full set of curricular resources as well as the organising framework – which were distributed well beyond the contributing schools and teachers and sustained by a group of core participants responsible for 'minding the system' (Gueudet et al. 2013). Likewise, recognising that the local insertion of resources into a digital learning shell makes considerable demands on teachers, Math-Mapper comes pre-populated with suitable curricular resources, so taking on a form closer to the contemporary e-textbook or digital curriculum programme. These trends indicate the continuing importance of externally developed systems of resources in supporting mathematics education in mainstream schools. In particular, it seems that, given the conditions under which many schools operate and teachers work, such systems are necessary to support efficient, coherent and comprehensive provision, while admitting a degree of substitution or supplementation according to local concerns and capacities. Equally, current developments indicate an important degree of innovation and diversification in the form that such resource systems take and in the character of the systematic organisation of resources that they provide.

Choppin et al. (2014) have found that contemporary digital curriculum programmes are broadly of two types. Major educational publishers have developed what the researchers termed 'digitised versions of traditional textbooks': these have structure and content similar to existing textbooks but in a digitised rather than printed form; and they are intended to be used in much the same way as traditional textbooks, under the direction of a teacher. Another type consists of what the researchers termed 'individual learning designs': these are devised to be used more directly by students as individualised study programmes, largely independent of the teacher, often with built-in assessments used to adjust the pacing and sequencing of content to the individual student user. This second type of digital curriculum programme can be seen as extending the type of approach pioneered by earlier traditions of programmed learning, individualised instruction, intelligent tutoring systems and integrated learning systems (Means 2007). In practice, however, it seems that teachers often appropriate such individualised digital programmes to create classroom resource systems which allow them to retain aspects of their role in which they are particularly invested, so that such systems prove complementary to teacher-led forms of instruction rather than a replacement for them (Ruthven 2018).

While curriculum programmes are, in principle, designed to be organised resource systems, it is now well recognised that, in practice, such designs can be re- or dis-organised as they are appropriated – and often repurposed to a degree – by users. Thus, recent research has given attention to the operational resource systems that teachers create for themselves and their classes, looking in particular at the associated development of their professional knowledge. Thus, I will now examine two of the main exemplars of this approach within recent research on mathematics education.

3.5 The Evolving Notion of 'Resource System' in the Structuring Features of Classroom Practice Framework

My own thinking about resource systems developed in the course of investigating the integration of digital tools and resources into everyday classroom practice. I recall, for example, the head of one school mathematics department commenting on the proliferation of computer-based resources being trialled in his department and expressing concern about effectively incorporating such a range into departmental curriculum schemes and familiarising staff and students with their varying operating principles. This reminded me of much earlier research contrasting the way in which expert and novice mathematics teachers made use of representations (Leinhardt 1989): whereas novices tended to introduce new representations for each new topic, expert teachers were more sparing in the range of representational devices that they employed and took pains to familiarise their pupils carefully with these devices as well as using them more intensively across a range of situations. Here, then, we see an economy of resource use emerging, whereby expert teachers attend to returns on the overheads of introducing a new resource. Indeed, in our own research, we found teachers embracing such economistic reasoning. For example, one teacher justified his decision to reserve dynamic geometry software only for teacher demonstration rather than having pupils use it for themselves in terms of it being 'a difficult program for the students to master... [and t]he return from the time investment... would be fairly small' (teacher quoted in Ruthven et al. 2008, p. 307).

3.5.1 The Structuring Features of Classroom Practice Framework

In the structuring features of classroom practice (SFCP) framework, then, 'resource system' refers to the various mathematical tools and curriculum materials in use in the classroom and to the way in which their use – individually and collectively – is organised and made functional. In particular, while new technologies broaden the range of tools and resources available to support school mathematics, they present the challenge of building a coherent resource system of compatible elements that function in a complementary manner and which participants are capable of using effectively. The fundamental hypothesis is that this is one of several structuring features of classroom practice which mediate the process through which teachers adapt their practice and develop associated professional knowledge.

In brief, the other structuring features (discussed more fully in Ruthven 2009) are the *working environment* of lessons, concerned with physical layout and class organisation, and including the classroom routines which enable lessons to flow smoothly; the available repertoire of activity formats that frame the action and interaction of participants during particular types of classroom episode, combining to create a prototypical *activity structure* for each style of lesson; and the teacher's *curriculum script* for teaching particular mathematical topics, a loosely ordered model of goals, resources and actions, interweaving mathematical ideas to be developed, appropriate tasks to be undertaken and potential student responses to be anticipated and incorporating variant expectancies of events and alternative courses of action. Finally, as noted above, teachers operate within a *time economy* in which they seek to optimise the rate at which the physical time available for classroom activity is converted into a didactic time measured in terms of the advance of knowledge.

3.5.2 A Case Study of a Teacher's Resource System in Evolution

In the main paper outlining SFCP (Ruthven 2009), this framework was illustrated by an example – developed from an earlier study (Ruthven et al. 2008) – of the evolving classroom practice of a mathematics teacher in the process of incorporating use of dynamic geometry software. His intention was to complement established construction tasks which made use of classical tools by introducing new tasks employing dynamic software. The rationale for the double instrumentation involved in creating such a classroom resource system was twofold: first, to strengthen attention to the geometric ideas underpinning constructions through their mediation by the software in terms of its named and constrained geometrical operations and, second, to give students experience of finding geometric rules and patterns through exploring a dynamic figure in ways impossible with static diagrams.

In many respects, the intentions behind this coordinated use of classical then digital tools were realised, producing a corresponding enhancement of the classroom resource system. Nevertheless, the teacher also experienced some discontinuities and diversions. First, he considered the correspondence between classical and digital techniques to be imperfect in some important respects, reducing the desired congruence between old and new tools: he had not yet found an effective resolution of this tension. Equally, the teacher experienced other issues which needed to be taken in hand if the classroom resource system was to function effectively. In resolving these, he developed new techniques and norms, extending his professional knowledge accordingly. For example, he developed knowledge not just of how the nuances of software operation might derail students' attempts at construction but also of how such difficulties might be turned to advantage in reinforcing the mathematical focus of the task. Equally, recognising that students might not appreciate the geometrical significance of the invariant properties of a figure, the teacher was developing strategies for addressing this, notably through exploiting the distinctive affordances of dragging a dynamic figure. In both these respects, then, the teacher was building professional knowledge contributing to a more effective functioning of the expanded classroom resource system. More prosaically too, the teacher was finding that students could be deflected from the mathematical focus of a task by the ease of experimenting with the presentational options provided by the software: he sought to manage this by showing students mathematically appropriate use of differing fonts and colour coding, an example of securing a more satisfactory functioning of the classroom resource system by establishing norms and techniques for the use of new tools.

3.5.3 A Comparative Study of the Resource Systems of Differentially Experienced Teachers

In a later study, the SCFP framework was applied more directly to investigation of teaching practices involving use of dynamic geometry software (Bozkurt 2016; Bozkurt and Ruthven 2017). Here, I will give a comparative sketch of the classroom resource systems established to teach the topic of transformations by two teachers, both with around 20 years of teaching experience, but differing markedly in their experience of using technology. First some similarities. Both teachers chose to have students make use of the software to tackle assigned tasks (in contrast to the example mentioned earlier of its use being restricted to teacher demonstration to the whole class). Equally, both teachers took a just-in-time approach to developing students' technical skills, introducing them to any unfamiliar features of the software immediately prior to tasks requiring their use. In both cases too, the resources in play comprised prepared dynamic files accompanied by printed worksheets giving students instructions on how to use the files and prompting them to record predictions and report findings. Finally, as this structuring of worksheets indicates, in both cases the resource system was designed to support processes through which the worksheet instructions prompted students to make a mathematical prediction and then guided them in using the dynamic file to test their prediction and generate feedback on it. In these respects, then, the two teachers followed similar approaches to making the digital tool part of a functioning classroom resource system.

However, there were also some important differences in the classroom resource systems that the teachers established. A first difference was in the provenance of the resources used. Whereas the most experienced teacher used his own file/worksheet duos, refined over a lengthy period, the least experienced teacher adopted a collection of duos found online, using them initially without modification. However, in the light of her experience of working with these borrowed duos, the least experienced teacher then adapted the worksheet for future use. There were also differences in the degree of task closure and direction that the teachers sought to achieve through their duos. When the least experienced teacher subsequently modified the worksheet part of her borrowed duos, she altered the wording of instructions so as to direct students more explicitly towards a particular solution envisaged in their design. By comparison, the task environments that the most experienced teacher provided were devised to permit a range of solution strategies: and while the dynamic files were tightly constrained, this served to reduce the need for direction in the worksheet while leaving open the possibility of different approaches. Finally, there were differences in the status that the teachers accorded to the two media. The least experienced teacher was concerned that students 'did not have enough practice on paper to put into practice what they had actually seen on the computer', and this led her to add two further worksheets of solely pen-and-paper tasks for this purpose. For her, then, the dynamic software served simply as a pedagogical aid to introduce new mathematical ideas, whereas the experienced teacher treated it as a more central tool for students' mathematical work. In his lessons, students continued to work within the dynamic software environment, with the teacher projecting selected screens to support whole class discussion of the different strategies that they exemplified. Nevertheless, while differing in the balance between conventional and digital media, as in the degree of task closure and direction, both teachers clearly made refinements to the classroom resource system which were intended to make it function more closely in accord with their own didactical preferences. In both cases, then, we see evidence of a process of professional adaptation – albeit at different stages in incorporating the use of dynamic software.

The SFCP framework in its present form has used the idea of classroom resource system in a loosely defined manner. This has had the advantage of ensuring that the construct is well grounded empirically, through allowing flexibility in identifying relevant phenomena and accommodating them. However, as our knowledge of such phenomena grows, particularly across a wider range of educational contexts, it would be beneficial to demarcate the construct in a more precise manner, breaking it down into components and clarifying their interrelation.

3.6 The Evolving Notion of 'Resource System' in the Documentational Approach to Didactics Framework

Other chapters in this book give detailed consideration to the documentational approach to didactics (DAD) (see Chaps. 2, 5 and 13). Here, then, I will focus specifically on its notion of a resource system. Nevertheless, it is important to start by emphasising three broader points. The first is that the DAD adopts an expansive notion of resource as comprising not just material but human nonmaterial assets. The second point is that the primary concern of the DAD to date has been with the resource systems of individual teachers (even if it acknowledges the part that other teachers and collectives play in shaping such systems) over the whole span of their professional activity (rather than only in the classroom or solely relating to a particular class or topic). The final important point is that – in the psychologically influenced DAD – a crucial distinction is made between an artefactual resource and the result of its appropriation (often in combination with other resources) to form an instrumental document.

3 The Construct of 'Resource System' as an Analytic Tool

This specialised use of 'document' refers to the resource(s) in play plus an associated utilisation scheme, the latter conceived as consisting of observable usages and not-directly-observable operational invariants governing these. Gueudet and Trouche illustrate their idea of a document with reference to a particular class of professional situations – delineated as 'propose homework on the addition of positive and negative numbers'– as follows:

> For this class of situations, a given teacher gathers resources: textbooks, her own course, a previously given sheet of exercises… She chooses among these resources to constitute a list of exercises, which is given to a class. It can then be modified, according to what happens with the students, before using it with another class during the same year, or the next year, or even later. The document develops throughout this variety of contexts. The operational invariants can be very general, like 'the homework must be extracted from the textbook', or more precisely linked with the mathematical content, like: 'the additions proposed must include the cases of mixed positive and negative numbers, and of only negative numbers,' etc. These operational invariants can be inferred from the observation of invariant behaviors of the teacher for the same class of situations across different contexts. They are teacher beliefs, and are both driving forces and outcomes of the teacher's activity, instrumented by a set of resources. (Gueudet and Trouche 2009, p. 205)

In particular, then, we should note that more generic operational invariants will be in play across multiple classes of professional situation. Thus the DAD posits that the documents that a teacher establishes, in response to the range of classes of professional situations that she/he encounters, constitute a system structured by professional activity. This leads to the fundamental hypothesis of the DAD that each teacher develops a structured documentation system which evolves over time with that teacher's professional practice.

Accordingly, early formulations of the DAD avoided the term 'resource system', emphasising that:

> each resource must be viewed as a part of a wider 'set of resources' (used here instead of 'resource system' which suggests an a priori structure of the resource sets). (Gueudet and Trouche 2009, p. 200)

In due course, however, the DAD embraced the term, while maintaining the crucial distinction between artefactual resource and instrumental document:

> The resource system of the teacher constitutes the 'resource' part of her documentation system (i.e. without the scheme part of the documents). (Gueudet and Trouche 2012, p. 27)

The rationale for considering this too to be a system lies in a wider structure made visible by the renewal of resources over time (leading to a reconfiguration of activity and to a renewal or abandonment of other resources):

> [E]ach 'renewing' of a resource impacts on other teacher resources, and may have different outcomes for what we name teacher resource system—the word 'system' is purposefully chosen to emphasize that this system is highly structured, the structure being linked, more or less explicitly, to teacher activity. (Gueudet et al. 2013, p. 1004)

Such structuring of the resource system may be attributable to the structure of the documentation system: for example, through the influence of generic operational invariants:

> Identifying [the] documentation system allows, for example, understanding the adoption or rejection of resources by the teacher (a new resource is more likely to be integrated if it matches other resources already present in the teacher's resource system). (Gueudet et al. 2014, p. 142)

However, one method characteristic of the DAD suggests other types of structuring of a teacher's resource system. In this method the researcher asks the teacher to draw a schematic representation of the structure of the resources that she/he uses, so generating what that DAD terms a schematic representation of the resource system (Gueudet and Trouche 2012, p. 28). Typically, it seems the process of eliciting such representations brings out socio-spatio-temporal-material dimensions of the relatively immediate organisation of teachers' work. In one study, a teacher's representation of her resource system identifies four 'zones' with which resources are associated: her work at home, her work at school without students, her work at school in the classroom with her students and her work in in-service training collectives (Gueudet and Trouche 2012, p. 35). In another study a teacher's representation of her resource system is configured first by worksite (home or school, linked by USB key) then, within site, by the places where resources are kept (shelves, bedroom or computer, and cupboard or computer, respectively) and finally, at home, by resource form (e-mails, books, scientific journals, paper folders, digital folders) (Gueudet et al. 2013, p. 1008). Another teacher groups resources, first, according to function (lesson preparation or communication with pupils and parents), then, for lesson preparation, according to form (audio-visual and online resources, games and similar activities) and status (the adopted textbook, other textbooks) or provenance (her own, from her colleagues) (Gueudet et al. 2013, p. 1010).

The DAD framework, then, incorporates two perspectives on teacher resource systems: one deriving from a theorised notion of teacher documentation with a particular focus on utilisation schemes and another originating from teachers' own representations of the structure of their resources, evoking varied aspects including the socio-spatio-temporal organisation of their work as well as the perceived form and function of the resources available to them. Clarifying the relationship between these perspectives represents one fruitful area for development of the DAD. It would also be interesting to explore congruences, complementarities and conflicts between the DAD and theories of distributed cognition and situated knowledge which offer alternative – but similarly socioculturally informed – accounts of the organisation and development of professional knowledge.

3.7 Conclusion

It is clear, then, that ideas of 'resource system' differ considerably in the ways in which they demarcate 'resources' and formulate 'system'. Equally, closer examination shows that different perspectives situate 'resource system' in contrasting ways: as adhering to a particular type of agent (teacher, student, designer) or as intervening between such agents; as relating to a specific educational entity (especially the classroom, the course or the lesson) or as ranging across and beyond these. Professionals and researchers have clearly found each of these variations useful for some purpose: an implication is that we could benefit from an expanded notion of 'resource system' which acknowledges all these dimensions and encourages users of the term to take more explicit account of them in framing their thinking about a particular issue and in describing and justifying that framing.

It would be remiss, however, not to conclude by emphasising the value of existing constructs of resource system in analysing the work of teaching. Collectively they highlight the central role that resources play in such work, illuminating the dynamic between designers, teachers and students in developing and refining resources and the manner in which they are used. Within the research field, particular attention has been given to resource systems as they relate to teachers. Of course, the motivation for developing the structuring features of classroom practice (SFCP) framework was very explicitly to better understand the adaptation of teachers' professional knowledge. Equally, the intention of the established body of studies using the documentational approach to didactics (DAD) framework has been to study resource systems as a phenomenon of teacher cognition. Accordingly, both approaches rely heavily on methods using teacher informants. There is scope, then, to develop approaches which take account of other perspectives[2] and introduce more comprehensive theoretical framings.

References

Adler, J. (2000). Conceptualising resources as a theme for teacher education. *Journal of Mathematics Teacher Education, 3*(3), 205–224.

Barrow-Green, J. (2006). Much necessary for all sortes of men': 450 years of Euclid's *Elements* in English. *BSHM Bulletin: Journal of the British Society for the History of Mathematics, 21*(1), 2–25.

Beswick, N. (1974). Library resource Centres: A developing literature. *Journal of Librarianship, 6*(1), 54–62.

Bozkurt, G. (2016). *Teaching with technology: A multiple-case study of secondary teachers' practices of GeoGebra use in mathematics teaching.* Unpublished PhD thesis, University of Cambridge.

Bozkurt, G., & Ruthven, K. (2017). Teaching with GeoGebra: Resource systems of mathematics teachers. In G. Aldon & J. Trgalová (Eds.), *Proceedings of the 13th International Conference on Technology in Mathematics Teaching [ICTMT 13]* (pp. 216–223). Lyon: École Normale Supérieure de Lyon/Université Claude Bernard Lyon 1.

Brock, W. H. (1975). Geometry and the universities: Euclid and his modem rivals 1860–1901. *History of Education, 4*(2), 21–35.

Brown, M. (1989). Graded assessment and learning hierarchies in mathematics – An alternative view. *British Educational Research Journal, 15*(2), 121–128.

Cajori, F. (1910). Attempts made during the eighteenth and nineteenth centuries to reform the teaching of geometry. *American Mathematical Monthly, 17*(10), 181–201.

---

[2] As, for example, does recent research using the documentational approach to study the use of digital resources by students in higher education (Gueudet & Pepin 2018).

Chemla, K. (Ed.). (2012). *The history of mathematical proof in ancient traditions*. Cambridge: Cambridge University Press.

Choppin, J., Carson, C., Borys, Z., Cerosaletti, C., & Gillis, R. (2014). A typology for analyzing digital curricula in mathematics education. *International Journal of Education in Mathematics, Science, and Technology, 2*(1), 11–25.

Confrey, J., Gianopulos, G., McGowan, W., Shah, M., & Belcher, M. (2017). Scaffolding learner-centered curricular coherence using learning maps and diagnostic assessments designed around mathematics learning trajectories. *ZDM – Mathematics Education, 49*(5), 717–734.

de los Arcos, B., Farrow, R., Pitt, R., Weller, M., & McAndrew, P. (2016). Adapting the curriculum: How K-12 teachers perceive the role of open educational resources. *Journal of Online Learning Research, 2*(1), 23–40.

Durell, C. V. (1939). *A new geometry for schools*. London: Bell.

Gibbons, R. (1975). An account of the Secondary Mathematics Individualized Learning Experiment. *Mathematics in School, 4*(6), 14–16.

Gillespie, R. J., & Humphreys, D. A. (1970). The application of a learning resource system in teaching undergraduate chemistry. *Pure and Applied Chemistry, 22*(1-2), 111–116.

Graystone, J. A. (1978). The role of the teacher in resource based learning: Towards a conceptual framework. *British Educational Research Journal, 4*(1), 27–35.

Gueudet, G., & Pepin, B. (2018). Didactic contract at university: A focus on resources and their use. *International Journal of Research in Undergraduate Mathematics Education, 4*(1), 56–73.

Gueudet, G., & Trouche, L. (2009). Towards new documentation systems for mathematics teachers? *Educational Studies in Mathematics, 71*(3), 199–218.

Gueudet, G., & Trouche, L. (2012). Teachers' work with resources: Documentational geneses and professional geneses. In G. Gueudet, B. Pepin, & L. Trouche (Eds.), *From text to 'lived' resources: Mathematics curriculum materials and teacher development*. New York: Springer.

Gueudet, G., Pepin, B., & Trouche, L. (2013). Collective work with resources: An essential dimension for teacher documentation. *ZDM – Mathematics Education, 45*(7), 1003–1016.

Gueudet, G., Buteau, C., Mesa, V., & Misfeldt, M. (2014). Instrumental and documentational approaches: From technology use to documentation systems in university mathematics education. *Research in Mathematics Education, 16*(2), 139–155.

Heath, T. L. (Ed.). (1908). *The thirteen books of Euclid's Elements*. Cambridge: Cambridge University Press.

Howsam, L., Stray, C., Jenkins, A., Secord, J. A., & Vaninskaya, A. (2007). What the Victorians learned: Perspectives on nineteenth-century schoolbooks. *Journal of Victorian Culture, 12*(2), 262–285.

Leinhardt, G. (1989). Math lessons: A contrast of novice and expert competence. *Journal for Research in Mathematics Education, 20*(1), 52–75.

Means, B. (2007). Technology's role in curriculum and instruction. In F. M. Connelly (Ed.), *The Sage handbook of curriculum and instruction* (pp. 123–144). London: Sage.

Pepin, B., Choppin, J., Ruthven, K., & Sinclair, N. (2017). Digital curriculum resources in mathematics education: Foundations for change. *ZDM – Mathematics Education, 49*(5), 645–661.

Povey, H. (2014). The origins and continued life of SMILE mathematics. *Mathematics Teaching, 241*, 5–6.

Quadling, D. (1996). A century of textbooks. *Mathematical Gazette, 80*(487), 119–126.

Recker, M. M., Dorward, J., & Nelson, L. M. (2004). Discovery and use of online learning resources: Case study findings. *Educational Technology & Society, 7*(2), 93–104.

Rouse Ball, W. W. (1908). *A short account of the history of mathematics* (4th ed.). London: Macmillan.

Ruthven, K. (2009). Towards a naturalistic conceptualisation of technology integration in classroom practice: The example of school mathematics. *Education & Didactique, 3*(1), 131–149.

Ruthven, K. (2018). Instructional activity and student interaction with digital resources. In L. Fan, L. Trouche, C. Qi, S. Rezat, & J. Visnovska (Eds.), *Research on mathematics textbooks and teachers' resources: Advances and issues. ICME 13 monograph* (pp. 251–275). Cham: Springer.

Ruthven, K., Hennessy, S., & Deaney, R. (2008). Constructions of dynamic geometry: A study of the interpretative flexibility of educational software in classroom practice. *Computers & Education, 51*(1), 297–317.

Zhao, Z., Cook, J., & Higgen, N. (1996). Online learning for design students. *ALT-J, 4*(1), 69–76.

Chapter 4
How Did Mathematics Masters Work Four Thousand Years Ago? Curricula and Progressions in Mesopotamia

Christine Proust

Abstract Education in Mesopotamia is remarkably well documented. The reason for this abundance of sources is the nature of the writing support that was used in the Ancient Near East, namely, clay, an indestructible material that has survived from antiquity to the present day. School exercises have been found by the tens of thousands during archaeological excavations in Iraq, Syria, and Iran. The work of masters left traces on many documents, for example, mathematical exercises for beginners or sets of problems for advanced students. These traces allow us to partly reconstruct the organization of teaching. In this paper, I focus on didactical structures conveyed by sets of mathematical texts from diverse levels of education. I show the diversity of these structures, distinguishing, for example, the curricula produced by long-term institutional mechanisms, from progressions reflecting specific teaching projects of masters. I try to grasp the mathematical notions conveyed by the different didactical structures. To do this, I rely on homogeneous sets of documents produced by quite well-identified communities of students or masters. A discussion on the relevance of the concept of "resource system" in the context of scribal schools is proposed in conclusion.

Keywords Cuneiform mathematics · Old Babylonian period · Nippur · Scribal school · Curriculum · Progression · Sexagesimal place-value notation · Metrological table · Procedure

---

This chapter originates from a lecture given to the Re(s)sources 2018 International Conference. Video at http://video.ens-lyon.fr/ife/2018/2018-05-28_004_Ressources2018_Christine_Proust_v1.mp4

C. Proust (✉)
Laboratoire SPHERE (UMR 7219), CNRS & Université Paris Diderot, Paris, France

© Springer Nature Switzerland AG 2019
L. Trouche et al. (eds.), *The 'Resource' Approach to Mathematics Education*,
Advances in Mathematics Education,
https://doi.org/10.1007/978-3-030-20393-1_4

4.1 The Scribal Schools

Schools probably existed in Mesopotamia from the invention of writing around the mid-fourth millennium before the Common Era (hereafter BCE). At the beginning of the second millennium, the number of schools exploded, and literacy increased significantly. A growing part of the urban elites were educated from childhood in writing, reading, accounting, and arithmetic.

Texts written by students on clay tablets, or produced for them, have come down to us in abundance. The work of masters left traces on these documents used or produced in pedagogical activities, which allow modern historians to partly reconstruct the way in which teaching was organized. In this chapter, I focus on didactical structures conveyed by several sets of texts that I selected for this purpose. I show the diversity of these structures, distinguishing curricula, produced by long-term institutional mechanisms, from progressions, reflecting specific teaching projects elaborated by masters.[1]

School exercises have been found in many places in the Near East, mainly in the regions which are today included in Iraq, Iran, and Syria. However, two sites of the Euphrates Valley have been particularly prolific: Nippur, the most important cultural center of the time situated in Southern Mesopotamia, where tens of thousands of school tablets were excavated during the twentieth century by American teams, and Mari, an ancient political and economic capital located near the border between Syria and Iraq, where a school was discovered in 1998 by a French team. Other important school archives were found in Central and Southern Mesopotamia, for example, in Ur, Uruk, Larsa, Sippar, Susa, and others. See map in Fig. 4.1.

Most of these school tablets are dated to the Old Babylonian period (early second millennium BCE). The abundance of Nippur's sources provides a well-documented portrait of education in these schools. Moreover, Nippur played an essential role in the development of schooling in Mesopotamia, and, during a large part of the third and second millennia BCE, Nippur was the place *par excellence* for the transmission of scholarly traditions (Michalowski 2012, Veldhuis 1997). For these archaeological and historical reasons, I will firstly focus on Nippur.

Most of the school texts are written in Sumerian, a language which was spoken in Southern Mesopotamia during the third millennium BCE and disappeared as a mother-tongue probably before the beginning of the second millennium. Sumerian was gradually replaced by Akkadian, a Semitic language. However, cuneiform signs representing Sumerian words (sumerograms) were used in scholarly texts until clay was abandoned as a writing support in the first centuries of the Common Era. In the Old Babylonian period, Sumerian was the language of scholarship and schooling despite the fact that this tongue was no longer spoken.[2]

---

[1] Here and elsewhere in the chapter, the term "master" is preferred to the term "teacher" to emphasize the broad social role of scholars who were involved in the transmission of knowledge in the context of scribal schools. For more arguments, see Proust (2014).

[2] For a discussion on the complex relationship between language and writing, see, for example, Rubio (2007).

4 How Did Mathematics Masters Work Four Thousand Years Ago?

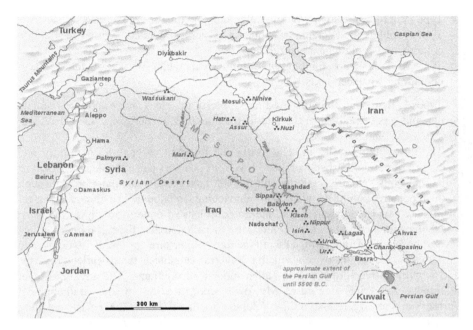

Fig. 4.1 Map of the Near East with main ancient cities. (Source: Wikipedia) (https://en.wikipedia.org/wiki/Mesopotamia, consulted 01/11/2018, GNU Free Documentation License)

The teaching in scribal schools included cuneiform writing, Sumerian literature, accounting and mathematics. Mathematical tablets represent broadly 10–20% of the school texts, which shows that mathematics had a significant, but not dominant, place in education. According to Veldhuis, the curriculum in Nippur schools was organized into three levels that he termed as elementary, intermediate, and advanced.[3] The different levels of education are evidenced by thousands of school tablets, including many duplicates which reflect the standardized character of the curriculum, and the importance of memorization (Veldhuis 1997; Delnero 2012; Proust 2015). These three levels correspond not only to specific texts but also to characteristic tablet shapes, which have been classified by Assyriologists as follows:

- Type I tablets are large (ca. 15 × 20 cm), rectangular, and multi-column and contain a long text beginning on the obverse (the side of the tablet, generally quite plane, written first) and continuing on the reverse (the side of the tablet, generally convex, written second).
- Type II tablets are also large and rectangular; however, unlike in type I tablets, the texts on the obverse and the reverse are different.
- Type III tablets are small and contain a short extract of texts contained in type I tablets.

---

[3] In the following, mathematical texts of elementary and intermediate level are referred to as "exercises."

64   C. Proust

- Type IV tablets are square or lenticular and contain a short exercise.
- Type S tablets are rectangular, sometimes very elongated, written in a single column, and contain an advanced text.
- Type M tablets are large multi-column rectangular or square tablets, also containing advanced texts.

Types I, II, III and IV were used in Nippur in the elementary and intermediate levels, and types S and M in the intermediate and advanced levels (Delnero 2010; Tinney 1999; Veldhuis 1997).

The curriculum set up in schools for the learning of cuneiform writing and Sumerian literature has been studied by various scholars since the decipherment of Sumerian. Niek Veldhuis' landmark thesis (Veldhuis 1997) was a major breakthrough in the reconstruction of the elementary curriculum in Nippur. The elementary level of literacy consisted essentially in memorizing lists of cuneiform signs, Sumerian vocabulary, and grammatical structures, the so-called lexical lists. The intermediate level consisted in applying the elementary repertoire of signs, words, and grammatical paradigms by reproducing Sumerian sentences, the so-called proverbs, and administrative forms, the so-called models of contracts. The advanced level addressed Sumerian literature. My own reconstruction of the mathematical curriculum was largely inspired by Veldhuis' methods (Proust 2007). The teaching of mathematics reproduced the same general organization: lists and tables memorized in the elementary level, and exercises applying these lists and tables in the intermediate level. However, in Nippur, the advanced level is much less well documented in mathematics than in Sumerian literature.[4]

In the first part of this chapter, I analyze how mathematical exercises of elementary level had been designed by the masters, in which order these exercises were offered to the pupils, and the mathematical significance of this order. These questions have already been addressed in recent publications, and I will limit myself to summarizing some important results (Proust 2007; Robson 2001). Moreover, as the elementary level provided the young scribes with fundamental arithmetical and metrological tools, this brief overview will be an introduction to the second and third parts dealing with the upper levels.

The exercises in the intermediate level are quite well known, but the order in which they were addressed is not clear. Indeed, the exercises are dispersed over many small tablets which are not connected to each other in a clear way. Nevertheless, in a second part, I will try to analyze some possible teaching structures evidenced by a group of exercises dealing with the evaluations of the surface of a square from Nippur. The advanced level is poorly known in mathematics. However, a group of texts from the same provenience, perhaps the Southern city of Larsa, which were probably written within the same community of masters, brings some light. In a third part, I rely on this small corpus to advance some hypotheses on how the

---

[4] A specific study of intermediate and advanced level of education in Nippur is still lacking. I began this study in (Proust in press-b). Scribal schools, especially those in Nippur, probably offered different trainings depending on the professions prepared by the young scribes and their future social level (*ibib*; Middeke-Conlin, forthcoming).

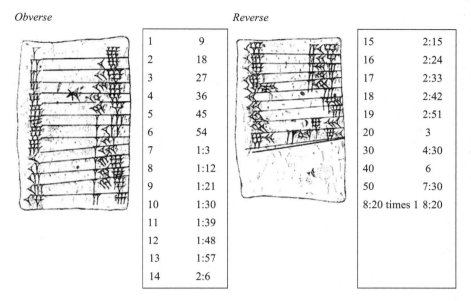

Fig. 4.2 Copy and translation of HS 217a (Hilprecht, 1906, no 15)

teaching of solving linear and quadratic problems had been thought about by the masters of this community. The conclusion will question the specific role of masters in structuring the teaching sequences of different levels.

4.1.1 The Sexagesimal Place-Value Notation

Cuneiform mathematics has a peculiarity that makes it quite original in comparison with other ancient traditions: the use of a sexagesimal place-value notation. Given the pivotal role played by this notation in mathematical training, an explanation of this system is required beforehand. Let us observe, for example, the notation of numbers in a school tablet translated in Fig. 4.2.[5]

In the left-hand column, we read: one wedge (𒁹), two wedges (𒈫), and so on until nine wedges (𒐚), one chevron (𒌋), which represents ten wedges, and so on. We recognize the sequence of numbers 1, 2, and so on; 10, 11, 12, and so on; and 19, 20, 30, 40, and 50. In the right-hand column:

- In front of 1, we read nine wedges, that is, the number 9.
- In front of 2, one chevron and eight wedges, that is, the number 18.
- In front of 3, the number 27, and so on.

---

[5] Tablet HS 217a from Nippur is now kept at the University of Jena and was published in (Hilprecht 1906; Proust 2008), photo at https://cdli.ucla.edu/P254585

It is clear that this tablet contains a multiplication table by 9. Thus, in front of 7, we expect 63, but we see one wedge, a space, and three wedges. It means that the "sixty" of "sixty-three" is represented by a wedge in the left position. We see that the notation uses the base 60 and a positional principle, exactly in the same way as we represent 1 min 3 s by the number 1:3. This is the so-called sexagesimal place-value notation (hereafter SPVN). Let us continue the reading: in front of 20, we expect 20 times 9, that is, 180, that is, 3 times 60. Indeed, we see three wedges. But the notation on the clay does not indicate that these wedges represent sixties, and not units. The "3" in front of 20 is the same as the "3" in the third line.

We see that the cuneiform sexagesimal place-value notation does not indicate the position of the units in the number. 1, 60, 1/60, and all powers of 60 are noted in the same way, a wedge. The notation is "floating." With this example, we see the three main properties of the notation of numbers used in multiplication tables: this notation is sexagesimal, place-valued, and floating.

By analogy with the modern sexagesimal place-value notation used for time, I separate the sexagesimal digits by colons in transliterations, translations, and commentaries. But the difference between ancient and modern notations must be kept in mind: the most important of these differences is that the ancient notation is floating, unlike the modern notation.

4.2 The Elementary Curriculum and Its Mathematical Meaning

4.2.1 Order of Texts

The evidence for the way in which the teaching material was sequenced and ordered is abundant and varied, and this alone proves the importance accorded to the order of carrying out exercises by the ancient masters.

Type I tablets provide a first kind of evidence. For example, the type I tablet from Nippur HS 249+ contains an enumeration of measurement values in increasing order.[6] The enumeration begins as follows (here, the *gin* is a capacity unit of about 17 ml – see Appendix for more information on metrological systems):

1 *gin* grain
2 *gin*
3 *gin*
4 *gin*
Etc.

---

[6]The tablet is composed of two fragments, HS 249 and HS 1805, now kept in the Hilprecht Collection at the University of Jena, and was published in Proust (2008), with photo, copy, transliteration, and translation; the photo is available online at https://cdli.ucla.edu/P388149

4 How Did Mathematics Masters Work Four Thousand Years Ago?

After the list of capacity measurements, the enumeration continues with weight, surface, and length measurements (these enumerations are called "metrological lists"). In many other instances, we find several metrological lists which are put together on the same tablet; in all cases, we observe the same order, namely, capacity, weight, surface, and length.

In the same way, all the numerical tables which were to be learnt during the elementary level are sometimes found together on the same type I tablets, such as Ist Ni 2733, from Nippur.[7] These numerical tables are the following, in this order:

> The table of reciprocals, multiplication tables by 50, 45, 44:26:40, 40, 36, 30, 25, 24, 22:30, 20, 18, 16:40, 16, 15, 12:30, 12, 10, 9, 8:20, 8, 7:30, 7:12, 7, 6:40, 6, 5, 4:30, 4, 3:45, 3:20, 3, 2:30, 2:24, 2, 1:40, 1:30, 1:20, 1:15, a table of squares and a table of square roots.

Whenever several numerical tables are put together on the same tablet, we observe the same order.

The enumerations of measurement values provided by metrological lists and numbers in sexagesimal place-value notation provided by numerical tables are connected in another genre of texts produced in the framework of elementary education, the so-called metrological tables. For example, in the type I tablet (CBS 8139+),[8] we recognize the items enumerated in metrological lists, with, in front of each item, a number written in sexagesimal place-value notation. The text begins with the metrological table of capacities:

1 *gin* grain	1
2 *gin*	2
3 *gin*	3
4 *gin*	4
Etc.	

After the list of capacity measurements, the enumeration continues with metro-logical tables of weights and surfaces. In the case of metrological tables too, when-ever several tables are put together on the same tablet, we observe the same order, namely, capacity, weight, surface, length, and heights.[9] The order of the lists and tables in type I tablets is thus extremely stable. In sources from other proveniences, we observe the same order as in Nippur.

Sometimes, only one metrological list or table or numerical table is written on a tablet, as in tablet HS 217a containing a multiplication table by 9 (Fig. 4.1). At the end of this table, after the last product which gives 9 times 50, an additional line gives the first line of the multiplication table by 8:20. In the order evidenced by type I tablets (such as Ist Ni 2733 just mentioned), the multiplication table by 8:30

---

[7] Tablet Ist Ni 2733 is now kept at the Archaeological Museum of Istanbul, and was published in Proust (2007), photo https://cdli.ucla.edu/P254643

[8] The tablet is composed of two fragments, CBS 08139 and N 3959, now kept in the Babylonian Section at the University of Pennsylvania Museum, and not yet published; the photo is online at https://cdli.ucla.edu/P263039

[9] The correspondence of measurement values and SPVN is different for length and height because of the definition of the volume units. See more explanation in (Proust, forthcoming).

68 C. Proust

appears to follow the multiplication table by 9. This additional item is thus a catch line, that is, the first line of the following text in the curricular order. Individual metrological lists or numerical tables are frequently followed by a catch line, indicating the position of this list or table inside the set it belongs to.

4.2.2 Reconstructing the Curriculum

We have observed a fixed order for the items inside the sets of metrological lists, metrological tables, and numerical tables. Are these three sets also rigidly ordered relative to one another? This question can be answered by examining the so-called type II tablets, that is, as mentioned above, tablets containing different texts on the obverse and the reverse. For example, the obverse of tablet HS 1703 contains a lexical list of names of professions and the reverse a metrological list of capacities.[10] It has been shown that the inscription on the obverse of type II tablets is a model that was written by a master or an advanced student to be reproduced by a pupil in order to memorize it and that the text on the reverse corresponds to sections of lists or tables memorized in a previous stage of the curriculum (see, for example, Civil 1985 and Veldhuis 1997). Thus, the type II tablets contain two texts which can be ordered in the curriculum: first, the text written on the reverse and second, the text written on the obverse. Systematically comparing the texts written on the hundreds of known type II tablets, Niek Veldhuis (1997) reconstructed the literacy curriculum. I applied the same method to mathematical texts (Proust 2007). As a result of these statistical comparisons, it is clear that the metrological lists were learned first, and then the numerical tables. Metrological lists and tables are difficult to compare with each other because they never appear associated on the same type II tablet. This could reflect differentiations in training and perhaps even the existence of specializations in different fields such as literature, mathematics, or accounting. As many type II tablets contain both lexical and mathematical texts, connections between the two curricula can be established.

On the basis of these observations, the mathematical curriculum in Nippur can be reconstructed as schematized in Fig. 4.3.

4.2.3 Metrological Tables: Numbers and Measurement Values

As we can see, elementary mathematical learning focussed on the assimilation of measurement units, numbers written in sexagesimal place-value notation, and the relationship between these two kinds of mathematical entities. A deep understanding of these fundamental pillars was needed by the students of scribal schools (and is

---

[10] Tablet HS 1703 from Nippur is now kept at the University of Jena and was published in (Proust 2008); photo at https://cdli.ucla.edu/P229902

4 How Did Mathematics Masters Work Four Thousand Years Ago?

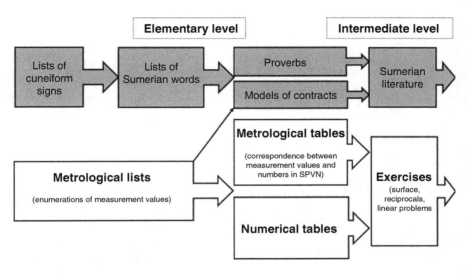

Fig. 4.3 Elementary and intermediate levels of education in Nippur

needed today by the present author and her readers) in order to penetrate the meaning of the mathematical methods used in procedures at the more advanced levels. A close observation of a metrological table will allow us such understanding.

A strict correspondence between measurement values and numbers in SPVN is established through the metrological tables. For example, the metrological table from Nippur (HS 241)[11] shows a correspondence between length measurements and numbers in SPVN (Fig. 4.4).

The measurement value 1 *šu-si* (1 finger, about 1.6 cm) corresponds to the number 10; hence, 2 *šu-si* corresponds to the number 20, etc., 5 *šu-si* to the number 50. For 6 *šu-si*, we expect 60, but we see instead the number "1." As in the multiplication tables, a wedge represents 1, as well as 60 or 1/60. We see again the floating character of the notation. The last item in the table states that 2 *kuš* (2 cubits, about 1 m) corresponds to the number 10. The measurement value 2 *kuš* is sixty times larger than 1 *šu-si*; thus, the number corresponding to 2 *kuš* is 60 times 10, that is, 10 in floating notation. In the right-hand column, we see the same numbers re-occurring cyclically.

---

[11] Tablet HS 241 from Nippur is now kept at the University of Jena and was published in (Hilprecht 1906; Proust 2008), photo at https://cdli.ucla.edu/P388160

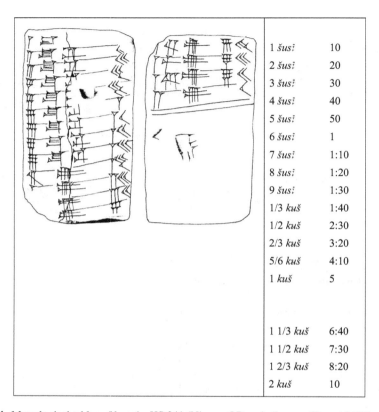

Fig. 4.4 Metrological tables of lengths HS 241 (Nippur, OB period), copy (Proust 2008)

4.2.4 Conclusion on the Elementary Level

To sum up, the first level of mathematics in scribal schools, at least in Nippur, consisted essentially in memorizing a strongly coherent and structured set of lists and tables. The numerous duplicates of these lists and tables attested in Nippur and elsewhere do not exhibit significant variations, neither in their order nor in their composition, which shows a high level of standardization of elementary education.

The "exercises" proposed for the student at this level were limited to the reproduction by heart of extracts of lists and tables and did not lead to the solving of problems. The goal was only the assimilation of the elementary tools needed for quantification and operations (multiplication and reciprocals). At this stage, the mathematical world was grounded on two different kinds of mathematical entities: firstly, measurement values enumerated in metrological lists and secondly, numbers in sexagesimal place-value notation, on which multiplications and reciprocals operate according to numerical tables. These two kinds of mathematical entities, while distinct, are closely connected by the metrological tables (see Appendix for an overview of the metrological systems and correspondences with SPVN). The nature of this connection is a key issue, which is illuminated by some of the intermediate level exercises.

4 How Did Mathematics Masters Work Four Thousand Years Ago? 71

4.3 Intermediate Level in Nippur: Basics of Arithmetic and Metrology

Following the elementary level, that is, the memorization of metrological and numerical tables, the students in scribal schools, at least probably the minority engaged in the study of mathematics, were trained to use these tables to solve problems. These exercises were noted on small round or square tablets, the so-called type IV tablets, which look very different from the tablets used in the elementary level (types I, II, and III). The type IV tablets from Nippur exhibit a strongly coherent set of exercises solving three classes of problems: how to calculate the surface of a square, how to compute a reciprocal, and how to solve linear problems (Proust 2007: sect. 6.1, 6.2, and 6.4).

4.3.1 Evaluating a Surface: Order of Magnitude and Calculation

Among the intermediate level exercises, the evaluations of surfaces are of special interest as they explain the articulation between the two kinds of mathematical entities: measurement values and numbers in SPVN. A dozen exercises of similar content and layout devoted to the evaluation of the surface of a square were found in Nippur. All have the same layout: on the top-left corner, there are three numbers in SPVN; on the bottom-right corner, there is a small problem text providing the statement and the answer. For example, in one of these exercises, UM 29-15-192,[12] the numbers noted on the top-left corner are 20, 20, and their product 6:40.

20
20
6:40

The statement noted on the bottom right corner is the following:

2 *šu-si* the side of a square
How much is the surface?
Its surface is 1/3 *še*.

What is the relationship between the numbers written on the top left (20 and 6,40) and the length and surface measurements written on the bottom right (2 *šu-si* and 1/3 *še*)? This relationship is exactly that established by the metrological tables (Table 4.1).

The content and layout of the tablet suggest that the process of evaluation of the surface included the following steps:

---

[12] Tablet UM 29-15-192, from Nippur, is now kept at the University of Pennsylvania Museum and was published by Neugebauer and Sachs (1984), photo at https://cdli.ucla.edu/P254900

72   C. Proust

Table 4.1 Metrological tables used in UM 29-15-192

First items on the metrological table of length HS 241[a]		First items of the metrological table of weight (and surface) MS 2186[b]	
		(1/3 *še*	6:40)
1 *šu-si*	10	1/2 *še* silver	10
2 *šu-si*	20	1 *še*	20
3 *šu-si*	30	1 1/2 *še*	30
4 *šu-si*	40	2 *še*	40
5 *šu-si*	50	2 1/2 *še*	50
6 *šu-si*	1	3 *še*	1

[a]Quoted above
[b]Tablet in the Schøyen Collection (Friberg 2007, p. 119), from unknown provenience, probably from Southern Mesopotamia. Although it does not come from Nippur, I quote this tablet here because it is in excellent condition and contains the same sequence as in many Nippur sources. The photo is available online (https://cdli.ucla.edu/P250902)

- First, the length measurements are transformed into floating numbers in sexagesimal place-value notations using the metrological table of lengths; indeed, the second item of this table provides the number 20 as corresponding to the length of the side 2 *šu-si* (c.a. 3.2 cm).
- Second, the number 20 is multiplied by itself using the multiplication tables, which gives 6:40.
- Third, the product 6:40 is transformed conversely into the corresponding surface measurement, 1/3 *še,* using a metrological table for surfaces.

The third step required special skills. Indeed, due to the floating character of the notation, as noted above, the same number in SPVN appears cyclically in the metrological tables. For example, the number 6:40 corresponds to 1/3 *še*, and also to 20 *še* which is sixty times larger, and so on. Thus, the choice of the relevant cycle of the metrological tables to be considered required mental monitoring of the order of magnitude of the expected result.[13]

The nature of the metrological tables is now clearer: they do not provide equalities between quantities and numbers in SPVN (the number 1 cannot be "equal" both to 3 *še* and to 1 *gin*), but a correspondence.[14] This correspondence is not bi-univocal

---

[13] Other skills are specifically related to the choice of the measurement value of the side. This side is small (2 *šu-si*, c.a. 3.2 cm); thus the expected area is smaller than the smallest measurement value which appears in the tables of surfaces ($^1/_3$ *sar*, c.a. 12 m²). The portion of the table to be used would be that of sub-units of the *sar*, i. e., the *gin* and the *še*, which appear only in tables for weights (hence the indication "silver" in the first item of the table translated in Table 1). But even in this portion, the smallest value ($^1/_2$ *še*, c.a. 15 cm²) is still too large, and an extrapolation to a smaller value (1/3 *še*, c.a. 10 cm²) is needed (see item in parenthesis in Table 4.1). What is interesting is that these difficulties seem to be intentional. Indeed, each of the evaluations of surfaces of the same kind found in Nippur mobilizes specific skills linked to the choice of the measurement value of the side. The meaning of these variations has been analyzed by de Varent (2018).

[14] Neugebauer and Sachs (1984, p. 248), who published this text, propose a different interpretation of the nature of the numbers. They do not make any connection with elementary mathematical

4 How Did Mathematics Masters Work Four Thousand Years Ago?

since several different measurement values correspond to the same number in SPVN (e.g., 3 *še* and 1 *gin* correspond to 1). This means that the reading of the table from left to right is straightforward, but the reading from right to left is only local. The selection of the relevant cycle when reading the metrological table from right to left, that is, the control of the orders of magnitude, appears to be one of the main skills that was developed in the intermediate level. The set of exercises devoted to the evaluation of the surface of a square shows how the training was carried out: the variation of the length of the side of the square allows all the aspects of the use of metrological tables to be explored (de Varent 2018).

The nature of the numbers in SPVN is also clearer: these numbers are the elements on which the multiplications apply. Numbers in SPVN appear to have been used as a calculation device, not to express quantities.[15] A specific arithmetic was developed inside the universe of floating numbers in sexagesimal place-value notation, with specific operations, multiplications and divisions, and specific algorithms, the most important being the method of factorization.

The fact that numbers in SPVN do not convey absolute quantitative information is one of the most essential aspects of school mathematics, even if quite puzzling for a modern observer. Another striking feature is that there is no trace of addition or subtraction in elementary and intermediate mathematical exercises. Additions and subtractions are operations that require the positions of the numbers to be identified with respect to each other and therefore could hardly be applied to floating numbers. Contrariwise, additions and subtractions are omnipresent in economic and administrative documents, where these operations apply on quantities, namely, measurement values and counting of discrete elements. Everything happens as if, in the school world, addition and subtraction did not belong to the field of mathematics, but only to the field of accounting.[16]

4.3.2 Curriculum in Mesopotamia

The picture of the curriculum which emerges from Nippur sources is quite clear. Is the curriculum the same in other cities? It is difficult to describe the mathematical education in the other schools with so much detail because, as mentioned above, sources are much more scarce than in Nippur, with the notable exception of Mari (Nicolet 2016). Moreover, the key evidence about the curriculum is provided by

---

education, which was not well known at that time. Their interpretation is grounded on the implicit assumption that the relationships between the measurement values and the numbers in SPVN are *equalities* (e.g., that 2 *šu-si* is considered to be *equal* to 20, and thus this later number is understood as 0;0,20 *ninda*). A similar text was recently analyzed in exactly the same manner by (Robson 2008) (p. 9).

[15] Written numbers were probably representations of a calculation tool based on token. See discussion on the role of such device in schools in (Trouche 2016).

[16] Note that, in Sumerian literary texts, the terminology distinguishes calculation (šid) and accounting (niggas).

type II tablets, but the type II tablets are rare out of Nippur. While the order of mathematical school exercises from other cities is difficult to detect, their content is not fundamentally different from those from Nippur, at least as far as the elementary level is concerned.

As for the intermediate level, a greater variety of exercises can be observed. We find in other cities, especially Ur in Southern Mesopotamia, a lot of examples of calculations similar to those found in Nippur, such as the calculation of reciprocals by the method of factorization, but also calculations of areas of circles or of trapezoids, or calculations of volumes, as well as tables of numbers which provide the solutions to a great variety of linear problems. The important point is that, as those from Nippur, all of these exercises belong to the multiplicative field in the sense that they involve only multiplications and divisions.

4.4 Some Light on Advanced Mathematical Education

How does advanced mathematical education fit into this landscape? The main issue is the identification of texts reflecting advanced mathematical education.[17] Teaching texts for the advanced level are often hard to distinguish from exercises for intermediate level or from scholarly mathematical texts.[18]

4.4.1 Sources

However, structures reflecting an advanced pedagogical project for teaching specific notions can be detected in some corpuses. This is the case for a group of several tablets with similar content dated to the Old Babylonian period and probably found at the same place. They are now kept at Yale University.[19] All of them are single-column tablets, sometimes very elongated. All of them contain a list of problem statements with no explanation on the resolution methods, and for this reason they were called "catalogue texts" by Høyrup (2000, p. 3; 2002, p. 9). In most of them the text ends with a sub-script, a "colophon," providing the number of statements as well as, in some instances, the theme of the problem (rectangle, stone, canal, or excavation). The texts are written using only sumerograms.[20] Some features of the

---

[17] By contrast, the texts that were used for advanced literary education are well known. See, for example, Delnero (2010) and Tinney (1999).

[18] See more discussion on the identification of teaching texts in Bernard and Proust (2014) and Proust (2012b).

[19] YBC 4612, YBC 6492, YBC 4607, YBC 4652, YBC 4657, YBC 5037, YBC 4666, and YBC 7164. These tablets were published by Neugebauer and Sachs (1945). For the provenience and date, see ibid as well as discussion in Høyrup (2002, Ch. 9) and Proust (2012a).

[20] Sumerograms are cuneiform signs representing Sumerian words. The writing system adopted to represent the Sumerian language was ideographic: the signs represent words. By contrast, the writ-

4 How Did Mathematics Masters Work Four Thousand Years Ago? 75

Table 4.2 Catalogue text C (YBC 4657) and related procedure texts.

Text	Tablet	Content	Corresponding statements in C	Colophon
Catalogue text C	YBC 4657	31 problem statements on trenches		31 sections on trenches
Procedure text Pa	YBC 4663	8 problems with procedures	1-8	No colophon
Procedure text Pb	lost	10 problems with procedures	9-18	
Procedure text Pc	YBC 4662	10 problems with procedures	19-28	No colophon

tablets, such as the shape, the presence of a colophon and the use of sumerograms, strongly evoke a teaching context.[21] In the following, we see how the content and organization of the problems in these tablets may reflect a pedagogical project.

Among the tablets containing catalogue texts, one is of special interest, YBC 4657. Indeed, the problems stated in this catalogue are solved in other tablets containing detailed explanations on the steps to be followed (procedures). Two of these procedure texts associated with catalogues are known, YBC 4663 and YBC 4662. Problems 1 to 8 in catalogue YBC 4657 are solved in YBC 4663, problems 19 to 28 in the same catalogue are solved in YBC 4662, and in between, problems 9 to 18 were probably solved in a procedure text noted in a tablet which did not reach us, as summarized in Table 4.2.[22]

The problems enumerated in catalogue C (YBC 4657) deal with the same situation, the dimensions of a trench to be excavated and the cost of this work. Some of the problems are linear, that is, they can be solved by a succession of multiplications and divisions, and others are quadratic. To underline some of the didactical features of these texts, I first examine the way in which problems 1, 2, and 7 are solved in the procedure text Pa (YBC 4663); second I analyze the structure of the whole set of problems in the catalogue.[23]

---

ing system adopted to represent the Akkadian language was phonetic: the signs represent syllables of the words.

[21] In literary education in Nippur, elongated single-column tablets (type S) are characteristic of the advanced level of education (Delnero 2010; Tinney 1999). For the meaning of the colophon as reflecting a teaching context, see Proust (2012a).

[22] My numbering of the texts (C, Pa, Pb, and Pc) is a simplification of the numbering I adopted in other publications, where these same texts appear as C5, P5a, P5b, and P5c (Proust 2012a, in press-a).

[23] In this presentation, I only focus on didactical aspects of the texts; for a deeper analysis of the content, in particular on the strategy adopted to prove the procedures, see Proust in press-a.

76 C. Proust

4.4.2 Three Fundamental Mathematical Methods Used in Procedures

Problem 1: which basic tools?

Pa (YBC 4663) #1 Obverse[24]

1.	A trench. 5 ninda is its length, 1 1/2 ninda (is its width), 1/2 ninda is its depth, 10 <gin > is the volume of the work assignment, 6 še [silver is the wage of the hired man].
2.	The base, the volume, the (number) of workers and the silver are how much? You, in your procedure,
3.	The length and the width cross, 7:30 it will give you.
4.	7:30 to its depth raise, 45 it will give you.
5.	The reciprocal of the work assignment detach, 6 it will give you. To 45 raise, 4:30 it will give you.
6.	4:30 to the wage raise, 9 it will give you. Such is the procedure.

The procedure opens and closes with a frozen formula "You, in your procedure," and "Such is the procedure" (lines 2–6). As in the catalogue, the writing of the statement uses only sumerograms, but unlike in the statement, the writing of the procedure uses mainly syllabic Akkadian words (underlined in the translation)

At first glance, two features are striking: in the statement, written with sumerograms, the data appear as measurement values (5 *ninda,* etc.). In the procedure, written in Akkadian, the numbers appear only in SPVN (7:30, etc.). Thus, the same question arises as in the example of the evaluation of the surface of the square above: what is the relationship between the measurement values given in the statement, and the numbers used in the procedure? Not surprisingly, the answer is the same: this relationship is that provided by the metrological tables. These correspondences are the following (see Appendix):

- 5 *ninda* corresponds to 5 in the metrological table of lengths,
- 1 1/2 *ninda* corresponds to 1:30 in the metrological table of lengths,
- 1/2 *ninda* corresponds to 6 in the metrological table of heights,[25]
- 10 *gin* corresponds to 10 in the metrological table of volumes,[26]
- 6 *še* corresponds to 2 in the metrological table of weights.

Then, the procedure operates only on these numbers in SPVN and produces numbers in SPVN. The operations are the following:

---

[24] My translation. The lines numbers were added by the modern editors. I underlined the words written in syllabic Akkadian.

[25] The numbers corresponding to the vertical dimensions are not the same as the numbers corresponding to the horizontal dimensions because of the definition of units of volume in the school context. See Neugebauer and Sachs (1945) (p. 5) and for more details and bibliography (Proust forthcoming).

[26] The metrological table of surfaces served also as metrological table of volumes (Proust forthcoming).

4 How Did Mathematics Masters Work Four Thousand Years Ago?

- Line 3   5 × 1:30 gives 7:30 (the base)
- Line 4   7:30 × 6 gives 45 (the volume).
- Line 5   45 ÷ 6, that is, 45 × recip(6), that is, 45 × 10 gives 4:30 (the number of workers)
- Line 6   4:30 × 2 gives 9 (the total salary)

The outputs could be transformed into measurement values as follows:

- 7:30, which corresponds to 7 1/2 *sar* in the metrological table of surfaces
- 45, which corresponds to 45 *sar* in the metrological table of volumes
- 4:30, which corresponds to 4 × 60 + 30 workers
- 9, which corresponds to 9 *gin* in the metrological table of weights.

These transformations are not explicit in the text, but they would be required in order to answer the questions asked in the statement: What are the base, the volume, the number of workers, and the amount of silver?

This problem wears the same didactic clothes as UM 29–15-192, the evaluation of the surface of a square analyzed above. In both cases, the two different kinds of mathematical entities are distributed in two different parts of the texts: in our problem, the measurement values are given in the statement, and the numbers in SPVN are placed between the opening formula ("you, in your procedure") and the closing formula ("that is the procedure"). Moreover, the distribution of the two kinds of mathematical entities is underlined by a change in writing system, sumerograms in the statement, syllabic Akkadian in the procedure. In both cases, the operations are multiplications (or divisions, which are multiplications by a reciprocal). In both cases, the correspondence between the measurement values and the numbers in SPVN is that provided by the metrological tables. Almost all of the metrological tables that had been memorized in elementary education are activated in turn in this problem: lengths, heights, surfaces, volumes, and weights.

As only multiplications and divisions are to be performed, the procedure does not require the position of the numbers in SPVN with respect to each other to be fixed. The floating notation is not a disadvantage; on the contrary, it confers a great simplicity to the calculation.

Problem 2: losing the meaning
Pa (YBC 4663) #2 Obverse

7.	9 gin is the silver for a trench, 1 1/2 ninda (is its width), 1/2 ninda is its depth, 10 (gin) is the volume of the work assignment, 6 še (of silver) is the wage.
8.	Its length is how much? You, in your procedure, the width and the depth cross.
9.	9 it will give you. The reciprocal of the work assignment detach.
10.	(and) to 9 raise, 54 it will give you.
11.	54 to the wage raise, 1:48 it will give you.
12.	The reciprocal of 1:48 (detach), 33:20 it will give you. 33:20 to 9, the silver, raise.
13.	5 it will give you. 5 ninda is its length. Such is the procedure.

Problem 2 seems very similar to problem 1. The difference is that the total salary is given (9 *gin*), but not the length of the trench, which is to be found. The other data are the same. The preliminary task, transforming the measurement values given in the statement into numbers in SPVN using metrological tables is the same as in problem 1. Then, the procedure prescribes a succession of operations:

- Lines 8–9   1:30 × 6 gives 9 (corresponding to a vertical surface).
- Lines 9–10   9 ÷ 10, that is, 9 × recip(10), that is, 9 × 6, gives 54 (this number does not correspond to any quantity).
- Line 11   54 × 2 gives 1:48 (this number does not correspond to any quantity).
- Lines 12–13   9 ÷ 1:48, that is, 9 × recip(1:48), that is, 9 × 33:20 gives 5 (corresponding to the length 5 *ninda*).

The apparently slight differences between problems 1 and 2, the order of the data, have a strong consequence: as we see, it is no longer possible to give a meaning to each step. The calculation seems to be done blind, but at the end it gives the correct result, 5. Unlike in problem 1, the question in problem 2 asks only the length, not other intermediate magnitudes. The layout adopted in problem 1, that is, one operation per line, is abandoned here. Thus, it seems that the reasoning has a different basis. To understand this procedure, let us compare the calculation flow in problems 1 and 2. The procedure in problem 1 can be described, in modern representation, by the following succession of arithmetical operations, to be executed from left to right (I replace the announcement of the output "it will give you" by an arrow; recip(x) means "the reciprocal of x").

$$5 \times 1{:}30 \times 6 \times \text{recip}(10) \times 2 \to 9$$

This calculation flow corresponds to the general procedure schematized below:

$$\text{length} \times \text{width} \times \text{depth} \times \text{recip(assignment)} \times \text{wage} \to \text{silver},$$

In which each of the steps, if we operate from left to right, has a meaning.

The same representation applied on problem 2 produces the following calculation flow:

$$[1{:}30 \times 6 \times \text{recip}(10) \times 2]\text{recip} \times 9 \to 5$$

Corresponding to this procedure:

$$[\text{width} \times \text{depth} \times \text{recip(assignment)} \times \text{wage}]\text{recip} \times \text{silver} \to \text{length}$$

Considering both representations, the arithmetical structure of the procedure in problem 2 can be compared to that in problem 1:

Procedure 1:   **length × width × depth × recip(assignment) × wage** → silver
Procedure 2:   **[width × depth × recip(assignment) × wage]**recip × silver → length

4 How Did Mathematics Masters Work Four Thousand Years Ago?

We see that the procedure in problem 2 uses a subroutine of procedure 1 (in bold above). If we represent the result of the subroutine by A, procedure 1 can be reduced to the following structure:

length × A → silver

And procedure 2 can be reduced to the following structure:

[A]recip × silver → length

The structure of procedure 1 is made similar to the calculation of the area of a rectangle, the sides of which are the length and A. Procedure 2 is thus a reverse problem: find a side of a rectangle knowing its area and the other side.

To sum up, the second problem, despite its resemblance to the first problem, is completely different in nature. The procedure does not rely on steps which are meaningful, but on the configuration of the rectangle, a side of which is a subroutine of procedure 1. Problems 3 to 6 are variants of problem 2 by circular permutations of the data.

Problem 7: how to deal with addition and subtraction?
Pa (YBC 4663) #7 reverse

0.	9 gin is the silver for a trench.
1.	The length and the width I added, it is 6:30. ½ ninda [is its depth].
2.	10 gin is the work assignment, 6 še (silver) is the wage. Its length and its width how much?
3.	You, in your procedure, the reciprocal of the wage detach.
4.	To 9 gin, the silver, raise. 4:30 it will give you.
5.	4.30 to the work assignment raise. 45 it will give you.
6.	The reciprocal of its depth detach. To 45 raise. 7:30 it will give you.
7.	½ of the length and the width which I added break. 3:15 it will give you.
8.	3:15 cross itself. 10:33:45 it will give you.
9.	7:30 from 10:33:45 tear out.
10.	3:3:45 it will give you. Its equal-side take.
11.	1:45 it will give you. To the one append, from the other cutoff.
12.	The length and the width it will give you. 5 (ninda) is the length, 1 1/2 ninda is the width.

Problem 7 introduces a new type of data, the sum of the length and the width (line 1: "The length and the width I added, it is 6:30"). The statement also gives the total salary (9 *gin*), the depth (½ *ninda*), the assignment (daily work 10 *gin*), and the daily salary (6 *še*). These data allow the base of the trench to be calculated (line 3 to 6): the base is 7:30. The problem has been transformed into the following: find the length and the width knowing their sum (the length added to the width is 6:30) and their product (the surface corresponds to 7:30). This is a quadratic problem which will serve as a reference for the other problems on the tablet (see Fig. 4.5)

Fig. 4.5 Representation of the quadratic situation of Pa (YBC 4663), problem 7

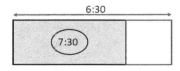

The procedure solves this problem by the so-called completion of the square method.[27] I do not go into the procedure in detail, but just underline the fact that, at some point in the process, a subtraction on numbers in SPVN is performed:

7:30 from 10:33:45 tear out.

Excluded from elementary and intermediate mathematical education, the addition and subtraction of numbers in SPVN are introduced at the advanced stage in order to solve quadratic problems. These operations would need more information on the numbers that the text does not provide.[28] The important point to be highlighted is the way in which the addition and subtraction of numbers in SPVN are treated in the program of teaching: operations that are impossible in the elementary level acquire a meaning in the context of quadratic procedures. Problem 8 is similar, but the difference of the length and the width is given instead of their sum, which leads to a second kind of reference quadratic problem. As we see, problems 7 and 8 introduce new methods: transforming a problem in order to obtain a reference quadratic problem, solving the two models of quadratic problems, working with addition and subtraction of numbers in SPVN.

4.4.3 The Mathematical Methods Introduced in the Procedure Text

To sum up, procedure text YBC 4663 starts by relying on tables and tools learnt in the elementary and intermediate levels and progressively introduces new mathematical methods in order to address the following issues:

- How to find a magnitude, here the total salary, in linear situations by calculating intermediate magnitudes, here the base, the volume, and the number of workers (problem 1).
- How to find a magnitude by using a subroutine of a reference linear problem, the steps of which are meaningful (problems 2–6).
- How to transform a quadratic problem in order to obtain a reference quadratic problem: here find the length and the width knowing their sum or difference and their product.

---

[27] For this method in general, see Høyrup (2002); for more explanation on this particular problem, see Proust in press-a.

[28] See Proust (2016) for an analysis of the particular skills required to perform operations in the quadratic procedures.

4 How Did Mathematics Masters Work Four Thousand Years Ago?

– How to solve such a quadratic problem using geometrical representations, how to deal with addition and subtraction of numbers in SPVN (problem 7 and 8).

These methods are applied in the other procedure texts related to catalogue C and beyond in Old Babylonian mathematics, and they constitute the fundamental toolbox for solving linear and quadratic problems.

4.4.4 Didactical Structure of Catalogue YBC 4657

We have just seen how the set of problems 1–8 in procedure text Pa (YBC 4663), which corresponds to statements 1–8 in catalogue C (YBC 4657), relies on elementary and intermediate level education and progressively introduces new tools. Are the other problems listed in the catalogue organized into similar sets? Some observations, synthetized in Table 4.3, can be made.

If we look at both the situation described in the problems listed in catalogue C and the nature of the problems, a second set of problems appears: problems 9–21 deal with the same situation, a trench the dimensions of which are given or to be found. This second set is composed of 4 linear problems (9–12), and 9 apparently quadratic problems (13–21). The linear problems are similar to problems 1–6 in the first set. The quadratic problems 13–14 are also similar to problems 7–8 in the first set. Problems 15–18 seem to be quadratic as the sum or the difference of the length and the width are given in the statement. However, simple transformations reduce the problems to linear problems (it is clear for 15–16, probable for 17–18, which are damaged). The three last problems in the second set, 19 to 21, are quadratic problems. These problems can be reduced to reference quadratic problems solved in the first set of problems, but this reduction is more technical because it involves fractions. We see that this second set of problems introduces new elements of complexity in quadratic problems: how to reduce a problem that appears to be quadratic into a linear problem and how to work with fractions. The linear problems are simpler than in the first set.

A third set is composed of problems 22 to 30. The situation is related to the same trench as before with the same numbers of workdays necessary to dig this trench, but unlike in the first and second set, there is no mention of the salaries. This third set begins with a series of linear problems. These linear problems seem to be similar to the previous ones: the procedures rely on the subroutines in a reference linear problem, the steps of which are meaningful. However, there is a significant difference: this reference linear problem is not given; the reader has to reconstruct it in order to obtain the subroutines.

To sum up, catalogue YBC 4657 is composed of three sets of problems structured in the same way: a sequence of linear problems followed by a sequence of quadratic problems. All the problems concern the same situation. The fundamental methods are introduced in the first set, and the other sets, while they rely on these fundamental methods, progressively introduce new tools. The structure of this catalogue evokes

82   C. Proust

Table 4.3 Content of problems listed in catalogue C (YBC 4657) and related procedure texts (Pa = YBC 4663, lost Pb, and Pc = YBC 4662)

Catalogue C	Procedure texts	Concrete situation	Nature of the problem	Tools
#1	Pa #1	Dimensions of the trench and cost in silver	Linear	Reference linear problem (steps meaningful)
#2-6	Pa #2-6	Dimensions of the trench and cost in silver	Linear	Subroutine of the reference linear problem
#7-8	Pa #7-8	Dimensions of the trench and cost in silver	Quadratic	Reference quadratic problems 1 and 2
#9	Lost #1	Dimensions of the trench	Linear	Reference linear problem (steps meaningful)
#10-12	Lost #2-4	Dimensions of the trench	Linear	Subroutine of the reference linear problem
#13-14	Lost #5-6	Dimensions of the trench	Quadratic	Reference quadratic problem 1 and 2
#15-18	Lost #7-10	Dimensions of the trench	False quadratic	Quadratic reduced to linear
#19	Pc #1	Dimensions of the trench	Quadratic	Reference quadratic problem 1
#20	Pc #2	Dimensions of the trench	Quadratic	Linear portion with fractions. Reference quadratic problem 2
#21	Pc #3	Dimensions of the trench	Quadratic	Linear portion with fractions. Reference quadratic problem 2
#22-28	Pc #4-10	Dimensions of the trench and workdays	Linear	Subroutine of a reference linear problem not given
#29		Dimensions of the trench and workdays	Quadratic	Reference quadratic problem 1
#30		Dimensions of the trench and workdays	Quadratic	Reference quadratic problem 2
#31		Dimensions of another trench and cost in grain	Linear	Cath line?
Colophon		"31 sections (about) trenches"		

a progressive program of teaching designed by masters of scribal schools in order to explain how to solve a variety of linear and quadratic problems. This program is organized into three cycles, the second and the third cycles reproducing the first, while enriching it. In a way, the catalogue reflects a **spiral progression**.[29]

---

[29] The concept of "spiral" curriculum (or progression, or method, or plan, or learning) emerged among educators such as Johann Heinrich Pestalozzi (1746–1827), August Wilhelm Grube (1816–1884), or David Eugene Smith (1860–1944) during the nineteenth century and early twentieth century (Smith 1904, 38; Bidwell and Clason 1970). This idea was revived later, for example, by

4 How Did Mathematics Masters Work Four Thousand Years Ago? 83

This progression is distinct from the curriculum that governs elementary education in the sense that it is a set of problems intentionally constructed by individuals, a master or group of masters, with the aim of teaching students specific methods to solve specific problems. The progression is more clearly the result of a teaching project lead by individuals than the elementary curriculum is.

4.4.5 Spiral Progression at the Scale of the Whole Set of Catalogue Texts

Let us now consider the whole set of mathematical catalogues kept at Yale from which our catalogue C is extracted (see list in note 23). Does this whole set of catalogues exhibit a didactical structure similar to that found in catalogue C? The analysis of the other catalogues cannot reach a comparable level of detail as that of catalogue C as only procedure texts related to catalogue C have come down to us. I limit myself to some remarks only, a deeper study still needing to be done.

First remark: the last problem in catalogue C (the 31st) deals with a trench different from that of the other problems in the text and appears to be a catch line, that is, the first problem of another catalogue. This other catalogue may be found in the Yale tablet numbered YBC 5037. Indeed, the final problem enumerated in catalogue C and the first on YBC 5037 are similar, even if they differ on some minor points, for example, the fact that the salary is paid in grain in the former, but in silver in the latter. Catalogue YBC 5037 contains 44 problem statements, also dealing with a trench and diverse related concrete parameters. This catalogue too contains cycles, some of which are similar to those in catalogue C, and others focus only on quadratic problems and introduce new methods. Thus, catalogue YBC 5037 appears to be a continuation of catalogue C. The progression detected in catalogue C appears to be a part of a broader spiral progression encompassing the sequence of problems listed in several catalogues (C, YBC 5037, and perhaps in other catalogues that have not come down to us).

Second remark: two of the mathematical catalogues kept at Yale deal with "fields," that is, rectangles. For example, in catalogue YBC 4612, 15 statements give the length and the width of rectangles and ask for the areas or, conversely, give the area and a side of a rectangle and ask for the other side. We observed above that some of the linear problems in our catalogue C are based on the fundamental configuration of the rectangle: the direct problem, given the sides of a rectangle, finds its area, and the two reverse problems, given the area and the length (respectively, the width), find its width (respectively, its length). Thus, the sequence of problems on fields listed in catalogue YBC 4612 may have constituted one of the first cycles of a larger progression, including our catalogue C and its possible continuation, catalogue YBC 5037.

Jerome Bruner in years 1960 and has become very popular in recent years in French educational institutions.

4.5 Didactical Structures and Resource Systems

In the previous sections, three different didactical structures have been brought to light; they are summarized in Table 4.4.

I conclude this overview of didactical structures sets up for different levels of mathematics education in Southern Mesopotamia by some remarks on the way in which these structures may reflect "resource systems." The concept of "resource system" developed by Kenneth Ruthven in this volume (Chap. 3) can hardly be used with exactly the same meaning in analyzing ancient teaching practices because of the difficulty to transfer to ancient societies conceptual tools shaped for tackling modern realities. Moreover, our knowledge of ancient scribal schools depends on a randomly selected corpus of written documents which came down to us. These documents represent a small proportion of the production of ancient schools and convey only tiny traces of unwritten practices. However, the concept of "resource system" may be relevant in the present discussion as it draws the attention on the multiple facets of teaching environments, actors, and practices. In the following, a "resource system" is understood as a nexus of written documents, memorized knowledge, computation devices, and other more nebulous elements of a mathematical culture shared by communities of scribes. I limit the present conclusion to some remarks on how masters used, created, and organized "resource systems" in the context of the different levels of mathematics education

The first of the three didactical structures summarized in Table 4.4 is the rigid curriculum governing elementary education in Nippur. The first level of mathematical education was not based on active mathematical training such as solving problems, but rather on learning lists and tables by heart. Prototypes of these lists and tables were probably shaped before the Old Babylonian period. Indeed, traces of the use of metrological and numerical tables have been detected in administrative and economic texts produced in the context of the centralized states at the end of the 3rd millennium for quantification of surfaces of lands, volumes of canals, quantities of work, value of goods, and other quantities.[30] These prototypes were possibly reformatted, but not fundamentally changed, in the context of scribal schools. The

Table 4.4 Didactical structures

Level	Place	Tablet type	Structure	Content
Elementary	Nippur	I, II, III	Standard curriculum	Metrological and numerical lists and tables
Intermediate	Nippur	IV	Small variations	Exercises: surface of squares, reciprocals, small linear problems
Advanced	South	S	Spiral progression	Linear and quadratic problems

---

[30] See more details on the computation and quantification practices in the third millennium, especially in administrative and economic contexts, in Chemla et al. (forthcoming).

written materials produced for or by elementary education do not appear as pedagogical artifacts designed by masters, but rather as the by-product of social and intellectual processes.[31] It is difficult to identify which role was played by specific individuals or communities in this process. However, the high stability of lists and tables used in elementary education, both geographically and chronologically, suggests that this role was minor. To sum up, the material used in the elementary level of mathematics education probably had been inherited from traditions handed down from generations to generations since the end of the third millennium. These traditions have taken the form of a fixed set of lists and tables transmitted without significant changes, in a rigid order, mainly by memorization. As far as the elementary level is concerned, the "resource system" seems to have been shaped more by tradition than by individual involvement or intentional decision of some masters

The second didactical structure is exemplified in Nippur by the set of exercises based on small variations that was proposed to intermediate level students. The goal of these exercises was to learn to solve three classes of problems: evaluating surfaces of squares, computing reciprocals, and solving in tabular layout some simple linear problems. These exercises relied on the use of tables memorized in the elementary level and on the use of a calculation device for performing multiplications. Some of these exercises may be understood as parts of pedagogical projects. For example, the set of exercises dealing with the evaluation of surfaces of squares seems to have been shaped by a master or a group of masters in order to explore all the facets of the use of metrological tables, especially the reverse reading of tables for surfaces (transforming numbers in sexagesimal place-value notation into measures of surface). This exploration is implemented by the variations of the measurements of the sides of the squares. As shown by de Varent (2018), the choices of the measurement of the sides expose the students to the numerous issues raised by the use of metrological tables (choice of the correct cycle, extrapolation, interpolation, circulation in the tables) and by performing multiplications. In the same way, a pedagogical project can be detected in the set of exercises dealing with the computations of reciprocals. However, unlike in catalogues and procedure texts, the exercises are isolated on separate tablets. The order in which they were proposed to the students is thus hard to reconstruct. To sum up, the material used or produced by masters for mathematics training of intermediate level is composite. It includes templates of a limited set of exercises, mainly computing a reciprocal, evaluating surfaces of squares, and solving basic linear problems, displayed in fixed layout and based on fixed algorithms. These templates seem to have circulated among schools in the Ancient Near East during the Old Babylonian period, since some of them, for example computing a reciprocal, are attested in most of the Southern schools as well as far away from Nippur, for example, in Mari. However, unlike elementary level exercises, intermediate level exercises do not include duplicates. Within the limits imposed by the use of a fixed set of templates, masters seem to have been free to apply their own pedagogy by choosing the data for these exercises. All in all, several

---

[31] In the same way, multiplication tables which are learnt today in elementary education have a long history.

processes seem to have influenced the way in which masters shaped their resource system for intermediate education. Among these processes, are the traditions inherited from masters of previous generations, the circulation of information between schools, possible evolution or improvement of calculation devices, and individual involvement, for example, in the choices of the data of the exercises

The third didactical structure is illustrated by the set of mathematical catalogues and related procedure texts kept at Yale. The provenience of these texts is unknown, thus these texts cannot be connected directly with the material from Nippur. However, these texts are grounded on the elementary and intermediate mathematical knowledge evidenced by school texts from Nippur. The same knowledge is documented in Larsa – where the catalogues may come from. The structure of the list of problems in the catalogues (e.g., YBC 4657), the solution of which being provided by two procedure texts which have come down to us (YBC 4663 and YBC 4662), evokes a spiral progression elaborated by a master or a community of masters in order to teach the methods for solving a large variety of linear and quadratic problems. Unlike the elementary curriculum, this progression more clearly reflects choices made by masters. Here, the resource system can hardly be described in all its complexity. It certainly included the basic mathematical knowledge – mediated by written texts, memorized tables, and technical skills – instilled to scribes during the first stages of their education. It involved also scholarly mathematical elaborations which were circulating, in written or oral form, among masters of the different schools, such as the procedures of solving quadratic problems. It also testimonies a didactical reflection on the transmission of these mathematical elaborations. The catalogues and associated procedure texts reflect the implementation of a spiral progression designed by masters for this transmission. Another facet of the transmission project may be the creation of the first libraries, evidenced by the colophons of the catalogues (Proust 2012a). To sum up, unlike in elementary level, the teaching practices related to advanced mathematics education were not governed only by perpetuating the tradition. The spiral progression appears to be an innovative pedagogical method, intentionally though by masters

Appendix

The diagrams below represent the metrological systems and correspondences with SPVN according to Old Babylonian sources from Nippur. The arrows represent the factors between different measurement units (e.g., *gin* ←180− *še* means 1 *gin* is equal to 180 *še*); the numbers below the units are the numbers in SPVN that correspond to these units in the metrological tables (e.g., 20 below *še* means that 1 *še* corresponds to 20 in metrological tables).

Length and other horizontal dimensions (1 *ninda* represents about 6 m):

ninda	←12−	*kuš*	← 30−	*šu-si*
1		5		10

4 How Did Mathematics Masters Work Four Thousand Years Ago?

Heights and other vertical dimensions (1 *ninda* represents about 6 m):

ninda	←12−	*kuš*	← 30−	*šu-si*
5		1		2

Surface and volume (a surface of 1 *sar* is that of a square of 1 *ninda*-side; a volume of 1 *sar* is that of a rectangular cuboid of 1 *sar*-base and 1 *kuš*-high):

gan	←100−	*sar*	←60−	*gin*	←180−	*še*
1:40		1		1		20

Weight (1 *mana* represents about 500 g):

mana	←60−	*gin*	←180−	*še*
1		1		20

References

Bernard, A., & Proust, C. (Eds.). (2014). *Scientific sources and teaching contexts throughout history: Problems and perspectives*. Dordrecht/Heidelberg/New York/London: Springer.

Bidwell, J. K., & Clason, R. G. (Eds.). (1970). *Readings in the history of mathematics education*. Washington, DC: National Council of Teachers of Mathematics.

Chemla, K., Keller, A., & Proust, C. (Eds.). (forthcoming). *Cultures of computation and quantification in the Ancient World*. New York: Springer.

Civil, M. (1985). Sur les "livres d'écoliers" à l'époque paléo-babylonienne. In J.-M. Durand & J.-R. Kupper (Eds.), *Miscellanea Babylonica, Mélanges offerts à M. Birot* (pp. 67–78). Paris: RC.

De Varent, C. (2018). *Pluralité des concepts liés aux unités de mesure. Liens entre histoire des sciences et didactique, le cas de l'aire du carré dans une sélection de textes anciens*. PhD. Paris: Université Paris Diderot.

Delnero, P. (2010). Sumerian Extract Tablets and Scribal Education. *Journal of Cuneiform Studies, 62*, 53–69.

Delnero, P. (2012). Memorization and the transmission of sumerian literary compositions. *Journal of Near Eastern Studies, 71*, 189–208.

Friberg, J. (2007). *A remarkable collection of babylonian mathematical texts* (Vol. I). New York: Springer.

Hilprecht, H. V. (1906). *Mathematical, Metrological and Chronological Tablets from the Temple Library of Nippur*. Philadelphia: University of Pennsylvania.

Høyrup, J. (2000). The finer structure of the Old Babylonian mathematical corpus. Elements of classification, with some results. In J. Marzahn & H. Neumann (Eds.), *Assyriologica et Semitica. Festschrift für Joachim Oelsner anläßlich seines 65* (pp. 117–178). Münster: Ugarit Verlag.

Høyrup, J. (2002). *Lengths, Widths, Surfaces. A Portrait of Old Babylonian Algebra and its Kin*. Berlin & Londres: Springer.

Michalowski, P. (2012). Literacy, schooling and the transmission of knowledge in early mesopotamian culture. In W. S. van Egmond & W. H. van Soldt (Eds.), *Theory and practice of knowl-*

edge transfer. Studies in school education in the Ancient Near East and beyond (pp. 39–57). Leiden: PIHANS.

Middeke-Conlin, R. (forthcoming). *The making of a scribe: Errors, mistakes, and rounding numbers in the Old Babylonian kingdom of Larsa.* New York: Springer.

Neugebauer, O., & Sachs, A. J. (1945). *Mathematical cuneiform texts.* New Haven: American Oriental Series & American Schools of Oriental Research.

Neugebauer, O., & Sachs, A. J. (1984). Mathematical and metrological texts. *Journal of Cuneiform Studies, 36,* 243–251.

Nicolet, G. (2016). *La 'Maison aux tablettes' et l'enseignement à Mari à l'époque paléobabylonienne* Université de Genève.

Proust, C. (2007). *Tablettes mathématiques de Nippur (with the collaboration of Antoine Cavigneaux).* Istanbul: Institut Français d'Etudes Anatoliennes, De Boccard.

Proust, C. (2008). *Tablettes mathématiques de la collection Hilprecht (with the collaboration of M. Krebernik and J. Oelsner).* Leipzig: Harrassowitz.

Proust, C. (2012a). Reading colophons from Mesopotamian clay-tablets dealing with mathematics. *NTM Zeitschrift für Geschichte der Wissenschaften, Technik und Medizin, 20*(3), 123–156.

Proust, C. (2012b). Teachers' writings and students' writings: school material in Mesopotamia. In G. Gueudet, B. Pepin, & L. Trouche (Eds.), *From text to 'Lived' resources: Mathematics curriculum materials and teacher development* (pp. 161–179). New York: Springer.

Proust, C. (2014). Does a master always write for his students? Some evidence from Old Babylonian Scribal Schools. In A. Bernard & C. Proust (Eds.), *Scientific sources and teaching contexts throughout History: Problems and perspectives* (pp. 69–94). New York: Springer.

Proust, C. (2015). La chanson des mathématiques dans l'*Edubba.* In M. C. Bustamante (Ed.), *Scientific writings and orality* (pp. 19–49). Turnhout: Brepols (Archives Internationales d'Histoire des Sciences).

Proust, C. (2016). Floating calculation in Mesopotamia (translation of "Du calcul flottant en Mésopotamie", 2013). *Cuneiform Digital Library Preprints (CDLP), 05.*

Proust, C. (forthcoming). Volume, brickage and capacity in Old Babylonian mathematical texts from southern Mesopotamia. In K. Chemla, A. Keller, & C. Proust (Eds.), *Cultures of computation and quantification.* Heidelberg/New York: Springer.

Proust, C. (in press-a). Algorithms through sets of problems in Old Babylonian cuneiform texts: Steps without meaning. In C. Proust, M. Husson, & A. Keller (Eds.), *Practices of Reasoning in Ancient Mathematics and astral sciences.* New York: Springer.

Proust, C. (in press-b). In M. Rutz & J. Steele (Eds.) *A diachronic picture of mathematics in Nippur, from Sargonic to Late-Babylonian periods.* Scholarship in Nippur.

Robson, E. (2001). The tablet house: A scribal school in Old Babylonian Nippur. *Revue d'Assyriologie, 95,* 39–66.

Robson, E. (2008). *Mathematics in Ancient Iraq: A social history.* Princeton: Princeton University Press.

Rubio, G. (2007). Writing in another tongue: Alloglottography and scribal antiquarianism in the Ancient Near East. In S. L. Sanders (Ed.), *Margins of writing, origins of cultures: Unofficial writing in the ancient Near East and beyond* (pp. 33–70). Chicago: The Oriental Institute.

Smith, D. E. (1904). *The teaching of elementary mathematics.* New York: The MacMillan Company.

Tinney, S. (1999). On the curricular setting of Sumerian literature. *Iraq, 61,* 159–172.

Trouche, L. (2016). The development of mathematics practices in the Mesopotamian Scribal Schools. In J. Monaghan, L. Trouche, & J. M. Borwein (Eds.), *Tools and mathematics: Instruments for learning* (pp. 117–138). New York: Springer.

Veldhuis, N. (1997). *Elementary Education at Nippur, The Lists of Trees and Wooden Objects* (Ph. D. dissertation), University of Groningen, Groningen.

Chapter 5
Reflecting on a Theoretical Approach from a Networking Perspective: The Case of the Documentational Approach to Didactics

Michèle Artigue

Abstract This chapter analyses the emergence and development of the documentational approach to didactics (DAD), paying specific attention to the theoretical sources and connections having inspired its progressive elaboration. After introducing the two main conceptual tools used for this analysis, the scale of networking strategies between theories (Bikner-Ahsbahs, A., & Prediger, S. (2008). Networking of theories – An approach for exploiting the diversity of theoretical approaches. In B. Sriraman & L. English (Eds.), *Theories in mathematics education* (pp. 483–506). New York: Springer) and the idea of research praxeology (Artigue M, Bosch M, Gascón J, Bosch M et al. Centre de Recerca Matemàtica, Barcelona, 2011), the chapter proposes a chronological analysis with two main sections, respectively, devoted to the emergence and development of this approach. This analysis, based on the main publications associated with DAD, shows the respective roles played in the dynamics of this approach by the rapid emergence and stabilization of a full research praxeology and, at the same time, the impressive number of connections established with a diversity of theories in no more than one decade. These characteristics give DAD a specific identity. The chapter ends by establishing a connection with the international Lexicon project.

Keywords Documentational approach to didactics · Networking of theories · Scale of networking · Research praxeology · Anthropological theory of the didactic · Lexicon project

---

This chapter originates from a lecture given at the Re(s)sources 2018 International Conference. Video at http://video.ens-lyon.fr/ife/2018/2018-05-29_006_Ressources2018_Michele_Artigue_v1.mp4.

M. Artigue (✉)
LDAR (EA4434), Université Paris-Diderot, UA, UCP, UPEC, URN, Paris, France

© Springer Nature Switzerland AG 2019
L. Trouche et al. (eds.), *The 'Resource' Approach to Mathematics Education*,
Advances in Mathematics Education,
https://doi.org/10.1007/978-3-030-20393-1_5

5.1 Introduction

One decade ago, the documentational approach to didactics (DAD) was just emerging. Since then, it has developed and matured, benefitting from the collaborative work and contributions of researchers with different research background and perspectives and different theoretical approaches. For this reason, it seems to me interesting to reflect on the development of this approach with the conceptual and methodological tools provided by what is today known as 'networking of theories' (Bikner-Ahsbahs and Prediger 2014). In this chapter, I develop a first attempt in this direction that has taken the form of an enquiry using a selection of publications related to the documentational approach to didactics (DAD in the following) as resources. I hope that this reflection will offer an insightful and original perspective on this very dynamic approach and the research it has nurtured in the last decade.

In the first section, I introduce the networking of theories and especially the two main conceptual tools that I use in this chapter: the networking scale (Bikner-Ahsbashs and Prediger 2008), on the one hand, and the idea of research praxeology (Artigue et al. 2011; Artigue and Bosch 2014), on the other hand. In the second and third sections, I use this networking perspective to analyse the development of DAD, thus paying specific attention to its theoretical sources and to the theoretical connections progressively built in it. I then introduce a new and promising connection with the international Lexicon project[1], before concluding with some final comments.

5.2 An Introduction to the Networking of Theories

The networking movement resulted from the increasing international awareness that the issues raised by theoretical diversity were insufficiently addressed at the global level of the mathematics education community, inducing theoretical fragmentation. From the start of this century, one can notice different incentives, especially at the European level:

- European projects such as the European Research Team TELMA created in 2003 within the Network of excellence Kaleidoscope and then the project ReMath (Artigue 2009; Kynigos and Lagrange 2014).
- The plenary sessions organized on this issue at the CERME congress, in 2005, and the resulting creation of a specific CERME working group on theoretical approaches and their comparison, which has been active since this time as shown by the synthesis (Kidron et al. 2018).
- The creation of the so-called Bremen Group at the same CERME that highly contributed to this working group and co-authored the book (Bikner-Ahsbahs and Prediger 2014) mentioned above.

---

[1] http://www.lexicon.iccr.edu.au (accessed 2018/07/14).

As made clear by these references, since 2005, a lot has been achieved in order to address the challenge of theoretical diversity. Empirical research has developed, comparing theoretical approaches and their influence on research problématiques, methodologies and results, exploring possible connections and complementarities. Conceptual tools and specific methodologies have emerged such as the methodology of cross-experimentation implemented in ReMath. In what follows, as announced, I focus on two of these conceptual tools: the *networking scale* and the concept of *research praxeology*.

5.2.1 The Networking Scale

The networking scale was established in the first steps of the networking enterprise. As explained in Bikner-Ahsbahs and Prediger (2008), it aims at showing the diversity of forms that connections between theories can take and at ordering these between two extremal positions expressing, respectively, a total absence of relationship and a global unification. As shown in Fig. 5.1, it distinguishes between eight intermediate positions regarding the degree of integration. These positions appear in a linear order, structured into pairs such as understanding others and making understandable, comparing and contrasting, etc.

The meaning of these terms is clarified by the authors, pages 492–497. For instance, it is pointed out that the combining and coordinating strategies 'aim at a deeper insight into an empirical phenomenon'. Coordinating means that 'a conceptual framework is built by well-fitting elements from different theories' and supposes the complementarity of the theoretical approaches involved, while combining means that 'the theoretical approaches are only juxtaposed according to a specific aspect'. The combining strategy can thus involve theories with some conflicting basic assumptions. Integrating locally and synthesizing, for their part, label a pair of strategies focusing 'on the development of theories by putting together a small number of theories or theoretical approaches into a new framework'. Synthesizing corresponds to the case when 'two (or more) equally stable theories are taken and connected in such a way that a new theory evolves', while locally integrating corresponds to the frequent case when 'the theories' scope and degree of development is not symmetric, and there are only some concepts or aspects of one theory integrated into an already more elaborate dominant theory'. In this chapter, in line with

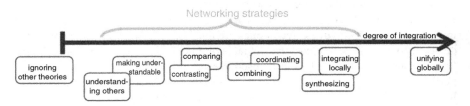

Fig. 5.1 Networking scale (Bikner-Ahsbahs and Prediger 2008, p. 492)

these definitions, I will use the words combining and coordinating when several theories are jointly used to make sense of empirical data or phenomena, and the words synthesizing and locally integrating when theoretical development is aimed at. However, I will use the word locally integrating each time there is some dissymmetry in the connection, even for theories having a similar state of development. The scale proposes a linear order, but:

> it must be emphasized that it is not easy to specify globally their exact topology, since the degree of integration always depends on the concrete realizations and networking methodologies. (ibidem, p. 492)

Moreover, researchers who try to connect theories usually combine several strategies. I will add that, for all those involved in the networking enterprise, a unified theory of mathematics education is not the Holy Grail they are pursuing. On the contrary, they are convinced that theoretical diversity is a normal state for this scientific field, and that diversity should not be interpreted as a sign of scientific immaturity:

> Since mathematics learning and teaching is a multi-faceted phenomenon which cannot be described, understood or explained by one monolithic theory alone, a variety of theories is necessary to do justice to the complexity of the field. (ibidem, p. 484)

5.2.2 Research Praxeologies

The concept of research praxeology was introduced more recently. It was first presented at CITAD3, the third congress on the anthropological theory of the didactic (ATD), in 2009 (Artigue et al. 2011), and then refined in Artigue and Bosch (2014). The basic idea is to consider that the model of praxeologies that ATD uses to model human practices might be useful to approach the issue of connection between theories, by making clear that theories emerge from research practices and condition these in return and that connection between theories involve thus necessarily much more than the theories themselves. They cannot be productively established by just looking for connections between theoretical discourses.

As is the case for any type of praxeology, research praxeologies are made of two blocks: a practical block and a theoretical block. The practical block is made of research tasks and research techniques or methods used in order to solve these tasks. A priori, praxeologies can be associated with any type of task that research leads to, from the elaboration of research questions to the communication of research results. However, in this chapter, I will limit myself to research tasks in form of research questions or problématiques. Techniques are thus the research techniques or methods used to address these questions. What is often called methodology in the literature includes both methods and a discourse describing them and justifying the pertinence of their use. In the praxeological model, this discourse is thus part of the logos block. This logos block indeed is made of the technological discourse used to

5 Reflecting on the Documentational Approach from a Networking Perspective

describe, explain and justify research methods and of the theories that back up this technological discourse.

ATD emphasizes the dynamic dimension of praxeologies, and this is indeed the case for research praxeologies:

> Research praxeologies, as any other praxeological form, are living entities that evolve and change, which affect at the same time their four components and their interactions. The evolution of the practical block $[T/\tau]$ produces new theoretical needs that make the block $[\Theta/\theta]$ progress and, reciprocally, the evolution of concepts, interpretations, or ways of thinking and the emergence of new results lead to the construction of new techniques and the formulation of new problems. (Artigue and Bosch 2014, p. 253)

In fact, the technological level plays here:

> the "transactional role" of including the first results obtained in the practical block as preliminary descriptions of regular facts and phenomena, then transferring the most robust of these results to the theoretical block in the form of new principles to add and new germs of methodologies and problems. (ibidem, p. 253)

For this reason, when introducing the concept of research praxeology, we gave a specific role to discursive constructions in terms of didactic phenomena that research makes emerge. These are part of the technological discourse and an essential ingredient of the dynamics of research praxeologies, and of the dialectics between the practice and logos block of praxeologies underlying this dynamics. For instance, the identification of didactic phenomena is often the source of new research questions aiming at their more systematic study; they can be the source of new research methods, as was the case for the phenomenon of didactic transposition (Chevallard 1985). Once consolidated, they can become part of existing theories, as was the case for the phenomenon of didactic contract which, first identified in the study known as the Gael's case, became then a fundamental concept of the theory of didactical situations (Brousseau 1997). They can even become the basis of a new theory as was the case for the phenomenon of didactic transposition.

The dynamics of research praxeologies also results from their progressive structuration from point praxeologies associated with a precise type of research question to local praxeologies grouping point praxeologies sharing the same technological discourse, and then regional and even global praxeologies sharing the same theoretical discourse. Considering connections between theories, this structuration is especially important, because even if a theoretical construction generally emerges as attached to a specific problématique – a point praxeology – as far as theories develop, they become an umbrella for many different research praxeologies and unify these at a regional level at least.

These constructions have shaped my enquiry. The notion of research praxeology led me to approach the emergence and development of DAD as the emergence and progressive structuration of a coherent set of research praxeologies. The scale of networking made me sensitive to the diversity of possible forms of establishing connections between theoretical approaches and constructs. The combination of these tools allowed me to analyse the development of DAD and of its connections with other approaches in the light of the conditions and constraints shaping research praxeologies as a whole, and not just their theoretical components. This combination also led me to envisage the development of connections as a bi-directional process, considering the connections established by the founders of the approach and their close collaborators and, at the same time, those built by researchers coming to DAD with well-established theoretical approaches, possibly very distant from DAD.

5.3 The Emergence of Documentational Approach to Didactics

5.3.1 The Emergence of a Full Research Praxeology

The first publications regarding the DAD, which was not named as such at the time, are the course given by Gueudet and Trouche at the XIVe Summer School of Didactics in 2007 (Gueudet and Trouche 2009a) and the article by the same authors (Gueudet and Trouche 2009b). These publications make clear that the emergence of DAD is situated within a continuous and coherent progression of research praxeologies. It takes place within a continuum that started with the development of the instrumental approach in the context of CAS technology, focusing on students' learning processes (Guin and Trouche 2002). This approach was then extended to other technologies: spreadsheets, dynamic geometry systems and e-exercises bases, the last one having played a special role in the emergence of DAD through research involving the resources produced by the association Sésamath and teachers active in this association (Gueudet 2006). It progressively incorporated the teacher into the picture. This new extension led to new theoretical constructions, in terms of instrumental orchestration (Trouche 2003), double instrumental genesis (Haspekian 2008) and then geneses of use (Abboud-Blanchard & Vandebrouck 2014), especially thanks to the GUPTEn (Genèses d'usages professionnels des technologies par les enseignants) project (Lagrange 2013). The emergence of DAD also situates in the continuity of the SFODEM project of collaborative development of resources (Guin & Trouche 2005), as explained in the first two publications. Both research contexts contributed to attract Gueudet's and Trouche's attention to the documentation work of mathematics teachers, and to consider it as an essential component of teachers' practices needing to be more systematically addressed, especially in the light of the important changes induced by technological evolution. They also led these two researchers to consider that teachers' documentation work offers a unique window on their professional development, and thus to tightly link these two issues.

We have thus at the origin of DAD both an evolution of research problématiques and an evident theoretical continuity. Rabardel's instrumental approach is, indeed, the main theoretical framework, with the distinction between *artefact* and *instrument*, the notion of *instrumental genesis*, the associated dual processes of *instrumentalization* and *instrumentation* and *schemes of utilization*. This frame-

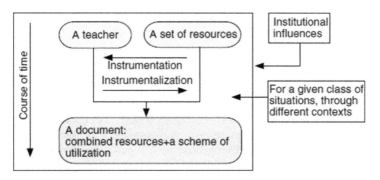

Fig. 5.2 Schematic representation of a documentational genesis

work is adapted to the new problématique, leading to the distinction between a *resource* and a *document*, which reflects the distinction between artefact and instrument, the notion of *documentational genesis* which reflects the notion of instrumental genesis and the associated schemes of utilization with their characteristics in terms of *classes of situations*, *rules of action* and *operational invariants*. These are expressed in terms of professional knowledge and different from those previously identified in instrumental geneses. The theoretical filiation is made clear in the schemas proposed in these first texts as the one in Gueudet and Trouche (2009b, p. 206), reproduced in Fig. 5.2.

The authors, however, point out a distinction with previous research work using Rabardel's perspective to approach technological integration: the dialectical relationship between resources and documents, which gives some specificity to the dynamics of documentational geneses:

> Documentational genesis must not be considered as a transformation with a set of resources as input, and a document as output. It is an ongoing process. ... A document developed from a set of resources provides new resources, which can be involved in a new set of resources, which will lead to a new document etc. Because of this process, we speak of the *dialectical* relationship between resources and documents. (Ibidem, p. 206)

Referring to Rabardel and Bourmaud (2005), they also hypothesize that 'a given teacher develops a structured documentation system, and that this documentation system and the teacher's professional practice evolve together' (ibidem, p. 211), thus the window offered on teachers' professional development. In fact, through the study of the teachers' documentational work, the new problématique aims at a better understanding of their professional activity and development.

To work out this new problématique, specific methods are needed, allowing researchers to access the documentational work of teachers which takes place mainly outside the classroom and even outside the school institution, in France at least. In fact, the experience gained through the study of the teachers' use of the e-exercise base Mathenpoche (MEP) for Gueudet and the SFODEM project for Trouche supports this methodological construction. Quite soon, a specific methodology emerges and is given a name: *reflective investigation* (Gueudet and Trouche 2010b). This is based on four principles (Gueudet and al. 2012, pp. 27-28)[2]:

– A principle of *long-term follow-up*. Geneses are ongoing processes and schemes develop over long periods of time. This indicates the need for long-term observation, within practical constraints.
– A principle of *in- and out-of-class follow-up*. The classroom is an important place where the teaching elaborated is implemented. [...] However, an important part of teachers' work takes place beyond the students' presence – at school, at home, in teacher development programs, etc. We pay attention to all these different locations.
– A principle of *broad collection* of the material resources used and produced in the documentation work, throughout the follow-up.
– A principle of *reflective follow-up* of the documentation work. We closely involve the teacher in the collection of data, with the pragmatic aim of broad collection and in-class and out-of-class follow-up previously discussed. The active involvement of the teacher yields a *reflective* stance.

Moreover, a specific methodological tool is created, to explore the resource system of teachers, that is to say the resource part of her documentational system (i.e. documentation system without associated schemes): the SRRS (*Schematic Representation of Resource System*).

Another important point is that, already in these first texts, the emerging construction claims its theoretical nature. For instance, in the introductory part of Gueudet and Trouche (2009b), one reads (p. 199):

> The generalized availability of digital resources for mathematics teachers entails a complete metamorphosis of curriculum material (Remillard 2005). It also yields a deep change in teachers' professional knowledge and development.
> We propose here a theoretical approach aiming at illuminating the consequences of this phenomenon.

These texts thus clearly show the emergence of a full research praxeology. Its practical block is organized around a main type of task: investigating teachers' practices and professional development through the identification of their documentation systems and the evolution of these, using case studies obeying the technique of reflective investigation, and its theoretical block combines explicit technological and theoretical components. I hypothesize that the context of this emergence, a course given at the French Summer school of didactics of mathematics, with the expectations associated to such an object, has certainly fostered the high level of explicitation observed already at this early stage.

Quickly, this research praxeology produces interesting results. It makes clear the complexity of teachers' systems of resources, the teachers' agency and authorship at stake in personal and collective documentational geneses, confirming the

---

[2]To avoid translation, we use the English description of the method provided in Gueudet et al. (2012), which is very close to the French description in Gueudet and Trouche (2010b).

5 Reflecting on the Documentational Approach from a Networking Perspective

ergonomic principle that conception goes on in usage and blurring the distinction between designers and users. It confirms the hypothesis that technological evolution substantially changes the documentational work of teachers. It also confirms that documentational activity is both *productive* and *constructive* and opens a window on teachers' professional development to which it substantially contributes.

5.3.2 Theoretical Connections

What about theoretical connections beyond the fundamental one with cognitive ergonomy? There is no doubt that this new problématique does not emerge in a *vacuum*. Various research fields can be connected to it and be source of inspiration: textbook research, analysis and use of curriculum material and teacher knowledge and professional development, to mention just a few beyond the area of research on technological integration at the origin of the instrumental approach.

In fact, from this early stage, many authors are mentioned and some connections emerge. For instance, in Gueudet and Trouche (2009b) one finds explicit reference to Adler's conception of resources (Adler 2000), Remillard's participative approach of the use of curriculum resources (Remillard 2005), Ball, Hill and Bass's model of mathematics knowledge for teaching (Ball et al. 2005) and Ball and Cohen's view of professional development (Ball and Cohen 1996). The authors also stress the proximity of their perspective with Ruthven's research on technological integration (Ruthven 2007). In terms of scale of networking, the main connection is, without any doubt, the connection with Adler's conceptualization of resources, considering that 'resources for school mathematics extend beyond basic material and human resources to include a range of other human and material resources, as well as mathematical, cultural and social resources' (Adler 2000, p. 210). This conceptualization explicitly shapes the vision of resources proposed in this paper:

> We use the term resources to emphasize the variety of artifacts we consider: a textbook, a piece of software, a students' sheet, a discussion with a colleague, etc. (Gueudet and Trouche 2009b, p. 205)

The connection becomes more explicit in Gueudet and Trouche (2010b), where the notion of resource is properly defined (p. 57):

> As announced in the introduction, *resources* is a primary term in this book, taking on different values throughout the chapters. The one we are retaining here is close to Adler's positions (Chap. 2): everything that is likely to re-source the teachers' work. (author's translation)

We thus observe a case of local integration, which has, of course, an evident influence on the methodological part of DAD research praxeologies. The book (Gueudet and Trouche 2010a), in fact, provides more information about theoretical connections. Moreover, the diversity of background of the 23 authors opens the analysis of connections in two directions: on the one hand, the connections established by Gueudet and Trouche in the two chapters they co-author (Gueudet and Trouche

2010b, 2010c), and on the other hand, the connections established by other authors with different backgrounds.

5.3.2.1 Theoretical Connections Established by Gueudet and Trouche

In Chap. 4 (Gueudet and Trouche 2010b), various authors are mentioned, and links are made with other chapters of the book, but few connections are really worked out. For instance, Remillard's research on the use of curriculum material is mentioned, but the categories she has introduced – *mode of destination, form of destination* and *mode of engagement* – and the associated sub-categories are not connected with DAD; the fact that teachers both are shaped by curriculum resources and shape these in return is not explicitly connected to the instrumentation and instrumentalization dimension of documentational geneses.

However, an example of local integration can be observed when, in line with Rabardel and Bourmaud (2005), the authors try to connect teachers' systems of documents and systems of activities. The nine categories of activities selected are explicitly inspired by the *study moments* of ATD (Chevallard 2002).

> We have adopted the essential criteria of purpose of the action proposed by Rabardel and Bourmaud (ibidem), which is well suited to our intention to capture the teacher's activity as a whole, and we have relied on the *study moments* (Chevallard 2002). (Gueudet and Trouche 2010b, p. 67). (author's translation)

Among the nine categories of activities, one finds indeed the following categories:

- Preparing and setting up introductory activities.
- Preparing and setting up syntheses.
- Preparing and setting up drill and practice.
- Preparing and setting up assessment.

These can be related to the six moments of study of Chevallard's model (first encounter with a praxeology and formulation of the tasks to be carried out, exploration of the tasks and emergence of a technique to carry out these, elaboration of a theoretical environment, institutionalization and evaluation).

In Chap. 11 devoted to the collective documentational work of teachers (Gueudet and Trouche 2010c), another theory is obviously influential, that of communities of practice (CoP) due to Wenger (1998). Categories used to define community of practices – *shared engagement, common project, active participation, reification* and *shared repertoire* – are explicitly used in the data analysis and productively coordinated with the basic tools of the DAD. Considering two particular cases of CoP organized around the production of educational resources, the association of teachers Sesamath and groups involved in the design and implementation of teacher professional development activities within the national Pairform@nce program, the authors show how the genesis of a CoP and the genesis of its system of resources, seen as part of its shared repertoire, intertwine. From this connection also emerge new theoretical constructs, that of *community documentational genesis* and *community resource system.*

5.3.2.2 Theoretical Connections Established by Other Authors

In the other chapters of the book, one also notes many cross-references, but once again rather few advanced forms of networking, which is not surprising in this emerging state of DAD. In most chapters, the main purpose seems to make understandable another approach. This is clearly the case, for instance, for the chapters respectively authored by Adler, Bachimont and Remillard.

While focused on JATD (Joint Action Theory in Didactics), the chapter authored by Sensevy (2010) goes further as it aims at understanding how documentational genesis conditions joint action in situ, especially through the ways it contributes to forming the initial teacher's *didactic intentionality*. Using three empirical studies relying on JATD, Sensevy illustrates forms that this conditioning can take and makes clear the influence in return of action in situ on documentational geneses. Moreover, claiming that the concepts of *style of thought* and *thought collective* due to Fleck (2005) are essential to our understanding of didactic intentionality and documentational genesis, he opens to a priori promising connections. In fact, Fleck's theory was already evoked in Gueudet and Trouche (2008, pp. 18-19) as a possible theoretical resource to approach the collective dimension of documentational work. In this article, they explain why the connection with the theory of CoP seems to them more appropriate to approach the types of collectives they study. However, it is worth noticing that the connection with Fleck's conceptualization has been recently developed in Rocha (2018) whose research questions the way teachers' collective work helps them design resources requested by curricular changes.

Other forms of networking can be identified in the different chapters: comparing and contrasting, combining and coordinating and even locally integrating. I exemplify them below, through a selection of examples.

The chapter co-authored by Maracci and Mariotti (2010), for instance, offers the first type of connection. A priori, the situation is favourable as Rabardel's instrumental approach is part of their theoretical framework. It is combined with the theory of semiotic mediation (TSM) situated within a Vygotskian perspective jointly developed by Bartolini Bussi and Mariotti (2008). However, despite this theoretical proximity, the research praxeologies remain distant, and the authors contrast them, making clear that they are interested in instrumental geneses, but not in documentational geneses. In fact, their research problématique focuses on the way teachers make a technological artefact an instrument of semiotic mediation for students, especially through the orchestration of classroom collective discussions.

As they write, at the end of the chapter, coming back to the similarities and differences with the documentational approach:

> In both cases, the stake is the study of geneses. However, in the case of TSM, one considers as much the students' geneses as the teacher's genesis while the documentational approach focuses more on the teacher. Moreover, by referring to TSM, our aim is not to describe all

the schemes developed by the teacher in connection with the use of the artefact: in the case of an instrument of semiotic mediation, we only retain the schemes that make sense from the point of view of semiotic mediation. (Mariotti & Maracci 2010, p. 105, author's translation)

An example of coordination/combination is the chapter authored by Vandebrouck. In this chapter, the theoretical reference is the double approach, didactic and ergonomic, to teaching practices, jointly initiated by Robert and Rogalski (2002) (see Vandebrouck (2013) for a reference in English). As Rabardel's construction, this approach is based on activity theory (AT), which should a priori favour the connection with DAD. For instance, categories such as the distinction between the *productive* and *constructive* dimensions of activity coming from AT and their dialectic relationships are shared with DAD. Moreover, Vandebrouck is familiar with the notion of instrumental genesis that he has contributed to extend to the teacher, as mentioned above. However, once again, research problématiques are rather distant. The double approach aims at understanding teacher practices, their coherence and stability and their variability and evolution, through the way teachers organize their students' mathematical activity (*cognitive component* of the model), and mediate it in the classroom (*mediative component*), and the way *social, institutional* and *personal* components influence these. As pointed out by Vandebrouck, researchers relying on this approach use a methodological detour, focusing on the analysis of the couples (tasks, *déroulement*). The author hypothesizes that this kind of analysis should allow the characterization of documentational geneses:

A teacher's documentational geneses also bring about stability and evolution. Approaching them in terms of components of practices is both restrictive, since only classroom activity serves as a basis for the analysis – even if the determinants are ultimately taken into account – and more general than is done in the documentational approach: the resources mobilized by teachers are the evolutions of these couples, interpreted in terms of stability and evolution of the five components, which allow us to characterize the documentational geneses in this chapter. (Vandebrouck 2010, p. 256, author's translation)

The two case studies presented in this chapter, however, show that the task is not so obvious due to the distance between research praxeologies. Even if this is not mentioned by the author, the fact, for instance, that the language of schemes, essential in DAD, is not used in this chapter, limits the characterization of documentational geneses, making clear that more research is needed in order to properly connect documentational geneses and the components of teachers' practices, as is concluded by the author.

One chapter in the book goes further along the connection scale reaching a state of local integration: the chapter authored by Trgalová studying teachers' didactic decisions in relation with their documentation. For this study, the author connects DAD with the model of teacher activity developed by Margolinas (2002) and Balacheff's cK¢ model of conceptions (Balacheff 1995), two constructions already connected by these two authors to analyse teachers' didactic decisions in (Balacheff and Margolinas 2005). Margolinas' model distinguishes between five levels of situation for the teacher, from the level − 1 (observation of students' activity) to the level + 3 of the values and conceptions of teaching/learning regulating her/his global educative project.

For this study, Trgalová uses data from Lima's doctoral thesis (Lima 2006) that she co-supervised with Balacheff. These data come from the following task: teachers were asked to design a session for the teaching of line symmetry (level + 1: situation of project), and they were proposed a set of resources made of students' productions to a diagnostic test and of 18 tasks. The proposals of two teachers are analysed, first using cK¢ to connect their diagnostic of students' productions and their didactic choices in the design of the session and reconstructing the teachers' intentions. Then, the same data are approached through the lens of DAD, considering the work asked to these teachers as a documentational work. Elements of documentational geneses and emergence of the associated schemes are identified with their rules of action and hypothesized operational invariants in the form of professional knowledge. Finally, the conclusion of the chapter efficiently synthesizes these analyses, in a discourse integrating those proper to the three theoretical frameworks used. This is the reason why this case, in my opinion, shows an example of productive theoretical coordination opening the way to local integration. There is no doubt that, in this particular case, the research methodology used in Lima's thesis, which stimulates some form of documentational work, makes the connection more practicable than in the two previous cases.

We thus observe that, from its emergence, the documentational approach has been submitted to different theoretical influences and began to forge links with a diversity of approaches. All these examples also confirm the importance of thinking in terms of praxeologies as a whole when discussing potential/effective theoretical networking.

5.4 The Development of the Documentational Approach to Didactics

A second book came out in 2012, in English (Gueudet et al. 2012), making the documentational approach and its situation within the global area of research on resources more accessible to an international audience. New authors were included, as well as reactors. This second book was co-edited by Gueudet, Trouche and Pepin, a specialist of textbook research who was tightly collaborating with the founders of DAD since 2010. In 2013, the volume 45.7 of *ZDM* entitled *Re-Sourcing Teacher Work and Interaction: New Perspectives on Resource Design, Use and Teacher Collaboration* was again co-edited by Pepin, Gueudet and Trouche. A Topic Study Group (TSG 38) was organized at ICME-13 in 2016 on issues related to mathematics teaching and learning resources (Fan et al. 2017) resulting again in a book published by Springer (Fan et al. 2018). A number of articles and master and doctoral theses defended or in preparation must be added to these books and special issues. These publications and the number of submissions to the ICME TSG show the increasing interest in the study of resources and of their personal and collective use, and in the evolution of these in the digital era. They also show the consolidation and increasing influence of DAD among the different theoretical perspectives used in this area of research.

5.4.1 Evolution of DAD

The evolution of DAD is well described in the chapter of this book authored by Gueudet (Gueudet, this volume). For the close outsider of the DAD community that I am, some characteristics of this evolution are especially interesting.

5.4.1.1 The Rapid Stabilization of the Theoretical Core of DAD Research Praxeologies

This rapid stabilization of the theoretical core of DAD is evident when reading the presentation of it in research papers and book chapters, and looking at associated schematizations. For instance, in the chapter (Gueudet and Trouche 2012), after anchoring more clearly their work in activity theory (pp. 23-24), the authors come back to the vision of resources developed by Adler in terms of re-sourcing (p. 24), stress the origin of the documentational approach in Rabardel's instrumental approach (p. 25) and reproduce the schema in Fig. 5.1 (p. 26). They then introduce the fundamental concepts of resource system and documentation system (p. 27), as was the case in Gueudet and Trouche (2010b), and conclude this section by saying that they have presented there the theoretical constructs framing their research.

Similar presentations can be found in the theoretical sections of articles recently published. This is, for instance, the case in Sabra (2016) studying the relationships between personal and collective documentation, the theme of his doctoral thesis. His theoretical framework coordinates the documentational approach, Margolinas' model mentioned above and CoP. The presentation of the documentational approach is made in reference to (Gueudet and Trouche 2008, 2009b; 2010). We are told that it is an extension of the instrumental approach, then the distinction between resource and document (the document having two components: the recombined resources and a scheme of utilization) is introduced together with the notion of documentational genesis. The author adds that a scheme of utilization is itself made of two parts: its observable part and its invisible part, constituted of operational invariants, which can be generally expressed in terms of knowledge for teaching mobilized in different contexts of activity.

This is also the case in Pepin et al. (2017) where the documentational approach is put at the service of understanding mathematics teaching expertise through a case study involving three Chinese mathematics teachers. One can read in the section entitled Theoretical Framework (pp. 260-261):

5 Reflecting on the Documentational Approach from a Networking Perspective

We draw in this paper on the *documentational approach to didactics* (Gueudet, Pepin & Trouche 2012; Gueudet & Trouche 2009), which acknowledges the central role of *resources* for teachers' work. In particular, this approach emphasizes the dialectic nature of the relationships between teachers and resources; and the core concept of a teacher's *resource system*.

Follows a clarification of the meaning to be given to the word resource, the introduction of the notions of instrumentation, instrumentalization and genesis, with explicit reference to Rabardel, and of the notion of document:

> this consists of the resources adapted and re-combined/designed; the implicit and intended usages of these resources; and the mathematical knowledge guiding these usages (content knowledge PCK; knowledge about these resources). We name this hybrid entity a *document*, as something documenting a teacher's activity, and we name the process, leading from a set of resources to a document, *documentational genesis*. (ibidem, p. 260)

It must be noticed that the word scheme is not explicitly used in this text, but one can read it between the lines, operational invariants being expressed in terms of knowledge. The documentational genesis is illustrated by the following schema (p. 261) (see Fig. 5.3), and then the notion of teacher resource system is introduced.

Thus, even if some variations are present and despite the fact that undeniable evolutions have taken place, what is considered the core of DAD is the same as it was in the first publications associated with this approach, and these are used as reference texts.

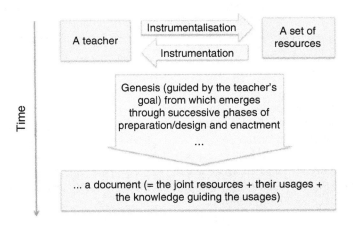

Fig. 5.3 A schema of documentational genesis (Pepin et al. 2017)

5.4.1.2 The Privileged Status of the Methodology of Reflective Investigation with the Associated SRRS Tool, Emblematic of DAD

Another striking point is how the methodology of reflective investigation has become an emblematic methodology of DAD research praxeologies, together with the associated SRRS tool. In the previous section, we outlined the four principles it relies on. In line with these principles, a diversity of data is systematically collected when investigating teachers' documentational geneses and systems of resources, and they need to be triangulated. For instance, for the teachers involved in the empirical study presented in Gueudet and Trouche (2010b), the global device was presented to the teachers involved at a first meeting; then these teachers answered a biographic questionnaire and they were also asked to fill a logbook during 3 weeks; all material resources used and produced in the classroom selected during the 3 weeks were collected; a lesson was observed and audio- or videotaped for each teacher; and three interviews were organized at the teachers' home, one at the beginning of the process and the two others before and after the classroom observation. Moreover, the teachers were asked to draw a representation of their system of resources, the SRRS. Of course, the methodology of reflective investigation offers some variation according to the research questions investigated. Additional tools also have been introduced, such as the *reflective mapping of a teacher's documentational trajectory* (RMTDT) introduced in Rocha (2018). However, reading articles and theses, this is clear that case studies obeying this methodology of reflective investigation with the associated types of data collected and visual tools have become emblematic of the research praxeologies based on DAD.

For instance, if we come back to the two recent articles already mentioned, Sabra writes (p. 64) in a methodological section entitled *Méthodologie d'investigation réflexive et prolongements* (Methodology of reflective investigation and extension):

> The proposed tools are based on the methodology of reflective investigation (Gueudet & Trouche, 2010b) with extensions. They can be adapted, if needed, to the working conditions of the teacher and the community. (author's translation)

Among the tools associated with this methodology, he distinguishes: the interviews carried out at home three times during the following period, the questionnaires at the beginning and end of the process, the logbooks, the SRRS and the classroom observations. He extends these in order to take into account the community documentation, with, for instance, what he calls the PAS (*petit agenda de suivi*) to trace the *documentation incidents* that take place at the community level during the realization of the common project.

In Pepin et al. (2017), in a similar way, to investigate the resource systems of three selected teachers regarded as experts by the educational authorities, the researchers combine reflective interviews, observations in situ – on how the teachers work in their respective TRG (Teacher Research Group), how they participate in school activities, and how they use their resources in classroom instruction – and the drawing of SRRS.

5.4.1.3 The Extension and Diversification of Research Problématiques

In the two previous paragraphs, I have pointed out some forms of stability occurring both at the level of the practical and theoretical block of DAD research praxeologies. These certainly contribute to the identity of DAD. However, another striking characteristic for an approach that only emerged a decade ago is the extension and diversification of the research problématiques it supports and, non-independent of it, the diversity of researchers that contribute to it. The study of teachers' documentational work is no longer reserved to the mathematics domain. It also regards the documentational work of science teachers (physics, chemistry, biology) as shown by Hammoud (2012), Shaaban et al. (2015) and Tuffery-Rochdi (2016). It has extended to all levels of schooling from kindergarten (Besnier and Gueudet 2016) to university level (Gueudet et al. 2014), and to interdisciplinary work (Prieur 2016). Thanks to international collaboration, it is no longer limited to the study of personal and collective documentational geneses of French teachers. As evidenced by the International Conference Res(s)ources 2018 to which contributed researchers from 23 different countries covering all continents, and the workshop for doctorate and post-doctoral students that followed it gathering about 50 participants, this extension of domains and contexts highly contributes to the dynamics of research praxeologies.

For instance, the article (Pepin et al. 2017) already mentioned shows an extension of the problématique certainly influenced by the Asiatic context. The study of documentational work is put at the service of understanding mathematics teaching expertise. More precisely, the research study focuses on these three questions (p. 258):

- How do three Chinese 'expert' mathematics teachers describe their resource system, which kinds of resources do they use in/for their daily practice?
- How do the three case teachers perceive expertise in teaching mathematics, and how to develop such expertise?
- What are the characteristics of the three teachers' resource systems, and in which ways they characterize mathematics teaching expertise?

The results are very interesting. They show that the three expert teachers involved in the study, with different profiles, have quite different resource systems. However, the three of them emphasize the collective aspect of developing and more importantly of sharing resources to improve instructional practices. The analyses make visible the role played in this sharing and development of expertise:

- By the Teaching Research Groups (TRG) to which the teachers belong, a compulsory practice in China.
- By what is called QQ discussion groups, QQ being an instant messaging software, available at school, district and city levels.
- By public lessons, also a traditional form of professional development in China as in other Asiatic countries such as Korea and Japan, internationally known as

Lesson Study (Isoda et al. 2007), which is now systematically studied and disseminating worldwide.

According to the authors, the research also shows the existence of a clear notion of mathematics teaching expertise institutionally acknowledged in China, thus a clear professional identity. However, this does not prevent the three teachers to have different perceptions of what expertise exactly means and of how it can be developed, despite the fact that they agree on the importance of professional learning experiences and support offered by expert colleagues. Thus the authors conclude that:

> the lens of resources provides an useful tool for examining mathematics teaching expertise, making it possible to bring to the surface different aspects of expertise by linking teaching to the materials with which teachers interact and work on a daily basis. (ibidem, p. 272)

The opening to new contexts also opens the way to comparative research, and to the insights gained by looking at one culture from the outside that comparative research provides. For instance, (Pepin et al. 2013) compare the documentational work and resource systems of Norwegian and French teachers.

The increasing cultural diversity of researchers contributing to DAD also leads to new theoretical connections, and we develop this point in the next section.

5.4.2 The Reinforcement and Diversification of Theoretical Connections

When preparing the plenary lecture at the origin of this chapter, I asked Luc Trouche a selection of references that would be useful for me to consider in order to approach this issue of theoretical connections. I received a list of *theoretical crossings* with, for each of them, one or two references.[3] The list mentioned the 13 following approaches: communities of practice, theory of Fleck on thought collectives, design-based research, Remillard's approach, approaches for research on curriculum material, cultural historical activity theory, double approach of teachers' practices, computer sciences, information and communication sciences, 'webbing' approaches, theory of social creativity, constructionism and meta-didactical transposition approach. Some of these connections have been active since the emergence of DAD and have been already mentioned; other have emerged more recently, as, for instance, the connections with constructionism and the theory of social creativity which emerged in the context of the European project MC2.[4] Moreover, it is interesting to notice that, among the 13 publications listed, only three are not co-authored. In this chapter, I cannot make justice of the affordances of so diverse theoretical connections, but I will address successively the two types through a few examples.

---

[3] Other connections could have been mentioned, for instance, connection with JATD that has developed since 2010, as shown for instance by Goujon's doctoral thesis (2016).

[4] http://www.mc2-project.eu (accessed 2018/07/13)

5.4.2.1 Reinforcement of Existing Theoretical Connections

I will use the papers by Gueudet and Vandebrouck (2011) and Sabra (2016) to approach the evolution of theoretical connections already present in the paper by Gueudet and Trouche (2010a). This choice will allow me to compare with the chapter authored by Vandebrouck (2010) alone discussed in the previous section.

The paper by Gueudet and Vandebrouck (2011) was published just 1 year after the one by Vandebrouck (2010). DAD and the double approach of teachers' practices were thus in a similar state of development. However, the level of theoretical connection is much more elaborated. In fact, the distance observed here confirms the experimental evidence I have gained from my long-term work on theoretical networking, regarding what is made possible by the collaboration between researchers having different theoretical cultures when compared to the connections that a single researcher involved in a particular culture can build. As explained in the paper by Artigue and Bosch (2014), deep theoretical connection cannot be achieved just by reading and trying to understand the publications of researchers from another culture. It requires specific conditions of study that allow researchers to enter into the intimacy of research praxeologies they are not familiar with, to experience the dialectic links between their practical and theoretical blocks and also to access the craftsmanship dimension of these research praxeologies. Research collaborations create the *adidactic antagonist milieus*, with the meaning given to this term in the theory of didactical situations (Brousseau 1997), allowing them to test their interpretations and hypothetical connections. Researchers who are natives of other cultures, or have already integrated the theories at stake into their research praxeologies, are essential ingredients for constituting such antagonist *milieus*.

In the paper by Gueudet and Vandebrouck (2011), the authors first advocate the necessity of crossing different approaches in order to understand the complexity of phenomena of technological integration, referring to different authors for that purpose. They then explain their choice to focus on the documentational approach and the double approach because these are 'cousin' approaches, and they detail their common basis in activity theory and cognitive ergonomics we have already stressed. Research regarding the integration of digital technologies into mathematics education is also more globally considered with, for instance, Ruthven's model of structuring characteristics of teaching practices (Ruthven 2007) and the extension of the instrumental approach towards teachers in terms of double instrumental genesis and geneses of use, already mentioned. Then the two approaches and two associated case studies are separately presented because, as pointed out by the authors, the two approaches differ in their methodological approaches. However, the case studies have been selected to present some commonalities favouring the comparison.

I recognize here conditions that I can interpret with my networking lens: productive networking activity requires the development of methods that both preserve the integrity of the theoretical frameworks at stake and create conditions for building and discussing possible connections, that is to say the development of meta-level praxeologies that allow to take our respective research praxeologies as objects of comparative study, what we did in TELMA, in ReMath and in the Bremen group.

After these separate presentations, a substantial part of the article (pp. 299-310) is devoted to the comparison of the two approaches and to their coordination in the analysis of the two case studies. The comparison is organized along the following lines, pointing out similarities and differences:

- Comparison of objects of study: proximity in the focus on the teachers' activity, but differences in the way this activity is approached through resources and documentational work/preparation of tasks and their implementation in classroom.
- Comparison of the study of the dialectics between stabilities and evolutions in teachers' practices: it must be noticed that, contrary to what was the case in Vandebrouck (2010), the fact that the use of the language of schemes in DAD creates a substantial distance with the analysis in terms of cognitive and mediative components of the double approach is pointed out (p. 301).
- Proximity induced by the inscription of the two approaches in the didactics of mathematics with its epistemological sensitivity, but differences induced by the orientation of task analysis towards the potential activity of students in the double approach.
- Comparison of the way the determinants of teachers' work are taken in charge: proximity created by the wide perspective adopted towards the teachers' work, but different roles given to students' activity and interaction between teacher and students; links are proposed between the mediative and cognitive components in the double approach on the one hand and rules of action in DAD on the other hand and between the personal component and operational invariants.

Then, the coordinated analysis of the two case studies makes clear the complementarity of the two approaches, which is then more generally discussed in the specific context of technological integration, together with its implication in terms of teacher education and professional development.

In Sabra's paper devoted to the study of relationships between the personal and the collective dimensions of teachers' documentational work, taking as an example the case study of a Sesamath collective engaged in the design of a digital textbook for grade 10 and the specific theme of functions, DAD is combined with CoP and Margolinas' structured model of situation/activity already combined with DAD in Trgalová (2010). This theoretical combination leads Sabra to the notions of *community knowledge* (the knowledge shared and validated by a community in the frame of a common project), *community resources* (the resources at stake in a community, mobilized in the processes of reification and participation) and that of *community documentation* (a game of dynamic interactions developing between community activities, community knowledge and community resources) complementing the notions of *community system of resources* and *community documentational genesis* introduced in the paper by Gueudet and Trouche (2010c), and to connect these with the positive levels of the Margolinas' model. The schema (p. 58) reproduced in Fig. 5.4 synthesizes the partial integration operated between the three theoretical frameworks.

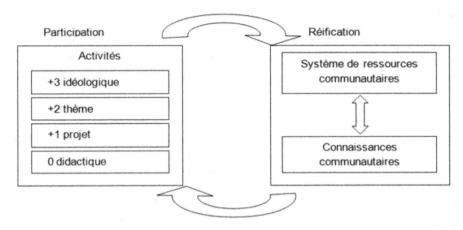

Fig. 5.4 Representation of the relationship between the processes of participation and reification in a CoP

This integrated structure is used to answer the following two research questions:

Q1: How to identify the impact of a teacher's involvement in a collective on his or her individual practices, at theoretical and methodological levels?

Q2: What role does the mathematical knowledge to be taught play in the building of a relationship between the individual and the collective aspects of the work of mathematics teachers? (author's translation).

The research shows the important role played, in the personal-collective relationships investigated, by specific phenomena that the author calls *community documentational incidents*, and defines as breakdowns or moves in the community documentation resulting from the integration of a resource in the community resource system, unexpected for at least a part of the community. This phenomenon appears as a new element of technological discourse that, if consolidated through its use in further research by the DAD community, might enter the theoretical component of DAD research praxeologies in the future.

Some readers could consider that this second example is a counterexample to the claim made above regarding the necessity of collaboration between researchers with different theoretical backgrounds for making possible deep theoretical connections. In fact, in this precise case, connections are favoured by the fact that Margolinas' model is a familiar model in the French didactic community which Sabra belongs to, and also because this community is more and more familiar with Wenger's theoretical approach, an approach, moreover, connected to DAD since its emergence. However, there is no doubt for me that joint work with Margolinas on the issues at stake and data collected would enrich and perhaps question the connections established here.

5.4.2.2 Emergence of New Theoretical Connections

To illustrate these connections, I will also consider two recent publications, first, a paper connecting DAD with CHAT (cultural historical activity theory) (Gueudet et al. 2016) and, second, a paper connecting DAD with more distant perspectives (Kynigos & Kolovou 2018).

In the paper by Gueudet et al. (2016), the team investigates the influence of the new digital opportunities offered by platforms and discussion lists on the design work of teacher collectives. Once again, the Sésamath association of teachers is considered, more precisely its collective design, from 2009 to 2013, of the chapter on functions of an e-textbook for grade 10. It is postulated that both the new digital means and the digital nature of e-textbooks facilitate the collective design by large groups of authors, and challenge the usual divide between designers and users. From a theoretical perspective, DAD is combined with CHAT (Engeström 2001), the two theories being seen in a relation of complementarity:

> For our study, we consider that CHAT complements the documentational approach. The two approaches share a focus on goal-directed activity and an interest in experience over time (history and culture versus genesis and scheme). CHAT gives more means for analyzing the evolution of communities; the documentational approach gives more means for analysing the evolution of their documentation systems. (Gueudet et al. 2016, p. 191)

The analysis developed makes clear this complementarity. In this long-term design process, three moments are distinguished, and the system of activity of what the authors call the e-textcom community is analysed in reference to the paradigmatic schema of CHAT for each of these moments (see, for instance, Fig. 5.5

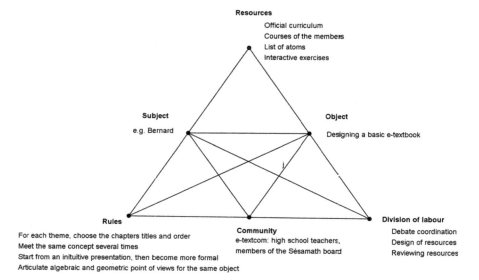

Fig. 5.5 A representation of the e-textcom activity system, third moment

5 Reflecting on the Documentational Approach from a Networking Perspective

corresponding to the third moment, p. 199). CHAT leads the authors to pay specific attention to the tensions occurring in these activity systems. For instance, the tension between the object of activity 'designing a toolkit-type textbook' and the will to organize resources in a coherent way associated with the belief that 'not all learning paths are equivalent' in the first moment or the tension between the respective authors' visions of appropriate teaching progression on the theme of functions in the third moment. As shown by the authors, these tensions and the way they are dealt with play an essential role in the process of collective documentational genesis they investigate and help us make sense of the resulting collective document, eventually not a toolkit-type textbook but a more classical e-textbook with interactive exercises and resources.

We observe here a new and productive theoretical connection complementing the affordances of the connection with the theory of CoP active in DAD since its emergence for approaching the collective dimension of documentational geneses. There is no doubt that this connection is facilitated by a common background in activity theory.

This is no longer the case for the second extension we consider now proposed in the paper by Kynigos and Kolovou (2018). The authors report on a study that took place within the European project MC2 mentioned above, focused on the collaborative design of resources supporting students' creative thinking. More precisely, the study investigates the design of a *c-book* (c for creative) on curvature by mathematics teachers working in collectives mixing a diversity of expertise. The study is informed by four theoretical perspectives, social creativity, constructionism, boundary crossing (BC in the text) and documentational approach (DA in the text), that the authors organize in a nested structure. As they explain (p. 148):

> We thought of social creativity being our focal point, and constructionism enhanced by the other two constructs, BC and DA, as being the tools to think of the former. Our connections thus had a sense of directionality and complementarity, as shown in the subsequent sections.

More precisely, on the one hand, the malleability of constructionist artefacts leads to consider these as *boundary objects* facilitating boundary crossing between designers involved in CoI (communities of interest) around a common project, thus communication and shared understanding between the different communities part of the CoI. On the other hand, the collaborative design activity involving teachers as designers of creative educational resources is seen as a process 'that is expected to trigger documentational geneses' (ibidem, p. 151).

This integrated structure is used to analyse the design of the c-book on curvature by a specific CoI of seven members with complementary expertise: mathematics, mathematics education, creative writing, computer-mediated communication and the design of digital books for mathematics education. The fine-grained analysis of the data collected using the facilities offered by the c-book environment developed for the MC2 project especially relies on the identification of *critical episodes* and *paths of socially creative ideas*. It shows how creativity emerges along the mathematics teachers' design process in this particular context, and the theoretical integrated structure helps understand the role played by the characteristics of this particular context combined with the potential offered by the tools developed and used in the MC2 project, and draw more general lessons from this particular case study. There is no doubt for me that the experience gained by one of the co-authors in theoretical connection through his participation to the projects TELMA and ReMath, mentioned in the second section of this chapter, has contributed to such achievements.

All these examples show a landscape of research praxeologies associated with DAD increasing in scope, connections and complexity. I complement this landscape by evoking an extension still in an embryonic stage, inspired by the Lexicon international project.

5.5 An Extension Inspired by the Lexicon Project

The Lexicon project aims at identifying and comparing the pedagogic-didactic lexicons that experienced teachers use in different languages and cultures to speak and exchange about what happens in mathematics classrooms. It was motivated by two main concerns (Clarke 2017):

- The limitations resulting from the hegemony of the English language in international communication in mathematics education, a limitation to which David Clarke, who launched this project, became especially aware when leading the Learners' Perspective Study, a comparative study involving 16 countries.
- The fact that, in many countries, the teaching profession seems still lacking a well-established professional language and that progressing towards a shared professional lexicon in which terms have a precise and agreed meaning would be an important step in that direction.

This project piloted by David Clarke and Carmel Mesiti from the University of Melbourne gathers partners from ten countries, Australia, Chile, China, Czech

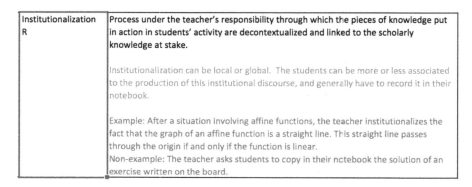

Fig. 5.6 Example of Lexicon term: Institutionalization

5 Reflecting on the Documentational Approach from a Networking Perspective

Republic, Finland, France, Germany, Japan, USA and Korea, that joined the project more recently. At this stage, ten lexicons have been built by mixed teams of researchers and expert teachers in each country, a predominant voice being given to the teachers, along a 3-year iterative process involving an increasing number of reviewers. Each lexicon proposes a structured list of terms with a definition/description, examples and non-examples, in original language and with approximate translation into English. For instance, the French lexicon is made of 115 terms and Fig. 5.6 gives an example in the English version.

The project has entered now its second phase devoted to the comparison of lexicons, the understanding of similarities and differences observed and the reflexion on how the different lexicons, seen as dynamic entities, can mutually enrich from these comparisons and on their possible contribution to teacher preparation and professional development activities (Artigue et al. 2017; Clarke et al. 2017).

Focused on classroom activity, the Lexicon project does not take in charge all dimensions of teachers' professional activity. Thus, the idea of developing a similar work investigating the terminology that teachers use in different countries and cultures to speak and exchange about their documentational activity. The preparation by Luc Trouche, Maryna Rafalska, Ulises Salinas, Karima Sayah, Hendrik van Steenbrugge and Chongyang Wang of a workshop associated with the Res(s)ources 2018 Conference was an opportunity to start working in this direction. Teacher interviews were organized by young researchers in eight different countries and languages, and the data were presented and jointly discussed in the workshop. Of course, this is just a first step, and my experience of the Lexicon project makes me aware of the distance separating a particular case study or a few case studies from what has been necessary to build and reasonably validate the ten lexicons we have produced, in the current state of maturity of teacher professional language. However, the enterprise seems promising. If pursued it will make emerge new research praxeologies both for producing *documentational lexicons* and for answering the new questions that this production and the comparison with the existing lexicons will necessarily raise. For instance, will we observe in this context similar difficulties to those at the origin of the Lexicon project? Will we observe the same diversity in lexicons, in terms both of structure and content? How to explain similarities/differences?

Reading Pepin et al. (2017), my attention was attracted by the following methodological comment (p. 263):

> After transcribing (in Chinese) and translating (in English) the interviews, we realized that our reflections on translations were actually reflections on the theoretical choices made. In order to enhance the conceptual equivalence of notions when translating (e.g. Hantrais & Mangen, 1996), several steps were taken [...] We contend that the translation of Chinese texts into English needed delicate work of negotiation and comparing understandings, leading to a deeper understanding of the main concepts at stake (e.g. 'resources', 'collective work')

This comment let me think that, yes, linguistic issues have entered the game and need to be addressed as far as DAD disseminates internationally, crossing languages and cultures, as is the case today. As is the case for the Lexicon project, this will certainly be the source of new theoretical connections.

5.6 Concluding Remarks

In this chapter, I have tried to use networking lenses and the concept of research praxeology to study the emergence and development of the approach of the documentational work of teachers known today as DAD – the documentational approach to didactics. This approach is quite recent, as the first texts attached to it were published just a decade ago. However, in the last 10 years, it has generated an impressive number of research studies and projects and attracted the interest of researchers worldwide. The diversity of interest and background of those who have contributed to it has resulted in a theoretical construction unifying today a wide diversity of research praxeologies, which a priori makes the choice of networking lenses well adapted. The concept of research praxeology, for its part, obliges the researcher to consider research practices, their evolution and their outcomes, through the dialectical and dynamic evolution of their practical and theoretical blocks, without giving priority to one over the other. As I have tried to express in this chapter, these conceptual and methodological tools helped me to make sense of this approach and of its outcomes, to approach its dynamics.

Of course, by shaping my inquiry, these choices have conditioned the vision I give of DAD, its emergence and evolution, making it a vision among many others possible but, I hope, an insightful vision for all those interested in this approach. I have to add that I carried out this inquiry in an outsider position, as DAD is not part of my research praxeologies, but I would say a close outsider due to my investment in the emergence and development of the instrumental approach and my long-term collaboration with some main actors of this approach. What I propose is thus an outsider personal vision. This is also a very partial vision. Writing this chapter, I was obliged to make a drastic selection among the different sources I have accessed, studied and could have used. Emphasizing some characteristics, I made some other less visible, for instance the methodological evolution of this approach and the different phenomena that, in the future, could enter its theoretical core. My hope is that this chapter, despite its limitations, will help newcomers to this approach to enter it in a structured and reflective way, and also that it will lead those already familiar with it to look at it with fresh eyes.

References

Abboud-Blanchard, M., & Vandebrouck, F. (2014). Geneses of technology uses: a theoretical model to study the development of teachers' practices in technology environments. In B. Ubuz, Ç. Haser, & M. A. Mariotti (Eds.), *Proceedings of the Eighth Congress of the European Society*

5 Reflecting on the Documentational Approach from a Networking Perspective 115

for Research in Mathematics Education (pp. 2504–2514). Ankara: Middle East Technical University and ERME.

Adler, J. (2000). Conceptualising resources as a theme for teacher education. *Journal of Mathematics Teacher Education, 3*, 205–224.

Artigue, M. (Ed.). (2009). Connecting approaches to technology enhanced learning in mathematics: The TELMA experience. *International Journal of Computers for Mathematical Learning, 14*(3).

Artigue, M., & Bosch, M. (2014). Reflection on networking through the praxeological lens. In A. Bikner-Ahsbahs & S. Prediger (Eds.), *Networking of theories as a research practice in mathematics education* (pp. 249–266). New York: Springer.

Artigue, M., Bosch, M., & Gascón, J. (2011). La TAD face au problème de l'interaction entre cadres théoriques en didactique des mathématiques. In M. Bosch et al. (Eds.), *Un panorama de la TAD. Actes du troisième congrès de la TAD* (pp. 33–56). Barcelona: Centre de Recerca Matemàtica.

Artigue, M., Novotná, J., Grugeon-Allys, B., Horoks, J., Hospesová, A., Moraová, H., Pilet, J., & Žlábková, I. (2017). Comparing the professional lexicons of Czech and French mathematics teachers. In B. Kaur, W. K. Ho, T. L. Toh, & B. H. Choy (Eds.), *Proceedings of PME 41* (Vol. 2, pp. 113–120). Singapore: PME.

Balacheff, N. (1995). Conception, Connaissance et Concept. *Didactique et technologies cognitives en mathématiques. Séminaires 1994–95* (pp. 219–244). Grenoble: Université Joseph Fourier.

Balacheff, N., & Margolinas, C. (2005). cK¢ Modèle de connaissances pour le calcul de situations didactiques. In A. Mercier & C. Margolinas (Eds.), *Balises en Didactique des Mathématiques* (pp. 75–106). Grenoble: La Pensée Sauvage éditions.

Ball, D. L., & Cohen, D. K. (1996). Reform by the book: What is-or might be-the role of curriculum materials in teacher learning and instructional reform? *Educational Researcher, 25*(9), 6–8, 14.

Ball, D. L., Hill, H. C., & Bass, H. (2005). Knowing mathematics for teaching. Who knows mathematics well enough to teach third grade, and how can we decide? *American Educator, 30*(3), 14–46.

Bartolini Bussi, M., & Mariotti, M. A. (2008). Semiotic mediation in the mathematics classroom: Artefacts and signs after a Vygotskian perspective. In L. English et al. (Eds.), *Handbook of international research in mathematics education* (pp. 750–787). New York: LEA.

Besnier, S., & Gueudet, G. (2016). Usages de ressources numériques pour l'enseignement des mathématiques en maternelle: orchestrations et documents. *Perspectivas em Educação Matemática, 9*(21), 978–1003. http://seer.ufms.br/index.php/pedmat/article/view/2215/2279.

Bikner-Ahsbahs, A., & Prediger, S. (2008). Networking of theories – An approach for exploiting the diversity of theoretical approaches. In B. Sriraman & L. English (Eds.), *Theories in mathematics education* (pp. 483–506). New York: Springer.

Bikner-Ahsbahs, A., & Prediger, S. (Eds.). (2014). *Networking of theories as a research practice in mathematics education*. New York: Springer.

Brousseau, G. (1997). *Theory of didactical situations in mathematics*. Dordrecht: Kluwer Academic Publishers.

Chevallard, Y. (1985). *La transposition didactique*. Grenoble: La Pensée Sauvage éditions.

Chevallard, Y. (2002). Organiser l'étude. In J.-L. Dorier, M. Artaud, M. Artigue, R. Berthelot, & R. Floris (Eds.), Actes de la Xème Ecole d'été de didactique des mathématiques (pp. 3–22, 41–56). Grenoble: La Pensée Sauvage éditions.

Clarke, D. J. (2017). Using cross-cultural comparison to interrogate the logic of classroom research in mathematics education. In B. Kaur, W. K. Ho, T. L. Toh, & B. H. Choy (Eds.), *Proceedings of PME 41* (Vol. 1, pp. 1–13). Singapore: PME.

Clarke, D., Mesiti, C., Cao, Y., & Novotna, J. (2017). The lexicon project: Examining the consequences for international comparative research of pedagogical naming systems from different cultures, In T. Dooley, & G. Gueudet (Eds.). *Proceedings of the Tenth Congress of the*

European Society for Research in Mathematics Education (CERME10, February 1 – 5, 2017) (pp. 1610-1617). Dublin: DCU Institute of Education and ERME.

Fan, L., Trouche, L., Qi, C., Rezat, S., & Vinovska, J. (2017). Topic study group no. 38. Research on resources (textbooks, learning materials, etc.). In G. Kaiser (Ed.), *Proceedings of the 13th international congress on mathematical education* (pp. 561–564). New York: Springer.

Fan, L., Trouche, L., Qi, C., Rezat, S., & Vinovska, J. (Eds.). (2018). *Research on mathematics textbooks and teachers' resources. Advances and issues. ICME-13 Monograph.* Cham: Springer.

Fleck, L. (2005). Genèse et développement d'un fait scientifique. In *Les Belles-lettres*. Paris.

Goujon, C. (2016). *Didactisation de pratiques de savoir scientifiques, transactions avec des publics scolaires et non scolaires. Des scientifiques, de leur laboratoire à la Fête de la science.* PhD. Rennes, France: Université de Bretagne Occidentale. https://hal.archives-ouvertes.fr/tel-01692314/document

Gueudet, G. (2008). Learning mathematics in class with online resources. In C. Hoyles, J.-B. Lagrange, L. Hung Son, & N. Sinclair (Eds.), *Proceedings of the 17th ICMI Study Conference "Technology revisited"* (pp. 205–212). Hanoi: Hanoi University of Technology.

Gueudet, G., & Trouche, L. (2008). Du travail documentaire des enseignants: genèses, collectifs, communautés. Le cas des mathématiques. *Education & Didactique, 2*(3), 7–34.

Gueudet, G., & Trouche, L. (2009a). Vers de nouveaux systèmes documentaires des professeurs de mathématiques ? In I. Bloch & F. Connes (Eds.), *Nouvelles perspectives en didactique des mathématiques. Cours de la XIVᵉ école d'été de didactique des mathématiques* (pp. 109–133). Grenoble: La Pensée Sauvage éditions.

Gueudet, G., & Trouche, L. (2009b). Towards new documentation systems for mathematics teachers? *Educational Studies in Mathematics, 71*(3), 199–218.

Gueudet, G., & Trouche, L. (Eds.). (2010a). *Ressources vives. Le travail documentaire des professeurs en mathématiques.* Rennes/Lyon: Presses Universitaires de Rennes et INRP.

Gueudet, G., & Trouche, L. (2010b). Des ressources aux documents, travail du professeur et genèses documentaires. In G. Gueudet & L. Trouche (Eds.), *Ressources vives. Le travail documentaire des professeurs en mathématiques* (pp. 57–74). Rennes/Lyon: Presses Universitaires de Rennes et INRP.

Gueudet, G., & Trouche, L. (2010c). Genèses communautaires, genèses documentaires: histoires en miroir. In G. Gueudet & L. Trouche (Eds.), *Ressources vives. Le travail documentaire des professeurs en mathématiques* (pp. 129–145). Rennes/Lyon: Presses Universitaires de Rennes et INRP.

Gueudet, G., & Trouche, L. (2012). Teachers' work with resources. Documentational geneses and professional geneses. In G. Gueudet, B. Pepin, & L. Trouche (Eds.), *From text to 'Lived' resources: Mathematics curriculum materials and teacher development* (pp. 23–41). New York: Springer.

Gueudet, G., & Vandebrouck, F. (2011). Technologie et evolution des pratiques enseignantes: études de cas et éclairages théoriques. *Recherches en Didactique des Mathématiques, 31*(3), 271–314.

Gueudet, G., Pepin, B., & Trouche, L. (Eds.). (2012). *From text to 'Lived' resources: Mathematics curriculum materials and teacher development.* New York: Springer.

Gueudet, G., Buteau, C., Mesa, V., & Misfeldt, M. (2014). Instrumental and documentational approaches: From technology use to documentation systems in university mathematics education. *Research in Mathematics Education, 16*(2), 139–155.

Gueudet, G., Pepin, B., Sabra, H., & Trouche, L. (2016). Collective design of an e-textbook: teachers' collective documentation. *Journal of Mathematics Teacher Education, 19,* 187–203.

Guin, D., & Trouche, L. (Eds.). (2002). *L'instrumentation de calculatrices symboliques: un problème didactique.* Grenoble: La Pensée Sauvage éditions.

Guin, D., & Trouche L. (2005). Distance training, a key mode to support teachers in the integration of ICT ? Towards collaborative conception of living pedagogical resources. In M. Bosch (Ed.), *Proceedings of the Fourth European Conference on Research on Mathematics Education* (pp. 1020–1029), FUNDEMI IQS—Universitat Ramon Llull.

5 Reflecting on the Documentational Approach from a Networking Perspective

Hammoud, R. (2012). *Le travail collectif des professeurs en chimie comme levier pour la mise en oeuvre de démarches d'investigation et le développement des connaissances profession-nelles. Contribution au développement de l'approche documentaire du didactique.* PhD. Lyon, France: Université Lyon 1, https://tel.archives-ouvertes.fr/tel-00762964/document

Haspekian, M. (2008). Une genèse des pratiques enseignantes en environnement instrumenté. In Vandebrouck (Ed.), *La classe de mathématiques: activités des élèves et pratiques des enseignants* (pp. 293–318). Toulouse: Octares.

Isoda, M., Stephens, M., Ohara, Y., & Miyakawa, T. (2007). *Japanese lesson study in mathematics. Its impact, diversity and potential for educational improvement.* Singapore: World Scientific.

Kidron, I., Bosch, M., Monaghan, J., & Palmér, H. (2018). Theoretical perspectives and approaches in mathematics education research. In T. Dreyfus, M. Artigue, D. Potari, S. Prediger, & K. Ruthven (Eds.), *Developing research in mathematics education. Twenty years of communication, cooperation and collaboration in Europe* (pp. 254–275). New York: Routledge.

Kynigos, C., & Kolovou, A. (2018). Teachers as designers of digital educational resources for creative mathematical thinking. In L. Fan, L. Trouche, C. Qi, S. Rezat, & J. Visnovska (Eds.), *Research on mathematics textbooks and teachers' resources: Advances and issues. ICME-13 monograph* (pp. 145–164). Cham: Springer.

Kynigos, C., & Lagrange, J.-B. (Eds.) (2014). Special issue: Representing mathematics with digital media: Working across theoretical and contextual boundaries. Educational Studies in Mathematics 85(3).

Lagrange, J.-B. (Ed.). (2013). *Les technologies numériques pour l'enseignement: usages, dispositifs et genèses.* Toulouse: Octarès.

Lima, I. (2006). *De la modélisation des connaissances des élèves aux décisions didactiques des professeurs: étude didactique dans le cas de la symétrie orthogonale.* Doctoral thesis. Université J. Fourier, Grenoble.

Margolinas, C. (2002). Situations, milieu, connaissances: analyse de l'activité du professeur. In J.-L. Dorier, M. Artaud, M. Artigue, R. Berthelot, & R. Floris (Eds.), *Actes de la XIe Ecole d'été de didactique des mathématiques* (pp. 141–156). Grenoble: La Pensée Sauvage éditions.

Mariotti, M. A., & Maracci, M. (2010). Un artefact comme instrument de médiation sémiotique: une ressource pour le professeur. In G. Gueudet & L. Trouche (Eds.), *Ressources vives. Le travail documentaire des professeurs en mathématiques* (pp. 91–107). Rennes/Lyon: Presses Universitaires de Rennes et INRP.

Pepin, B., Gueudet, G., & Trouche, L. (2013). Investigating textbooks as crucial interfaces between culture, policy and teacher curricular practice: Two contrasted case studies in France and Norway. *ZDM - Mathematics Education, 45*(5), 685–698.

Prieur, M. (2016). *La conception codisciplinaire de méta ressources comme appui à l'évolution des connaissances des professeurs de sciences. Les connaissances qui guident un travail de préparation pour engager les élèves dans l'élaboration d'hypothèses ou de conjectures.* PhD. Lyon, France: Université de Lyon, https://hal.archives-ouvertes.fr/tel-01364778v2/document

Rabardel, P., & Bourmaud, G. (2005). Instruments et systèmes d'instruments. In P. Rabardel & P. Pastré (Eds.), *Modèles du sujet pour la conception. Dialectiques activités développement* (pp. 211–229). Toulouse: Octarès.

Remillard, J. (2005). Examining key concepts in research on teachers' use of mathematics curricula. *Review of Educational Research, 75*(2), 211–246.

Robert, A., & Rogalski, J. (2002). Le système complexe et cohérent des pratiques des enseignants de mathématiques: une double approche. *Revue Canadienne de l'Enseignement des Sciences, des Mathématiques et des Technologies, 2*(4), 505–528.

Rocha, K. (2018). Uses of online resources and documentational trajectories: The case of Sésamath. In L. Fan, L. Trouche, C. Qi, S. Rezat, & J. Visnovska (Eds.), *Research on mathematics textbooks and –13 teachers' resources: Advances and issues. ICME-13 monograph* (pp. 235–258). Cham: Springer.

Ruthven, K. (2007). Teachers, technologies and the structures of schooling. In D. Pitta-Pantazi & G. Philippou (Eds.), *Proceedings of the fifth congress of the european society for research in mathematics education* (pp. 52–67). Larnaca: University of Cyprus and ERME.

Sabra, H. (2016). L'étude des rapports entre documentation individuelle et collective: incidents, connaissances et ressources mathématiques. *Recherches en Didactique des Mathématiques, 36*(1), 49–96.

Sensevy, G. (2010). Formes de l'intention didactique, collectifs, et travail documentaire. In G. Gueudet & L. Trouche (Eds.), *Ressources vives. Le travail documentaire des professeurs en mathématiques* (pp. 147–161). Rennes/Lyon: Presses Universitaires de Rennes et INRP.

Shaaban, E., Khalil, I., & Trouche, L. (2015). Interactions between digital resources and biology teachers' conceptions about genetic determinism: A case study of two Lebanese teachers. *International Journal of Science and Research, 4*(10), 1190–1200.

Trgalová, J. (2010). Documentation et décisions didactiques des professeurs. In G. Gueudet & L. Trouche (Eds.), *Ressources vives. Le travail documentaire des professeurs en mathématiques* (pp. 271–291). Rennes/Lyon: Presses Universitaires de Rennes et INRP.

Trouche, L. (2003). *Construction et conduite des instruments dans les apprentissages mathématiques: nécessité des orchestrations*. HDR. Paris: Université Paris Diderot-Paris 7. https://telearn.archives-ouvertes.fr/file/index/docid/190091/filename/Trouche_2003.pdf

Trouche, L., & Pepin, B. (2014). From instrumental to documentational approach: Towards a holistic perspective of teachers' resource systems in higher education. *Research in Mathematics Education, 16*(2), 156–160.

Tuffery-Rochdi, C. (2016). *Les ressources au cœur des pratiques des enseignants de mathématiques. Le cas de l'enseignement d'exploration MPS en seconde*. PhD. St Denis, France: Université de La Réunion, https://tel.archives-ouvertes.fr/tel-01391464/document.

Vandebrouck, F. (2010). Ressources et documents, le cas de la démarche expérimentale en mathématiques. In G. Gueudet & L. Trouche (Eds.), *Ressources vives. Le travail documentaire des professeurs en mathématiques* (pp. 253–269). Rennes/Lyon: Presses Universitaires de Rennes et INRP.

Vandebrouck, F. (Ed.). (2013). *Mathematics classrooms: Students' activities and Teachers' practices*. Rotterdam: Sense Publishers.

Wenger, E. (1998). *Communities of practice. Learning, meaning, identity*. New York: Cambridge University Press.

Part II
A Comparative Perspective

Chapter 6
Mathematics Teachers as Curriculum Designers: An International Perspective to Develop a Deeper Understanding of the Concept

Birgit Pepin, Michèle Artigue, Verônica Gitirana, Takeshi Miyakawa, Kenneth Ruthven, and Binyan Xu

Abstract In this chapter, we investigate the notion of "teachers as curriculum designers" from the literature and from six international perspectives. This is done in order to (1) develop a deeper understanding of the concept, and (2) provide an international perspective and illustrations of the different facets of teacher design. Based on this investigation, we could identify different modes of teacher design: from teacher *d*esign activities at micro level (e.g., lesson preparation alone or in small groups), over those at meso level (e.g., *D/d*esigning in collectives of colleagues for the purpose of use by others), to *D*esign at macro level (e.g., involvement in the design of national frameworks by professional design teams for the use of many others). More generally, we claim that the often casually used term of "teacher design" has different meanings in different contexts and that teacher design activities may be for different purposes and for different expected end results. A major distinction is whether the design is more oriented towards the process, or the product. We argue that the most promising form of teacher design might lie at the

---

B. Pepin (✉)
Eindhoven University of Technology, Eindhoven, The Netherlands
e-mail: b.e.u.pepin@tue.nl

M. Artigue
Université Paris-Diderot, Paris, France

V. Gitirana
CAA - Núcleo de Formação Docente, Federal University of Pernambuco, Caruaru, PE, Brazil

T. Miyakawa
Waseda University, Tokyo, Japan

K. Ruthven
University of Cambridge, Cambridge, UK

B. Xu
East China Normal University, Shanghai, China

© Springer Nature Switzerland AG 2019
L. Trouche et al. (eds.), *The 'Resource' Approach to Mathematics Education*,
Advances in Mathematics Education,
https://doi.org/10.1007/978-3-030-20393-1_6

crossroads between product and process orientation, with connections between the two. This has implications for teacher education and professionalism.

Keywords Mathematics teacher design · Curriculum designer/s · International perspective/s

6.1 Introduction

In previous research (e.g., Margolinas 2014; Pepin et al. 2013; Remillard 2005), mathematics teacher interaction with resources has been discussed. It has become clear that teachers interact with (curriculum) resources in different ways (e.g., adaptation, appropriation), and one of the forms of interaction has been labelled as "design" (e.g., Brown 2009; Pepin et al. 2017a). At the same time, the term "design" is used differently by different educationists, which in turn creates the need for clarity and a better conceptualization: What are the dimensions of "teacher design? What does it entail (e.g., compared to the teacher as a "user" of materials)? A common "language" is needed that we can share when discussing mathematics "teacher design."

At the "Res(s)ources 2018" conference (at the French Institute of Education (IFÉ) in Lyon in May 2018), international scholars (the authors of the paper) were invited to participate in the panel discussion "Mathematics Teachers as Designers: An International Perspective," to provide illustrative examples of "teacher design" in different contexts. The aim was to explore the notion of "teachers as designers" in different international contexts, in order to develop a deeper understanding of the concept. After the conference, (1) a literature review was conducted on the notion of the "teacher as curriculum designer" and (2) the participants were invited to contribute their respective "cases" in writing. These two sets of sources formed the basis for our investigation and analyses, which in turn helped us to re-conceptualize "teacher design" and provide illustrations of its different facets in different international contexts.

In this conceptual chapter (and after a short introduction), we report, first, on a review of the literature with respect to three notions (teacher design and teacher design capacity; modes of teacher design work; and curriculum design). Second, (a) the development of the six international perspectives (and cases) is explained and (b) the findings from the investigation of the cases are presented in a table and discussed. Third, we draw conclusions by reflecting on the findings, attempting to nuance and re-conceptualize teacher design, and we outline implications of the investigation.

6.2 Conceptualizations of the Mathematics Teacher as Designer

In previous curriculum renewals, teachers have often been the "implementers" of the curriculum that was mandated and/or designed by the ministries (and their agencies). For decades, scholarship on factors affecting curriculum implementation has pointed to the importance of involving teachers, to varying degrees, in shaping the learning scenarios and trajectories in their own classrooms (e.g., Ben-Peretz 1990). More recently, in many countries worldwide (e.g., Australia, Canada, China, France, the Netherlands, Scotland, Singapore), a new wave of curriculum renewal has been initiated by the respective ministries and conducted/carried out by their curriculum development agencies. Distinctively, and unlike most earlier curriculum changes, teachers have been more included than before. While the benefits of teacher involvement in curriculum design (albeit not at macro/national level) are acknowledged in the literature (e.g., Priestley et al. 2017), far less is known about shaping that involvement to yield expected benefits. At the same time, recent technological developments (e.g., new web-based curriculum resources) have changed the nature of teacher design work. Teachers design, redesign, customize, and appropriate not only conventional but also digitally enhanced learning materials, curriculum resources, and activities. Moreover, they are often (co-)designers of their own (school and classroom) curriculum and the associated and envisaged student learning trajectories.

In this section, we bring together the research literature under the following three themes: (a) teachers as designers and teacher design capacity; (b) modes of teacher design work/activity; and (c) curriculum design, representations, and structure. This allows us to better frame our view on the different aspects of teacher design and curriculum.

6.2.1 The Notions of Mathematics Teacher Design and Teacher Design Capacity

There has been considerable research carried out in the field of teacher design (e.g., in curriculum studies; instructional design with regard to technology enhanced learning), more recently with regard to how design is conceptualized within teachers' work and practice (Huizinga 2009; Nieveen and van der Hoeven 2011). Selected studies (within the domain of mathematics education) emphasize the relational aspects of design work (e.g., Pepin et al. 2017a) or teacher curriculum design within the context of educational reform and change (e.g., Trouche et al. 2019), to name but a few.

We take as a starting point a very broad notion of design that includes the processes of appropriating and/or actually developing specific resources for teaching or learning. Recent mathematics education research reveals how individual teachers select, adapt, appropriate, combine, or redesign different curriculum resources (e.g., Pepin et al. 2013) for their personal use and enact the different curriculum elements in their teaching practice (e.g., Remillard 2005). However, depending on the context in which the design work takes place, we also need to consider "larger design," that is, when mathematics teachers are part of national design teams for the renewal of the national curriculum. Hence, we contend that these two notions of teacher design may lie on a continuum. For the moment, we understand "teacher design" as including both (at each end of the spectrum) and as work that involves the interaction between individual and collective capacities and environmental conditions/support (Pepin et al. 2017a; Priestley et al. 2017).

The following quote by Priestley et al. (2017) serves as a point of departure for how teacher curriculum design is leaning on teacher agency:

"The main distinctive factor is that agency [and teacher design work] involves intentionality, the capacity to formulate possibilities for action, active consideration of such possibilities and the exercise of choice. But it also includes the causative properties of contextual factors – social and material structures and cultural forms that influence human behavior – which is why, as mentioned, a full understanding of agency must consider how individual capacity interplays with contextual factors." (Priestley et al. 2017, p. 23).

In an earlier study, we reviewed literature on teacher expertise and teacher design in mathematics education and curriculum studies, to develop a refined understanding of teacher design capacity (Pepin et al. 2017a). In that study teacher design capacity was defined to include the following components:

- An orientation, a goal, or point/s of reference for the design:

  - To know the "status quo" (e.g., what do students know, which problems they do have in terms of misconceptions), as well as what teachers are aiming for in terms of their mathematical-didactical design.
  - To understand the larger (e.g., national curriculum guidelines) and the smaller picture (e.g., learning trajectory for a particular mathematical topic) of their design with respect to the curriculum (e.g., a task/activity; a lesson; a lesson sequence, e.g., for a particular grade).
  - To discern where it fits in the short (i.e., for a lesson cycle) as well as the long term (i.e., connecting topic areas across grades).

- A set of design principles, which must be firm but flexible: a teacher needs a set of "universals" for the design, or principles, which are evidence-informed (e.g., from own practice, or based upon research) and supported by justification for their choices. We call those robust principles. At the same time, these principles must be flexible enough, i.e., didactically flexible, to adapt to new challenges and contexts, so that the teacher's frame of reference can grow and expand, perhaps cover new areas, or differentiate/validate within the existing frame.

6 Mathematics Teachers as Curriculum Designers

- "Design-in-action" type of implicit understandings, reflections, and realizations: a teacher needs to be able to generate relationships or informed potential lines of action, which are often not observable and which develop in the course of instruction.

This "definition" has only partly been helpful, as it provides an ambitious, idealized image of teacher design capacity. The reality is often quite different, and this raises questions about its possible use in practice.

Hence, starting by using the term "design" more broadly (e.g., to include the individual and the "larger" design), we propose the following dimensions as parts of the notion of "teacher design":

- Intentionality dimension: deliberate, goal-directed mental activity/thinking, definition of a clear goal (probably due to an actual "problem"/rationale).
- (Degree of) Novelty dimension: positioned on the continuum between (on one extreme) slight adaptations of current practices, to (at the other extreme) developing a new curriculum resource (e.g., textbook) or scheme of work from scratch
- Approach dimension: strategies, styles, design approaches.
- Time (duration) dimension: depending on the context, on a time continuum between hourly design session/s, to a long-term professional development design activity.
- Individual/collaborative ("teaming") dimension: from individual teacher design (in school, or at home) to professional teacher design teams.
- Audience/use dimension: for the/one teacher's own teaching; for all mathematics teachers in the school (site-specific design); for the whole regional/national teaching staff (generic design).
- Context dimension:

  - Design space/environment: at home, school, or Internet.
  - Resources: resources and tools available in the national/school context and used for the design.

We will refer to this analytical frame for the analysis of our cases. In theoretical terms, it leads us to explore the nature of teacher design work and its different modes.

6.2.2 Modes of Teacher Design Work

Teacher design work can vary in character and take on different forms. Teachers often work alone, or they work in teams; they may take on various roles: that of redesigner of existing materials and activities, or as co-designers, for example. Without claiming to be exhaustive, in this section we first review the literature (e.g., in mathematics education; instructional science; technology-enhanced learning sciences), where we mainly found two modes: *teachers as designers in terms of customization for own teaching* and *teachers as participatory designers (in small local or large national teams).* Second, we reflect "across" the two modes pointing to particular affordances and constraints. Moreover, we contend that, at least theoretically, there are four different modes of teacher design work.

6.2.2.1 Teacher Customization for Their Own Teaching

Teachers can contribute to the curriculum in different ways: they may be enactors of the curriculum, that is, they implement ready-made materials (and more or less align with the designers' intentions). Equally, they may use ready-made materials "creatively": they use given materials to try out new activities and improvise in the moments of enactment. Another way would be to redesign mathematics curriculum materials via making small, systematic changes or adjustments, mostly based on their earlier experiences in class (e.g., Remillard 2005). Even when they use the same curriculum materials (e.g., textbooks), they frequently adapt these to accommodate the varied needs of their students. At times this is also done when teaching in class (e.g., "design-in-use," Pepin et al. 2013), as in-the-moment decision/s. Indeed, it appears that materials that yield to teachers' modifications better respond to the changing needs of the classroom, and to its constraints and resources.

It is known that teachers redesign curriculum materials for various reasons: to better align them with their teaching goals or styles, to respond to different students' needs or different classroom situations (e.g., Brown and Edelson 2003). Their customizations may serve to align materials to changing content standards, or to add details that address their students' or local communities' interests, or to adapt the level of challenge to suit individual abilities, to name but a few (Matuk et al. 2015). There are of course often also practicality-related concerns, which hinder or support teachers' (re-) design of curriculum materials (see framework of Ruthven 2014).

6.2.2.2 Teachers as Participatory Designers/Partners in Task Design

Teacher involvement in curriculum (e.g., mathematical tasks and activities) design has a long tradition, in particular in mathematics education, where teachers have been designing mathematical tasks (e.g., Instituts de Recherche sur l'Enseignement des Mathématiques network in France, see Trouche (2016); Sésamath association in France, see Gueudet et al. (2016); see also Pepin and Jones (2016)). However, although it is said to foster implementation of curriculum reforms, teachers often encounter various problems while designing, related to conditions set for the design process, and they often lack the knowledge and skills needed to enact design processes.

The expertise required to enact curriculum design has been described by various scholars (e.g., Huizinga 2009, Nieveen and Van der Hoeven 2011). They use different labels to describe elements of the same concept, including curriculum design competencies (e.g., Huizinga 2009), instructional design competencies (e.g., Richey et al. 2001), and design expertise (Huizinga 2009). For Huizinga (2009), design expertise consists of three aspects (curriculum design expertise; subject matter knowledge; pedagogical content knowledge), and it includes analysis, design, development, implementation, and evaluation skills.

In collaborative design, teachers often create new or adapt existing materials in teams, because they are intrinsically interested in designing curriculum materials, or to comply with the intentions of the curriculum designers and with the realities of their context. Often, external experts are involved in the process, and they are expected to provide the team with recent, up-to-date insights, for example, concerning the underlying rationale for particular curriculum changes, or in terms of recent research outcomes related to the intended design. The collaborative process is said to provide opportunities for teachers, for example, to reflect on intentions of a particular reform, and to develop materials that correspond to their needs within the reform context (Voogt et al. 2015). The interaction with peers and experts is expected to deepen and challenge (1) teachers' beliefs, (2) their practice, and (3) their goals for student learning (Borko 2004). These three points link to the main activities of a Teaching Research Group (TRG), a format for teacher design institutionally established in China.

Yuan and Li (2015) report on particular practices in teams:

> During a typical [collaborative] activity, two or more teachers teach a common topic to different groups of students with distinct lesson designs, while their fellow teacher participants observe each of these lessons. After all lessons are completed, all teachers involved gather to discuss the lesson designs and classroom teaching practices, make comments and suggestions for future revisions and improvements. (p. 568)

Borko (2004) also argues that in order for collaborative curricular design processes to have the potential to contribute to teacher learning, these must be well-scaffolded. In addition, the curricular materials resulting from the design process must be based on recent knowledge of good practice and considered by teachers to be usable in their contexts (Penuel et al. 2007).

6.2.2.3 Reflecting "Across" the Two Modes

Across the various modes of teacher design work, individuals and teams work differently to inform both the processes and the products of design. While teachers sometimes design in "multiple expert teams" (e.g., university-based mathematicians; mathematics teacher educators; mathematics school teachers – see Jackson et al. 2015; Penuel et al. 2007), teacher design work is often small scale and close to practice. According to the literature, it typically involves (a) critical reflection on and redesign of one's personal practice, which teachers find insightful (e.g., Pepin et al. 2017a); (b) adaptation based on research evidence (e.g., Cobb and Jackson 2015) (this typically plays a very modest role in a teacher's design work, unless s/he works with teacher design teams with external (research) support); and/or (c) team design within one organization/school (e.g., Yang 2009).

Moreover, there are various reasons why teachers may become involved in design work. First, they want to design artifacts that can provide resources tailored for use in specific classrooms with particular learners, in order to improve their student learning (Pepin et al. 2017b), hence closely related to their daily instructional/pedagogical practices. Second, teachers often engage in design to adapt to curriculum reforms (Trouche et al. 2019). Third, teacher involvement in the design of (innovative) products may be sought, by external agencies (e.g., education ministries), to increase their practicality. Fourth, teachers may value engagement in particular design work, as it is likely to yield increased ownership and commitment for implementation (e.g., Cviko et al. 2014). Finally, teacher design work can provide a rich, authentic, and practical context for teacher learning and professional development about mathematics, curriculum materials, and/or technology suitable for a particular content (e.g., Koehler and Mishra 2005).

Research (e.g., Cobb and Jackson 2015) has shown that support and external expertise are likely to be beneficial to both the processes and the products of teacher design, especially when focused on how to structure work in teams, on substantive vision, and on process guidance. Moreover, to establish and maintain the substantive focus for design, a shared vision is essential (Gueudet et al. 2013). Conversations about vision and goals stimulate teachers to apply their didactical knowledge, especially when tackling new topics (Gueudet et al. 2016). Research has demonstrated that high-quality process support, in addition to substantive support, is crucial for design success (Jackson et al. 2015).

Looking across the modes reported in the literature, teacher design can be seen in (at least) two dimensions: (1) individual/collaborative ("teaming") dimension, from working alone (single) to working in a collective, and (2) "use" dimension – from "for own use" (for his/her teaching; site-specific) to use by others (generic) (see Table 6.1). This alerted us to suggest that there are potentially (and theoretically) four different modes of teacher design – we denoted these with d-esign, d/D-esign, D/d-esign, and D-esign, where, for each dimension, d is a marker of narrower scope and D of broader scope; and in combining dimensions signal situations where the scope of use/teaming differs.

Table 6.1 Two dimensions of teacher design

Use/teaming	Working/designing alone	Working/designing in a team
Designing for own use/ teaching	A teacher designing on his/her own for his/her own teaching (e.g., lesson preparation at home)	Teachers designing in a team (e.g., of colleagues in same school) for their own teaching
	d	D/d
Designing for use by others	Teachers designing on their own/alone for use by others (e.g., expert teachers/ professional designers)	Teams of teachers/experts designing for use by others (e.g., teams of professional designers)
	d/D	D

6.2.3 Curriculum Levels, Representations, and the Spider Web

In most international contexts, the "curriculum" is seen as a "plan for learning," and each country's National Curriculum provides its plan for what the country values their students/pupils to learn. At the same time, it is important to note that the curriculum "works" at specific curriculum levels, in particular contexts, and it has particular representations.

First, in terms of curriculum levels, it is noteworthy that, at different curriculum levels, particular "products" may be identified (Van den Akker 2003) (Table 6.2).

These levels are important for our analytical/conceptual frame, in particular the meso and micro level, as these are closest to the teachers' work. At the same time, the "higher" curriculum levels affect the "lower" ones, as they set the context for the work of teachers. For example, the national curriculum and national examination programs, at macro level, are part of the context in which teachers work and design in/for their teaching (at meso and micro level). Another example is textbooks: textbook authors typically take the macro frameworks (including innovations and reforms) into account when producing textbooks. It is also worth noting that curriculum products vary greatly in their nature and scope, also depending on the audience. Examples are textbooks, in some contexts approved and used nationwide, as compared to lesson/teaching plans which are typically site-specific and used by one or several teachers for their own practice.

Second, the curriculum can be represented in different forms. Curriculum research (e.g., Goodlad 1979; van den Akker 2003) typically distinguishes between the following curriculum representations (Table 6.3).

The division into six representations is especially useful for our analysis of the processes (and the outcomes) of curriculum innovations (e.g., the French case). For our purpose of investigating "teacher design" of the curriculum, this distinction of forms emphasizes the different layers of the curriculum concept and demonstrates the often-substantial discrepancies between the various forms.

Table 6.2 Curriculum levels and curriculum products (Thijs and Van den Akker 2009, p. 9)

Level	Description	Examples
Supra	International	Common European framework of references for languages
Macro	System, national	Core objectives, attainment levels
		Examination programs
Meso	School, institute	School program
		Educational program
Micro	Classroom, teacher	Teaching plan, instructional materials
		Module, course
		Textbooks
Nano	Pupil, individual	Personal plan for learning
		Individual course of learning

Table 6.3 Curriculum representations (Thijs and Van den Akker 2009, p.10)

Intended	Ideal	Vision (rationale or basic philosophy underlying a curriculum)
	Formal/ Written	Intentions as specified in curriculum documents and/or materials
Implemented	Perceived	Curriculum as interpreted by its users (especially teachers)
	Operational	Actual process of teaching and learning (also: Curriculum-in-action)
Attained	Experiential	Learning experiences as perceived by learners
	Learned	Resulting learning outcomes of learners

Third, curriculum theory often uses the so-called curricular spider web (van den Akker 2003) to denote the close connection between aims and content of learning and the other aspects (e.g., assessment, resources, teacher role) of the curriculum (as the plan for learning). The core and the nine threads of the spider web refer to the ten parts of a curriculum, each concerning an aspect of learning and the learning program for pupils (see Table 6.4).

At the same time, visualizing the relationship between the various aspects as a spider web also indicates the fragility of the relationships: if a teacher designs taking only assessment into consideration (and neglecting the other aspects), it is likely that the web is pulled into one direction and may possibly break; hence, the plan for learning will most likely lack consistency and coherence.

In a previous paper, we had amended these 10 questions for our purpose, to investigate "teacher design" (see Pepin et al. 2017a, b) from a curriculum perspective (Table 6.5).

This frame has been helpful for comparing teacher design, in particular when we compared collective and individual aspects of teacher design, and which audience the design was aimed at.

Of course, teacher curriculum design/innovation can start with any component. Traditionally, the learning content has received the most attention. However, over the past decades, new insights about learning mathematics, and about resources beneficial for learning mathematics, have provided sources of inspiration for innovative practices. It is known that textbooks have been a significant component of the curriculum (and "stirrer") for a long time (e.g., they provided guidance for teachers), and recent opportunities provided by digitalization offer new impulses for innovations. The time factor is a classical object of curriculum discussions: How is the always scarce amount of time distributed across domains and learning tasks? In our quest for teacher design, it raises the question of how much time teachers get to design their own curriculum.

It is clear that the relevance of the ten components varies for the five curriculum levels mentioned earlier. For our purpose, that is, the study of "teacher design," the micro and meso levels (see Table 6.2) are clearly the most relevant ones. At the same time, all other levels, and in particular the macro and nano levels, clearly play a role for teachers as designers. In addition, the consistency and coherence between objectives and content on the one hand, and pedagogical considerations, assessment, and

6 Mathematics Teachers as Curriculum Designers 131

Table 6.4 Curriculum components in question form (Thijs and van den Akker 2009, pp. 11/12)

Component	Core question
Rationale	Why are they learning?
Aims and objectives	Towards which goals are they learning?
Content	What are they learning?
Learning activities	How are they learning?
Teacher role	How is the teacher facilitating their learning?
Materials and resources	With what are they learning?
Grouping	With whom are they learning?
Location	Where are they learning?
Time	When are they learning?
Assessment	How is their learning assessed?

Table 6.5 Teacher design components in question form (Pepin et al. 2017a, pp. 801–802)

Component	Core question
Rationale	Why are teachers designing? – e.g., dissatisfaction with textbook; to become less dependent on the textbook; to make teaching more varied
Aims and objectives	What are their aims and goals? – e.g., to prepare a series of exemplary lessons for particular topic areas
Audience	What is the audience? – e.g., fellow teachers; teachers nationwide; students
Content	What are they designing? – e.g., lessons; assessment questions
Activities	How are they designing? – e.g., design approaches; sequences; strategies; styles
Materials and resources	What are the resources and tools used for the design? – e.g., resources used
Grouping	With whom are they designing? – e.g., in a group; individually; team membership
Location	Where are they designing? – e.g., in school; on the internet – The design environment
Time	When are they designing? – e.g., how long does the design take
Assessment	How is the design evaluated? – e.g., expert appraisal; peer appraisal; observation/interviews of/with users; assessing learning results

the nature of resources used, on the other hand, are of great importance at these levels. At school and classroom levels, nearly all components play a role. Here, overall consistency is of crucial importance for successful and sustainable implementation of innovative designs.

6.3 International Perspectives

In this section, we (a) report on the development of the six international "cases" and (b) present and discuss the findings from the investigation of the cases.

6.3.1 The Development of the Cases

The overall purpose of our investigation was to identify different facets of the commonly used constructs of "teacher design" or "teachers as curriculum designers" in order to develop a more nuanced understanding of the concept. To structure our panel discussion, and subsequently our cases, we took into consideration our knowledge of previous mathematics education research on teacher design. Making the investigation feasible, we opted for the three (what we judged as) most important questions/lines, in order to investigate the phenomenon "mathematics teacher as curriculum designer" in different international contexts. The panelists were given the following questions:

- Why are teacher design activities relevant? Why would they design?
- What would teachers design? What are the most interesting/challenging design tasks?
- How would teachers design? What sorts of design approaches would they use, and under which conditions?

In practical terms, in the first stage each panelist (separately) wrote up "his/her case" (broadly structured by the three questions) related to their experiences in their contexts, in addition to a description of each context. As it turned out, the cases included important additional information. In the second stage, the first author (alerted by the previous findings from the literature) sent the table she had produced (based on the individual case stories) to the case authors for validation, together with the first version of the paper. Subsequently, case authors amended and validated their cases. For an overview, we have collected the findings in Table 6.6.

More precisely, the cases were analyzed based on our knowledge of

1. The notion of "teachers as curriculum designers," which included both curriculum design theory/research (e.g., Nieveen and van der Hoeven 2011) and mathematics education research (e.g., Pepin et al. 2017a, b), and our previously stated two dimensions of "teacher design" (see Table 6.1).
2. The different modes of teacher design work (see Table 6.1).
3. Curriculum design, more precisely, the spider web (e.g., van den Akker 2003; Thijs and van den Akker 2009).

We note here that the previous identification of modes (see Table 6.1) was theoretical, whereas the analysis allowed to identify only three of the four modes: D, D/d, and d could be identified (see next section).

6.3.2 Discussion of Findings from Cases

In this section, we present our findings (based on the cross-case analyses – see Table 6.6), and we distinguish between four main claims.

6 Mathematics Teachers as Curriculum Designers

Table 6.6 Findings from the cases

Country		Context	Why	What	How
France	D	IREM groups across France; Sésamath	Support of innovations/reform/renewal of curriculum	Production of resources for teaching and teacher education	Didactical engineering in collectives (teachers, teacher educators, university mathematicians, didacticians)
				Tasks and didactic situations	
	d	Teachers in schools	Translate the National Curriculum into teaching (resources) in schools adaptation	Development of curriculum progressions	Teachers' personal work
					Lesson preparation in teacher groups/collectives (thematic groups)
					Building on a variety of resources
England	D	"National regulation" of curriculum and assessment specifications by government agencies	"School improvement" through setting national standards aimed at establishing sound provision and raising performance in system-wide national and international assessments	Official documentation setting out national specifications for curriculum coverage and learning progression	Official documentation prepared by government agencies, with input from working groups
		"Free market" in curricular resources developed by multiple commercial and non-commercial organizations and individuals		Curricular resources (including complete curriculum schemes) promoted nationally by various organizations	Curricular resources developed by multiple commercial and non-commercial organizations and individuals
	d	"Curriculum resourcing" by teachers in school departments, working collectively and individually	"Local customization" aimed at assembling curricular resources well suited to staff and students of school, and addressing issues of "school improvement"	Mandated production of "schemes of work" for the school/department to create a system of classroom resources for "curriculum coverage"	Collective and/or individual creation of teaching sequences for "schemes of work" through selection, and adaptation of classroom resources from a variety of sources

(continued)

Table 6.6 (continued)

Country		Context	Why	What	How
Japan	D/d	Lesson study and open lesson	Process of designing is seen as teacher professional development, to better understand the National Curriculum and curriculum materials (e.g., approved textbooks)	Preparing a series of lessons including one lesson demonstrated to the colleagues	Individual and collective work with colleagues (from own and/or neighboring schools) (e.g., for analysis of textbook and teacher guide – This process is named "kyōzai-kenkyū")
			Improvement of teaching as a school mission	Preparing lesson plan	Analysis, exploration of variety of resources: Internet, workbook, textbook
			Implementation of renewed curriculum		
	d	Individual teachers (or groups of two teachers, e.g., for "team teaching")	Lesson/teaching preparation	Appropriation of curriculum progression and teaching materials	Individual work (e.g., for "kyōzai-kenkyū")
				"Bansho" and questions	Reliance on textbook and teacher guide
China	D/d	Structured system from top down composed of – TROs (teaching research office): They play the role of giving administrative and professional guidance; they often work with teams of professional researchers, and play an important role in bridging the gap between teaching theories and instructional practice. – Same-school TRGs (teaching research Group – Teachers in same school/year group)	Study classroom teaching	Lesson plans and progressions	TROs are powerful middlemen for conducting school-based teaching research activities
			Increase quality of education	Content	
			Implement curriculum reforms	Teaching method/s	
			Work out lesson plans (also progression over a particular period) and teaching methods (one approved textbook)	Problems/activities	In TRGs (and working with expert teachers), in particular TGRs/groups which include school teachers, expert teachers in school and researchers from universities
			Design for teaching and learning is conceived as training for teachers, so that they become "researchers of classroom teaching"	Action research focused on practical teaching problems	

	D/d and d	Individual teachers (e.g., in preparation for TRG work)	Sharing teaching resources collected by individual teachers	The major work of the LPG (lesson preparation group) is about arranging each unit of mathematics content, preparing lesson, and sharing teaching resources collected by individual teachers	Teachers from the same grade and same subject are encouraged to build a LPG (lesson preparation group), which is led by an experienced teacher
		Teachers from the same grade and same subject are encouraged to build a LPG (lesson preparation group) which is led by an experienced teacher			
Brazil	D	A national project of textbooks to evaluate and write a guide for textbooks for state school teachers, coordinated by the national ministry of education involving researchers and teachers in the evaluation process	To support teaching in and amend the materials for the different regions	To evaluate textbooks and design meta-resources	In teams (consisting of teachers, teacher educators and sometimes researchers) who meet online and in person
	D/d and d	Collective of teacher educators and individual teachers	Reflection and amendment of materials	Adapting existing materials/ textbooks	Individual and in collectives (within a school or neighboring schools)
			To cope with diversity	Re-creating activities with respect to social context/cultural context	
			Authoring of materials for teachers' own development		
Netherlands	D	SLO- Centre for Curriculum Development (for all school subject areas)	Support curriculum reforms	(proposals for) curriculum frameworks at national scale	Consult/co-design with experts, teacher educators, teachers (in interaction with)
		Variety of textbook publishers	Curriculum innovations	Textbook production	
				Exemplary materials (within those frameworks) to inspire/ stimulate teachers and textbook publishers	
	D/d and d	D/d TDTs (teacher design team)	Get good/better pupil attainment and school results	Adapt existing materials for their teaching e.g., ICT in maths; create concept-context materials	Teams of teachers (sometimes also teacher educators) in TDTs
		d individual teachers	Professional development/ learning	Prepare lessons	Individual teachers (at home)

1. Different contexts allowed for different *modes of teacher design*, and these were linked to different design spaces at different curriculum levels. We could identify at least three *design modes* (and they are not hierarchically organized):

   (a) At macro (system, national) level, teams of experts (e.g., in ministries, or expert centers or task forces) worked on the design of a national curriculum, which included not only mathematical content (for each age group) but often also didactical considerations and particularly pertinent activities and tasks (e.g., French context). These teams of experts rarely included classroom teachers (teachers were more often consulted to react on drafts than involved as active designers of national frameworks), and mainly consisted of subject and subject didactics experts and professional curriculum designers. This type of mathematics curriculum design is for generic use, and we have proposed (in Table 6.1) to denote it capital D: *"D-esign."*

   (b) At meso level (school, institute), different scenarios offered opportunities for teacher design, and at this level classroom teachers were typically involved. For example, in England, mathematics teachers in school departments would work individually or collectively on "curriculum resourcing" for their respective school/department. This included "local customization" aimed at assembling curricular resources well suited to staff and students of their school and at addressing issues of "school improvement." Teachers would typically be expected to produce "schemes of work" for their school's mathematics department, to create a system of classroom resources to "cover" the official curriculum. This would be done, either individually or collectively, by creating teaching sequences for the "schemes of work" through selection and adaptation of classroom resources from a variety of sources, including those published by a host of commercial and non-commercial organizations, as well as others exchanged more informally. Except for sporadic professional development courses (provided by various organizations), there was little further help to "interpret the official curriculum" and to design tasks, activities, and learning lines for students.

   In France, it appeared that regionally established IREM groups, and associations such as Sésamath, bridged the gap between the nationally offered curriculum/innovations (including guidelines to the curriculum) and teaching in schools. These associations of "experts" (part-time teachers/part-time teacher educators, university mathematicians, didacticians) designed resources for mathematics teaching and teacher education, in particular those in support of curriculum innovations. Particular practices and theories were evident, such as "didactical engineering" and "didactic situations," which reflected a common theoretical underpinning and the importance of sharing a common language on (curriculum) design tasks among designers.

   In Japan, Lesson Study at school level (Fernandez and Yoshida, 2004; Isoda et al. 2007; Stigler and Hiebert 1999) included the processes of designing a series of lessons and of teaching one of them as an open lesson, by one teacher. This was done for the sake of professional development for this teacher (who designed the lessons), as well as for the colleagues who participated in the observation and discussions. The main aim was to better understand the national curriculum (including reforms) and the use of particular materials, as well as to improve the teaching and learning in their school.

In China, similar practices were evident at (1) city and (2) school level: (1) At city level, the Teaching Research Offices (TROs) were powerful middlemen for the conduct of school-based teaching research activities, and they invited teachers from schools to participate in designing series of guidance/support materials (e.g., teaching guidance, standard implementation guidance, examination guidance). (2) At school level, Teaching Research Groups (TRGs) were common. In TRGs, classroom teachers would design curricular/lesson plans and instruction and analyze the quality of particular materials, in short, act as "researchers of classroom teaching." These groups would often include one "expert teacher" who was expected to mediate recent research, and reforms, into the practice of teaching (e.g., Pepin et al. 2017a, b; Yang 2009).

In Brazil, despite a large program of textbook evaluation and distribution, teams of didacticians and teachers felt the need to redesign and amend particular materials, in order to manage the regional diversity of students (e.g., Gitirana et al. 2013; Silva and Lima, 2017).

In the Netherlands, teacher design teams (TDTs) would group teachers and didacticians around particular themes, often themes related to particular/recent curriculum revisions (e.g., reasoning and proof) or persistent problems in mathematics teaching (e.g., integration of ICT, Drijvers et al. 2010).

These kinds of teacher design are characterized by the following: teachers work alongside experts and teacher educators, and the products are also for "generic" use. We have denoted this kind of teacher design by "*D/d*"-*design* (or "*d/D-esign*"), and we found it difficult to distinguish between the two, at least in our cases. For this reason, Table 6.6 only includes D/d. This kind of teacher design appears to offer a bridge between the generic and direct use in class. By "generic" we mean here that the use was broader than strictly own classroom use (in principle available to a wider audience of users) and often included professional development elements (in some cases explicitly).

(c) At micro level (classroom), the individual teacher (or a small group of teachers) designs his/her curriculum, including teaching plan/s, instructional materials, and the curricular progressions/learning lines for his/her students. This was particularly evident in the French context, where individual teachers "designed," that is, adapted and translated the national curriculum in their mathematics teaching in schools, building on a variety of resources. Another example was the Japanese case, where the individual teacher designed their lessons, including setting goals, content, and how to use particular mathematical tasks. The board work ("bansho"; see Yoshida 2005; Tan et al. 2018) and questions for students were also specially designed. The textbook and teacher guide were carefully explored and analyzed for the teaching design – this process was named "kyōzai-kenkyū" (e.g., Watanabe et al. 2008; Fujii 2015). This micro design comes very close to what could always be considered as the "natural" part of teachers' work: lesson preparation. This teacher design has been denoted (in Table 6.1) with a small d: "*d-esign.*"

In several (but not all) of the case contexts rather immediate classroom use was a partial goal, and the immediate and broader goals were closely connected (e.g., Japan, China). In these cases, it would be difficult to distinguish between D/d and d for the design mode. Moreover, it seemed that in some contexts there was hardly any individual teacher design (for individual use); it all took place in teams and for use by all team colleague teachers. For example, in China, Lesson Preparation Groups (LPGs), consisting of a small number of individual teachers, were introduced which could provide in particular novice mathematics teachers with clear structures of mathematical content for each curriculum unit and a concrete plan of how to implement each lesson.

Of course, teacher design does not stop with out-of-class preparation but could also include teacher "design-in-use," that is, the in-the-moment decisions that teachers make in the classroom. As our cases did not provide evidence for such "design-in-use," we have not analyzed this further.

It is worth noting that teacher *d*-esign tasks were, of course, expected of single teachers in all contexts – this was part of their "traditional" responsibilities. However, the degree of guidance varied: from little guidance (e.g., English context) to institutionalized support, e.g., by colleagues (The Netherlands), or colleagues and experienced teachers (France, Japan), or colleagues and "expert teachers" (China).

2. It was interesting to note *that D-esign, D/d-esign* (or *d/D-esign*), and *d-esign* were underpinned by mathematical educational/didactical theory, and theory brought into the designs, but to a greater or lesser extent: In the French context, the knowledge of "didactical engineering" (Artigue 2015) and its main roots in Brousseau's theory of "didactical situations" (Brousseau et al. 2014) seemed to be supporting the design processes, whereas, in the English context Anglo-Saxon/American research-based reform movements (e.g., assessment for learning) including their didactical dimensions, it seemed to be guiding teachers' design efforts. In Japan, the theories and practices of Lesson Study appeared to support the design activities (e.g., Miyakawa and Winsløw 2009), and equally the design activities in TRGs (in China) were supported by theoretically underpinned practical knowledge made "digestible" by experts. In the Brazil example, there has been an emphasis on the French didactic tradition to support teacher curricular design.

3. In terms of *design groups*, they were linked to *design spaces* and would vary in size and participants:

   • A single mathematics teacher, perhaps working with a colleague, in or out of school.

6 Mathematics Teachers as Curriculum Designers

- Several mathematics teachers working together on a particular theme/topic/materials/teaching process at local or regional level (e.g., Teacher Research Groups; Lesson Study; Teacher design teams – TDTs).
- Mixed group of teachers, teacher educators/didacticians, university mathematicians, researchers designing at regional level (e.g., IREM).
- Expert groups designing at institute level (e.g., National Institute for Curriculum Development, often teaming up with other experts, subject didacticians, etc.) or ministry (e.g., national ministries).

In terms of curriculum *design spaces*, this ranged from schools (where *d*esign work with colleague teachers took place), over spaces at regional or national organizations or over the web (where *D/d*esign activities took place, e.g., Sésamath, see Gueudet et al. 2016), to ministries and national curriculum institutes (where the *D*esign of national curriculum frameworks and guidelines were situated). However, it is noteworthy that all three modes of design increasingly included classroom teachers' involvement, and the preferred mode of communication, also for practical reasons, was often via the web.

Viewing *design spaces* in a non-literal sense, there appeared to be (at least traditionally) three design spaces: the "national" *D*esign space with its design of the national curriculum and (sometimes approved) textbooks; the "collective" *D/d*esign space with its activities in order to help teachers "digest" curriculum innovations; and the "individual" *d*esign space where individual teachers design their lessons. In recent years, however, a new more dynamic space has been opened for teacher design: the "interactive" *D/d*esign space, which permeates groups and traditional meeting places. In several countries (e.g., France, the Netherlands), *D/design platforms* have been developed where teachers can design with colleagues and experts and with their students.

4. It is also noteworthy that different contexts used, and produced, different resources for the design processes: whereas in England, although *textbooks* continued to be published, they did not seem to be highly valued as curriculum resources (and there was a "free market" in classroom resources developed by multiple commercial and non-commercial organizations and individuals). However, in China and Japan textbooks were highly valued, and they were approved (by the ministry), which made them the main object of and guideline for design. It appeared that in these two contexts teachers (designed and) analyzed textbooks, in order to understand how to align with the national guidelines expressed in the textbook. In the French context teachers appeared to be doing a considerable amount of design work: at classroom preparation/design level with a variety of textbooks and other resources; at Design level in associations (e.g., Sésamath textbooks/resources produced "by teachers for teachers"). In the Dutch context textbooks were used extensively (and "page-by-page") by mathematics teachers in class. However, in the teacher design teams (TDTs), textbooks rarely guided teachers: textbooks seemed to be for the "bread-and-butter" teaching (where hardly any preparation was needed), whereas designing for innovative

teaching seemed to be regarded as "creative." In Brazil, the textbook has been central for teachers' *d*esign activities, and teachers "trust" the textbook, as it has been analyzed by ministry specialists committee (comprising of mathematics teachers, mathematics and statistics teacher educators, and mathematicians).

6.4 Conclusions

Our claim is, first, that the term "teacher design" is often used casually, with little understanding of the different facets of "teacher design" and/or demarcation between the levels/characteristics of "teacher design" depending on the context/site, (number of) participants and "teaming," and the audience and use of the design. We contend that what we term as "teacher design" activities can be regarded to lie on the crossroads between two dimensions: the "teaming" dimension (from working alone (single) to working in a collective) and the use dimension (from own use (for his/her teaching; site-specific) to use by others (generic)) (see Table 6.1). Theoretically, this resulted in four modes of teacher design:

- Teacher *d*esign activities at micro level (e.g., lesson preparation for own teaching).
- Teachers *d/D*esigning on their own/alone for use by others (e.g., expert teachers/ professional designers) – we could not identify this mode in our cases, although there were often expert teachers involved in collective design.
- Teacher *D/d*esign activities at meso level (e.g., designing in collectives of colleagues).
- Teacher *D*esign at macro level (e.g., teams of teachers/experts designing for use by others, involvement in the design of national frameworks).

It is important to note that the *d* or *D* should not denote a hierarchical level, diminishing the importance of the d work – perhaps different terms can be found to denote *D, D/d,* and *d* work, or indeed further differentiation could be found.

Second, our international contexts illustrate that teacher design activities may be for different purposes, and for different expected end results. In the Japanese and Chinese contexts, the design activities were (beyond the immediacy of the lesson) for the purpose of teacher professional development, as an effective means of professional learning, in mathematics/subject teacher collectives (supported predominantly by experts). In the Brazilian, Dutch, English, and French contexts, the purpose of teacher design was for designing an artifact or a product. Hence, in one context, the aim was *process-orientated*, while in the other, it was *product-orientated*, and it could be linked to the mode of design characteristic for the context. We contend that the most promising form of teacher design might lie at the crossroads between product and process orientation, where more connections can be found between the two (what are now often two separate worlds).

Third, we claim that such connections could be provided by what we call *digital design platforms*. They have the potential of providing, as affordances, interactions between different dimensions of teacher design. In previous research, we have shown that e-textbooks (Pepin et al. 2016) provide such connections: between teachers and designers and between teacher colleagues (e.g., Sésamath – see Gueudet et al. 2016). More recently, such digital platforms have been created (e.g., in the French and Dutch contexts); we are in the process of analyzing which connections are actually made by such platforms, in other words in which ways they may support teacher design. Such *digital design platforms* are a strong promise for enhancing mathematics teacher design work.

The chapter focuses on one aspect of the recent changes in expectations for teachers' work, often outside the classroom: the teacher as a designer of the curriculum (at different levels). These changes presuppose a new kind of professionalism and imply new/different professional development needs, related to aspects of the design work: while previously teachers "only" had to prepare their own lessons and most of this design was embedded in practice, now they are expected to work in teams and/or design for a wider audience (e.g., colleagues). Seeing curriculum development and the designing of school curricula as a "normal" practice, which is different from teaching in the classroom, opens new ways of seeing teacher professionalism and expertise. Moreover, it has implications for organizing (pre- and in-service) teacher education programs.

References

Artigue, M. (2015). Perspective on design research: The case of didactical engineering. In A. A. Bikner, K. Knipping, & N. Presmeg (Eds.), *Approaches to qualitative research in mathematics education* (pp. 467–496). Dordrecht: Springer.

Ben-Peretz, M. (1990). *The teacher-curriculum encounter: Freeing teachers from the tyranny of texts*. Albany: SUNY Press.

Borko, H. (2004). Professional development and teacher learning: Mapping the terrain. *Educational Researcher, 33*(8), 3–15.

Brousseau, G., Brousseau, N., & Warfield, G. (2014). *Teaching fractions through situations: A fundamental experiment*. Dordrecht: Springer.

Brown, M. W. (2009). The teacher-tool relationship: Theorizing the design and use of curriculum materials. In J. T. Remillard, B. A. Herbel-Eisenmann, & G. M. Lloyd (Eds.), *Mathematics teachers at work: Connecting curriculum materials and classroom instruction* (pp. 17–36). New York: Routledge.

Brown, M., & Edelson, D. (2003). *Teaching as design: Can we better understand the ways in which teachers use materials so we can better design materials to support their changes in practice*. Evanston: Centre for Learning Technologies in Urban Schools (design brief).

Cobb, P., & Jackson, K. (2015). Supporting teachers' use of research-based instructional sequences. *ZDM – Mathematics Education, 47*, 1027–1038.

Cviko, A., McKenney, S., & Voogt, J. (2014). Teacher roles in designing technology-rich learning activities for early literacy: A cross-case analysis. *Computers & Education, 72*, 68–79.

Drijvers, P., Doorman, M., Boon, P., Reed, H., & Gravemeijer, K. (2010). The teacher and the tool: Instrumental orchestrations in the technology-rich mathematics classroom. *Educational Studies in Mathematics, 75*(2), 213–234. https://doi.org/10.1007/s10649-010-9254-5.

Fernandez, C., & Yoshida, M. (2004). *Lesson study – A Japanese approach to improving mathematics teaching and learning*. Mahwah: Lawrence Erlbaum.

Fujii, T. (2015). The critical role of task design in lesson study. In A. Watson & M. Ohtani (Eds.), *Task design in mathematics education* (pp. 273–286). Cham: Springer.

Gitirana, V., Teles, R., Bellemain, P.B., Castro, A., Andrade, Y., Lima, P., & Bellemain, F. (2013). *Jogos com sucata na Educação Matemática*. Recife-NEMAT: Editora Universitária da UFPE.

Goodlad, J. I. (1979). *Curriculum inquiry. The study of curriculum practice*. New York: McGraw-Hill.

Gueudet, G., Pepin, B., & Trouche, L. (2013). Collective work with resources: An essential dimension for teacher documentation. *ZDM – Mathematics Education, 45*(7), 1003–1016.

Gueudet, G., Pepin, B., Sabra, H., & Trouche, L. (2016). Collective design of an e-textbook: Teachers' collective documentation. *Journal of Mathematics Teacher Education, 19*(2), 187–203.

Huizinga, T. (2009). *Op weg naar een instrument voor het meten van docentcompetencies voor het ontwikkelen van curricula [Towards an instrument to measure teacher competencies for the development of curricula]*. Enschede: University of Twente.

Isoda, M., Stephens, M., Ohara, Y., & Miyakawa, T. (Eds.). (2007). *Japanese lesson study in mathematics: Its impact, diversity and potential for educational improvement*. Singapore: World Scientific Publishing.

Jackson, K., Cobb, P., Wilson, J., Webster, M., Dunlap, C., & Applegate, M. (2015). Investigating the development of mathematics leaders' capacity to support teachers' learning on a large scale. *ZDM – Mathematics Education, 47*, 93–104.

Koehler, M. J., & Mishra, P. (2005). What happens when teachers design educational technology? The development of technological pedagogical content knowledge. *Journal of Educational Computing Research, 32*(2), 131–152.

Margolinas, C. (2014). *Task design in mathematics education. Proceedings of ICMI Study 22*. ICMI Study 22, Oxford, United Kingdom, 2013. 978-2-7466-6554-5. Accessed October 2018 at https://hal.archives-ouvertes.fr/hal-00834054v3/document

Matuk, C. F., Linn, M. C., & Eylon, B. S. (2015). Technology to support teachers using evidence from student work to customize technology-enhanced inquiry units. *Instructional Science, 43*(2), 229–257.

Miyakawa, T., & Winsløw, C. (2009). Didactical designs for students' proportional reasoning: An "open approach" lesson and a "fundamental situation". *Educational Studies in Mathematics, 72*(2), 199–218.

Nieveen, N., & van der Hoeven, M. (2011). Building the curricular capacity of teachers: Insights from the Netherlands. In P. Picard & L. Ria (Eds.), *Beginning teachers: Challenge for educational systems. CIDREE Yearbook 2011* (pp. 49–64). Lyon: ENS de Lyon, Institut Français de l'Éducation.

Penuel, W., Roschelle, J., & Shechtman, N. (2007). Designing formative assessment software with teachers: An analysis of the co-design process. *Research and Practice in Technology Enhanced Learning, 2*(1), 51–74.

Pepin, B. & Jones, K. (Eds.) (2016). Mathematics teachers as partners in task design. Double Special Issue of *Journal of Mathematics Teacher Education* 19(2 &3).

Pepin, B., Gueudet, G., & Trouche, L. (2013). Re-sourcing teacher work and interaction: A collective perspective on resource, their use and transformation. *ZDM – Mathematics Education, 45*(7), 929–943.

Pepin, B., Gueudet, G., Yerushalmy, M., Trouche, L., & Chazan, D. (2016). E-textbooks in/for teaching and learning mathematics: A disruptive and potentially transformative educational technology. In L. English & D. Kirshner (Eds.), *Handbook of research in mathematics education* (3rd ed., pp. 636–661). London: Taylor & Francis.

Pepin, B., Gueudet, G., & Trouche, L. (2017a). Refining *teacher design capacity:* Mathematics teachers' interactions with digital curriculum resources. *ZDM - Mathematics Education, 49*(5), 799–812. https://doi.org/10.1007/s11858-017-0870-8.

Pepin, B., Xu, B., Trouche, L., & Wang, C. (2017b). Developing a deeper understanding of *mathematics teaching expertise*: An examination of three Chinese mathematics teachers' resource

6 Mathematics Teachers as Curriculum Designers

systems as windows into their work and expertise. *Educational Studies in Mathematics, 94*(3), 257–274. https://doi.org/10.1007/s10649-016-9727-2.

Priestley, M., Biesta, G., & Robinson, S. (2017). *Teacher agency: An ecological approach.* London: Bloomsbury Academic.

Remillard, J. T. (2005). Examining key concepts in research on teachers' use of mathematics curricula. *Review of Educational Research, 75*(2), 211–246.

Richey, R. C., Fields, D. C., & Foxon, M. (2001). *Instructional design competencies: The standards.* ERIC Clearinghouse on Information & Technology, Syracuse University, 621 Skytop Rd., Suite 160, Syracuse, NY 13244–5290.

Ruthven, K. (2014). Frameworks for analysing the expertise that underpins successful integration of digital technologies into everyday teaching practice. In A. Clark-Wilson, O. Robutti, & N. Sinclair (Eds.), *The mathematics teacher in the digital era* (pp. 373–393). Dordrecht: Springer.

Silva, J. P., & Lima, I. M. S. (2017). Atividades Matemáticas propostas por Professores que ensinam na EJA Campo ? Ensino Médio. *Revista Paranaense de Educação Matemática, 6,* 246–268.

Stigler, J. W., & Hiebert, J. (1999). *The teaching gap: Best ideas from the world's teachers for improving education in the classroom.* New York: Free Press.

Tan, S., Fukaya, K., & Nozaki, S. (2018). Development of bansho (Board Writing) analysis as a research method to improve observation and analysis of instruction in Lesson Study. *International Journal for Lesson and Learning Studies, 7*(3), 230–247.

Thijs, A., & Van den Akker, J. (2009). Curriculum in development. In *Enschede.* Dordrecht: SLO.

Trouche, L. (2016). Didactics of mathematics: Concepts, roots, interactions and dynamics from France. In J. Monaghan, L. Trouche, & J. Borwein (Eds.), *Tools and mathematics: Instruments for learning* (pp. 219–256). New York: Springer.

Trouche, L., Gitirana, V., Miyakawa, T., Pepin, B., & Wang, C. (2019). Studying mathematics teachers interactions with curriculum materials through different lenses: Towards a deeper understanding of the processes at stake. *International Journal of Educational Research 93,* 53–67, Retreived on February 21st at https://doi.org/10.1016/j.ijer.2018.09.002.

Van den Akker, J. (2003). Curriculum perspectives: An introduction. In J. van den Akker, W. Kuiper, & U. Hameyer (Eds.), *Curriculum landscapes and trends* (pp. 1–10). Dordrecht: Kluwer Academic Publishers.

Voogt, J., Laferrie're, T., Breuleux, A., Itow, R., Hickey, D., & McKenney, S. (2015). Collaborative design as a form of professional development. *Instructional Science, 43*(2), 259–282. https://doi.org/10.1007/s11251-014-9340-7.

Watanabe, T., Takahashi, A., & Yoshida, M. (2008). Kyozaikenkyu: A critical step for conducting effective lesson study and beyond. In F. Arbaugh & P. M. Taylor (Eds.), *Inquiry into mathematics teacher education* (AMTE monograph series) (Vol. 5, pp. 131–142). San Diego: Association of Mathematics Teacher Educators.

Yang, Y. (2009). How a Chinese teacher improved classroom teaching in teaching research group: A case study on Pythagoras theorem teaching in Shanghai. *ZDM - Mathematics Education, 41*(3), 279–296.

Yoshida, M. (2005). Using lesson study to develop effective blackboard practice. In P. Wang-Iverson & M. Yoshida (Eds.), *Building our understanding of lesson study* (pp. 93–100). Philadelphia: Research for Better Schools.

Yuan, Z., & Li, X. (2015). "Same content different designs" activities and their impact on prospective mathematics teachers' professional development: The case of Nadine. In L. Fan, N.-Y. Wong, J. Cai, & S. Li (Eds.), *How Chinese teach mathematics. Perspectives from insiders* (pp. 567–589). Singapore: World Scientific Publishing.

Chapter 7
Teachers' Collective Work Inside and Outside School as an Essential Source of Mathematics Teachers' Documentation Work: Experiences from Japan and China

Takeshi Miyakawa and Binyan Xu

Abstract This chapter aims to report the results of a comparative study of teachers' documentation work in China and Japan, as well as to share some East Asian experiences that are less accessible to Western researchers. The Chinese case is gathered from teachers' collective work carried out inside school, and the Japanese case is taken from the group activities of a local mathematics teachers' association outside school. We analyze in each case teachers' documentation work as well as resources associated with such work. The comparison of the results of the analyses elucidates the commonalities between the two cases, such as the importance of textbook as a resource and the *practice-based* and *research-oriented* professional development, albeit the differences of contexts and institutional frameworks inside and outside school. We lastly discuss the perspectives for future research on the teachers' collective work with resources.

Keywords Mathematics teachers · Collective work · International perspective

---

This chapter originates from a lecture given at the Re(s)sources 2018 International Conference available at http://video.ens-lyon.fr/ife/2018/2018-05-30_007_Ressources2018_T-Miyakawa_B-Xu_v1.mp4

T. Miyakawa (✉)
Waseda University, Tokyo, Japan
e-mail: tmiyakawa@waseda.jp

B. Xu
East China Normal University, Shanghai, China

© The Author(s) 2019
L. Trouche et al. (eds.), *The 'Resource' Approach to Mathematics Education*,
Advances in Mathematics Education,
https://doi.org/10.1007/978-3-030-20393-1_7

7.1 Teachers' Collective Work and Resources from an International Perspective

Today collective actions by teachers inside and outside school receive particular attention in mathematics education research (cf. Goos 2014; Jaworski 2014; Hart et al. 2011; Gueudet et al. 2013). A wide range of collective work is carried out in different parts of the world for different purposes: the collective development of resources for preparing day-to-day teaching, collective online writing of textbooks in France (Gueudet et al. 2016), Japanese lesson studies (Fernandez and Yoshida 2004; Isoda et al. 2007; Stigler and Hiebert 1999), Chinese Teaching Research Groups (Wang 2012; Gu and Wang 2003) for school-based professional development, and working groups in mathematics teachers' associations, to name but a few.

Resources such as teaching materials, lesson plans, and textbooks play a crucial role for any teacher collective work. Preparing lessons requires the teachers to investigate and develop multiple resources. Teachers' work cannot be dissociated from the use of resources. This is the rationale of the documentational approach to didactics (Gueudet and Trouche 2009), which investigates teachers' work and its evolution through the usage of resources.

In this chapter, we present a comparative study of teachers' documentation work in China and Japan from an international perspective. Our objective is to share selected illustrations of teachers' work that are less accessible to researchers outside China and Japan, and to provide some insights and questions to be investigated in future research. It will illustrate that China and Japan share a common culture which emphasizes integration and harmony and reflects the social orientation of its people.

The Chinese case is gathered from teachers' collective work carried out inside school, and the Japanese case is taken from the group activities of a local mathematics teachers' association outside school. These two cases are complementary to each other, in terms of the two kinds of teachers' collective work in East Asia, inside and outside school. Based on these two illustrative examples, we contend that teachers' collective work inside and outside school is an essential source of mathematics teachers' documentation work.

Teachers' work is complex and includes a variety of activities. In order to frame and organize our analysis of teachers' documentation work in the Chinese and Japanese cases, we share the view of the documentational approach to didactics. We rely especially on the idea that a *document* consists of (1) *resources* as artifacts and (2) a *scheme of utilization* on how to use these resources (Gueudet and Trouche 2009). "Scheme" in this case means "the invariant organization of activity for a certain class of situations" (Vergnaud 2009, p. 88), and it consists of four components: *goals*, *rules*, *operational invariants*, and possibilities of *inference*. Here we focus on the idea that the utilization scheme is specific to a certain class of situations. That is to say, if the situation was different, there would be another way to use the same resource. Through our examples of teachers' collective work in China and Japan, we will identify different classes of situations, inside and outside school, requiring different utilization schemes, hence different teacher documentation work.

The guiding questions in this chapter are the following:

- What kinds of teachers' collective work are carried out, and in which ways?
- What kinds of resources are used and/or developed in the process, and in which ways?

The first question is intended to identify different classes of situations, while the second question aims to reveal the kinds of resources at stake and the related utilization schemes. In order to answer these questions, we carry out a comparative study between the Chinese case inside school (Sect. 7.2) and the Japanese case outside school (Sect. 7.3). In both cases, we present first institutional frameworks that create formally or informally opportunities for mathematics teachers to work together. It will show different structures of institutional framework in Japan and in China that should provide with various forms of teachers' collective work. In order to clarify such teachers' collective work, we will analyze one typical case from each, and elucidate teachers' documentation work as well as resources associated with such work. Finally, through the comparison of the results obtained in the case studies, we discuss the commonalities and differences between the two cases, as well as the perspectives for future research on teachers' collective work with resources (Sect. 7.4).

7.2 Inside School: The Chinese Case

Normally, Chinese teachers could and would work together inside schools because there are different kinds of working units that support teachers' collaborative works. Such working units support and contribute to teachers' professional development. In such professional development groups/units, teachers work collectively and with different resources. In the following, we explore mechanisms and development of teachers' work in such collectives in China.

7.2.1 Context and Institutional Frameworks for Teachers' Work

Entering the twenty-first century, the Chinese government has directed education to develop tasks to deepen education reform, to optimize the education structure, and to push forward the implementation of quality education (Pan 2005). Ministry of Education (MOE) published the Chinese mathematics curriculum standards (MOE 2001, 2003). Accordingly, standard-based textbooks were developed. At the same time, the curriculum reform suggested that teachers should not stick to such

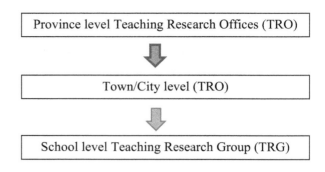

Fig. 7.1 Network of teachers' collective work in China

published textbooks; to the contrary, teachers would need to be able to reorganize textbooks and collect additional resources for mathematics teaching.

The curriculum reform and its implementation have generated much attention and discussion. How to work with and orchestrate abundant teaching resources, including textbooks, became teachers' essential work again. That means teachers are encouraged to be involved in the generation of teaching resources. This standard-based reform has been studied from international perspectives (e.g., Li 2007) as well as Chinese perspectives (e.g., Cao et al. 2006; Sun 2013). Sun (2013) mentioned that teaching materials are the basic foundation of teaching activities. He discussed the variety of teaching materials used by teachers collectively.

In China, teachers' collective work is aimed at enhancing student learning and teaching quality. One of the main tasks pays attention to school-based research. In order to help teachers to do research based on their teaching practical problems, a "three-level-institution" network was constructed by the government (see Fig. 7.1).

This is a top-down approach. From a macro point of view, it reflects an advantage of China's education system by playing an important role in managing and guiding school-based teaching research activities (Yang et al. 2013). The two teaching research officers (TROs) play the role of administration and professional guidance. From a micro point of view, in addition to researchers in higher learning institutions and school teachers, TROs[1] enlarge the team of professional researchers and play an important role in bridging the gap between teaching theories and instructional practice. TROs are powerful middlemen in the conducting of school-based teaching research activities. In this chapter, we focus on such research activities, which, in fact, are carried out in different typical teachers' collective work groups. In addition some new forms of collective work were developed in order to amend shortage of typical groups. One of the new forms would be analyzed.

---

[1] They work at TROs, called in Chinese 教研员. Normally they used to be experienced teachers and know development of certain educational theories very well. They provide school teachers with administration and professional guidance.

7.2.2 A Framework inside School: School-Based Groups of Teachers' Collective Work

In China, each school sets up different kinds of teachers' collective work groups. It includes *Lesson Preparation Group* (LPG), called in Chinese 备课组, *Teaching Research Group* (TRG) called in Chinese 教研组 and *Research Project Group* (RPG) called in Chinese 课题组. The three types of groups have different functions, at the same time they are integrated and implement a complex program.

7.2.2.1 Teachers' Documentation Work in LPG

Teachers from the same grade and same subject gather to build a LPG which is led by an experienced teacher. Generally speaking, working in mathematics LPG can provide each mathematics teacher, especially novice teachers, with a clear structure of mathematics content for each unit and a concrete plan on how to implement each lesson. LPGs contribute to improving teaching practices and enhancing teaching effectiveness.

For Chinese teachers, textbooks are the most important resources in the mathematics classroom. One of teachers' essential work in China is to navigate and study textbooks in order to design instruction. Related to the LPG, there are two parts of resources that teachers may use: one is school related (e.g., the textbook, teaching guidance books, curriculum standards, organized in-service training); the other refers to teachers' individual experiences, including self-learned resources (e.g., own collection of books). In the digital age, most experiences derive from online resources, or from journals for mathematics teaching and learning. Often such individual resources play a role while teachers need to extend or deepen their understanding of school-related resources. In LPGs both kinds of resources are used while teachers prepare lessons (Fig. 7.2).

7.2.2.2 Teachers' Documentation Work in TRGs

The TRG is a popular group where teachers improve their teaching through collective study of practical problems. In the *Secondary School Teaching Research Group Rulebook (draft)* issued by Ministry of Education (MOE) in 1957, the function of the TRG was described.

The TRG is responsible for all mathematics teachers' professional development in the school (Fan et al. 2015). In TRGs teachers from the same subject in the school gather led by a subject head. It has three general foci: firstly, the TRG focuses on discussing teaching practices, including instructional design, mid-semester examination, and school-based open lesson. Secondly, the TRG orients on school-based research questions which reflect crucial teaching activities or misconceptions/problem areas, for example, how to improve geometrical under-

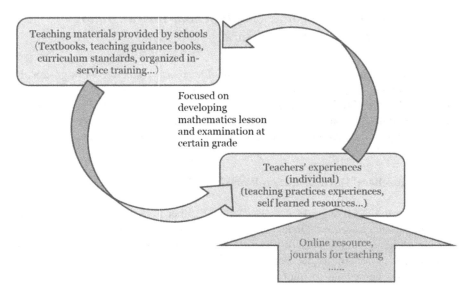

Fig. 7.2 Resources structure related to LPG

standing with support of dynamic software or how to design mathematics lesson based on students' mathematical mistakes from their homework. Based on such research questions, the TRG tries to propose school-based research projects collectively. In order to encourage teachers or the TRG to implement projects, some schools also set up special project funding that can be applied for by teachers. The third role of the TRG is to be in charge of connecting city-level TROs. The TROs provide teachers with opportunities to participate in teaching evaluation, teaching competition, or participate in other tasks, which are assigned by city-level TRO. TRGs play an important role to help teachers to prepare collectively teaching competition.

Since the TRG undertakes different kinds of teachers' collective work, teachers within TRG utilize various resources as well as develop new resources. Teachers mainly use three types of resources, two of them are in accord with resources from the LPG. We can observe that the most important and valuable resources refer to resources generated at city-level TRO, including teaching evaluation, teaching competition, as well as research theories or methods from experiences with university researchers or researching institutes. Teachers' documentation work in TRGs happens in relative open environments, TRGs have good opportunities to interact with teaching practice groups from other schools, research groups from universities, and teaching administration groups. Working as a team, teachers in the TRG collect abundant information from those groups and may convert them into teaching resources. Figure 7.3 illustrates the resource system operated in TRGs.

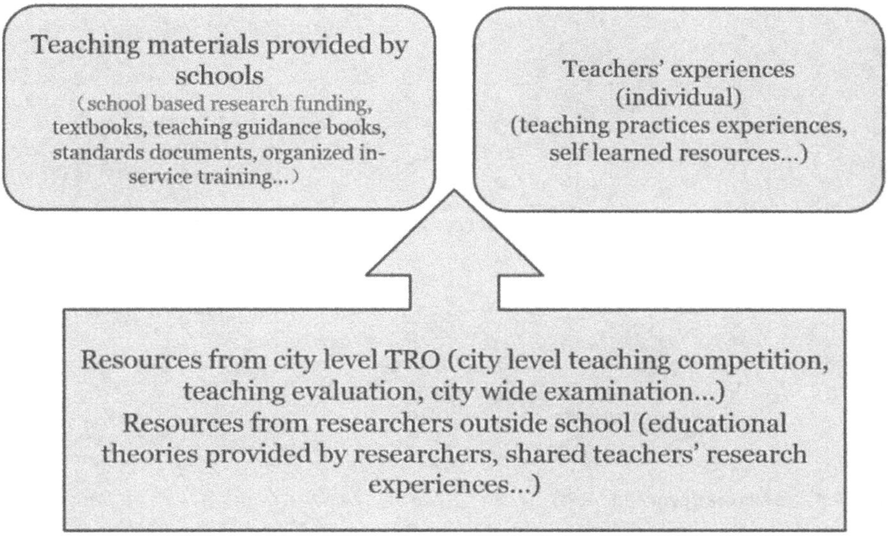

Teaching materials provided by schools
(school based research funding, textbooks, teaching guidance books, standards documents, organized in-service training...)

Teachers' experiences (individual)
(teaching practices experiences, self learned resources...)

Resources from city level TRO (city level teaching competition, teaching evaluation, city wide examination...)
Resources from researchers outside school (educational theories provided by researchers, shared teachers' research experiences...)

Fig. 7.3 Resource operated in TRG

7.2.2.3 Teachers' Documentation Work in RPG

Inside schools in China, there exists a working group called Research Project Group (RPG) that is led by a director of research in the school. The RPG aims at experiencing or implementing whole research projects, including literature review or analyzing practical teaching problems, design of research proposals according to particular research framework. RPGs also apply for research project funding at the city level, or province level, or national level.

In addition, the RPG has other opportunities to undertake a sub-project assigned by a research group outside school. For example, some schools got a sub-project of a national project, "construction of an innovative model to promote teacher professional development." One of the sub-projects may focus on a case study of mathematics teacher professional development. In order to finish such sub-project, the RPG would invite experts from outside school and discuss research methods, or research frameworks.

In RPGs teachers can have different resources that support teachers to do research related to teaching practices as shown in Fig. 7.4. Because practical problems are derived from all kinds of school-based activities, resources that RPG members use can be divided into three categories: developmental programs or previous research experiences at school level; teaching and learning practices at teacher individual level; and educational theories, relevant publications, research methods at theoretical level. The RPG teachers learn to manipulate different resources targeted.

Such structured mechanisms ensure that teachers experience collective working culture at schools. But often Chinese teachers express more "collective voice" than their individual voice. Such "collective work" cannot fully reflect requirements/needs of individual teachers for their professional development.

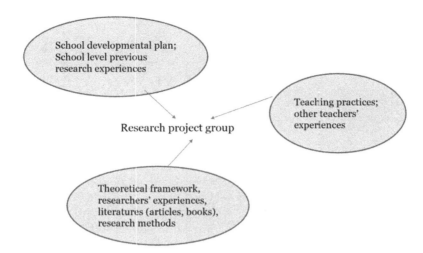

Fig. 7.4 Resources operated in RPG

7.2.3 A Case Study: A New Model of Teachers' Collective Work

Facing challenges of curriculum reform, school-based teaching research has been developed. School-based teaching research activities are not isolated; in other words, many schools open their doors and welcome or invite experts from outside. The boundaries of Teaching Research Group and Research Project Group become vague. Experts from city-level TRO or university researchers are actively involved in school-based research activities. Teachers have more opportunities to interact with academic colleagues. Teachers' collective work is full of thinking and enthusiasm.

7.2.3.1 Collaboration Research Group Model

Hereon we introduce one of new models of teachers' collective work. This model is called Collaboration Research Group (CRG), in Chinese called 合作研究组, whose general nature is collaboration and sharing. The core ideas of the CRG target at researching for improving teaching, and thinking for enhancing development. This model has been established and implemented at schools for the past 10 years (Ye and Si 2017).

Members of CRG consist of school teachers, researchers from universities, and experts from city-level TRO. The three groups of members play different roles, respectively, while working and sharing collectively in CRG. School teachers will initiate research questions based on their teaching practices. Researchers provide with theoretical framework related to practical research questions and expound relevant theories to school teachers and TRO experts. School teachers will work

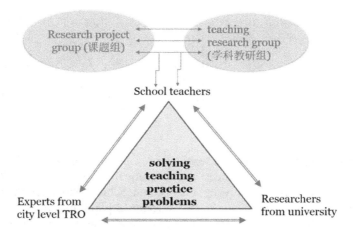

Fig. 7.5 Structure of Collaboration Research Group (CRG) in school

together with TRO experts and discuss how to apply theories into practices and design classroom teaching based on new theoretical perspectives. Researchers will observe and comment teaching practice designed by school teachers and TRO experts, and then will construct methods to evaluate function of CRG.

Only when school leaders attach importance to teacher professional development and encourage collaborative research working, they set up such CRG in schools. This is a research project-driven organization, instead of permanent administrative unit in school. The expectation of schools for CRG is that teaching practice problems should be explored. Figure 7.5 illustrates the structure of CRG.

7.2.3.2 A Case of Implementing Collaboration Research Group

In one middle school of Zhejiang province, one of the key tasks of this school is to support teachers' professional development. One CRG has been set up in this school, with emphasis on exploring, analyzing, evaluating and improving mathematics teaching behaviors.

Firstly, one researcher from university and one expert from city-level TRO were invited by the school; they worked together with leaders from school-based TRG and RPG, in order to investigate mathematics classroom teaching and make decision on teaching problems driven research questions. The particular project was that how to understand and analyze mathematics classroom teaching based on video analysis. They believe that teachers will improve their teaching practice through engaging in such project.

Secondly, teachers who have interest in such topics were invited to work together with researchers; then the CRG is organized. At the beginning, all CRG members shared their own ideas focused on this topic, and then the researcher gave advises to participating teachers to design a practical research project.

Fig. 7.6 Pictures in Lesson 1

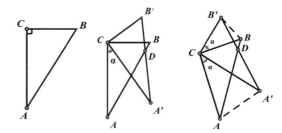

Subsequently, researchers and teachers took on different roles. Researchers brought their research experiences and theoretical viewpoints into CRG, suggested one framework for analyzing classroom teaching, explained the theoretical background of the framework, and introduced particular analysis methods and tools. Teachers explained important or difficult mathematics content while teaching mathematics and designed lesson plan focused on concrete mathematics topics.

In the following, we show how teachers and researchers worked together. CRG focused on two mathematics lessons which had same mathematics topic, but different teaching strategies.[2] To design and implement the both lessons aimed at exploring characteristics of reviewing lesson of geometric for grade 9, and discussing how to embody mathematics core competencies in the classroom teaching.

7.2.3.3 Two Lessons of the Same Topic

Lesson 1 focused on e*xploration of a rotational question, general repertory of geometric inquiry, made by S*; Lesson 2 was about g*eometry exploration journey, made by Y.*

S designed three inquiring tasks for Lesson 1.

- Task 1: As pictured (Fig. 7.6), in $\triangle ABC$, $\angle C = 90°$, $\angle A = 30°$, if we let $\triangle ABC$ rotate 30° counterclockwise around point C to get $\triangle A'B'C'$, what can you find from the image? (Please draw the image first.)
- Task 2: If we change the angle of rotation into α ($0° < \alpha < 45°$), do the conclusion from task 1 change?
- Task 3: When $\triangle ABC$ is a general triangle, what have you found?

The teacher S (Fig. 7.7) gave conclusion of the lesson related to general repertory of geometric inquiry as follows:

---

[2] "Same mathematics topic, but different teaching strategies (同课异构)" is a particular teaching research activity in China. It means, focusing on one mathematics topic, teachers will design two different lessons using different methods, so that teachers can discuss or explore these lessons.

Fig. 7.7 Lesson 1 by S

Fig. 7.8 Pictures in Lesson 2

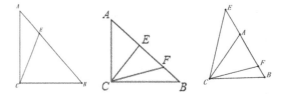

1. To determine the research objects (geometry elements—determine problems).
2. To explore the research contents (explore the invariant relationship in change, the relationship between geometric elements).
3. Inductive research methods (which were useful for solving tasks using special or general methods).

Y designed three tasks for students' inquiring for Lesson 2.

- Task 1. In Fig. 7.8, in the isosceles right triangle ABC, point E is a moving point on AB. Which relation existed between AE and BE?
- Task 2. In Fig. 7.8 in $\triangle ABC$, $\angle ACB = 90°$, $AC = BC$, points E and F are two moving points on AB, and $\angle ECF = \angle A$. Which relation exited between AE and BE?
- Task 3. If $\angle ACB = 90°$ is changed to $\angle ACB = \alpha$ ($0° < \alpha < 90°$), other conditions remain unchanged. Do the above conclusions still exist?

Figure 7.9 showed that Y explained these three inquiring tasks.

Fig. 7.9 Lesson 2 by Y

7.2.3.4 Discussion After the Two Lessons

After implementing both the lessons, members of CRG shared their ideas and comments focused on the lessons. At first, according to the observation, the researcher Ye interpreted that these two lessons fully embodied the nature of the ninth grade review of geometry. He commented that these lessons grasped the object of geometry, used special-to-general thinking to explore the relationship between elements in the figures, so to find unique and concise conclusions.

He analyzed the differences of both lessons. Firstly, he observed the differences related to content. He said, for Lesson 1, the triangle ABC itself rotates. The two triangles (triangle ABC and triangle A'B'C') given here are two same triangles. The tasks evolve as follows: from determined angle rotation to any angle rotation; from isosceles right triangle to general triangle. For Lesson 2, we choose the moving point on one side of triangle ABC. The two given triangles (triangle ABC and triangle EFC) are probably not the same here. The tasks evolve as follows: from one moving point to two moving points; from isosceles right triangle to right triangle.

He also analyzed the difference related to instructional design. Teacher S uses this task to let students experience the process of how to explore the relations with moving points. The purpose of this task is to teach students the steps of exploring geometry relations: determine the objects (geometry elements), explore the contents, and generate the methods. So the task is used by teachers' guiding. For Lesson 2, she pointed out that this task is more open for students. The teacher Y hadn't demonstrated any conclusions before the class. So during the teaching process, the teacher decides or changes her way to teach based on the different responses given by the students. Which means teacher would use different teaching methods when working with different students. Students are more initiative to decide what to explore when working with the task.

The expert from TRO gave also comments, and teachers explained and reflect their teaching purpose. Such dialogues between members of CRG improve the teachers' professional development effectively.

There is a researcher (Sun) from the Zhejiang Provincial Teaching and Research Office who gave a high evaluation of these two lessons from the necessity, objective, structure, and effectiveness of a class. He encouraged school teachers to maintain such an atmosphere of teaching and research, trying and innovating, and to provide teachers meta motivation for quality education, teaching, and research.

In this case, school leaders were also concerned with CRG activities. The leader of mathematics TRG Lv represented other participating mathematics teachers. He said that he has learned a lot from the activities. After reviewing the original features of the lesson and geometry class, he must apply the ideas and methods learned from the activities to ordinary teaching practice, live up to the guidance and expectation of experts and predecessor.

7.2.4 Summary of Teachers' Collective Work Inside School

Traditionally, in Chinese schools, there are different kinds of structured organizations (groups) where teachers can work collectively. They discuss and modify lesson plans, design examinations, share additional teaching resources, or study teaching practice problems and improve instructional quality. It is difficult to image that teachers can develop effective plans, tests or other resources, without collective work. Fortunately, school-based teacher collective work has expanded. Some research projects driven by collective work were carried out. Teachers, university researchers, and experts from other organization have had opportunities to gather at schools, and to undertake different tasks. Especially, researchers could share their research experiences and theoretical consideration with teachers, and in turn teachers' practical experiences were enriched with underpinning theory.

7.3 Outside School: The Japanese Case

Japanese lesson study is well documented in the educational literature (written in English) as a format for teachers' collective work (Fernandez and Yoshida 2004; Isoda et al. 2007; Stigler and Hiebert 1999). Apart from it, one may find other kinds of formats for teachers' collective work outside school. One of them is organized by the local teachers' association, through monthly or biweekly meetings, where teachers get together, share, and discuss their teaching experiences and eventually carry out a lesson study project. This section presents the documentation work in teachers' meetings in Japan through two kinds of resources, *lesson plans* and *practice research reports*, in order to illustrate how teachers' collective work contributes to the sharing and development of their practice and knowledge.

7.3.1 Context and Institutional Frameworks for Teachers' Work

In Japan, the Ministry of Education, Culture, Sports, Science and Technology (MEXT) determines the educational system, which is applied to all parts of the country and guarantees quality education. Until the end of lower secondary school education, the single-track system is adopted and all students are in a position to receive almost the same quality of education either in a city or in a rural area. The national curricula written by MEXT determine the number of hours dedicated to each subject and the teaching content (cf. MEXT 2008).

Concerning the teachers' work, there are different institutional frameworks, as in Chinese cases, that allow teachers to work collectively or individually inside and outside school. We classified them in Table 7.1 according to geographical levels, which also implies the different levels of educational management (see also Miyakawa and Winsløw 2017). In Japan, the board of education at the city level manages the public primary and lower secondary schools, and the board of education of the prefecture manages the administration related to the education of all cities, including upper secondary school.

Japanese teachers spend most of their working hours in school not only for preparing and teaching classes, but also for undergoing professional development such as lesson studies. At the city level, the board of education and teachers' associations provide teachers with opportunities for professional development. In this section, we take up the activities of teachers' associations at this local level.

Table 7.1 Institutional frameworks of the different levels

Level	Institutional frameworks of teachers' work
Nation	Ministry of Education National Center for Education Associations of math teachers Commercial companies
Prefecture(s)	Board of Education Education center Teacher training university Schools attached to the university Associations of math teachers
City(s)	Board of Education Associations of math teachers
School	Schools

7.3.2 A Framework Outside School: Local Teachers' Association

In most Japanese cities, there exists a local voluntary association for mathematics teachers, which provides a place for them to work together and to improve their teaching practices. Such associations exist not only for mathematics but also for other subjects like science, history, and Japanese. In Jōetsu, a relatively small city in Japan, there is an association for primary and middle school mathematics teachers called *Jōetsu sūgaku kyōiku kenkyūkai* (Research Association for Mathematics Teaching in Jōetsu). Teachers take part in activities of this association without any obligation or reward. Different kinds of activities are proposed: monthly meetings, lectures by invitees (e.g., researchers, expert teachers), an annual congress, workshops for teachers, publication of a bulletin or book, and so forth. Our focus in this section is the teachers' documentation work in monthly meetings.

The monthly meeting of this association is held in the evening. It is open not only to the association members but also to anyone interested in discussing mathematics teaching. There are usually 10–15 different kinds of participants: teachers from primary and middle school, educational advisors, school principals (ex-math teachers), university professors, pre-service teachers (students), etc.

The meeting is devoted to two topics—with 45–60 minutes for each—brought up by two teachers. The presenting teacher always brings a material or a handout as a resource and distributes it to the participants. There are two kinds of resources. The first one is the *lesson plan* that describes the details of the designed lesson which will be taught in the classroom for different purposes, such as an *open research lesson*[3] in the context of school-based professional development. The second resource is the teaching *practice report* which describes the results of teaching practices that have taken place in the classroom. In general, these are the two principal resources that Japanese teachers develop and share in their ordinary activities inside and outside school. They are easily accessible on the websites managed by the educational center of the board of education.

7.3.3 A Case Study: Monthly Meetings

We go into the details of teachers' work promoted in the monthly meetings of local teachers' association. A case study is carried out through the analysis of the two types of resources discussed above, *lesson plan* and *practice report*. For each type of resources, we first present a lesson plan/practice report distributed at a monthly meeting with a brief analysis of its role, and then identify teachers' work associated

---

[3] This is a lesson, called in Japanese *kōkai-jugyō* (*kōkai* means open or public), which is demonstrated to the colleagues of same school or the teachers of other school (cf. Miyakawa and Winsløw 2013). This is very often a part of lesson study or considered as a lesson study.

with it with a special focus on the resources used. We also present the discussion at a monthly meeting in order to clarify the nature of teachers' work and the resources involved.

7.3.3.1 Lesson Plan and Its Roles

The lesson plan is the most familiar resource since the preservice teacher training and throughout the profession of Japanese teachers. In a monthly meeting, the participants were discussing mathematics teaching with a lesson plan, which is given in Fig. 7.10. An individual primary school teacher was preparing this lesson plan for an open research lesson scheduled for the following month, and presented it as a material to be discussed at this meeting.

This plan consists of two A4 pages, and has a lot of text. At the top of the left page is the title, "View from inside a box" (first author's translation). The lesson plan is for a class on space geometry in grade 2 mathematics and proposes activities for the pupils (7–8 years old) that involve creating a big box or polyhedron, as shown in Fig. 7.11, so that they can feel and enjoy the breadth of the space from inside the box.

The lesson plan on the left-hand side consists of four sections: (1) Goal of activities; (2) Intentions of activities; (3) Actual state of the children; and (4) Characteristics of these activities. The first page is therefore describing the goal of teaching and its rationale with respect to the actual state of the pupils in the class. The second page (on the right-hand side of Fig. 7.10) is devoted to an explanation of one specific lesson, which would be demonstrated at the presenting teacher's school. One section devoted to a whole page is titled "5) About this lesson" and consists of three subsections: (1) Goal of this lesson, (2) Characteristics of this lesson, and (3) Progression of the class. Here, a goal is given again, since the goal of a single lesson is usually different from the overall goal of a unit. Further, the explanation of and justification for this lesson are given. Then, a table is used to describe the teaching process along with the timing, the expected pupil behaviors, and the teacher's instructional moves.

The lesson plan plays several roles. A principal role one may identify from the example above is to share with participants or readers the teaching practices of the designed lesson, as well as the teacher's ideas behind the series of lessons and the setting of these lessons. Further, a lesson plan is a tool for a teacher to justify and convince them of his/her choices. This is the reason why a lot of texts are necessary in the lesson plan, as seen in Fig. 7.11. Such a detailed lesson plan with justification would not be necessary if the designed lessons had already been shared with colleagues (such as in collaborative designing).

In contrast, the table showing the teaching process of the single lesson is relatively short. This implies that the lesson plan is a guide for participants or readers to help them understand the overall structure and activities of the lesson, rather than a guide for the presenting teacher on what to do during teaching. In general, the description of the lesson in the lesson plan does not provide precise teacher's

Fig. 7.10 Lesson plan distributed at a monthly meeting. (Kimura 2015)

Fig. 7.11 Pictures taken during the open research lesson that took place later

instructions in the classroom. The teacher may prepare, apart from the lesson plan to be distributed, a memo to remind himself/herself what to say.

In Japan, a lesson plan therefore targets others rather than the teacher. This is one of the reasons why some Japanese scholars propose calling this resource a "lesson proposal" instead of a "lesson plan" (Fujii 2015). It should also be noted that the format of lesson plans depends on the school. Some schools might ask for a longer plan including more precise descriptions of the teaching process. One may find several examples of Japanese lesson plans in English literature (Fernandez and Yoshida 2004; Takahashi 2005; Miyakawa and Winsløw 2013; Miyakawa 2015).

7.3.3.2 Teachers' Work Associated with Lesson Plans

What kinds of teachers' work are associated with this lesson plan in addition to the collective discussions at the monthly meeting? The lesson plan and the discussion in the meeting imply teacher's different kinds of work (in terms of the use of resources), which are generally carried out in Japan for developing a lesson plan. They are as follows:

- Understanding the goals.
- Designing tasks.
- Designing lessons.
- Writing a lesson plan.

Since mathematics classes are based on the national curriculum, the Japanese teacher is first of all required to understand the goals of a given unit and its lessons, through an analysis of the curricular resources, in particular the textbooks. This work before (or while) designing tasks is often called *kyōzai-kenkyū*, which literally means the study of teaching materials (*kyōzai*) (cf. Watanabe et al. 2008). It is noteworthy that the textbook has a special status as a resource for Japanese teachers. It should be approved by the ministry of education, and its use is compulsory by the Japanese regulation. The teacher covers almost all the materials given in the textbook (e.g., Becker et al., 1990). This is a reason why the textbook analysis is one of primary activities for preparing lessons. This was also the case for the teacher who wrote the lesson plan above. In fact, in the discussion of the monthly meeting, participants discussed what the textbook intends to teach.

The next work, *designing tasks*, involves coming up with tasks to be implemented in a series of lessons, through the exploration of different resources such as the internet, textbooks, and professional journals. This work is often called *kyōzai-kaihatsu*, which literally means the development (*kaihatsu*) of teaching materials. The teacher of the meeting invented the tasks that could not be found in the textbook.

Designing lessons refers to the development of the process or progression of teaching with the designed tasks. The resources necessary for this work tend to focus more on concrete teaching and learning actions or experiences in the classroom, such as learners' behaviors. This work is sometimes (not so often comparing to the above two kinds of work) called *jugyō-kaihatsu* in Japan, which means the development of lessons.

Writing a lesson plan can be a different task from the three previous ones; it forces the teacher to explicitly formulate the ideas behind the lessons.

The distinction between these four kinds of work and the utilization of each term are not clear-cut in the Japanese educational community. They may overlap in some ways: *kyōzai-kenkyū* may at times include *kyōzai-kaihatsu,* and vice versa; *jugyō-kaihatsu* may include the two former kinds of work.

It is also important to note that these four kinds of work are required especially in a lesson study or meetings with colleagues like the one documented in this chapter. In a day-to-day lesson, Japanese teachers often use the tasks given in the textbooks, and they will not write out a lesson plan like the one in Fig. 7.10, while an understanding of the teaching goals is always necessary.

7.3.3.3 Practice Report and Its Roles

Another monthly meeting was devoted to a discussion of the teaching practice report that would be presented at a regional congress for teachers several months later. What we call a *practice report* here is a report that a teacher writes after his/her teaching practices; it is called *jissen-hōkoku* in Japanese (*jissen* and *hōkoku* denote "practice" and "report," respectively). It is written either in the context of a lesson study or as a part of individual or collective action research. As noted earlier, there are teachers' associations at different institutional levels. These associations organize the annual congress for the teachers to share their teaching practices. A teacher is sometimes asked to present their practice report at a congress or publish it in a professional journal. So, the activity of this monthly meeting was a preparation for the teachers who were to give oral presentations at the regional congress. A detailed analysis of how the activities of local associations relate to the activities of regional congresses is given by Miyakawa and Winsløw (2017). In this section, we will provide another example and an analysis from the perspective of teachers' documentation work.

A primary school teacher prepared a practice report for a monthly meeting (Fig. 7.12). This report consisted of six A4 pages and presented the results of his teaching practices carried out in grade 6 mathematics classes on the geometric unit on enlarged and reduced figures. According to him, this was the result of a lesson study carried out as school-based professional development. The structure of the report with our translations of section titles is given in Fig. 7.13. The title is given at the top of the first page. There is a section on the rationale for the selected theme (Section 1), and a "research hypothesis" is given (Section 2). The main part is Section 4. Four and a half pages are devoted to describing the teaching practices of the sequence of lessons. He selected some sessions and explained how the lessons had unfolded. He then concluded with the results and further issues (Section 5), followed by a reference list (only two sources are listed).

The report looks like a scientific paper. The term "research" (*kenkyū* in Japanese) is often used. This is because such kind of teacher's work is often regarded in Japan as research called "practice research" (*jissen-kenkyū*; see Miyakawa and Winsløw 2017). A lesson study is also considered to be a kind of practice research.

In this practice report, the teacher proposed a process of learning in the classroom that includes verbalization of the problem solving method, and posited the hypothesis that this activity would deepen students' understanding of geometric figures. One can see the main idea of his *research* in a diagram (Fig. 7.14); it shows the process and structure of pupils' learning, including the verbalization of the solving method during group work.

Fixing a hypothesis allows the teacher to focus on a specific aspect of the complex mathematics lesson. Further the scientific report format requires the teacher to deeply reflect on and investigate their teaching practices. In Section 4, for the description of the teaching practices, the presenting teacher identified the remarkable events, and described the learning process how the verbalization affected pupils' activities in the classroom.

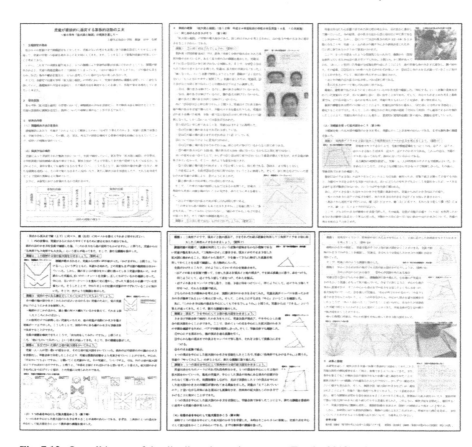

Fig. 7.12 Overall image of the distributed practice report. (Tanaka 2013)

The role of practice reports for the community of mathematics teachers is to share with colleagues or readers teaching practices and the ideas behind them. As in the case of the lesson plan, the practice report distributed at the monthly meeting targeted first the participants who did not know the presenting teacher's teaching practices, and second, the participants in the regional congress scheduled some months later. This resource provided participants with a specific subject to discuss and reflect on with concrete instances of mathematics teaching in a classroom.

The practice reports developed for and at the meetings are disseminated through oral presentations at the congress, and eventually through professional journals or books, becoming a resource to be explored in other practice research in different places. It should also be noted that the writing of a practice report is often a part of the professional development of an individual teacher. This role is discussed below in terms of the teacher's associated work.

7 Teachers' Collective Work Inside and Outside School 165

Title: Mathematical activities in which children are motivated to participate: through the teaching practices of a grade 6 lesson: "Enlarged and reduced figures"

1. Reasons for the choice of this theme
2. Research hypothesis
3. Research content
(1) Verbalization of the problem solving method
(2) Discussion of the problem solving method
4. Overview of teaching practices: "Enlarged and reduced figures"
(1) Let's look for items of the same shape (Session 1)
(2) Let's draw an enlarged figure on the grid sheet (Session 3)
(3) Let's draw an enlarged figure using a specific center point (Session 7)
(4) Let's draw an enlarged figure using any center point (Session 8)
5. Results and further issues
References

Fig. 7.13 Structure of the practice report with translated section titles

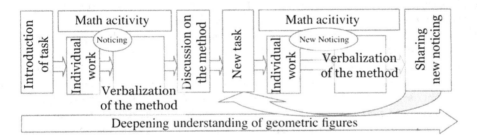

Fig. 7.14 Diagram of the lesson flow (translated by the first author)

7.3.3.4 Teacher's Work Associated with the Practice Report

As in the case of a lesson plan, one may identify, based on the practice report, different kinds of documentation work by the teacher, which include the tasks associated with the lesson plan we discussed in the previous section. In addition to those for the lesson plan, the teacher must carry out the teaching in the classroom and the collection of data, analyze or reflect on his own teaching, and write a practice report.

The analysis in the practice report is not as rigorous as in a scientific paper, but is the result of a "sincere reflection" by the teacher on what happened in the series of lessons. In fact, the analysis given in the practice report above was principally based on the pupil's worksheets and the teacher's memories (he regretted in the meeting that he had not audiotaped the discussions in the classroom). The main task in writing a practice report is objectifying the teacher's own teaching, and summarizing and formalizing the main events in the lessons containing the pupils' work. Such work is rare in day-to-day teaching in Japan. The teacher usually relies on the textbooks and does not have enough time to reflect on his/her own teaching practices. Practice research creates situations that require the utilization of resources which are different from those used in the preparation of ordinary lessons. It is therefore an opportunity for teachers to better understand their own teaching, and to develop their professional skills and knowledge. Additionally, like in the case of a lesson plan, the teacher's collective work either as part of the discussion at the monthly meeting or as part of the oral presentation at the congress plays a crucial role in triggering this documentation work.

7.3.3.5 Discussion at a Monthly Meeting

We present here briefly what happens in the discussion of monthly meeting of the local teachers' association, and analyze teachers' work. In general, in any monthly meeting, there is a participant who moderates the session; the presenting teacher first explains his designed lesson in the case of a lesson plan, or his implemented lessons in the case of a practice report; then, the participants ask questions to understand the lesson and make comments to provide some helpful ideas.

The monthly meeting for the practice report above (Fig. 7.12) was held with a dozen or so participants of different kinds: primary and middle school teachers, university researchers, and pre-service teachers. The presenting teacher first took 15 minutes to explain his report, followed by 45 minutes of questions and comments from the participants. His explanation followed the structure of a distributed report, concluding with the issues that he identified. In the discussion, the moderator initially proceeded from the first page in order, soliciting questions and comments from the participants along the way, but partway through the process, the discussion gave way to an opinion-exchange session covering the entire document. The questions and comments offered can be roughly summarized as follows:

- The terminology of mathematics education (e.g., mathematical activities).
- The writing method of the teaching practice report.
- The content of the report: Consistency of the report (title and content), suggestion of some complementary contents ("you should add…").
- The participants' experience of teaching practices of the similar units.
- The pupils' behaviors and actions during the lesson; issues/problems faced by the teacher (aspects where the lesson did not go well).
- Its relationship with other teaching contents in primary and middle school.
- Suggestions for teacher's instruction, teaching materials, tasks, etc.
- Suggestions for new foci or themes of practice research.

As is apparent, a wide range of topics were discussed and considered. The principal (material) resource for the discussion was the practice report prepared by the presenting teacher. Further, the participants shared a lot of *cognitive resources*, the experiences of different kinds of participants. This is a specificity of this monthly meeting. The participants bring, according to their expertise, a variety of experiences to the discussion, and *re-source* each other. For example, an experienced teacher provided his experiences how to write a practice report and how to present it at a teachers' congress; a middle school teacher shared his experience of the similar topic (similar figures) and suggested to check the middle school textbooks; a primary school teacher brought up a perspective on the phrase "mathematical activities" in the title of the report, which is a concept emphasized in the Japanese national curriculum (MEXT 2008), and suggested that there had been insufficient consideration from that perspective; a university researcher shares the idea of additive reasoning and multiplicative reasoning as a related theme for the practice research.

It should also be noted that the teachers' collective work at such meetings is usually collaborative rather than cooperative, in the sense that the participants make different comments and do not necessarily look for a consensus. The presenting teacher receives these comments as resources for further reflections. This is also the case for the discussion on lesson plans. Principally in Japan, the teacher is charged with deciding what task will be used and how to teach in the open research lesson.

7.3.4 Summary of Teachers' Collective Work Outside School

Teachers' collective work in associations outside school in Japan is very often intended for the development and sharing of teaching practices through *lesson plans* and *practice reports*. These resources are slightly different from the usual resources for classroom use, such as mathematical tasks and student worksheets. They serve to open up discussions with other teachers and to lead to sharing and acquiring ideas for use in future teaching practices. Further, developing such resources is a critical process that requires associated documentation work. Teachers' collective work is crucial here in the sense that it triggers teachers' individual documentation work for the sake of their professional development.

7.4 Discussion and Perspective

In this chapter, we have shared teachers' collective work inside (China) and outside (Japan) school in China and Japan. We discuss here the commonalities and differences based on the comparison of our two cases, in terms of the teachers' collective work and the resources associated with such work. In addition, we provide perspectives for future research on the teachers' documentation work.

Table 7.2 Comparison of the two cases

	CRG: a Chinese case inside school	Monthly meetings: a Japanese case outside school
Institutional frameworks	School Teaching research Office (TRO) of different levels University	Local mathematics teachers' association
Teachers' work	Development of lessons, based on individual/collective practice-based activities (analyzing curricular material, designing, implementing, and analyzing lessons) Research-oriented activities Discussion on teaching practices and their theoretical framework	Development of lesson plans or practice reports, based on individual/collective practice-based activities (analyzing curricular material, designing, implementing, and analyzing lessons) Research-oriented activities Discussion on teaching practices
Resources	Teaching materials (textbook, guideline, books, etc.) Research literature (theoretical framework, research method, etc.) Cognitive resources of different participants (experience teachers, university researchers, etc.) Publication opportunities in professional journals (associations or private publishers), proceedings	Lesson plans and practice reports Teaching materials (textbook, guideline, books, etc.) for the development of lessons Cognitive resources of different participants (experience teachers, university researchers, etc.) Publication opportunities in professional journals (associations or private publishers), proceedings

7.4.1 Comparison: Commonalities and Differences

We first summarized the results of the two case studies in Table 7.2. As these cases are in the very different educational contexts (inside and outside school), the table of comparison suggests the complementarities of teachers' documentation work in East-Asian countries, rather than the differences between China and Japan. The comparison does not mean therefore that the teachers' work and resources in China do not exist in Japan, or vice versa, but they are specific to each case regardless of country.

In both countries, different institutional frameworks at the different levels—ranging from school to national level—provide teachers with opportunities to work together. In the case of CRG, it is noteworthy that the university is involved as a principal sector, in addition to TRO which officially carries out TRG in a top-down approach. In contrast, the monthly meeting organized by the local teachers' association is a result of bottom-up action by voluntary teachers, which promotes in addition teachers' work in the associations of regional and national levels.

Regarding the teachers' work, China and Japan adopt a form of *practice-based* professional development, including the designing and implementation of teaching practices, instead of a form of lecture or workshop which is sometimes dissociated from the usual teaching practices with students. Remarkably, the *research-oriented* work is promoted, and the term "research" is very often used in both countries.

Teachers' work is considered to be a kind of research work focused on practical problems faced in teaching.

Further, there is a close relationship between the university researchers and the school teachers. The CRG Model in China and the monthly meeting in Japan both involve researchers from university, who bring cognitive resources into schools such as research experiences and theoretical viewpoints developed in mathematics education research. Moreover, the diversity of participants, which is a commonality in the two cases, is a critical aspect in order to enrich cognitive resources shared in the teachers' collective work.

In terms of resources, in both countries, the textbook occupies a prominent place among teachers' resources, and the study of textbooks is one of the essential works for teachers. In addition, it is noteworthy that the teacher communities are equipped with the publication infrastructure of professional journals or books that allow for the teachers to disseminate their work and hence to "re-source" other teachers.

7.4.2 Perspectives for Future Research

While teachers' collective work exists all over the world, the nature of collective work and the formats that promote such work differ based on the countries. We consider that the differences and commonalities between Eastern and Western countries in terms of collective work and associated resources are still to be further investigated. We discuss here the perspectives for future research in this respect through the Chinese and Japanese cases.

We consider, first, the need for a closer analysis of teachers' collective work in East Asian countries. This is, for instance, the case for the lesson study which is well known today and practiced in different places outside Japan (Hart et al. 2011; Lewis and Hurd 2011). The analysis of teachers' work in Japanese lesson study is still limited. In fact, while the collective work is very often emphasized in lesson study, there are a lot of associated individual work, and we do not yet understand how individual work is combined with the collective work, and how these different documentation work practices affect teachers' professional learning. The detailed lesson plan presented in this chapter would not make sense without such understanding. This need for closer analysis is also the case for Chinese teachers' collective work. We observed in China that teachers would sometimes follow the "collective voice," instead of expressing their own "voice". It will be important to go into the detail how teachers maintain their own identity while working collectively, in order to deeply understand how the collective work supports teacher learning.

Second, while we use similar resources with similar terms in Eastern and Western countries, their roles and functions and the associated teacher's work may be different, and it is necessary to carry out a closer analysis of such resources and teacher's documentation work. For example, in the case of textbooks, while we referred to the importance of textbook in East Asian countries, the textbook is usually a most important resource for teacher in any country (Pepin and Haggarty 2001; Pepin et al. 2013; Mullis et al. 2012). However, the way this resource is used may vary from country to country, that is to say, there are different *utilization schemes* related to the textbook. As mentioned above, the deep and thoughtful analysis of textbooks is an ordinary and essential practice for Chinese and Japanese teachers. We also observed that teachers in China paid attention to students' cognitive development while using textbooks. This is, to some extent, due to the specific status of textbooks in East Asian countries: the textbooks should be approved by the government and their use made compulsory.

In such analyses on teachers' documentation work in East Asian countries, it is important to not only identify the differences between Western and Eastern countries, but to reveal the cultural elements that make such differences. Teachers' work is affected and shaped by several elements. A new system from a country cannot be transposed to another country without adaptation and appropriation. It is necessary therefore not only to learn from other countries, but also to understand, as researchers, the mechanism of teachers' documentation work in our own country, in order to improve teacher professional development and, consequently, improve teaching practices in the classroom.

Acknowledgements The work presented in this paper was partially supported by JSPS KAKENHI (JP15KK0113) to the first author.

References

Becker, J. P., Silver, E. A., Kantowski, M. G., Travers, K. J., & Wilson, J. W. (1990). Some observations of mathematics teaching in Japanese elementary and junior high schools. *Arithmetic Teacher, 38*(2), 12–21.

Cao, Z., Seah, W., & Bishop, A. (2006). A comparison of mathematical values conveyed in mathematics textbooks in China and Australia. In F. K. S. Leung et al. (Eds.), *Mathematics education in different cultural traditions: A comparative study of East Asia and the west* (pp. 483–493). New York: Springer.

Fan, L., Miao, Z., & Mok, A. (2015). How Chinese teachers teach mathematics and pursue professional development: Perspectives from contemporary international research. In L. Fan et al. (Eds.), *How Chinese teach mathematics. Perspectives from insiders* (pp. 43–72). Singapore: World Scientific.

Fernandez, C., & Yoshida, M. (2004). *Lesson study – A Japanese approach to improving mathematics teaching and learning*. Mahwah: Lawrence Erlbaum.

Fujii, T. (2015). The critical role of task design in lesson study. In A. Watson & M. Ohtani (Eds.), *Task design in mathematics education* (pp. 273–286). Cham: Springer.

Goos, M. (2014). Communities of practice in mathematics teacher education. In S. Lerman (Ed.), *Encyclopedia of mathematics education* (pp. 82–84). Dordrecht: Springer.

Gu, L. Y., & Wang, J. (2003). Teachers' professional development in action education. *Curriculum-Textbook-Pedagogy, 1*(2), 2–10.

Gueudet, G., & Trouche, L. (2009). Towards new documentation systems for mathematics teachers? *Educational Studies in Mathematics, 71*(3), 199–218.

Gueudet, G., Pepin, B., & Trouche, L. (2013). Collective work with resources: An essential dimension for teacher documentation. *ZDM – Mathematics Education, 45*(7), 1003–1016.

Gueudet, G., Pepin, B., Sabra, H., & Trouche, L. (2016). Collective design of an e-textbook: Teachers' collective documentation. *Journal of Mathematics Teacher Education, 19*(2), 187–203.

Hart, L. C., Alston, A., & Murata, A. (Eds.). (2011). *Lesson study research and practice in mathematics education. Learning together*. Dordrecht: Springer.

Isoda, M., Stephens, M., Ohara, Y., & Miyakawa, T. (Eds.). (2007). *Japanese lesson study in mathematics: Its impact, diversity and potential for educational improvement*. Singapore: World Scientific Publishing.

Jaworski, B. (2014). Communities of inquiry in mathematics teacher education. In S. Lerman (Ed.), *Encyclopedia of mathematics education* (pp. 76–78). Dordrecht: Springer.

Kimura, T. (2015). *Hako kara miruto* [Viewing from inside box]. Document distributed at the monthly meeting of research Association for Mathematics Teaching in Jōetsu on 5th May, 2015.

Lewis, C., & Hurd, J. (2011). *Lesson study step by step: How teacher learning communities improve instruction*. Portsmouth: Heinemann.

Li, Y. (2007). Curriculum and culture: An exploratory examination of mathematics curriculum materials in their system and cultural contexts. *The Mathematics Educator, 10*(1), 21–38.

MEXT. (2008). *Course of study: Arithmetic*. Retrieved from http://www.mext.go.jp/en/policy/education/elsec/title02/detail02/1373859.htm

Ministry of Education, People's Republic of China. (2001). *Mathematics curriculum standard for compulsory education (the trial version)*. Beijing: Beijing Normal University Press.

Ministry of Education, People's Republic of China. (2003). *Mathematics curriculum standard for senior secondary schools (the trial version)*. Beijing: Beijing Normal University Press.

Miyakawa, T. (2015). What is a good lesson in Japan? An analysis. In M. Inprasitha et al. (Eds.), *Lesson study: Challenges in mathematics education* (pp. 327–349). Singapore: World Scientific.

Miyakawa, T., & Winsløw, C. (2013). Developing mathematics teacher knowledge: The paradidactic infrastructure of "open lesson" in Japan. *Journal of Mathematics Teacher Education, 16*(3), 185–209.

Miyakawa, T., & Winsløw, C. (2017, Online first). Paradidactic infrastructure for sharing and documenting mathematics teacher knowledge: A case study of "practice research" in Japan. *Journal of Mathematics Teacher Education, 22*, 281–303.

Mullis, I. V. S., Martin, M. O., Foy, P., & Arora, A. (2012). *TIMSS 2011 international results in mathematics*. Boston: Boston College/IEA.

Pan, M. (2005). On core competitive power in the 21st century in China: Rational structure of "education and talent". *China Higher Education Research, 3*, 1–2.

Pepin, B., & Haggarty, L. (2001). Mathematics textbooks and their use in English, French, and German classrooms: A way to understand teaching and learning cultures. *ZDM – Mathematics Education, 33*(5), 158–175.

Pepin, B., Gueudet, G., & Trouche, L. (2013). Investigating textbooks as crucial interfaces between culture, policy and teacher curricular practice: Two contrasted case studies in France and Norway. *ZDM – Mathematics Education, 45*(5), 685–698.

Stigler, J. W., & Hiebert, J. (1999). *The teaching gap: Best ideas from the world's teachers for improving education in the classroom*. New York: Free Press.

Sun, X. (2013). Trends in mathematics education in contemporary China. In J. Wang (Ed.), *Mathematics education in China: Tradition and reality* (pp. 303–322). Singapore: Gale Asia.

Takahashi, A. (2005). Tool for lesson study: Template for a lesson plan. In P. Wang-Iverson & M. Yoshida (Eds.), *Building our understanding of lesson study* (pp. 63–64). Philadelphia: Research for Better Schools.

Tanaka, Y. (2013). *Jidō ga iyoku-teki ni tsuikyū suru sansū-teki katsudō no kufū: dai 6 gakunen "kakudai-zu to shuku-zu" no jissen wo tōshite* [Mathematical activities in which children are motivated to participate: The teaching practices of a grade 6 lesson "enlarged and reduced figures"]. Document distributed at the monthly meeting of research Association for Mathematics Teaching in Jōetsu on 31st July, 2013.

Vergnaud, G. (2009). The theory of conceptual fields. *Human Development* 52(2), 83–94.
Wang, J. P. (2012). *Mathematics education in China: Tradition and reality*. Singapore: Cengage Learning Asia Pte Ltd.
Watanabe, T., Takahashi, A., & Yoshida, M. (2008). Kyozaikenkyu: A critical step for conducting effective lesson study and beyond. In F. Arbaugh & P. M. Taylor (Eds.), *Inquiry into mathematics teacher education* (pp. 131–142). San Diego: Association of Mathematics Teacher Educators.
Yang, Y., Li, J., Gao, H., & Xu, Q. (2013). Teacher education and the professional development of mathematics teachers. In J. Wang (Ed.), *Mathematics education in China. Tradition and reality* (pp. 205–238). Singapore: Cengage Learning Asia Pte Ltd.
Ye, L., & Si, H. (2017). *Study and practice of "PET" collaboration model based on teacher professional development. The Inservice Education and Training of School Teachers* (Vol. 2, pp. 9–12).

Open Access This chapter is licensed under the terms of the Creative Commons Attribution 4.0 International License (http://creativecommons.org/licenses/by/4.0/), which permits use, sharing, adaptation, distribution and reproduction in any medium or format, as long as you give appropriate credit to the original author(s) and the source, provide a link to the Creative Commons licence and indicate if changes were made.

The images or other third party material in this chapter are included in the chapter's Creative Commons licence, unless indicated otherwise in a credit line to the material. If material is not included in the chapter's Creative Commons licence and your intended use is not permitted by statutory regulation or exceeds the permitted use, you will need to obtain permission directly from the copyright holder.

Chapter 8
Teachers' Use of Mathematics Resources: A Look Across Cultural Boundaries

Janine T. Remillard

Abstract This chapter is written as a reflection on my encounters with the growing body of research on mathematics teachers' use of resources, focusing on the documentational approach and its impact on my research. I begin by detailing my first encounter with the documentational genesis framework in 2008, introducing me to new language, frameworks, and colleagues from a different cultural context. I then describe two subsequent research projects I have undertaken, one in the USA and the other involving four contexts: Finland, Flanders (Belgium), Sweden, and the USA. These projects have allowed me to refine and deploy the participatory perspective in relation to the documentational approach and have contributed to my understanding of teachers' interactions with mathematics curriculum resources. I conclude by offering four propositions for research on teachers' interactions with curriculum resources; the first three reflect the theoretical perspectives of the documentational framework. The fourth reflects findings from my research.

Keywords Curriculum use; Participatory perspective · Documentational genesis · Mathematics teachers · Curriculum resources · Cross-cultural research

---

The work of this chapter was supported in part by the National Science Foundation under grant nos. 0918141 and 0918126 and the Swedish Research Council. Any opinions, findings, conclusions, or recommendations expressed herein are those of the author and do not necessarily reflect the views of the funders.

This chapter originates from a lecture given to the Re(s)sources 2018 International Conference. Video in English is available at https://www.canalu.tv/video/ecole_normale_superieure_de_lyon/teachers_use_of_mathematics_resources_a_look_across_cultural_boundaries.45771

J. T. Remillard (✉)
University of Pennsylvania, Philadelphia, PA, USA
e-mail: janiner@upenn.edu

© Springer Nature Switzerland AG 2019
L. Trouche et al. (eds.), *The 'Resource' Approach to Mathematics Education*,
Advances in Mathematics Education,
https://doi.org/10.1007/978-3-030-20393-1_8

8.1 Introduction

The subtitle of this chapter, *A Look across Cultural Boundaries*, has two meanings. The first meaning has to do with the way ideas cross cultural boundaries and build on one another, for the better. The second has to do with undertaking research across cultural boundaries, which raises new methodological challenges. In this chapter, I address both these issues. In Sect. 8.2, I add to Gueudet's historical sketch of the emergence of the Documentational Approach to Didactics (DAD) (see Chap. 2), offering a picture from the other side of the Atlantic Ocean. I describe what I refer to as my documentational trajectory as a researcher in the USA and, in particular, the impact that encountering the documentational perspective had on my research and, hopefully, on similar research in the USA. I was introduced to new language and frameworks, which resonated with my work and shared similar foundational roots. In Sect. 8.3, I delve more deeply into my recent research and, in so doing, I identify some key differences between my work and the DAD work. I also briefly discuss findings from this research and its contribution to this wider body of work. In Sect. 8.4, I share insights from an initial effort to study teachers' documentational work in a cross-cultural context, which surfaces new issues and questions about cross-cultural approaches to research on teachers' resource use. Finally, from the perspective of these varied bodies of work, I conclude with a reflection on the contributions of the documentational approach and related frameworks to the field.

8.2 A Researcher's Documentational Trajectory

I first encountered the documentational approach in 2008, when Ghislaine Gueudet contacted me, inviting me to contribute a chapter to a book she and Luc Trouche were editing (Gueudet and Trouche 2010). Over email, and with the generous translational skills of Kenneth Ruthven, they introduced me to the Documentational Approach to Didactics. They had discovered my work through an earlier published review of research (Remillard 2005) and found a number of synergies. They also shared with me their article, published in *Educational Studies of Mathematics* (Gueudet and Trouche 2009), in which they lay out their approach. Their discovery of my work and their subsequent reaching out to me turned out to be a turning point for my research.

Since the mid-1990s, I had studied how teachers interact with and use mathematics curriculum materials to design and enact instruction, the factors that influenced this work, and how engaging in these practices can lead to new learning and new practices for teachers (Remillard 1999, 2000; Remillard and Bryans 2004). Through this work, I had begun to conceptualize this aspect of teachers' work as a dynamic, interactive, and multiphased process of meaning making and enactment. At the same time, I observed that researchers and practitioners in the USA often thought about curriculum material use as a straightforward process of implementation. Teachers simply picked materials up and used them.

During this period, mid-1990s–early 2000s, there was a great deal of interest in new mathematics curriculum materials among US researchers. In response to the publication and influence of the *Curriculum and Evaluation Standards for School Mathematics*, published by the National Council of Teachers of Mathematics (NCTM 1989), mathematics education was undergoing significant reform. Newly developed curriculum materials, designed to align with the goals of the NCTM Standards, were being adopted by school districts and used by teachers across the country. Because they represented a shift in approach to teaching mathematics—greater emphasis on problem solving, reasoning, and conceptual understanding and decreased emphasis on rules and procedures taught in isolation—there was substantial interest in studying how teachers used these materials and measuring their "effects" on student learning.

My reading of much of the research being undertaken at this time led me to two related observations. First, it appeared that researchers were conceptualizing and measuring curriculum use in substantially different ways. Some, for example, thought about curriculum use as following or subverting, that is, teachers' curriculum use could be explored through a fidelity lens. Others thought of it as a process of interpretation. Rather than considering the extent to which teachers followed the written curriculum guide, these researchers asked *how* they used it. This latter perspective was influenced by research on teacher beliefs and knowledge and key factors that influenced teacher actions (see Remillard 2005 for more detail on different conceptualizations of curriculum use). Second, I found that much of the research on teachers' use of curriculum materials was under-theorized. In other words, the field had not developed or identified a theoretical foundation to support many of its empirical approaches. I concluded that the field would benefit from a theory that explains what happens when teachers use curriculum materials. In fact, I argued that the many conflicting findings in this body of research might be explained by the fact that curriculum materials and their use were under-theorized and under-conceptualized (Remillard 2005).

I was particularly interested in understanding the process by which teachers interacted with these resources. In my research, I had found differences in the parts of curriculum materials teachers read, the purposes of their reading, the components they used, modified, or ignored, and how they thought about the type of tool a published teacher's guide might be for them (Remillard 1999, 2000; Remillard and Bryans 2004). I also found that features of the materials mattered for how teachers used them, as did the context in which they were being used (Brown 2009; Remillard 2005).

I was drawn to Vygotskian-inspired theories of human tool-use and mediated action to develop a theory to explain teachers' interactions with curriculum resources. From this perspective, all human activity is mediated by tools or artifacts, which themselves are products of human activity (Vygotsky 1978) or what Wertsch (1998) referred to as "sociocultural evolution." Teachers participate with curriculum resources when they plan lessons. And the product of this activity, the planned curriculum, is shaped by the agent and the tool. "Any attempt to reduce the account of mediated action to one or the other of these elements," as Wertsch explained, "runs the risk of destroying the phenomenon under observation." This understanding of the teacher-curriculum relationship is at the heart of the participatory perspective for studying teachers' work with curriculum resources (Remillard 2005). In short, examining teachers' work with curriculum resources requires taking into account how teachers interact with resources, as well as how these interactions are mediated by both the teacher and the materials.

Having developed a model that seeks to capture the complexity of teachers' interactions with curriculum materials to develop and enact instruction, I was struck by the insufficiency of the English term "use" to describe it. I found myself saying, "when I say teachers *use* curriculum materials, I am referring to a whole set of practices, including selecting, purposefully reading, interpreting, drawing from, modifying, and reflecting on in order to design one's plan.

When Ghislaine and Luc contacted me in 2008, I was struck to find that the French had a term to describe this work: *travail documentaire*, which literally means "to work with documents." As Ghislaine explained in an email, "The word *documentation* in French describes both a set of documents, and an activity aiming at elaborating such a set (searching for documents, but also building them). Travail documentaire "is synonymous with this last meaning of documentation." She also explained that even a teacher's work elaborating a plan from an "idea evoked in a conversation with a colleague" is also considered documentation work (email, May 27, 2008). Kenneth Ruthven further explained specific framing aspects of Ghislaine and Luc's work, including the notion of documentational genesis, which distinguishes between available resources and documents developed by teachers through this process. Through reading their work (Gueudet and Trouche 2009), I came to understand how their work drew on Rabardel's (1995) instrumental approach, which differentiates between artifact and instrument. Instruments are built from artifacts by a subject through goal-directed activity. He called this the process of *instrumental genesis*. Similarly, when using resources to design instructional plans, Gueudet and Trouche propose that teachers are engaged in a process of documentational genesis, that is, transforming resources into documents.

This discovery was pivotal for me. I saw a number of connections to the ideas I had been developing. Most notably, Gueudet and Trouche (2009) were offering a theoretically grounded description of teacher's work with curriculum (and other) resources. Moreover, the foundational ideas underlying their model could also be traced to Vygotsky's work. In his introduction to the instrumental approach, Rabardel (1995) notes that, according to Vygotsky, the use of instruments is one of the fundamental forms of cultural behavior (the other is human language). Through goal-oriented use of artifacts, humans transform them into tools or instruments. So, despite some differences in our approaches, the documentational approach and the participatory perspective share the view that the human (and didactic) activity of using resources to design instructional plans (or documents) must be understood as a transformational and generative process. (See Table 8.1 for summary of key concepts.)

8 Teachers' Use of Mathematics Resources: A Look Across Cultural Boundaries

Table 8.1 Comparison of key concepts in documentational and participatory perspectives

	Documentational approach	Participatory perspective
Conception of resources	A variety of possible artifacts (including textbooks, software, conversations with colleagues)	Cultural tools; curriculum resources designed to support teachers' instructional design
Conception of teacher's role	Teacher is a designer who, guided by a goal, transforms resources into documents	Collaborator with curriculum resources to design and enact instructional episodes
Products of work	Documents	Teacher-intended and enacted curriculum
Theoretical foundation	Vygotsky: generation of instruments Rabardel: instrumental genesis	Vygotsky: human tool use Wertsch: mediated action
Focus of research	Teachers' goal-directed work with documents (travail documentaire); how teachers search for and use resources to create documents (resource + scheme of utilization)	How teachers interact with resources; teacher and curricular factors that mediate these interactions

My exchange with Luc and Ghislaine also highlighted both the limitations and possibilities of language to express concepts precisely. As I mentioned previously, I found English terms, like "use," insufficient for describing the work teachers do with curriculum resources. The rich meanings of "travail documentaire" and "documentational genesis" seemed substantially more robust. I began to use these terms in talks and writing to express my ideas more clearly.

Most meaningfully, this exchange opened new doors for me. It led to an ongoing collaborative exchange with Luc and Ghislaine and eventually others, including Kenneth Ruthven and Birgit Pepin. I had the opportunity to contribute two chapters, one in French and one in English, to edited volumes they were developing (see Remillard 2010, 2012). Over the years since, our collaboration has evolved through conference presentations and writing projects and has expanded to include a number of other graduate students and researchers. I continue to benefit and learn from their ideas and the opportunity to think from a different point of view. As is evident in the sections that follow, my subsequent work has been influenced by my encounters with the documentational approach and cross-cultural lenses.

8.3 Studying Teachers' Documentational Work from a Participatory Perspective

I now turn to a discussion of subsequent research I have undertaken with colleagues, which has been influenced by my developing understanding of the documentational approach. Guided by a participatory perspective, my work has focused on examining teachers' interactions with mathematics curriculum resources in order to conceptualize teacher capacity to make productive use of resources. As discussed above, the participatory perspective and the Documentational Approach to Didactics

(Gueudet this volume) have similar roots in sociocultural theory and interest in mediated use of artifacts and production of new tools (instruments). One difference, however, is the primary focus within the participatory perspective on teacher-resource interactions and the mediating agency of the resources as artifacts of culture. Whereas the documentational approach places the teacher's goal-directed activity at the center of its analysis, the participatory perspective places the teacher's interactions with resources at the center and assumes that both the teacher and resources have mediating influence (see Table 8.1). This perspective has led me to examine potentially influential characteristics of resources, as well as influential characteristics of teachers using them. Other ways that my work has differed from much of the DAD research are that (a) I focus on elementary teachers (in the USA, that is, kindergarten through grade 6) and (b) I examine teachers' interactions with mathematics curriculum resources designed to guide their instructional decision making. As I discuss below, these features have important implications for my primary focus on teacher capacity.

8.3.1 Studying Elementary Teachers

Perhaps on account of my own experience as an elementary teacher using curriculum resources in the 1980s, I am particularly interested in studying elementary teachers. Understanding distinguishing characteristics of this group of teachers, especially how they differ from secondary mathematics teachers, is important for contextualizing the research. Throughout the USA and in many other countries, teachers of children between the ages of 5 and 10 or 11 are responsible for teaching all or many school subjects. Consequently, elementary teachers have less time to devote to planning mathematics lessons than their secondary colleagues do. Furthermore, it is not uncommon for elementary teachers to have limited mathematics knowledge. In the USA, elementary teachers are not expected to have extensive content expertise in mathematics, and the trend is for this group to favor literacy over mathematics. Together, limited content knowledge and responsibility for multiple subjects increase the likelihood that elementary teachers will rely on primary curriculum programs to guide their mathematics instruction. For this reason, a perspective that examines the agency and influence of the resources being used, as well as teachers' purposes and individual characteristics, is highly relevant.

In many places around the world, the elementary mathematics curriculum and curriculum resources have undergone substantial change over the last 25 years. In the USA, the change began in the early 1990s, in response to the publication of the NCTM standards in 1989. Subsequently, the emphasis on conceptual understanding, problem solving, and mathematical reasoning have become foundational ideas in other national curricula (Boesen et al. 2014).

8.3.2 Focusing on Mathematics Curriculum Resources

Today, teachers have access to a range of resources, both print and digital, that they are likely to use to design and enact instruction. I use the term *curriculum resources* to refer to print or digital artifacts designed to support a program of instruction and student learning over time. I use this term to distinguish curriculum resources from the broader category of *instructional resources,* which refers to artifacts provided to, appropriated by, or generated by teachers to guide or support classroom instruction. Instructional resources include curriculum resources, as well as others that are not curricular in nature (see Fig. 8.1).

The term curriculum, derived from the Latin word for course or race, refers to the pathway on which learners are guided. Resources that attend to sequencing or mapping students' learning over a period of time, such as a lesson sequence, a set of lessons, a year of instruction, or more, I argue, are curricular in nature. This characteristic of sequencing is an important component of curriculum resource design, as it proposes an intended learning progression for particular mathematical domains. Choppin (2011) has identified these learning sequences as a critical element of many curriculum programs that are not always made visible to the teacher. Sleep (2009) names identifying learning sequences as an important feature of content-specific curriculum knowledge. Elsewhere, I have argued that sequencing or curriculum mapping (Remillard 2016) is an under-appreciated aspect of curriculum design and curriculum knowledge.

I think of the domain of curriculum resources as including two types of resources worthy of consideration. Student texts and tools are typically designed for the students' consumption (Fan et al. 2013) and interaction. Student textbooks might include exercises, problems, and other tasks for students to undertake, along with worked examples and definitions. This subcategory also includes digital tools designed for students to interact with. Curriculum resources also include guidance and support prepared specifically for the teacher. In the USA and a number of other countries, curriculum programs include a teacher's guide, which is written to communicate to teachers and support them in shaping lessons, monitoring student progress, and providing additional support (Remillard 2018a; Remillard et al. 2016).

Instructional Resources		
Resources provided to, appropriated by, or generated by teachers to guide or support classroom instruction (Instructional resources include curriculum resources, as well as others that are not curricular in nature.)		
Curriculum Resources		
Designed to support instruction over time, attending to learning sequences and content mapping		
Curriculum Programs		Documents
Student texts and tools	Teacher's guide	Products of teachers' curriculum design work (Teacher-intended)
Designed for student consumption and interaction	Designed to support the teacher in designing instruction	

Fig. 8.1 Summary of terms differentiating instructional and curriculum resources

Digital capabilities have expanded the nature and purpose of curriculum support for teachers. In addition to supporting their instructional decision making and classroom enactments, digital resources might include tools to track student progress through online tasks or modules, analyze features of student work over time, provide digital professional learning, and connect teachers to others. Teacher's guides and textbooks are also accompanied by many additional resources, both print and digital. I refer to these full packages as curriculum programs.

Over the last two decades, I have been particularly interested in elementary teachers' use of mathematics teacher's guides. In the 1990s, some curriculum authors promoting pedagogical change used teacher's guides to communicate these new approaches to teachers. Some have considered the possibility that teacher's guides could be designed to support teacher learning, often referred to as educative curriculum materials (Davis and Krajcik 2005).

Drawing on the work of Gueudet and Trouche (2009), I note a third type of curriculum resource worthy of consideration, documents. Unlike those described above, which are designed for teachers' use, documents are the products of teachers' curriculum design (or documentational genesis) work. As Gueudet and Trouche note, documents are resources that have been imbued with the teacher's "scheme of utilization" and as such have become instruments. From this perspective, documents approximate (Fig. 8.1) what Remillard and Heck (2014) refer to as the teacher-intended curriculum, which includes the interpretations and decisions teachers make (with resources) in order to envision and plan instruction" (p. 711).

8.3.3 *ICUBiT Project: Understanding Pedagogical Design Capacity*

My research on curriculum programs over the last 10 years has focused on understanding components of teacher capacity needed to engage in productive documentational work and examining how features of teacher's guides contribute to this work. Much of this work took place under the umbrella of a study called Improving Curriculum Use for Better Teaching (ICUBiT), directed by Ok-Kyeong Kim and myself and funded by the National Science Foundation. An underlying assumption of this work is that productively using curriculum resources requires skill. Brown (2009) referred to this skill as pedagogical design capacity or PDC, the knowledge and skills involved in perceiving and mobilizing curriculum resources to design and enact instruction. PDC is critical to the work of using curriculum resources because these resources convey "rich ideas and dynamic practices through succinct shorthand" (p. 21) and in static form, from which teachers create instructional episodes.

The goal of the ICUBiT project was to conceptualize PDC, identify its properties, and develop ways to measure it for research purposes. Following a participatory perspective, we understood PDC to be distributed across an individual teacher and the curriculum resources she was using, in a specific context. This is the case

8 Teachers' Use of Mathematics Resources: A Look Across Cultural Boundaries

because different types of resources are likely to place different types of demands on teachers using them or they may support them in other ways.

Drawing on Brown's (2009) initial proposal, we thought of PDC as involving both *perceiving* and *mobilizing* curriculum resources to design and enact instruction. Through our analysis, we propose this work occurring in two phases: *preparation* and *enactment*. When preparing instruction, teachers *perceive* curriculum resources by (a) reading, (b) interpreting, and (c) evaluating the contents of curriculum resources in order to decide what to use and how to use it. Teachers interpret and evaluate what they read, using a variety of lenses and knowledge. Also, in the preparation phase, teachers *mobilize* what they read into plans for instruction. During enactment of instruction, teachers *perceive* and *mobilize* the activities of the lesson with respect to their instructional plans. They (a) read students and the class as a whole, (b) interpret students' actions, and (c) evaluate their work with respect to their mathematical goals; they mobilize curriculum resources and their own repertoires to shape the instructional episodes in the lesson. During enactment, teachers also make in-the-moment design decisions based on their perceptions and mobilization skills.

The notion of PDC aligns well with the documentational approach and other frameworks that view teachers as designers engaged in goal-directive, purposeful activity (Pepin et al. this volume; Pepin et al. 2017b). Thus, it is not surprising that many of the characteristics of PDC are reminiscent of those possessed by teachers described by researchers using DAD (Gueudet and Trouche 2009) or related approaches to examining teachers' work.

In order to understand how different teacher's guides contributed to PDC, we analyzed the teacher's guides of five commonly used curriculum programs for grades 3–5. As I discuss in a subsequent section, we examined the mathematical and pedagogical demands of the resources and the supports they provided to teachers. We also followed five teachers using each of the five programs, gathering data on their general approaches to using curriculum resources, how they used specific components of the guides to plan their lessons, and what happened during those lessons. In the following sections, I summarize several analytical activities and findings from this work related specifically to understanding PDC from a participatory perspective.[1]

8.3.3.1 Curriculum Resource Analysis

In order to understand how different teacher's guides contributed to PDC, we analyzed the teacher's guides of five commonly used curriculum programs for grades 3–5. The focus of our analysis was on both the mathematical and pedagogical demands the resources placed on teachers and the types of support they provided.

---

[1] The ICUBiT team included a number of graduate students and collaborators who contributed to data collection and analysis, including Ok-Kyeong Kim, Napthalin Atanga, Dustin Smith, Luke Reinke, Joshua Taton, Shari McCarty, and Hendrik van Steenbrugge.

Drawing on Stein and Kim's (2009) analysis, we hypothesized that programs that emphasized conceptual understanding and complex mathematical concepts and that posed cognitively demanding tasks would place greater mathematical demands on the teacher. We also hypothesized that pedagogical approaches that encouraged exploration, student generation of strategies, and classroom discourse would place greater pedagogical demands on teachers. In order to explore how different teacher's guides supported teachers, we looked for what many call "educative features" (Davis and Krajcik 2005; Pepin 2018). We coded how teacher's guides communicated with teachers, differentiating when they directed teacher actions from when they provided information about design principles, anticipated student ideas, mathematics concepts, or decision making (Remillard 2013).

Our full findings from this analysis will be reported in the forthcoming volume (Remillard and Kim forthcoming). Of significance, I note here that we found substantial variation in the quantity and type of communication across the five programs. All placed greater emphasis on directing teacher action than on communicating with teachers. The teacher's guides that were more pedagogically demanding tended to provide more educative supports, but they varied in the types of support or guidance they provided teachers. In subsequent analyses, we considered relationships between the types of supports provided and classroom enactments.

8.3.3.2 Articulating and Steering Toward the Mathematical Point

One type of support teacher's guides might provide teachers is what we refer to as mathematical purposing. Sleep (2012) argued that teachers must do two types of work when teaching mathematics: *purposing* involves identifying, detailing, and coordinating both the mathematical goals and the lesson activities and *steering* the instruction toward the mathematical learning goals in the moment. Sleep also emphasized that instructional activities that comprise mathematics lessons found in curriculum resources or elsewhere do not in and of themselves communicate the intended mathematical learning goals. It is the role of the teacher to steer students toward the mathematical point by "deploying teaching moves during an activity's enactment in order to keep students engaged with the intended mathematics" (p. 938). Using a subset of data from the ICUBiT project (eight teachers using four curriculum programs), Remillard et al. (2019) drew on Sleep's conception of mathematical purposing to consider the extent to which curriculum authors clearly identified and elaborated learning goals and specified how the proposed activities related to those goals. Hypothesizing that this type of support might help teachers steer instruction toward the goals, we also analyzed the frequency with which teachers using different teacher's guides steered instruction toward the mathematical goals during the lesson.

Our analysis uncovered substantial variation in how curriculum authors communicated and supported lesson goals. We also found a correlation between the depth to which the goals were communicated in the teacher's guides and the extent to which teachers steered the instruction toward the goals. Most lesson guides, for example, typically included four to five goals but provided purposing support for just two to three. Teachers generally steered toward two to three goals per lesson, and they steered more heavily toward goals that received more purposing support in the teacher's guides. Even though this analysis did not consider how closely the teacher read different components of the teacher's guides, the findings suggest that purposing supports in teacher's guides might help teachers attend to key mathematical points during instruction.

8.3.3.3 Knowledge of Curriculum Embedded Mathematics

Our analysis of elementary teacher's guides also allowed us to consider one component of PDC: how teachers might deploy different types of mathematical knowledge to read, interpret, use mathematical tasks, instructional designs, and representations in mathematics curriculum guides. Remillard and Kim (2017) proposed the term *Knowledge of Curriculum Embedded Mathematics* (KCEM) to refer to the mathematical knowledge teachers activate when using curriculum resources. The KCEM framework is situated within existing research on content-specific teacher knowledge (e.g., Ball et al. 2008; Mason and Spence 1999; Rowland 2013; Shulman 1986, 1987) and follows Sleep's (2012) assertion that instructional activities and representations do not necessarily make explicit their underlying meanings or mathematical learning goals.

Through analysis of the five mathematics teacher's guides, we identified elements of curriculum resources teachers interact with when using them to plan instruction, including goal statements, tasks, and representations. From these components, we proposed four overlapping dimensions of KCEM: *foundational mathematical ideas, representations and connections among these ideas, problem complexity,* and *mathematical learning pathways.* These dimensions identify mathematical components of designed curriculum resources that teachers must interpret and navigate when using them to design instruction. These findings were complemented by interviews of teachers using curriculum guides to plan lessons, uncovering how they interacted with different elements of their guides.

8.3.3.4 Conceptualizing Pedagogical Design Capacity: An Illustrative Case

As mentioned earlier, the ultimate goal of the ICUBiT research project was to conceptualize and develop a deeper understanding of PDC or the capacity involved in perceiving and mobilizing curriculum resources to design and enact instructional episodes (Brown 2009). Below I briefly describe one illustrative case of our analysis to this end.

In Remillard (2018a), I discuss the case of Maya Fiero's interactions with her mathematics teacher's guide to plan and enact a lesson in her fourth-grade classroom. Ms. Fiero was using *Mathematics in Focus* (MiF) (Kheong et al. 2010) for the second year, and much of the program's approach still seemed unfamiliar to her. MiF was a modified version of one of the mathematics programs used in Singapore, developed by Marshall Cavendish and sold for use in the USA. In addition to analyzing the mathematical and pedagogical approach taken in MiF and how the authors communicate to teachers, we analyzed the teachers' reading of the guide, several enacted lessons, and a pre- and post-observation interview.

Analysis of the teacher's guide indicated a general lack of transparency about key mathematical and pedagogical concepts. MiF tended to present complex mathematical concepts using approaches not typical of instructional approaches used in the USA. One lesson analyzed demonstrated an approach to multiplying any number by a multiple of ten. It guided students through steps of rewriting the original expression in equivalent forms in order to solve the following: 4×10 can be written as 4×1 ten and then 4 and 1 can be multiplied, resulting in 4 tens or 40. The curriculum authors provided minimal explanation or description of the rationale behind the instructional approach of the intended sequencing of the tasks. It communicates with teachers primarily through directing their pedagogical actions. It provides little in the way of transparency or other educative supports that might provide insights into the underlying mathematical ideas or design rationale.

In her reading of the teacher's guide, Ms. Fiero attended the overall mathematical approach but missed an important element of the curricular sequencing built into the designed lesson, including a trajectory from less complex to more complex ideas. In fact, she replaced a lesson warm-up that involved multiplying single-digit numbers by ten and one hundred with a practice involving multiplying one-digit numbers by two-digit numbers. During the lesson, students had difficulty with this new approach, and Ms. Fiero found herself spending much of the lesson struggling to help them understand a key equivalence: $4 \times 10 = 4 \times 1$ ten. They also had difficulty recognizing that 4×10 was indeed equivalent to 4 tens, a relationship that was at the heart of the warm-up she had decided to skip.

Through interviews with Ms. Fiero, we were able to speculate on her understanding of the mathematical and pedagogical approach in the lesson. Her grasp of the foundational mathematical ideas underlying the unfamiliar approach to multiplying by factors of ten appeared to be sufficiently strong. She saw the mathematical importance of restating the expressions in equivalent forms, the value of understanding the meaning of the equal sign, and the ways this approach was a precursor to algebraic manipulation. At the same time, she did not seem to appreciate the meaning of multiplication as iterating composite units nor did she fully understand the developmental progression needed for children to work flexibly within multiplicative structures (Ulrich 2015). As a result, Ms. Fiero did not recognize or find value in other components of the lesson aimed at helping students understand the meaning of multiplying composite units of ten. These possible gaps in Ms. Fiero's understanding of the development of multiplicative reasoning may help to explain why she underestimated the challenge it would present to students and did not interpret the warm-up activity as a useful precursor to the focal tasks of the lesson.

Looking at Ms. Fiero's interaction with the MiF teacher's guide from a lens of PDC, we see both underdeveloped understanding on her part and missed opportunities on the part of the curriculum authors. PDC is not a static capacity residing in individual teachers. It is mediated by characteristics of the resource. Some curriculum authors provide more transparency and explication than others to guide teachers' interpretations and assist them in anticipating student difficulties (Davis and Krajcik 2005; Stein and Kim 2009). My analysis of the excerpt of the MiF teacher's guide raises questions about the extent to which the curriculum resource was designed to support teachers to activate their PDC.

8.3.3.5   Summary of ICUBiT Findings and Next Steps

The findings described above highlight several points about elementary teachers' work with mathematics curriculum resources, which are supported by others not referenced here (Kim 2018; Remillard 2018b). Together, these points illustrate essential links between the DAD approach (Gueudet and Trouche 2009; Gueudet this volume), which views teachers as designers, and the participatory perspective, which draws attention to the mediating influence of resources and importance of the teacher-resource interaction. First, curriculum resources designed for teachers' use are not only complex and multifaceted but vary significantly in the types of demands they place on teachers and how they support their design work. Second, reading, interpreting, and transforming curriculum resources into instructional designs call on teachers to activate different types of mathematical and pedagogical knowledge. Third, the variation in curriculum resources appears to matter for how teachers use them when designing and enacting mathematics lessons. In short, the design of curriculum resources *for* teachers presents an opportunity (often missed) for authors to anticipate potential challenges for elementary teachers and provide support (see Dietiker and Riling 2018, e.g., of such an approach).

The ICUBiT study was located in the USA and examined teachers' interactions with resources that were print-centric. The substantial shifts in the availability of digital resources and related expansion of available instructional resources through the Internet over the last two decades, discussed in more detail in the following section, have increased the complexity of teachers' design work. In addition to leveraging curriculum resources designed for their use, elementary teachers find themselves navigating and integrating a landscape of new resources. It was in this context that cross-cultural research, described in the following section, emerged.

8.4   A Cross-Cultural Curriculum Research in Mathematics

In this section, I describe a shift in my research on teachers' documentational work to include a cross-cultural focus. This work evolved naturally, as I had increased opportunities to interact with researchers around the world. Given some substantial differences in the design of elementary curriculum resources around the world, this work provides more opportunities to consider how curriculum resource designs matter for teachers' interactions with them. I begin with an analysis of curriculum resources from three cultures. I then describe a cross-cultural study of teachers' interactions with print and digital resources in four cultures, which is currently underway.

8.4.1 Multimodal Cross-Cultural Curriculum Resource Analysis

In collaboration with Hendrik Van Steenbrugge and Tomas Bergqvist, I have continued to analyze how authors of elementary teacher's guides communicate with teachers, using a similar coding scheme described earlier, but this time, comparing guides from Flanders (Belgium), Sweden, and the USA (Remillard et al. 2016). More recently, Hendrik and I have broadened our analytical lens considerably to include a multimodal framework (e.g., Bezemer and Kress 2008, 2015). This approach considers how modes, such as arrangement, color, and prominence, communicate different ideas about teaching and learning mathematics, including locus of control of mathematical ideas and the roles of the teacher and the student (Remillard and Van Steenbrugge in preparation). Interestingly, even though the official mathematics curricula in Flanders, Sweden, and the USA share many similarities (Boesen et al. 2014), the subtle messages surfaced through our analysis about mathematics teaching and learning appear to differ. These differences may be rooted in different cultural traditions across these three contexts (Pepin and Haggarty 2001), a question I am currently pursuing in the Mathematics 3Cs study with colleagues from Belgium, Finland, and Sweden.

8.4.2 The Cross-Cultural Study of Mathematics Teachers' Curriculum Use

The Math 3Cs study emerged out of the analysis I described above and changes in teachers' interactions with curriculum resources in a digital environment. The last decade (or more) has seen remarkable changes in the domain of instructional resources. Both digitization of resources and the reach of the Internet have made this space much more dense (Pepin et al. 2017a, b; Remillard and Heck 2014). There is evidence to suggest that particular characteristics of digital resources put different demands on the teacher (Remillard 2016). Further, there has been an explosion of educational entrepreneurs and designers, including teachers, filling the Internet with all manner of potential resources made directly available to teachers who are expected to navigate this new terrain. With digitization comprehensive, static textbooks are a relic of the past; digital forms allow for multiple, interactive resources to be layered on top of one another, with options for differentiation and analytics. Finally, the globalization of the curriculum publishing industry and the fact that resources on the Internet are available to teachers throughout much of the world, regardless of their physical location or language, makes the need for studies on curriculum use set in cross-cultural contexts especially relevant (Haggarty and Pepin 2002).

It is in this digital context that the Math 3Cs study is located. Funded by the Swedish Research Council in 2017, the project is codirected by Hendrik Van Steenbrugge, Kirsti Hemmi, Heidi Krzywacki, and myself and is comprised of a cross-cultural team. Our aim is to examine elementary teachers' documentational work with print and digital resources to design and enact instruction in Finland, Flanders, Sweden, and the USA from a cross-cultural perspective. We are interested in how teachers access and have access to various resources, how they use them, factors that influence them, and the variation within and across cultural contexts.

In the section that follows, I explain the relevance of the Math 3C study and describe key elements of our methodological approach. I then discuss two cultural issues that have arisen in our methodological decision making. Because the study is currently in its early stages of development, I do not present findings at this time.

8.4.2.1 Why Look at Curriculum Resource Use Across Cultural Boundaries?

Although there is substantial interest in teachers' interactions with curriculum resources around the world, there have been relatively few research studies of teachers' curriculum resources work in cross-cultural contexts. Birgit Pepin's work has contributed substantially to our understanding in this area (Pepin et al. 2001; Pepin et al. 2013). We know that teaching is a cultural activity and that cultural scripts are hard to see from inside the culture (Stigler and Hiebert 1999). To this end, cross-cultural studies enable us to identify and characterize such cultural scripts and examine assumptions and practices that are often taken for granted by cultural insiders (Andrews 2007; Pepin and Haggarty 2001). Pepin and Haggarty go on to argue that mathematics textbooks represent culturally specific representations of what mathematics is valued and cultural traditions around mathematics teaching.

8.4.2.2 Study Design and Methods

The first phase of the four-year study involves interviews of 40 teachers, ten from each cultural region. Similar to the ICUBiT study, the Math 3Cs study uses published curriculum programs to guide initial data collection. We identified two print curriculum programs from each region that represented existing culture, policy, and reforms and held at least 10% market share. In each region, we attempted to find programs with contrasting features: one program that had been in use for a longer period and one that represented recent changes in the mathematical landscape of the region. Our intention was to use the two programs to understand both the variations within each region, as well as the commonalities within each region in comparison with other regions. As many of the researchers on our team had done other curriculum studies, we were able to select materials that we knew well to represent the older approaches in Flanders, Sweden, and the USA. The programs that were selected were:

- Flanders: Kompas (established) and Nieuwe Pluspunt (newer)
- Finland: Otava's Tuhattaituri (established) and Edukustannus (newer)
- Sweden: Matte Direkt (established) and Favorit matematik (newer, imported from Finland)
- USA: Everyday Mathematics (established) and Eureka! Math (newer)

All the programs have both digital and print components.

Following collectively agreed-upon criteria, we then identified five teachers using each of the two programs per context to interview. The first interview inquired about the teacher's experience with curriculum resources, approaches to using curriculum resources, and general beliefs about mathematics teaching and learning. The second interview asked the teacher to walk us through her planning of the most recent lesson. We are currently analyzing these two interviews for 40 teachers. As I discuss below, this emergent process has surfaced other cross-cultural challenges.

8.4.3 Addressing Cross-Cultural Challenges on a Cross-Cultural Research Team

Through the process of designing and analyzing interviews, our team has confronted and learned from several cross-cultural challenges related to the work. In seeking to understand and move through these challenges, we have consulted the work of other experts, including Paul Andrews (2007), David Clarke (2013), and Marilyn Osborn (2004).

8.4.3.1 Interview Development

The aim of the interviews was to understand how teachers wove print and digital resources together by starting with a lesson walk-through from the current day's lesson. This part of the interview protocol sparked an ongoing cross-cultural discussion among the researchers. In some regions, textbooks and teacher's guides are divided into discrete lessons, making it reasonable to ask teachers to describe how they plan and teach "a lesson." In other contexts, textbooks provide an overview of concepts and skills that students should master by the end of a week or unit; teachers plan at this level and determine what to cover each day in response to their students' progress. For these teachers, prompts such as, "which lesson will you be teaching tomorrow?" or "describe how you planned for today's lesson" might not make sense

(Clarke 2013). We ultimately decided to focus on the mathematics teaching that occurred on the day of the interview, recognizing that different terminology would need to be used to describe this in different contexts and that probes would address variations.

8.4.3.2 Linguistic Mapping

The team communicates in English, as all team members have mastery of English. That said, we are learning that commonly used terms have different meanings. For instances, words that are seemingly straightforward in their translation, such as "instruction," have different meanings when translated into different languages. One team member used the term instruction to refer to what was happening throughout a lesson under the teacher's guidance and orchestration. A Swedish member of the team translated this term into the Swedish as "genomgång," which refers to the part of a lesson when the teacher goes over or reviews material. We have discovered through our discussions that the English tendency to create nouns out of the gerund forms of verbs (e.g., teaching) is not common to other languages, especially Swedish and Finnish, which may use words with separate roots and meanings for the noun and verb forms of a practice. Thus, the terms "teaching" and "learning" do not always translate with similar meanings. This issue reflects Pepin's (2005) and Osborn's (2004) warnings that seeking linguistic equivalences (Warwick and Osherson 1973) is insufficient in cross-cultural research.

To address this challenge and in keeping with Osborn's (2004) and Pepin's (2005) recommendations that cross-cultural researchers seek conceptual equivalences, we have begun a multilingual glossary of key terms used by the research team. We will continue to add to this document and engage in ongoing discussion about their meanings. We have also agreed that we will not limit ourselves to English terms. As I discovered 10 years ago, it is possible, even likely, that some meanings we wish to express cannot be clearly communicated in the English language. For instance, the Russian term "Obuchenie" does not have a single, direct English translation. The term refers to an activity or interaction in which teachers and students are joint participants and is sometimes translated to English as *learning* and other times as *instruction*. The Finnish term *opetus* and Swedish term *undervisning* have similar meanings to the Russian term.

8.4.3.3 Analyzing Interviews

Our process for analyzing interviews, guided by Andrews (2007), has emerged as the team has worked through developing shared meanings of the terms we are using and of the different contexts in which the data are being collected. Once we collected and transcribed the interviews into their original language, we were faced with the significant challenge of analyzing them across the team. We wanted to avoid creating artificial equivalencies (Osborn 2004; Pepin 2005) but also believe that comparison and an outsider's perspective can identify hidden cultural scripts (Stigler and Hiebert 1999).

We began by developing common coding categories, which we applied and refined collaboratively with several American transcripts. Team members then undertook within culture coding of transcripts of those from their own region and in their native language for one teacher. Using the coded transcripts, they developed descriptive cases that characterized a single teacher's use of resources. The cases included illustrative quotes and images of resources captured during the interviews.

The team, then, read and discussed the cases, asking to clarify questions about the descriptions, the resources, and the context. Team members naturally made comparisons to their own context and interviews. These discussions have been a critical part of our developing methodology. Through them, we continue to collectively identify what needs to be explicitly described in the cases and surface taken-for-granted features of the case the author has missed, due to familiarity.

This process also allowed us to identify approaches that we determined should be applied to each case. For example, the Finnish team used a chart to list components of the Finnish teacher's guide and indicate which were used by the teacher and which were not. The team agreed that all cases should include such a chart. Further, through a discussion of the images of the teacher's guide included in the case, we were able to identify components that the researchers had unintentionally omitted from the chart.

The development and discussion of cases played several important roles in our cross-cultural analytical process. It allowed us to undertake initial, low-inference analysis by a cultural insider and make it available to the entire research team, giving the cultural outsiders access to one example of resource use with each program. Reading and discussing one another's cases allowed us to ask clarifying questions about the context, the resources, and the teachers' uses of them and consider similar or comparable elements in our own cases. The process also allowed us to identify missing elements, uncover additional insider assumptions, and arrive at common conventions for the cases (Andrews 2007).

Building on the prerequisite common understandings (Andrews 2007) already generated among the team during discussions of case and context descriptions, we have devised a more analytical approach to interpreting the interviews, which comprise our next step. The analytical approach involves careful analysis of the interviews in their native languages without developing full cases of each teacher. We also designed a three-step process, which uses insider-outsider perspectives to further these understandings and ensure a sound cross-cultural analytical approach. This work is currently underway, but not completed at the time of this writing.

8.4.4 Summary and Future Possibilities

The cross-cultural research team is in the midst of analyzing the Math 3C data at the time of this writing. Still, the process of undertaking cross-cultural research has extended our understanding of teachers' documentational work in our own contexts and in others. We anticipate that future findings will contribute to knowledge of teachers' documentational work, understanding of how this work is mediated by the context and different curriculum resources, and add precision to the language we use to describe this aspect of teaching practice.

8.5 Final Remarks

This chapter has been written at an important point of transition for my research and for the field. This volume represents a substantial coming together of mathematics education researchers from around the world, seeking to understand teachers' documentational work across different contexts and in a changing curricular landscape. I am fortunate to be part of this conversation. DAD, as a theoretical perspective and research approach, offers several propositions that have salience for this conversation. They are also foundational to my work. The first is the importance of grounding research on resource use in theoretical frameworks that offer sound and sufficiently robust explanatory mechanisms for the nature of teachers' work. Vygotsky-inspired frameworks have helped the field to characterize human activity in relation to artifacts and cultural tools and it is promising that they have become foundational to this work. The second proposition has to do with the complexity of teachers' documentational work. Gueudet (this volume) uses an illustration of a teacher with arms reaching for resources in many different directions to illustrate one aspect of the complexity of this work. But documentational genesis involves much more than incorporating multiple resources into one's lessons. It involves studying them, interpreting them, excerpting, and modifying them in the design process. The third proposition has to do with the transformational nature of using resources to design instruction. In the process of this design work, teachers imbue resources with purposeful schemes, which reflect their understandings, intents, and goals. I believe my work contributes a fourth proposition: the characteristics and design of the resources being used mediate this work. This final proposition has implications for the design of resources for teachers. This cross-cultural conversation and continuing research provide a platform to explore and extend these ideas around the world.

References

Andrews, P. (2007). Negotiating meaning in cross-national studies of mathematics teaching: Kissing frogs to find princes. *Comparative Education, 43*(4), 489–509.

Ball, D. L., Thames, M. H., & Phelps, G. (2008). Content knowledge for teaching: What makes it special? *Journal of Teacher Education, 59*(5), 389–407.

Bezemer, J., & Kress, G. (2008). Writing in multimodal texts: A social semiotic account of designs for learning. *Written Communication, 25*(2), 166–194.

Bezemer, J., & Kress, G. (2016). *Multimodality, learning and communication: A social semiotic frame*. New York: Routledge.

Boesen, J., Helenius, O., Bergqvist, E., Bergqvist, T., Lithner, J., Palm, T., & Palmberg, B. (2014). Developing mathematical competence: From the intended to the enacted curriculum. *The Journal of Mathematical Behavior, 33*, 72–87.

Brown, M. (2009). Toward a theory of curriculum design and use: Understanding the teacher-tool relationship. In J. T. Remillard, B. A. Herbel-Eisenmann, & G. M. Lloyd (Eds.), *Mathematics teachers at work: Connecting curriculum materials and classroom instruction* (pp. 17–36). New York: Routledge.

Choppin, J. (2011). Learned adaptations: Teachers' understanding and use of curriculum resources. *Journal of Mathematics Teacher Education, 14*, 331–353.

Clarke, D. (2013). *Cultural studies in mathematics education*. Paper presented at the Eighth Congress of the European Society for Research in Mathematics Education, Antalya, Turkey.

Davis, E. A., & Krajcik, J. (2005). Designing educative curriculum materials to promote teacher learning. *Educational Researcher, 34*(3), 3–14.

Dietiker, L., & Riling, M. (2018). Design (in)tensions in mathematics curriculum. *International Journal of Educational Research, 92*, 43–52.

Fan, L., Zhu, Y., & Miao, Z. (2013). Textbook research in mathematics education: Development status and directions. *ZDM – Mathematics Education, 45*(5), 633–646.

Gueudet, G. (this volume) Studying teachers' documentation work: Emergence of a theoretical approach. In L. Trouche, G. Gueudet, & B. Pepin (Eds.). *The 'resource' approach to mathematics education*. Cham: Springer.

Gueudet, G., & Trouche, L. (2009). Towards new documentation systems for mathematics teachers? *Educational Studies in Mathematics, 71*(3), 199–218.

Gueudet, G., & Trouche, L. (Eds.). (2010). *Ressources vives, le travail documentaire des professeurs en mathématiques*. Rennes: Presses Universitaires de Rennes.

Haggarty, L., & Pepin, B. (2002). An investigation of mathematics textbooks and their use in English, French and German classrooms: Who gets an opportunity to learn what? *British Educational Research Journal, 28*(4), 567–590.

Kheong, F. H., Sharpe, P., Soon, G. K., Ramakrishnan, C., Wah, B. L. F., & Choo, M. (2010). *Math in focus: The Singapore approach by Marshall Cavendish*. Boston: Houghton Mifflin Harcourt.

Kim, O. K. (2018). Teacher decisions on lesson sequence and their impact on opportunities for students to learn. In L. Fan, L. Trouche, C. Qi, S. Rezat, & J. Visnovska (Eds.), *Research on mathematics textbooks and 'teachers resources. Advances and issues. ICME-13 monograph* (pp. 315–339). Cham: Springer.

Mason, J., & Spence, M. (1999). Beyond mere knowledge of mathematics: The importance of knowing-to act in the moment. *Educational Studies in Mathematics, 38*, 135–161.

NCTM. (1989). *Curriculum and Evaluation Standards for School Mathematics*. Reston: Author.

Osborn, M. (2004). New methodologies for comparative research? Establishing 'constants' and 'contexts' in educational experience. *Oxford Review of Education, 30*(2), 265–285.

Pepin, B. (2005). Can we compare like with like in comparative education research? – Methodological considerations in cross-cultural studies in mathematics education. In B. Hudson & J. Fragner (Eds.), *Researching Teaching and Learning of Mathematics II* (pp. 39–54). Linz: Trauner Verlag.

8 Teachers' Use of Mathematics Resources: A Look Across Cultural Boundaries   193

Pepin, B. (2018). Enhancing teacher learning with curriculum resources. In L. Fan, L. Trouche, C. Qi, S. Rezat, & J. Visnovska (Eds.), *Research on mathematics textbooks and teachers' resources. Advances and issues. ICME-13 monograph* (pp. 359–374). Cham: Springer.

Pepin, B., & Haggarty, L. (2001). Mathematics textbooks and their use in English, French, and German classrooms: a way to understand teaching and learning cultures. *ZDM – Mathematics Education, 33*(5), 158–175.

Pepin, B., Gueudet, G., & Trouche, L. (2013). Re-sourcing teachers' work and interactions: A collective perspective on resources, their use and transformation. *ZDM – Mathematics Education, 45*(7), 929–943.

Pepin, B., Choppin, J., Ruthven, K., & Sinclair, N. (2017a). Digital curriculum resources in mathematics education: Foundations for change. *ZDM – Mathematics Education, 49*(5), 645–661.

Pepin, B., Gueudet, G., & Trouche, L. (2017b). Refining teacher design capacity: Mathematics teachers' interactions with digital curriculum resources. *ZDM – Mathematics Education, 49*(5), 799–812. http://rdcu.be/tmXb.

Pepin, B., Artigue, M., Gitirana, M., Miyakawa, T., Ruthven, K., & Xu, B. (this volume) Mathematics teachers as curriculum designers: An international perspective to develop a deeper understanding of the concept. In L. Trouche, G. Gueudet, & B. Pepin (Eds.). *The 'resource' approach to mathematics education.* Cham: Springer.

Rabardel, P. (1995). Les hommes et les technologies. Une approche cognitive des instruments contemporains. Paris: Armand Colin (English version at http://ergoserv.psy.univ-paris8.fr/Site/default.asp?Act_group=1).

Remillard, J. T. (1999). Curriculum materials in mathematics education reform: A framework for examining teachers' curriculum development. *Curriculum Inquiry, 29*(3), 315–342.

Remillard, J. T. (2000). Can curriculum materials support teachers' learning? *Elementary School Journal, 100*(4), 331–350.

Remillard, J. T. (2005). Examining key concepts in research on teachers' use of mathematics curricula. *Review of Educational Research, 75*(2), 211–246.

Remillard, J. T. (2010). Modes d'engagement : comprendre les transactions des professeurs avec les ressources curriculaires en mathématiques. In G. Gueudet & L. Trouche (Eds.), *Ressources Vives. Le travail documentaire des professeurs en mathématiques* (pp. 201–216). Rennes: Presses Universitaires de Rennes.

Remillard, J. T. (2012). Modes of engagement: Understanding teachers' transactions with mathematics curriculum resources. In G. Gueudet, B. Pepin, & L. Trouche (Eds.), *From text to 'lived' resources: Mathematics curriculum materials and teacher development* (pp. 105–122). New York: Springer.

Remillard, J. T. (2013, May). *Beyond the script: Educative features of five mathematics curricula and how teachers use them.* Paper presented at the annual meeting of the American Educational Research Association, San Francisco, CA.

Remillard, J. T. (2016). Keeping an eye on the teacher in the digital curriculum race. In M. Bates & Z. Usiskin (Eds.), *Digital curricula in school mathematics* (pp. 195–204). Greenwich: Information Age.

Remillard, J. T. (2018a). Examining teachers' interactions with curriculum resource to uncover pedagogical design capacity. In L. Fan, L. Trouche, C. Qi, S. Rezat, & J. Visnovska (Eds.), *Research on mathematics textbooks and teachers' resources: Advances and issues. ICME-13 monograph* (pp. 69–88). Cham: Springer.

Remillard, J. T. (2018b). Mapping the relationship between written and enacted curriculum: Examining teachers' decision making. In G. Kaiser (Ed.), *Invited lectures from the 13th international congress on mathematical education.* New York: Springer.

Remillard, J. T., & Bryans, M. B. (2004). Teachers' orientations toward mathematics curriculum materials: Implications for teacher learning. *Journal of Research in Mathematics Education, 35*(5), 352–388.

Remillard, J., & Heck, D. J. (2014). Conceptualising the curriculum enactment process in mathematics education. *ZDM – Mathematics Education, 46*(5), 705–718.

Remillard, J. T. & Kim, O-K. (2017). Knowledge of curriculum embedded mathematics: Exploring a critical domain of teaching. Educational Studies in Mathematics 96(1), 65–81 (view online: http://rdcu.be/qajL).

Remillard, J. T., & Kim, O. K. (forthcoming). *Comparing elementary mathematics curriculum materials: Implications for teachers and teaching.* New York: Springer.

Remillard, J.T., & Van Steenbrugge, H., (in preparation). A multimodal analysis of the voice of six teacher's guides from the United States, Flanders, and Sweden.

Remillard, J.T., Van Steenbrugge, H., & Bergqvist, T. (2016, April). *A cross-cultural analysis of the voice of six Teacher's guides from three cultural contexts.* Paper presented at the annual meeting of the American Educational Research Association, Washington, DC.

Remillard, J. T., Reinke, L. R., & Kapoor, R. (2019). What is the point? Examining how curriculum materials articulate mathematical goals and how teachers steer instruction. *International Journal of Educational Research, 93*, 101–117.

Rowland, T. (2013). The knowledge quartet: The genesis and application of a framework for analyzing mathematics teaching and deepening teachers' mathematics knowledge. *Journal of Education, 1*(3), 15–43.

Shulman, L. S. (1986). Those who understand: Knowledge growth in teaching. *Educational Researcher, 15*(2), 4–14.

Shulman, L. S. (1987). Knowledge and teaching: Foundations of the new reform. *Harvard Educational Review, 57*(1), 1–21.

Sleep, L. (2009). *Teaching to the mathematical point: Knowing and using mathematics in teaching.* Unpublished PhD. University of Michigan, USA.

Sleep, L. (2012). The work of steering instruction toward the mathematical point a decomposition of teaching practice. *American Educational Research Journal, 49*(5), 935–970.

Stein, M. K., & Kim, G. (2009). The role of mathematics curriculum materials in large-scale urban reform: An analysis of demands and opportunities for teacher learning. In J. T. Remillard, B. A. Herbel-Eisenmann, & G. M. Lloyd (Eds.), *Mathematics teachers at work: Connecting curriculum materials and classroom instruction* (pp. 37–55). New York: Routledge.

Stigler, J., & Hiebert, J. (1999). *The teaching gap: Best ideas from the world's teachers for improving education in the classroom.* New York: The Free Press.

Ulrich, C. (2015). Stages in constructing and coordinating units additively and multiplicatively (Part 1). *For the Learning of Mathematics, 35*(3), 2–7.

Vygotsky, L. S. (1978). *Thought and language.* Cambridge: MIT Press. (Original work published 1934).

Warwick, D., & Osherson, S. (Eds.). (1973). *Comparative research methods: An overview.* Englewood Cliffs: Prentice Hall.

Wertsch, J. V. (1998). *Mind as action.* New York: Oxford University Press.

Part III
New Resources Needed, Perspectives for Further Research

Chapter 9
Teachers' Resource Systems: Their Constitution, Structure and Evolution

**Jana Trgalová, Moustapha Sokhna, Cibelle Assis,
Mohammad Dames Alturkmani, Elisângela Espindola, Rim Hammoud,
and Karima Sayah**

Abstract An important facet of teachers' work, done outside the classroom, involves searching for, selecting, and gathering resources for lesson and assessment preparation, for inquiring about institutional requirements and constraints, and for professional development. Teachers' work with resources undergoes deep changes in the era of the development of digital technology that results in a profusion of digital resources available over the Internet. Moreover, various communities of teachers producing and sharing resources emerge, which impacts strongly their work with resources. This chapter contributes to the investigation of teachers' resource systems. Based on the contributions and discussions in Working Group 1 and drawing on the documentational approach to didactics, it aims at providing an insight into three aspects of teachers' resource systems: their constitution, structure, and evolution.

Keywords Resource system · Constitution of a resource system · Structure of a resource system · Evolution of a resource system · Documentational approach to didactics

---

J. Trgalová (✉) · K. Sayah
S2HEP EA4148, Claude Bernard University, Lyon, France
e-mail: jana.trgalova@univ-lyon1.fr

M. Sokhna
Cheikh Anta Diop University, Dakar, Senegal

C. Assis
Federal University of Paraíba, Rio Tinto, Paraiba, Brazil

M. D. Alturkmani
Ecole Normale Supérieure, Lyon, France

E. Espindola
Federal Rural University of Pernambuco, Recife, Brazil

R. Hammoud
Lebanese University, Beyrouth, Lebanon

© Springer Nature Switzerland AG 2019
L. Trouche et al. (eds.), *The 'Resource' Approach to Mathematics Education*,
Advances in Mathematics Education,
https://doi.org/10.1007/978-3-030-20393-1_9

9.1 Introduction

An important facet of teachers' work, done outside the classroom, involves searching for, selecting, and gathering resources for lesson and assessment preparation, for inquiring about institutional requirements and constraints, and for professional development. Teachers' work with resources undergoes deep changes in the era of the development of digital technology that results in a profusion of digital resources available over the Internet (Gueudet, Chap. 2, this book). Moreover, various collectives of teachers producing and sharing resources emerge, which impacts strongly their work with resources. Therefore, studying teachers' interactions with resources gains more and more interest in research in mathematics education, leading to the development of specific theoretical and methodological approaches.

Working group 1 (WG1) focused on issues related to this aspect of teachers' work paying particular attention to teachers' resource systems. Indeed, according to Gueudet and Trouche (2009), teachers' resources are not isolated but rather form a more or less structured system. The ways of how teachers constitute their resource systems were an issue tackled in WG1. Novice teachers, as well as teachers needing to teach a new topic for which they may not have yet adequate resources, provide a particularly relevant window on processes of resource system constitution. However, we consider also selecting a resource and integrating it into an existing resource system as a process of resource system constitution. Therefore, investigating the ways teachers search for, select, and integrate resources into existing resource systems, the origin of selected resources and criteria used to select these resources, and teachers' representations of "good" resources contribute to getting deeper insight into the processes of *constitution of teachers' resource systems*. Gueudet (Chap. 2, this book) highlights methodological difficulties when studying teachers' resource systems and claims in particular that "the issue of the structure of document system and resource system remains unresolved" (p. 23). Attempting to fill this gap, exploring the *structure of teachers' resource systems* was one of the aims of WG1 by investigating the components of the system (e.g., nature of the resources, their place in the system), the roles that some specific resources may play in teachers' documentation work, and the relations between components in the system. The integration of a new resource into an existing resource system impacts the latter, and consequently, the resource system evolves. *Evolution of teachers' resource system* was another aspect of interest for WG1 that led to explore how teachers' resource systems evolve and what are the levers of their evolution.

In the working group, 18 papers and 3 posters were presented and discussed. All of them addressed one or more of the three aspects related to resource systems mentioned above, namely, constitution, structure, and evolution of teachers' resource systems. This chapter is therefore organized around these three aspects, although we are aware that in reality, these aspects are rather related to each other and hardly separable. Section 9.2 outlines the theoretical frameworks and concepts used in the contributions. The contributions with respect to resource systems' constitution, structure, and evolution are synthesized in Sect. 9.3. The three subsequent Sects.

9.4, 9.5, and 9.6, are contributions from WG1 that help develop and discuss these three issues:

- The contribution of Cibelle Assis and Elisângela Espindola (Sect. 9.4), "Constitution of resource systems by prospective teachers – process of metamorphosis," is based on two WG1 contributions (Assis et al. 2018, Espindola and Trgalová 2018) and develops the notion of metamorphosis as process of constituting resource system of beginning teachers.
- The contribution of Rim Hammoud and Mohammad Alturkmani (Sect. 9.5), "Teachers' resource systems and their structure," extends the WG1 contribution (Hammoud and Alturkmani 2018) to shed light on structuring elements in teachers' resource systems – pivotal and structuring mother-resources.
- The contribution of Karima Sayah, (Sect. 9.6), "Evolution of a resource system: articulation of dynamic and static dimensions," extending the WG1 contribution (Sayah 2018a), mainly addresses the evolution of a teacher's resource system triggered by the integration of a new resource.

Concluding Sect. 9.7 summarizes main outcomes of the WG1 and outlines some perspectives in terms of needs for further theoretical and methodological developments within the documentational approach to didactics.

9.2 Theoretical Framework

The main theoretical framework referred to in this chapter is the documentational approach to didactics (DAD) developed by Gueudet and Trouche (2008, 2009, 2012). Gueudet (Chap. 2, this book) gives an overview of the emergence of the approach a decade ago and relates its evolution. In this chapter, the reader can find the definitions of the core concepts – documentation work, resources, documents, and documentational genesis – and we do not recall them here. We focus on the concept of resource system, which is at the center of this chapter, and present other notions related to this concept when studying the constitution, structure, and evolution of teachers' resource systems.

9.2.1 Resource System

From the outset of the development of the DAD, Gueudet and Trouche (2009) suggest that "each resource must be viewed as a part of a wider 'set of resources'" (p. 200); such a set is named *resource system*. According to Ruthven (Chap. 3, this book),

> [t]he central idea of a 'system' is one of organisation: the term may refer to some structure resulting from multiple entities being organised to form a functioning whole, or to some scheme or method which provides a basis for such organisation (p. 44).

The idea of a structure of a teacher's set of resources is stressed by Gueudet et al. (2013) who claim that "the word 'system' is purposefully chosen to emphasize that this system is highly structured, the structure being linked, more or less explicitly, to teacher activity" (p. 1004). In this chapter, we adopt the definition of a teacher's resource system that has been recently introduced by Trouche et al. (2018), viewing it as "the set formed by all the resources used by the teacher" (p. 40).

Following Ruthven (op. cit.), teachers' resource systems are composed of "multiple entities" (resources) organized "to form a functioning whole." In the attempt to highlight the structure of a resource system, Gueudet et al. (op. cit.) suggest that the latter is linked to teachers' professional activity. Nevertheless, defining relevant activity families seems to be a complex issue, as Gueudet reports (Chap. 2, this book). Indeed, while in the early studies, three families were identified ("design and organize the teaching," "participate to the school's organization," "reflect on his/her practice"), recently, nine families were brought to the fore:

1. Reflecting on his/her practice.
2. Planning.
3. Preparing and setting up introductory activities.
4. Preparing and setting up syntheses.
5. Preparing and setting up drill and practice.
6. Preparing and setting up assessment.
7. Manage the class and follow the students.
8. Participate in the school life.
9. Participate in collective work out-of-class (ibid., p. 27).

However, Gueudet admits that these activities have not been used by other researchers. In our report, we therefore limit ourselves to highlighting families of activities researchers consider when studying teachers' interactions with resources, without attempting to suggest any classification of these.

9.2.2 Constitution of a Resource System

In their daily practice, teachers develop a resource system that they constantly modify motivated by different goals (Gueudet and Trouche 2010), such as a desire of combining resources for (re)designing a lesson, (re)elaborating a task, or an assessment. These goals are related to different and specific moments of a lesson or related to different events of teachers' professional trajectory. This work is a dynamic process which includes searching for, selecting, and integrating resources whose result is always a process of *constitution of a resource system*.

By *constitution* of a resource system, we mean the *origin* of this system. This concept considers both constitution of a new resource system, in case of a novice teacher or a teacher starting teaching a new topic, and integration of new resources into the existing resource system. Therefore, our study on constitution of a resource system does not consider the impact of the integration of a resource on the teacher's resource system (this aspect is considered as evolution of the resource system, see Sect. 9.2.4) neither the components, roles of the resources, or relations between resources (these aspects are considered as constituting a structure of a resource system, see Sect. 9.2.3). Instead, we are interested in understanding how this process develops in the daily practice of the teachers considering their *contexts* and *sources*, what *selection criteria* are used for selecting and integrating resources into existing resource systems and what are teachers' *representations of the resources* that motivate their documentation work.

In relation to the constitution of teachers' resource systems, the concept of *metamorphosis* emerged in the WG1 discussions. It was introduced by Assis et al. (2018) who observed a process of a constitution of systems of resources by future teachers from resources they used during their initial teacher education. This concept is further elaborated and illustrated in two case studies in Sect. 9.4.

9.2.3 Structure of a Resource System

Based on the conceptualization of a resource system (see earlier), when investigating the *structure of a resource system*, we are interested in the *nature of resources* that compose the system, the *roles* resources play in teachers' documentation work, and the *relationships* between these resources.

Regarding the types of resources, teachers' resource systems are composed of a variety of resources. Gueudet and Trouche distinguish between *material* resources (e.g., teacher's notes in a book) and *nonmaterial* resources (e.g., verbal interactions with colleagues or with students); the latter are more difficult to access for a researcher. Remillard and Heck (2014) use the term *instructional materials* to refer to "resources designed to support or supplement instruction, including textbooks, curriculum guides, descriptions of mathematical tasks, and instructional software," which distinguishes them from other resources that were not designed for educational purposes. These conceptualizations show that there is no commonly accepted classification of resources, and they respond rather to the research purposes.

Within a resource system, some resources play a specific role. Gueudet (Chap. 2, this book) claims that "a given resource could be used by the teachers for different aims, corresponding to different activity families." Resources that are mobilized in several families of activity are called *pivotal resources*. In her research, Hammoud (2012) feels the necessity to distinguish between resources that are used by a teacher and resources that she produces in her documentation work, which leads the author to introduce two concepts: *mother-resources* that designate a set of available resources a teacher uses in order to prepare her teaching and *daughter-resource* that is a resource the teacher has elaborated from re-combining mother-resources and that is ready to be implemented in her class. Alturkmani (2015) introduces the concept of *structuring mother-resource,* which is a mother-resource (as defined by Hammoud) that contributes to structuring a teacher's documentation work from two points of view: first, it is around this resource that a daughter-resource devoted to

9.2.4 Evolution of a Resource System

The various meanings of the notions of resource, document, and system retained in this book converge on the idea that the term evolution is inherent to documentation systems. Three main reasons underpin this claim. The first reason will result in substituting the notion of *documentation system* for the term *resource system*. Indeed, according to Gueudet and Trouche (2009), unlike Ruthven (2007) who considers the resource system as an element of what he calls "the structuring context of the classroom practice," a different perspective should be taken by looking at the development of documents from the resources. This leads the authors to consider a *documentation system* instead of a *resource system*. The authors also claim that teachers develop a documentation system whose structure follows that of their professional activity. The second reason is based on a point which, according to Gueudet and Trouche (2008), is fundamental in the DAD, namely, that documentation systems are not rigid and they evolve permanently over time, in a dynamics fueled by documentational geneses.

The concept of documentational genesis allows to theoretically establish the articulation of and the continuity between the institutional processes of the design of artifacts or resources and the continuation of the design within the activities of use, resulting in an instrument or a document. *Instrumentation* processes participate in the overall design process by entering into a cycle: operating modes (planned by the designers), schemes of use (developed by the users), and new operating modes provided by the designers based on the schemes of use. *Instrumentalization* processes are part of a cycle parallel to the previous one: constituent functions of the artifact or resource (defined by the designers), constituted functions (by the users), and inscription of these constituted functions in a new generation of artifacts or resources (by the designers) (Fig. 9.1).

The third reason is that the evolution of the documentation systems and the development of teachers' knowledge feed one another, and it is the concept of *documentation mediation* that makes it possible to think of and analyze it (Sokhna and Trouche 2015). The authors introduce the term *documentation mediation* by extending that of *instrumental mediation*, which, for Rabardel (1999b, 2002), appears as a central concept for thinking and analyzing the modalities by which instruments influence the construction of knowledge. Indeed, Rabardel (2002) points out that:

> an instrument is unanimously considered as an intermediary entity, a medium term, or even an intermediary world between two entities: the subject, actor, user of the instrument and the object of the action. [...] The instrument's intermediary position makes it the mediator of relations between subject and object. It constitutes an intermediary world whose main

9 Teachers' Resource Systems: Their Constitution, Structure and Evolution

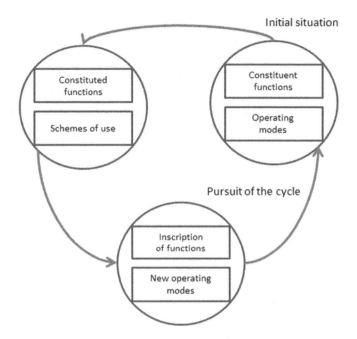

Fig. 9.1 Cycle of documentational genesis, according to Condamines et al. (2003, p. 8)

feature is being adapted to both subject and object. This adaptation is in terms of material as well as cognitive and semiotic properties in line with the type of activity in which the instrument is inserted or is destined to be inserted. (p. 63).

Rabardel calls *instrumental mediation* this mediation between the subject and the object. In line with these considerations, we complete the documentational approach theorization by introducing the notion of *documentation mediation* (Fig. 9.2) as a mediation of relationship between a teacher and a resource system through a document.

Moreover, according to Rabardel (1999a, 2002), artifacts or resources should not be analyzed as things but in the way they mediate the use. The author claims that the mediation triangle between subject, object, and tools and signs is only the tip of the iceberg. Less visible activity mediators – rules, community, and division of labor – constitute the foundation of the activity model proposed by Engeström (1987) within the activity theory (Fig. 9.3). The system is in continuous transformation, and the activity of the system is constantly rebuilding itself.

Rabardel (2002) describes mediation in four forms: *epistemic mediation* that is oriented toward the knowledge of the object, *pragmatic mediation* that is oriented toward the action, *reflective mediation* that is oriented toward the subject itself, and finally *interpersonal mediation* that is realized between subjects (Fig. 9.4). We refer to epistemic mediation when the object of the activity (in the sense of the theory of activity, Engeström 1987) is related to "preparing a lesson"; the mediations are pragmatic in the analysis of classroom situations; in the framework of a collaborative

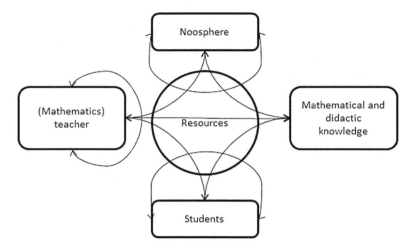

Fig. 9.2 Main documentation mediations between proactive noosphere (Chevallard (1982) calls noosphere the whole body of the society that presides over the didactic transposition: all actors intervening at the intersection of the education system and society, especially – and above all – parents, scientists, policymakers), the teacher, and the students (Sokhna 2006, p. 61)

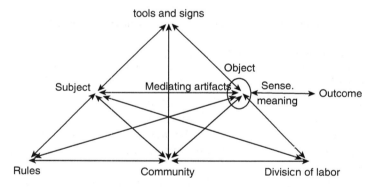

Fig. 9.3 The structure of an activity system (Engeström 1987, p. 78)

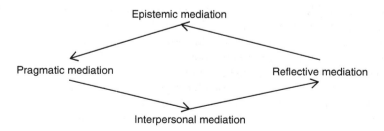

Fig. 9.4 Model of coordination of the four forms of mediation

9 Teachers' Resource Systems: Their Constitution, Structure and Evolution

work, the mediation is interpersonal, and finally, when the object of the activity is assessment of the teaching and learning, the mediation is reflective. These documentation mediations allow explaining and justifying methodological elements relying on DAD, such as reflective investigation (see Chap. 2, this book).

The documentation mediation, which should constitute the base of the documentation approach, is not often developed in mathematics education. Yet, in education, documentation mediations are at the heart of processes: at the upper didactic level (see Table 9.1 below), from the design of curricula to teachers who, after analyzing and interpreting the curricula, collect and design resources to "do their lessons," and at the lower didactic level, in the enactment of the resources by a teacher in her class and in the assessment phases (Chevallard 1998).

The study of evolution leading to identifying invariants in an evolutionary process is at the heart of the didactic activity. Brousseau (1997) considers introducing a mathematical notion not as a mere reformulation of knowledge to be taught, but through interacting with a system antagonist to the subject: a *milieu*. The *milieu* is thus a system that appropriately responds to the actions of the subject and forces her

Table 9.1 The structure of the *milieu* according to (Margolinas 2004, p. 81): M stands for *milieu*, E for student, P for teacher, and S for situation

M_{+3} M-Construction		P_{+3} P-Noosphere	S_{+3} Noosphere situation	
M_{+2} M-Project		P_{+2} P-Constructor	S_{+2} Situation of construction	Upper didactic level (niveau sur-didactique)
M_{+1} M-Didactic	E_{+1} E-Reflexive	P_{+1} P-Projecting	S_{+1} Situation of project	
M_0 M-Learning	$E_{0:}$ E-Student The student is learning	P_0 P-Teacher for the student	S_0 Didactic situation	
M_{-1} M-Reference	E_{-1} E-Learner The learner is acting and thinks about her action	P_{-1} P-Teacher in action	S_{-1} A-didactic situation	
M_{-2} M-Objective	E_{-2} E-Acting The student is acting and thinks about her action	P_{-2} P-Observing teacher	S_{-2} Reference situation	Lower didactic level (niveau sous-didactique)
M_{-3} M-Material (Usual problem)	E_{-3} E-Objective The student is the actor		$S_{-3}:$ Objective situation	

to mobilize the knowledge expected by the teacher. To better take into account the modeling of the evolution of the teacher's activities in the theory of didactical situations, Margolinas (2004) proposes *bottom-up* and *top-down* analyses of the teacher's situation. Table 9.1 suggested by Margolinas (ibid., p. 81), to which we add the different *milieus* of the student as stated by Brousseau (1986), as well as those of the teacher, is an illustration of the evolution of both resources and usages.

In this table, each line designates a cyclical process of the genesis (Table 9.1) of a milieu M_i, m_{i1} representing its initial state and its final state corresponding to m_{i3}. The transition from m_{i1} to m_{i3} will be dictated by m_{i2} which corresponds to the intermediate stage with the instrumentation and instrumentalization phases. To follow the cyclical evolution, m_{i3} then becomes $m_{i+1\,1}$, that is, the initial state of M_{i+1}. Thus for each m_{i1}, $i > -3$, the constituent functions of the *milieu* are $m_{i-1\,3}$ and the effective activity of the student E_i in interaction with $m_{i-1\,3}$ ($m_{-3\,1}$ being the material *milieu*). The knowledge shown or used by the teacher to manage the *milieu* constitutes a proof of a good level of her instrumentation.

However, it should be noted that the teacher works most often on a global organization, i.e., the activities of preparation do not often stop at one session but are related to several sequences or even several programs. The course that the teacher prepares for a level n is based on courses prepared at the level n-1 and allows to prepare the level $n + 1$. Thus, to complete the analysis tools present in Table 9.1, which draw on the lesson preparation with basically an evolution of a documentation system through epistemic and pragmatic mediations, it is necessary to take into account the interpersonal and reflective mediations.

9.3 Overview of the WG1 Contributions

In this section, we present a synthetic overview of the WG1 contributions organized around the three above-mentioned themes related to teachers' resource systems, namely, their constitution, structure, and evolution. For each of the themes, we recall the research questions that framed the group discussions and that structure the presentation of the issues raised and of the main findings.

9.3.1 Constitution of the Resource Systems

This section is devoted to discussing the issues related to the constitution of teachers' resource systems (as defined earlier). We start by recalling the questions related to this theme proposed to the WG1 participants and synthesizing WG1 contributions organized around these questions:

1. How do teachers search for resources and where do they get them from?
2. What criteria do they (explicitly or implicitly) use to select new resources?

9 Teachers' Resource Systems: Their Constitution, Structure and Evolution

3. How are these new resources integrated into the existing resource system?
4. What are teachers' representations of "good" resources? Do these representations differ according to the subject matter (mathematics, physics, etc.), school level (primary, secondary, tertiary), type of activities (lesson preparation, assessment, etc.), or other factors?

These questions address the following three topics: the origin of the selected resources (question 1), processes of selection and integration of resources (questions 2 and 3), and teachers' representations of "good" resources (question 4). In the sequel, we report how the theme of the *constitution of teachers' resource systems* was addressed in the WG1, highlighting aspects related to this topic and the above-mentioned questions.

9.3.1.1 The Origin of the Selected Resources

Here, we aim to answer the question: How do teachers search for resources and where do they get them from?

Analyzing the set of contributions, we observe that teachers can constitute their resource system influenced by the context in which they are engaged. It means that they get resources available or accepted from institutions or communities using this context as source for the constitution of their resource system. In order to illustrate this fact, we mention the contributions of Baştürk-Şahin and Tapan-Broutin (2018b), Hammoud (2018), Hamoud and Alturkmani (2018), Messaoui (2018), Espíndola and Trgalová (2018), and Assis et al. (2018).

Baştürk-Şahin and Tapan-Broutin (2018b) studied the activity of lesson preparation of four experienced Turkish mathematics teachers. Analyzing teachers' lesson documents, the authors mentioned *outer* factors which were taken into consideration by the teachers in order to develop this professional activity: country's national education strategies, exam system, and school instruction methods. Hammoud (2018) mentioned, as an example, the participation in a virtual community as an element for the constitution (and evolution) of teachers' resource system. In fact, the author highlights from the developed research that "the resources exchanged within the community seem to be the heart of [the teacher's] resources system" (ibid., p. 72).

Hammoud and Alturkmani (2018) compare two case studies in which they observed two teachers teaching physics and chemistry in France and two Lebanese chemistry teachers, respectively. They found differences in teachers' interactions with resources since the relationship with disciplines, the teaching activities, and the curriculum are not the same in both cases. They highlight how the curriculum in each country influences the resources of the teachers: in the case of French teachers, the resources used for teaching physics and chemistry are related to the design and implementation of experimental activities. These resources seem marginal for Lebanese teachers who use resources for teaching chemistry only and do not have laboratories necessary for implementing experimental activities at their disposal in the public schools.

Therefore, some WG1 contributions consider specific contexts where the constitution of a resource system is related to particular situations experienced by teachers for which they develop resources according to specific goals. In this case, such a set of new resources can give birth to a resource system. For example, Messaoui (2018) mentions the curriculum reform in France and the introduction of new topics, such as computational thinking in mathematics and technology. According to the author, this fact motivated secondary school teachers to search for new resources, especially digital ones. As a result, a new resource system must be constituted with resources that are specific to teaching computational thinking. Espíndola and Trgalová (2018) and Assis et al. (2018) explore how prospective teachers constituted their first resource system for teaching during a teacher training. In both cases, the authors observed the tutors' resources (i.e., resources of their teachers or supervisors from school or university) as an element of constitution of prospective teachers' resource systems in the context of the teacher education.

9.3.1.2 Selection and Integration of Resources

We address here two questions: What criteria do teachers (explicitly or implicitly) use to select new resources? How are these new resources integrated into the existing resource system?

Fofana and Sokhna (2018) point out that, in some countries, teachers can choose with more or less freedom programs and resources. In both cases, we are interested in deepening the understanding of the processes of integration of resources into teachers' resource systems through the criteria of resource selection. Although the criteria of selection and integration of resources are not at the center of the majority of the contributions, we refer to the research studies developed by Sokhna (2018), Fofana and Sokhna (2018), Baştürk-Şahin and Tapan-Broutin (2018a), Hammoud and Alturkmani (2018), Sayac (2018), Messaoui (2018), Sayah (2018a), and Salinas-Hernandez et al. (2018), in which criteria of selection of resources are mentioned more or less explicitly.

Analyzing the transition of the candidates into teachers and considering before and after a teaching experience, Baştürk-Şahin and Tapan-Broutin (2018a) observed a change in the criteria of selecting resources of these teachers passing from the quality of the visual aspect to the appropriateness with respect to the exam system. In other words, a resource must be in accordance with the exam system, and therefore, it is a criterion of choice of a resource. The same phenomenon was observed by Hammoud and Alturkmani (2018) who considered the case of textbooks. In their study, this resource was central for teachers at the beginning of their career. The authors explain this finding by the fact that these curricular resources constitute, for the teachers, a means to follow appropriately and apply the curriculum that is prescribed to them.

The study developed by Sayac (2018) highlights that, despite a large amount of available resources including Internet resources (45%), textbook (30%), and teacher's guide (27%), a majority of primary school teachers in France (73%) refer primarily to the skills targeted by official mathematics programs for producing assessment documents. It seems that the criteria of choice related to skills are more coherent with the goal of producing an assessment.

Sayah (2018a) observed a teacher's activity of selecting a Sésamath multiple choice questionnaire (MCQ) resource available online in order to develop an assessment about spatial geometry. This resource was chosen for various reasons such as diversity of kinds of activities presented in the Sésamath resource; the similarity of the subject to the program, making it possible to consider certain notions in the continuity of the program; the motivation that MCQ can enhance in students to reflect about the subject while they analyze the multiple answers. In this case, we observe criteria of selection of the MCQ resources of Sésamath linked to the curricular, instrumental, and documentational aspects.

Integrating a new resource into an existing resource system is, in some cases, difficult even for an experienced teacher. For example, Salinas-Hernandez et al. (2018) evoke a case of a teacher (former chemical engineer) with 40 years of teaching experience and regularly taking courses in the use of technology who was not able to take advantage of the dynamism of the GeoGebra environment to go beyond the traditional way of teaching and promote new mathematical knowledge. GeoGebra was a new resource, totally different from other resources in the teacher's resource system, which may explain the difficulty of its integration. This finding is in accordance with Gueudet's (2013) claim that "a new resource is easily integrated if it fits naturally with resources already present in the system" (p. 99, our translation). This case calls attention to a deeper perspective of the integration of a new resource into an existing resource system: how a teacher uses the new resource rather than simply observing the addition of a new one in the system.

Referring to Choppin (2005), Sokhna (2018) suggests two kinds of parameters of resource quality that can be used by teachers for choosing their resources: internal parameters that are associated with the resource function – reference, instrumental, ideological, cultural, documentational, and external parameters that are associated with the resource model – reusability, adaptability, collaboration, accessibility, sustainability, pedagogical relevance, and interoperability. This perspective illuminates a point of view about the criteria of selection and therefore of integration of resources that can be considered in the study about constitution of a resource system. Regarding these parameters, from the previously cited contributions, the internal parameters appear as predominant in the teachers' criteria of selection, varying between referential and instrumental functions.

9.3.1.3 Teachers' Representation of "Good" Resources

We address the set of questions: What are teachers' representations of "good" resources? Do these representations differ according to the subject matter (mathematics, physics, etc.), school level (primary, secondary, tertiary), type of activities (lesson preparation, assessment, etc.), or other factors?

We search for elements of answers to these questions in the contributions of Fofana and Sokhna (2018), Jameau and Le Hénaff (2018), and Van Steenbrugge et al. (2018). In general, this set of contributions indicates some elements for what "good" resources means: they can be conceived as convenient resources for teachers considering their daily practice (goals), context (instructional, professional), and also the possibility to transform them continuously according to each professional situation.

For example, Fofana and Sokhna (2018) mention that in Senegal there are no official resources for accompanying the development of the program. Consequently, teachers choose resources that they consider appropriate and coherent with the program. In addition, the authors claim that with the development of the resources on the web, some teachers choose resources that come from other cultures and other programs.

Jameau and Le Hénaff (2018) explore the use of resources within the context of Content and Language Integrated Learning (CLIL), which involves teaching of chemistry in English at high school in France. They investigate what are the criteria that guided a teacher in choosing a video resource, associated with the use of a fill-in-the gaps text. According to the authors, the criteria for choosing these "good" resources for CLIL teaching are mainly oriented toward the will to make her students practice spoken English (fluency in communication). In addition, the authors mention that the choice is partly in line with the institutional expectations as regards CLIL teaching, which is often described as an opportunity to develop students' fluency in a foreign language.

Van Steenbrugge et al. (2018) also study teachers' use of instructional resources from a cross-cultural perspective: the cases of Sweden and Flanders. In this contribution, the representation and use of the curriculum resources in both contexts, their similarities and differences, are explored. Both Swedish and Flanders teachers rely on their printed curriculum resources for sequencing of the content and to ensure coverage of the curricular aims and objectives as stated by the governing agencies. In addition, Swedish and Flanders teachers adapt, sometimes replace, and complement their main printed curriculum resources differently, based on a number of factors. In Flanders, for instance, teachers working with the curriculum program, in which lessons typically address more than one content domain, consistently critiqued how lessons were organized and modified the sequence within chapters, and structured lessons and even tests so that lessons and tests relate to a unique content domain. According to the authors, teachers related this to their experiences as to how students best learn mathematics, to their personal preferences (e.g., it is easy to work with a resource that has structured lessons per content domain), and stance to learning (e.g., structure is very important for students' learning). Adaptations in

Sweden reflect the prevailing practice (teachers working with the new curriculum resource have a tendency not to skip the tasks and exercises that students can work with on their own), and teachers working with the traditional curriculum resource extend or add a lesson instructional phase.

9.3.2 The Structure of Teachers' Resource Systems

This section is devoted to investigating the structure of teachers' resource systems. As we mentioned earlier, studying the structure of a resource system leads to focus on the *components* or *entities* composing the system, i.e., the various resources within the system, their *roles*, and the *relations* that organize these entities in a system. We start by exploring in particular the following research questions, based on a review of the WG1 contributions

1. How do the teachers structure their resource systems? Are there central or pivotal resources and what is their role?
2. What is the place of curricular resources (prescribed curriculum) and textbooks in teachers' resource systems?

From the brief outline of the core concepts presented in Sect. 9.2, we retain that teachers' activity systems and resource systems are inseparable. Studying teachers' resource systems thus requires identifying goals of teachers' activities. According to Gueudet (2013), analyzing teachers' resource systems is rather complex and requires a specific research methodology. Gueudet and Trouche (2010) elaborated such a methodology, called reflexive investigation, that associates teachers with data gathering, as they are the only ones having access to their resources and to activities carried out with these resources (Gueudet 2013). Research studies employing reflective investigation methodology are therefore qualitative, focusing on a limited number of teachers. This is the case of most of WG1 contributions. Although general results are difficult to draw from such studies, in what follows, we report findings that allow to get a deeper insight into the structure of teachers' resource systems, to highlight the existence of structuring elements in these systems, and to understand factors that impact their structure. Research studies discussed within the WG1 focus on documentational work of teachers teaching various subject matters (mathematics, physics, chemistry, language) in various countries. We can therefore compare to some extent teachers' resource systems and observe similarities and differences according to the cultural and institutional contexts.

9.3.2.1 Nature of Resources in Teachers' Resource Systems

In this section, we aim at highlighting what resources teachers use and in which professional activities.

Van Steenbrugge et al. (2018) report about a research they conducted in Sweden and Flanders (Belgium) aiming at better understanding what resources teachers use when they plan for and enact lessons. They focus especially on instructional resources, i.e., the resources designed to support curriculum enactment (p. 117) that include both "curriculum resources that sequence a particular content such as student textbooks and teacher's guides" and other resources "such as digital (online) applications" (ibid.). The authors found that both Swedish and Flanders teachers use their printed curriculum resource, which they complement by other resources, some of which are digital. The authors report a difference in the use of digital resources in Swedish and Flanders teachers: whereas most of the Swedish teachers use digital resources, which is supported by nationwide professional development projects, the use of digital resources by Flanders teachers, who are not supported by such programs, seems to depend on teachers' stance toward digital resources.

Fofana and Sokhna (2018) highlight that resources designed by educational agencies take a special place in teachers' resource systems, as they subject the teachers' work. This is the case of the prescribed curriculum, that is, the teachers' *primary resource*, according to the authors: "it shapes practices and make the teaching content official" (p. 65, our translation). However, for planning lessons, teachers use also secondary resources, such as textbooks or digital resources. The authors claim that some of these resources come from sources that are foreign to the national educational system, and thus, they do not adequately interpret the curriculum of this system, which may lead to inconsistency between the prescribed and the enacted curriculum.

Attempting to describe a structure of teachers' resource system, Sayah's (2018a) investigation approaches the latter from both static and dynamic points of view. The dynamic point of view leads to observing teachers' actions on resources, i.e., her documentation work, while the static point of view focuses on the nature of the mobilized resources. Sayah (2018b) introduces the term *primary resource* to refer to "any living institutional resource – what a teacher needs – to fulfill her didactic function" (p. 52, our translation). Note that the meaning of primary resource is different from the one used by Fofana and Sokhna (2018). The author specifies that these resources come from educational agencies (ministry of education) and "cannot be wronged or modified by the teacher" (ibid.). Textbook or teacher's guide are examples of primary resources in Sayah's sense. The author uses the term *intermediate* resource to refer to "any resource the teacher creates, designs from mother and primary resources" (p. 53, our translation), mother-resources referring to resources other than primary the teacher uses. According to the author, intermediate resources evolve over time within the system: they are created, modified, recombined, and adjusted, until they become *stabilized*. Thus, Sayah uses the terms primary, stabilized, and mother-resources, which she calls *resource taxonomy* from the static point of view (p. 52).

Textbooks and curricula appear as the most common resources in teachers' resource systems according to WG1 contributions. Other types of resources are also reported. For example, Hammoud and Alturkmani (2018), who conducted case studies with French physics teachers and with Lebanese chemistry teachers, found that interactions between a teacher and her colleagues or her students nourished the documentation work of the teachers interviewed. These resources can have various forms: discussions with colleagues and their resources, interactions with students in a classroom or with students taking private courses with the teacher, resources related to courses, or assessment of the latter. In the case of these teachers, such (nonmaterial) resources played a role of pivotal and structuring mother-resources (we further elaborate on this issue in Sect. 9.5). In her study of a virtual community of Lebanese chemistry teachers, Hammoud (2018) identified a variety of resources shared by the community: "photos, videos, digital textbooks, websites, course summary, lesson models, annual progression, exercises, assessments..." (p. 72).

Sayac (2018) investigates primary teachers' resource systems related to the activity of designing assessment for their mathematics classes. Based on the analysis of 600 responses to an online questionnaire, the author points out that resources used by teachers to design assessment are numerous and varied, among which the most widely used ones are curriculum (cited by 73% of teachers), Internet resources (45%), textbooks (30%), and teacher's guides (27%).

9.3.2.2 Central or Pivotal Resources and Their Roles

Several studies identified particular resources in teachers' resource systems playing specific role in teachers' activities. In their cross-cultural study, Van Steenbrugge et al. (2018) found that printed curriculum resources play a central role when teachers in Sweden and Flanders (Belgium) prepare their mathematics lessons; the authors call it "central curriculum resource" (p. 119). This resource is used by both Swedish and Flanders teachers "for sequencing of the content and to ensure coverage of the curricular aims and objectives as stated by the governing agencies."

Hammoud and Alturkmani (2018) highlight a specific role of interactions with colleagues and students in teachers' documentation work. In the case of a French physics-chemistry teacher, they observed that this teacher's discussions with two colleagues from a research group named SESAMES and their resources contributed to the development of the teacher's physics knowledge and supported the design of his daughter-resource that has a similar structure as SESAMES. The authors call such resources (discussions with peers and their resources) *structuring mother-resources* in physics. According to the authors, these resources appear also as pivotal in the teacher's resource system "since he relies essentially on this type of resources to organize his teaching in physics or chemistry" (p. 77). Similarly, in the case of two Lebanese chemistry teachers, interactions with students, especially those whom they tutored privately, as well as their productions, contributed to the development of teachers' professional knowledge and new daughter-resources for chemistry teaching. These resources thus constitute *structuring mother-resources* in chemistry. The authors stress that interactions also appear as a pivotal resource "because they are, on the one hand, involved in several types of teachers' activities: the preparation of lessons, exercises and assessments. On the other hand, more than an enrichment of the resource system, they seem to help restructure and reorganize the resource system of these teachers" (ibid.).

9.3.2.3 Place of Textbooks and Curricular Resources in Teachers' Resource Systems

As mentioned in the previous section, textbooks and other curricular resources have a privileged place in teachers' resource systems, at least at the beginning of their career, regardless of the subject matter and country. Given that curricular resources are in general aligned with the prescribed curriculum, this claim seems not to be surprising.

Thus, Assis et al. (2018) report that teaching experiences of a Brazilian prospective teacher whose documentation work they studied "were sourced by the work on and with particular resources (lesson plan model, textbooks, curriculum resources)" (p. 41). Espindola et al. (2018) also observed textbook and curricular resources besides specific websites in a resource system of an experienced Brazilian mathematics teacher. Baştürk-Şahin and Tapan-Broutin (2018b) cite textbooks as one of the foremost resources Turkish mathematics teachers use while preparing their lessons. The fact that textbooks are among the main resources teachers rely upon led Brazilian educational authorities to set up, in 2011, a National Textbook Program establishing an evaluative process of textbooks, which allows to approve or exclude textbooks and, at the same time, gives rise to the textbook guides that are intended to assist the teachers in the choice of books (Lima 2018).

Hammoud and Alturkmani (2018) moderate somehow this general claim about the place of the textbook in resource systems. Indeed, they found that, although the four teachers they observed used textbooks as a main mother-resource at the beginning of their career, they largely freed themselves from it later, leaving bigger place to digital resources in their resource systems. The authors thus claim that "the use of textbooks changes with the years of experience and professional development of the teacher: from a 'main' mother-resource to a 'secondary' mother-resource" (p. 76).

9.3.3 Evolution of Resource Systems

Recall that the two questions that framed discussions about the sub-theme related to the evolution of teachers' resource systems were:

1. How do teachers' resource systems evolve over time? Which professional practices make them evolve?
2. What are the levers of their evolution (experience, cultural environment, curricular changes, teachers' participation at professional development courses, etc.)?

9 Teachers' Resource Systems: Their Constitution, Structure and Evolution

The education system is a system open to society; endogenous or exogenous factors in schools that contribute to the professional development of teachers and to the evolution of resource systems can be considered. We will question their nature and their impact. First, we give a brief overview of the WG1 contributions that address, implicitly or explicitly, these questions. Then, we report a study conducted by Sayah (2018a) that sheds light on events triggering the evolution of a teacher's resource system (Sect. 9.6).

Most of the WG1 papers that have dealt with the sub-theme on evolution have rephrased, sometimes implicitly or sometimes explicitly, the above questions and have studied the evolution of the professional development of teachers in conjunction with the evolution of resources they use. However, in this section, only issues related to the evolution of the resource systems will be addressed.

Three issues were identified in WG1 contributions that provide elements of answers to the above questions: impact of collectives and of assessments on the evolution of teachers' resource systems and the concept of metamorphosis, already discussed in Sect. 9.3.1 from the perspective of constitution of a resource system.

9.3.3.1 Impact of Communities on the Evolution of Resource Systems

Baştürk-Şahin and Tapan-Broutin (2018a) found that a type of school (public or private in the Turkish context) and the curricular prescriptions may have an impact on teachers' sharing of resources with their colleagues and students. Indeed, the author observed that a student-teacher, Melodi, from a public school "was willing to share her resources and she was using digital resources to share resources with other teachers or teacher candidates" (p. 45), whereas a student-teacher, Esin, from a private school "is willing to share resources with her school colleagues, not the other teachers" (ibid.). A year after, when these student-teachers became teachers, different evolutions of sharing resources are observed: while Melodi cannot share resources with the students, this being strictly forbidden in public schools, Esin, working in a private school, shares all resources with her students. In their research, the authors used the reflective investigation methodology that, according to them, allows following the process closely: first, they analyze prospective teachers' lesson plans, and then, they observe the enactments of the lesson. After the lesson, they interview the teachers to discuss their way of teaching, ideas, and resource system that shape their lesson. During the interview, the teachers draw a schematic representation of their resource system. A year after, when the prospective teachers have become teachers, they are asked to observe a lesson they teach and factors that impact their teaching are discussed. It is interesting to note that documentation mediations shed another light of the teachers' activities and systems of resources.

The study shows the importance of interpersonal mediations. At stage 1, weak links between technological resources, represented by R1 in Fig. 9.5, and the other resources R2, R3, and R4 have given way, after interpersonal mediations, to stronger links (represented with bold arrows) in Esin's documentation system (stage 2). In this case, the community is an important lever of Esin's documentation system.

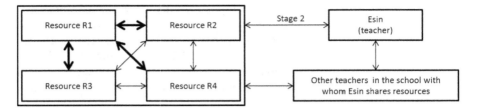

Fig. 9.5 Evolution of Esin's documentation system

In the study by Hammoud (2018), participation to a collective is also an important lever for a "deep" reorganization and restructuring of a beginning teacher's resource system, whereas in the case of an experienced teacher, participation to a virtual community leads only to a "local" evolution. It needs to be noted that, for the author, virtual community is considered as a point of articulation between the notion of community and technological tools (Daele and Charlier 2006). The virtual community of teachers is an interesting form of professional co-training, which, supported or not by the institution, offers its members significant opportunities for pedagogical innovation, information and knowledge sharing, personal expression, identity construction, and professional reflection. Building on technologies, Lebanese chemistry teachers created and animated, for about a year and a half, a professional group named "chemistry teachers of Lebanon." This community, created "by" teachers "for" teachers, promotes exchange, sharing of resources, and experience among teachers. So far, few studies have focused on the evolution of resources and the development of teachers' practices in these communities created by and for teachers outside strict institutional circuits. As Quentin (2012) pointed out, knowledge shared and created in teacher networks could be the source of a new professional identity and encourage the implementation of changes in professional practices. Hammoud (2018) addresses two questions:

1. What is the impact of chemistry teachers' participation in this virtual community on their documentation work?
2. How can this participation contribute to the evolution of their resource system and, more thoroughly, to their professional development?

To answer these questions, the author carried out an empirical study through an exploratory approach with mostly qualitative methodology. In the first phase, semi-directive interviews were conducted with four community members: a leader, a beginning teacher, and two experienced teachers. The teachers' vision, as well as their description of the context of the community, is privileged. The narrative inquiry (Clandinin and Connelly 1990), which involves the reconstruction of the experience of a person in relation to both the other and a social background, was adopted. After having clarified the purpose of her study to the leaders of this community, the author asked them to be added as a member of this community. This allows her to follow this community closely in order to better understand the interactions between the members and thus to better understand this community, its rules, its objectives, the frequency of exchanges, and the type of resources exchanged.

Of the two studies cited above, the epistemological analysis of the discipline is not taken into account. Yet, it can be hypothesized that the organization of the collective in the teaching of mathematics may be different from the one established for the teaching of chemistry. The resource system in experimental phases of chemistry with the purchase of the products, the laboratories, and the availability of the resources can have links which are of different nature compared to the links of the resource system in mathematics.

9.3.3.2 Impact of Assessment on the Evolution of the Resource Systems

In the past few years, in mathematics, in many OECD countries, average student achievement in the PISA study has been taken very seriously. The results of these assessments have impacted some education systems but have also given assessment a more prominent place in education. Baştürk-Şahin and Tapan-Broutin (2018a) showed that beginning teachers Melodi and Esin choose their auxiliary resources (i.e., resources that complement curricular resources) based on their relevance to the examination system. The examination system can therefore be considered as a lever for an evolution of resource systems (Fig. 9.6). It should be noted that pragmatic mediations offer another perspective in the study of the resource systems.

This study shows that a country's evaluation system can affect teachers' resources and their professional development. This finding confirms quantitative data collected in a survey of 1450 high school mathematics teachers (Abboud-Blanchard et al. 2015). Nearly 40% of participants came from France (572 participants) and 20% from Quebec (281 participants). The other countries most represented in number of participants are in order: Senegal (130 participants), Tunisia (111 participants),

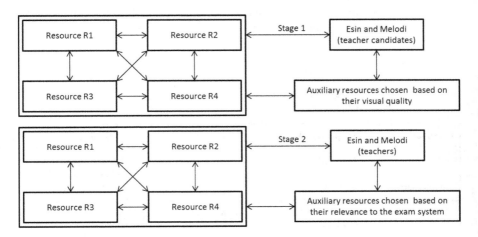

Fig. 9.6 Evolution of Esin's and Melodi's documentation systems

Switzerland (71 participants), Ivory Coast (63 participants), Belgium (49 participants), Morocco (28 participants), Vietnam (25 participants), and French-speaking Canada outside Quebec (24 participants). For these teachers, in terms of the resources used to guide and organize their course, the weight of official assessment tests is between 42% who consult them "systematically," 38% "often," and 14% "sometimes."

9.3.3.3 Metamorphosis of Teachers' Resource Systems

Assis et al. (2018) studied the elements of beginning teachers' resource systems and their "metamorphoses" (see also Sect. 9.3.1). The authors show that resources used for studying can be "metamorphosed" into teaching resources, and they explain what contributes to this evolution. This observation contrasts with the studies that are done during these phases of epistemic mediation. According to a study by Abboud-Blanchard et al. (2015), only 24% of the 1450 teachers surveyed used resources coming from in-service teacher training as resources for teaching. The study conducted by Assis et al. (2018) offers another reading. For these authors, "resource systems for teaching" (RST) may come from the *metamorphosis* of "resource systems for studying" (RSS); indeed, they observed that prospective teachers *metamorphose* their RSS into RST. The authors bring to the fore two factors that can influence this evolution of resource systems: the resources of an expert teacher who tutors the prospective teacher and the transitional resources, well integrated into the resource system of the latter, allow her to carry out her professional activities and, consequently, contribute to her professional development. This question of metamorphosis from RSS into RST is not common. Indeed, in recent years, questioning about the nature of mathematical training of teachers is done. Hache et al. (2009) situate this mathematical training on a scale of perspectives from 1 to 4 (Fig. 9.7): the closer we go to perspective 4, the more the mathematics are "dissected," "undone," and "detailed," whereas they are more and more "compressed," "condensed," and "compacted" when approaching perspective 1.

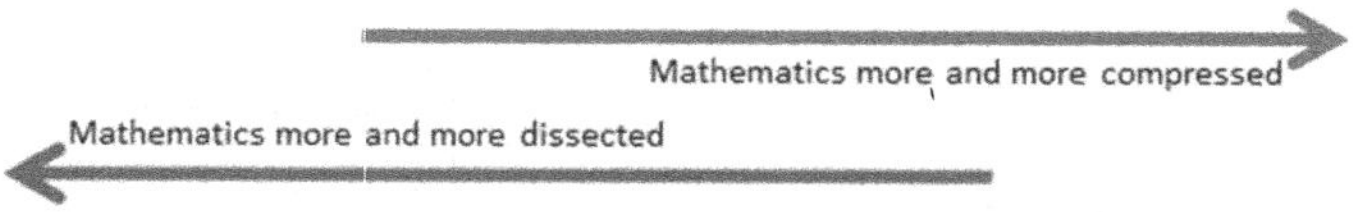

Perspective 4	Perspective 3	Perspective 2	Perspective 1
Working "school" mathematics	Working new mathematics, in relation to the school contents	Working academic mathematics, with systematic and explicit relation to content to be taught at school	Working academic mathematics taught at the university for a future mathematician

Fig. 9.7 Perspectives of the mathematical training of teachers. (Hache et al. 2009, p. 37)

The question of the metamorphosis of resources for studying into resources for teaching reveals the notion of distance between mathematics studied by prospective teachers and the mathematics they teach. It can be hypothesized that the greater the distance between mathematics learnt during the training and the mathematics to be taught, the more important are the modifications between resource systems.

To sum up, we notice that all studies on the evolution of resource systems converge on the importance of the role of communities. It has been shown, from the theoretical point of view, that the four mediations are interrelated. We can now add that these mediations are rather guided by interpersonal mediations when studying the evolutions of resource systems. Although all these studies have not specified triggering moments and events, we can hypothesize that this depends on the context within which the study is carried out, as well as of the instrumentation level of the user (beginning or experienced teacher) and the subject matter. This raises a second question: What is the impact of the evolution of resources of a teacher on her professional development and, vice versa, what is the impact of the teacher's professional development on the evolution of resource systems? An element of answer is found in the work of Essonnier and Trgalová (2018) for whom, based on a study on a socio-technological environment for the design of digital resources fostering creative mathematical thinking, the design process made the designers' professional knowledge and representations evolve. Their study draws on activity theory that explains the role of contradictions in the evolution of the activity and shows that contradictions need to be perceived as constituting the fundamental logic of the development.

9.4 Constitution of Resource Systems by Prospective Teachers: Process of Metamorphosis

Cibelle Assis and Eisângela Espíndola

This section is a result of the integration of two intertwined studies presented in the WG1: *Metamorphosis of resource systems of prospective teacher – from studying to teaching* by Assis et al. (2018), and *The documentational work in the initial formation of a mathematics undergraduate in training for the teaching of first-degree equation* whose authors are Espindola and Trgalová (2018). These studies are particularly interested in discussing how teachers start constituting their resource systems at the beginning of their careers during the mathematics teacher training courses.

Assis et al. (2018) hypothesize that prospective teachers perform a *metamorphosis* of their "resource systems for studying" into "resource systems for teaching" (RST). Espíndola and Trgalová (2018) state that the constitution of their resource systems is impacted by the resources they encountered in their training courses, on the one hand, and by the resource systems of their tutors (i.e., expert teachers in charge of accompanying the prospective teacher), on the other hand.

In order to better understand this issue of metamorphosis, we considered two case studies developed by the authors with two prospective teachers, Cecília and Severino. Each case study illustrates, in terms of a metamorphosis, the development of transitional resources (Cecília's case) and the influence of tutors' resources (Severino's case) as elements favorable to the process of constitution of prospective teachers' RST. The study of the metamorphosis in both cases emphasizes the origin of selected resources, the process of selection/integration, the representation of the resources, and constitution of a first resource system.

We organize this section in two parts. First, we situate the notion of the metamorphosis in the framework of the documentational approach (Gueudet & Trouche 2009). Next, we present the two case studies, their methodological choices, and results.

9.4.1 Metamorphosis of a Resource System: From Studying to Teaching

In this section, we present the notions of *resource system for studying*, *resource system for teaching*, and *metamorphosis* of the resource system of a prospective teacher. These terms allow to conceptualize the way prospective teachers constitute their resource systems in the context of a mathematics teacher training course. In accordance with the documentational approach to didactics, these terms refer mainly to the concepts of resources and documents, system of resources, and documentational work introduced by Gueudet and Trouche (2009, see also Chap. 2, this book).

Based on Besnier (2016) and Vergnaud (1993), Assis et al. (2018) distinguish, in the case of prospective teachers, two main classes of situations: studying situations and teaching situations. Studying situations comprise experiences related to studying any subject during the course, for example, mathematics, specific software, or how to prepare a lesson plan. In this case, a prospective teacher is focused on her own learning. Teaching situations are related to experiences in which teaching is a goal, being at the university or at school, with colleagues or students as a target. Therefore, in the context of the training courses, both situations can exist simultaneously during the development of a subject.

Corresponding to these two classes of situations, for a given prospective teacher, we consider a *resource system for studying* (RSS) and a *resource system for teaching* (RST). RSS comprises everything that supports prospective teacher's studying activity, and RST comprises resources that support her teaching. Depending on the situation in which a resource is used, it can be considered a resource either for studying or for teaching. Both sets of resources have their own structure, making them resource systems. In addition, there is coherence between them that leads to characterize the changes from RSS to RST as a *metamorphosis*. This process of change and constitution of a resource system for teaching from a system for studying is interrelated to the development of the teacher's professional knowledge. In addition, three dimensions of metamorphosis can be analyzed: the *content*, the *structure*, and the *nature*.

The content of a metamorphosis is analyzed through a material perspective of the resources. It means that a study is conducted whose goal is to identify material resources used during the development of a set of activities on a long- or short-term basis. To do this, the researcher tries to answer the following questions: Which resources? What kind of resources? What were they used for: teaching or studying? Practically, it means inferring a first version of both RSS and RST. Regarding studying situations and teaching situations, it is also possible to infer what resources belong to the RSS and to RST. A resource that belongs to both resource systems, i.e., a resource for studying that turned into a resource for teaching, is called a *transitional resource*. In addition, some *professional resources* such as curriculum resources or guide for teachers are new, unknown, or not yet explored by prospective teachers at school or at university course. These professional resources are also present in the RST.

The study of the structure of a metamorphosis reveals new relationships between resources and (re)establishment of their roles. It leads to answer the questions: resources for what? What roles for what resources? Following Besnier (2016), once the resources are organized according to specific blocks of activities related to classes of studying and teaching situations (e.g., accomplish a task or create a task with GeoGebra), the roles played by the resources and structural changes of RSS are inferred. Therefore, this analysis allows not only to identify resources but also to infer their roles: a particular role in a particular situation or in several situations, during a long or a short period of time. The presence of professional resources is identified when they were developed for new professional activities (e.g., designing a lesson or studying the curriculum itself) and, therefore, have a new role. In addition, an "old" resource such as a textbook can play a new role in a teaching situation.

Finally, the study of the nature of a metamorphosis aims to identify changes from the status "student" to the status "teacher" of a prospective teacher through the integration of resources in order to accomplish a professional activity. This leads to investigate what prospective teachers do with their resources and why. Such a study reveals schemes of utilization of the resources and the associated professional knowledge and developed competences. However, following Goigoux and Vergnaud (2005), studying the nature of a metamorphosis means studying professional schemes related to a teaching situation. We consider that a teaching situation can be considered as any didactic action of the teacher that comprises, for example, selecting, adapting, and structuring the resources and not only implementing them in the class.

The analysis of these three dimensions of a metamorphosis altogether allows to understand the way in which prospective teachers constitute their resource systems. Figure 9.8 represents an overview of the process of a metamorphosis.

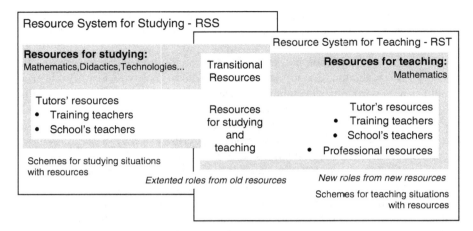

Fig. 9.8 Representation for metamorphosis of a RST from a RSS

This diagram can be adapted in accordance with the prospective teacher's activities analyzed in the study at stake. It highlights:

- The content dimension: tutor's resources, transitional resources, and professional resources as part of the RS.
- The structure dimension: the new roles or extension of old ones.
- The nature dimension: schemes associated with the uses of the resources in teaching situations. These three dimensions allow to analyze constitution of an RST from an RSS.

In the next two sections, we present two case studies in which the two prospective teachers constituted their resource systems for teaching a subject at the first time.

9.4.2 Cecília's Metamorphosis and Constitution of a Resource System for Teaching from a Resource System for Studying

Cecilia, a prospective teacher, was chosen because GeoGebra, dynamic geometry software, was previously identified as an element of both her RSS and RST. In addition, she developed some projects and subjects during her teacher training offered by the Federal University of Paraiba between 2012 and 2016.

The research methodology was organized in four phases. First, Cecilia was asked to build up her documentational trajectory (Rocha and Trouche 2017), and an interview was conducted in order to make a relation between events and important resources for her professional development mentioned in the trajectory. The interview carried out in November 2016 was audio and video recorded. Second, Cecilia was asked to send to the researchers, by email, some tasks previously developed with GeoGebra, both for studying and for teaching. This data collection was done in July 2017. The collected set of tasks was analyzed considering the documents she produced/used, such as lesson plans and worksheets, reports, as well as recordings of the implementation of some lessons at school in which the tasks and documents were enacted. This set of data, organized according to each task, was named *group of resources*. The videos of the lessons were analyzed in terms of schemes (Vergnaud 1993).

The combination of reflective data from Cecília and the researchers' inferences allowed to represent the RSS and RST from her engagement with activities supported by GeoGebra and to identify the roles played by the resources in that specific moment of the metamorphosis. Figure 9.9 is a representation of Cecília's inferred documentational trajectory. Briefly, we represent events (subjects and projects) related to studying (mathematics, technologies, and didactics) and teaching (mathematics) and resources used in these situations (technological, professional, and didactical).

Considering the *content* dimension, GeoGebra was identified in the Cecília's RST as a transitional resource and as a tutor's resource, once it was introduced by her teacher (tutor from the university). Some other resources, such as textbook and videos, were identified in her RSS. In addition, professional resources were observed in the RST, such as lesson plans, websites for mathematics teachers, official documents, or curriculum resources. An analysis of Cecília's engagement with curriculum resources is developed in Assis and Gitirana (2017).

An analysis related to the *structure* of the metamorphosis enables to infer the roles of resources and, therefore, of their uses. In the case of GeoGebra, its roles were expanded considering blocks of activities: they passed from *studying mathematics* or *following a task* into resources *to conceive, to structure tasks,* and *to support students' activity in a class.*

The study of the *nature* dimension comprised the study of Cecília's scheme *defining equilateral triangle with GeoGebra* regarding her activity in the classroom.

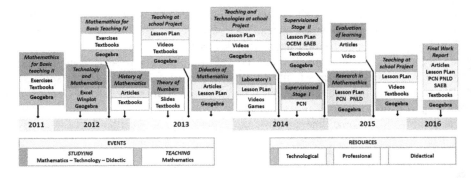

Fig. 9.9 Inferred representation of Cecília's documentational trajectory

This scheme revealed how Cecília relies on GeoGebra in order to get and create examples of triangles and to present to students at school a classification of triangles according to their sides.

From the analysis of the video of the lesson enacted in the classroom, *rules of action* (RA) could be inferred for the scheme of Cecilia, in which a pattern for her organization was observed: RA1, asking a question to the students about what is an equilateral triangle (reading the produced worksheet); RA2, insisting that the answers must be coherent with GeoGebra feedback (visual aspect for a construction done); RA3, waiting for and listening the students' answers and inference; RA4, reformulating the students' answers; and RA5, explaining the relationship between the procedure of construction and the equilateral triangle properties.

Considering the scheme, *operational invariants* related to the use of GeoGebra and dynamic geometry properties were identified, for example, each family of triangles (equilateral, isosceles, and scalene) has a different procedure of construction in GeoGebra; the construction procedure in GeoGebra uses mathematical properties; robust constructions in GeoGebra preserve the properties for each family of triangles (equilateral, isosceles, and scalene); each robust construction offers an unlimited number of triangles or examples. Some of these operational invariants are considered *as persistent* because they were present in Cecilia's scheme for studying (e.g., the identification of properties of the triangles can be performed from the analysis of several examples as in the textbook) and *flexible* due to the development of schemes for teaching through the integration of old and new resources (e.g., she knows that a robust construction done with GeoGebra offers an unlimited number of triangles, more than those present in the textbook).

In summary, the constitution of Cecília's RST was initially influenced by the resources used for studying mathematics, such as textbooks and GeoGebra supported by worksheets. These resources are considered transitional and were introduced by her tutors at the university. Other resources were integrated in Cecília's RS according to subjects; this is the case of professional resources (lesson plans, websites for mathematics teachers, official documents, or curriculum resources). We observed the influence of the institutional context (resources and tutors' resources) as a source for the constitution of an RS.

Regarding the use of GeoGebra for teaching triangle classification, the possibility of using dynamic geometry appears as a strong criterion of choice. In fact, possibilities to get examples and build triangles that can be moved by the students, possibilities for the students to infer and validate classifications of triangles, and possibilities for the students to use computers in mathematics classes are some of these criteria. Following these criteria, we observed a representation of GeoGebra as a "good" resource for working in the investigative perspective (inferences and validation) and, at same time, amplifying the possibilities of textbook use.

9.4.3 Severino's Metamorphosis and Constitution of an RST from an RSS

This section reports a study carried out by Espíndola and Trgalová (2018) motivated by the desire to improve a dialogue between the actors involved in the supervised teacher training: the two tutors – a supervisor (ST, an experienced teacher from the school) and an advisor (AT, a teacher from the university) – and a prospective teacher.

This study explores the influence of the indications of resources, guidance that the tutors offer to prospective teachers. It investigates the ways the prospective teachers in training reflect on their own documentational work, from their lesson plans to their implementation in the classroom. The question addressed is *how tutors' resources guide the process of constitution of the prospective teacher's resource system.*

The reflective investigation (Gueudet and Trouche 2010) was adopted as a methodological framework to follow Severino during the development of his activities in the course titled "supervised compulsory internship" (Estágio Supervisionado Obrigatório IV-ESO-IV) offered at the Federal University Rural of Pernambuco in Recife.

Severino's teaching activities in the framework of his internship were accompanied by a supervisor (ST) from the school and by an advisor (AT), a teacher educator from the university. Severino was engaged in the internship for 2 months: first, he observed ST in the classroom in order to become familiar with the students; and then he was expected to design and implement a mathematics lesson. The mathematical subject was about first-degree equations for the first year of high school of youth and adult education in Brazil. This subject was part of the progression of the school teacher's activities in this classroom.

The first analysis of the case study with Severino (Machado et al. 2018) revealed some challenges and limits of the choice and use of the resources for teaching considering the preservice teacher's autonomy and the experience of their tutors. These aspects have been a challenge in the initial teacher education and a fruitful investigative path to initial teacher education in the light of the documentational approach to didactics (Gueudet and Trouche 2010).

The notion of metamorphosis is used to investigate how Severino constituted his resource system for teaching based on tutors' resources. The research was organized in three phases. In the first stage, Severino's resource system was inferred by the researchers from Severino's documentational trajectory (Rocha and Trouche 2017). To understand this trajectory, Severino was asked to represent the events and their relationships with the important resources that he thinks affected his teacher training, considering his experience and performance in the teacher training course, at the school and in other training spaces. The interviews served to deepen the content and the structure related to his resources for studying and for teaching, as well as, the features of the process of the constitution of his RST.

In the second phase, a resource used by ST in the teaching of the first-degree equations was analyzed and its use in the classroom by the teacher was observed. The resource, named "first-degree equation exercises," was presented in a form of a list of exercises obtained from the web. This resource was shared by the teacher with Severino. Severino with his AT analyzed the resource in order to identify the mathematical organization (MO) of the theme "first-degree equations," drawing on the anthropological theory of didactics (ATD, Chevallard 1999).

The third phase of the research concerned the teaching practice in the ESO IV internship. A study was carried out on the nature of the metamorphosis taking into account the resources used by Severino in the design of a lesson plan about first-degree equations. In this phase, systematic interviews were carried out about the process of selecting the resources by Severino in which were identified, among other aspects, the goals, knowledge (operational invariants), and rules of action in relation to the schemes associated with this professional situation of designing a lesson plan.

The design of the lesson plan about first-degree equations had, as the main objective, to deepen students' learning. It was the first time that Severino faced a teaching situation about this mathematical subject. To guide Severino's activity, ST made available his resource called "*list of first-degree equation exercises*" that he used in the classroom.

In addition, under the guidance of AT and drawing on the work of de Araújo (2009) and Araújo and Santos (2010), Severino analyzed the mathematical organization present in the resource. Two types of tasks were identified: *T1, solving first-degree eqs.* (40 exercises), and *T2, solving problems with a first-degree equation* (nine exercises). In classroom observations, Severino found that ST proposed to students 10 exercises with T1:

- T1.1: $ax + b = c$ (e.g., $18x - 43 = 45$) – one exercise.
- T1.2: $ax + b = cx + d$ (e.g., $23x - 16 = 14 - 17x$) – four exercises.
- T1.3: $ax + b = cx$ – one exercise.
- T1.4: $A1(x) = A2(x)$, where A1 and A2 are expressions with x (e.g., $10-5(1 + x) = 3 (2x - 2) - 20$ – two exercises.
- T1.5: $ax = b$ (e.g., $4x = 8$) – two exercises.

and three exercises with T2:

- T2.1: problem that can be solved with an equation $ax + b = c$ (e.g., twice a number increased by 15 equals 49. What is this number?) – one exercise.
- T2.2: problem that can be solved with an equation $ax = c$ (e.g., the sum of a number with its triple equals 48. What is that number?) – two exercises.

The technique associated with T1 used by ST was "τNTC – neutralization of terms or coefficients" justified by the technology θ "principle of equivalence between equations" that refers to the theory Θ "rings of polynomials" (de Araújo 2009). For ST, such exercises would be essential for the revision of the subject, given the already known students' difficulties. When talking with Severino, ST also evoked a scale as a resource for teaching the technique τNTC.

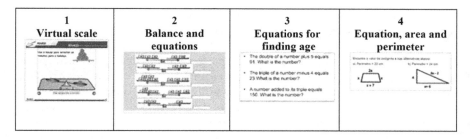

Fig. 9.10 New resources for teaching used by Severino

In particular, Severino had no knowledge about τNTC; rather he always used the technique τTTC "transposition of terms or coefficients" for solving first-degree equations during his studies about this subject. This fact triggered his interest in resources that would help students understand the τNTC. He thus chose resources that could fulfill this aim. Some of these resources were pointed out by AT in discussions with Severino: scientific publications as de Araújo (2009) and de Araújo and Santos (2010) drawing on ATD (Chevallard 1999) and curricular guidelines (Pernambuco 2012a, b). These resources were identified as professional resources and tutor's resources. From this moment on, Severino designed his lesson plan. We observed that ST's list of exercises and the professional resources were Severino's references to start his activity and to search for other resources that would support him in this professional situation.

Considering the goal of making students' learning of first-degree equations evolve, two classes of situations corresponding to two didactic moments of studying a mathematics theme (Chevallard 1998) were identified: *to conceive a moment of introduction and discovery* and *to conceive a moment of training*. For the first one, Severino used the resource "Virtual scale,"[1] and for the second one, he used three other resources found on the web: "Balance and Equations,"[2] "Equations for finding age,"[3] and "Equation, area, and perimeter"[4] from which he selected several questions. Figure 9.10 shows these resources.

In this set of resources (Fig. 9.10), the influence of the mathematical organization (τNTC and θ related to T1) identified in the ST's resource is visible. Indeed, Severino proposed two tasks with virtual scales (resources 1 and 2), and he chose problems already worked in class by ST about how to find age using equations (resource 3). The exercise involving area and perimeter (resource 4) was the only one different from those already proposed by ST.

In terms of metamorphosis, the analysis of the above-mentioned resources, their roles, and the reasons why Severino used them allowed to shed light on the process

---

[1] http://www.projetos.unijui.edu.br/matematica/fabrica_virtual/Antonio_miguel_e_Adilson_Sella/
[2] http://websmed.portoalegre.rs.gov.br/escolas/marcirio/expressao_numerica/aplicando_3.htm
[3] http://files.comunidades.net/profjosecarlos/equacao_do_1_grau.pdf
[4] http://interna.coceducacao.com.br/Arquivos/EstudoPontoCom/2011/downloaD_estudo-com98197.pdf

of constitution of his resource system for teaching. For each resource used (Fig. 9.10), it was possible to identify what guided the search for resources (how, why, and where) and, consequently, how Severino constituted his RST for the given class of situations. In other words, some aspects related to the nature of the metamorphosis can be brought to the fore in terms of operational invariants inferred from the analysis of the resources used in the lessons. For example, with the choice of the resource 1, "Virtual scale," Severino aimed to develop students' learning about the technique of neutralization of terms and coefficients (τNTC) for solving first-degree equations. The following operational invariants could be inferred from the analysis of the resource, as well as from interviews conducted with Severino: designing lessons related to the students' daily life (most of the students are workers who strive to attend classes at night and also they are tired after their working day); visualization of the balance and imbalance effects of the scale as a support for the understanding of the technique of neutralization of terms and coefficients in solving equations. Considering resource 2, "Balance and equations," the goal was to work on T1-type tasks (*solving equations of the first degree*). The following operational invariants could be inferred: it is necessary to propose tasks of type T1 because it is in accordance with the school teacher's guidance; the idea of the scale considers the τNTC technique; understanding of the additive and multiplicative principles is necessary in solving equations. The last two resources, "Equations for finding age" and "Equation, area, and perimeter," aimed at working on T2-type tasks (*solving problems with first-degree equations*). Operational invariants inferred for resource 3 are as follows: it is necessary to propose tasks of type T2 because it is in accordance with the school teacher's guidance; it is necessary to propose different types of tasks in order to make students' learning evolve; it is necessary to explore the transition from natural to algebraic language. Operational invariants inferred for the resource 4 are as follows: it is necessary to propose problems that articulate different fields of mathematics (e.g., algebra and magnitudes and measures), and it is necessary that students develop flexibility in the transition from figural language (trapezoid, triangle) to algebraic language.

In summary, the constitution of Severino's RST was initially sourced by the guidance of ST and his resources (list of exercises proposing first-degree equations and problems that can be solved with such equations, and the technique τNTC for solving equations). Then, Severino wished to use a balance as a resource for teaching. He thus started searching for resources to conceive a moment of introduction, discovery, and training. To do this, he used his knowledge about the mathematical subject and his conception of teaching and learning to select the four resources. In this process of constitution of his RS, the roles played by the tutors and their resources, being from the school or from the university, were decisive. As one of the researchers was also a tutor (AT), it seems relevant to question to what extent this double role could have impacted the reported research outcomes.

9.4.4 Concluding Remarks

In both case studies, the experiences lived in real teaching situations seemed to be one of the motors of the process of learning and professional development or, in other words, of the process of formation and evolution of prospective teachers' schemes that allowed to constitute their resource systems continuously.

The notion of metamorphosis turned out to be relevant and useful for analyzing the engagement of prospective teachers with resources and how this engagement can reveal aspects of their professional development, including constitution of a resource system, for instance, the evolution of uses of "old" resources, searching for new resources or developing new uses according to teaching goals; different levels of dependence or autonomy of prospective teachers with respect to their tutors and the tutors' resources; development of knowledge (mathematical, didactical, pedagogical, etc.) in the situations (studying and teaching); and its progress over time. Based on these considerations, we hypothesize possible differences between metamorphoses, which open a perspective for further research.

9.5 Teachers' Resource Systems and Their Structure

Rim Hammoud and Mohammad Dames Alturkmani

In their professional activity, teachers interact with a wide range of *resources*, in many ways, in diverse places and moments. An important facet of teachers' work, done outside the classroom, involves searching for, collecting, selecting, and transforming resources for lesson and assessment preparation. Teachers develop a *resource system* (Gueudet and Trouche 2010) that they constantly modify by adding new resources, modifying older ones, removing some resources, and reorganizing the links structuring this system. Interactions with resources are thus major elements in teachers' work. This section focuses on issues related to this aspect of teachers' work and develops a variety of perspectives on these interactions, on teachers' resources and their use, and more broadly on teachers' resource systems, their structure, and organization, as well as the impact of the teachers' interactions with some aspects of the curriculum of their country on their work with resources by crossing two case studies: the first is related to two professors teaching physics-chemistry in France, whereas the second case investigates two Lebanese chemistry professors' interactions with resources.

Indeed, in the tradition of French secondary education, physics and chemistry are closely associated, and they are integrated under the generic name of "physical and chemical sciences" or simply called "physical sciences." Therefore the same professor teaches both physics and chemistry. However, the Lebanese educational system does not combine physics and chemistry as it is the case in France. As such, Caillot (1994) claims that physics and chemistry are not so "sisters." Actually, these two disciplines have common points as well as differences, from epistemological or didactic points of view. Concerning commonalities, these disciplines use concepts such as mass, volume, or energy. The use of experience and modeling (Justi and Van Driel 2005; Martinand 1992) occupies an important place in both disciplines. Nevertheless, several studies point out specificities of each of these two disciplines (Johnstone 1993; Le Maréchal 1999; Tiberghien 2000, Robert and Treiner 2004; Kermen 2007; Houart 2009): physics and chemistry have differences in the nature of the knowledge mobilized, which implies specific didactic issues. In fact, chemistry is different from physics by its very strong relation to experimentation; the dialectics modeling-experimentation in chemistry is stronger than in physics because, on the one hand, of the great experimental diversity of chemical reactions and, on the other hand, of a relation to mathematics less accentuated and less abstract (Barlet 1999). According to this perspective, mathematical modeling is less present in chemistry than in physics and the dialectics "microscopic-macroscopic" and "modeling-experimentation" make the specificity of chemistry:

> the microscopic-macroscopic dialectics or modeling-experimentation is thus an epistemological characteristic as much as a didactic necessity: the deep understanding of macroscopic observables and quantitative data necessarily involves relevant representations of their microscopic aspects (Barlet 1999, p. 1440).

As a result, we assume that these differences reflect, from our point of view, differences between Lebanese and French teachers in their interactions with resources, in terms of their resource systems, since the relationship to the discipline, teaching activities, and curriculum is not the same in both cases. It is important to note, however, that we do not make here a comparison between the Lebanese and French curriculum and detail these two curricula, but rather we focus, among other things, on how teachers' interactions with some aspects of the curriculum of their country influence their documentation work and their resource systems.

9.5.1 Elements of the Documentational Approach to Didactics

We will not develop here the documentational approach to didactics (Gueudet and Trouche 2010) on which we rely, but we focus on the new concepts that have enriched this approach, namely, *mother-resource, daughter-resource,* and *structuring mother-resource.*

Like Adler (2000) and Gueudet and Trouche (2010), we give a very broad meaning to the term "resource": everything that contributes to the professor's teaching project, to the design of the material for this teaching, as well as to the reflection that supports this design (material resources, digital or not, but also socio-cultural resources such as interactions with students or discussions with colleagues). The teacher interacts with resources, selects them, and works on them (adapting, revising, reorganizing, etc.) within a process where design and enacting are intertwined. The expression *documentation work* (Gueudet and Trouche 2010) encompasses all these interactions.

Hammoud (2012) introduced two new concepts, namely, *mother-resources* and *daughter-resources*, that allow to distinguish between what the teacher uses to prepare his teaching (mother-resource) and what he produces and develops from the initial resources (daughter-resource). Describing a specific type of mother-resource, Alturkmani (2015) introduced the concept of *structuring mother-resource,* which is a mother-resource that helps structure the teacher's documentation work from two points of view: on the one hand, it is around this particular resource that the daughter-resource dedicated to this teaching is structured, and on the other hand, this resource induces new equilibrium in teacher knowledge and, thus, in the disciplinary and didactic affinities[5] of the teacher.

9.5.2 Research Questions and Methodological Elements

We focus here on the documentation work and the resource system of four teachers, two teachers of physics-chemistry in France and two chemistry teachers in Lebanon, to highlight commonalities and differences in their interactions with resources. In what follows, we formulate our research questions:

- How do teachers structure their resource systems? Does this structure differ between a physics-chemistry teacher in France and a chemistry teacher in Lebanon? In other words, what is the difference between the resources and, more broadly, the resource system, of a physics-chemistry teacher in France and a chemistry teacher in Lebanon?
- How do teacher's interactions with some aspects of the curriculum of his country affect his documentation work and his resource system?

To provide some answers to these questions, we have chosen a qualitative approach based on the *reflective investigation* methodology (Gueudet and Trouche 2012). Among the tools used in this methodology, we are interested here in three tools: interviews, *schematic representation of the resource system* (SRRS), and collection of resources. We conduct a semi-directive interview (Vermersch 1994), with each teacher aiming at approaching his documentation work and his resource system. For the interview, we note in the same way the occurrences of the types of activity and the resources mentioned. During the interview, we also organize a guided visit of the teacher's resources, where he presents a set of resources gathered to support his activity; we then collect all these resources. In relation to the "structuring mother-resources" for a specific content, we seek first to identify what the teacher uses as "mother-resources" to organize the teaching of this content and the

---

[5] Disciplinary affinity is defined by disciplinary interest and disciplinary awareness. Didactic affinity is defined by didactic interest and didactic awareness (Alturkmani et al. 2018).

structure of these resources. Among these, we attempt to identify the most important mother-resources for the teacher and for the teaching of this content. In this last category, we can distinguish two subcategories, namely, that the structuring mother-resource plays a special role in the disciplinary and didactic affinity and in the production of a new resource (Alturkmani et al. 2018). For example, reading an article by a teacher, related to the history of a discipline, allows him to understand the objects of the study of this discipline. This develops his awareness of this discipline ("structuring" character of the resource) and also allows him to produce a new resource ("maternal" character of the resource).

Moreover, based on the principle of *reflective follow-up* of the documentation work, we ask the teacher, during this interview, to make a schematic representation of his resource system (SRRS). It is indeed a representation in the double meaning of the term: on the one hand, it is an external representation, a schema that we can exploit to infer elements of structure of teacher's documentation work and resource system; on the other hand, it is an internal representation, in the sense that it allows us to see the way in which the teacher represents himself and wishes to present and communicate elements of organization of his work. Hammoud (2012) proposed an approach for analyzing SRRS on which we rely for the analysis of these schematic representations. Although it is a schematic representation, we consider that what is given to us is not just a simple schema, but elements of a relationship between resources, activity of the teacher, and elements on the use of these resources. The elements resulting from this schematic representation are then confronted with what is said during the interview and with other data, in particular the resources collected, to evidence elements of structure of the teacher's activity and of his resources. The interview thus stimulates the reflexivity of the teacher on the nature and structure of his resources.

9.5.3 Findings

In this section, we present the main results for the four teachers related to the place of the textbook in teachers' resource system, the impact of the teacher's interactions with some aspects of the curriculum of his country on his documentation work, the types of resources identified in relation to the type of teachers' professional activity, and the identification of particular resources, especially *structuring mother-resources* and *pivotal* resources (Gueudet and Trouche 2010) in the teachers' resource system, as well as the role of collectives as nourishing and enriching teachers' resource system. We designate the two French teachers by PC1 (he has an affinity for chemistry and 10 years of professional experience in high school) and PC2 (he has an affinity for physics and he has been teaching for 14 years in high school) and the two Lebanese teachers by C1 and C2 (C1 has 12 years of professional experience in middle school and C2 has 11 years of professional experience in middle and high school).

9.5.3.1 Similar Evolution Over Time of the Role of the Textbook as a Mother-Resource

Textbooks, as part of curricular resources, generally respect the curriculum imposed by the educational system of each country. Among the curricular resources, the textbook is commonly seen by the four teachers as the major curricular resource on which they tended to rely. In fact, we found that the four teachers used, at the beginning of their career, textbooks as a main mother-resource but largely deviated from it later. This use is justified by the fact that these curricular resources constitute, for them, a means to follow appropriately and apply the curriculum that is prescribed for them. Nevertheless, the use of textbooks changes with the years of experience and professional development of these teachers: from a "main" mother-resource to a "secondary" mother-resource.

9.5.3.2 Teachers' Resource System in Strong Connection with the Curriculum and Teachers' Professional Activity

In France, new programs in high school have been applied since 2010 following a curriculum reform. Changes have affected the teaching of physics-chemistry in various ways: this teaching is now structured by themes that make the two disciplines interact in connection with everyday life in order to motivate students. As a result, the physics and chemistry programs, because of their thematic entries, no longer distinguish chemistry from physics, and hence, these two disciplines are mixed within each theme. For example, for the teaching of physics-chemistry in grade 10, three thematic entries are considered, health, sport, and universe, and in each of these three themes, scientific concepts and contents related to physics and chemistry are taught. Moreover, in practical work, experimental approaches such as an inquiry approach are highly recommended. It is indeed the acquisition of skills that is recommended with the students' ability to mobilize them autonomously and to transfer them to different areas and situations in everyday life. Furthermore, in the teaching of physics and chemistry, the reduction of mathematical formulas is also advocated.

Because of the curriculum reform that has resulted in a thematic approach to teaching, we noticed that PC1 and PC2 do not distinguish in their resources the teaching of physics and that of chemistry. The reduction of mathematical formulas in the curriculum allowed PC1 to develop his disciplinary and didactic interest in physics. He puts much less emphasis on the mathematical aspect in the teaching of physical concepts. Depending on the disciplinary themes, PC1 and PC2 point out that, sometimes, they implement inquiry in their physics-chemistry teaching. Thus, this curriculum reform led to a particular documentation work for these teachers in order to integrate new resources and to reorganize resources already produced.

Since experimental activities occupy an important place in the French curriculum, we found that the place of practical work (so-called Lab work) is much more central in the professional activity of teachers in France than in Lebanon. Both PC1 and PC2 declare that they begin their teaching with experimental activities, and then they institutionalize the knowledge at the end of the session. The collection and guided visit of their resources show that resources related to this type of activity appear also central in the resource system of these teachers. On the other hand, the difficult conditions of the laboratories in the Lebanese public schools of C1 and C2 (no laboratory in C1 school, presence of a laboratory with a single bench in C2 school, lack of materials) and more importantly the fact that the Lebanese curriculum does not sufficiently emphasize, in its general objectives, the need to implement experimental approaches are the reasons that lead these teachers not to give an important place for the experimental activities in their teaching. Consequently, the documentation work and the resources of C1 and C2 related to this type of professional activity appear *marginal*. Hence, the use of resources, their importance, and their place in the resource system of these teachers appear strongly in relation to the type of their professional activity: for C1 and C2, the activities related to the "preparation of exercises" and "preparation of assessments" seem *dominant* compared to those related to "course design" and "development and implementation of an experimental activity." As a result, resources in relation to *dominant* types of activity appear in turn *dominant* and central in the resource system of these teachers.

9.5.3.3 Interactions with Colleagues or Students: A Structuring Mother-Resource

Beyond the curriculum and textbooks, the interactions between a teacher and his students, on the one hand, and the interactions between a teacher and his colleagues, on the other hand, are central resources that nourish the documentation work of the teachers interviewed.

We inferred that PC1 interactions with two colleagues from SESAMES[6] group and the resources of his colleagues contribute to the development of his physics knowledge and support the design of his daughter-resources. They thus appear as a *structuring mother-resource* in physics. Moreover, we noticed that the structure of his daughter-resources is identical to that of SESAMES group resources, which are presented as "models and activities." Therefore, the latter also appear as *pivotal resources* in his resource system, since he relies essentially on this type of resources to organize his teaching in physics or chemistry.

In parallel, the interactions of C1 and C2 with their students (and students' productions), especially with the students to whom they gave private lessons,[7] greatly enriched their resource systems. Indeed, the direct contact with these students and their resources (students' resources related to courses, exercises, and assessments

---

[6] The SESAMES group brings together researchers in science didactics and physics-chemistry teachers in middle or high school in order to develop resources for teaching: http://pegase.ens-lyon.fr/enseigner.php

[7] In Lebanon, a large number of teachers give private lessons to students in *after-school* learning *centers*.

given by their own teacher at school and which C1 and C2 collect during private lessons), and the close follow-up of their difficulties, allowed these teachers to develop their professional knowledge as well as new daughter-resources in chemistry. Therefore, it appears that the interactions of these teachers with these students constitute a *structuring mother-resource* in chemistry. These interactions also appear, beyond a structuring mother-resource, as a *pivotal resource* because they are, on the one hand, involved in several types of teachers' activities: the preparation of lessons, exercises, and assessments. On the other hand, more than an enrichment of the resource system, they seem to help restructure and reorganize the resource system of these teachers.

9.5.3.4 Role of Collectives as Nourishing and Enriching Teachers' Resource System

With technological and Internet development and, consequently, the proliferation of digital resources (including online resources, simulations, videos), the latter are increasingly occupying an important place in the resource system of the four teachers. In Lebanon, the two teachers specify a particular role for social networks (Facebook, WhatsApp, Telegram) in the diffusion of digital resources in chemistry: more particularly, C1 and C2 take part in a collective that consists of a group of Lebanese chemistry teachers gathering more than 1000 chemistry teachers in middle and high school through the Telegram application. This group allows sharing and exchange of all types of resources related to chemistry education and education in general (Hammoud 2018). We found that the resources of this group constitute a central resource in the resource systems of these teachers, particularly for the preparation of assessments.

Similarly, PC1 and PC2 are part of collectives involving teachers, outside their school, with a strong epistemological coherence: PC1 works with SESAMES group, that is distinguished by its point of view on science and models, and PC2 is involved in the GFEN group (Groupe Français d'Education Nouvelle translated as French Group of New Education) that is distinguished by a strong point of view on socio-constructivism and scientific work. We inferred that these two collectives support the documentation work of PC1 and PC2 and nourish their resource systems, stimulating, from the designed resources, the development of their *disciplinary* and *didactic affinity* (Alturkmani 2015).

9.5.3.5 Structure of Teachers' Resource Systems, as Seen Through the Schematic Representation of Their Resource System (SRRS)

The analysis of the SRRS of the teachers (here we consider only the schematic representations of PC1 and C2) allows us to further deepen the structure of their resource systems. Indeed, the resources collected, the SRRS, the guided visit of the

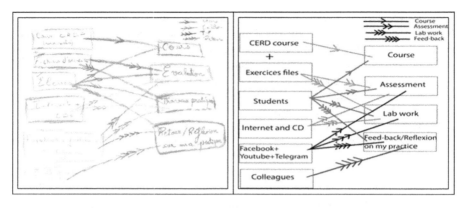

Fig. 9.11 SRRS of C2 (left: teacher's handwritten representation, right: our transcription and translation)

resources, and what was mentioned during the interview highlight the complementarity of these different methodological elements that we have used to bring closer, as much as possible, what these teachers say about their resource system and the reality of that system.

Comparing what we observed about the structure of C2 resource system and what he drew in his SRRS (see Fig. 9.11), we find that what is noted in the schematic representation goes beyond a simple enunciation of resources to highlight a connection between resources and types of C2 professional activities. Six poles appear to the left of this SRRS: "CERD[8] course" that refers to the official textbook; "Exercises files"; "Students"; "Internet and CDs"; "Facebook, YouTube, Telegram"; and "Colleagues." These poles refer to the resources likely to be mother-resources used by C2 to organize his teaching and to design daughter-resources. To the right of this SRRS, C2 shows, in the form of four poles, the types of professional activities as part of his chemistry teaching: "Course," "Assessment," "Lab work," and "Feedback/reflection on my practice."

What we want to emphasize through this SRRS is the importance of the pole "Student" as a resource that is mobilized by C2 for all types of the professional activities that he evokes in his SRRS. Actually, the four arrows that start from this pole and each reaching a pole characterizing a type of C2 professional activity show that this resource is a pivotal resource, as it is used by C2 for several goals of his professional activity.

As this SRRS shows, C2 reflection about his practice is widely based on his interactions with his colleagues. In addition, another collective dimension intervenes and nourishes the general reflection of C2 on his practice but also the design

---

[8] CERD: Center for Educational Research and Development (in French: Centre Régional de Documentation Pédagogique CRDP) is a public institution linked directly to the Minister of Education and Higher Education in Lebanon. This Center is responsible, among other things, for the production of textbooks and educational means. www.crdp.org

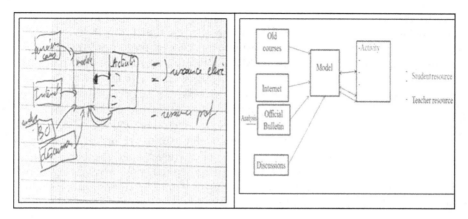

Fig. 9.12 SRRS of PC1 (left: teacher's handwritten representation, right: our transcription and translation)

of "assessment" and "Lab work" sessions. It concerns more particularly his exchanges with other colleagues through Facebook and foster the Telegram, which brings together, as we have already mentioned, a large number of chemistry teachers exchanging on their practices. More generally, it appears that the exchanges of C2 with other colleagues constitute a structuring element of his resource system. Moreover, what this SRRS reveals to us further strengthens our inferences: the results that we have highlighted previously are indeed corroborated by this SRRS insofar, as we have identified that, on the one hand, C2 interactions with his students constitute a pivotal resource and, beyond that, a structuring mother-resource and, on the other hand, his interactions with his colleagues within the collectives foster the enrichment of his resource system. This SRRS also supports the fact that online and digital resources (Internet, YouTube, CDs) play an important role in his resource system and nourish his documentation work.

Besides, the SRRS drawn by PC1 (Fig. 9.12) is consistent with what he said about his resources and his interactions with his colleagues during the interview.

Actually, we have previously pointed out that the two French teachers, PC1 and PC2, do not make a difference between their resources for teaching physics and those for teaching chemistry. This is supported by the fact that PC1 has drawn a single schema that represents his resource system for teaching both physics and chemistry. We have identified in this SRRS several types of resources and the links that organize them. These resources can be used by PC1 as mother-resources to design a new daughter-resource.

The heart of his documentation work is represented by a resource called "model," since the latter appears in the center of his SRRS, and several elements are directly linked to it. As the SRRS shows, PC1 organizes his resources in two parts: "model" and "activity." This organization comes to further support its consistency with that of SESAMES group resources. On the left of the SRRS, PC1 notes four poles that nourish the "model": the "old courses," the "Internet" sites, the "Official Bulletin,[9]" and the "discussions" with his colleagues in his school and in SESAMES group. These four poles with the "model" constitute the "teacher resources." Another pole, "activity," appears to the right of the SRRS and it forms, with the four poles that nourish the "model," the "student resources." As we can see in the SRRS, there is a reversible arrow and a double reversible arrow between the pole "activity" and the center "model." In other words, they influence each other. It seems that these two resources, "activity" and "model," constitute a structuring element of PC1 documentation work and resource system. This corroborates the results we have drawn that show SESAMES group resources as pivotal resources in PC1 resource system. Therefore, this SRRS further supports our findings on the importance of SESAMES group and the interactions of PC1 with colleagues in this group for his documentation work and the enrichment of his resource system.

9.5.4 Discussion and Conclusion

Using a theoretical framework allowing to study teacher documentation work, we focused on interactions between teachers and resources by considering two teachers in France and two other teachers in Lebanon. Through this study, we identified differences as well as common elements in the structure of the resource system of Lebanese and French teachers. Beyond comparison, our main objective was to understand the nature and contexts of resources and of teachers' resource system.

As our results show, textbooks remain the central curricular resources for teaching physics and chemistry in both countries. These resources are those that teachers use in their classrooms to apply the prescribed curriculum. Nevertheless, textbooks were the main mother-resource for the four teachers at the beginning of their career, but this resource became "secondary" with teachers' professional development and the proliferation of digital resources. The latter and among them resources accessible through the Internet are increasingly used and occupy a central position in the resource system of the four teachers. As the experience of these teachers grows, their openness to resources grows as well. We also found that teachers' resource system is in strong connection with the curriculum and teachers' professional activity. Indeed we have highlighted the influence of some aspects of the curriculum in each country on the documentation work and the resource system of the teachers: in the case of French teachers, the resources are used for the teaching physics-chemistry, with sometimes orientations toward one or the other discipline, and the resources related to the design and implementation of experimental activities are central. Nonetheless, these resources seem marginal for Lebanese teachers who use resources for teaching chemistry only. Hence, teachers' documentation work is supported but also constrained by the curriculum.

---

[9] The Official Bulletin of the French National Education publishes administrative acts: decrees, orders, memos, etc.

We have also highlighted a close relationship between the use of resources, their importance, and their place in the resource system of these teachers, on the one hand, and the type of teachers' professional activity, on the other. Furthermore, structuring mother-resources as well as pivotal resources have been identified in teachers' resource systems.

We have focused on the individual teachers' documentation work, but it is clear that they draw on resources developed by other teachers. Our results indicate that collective dimensions are always present in teachers' work. Interactions between the four teachers and their colleagues within collectives seem to hold an increasing place and have a potential role in teachers' work with resources and hence in supporting their resource systems.

Resources, their use, institutional conditions, and constraints certainly differ in the various contexts we have discussed. Studying interactions between teachers and resources helps deepen our understanding of such phenomena. It seems to us that all the teachers, whatever their specialty, carry out a documentation work which occupies, in all cases, an important part of their activity, but a specificity of this work seems to prevail. Neither the resources nor the uses are generic.

The results provide deeper insights into teacher's resource system and its structure. Turning to future development of a further deepening of the notions of resource system and its structure, it would be interesting to develop our results by producing digital supports in the form of webdocuments on the AnA.doc platform (Alturkmani et al. in press). This platform contains typical situations related to teachers' documentation work (preparation of a lesson, implementation, revision, etc.). A webdocument is a short analysis of a situation which allows to answer a specific question with illustrations (video or audio extracts, schematic representation images, etc.). For example, we could produce a comparative webdocument on the structuring mother-resources of the four French and Lebanese teachers. Additionally, beyond the tools and concepts that we have mobilized, it would be appropriate to rely on others developed in the context of the documentational approach: for example, the *documentation expertise* (Wang 2018) and the *documentational trajectory* (Rocha 2018) in order to identify the moments and the most important resources that have impacted teachers' documentation work and to analyze the professional development process of teachers over time in order to understand what events contribute to their design work and resource use, as well as the place of collective work in this process.

This chapter constitutes one step in an ongoing work, and the results outlined above need to be further investigated. Crucial questions emerge; investigating them might prove an important area for future research:

- We have identified in the case of a French teacher that the structure of his resources is identical to that of the collective in which he takes part. This raises the question of the link between the structure of the collective resource system and the structure of the individual resource system. How to describe these relations? What kinds of relations?

- Deepening the nature, content, and structure of a teacher's resource system: how to think about the structure of a resource system, based on which criteria? According to storage location, teacher's activity system, scientific content, forms and functions of resources, resource organization, grouping of resources based on usage, links between resources (and how they are connected), roles of resources, etc.?
- If the resource system is the set formed by all the resources used by the teacher, could we talk about and identify subsystems in this large system? Considering, for example, a classroom resource system as a subsystem? Identifying subsystems more functional than others and investigating how are the different subsystems interconnected?
- Following the previous perspective and following Hammoud (2012), could we distinguish, like mother-resource and daughter-resource, a mother-resource system and a daughter-resource system, containing what is already appropriated/used?

It would certainly be interesting to explore in future research by looking closer on all these issues and perspectives. Additional tools and models are definitely needed for description and analysis.

9.6 Evolution of a Resource System: Articulation of Dynamic and Static Dimensions

Karima Sayah

This section aims to analyze the structure of a mathematics teacher resource system, drawing on concepts already present in the documentational approach. We analyze this system from the static (resource taxonomy) and from the dynamic points of view (transformation, evolution) justified by the concept of schema related to a given situation.

An integration of Sésamath[10] resources took place in a mathematical workshop organized in an Algerian lower secondary school by a former inspector (coordinator of mathematics). We study the teacher's resource system drawing on concepts already present in the documentational approach (Gueudet and Trouche 2009). We highlight static and dynamic aspects of this system. Based on the reflexive investigation methodology, we propose a model of analysis of this system and thus approach its evolution.

---

[10] Sésamath is a French association of mathematics teachers who develop and share free resources for mathematics teaching in high school (Grades 6–10).

9.6.1 Theoretical Framework and Research Questions

We first present the fundamentals of the documentational approach that constitutes our main theoretical framework: the notions of resource, system of resources. Then we describe our approach to studying the structure of a resource system.

Gueudet and Trouche (2008) pay a particular attention to teachers' activity and mathematics teachers' documentation, particularly from the point of view of their collective documentation work and of their professional development. They consider that teacher's work is nurtured by resources available in the collective to create what is needed in order to accomplish his professional activities. According to the authors, a teacher, in his documentation work, has a set of resources of various kinds that will give birth, for a given class of situations, during a documentational genesis, to a document. The teacher's documentation work is considered as the driving force of a documentational genesis, which develops a new resource (composed of a set of selected, modified, recombined resources). Any documentational genesis, for a teacher, is a vehicle of professional development in the sense that the teacher acquires new knowledge, new skills, and new practices (Gueudet and Trouche 2008).

Like many other human activities, today's teaching activity is undergoing significant changes related to the generalization of the digital technology – the mathematics teaching is no exception – modifying the nature of the mediums, hence both the teacher resources and the conditions of their exploitation (Bachimont and Crozat 2004), their design, and sharing. As a result, the same resource can give birth to as many reconstructed views as the different contexts of consultation require. The use of technology by the educational actors (teachers and pupils) has made these resources ubiquitous for both the teacher and the pupil.

The documentational approach distinguishes a resource from a document (see also Chap. 2, this book). By resource, we designate all elements of a set (e.g., material, digital, notebooks, and Sésamath textbooks in the case of the mathematics teacher that we report about in this section). These elements constitute the ingredients, which are inputs that the teacher needs to create her own document, her output. This conception of the document takes place in a finite cycle that can return to the actions and to the resources at the input. A resource is what is available for the teacher: she appropriates it, transforms it, and adapts it in order to construct his document. Unlike the resource, a document has a teaching purpose, a didactic intent, to deal with a class of situations adapted to a context (e.g., to design activities on proportionality in grade 6, to integrate dynamic geometry activities with using dedicated software).

During her documentation work, the teacher has a variety of material and digital resources that, combined in different contexts, give birth to one or several documents in a process of a documentational genesis. The document resulting from this transformation must meet a didactic intention, the needs of the teacher, and the rules organizing its use. We adopt the definition given by Gueudet and Trouche (2010): the document is the fusion of recombined resources and its scheme of use.

For Vergnaud (1991), the scheme aims to describe the relationships between knowledge and activities in a given situation. He concludes that the scheme is also the result of a continuous process of adjustment and control of the action and of the development of knowledge. The document exceeds the meaning of a resource, by the synchronization between knowledge and activities in situation. We can thus consider a document defined as follows:

Document = Resources + usages + professional knowledge

Gueudet and Trouche (2009) distinguish two parts in a scheme: an observable part and an invisible part. For these authors, the observable part of the scheme is the regularities in the activities of teachers in various contexts, belonging to the same class of situation designated by these authors by the word *usages*. The invisible part represents essentially the teacher's knowledge. A document for these authors is.

Document = Recombined resources + scheme of use (Gueudet and Trouche 2010, p. 59).

In this research, we refer to the notion of scheme defined by Vergnaud as "an invariant organization of activity for a given class of situation" (2009, p. 36, our translation). Vergnaud describes the concept of *scheme* and encompasses it around its constituents: its purpose, sub-goals and expectations, rules of action, information taking and control, operational invariants (concept-in-action and theorem-in-action), and the possibilities of inference, which he generalizes by the organization of the activity. In the following section, we describe these elements for a better understanding of the concept of scheme. To define a scheme leads thus to:

> observe an activity in a situation and see how this activity is generated progressively, according to the previous actions, according to the information taken and to control, depending on the possible connections of the activity. And this requires finding the concepts-in-action and theorems-in-action that are mobilized (Vergnaud 2009, our translation).

In this research, we use the notion of scheme to approach the usage aspect of uses, thus approaching the dynamics of the resource system.

In order to analyze a teacher's resource system, we consider it at both static and dynamic levels. At the static level, we introduce the notion of *primary resource* and *stabilized resource* and give our definition of *mother-resource*. On the dynamic level, we introduce the notion of *intermediate resource, triggering event*, and resource *status* (active or standby).

9.6.1.1 Static Level of a Resource System

During the resource design process, we consider as a *primary resource* any living institutional resource – that the teacher needs – to perform its didactic function. In our case, these resources are provided by the ministry, and they cannot be in any way altered or modified by the teacher. These resources are considered essential resources for his function. We cite as example textbooks, guides accompanying the curricula. Such a resource cannot be modified; this is why we call this level static. Mother-resource introduced by Hammoud (2012) represents the set of initial resources that the teacher mobilizes to prepare a given teaching. We retain this definition, but we consider that these resources are optional and are not institutional (coming from the ministry of education), but they come from other institutions, which gives them a certain reliability and distinguishes them from other resources available in the teacher's resource system. We take as examples Sésamath resources, foreign textbooks, results of educational research, etc.

We introduce the notion of *intermediate resource* to designate any resource that the teacher conceives from his mother and primary resources. Whereas Hammoud (2012) attributes the concept of intermediate resource to any instance of the design of a daughter-resource, we consider as intermediate resource any resource that dynamically evolves in the system, being newly created, modified, recombined, and adjusted in an individual, or in the collective context (interactions between teachers or between teacher and students). This evolution continues, and we consider that the evolution of the intermediate resource over time tends toward stability, hence the notion of a *stabilized resource* (Fig. 9.13).

9.6.1.2 Dynamic Level of a Resource System

On the dynamic level, we consider as resource any living entity in the system (Guin and Trouche 2002). In this sense, a resource can only be living if it is active in this system. But it is also possible that some resources are inactive during a certain period, i.e., they do not undergo any action; we consider such resources as resources on *standby*. The use of such a resource is linked to a *triggering event* that changes it status to active resource. We assign this status of resource on standby also to any entity of the system that the teacher discovers before its use (Fig. 9.14).

To sum up, the structure of a mathematics teacher resource system can be viewed from two perspectives. From the static point of view, we identify primary institutional

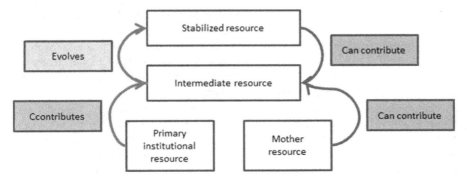

Fig. 9.13 Mathematics teacher's resource system

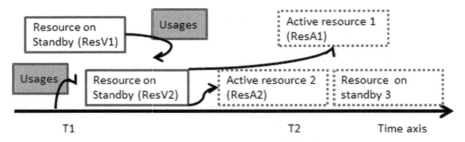

Fig. 9.14 Active and standby resources and transition from the latter to the former

resources (coming from the ministry of education) and optional institutional resources coming from other institutions (foreign textbooks, resources created by associations, etc.) and mother-resources. Dynamic point of view is characterized by the design, modification, and combination of resources. Two different statuses can be assigned to a resource: intermediate resource meaning that the resource evolves toward a stabilized resource. The latter will become part of the system and will possibly contribute to the design of new resources.

9.6.2 Analysis of Meriam's Resource System

In this section, we study the evolution of collective practices of Meriam, a mathematics teacher and its impact on the evolution of her resource system. Meriam teaches at IMTIYAZ, a private Arabic-speaking lower high school, which means that, according to the institutional rules, all subject matters are taught in Arabic. Mathematics teaching is no exception. However, writing and mathematical symbolism are left to right and in French letters. In this school, under the responsibility of the mathematics coordinator, a mathematical workshop (noninstitutional class) was organized, which served, for the teachers of the school, as an environment of discovery of the Sésamath resources. Considering these resources, we investigate what role the teacher community, gathered around these resources, plays in the evolution of Meriam's resource system and teaching practice.

The groups that we observed belong to two communities of practice (Wenger 1998): COP(ICT), a community of practice around the usage of digital Sésamath resources in institutional classes, and COP(Sésamath), around the usages of the Sésamath textbook. Meriam belongs to the latter.

Our methodology draws on reflexive investigation methodology (Gueudet and Trouche 2009) involving interviews, schematic representation of her resource system, and observations of the COP (Sésamath) during a working session aimed at selecting a Sésamath resource for teaching 3D geometry in Meriam's grade 6 class.

The teacher's schematic representation of her resource system shows the system in its entirety. We consider it as a *flow of resources* exchanged between *actors*. It does not show in any case the relations or the structure of the resources involved. From this schematic representation of her resource system, we tried to identify

9 Teachers' Resource Systems: Their Constitution, Structure and Evolution

Table 9.2 Meriam's resource dictionary

الموارد	التعريف بالمورد	Resource (our translation of the first column)	Type of the resource defined by the teacher (our translation)	Description of the resource provided by the teacher (our translation of the second column)
Primary resources				
البرنامج	نقصد بها المعلومات و المعارف التي يجب تلقينها للطفل خلال فترة معينة.	Program	External	Represents the information and knowledge to be learnt by the student during a certain period of time
منهاج	يشمل كل العمليات التكوينية التي يساهم فيها التلميذ بتأطير من المدرسة في فترة تعلم. مثال منهاج الرياضيات لقسم الثالثة متوسط	Curriculum	External	Includes all training processes in which the student contributes with the supervision of the school during the learning period.
التدرج السنوي	توزيع الجوانب التعليمية ومجمل نشاطات التعلم وفق مبدأ تدرج الزمن الدراسي حسب مستويات التعليم	Distribution	External	Distribution of educational aspects and the group of activities according to the teaching period and the school level
Intermediate resources				
المذكرة	ورقة عمل لسيرورةالحصة توضح تنظيم الوقت استبق الاحداث،تفاصيل الدرس، نشاط البحث، خلاصة المعرفة والتقويم.	Lesson plan	Internal	Worksheet for conducting of the lesson, specifies time management, anticipations of events, details of the lesson, research activity, synthesis of knowledge and evaluation.

material resources that Meriam has to perform her various tasks and that we named *the resource dictionary*. This dictionary (see Table 9.2) gathers all resources, their identification, and description; this will allow us to structure the system. This dictionary has been established by different data collection tools (different schematic representations, interviews). Meriam identifies her own resources as internal resources and the resources she receives from her colleagues as external ones.

Meriam's resources are not independent, rather they are interrelated and constitute a coherent system (Fig. 9.15). During the interviews and the different guided visits of her resource system, we tried to identify relations between her resources that we present in what follows:

- Pedagogical guide, textbook, teacher's guide, and the distribution are primary resources.
- The pedagogical guide develops the content of the textbook.

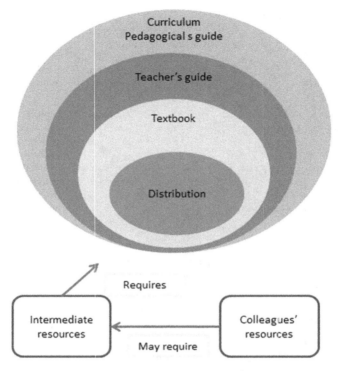

Fig. 9.15 Conceptual model of Meriam's resources under its static aspect

- The teacher's guide provides a detail of some activities, exercises, and problems from the textbook.
- The distribution corresponds to the overall content of the textbook, but the detail is related to the content of the pedagogical guide.
- The textbook is not the only teacher's resource for accomplishing her teaching tasks; other resources can be used, such as inherited intermediate resources, either individual or coming from collectives.
- The content of the lesson plan, assessment, and list of exercises is related to the content of the textbook and the distribution.

Any resource from Meriam's system can be described by an information sheet that allows to situate it in the system. The information contained in the sheet is:

- Its type: mother, primary, stabilized, or intermediate.
- Its origin: resource coming from a collective, individual or outside the school.
- Its status at a given moment: resource on standby or living.
- Its purpose: resource for assessment, for remediation, as a support of a lesson.

We described the *conceptual model* of Meriam's resource system under its static aspect considering only her material resources and their relations (Fig. 9.15). Figure 9.16 describes the dynamic aspect of this system.

9 Teachers' Resource Systems: Their Constitution, Structure and Evolution   247

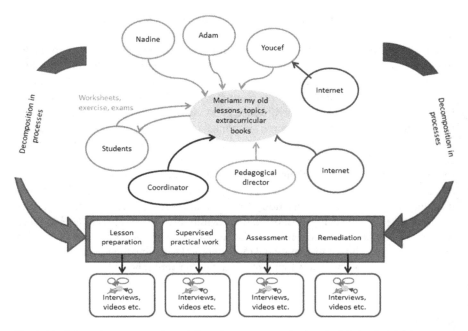

Fig. 9.16 Schematic representation of the subsystems constituting the Meriam's initial resource system

When reading her schema, Meriam explained the usage of her resources in relation to her activities. We identified, from her description of the system, four *processes* that constitute *triggering* moments of her interactions with her system (Fig. 9.16): *process of lesson preparation, process of preparation of supervised practical work, process of preparation of assessment*, and finally *process of preparation of remediation sessions* (Sayah 2018a, b). Each process represents the dynamics in the resource system: it enacts material resources and schemes of use of her resources. The professional development of the teacher (not developed in this text) was analyzed by the notion of schemes: we identified operational invariants (theorem in action and concept in action), and we followed their evolution through the different processes involved.

9.6.3 Concluding Remarks

Meriam's resource system has evolved during the period of its follow-up. Initially, Meriam relied on official documents (textbooks and pedagogical guides), and her interactions with the community mainly focused on the discussion of her intermediate resource. The work around Sésamath resources initiated work in two communities: COP(ICT) for the integration of Sésamath digital resources and the COP(Sésamath) for the appropriation of Sésamath resources in paper form.

The analysis of her resource system allowed us to structure it in its static aspect, by identifying the elements of her *resource dictionary* (what the teacher needs). These resources can be *active* or *on standby*, a *triggering event* can make a resource to change its status into the active one. For example, a Sésamath resource is on standby, its transition to active status is linked to a triggering event such as lack of institutional resources. This has led us to elaborate the *conceptual model of a resource* to describe the links between the resources of the system, hence the static aspect of the system. To approach the structure of the teacher's resource system leads to identify the processes related to these resources. We have decomposed Meriam's activity in *processes*: using our *conceptual model of usage of these resources*, we tried to deepen the analysis of her activity based on the notion of scheme. The analysis of the process of preparation of an assessment gave birth to the schemes: selection of a Sésamath resource, adaptation of a Sésamath resource, and translation of a Sésamath resource. The notion of scheme was mobilized for the analysis of the activity within the different processes and therefore of the teacher's interactions with the resources, both individual and collective. This allowed us to infer the operational invariants and to follow their evolution, or even approach the professional development of the teacher (not reported in the text).

9.7 Conclusion

This concluding section highlights first the most salient results presented in the WG1 contributions and elaborated in this chapter and, second, brings to the fore needs in terms of theoretical and methodological developments.

9.7.1 Teachers' Resource Systems: Salient Results

The WG1 discussions focused on teachers' resource systems in order to better understand how these are constituted, what is their structure and content, and how they evolve over time. These three aspects were mentioned explicitly in the call for contributions. Although they were separated in the call, in reality, they are strongly interrelated, which appears clearly in most of the WG1 contributions and in particular in Sayah's (2018a, b) contribution who suggests analyzing a teacher's resource system from a static point of view when the focus is on its content and structure and from a dynamic point of view when its evolution is under consideration.

In the anthropological theory of didactics, Chevallard (2002) introduces the notion of co-determination levels (Fig. 9.17) to identify conditions and constraints that impact teachers' actions and practices. Indeed, as Bosch (2010) says.

> the conditions that a teacher can create in her classroom and the constraints that determine her room for manoeuvre cannot be apprehended without seeing what happens beyond the classroom, in the institutions that overhang it and are constantly interacting with it (p. 19, our translation).

9 Teachers' Resource Systems: Their Constitution, Structure and Evolution

Fig. 9.17 Levels of didactic co-determination

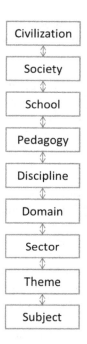

A lesson that a mathematics (*discipline*) teacher prepares concerns a mathematical *subject* (e.g., solve a first-degree equations) that is related to a *theme* (in the case of the French curriculum, "first-degree equations"), belonging to a *sector* (in the French curriculum, "numbers and calculation") and a larger *domain* (in our case, algebra). The various factors impacting teachers' documentation work and consequently the evolution of their resource systems can be looked at through the lenses of the levels of codetermination. For example, the alignment of resources with national educational strategies, exam system, and school instruction methods highlight the constraints of the levels of *pedagogy*, *school*, or even *society*. Similarly, communities that were reported as levers of the evolution of teachers' resource systems may be seen as the influence of the levels of *school* when the communities gather teacher from the same school or *society* otherwise (e.g., in the case of virtual communities). It appears therefore important to take into account the codetermination levels in order to better understand the conditions and the constraints that weigh on teachers' interactions with resources.

Aspects related to the constitution of resource systems were approached through the observation of processes of selection of resources that are subsequently integrated into a resource system. Observing prospective teachers or teachers at the beginning of their career appeared as particularly interesting and relevant with respect to the analysis of processes of constitution of resource systems. Results reported in this chapter show that tutors or mentors and their own resources, as well as resources that novice teachers encountered during their studies, play an important role in these processes. Indeed, these resources, which undergo a transformation called a *metamorphosis* by

Assis et al. (2018), are among the first ones around which novice teachers constitute their resource system. In this case, the authors call attention to *transitional resources*. Several motivational factors that conduct teachers toward constitution of a resource system were highlighted. These factors are linked to a variety of experienced teaching situations and teachers' knowledge. Phenomena related to the constitution of a system of resources (or at least a subsystem) can also be observed in experienced teachers. This occurs especially when the teachers face changes in their practices due to a curriculum reform or the integration of digital technology, for example. In some cases, teachers encounter difficulties with integrating novel resources into their existing resource system, as was the case reported by Salinas-Hernandez et al. (2018). A possible reason explaining such difficulties may be that the new resource is not consistent with the resources already present in the resource system (Gueudet 2013).

Contributions that focused on the content and the structure of teachers' resource systems highlight a privileged place of textbooks in teachers' resource systems, regardless of the subject matter or the school level. However, in some cases, the importance of the textbooks seems to diminish with the growing experience of teachers (Hammoud and Alturkmani 2018). Curricular resources, such as programs and other resources produced by ministry of education-related institutions, constitute also an important part of teachers resource systems. Some authors call these resources *primary* to stress their specific position within the resource systems (Fofana and Sokhna 2018; Sayah 2018a, b). Teachers' resource systems seem to contain particular resources around which the systems are structured. Alturkmani (2015) introduced the notion of *structuring mother-resource* to designate a resource that helps structuring daughter-resources (i.e., resources ready to be used in a classroom stemming from a mother-resource). Gueudet and Trouche (2010) designate by the term *pivotal* resource a resource involved in several types of teachers' activities, such as preparation of lessons, exercises, or assessments. These structuring elements would deserve further research in order to get deeper insight into their role within the resource system and the relations they have with other components.

Studies analyzing evolution of resource systems bring to the fore several factors that make the systems evolve. Among these, teachers' participation to communities appears as a driving force of teachers' professional development and, consequently, of the evolution of their resource system (Hammoud 2018; Essonnier and Trgalová 2018). Such participation causes deep reorganization and restructuring of resource systems mostly in the case of novice teachers. Sayah (2018a, b) considers the evolution of a resource system as its dynamic aspect characterized by the design, modification, and combination of resources, which is designated by the term *intermediate* resource evolving toward a *stabilized* resource.

9.7.2 Research Perspectives

Besides important results contributed by WG1 participants to the research on teachers' documentation work and their resource systems, the discussions within the working group evidenced the need for further clarification of concepts defined within the documentational approach and for further theoretical and methodological developments.

A number of new concepts were introduced by the authors of WG1 contributions, highlighting the need for further conceptualizations. Among these, we can mention an attempt to build a *taxonomy* of resources in order to distinguish between various types of resources (e.g., resources that are produced by official bodies related to policymakers and those that come from other sources, resources that are used and those that are at the teacher's disposal without being used). We can cite a concept of *structuring mother-resource* to qualify a structuring resource whose role is somewhat different from a pivotal resource. We can also mention the concept of *metamorphosis* that designate a specific process of constituting a resource system by novice teachers either from resources that the teachers used as students or from their tutors' or mentors' resources. The future will show whether these concepts will be taken up by other researchers and will continue to live.

It is important to note that some concepts, even those that have been defined some time ago and are widely used, seem to be understood in different ways. This is the case of the concepts of scheme or operational invariant. And conversely, some new terms introduced by different authors may have the same, or at least very similar, meaning, e.g., main, primary, institutional, or pivotal resource.

The complexity of phenomena related to teachers' professional activity; to processes of constitution, structuring, and evolution of their resource systems; and to their professional development require specific theoretical and methodological tools. In particular, analyzing the structure of a resource system appeared difficult and participants raised a need for models allowing capturing elements of such a system and relations between its components. The notion of scheme appeared also as very complex to use and a lack of methods for inferring schemes and for tracking their evolution was expressed. Participants also noted a difficulty to cope with a stability of observed phenomena, which is necessary for studying a structure of resource systems and inferring operational invariants, on the one hand, and the evolution of resource systems related to teachers' professional development, on the other hand.

It would certainly be interesting to explore in future research all these issues and perspectives.

References

Abboud-Blanchard, M., Caron, F., Dorier, J.-L., & Sokhna, M. (2015). Ressources dans l'espace mathématique francophone. In Theis L. (Ed.), *Pluralités culturelles et universalité des mathématiques : enjeux et perspectives pour leur enseignement et leur apprentissage – Actes du colloque EMF2015 – Plénières* (pp. 40–66). Alger: Université des Sciences et de la Technologie Houari Boumediene.

Adler, J. (2000). Conceptualising resources as a theme for teacher education, Journal of Mathematics Teacher Education 3, 205–224.

Alturkmani, M. D. (2015). *Genèse des affinités disciplinaire et didactique et genèse documentaire : le cas des professeurs de physique-chimie en France.* Thèse de doctorat. Lyon: École Normale Supérieure de Lyon.

Alturkmani, M. D., Trouche, L., & Morge, L. (2018). Étude des liens entre affinités disciplinaire et didactique, et travail de l'enseignant : le cas d'un enseignant de physique-chimie en France. *Recherches en Didactique des Sciences et des Technologies, 17,* 129–157.

Alturkmani, M.-D., Daubias, P., Loisy, C., Messaoui, A., & Trouche, L. (in press). Instrumenter les recherches sur le travail documentaire des enseignants : le projet AnA.doc. *Éducation & didactique.*

Assis, C., & Gitirana, V. (2017). An analysis of the engagement of preservice teachers with curriculum resources in Brazil. In G. Schubring, L. Fan, L., & V. Giraldo (Eds.), *Proceedings of the second international conference on mathematics textbook research and development* (ICMT2). Rio de Janeiro-RJ: Universidade Federal do Rio de Janeiro.

Assis, C., Gitirana, V., & Trouche, L. (2018). The metamorphosis of resource systems of prospective teacher: From studying to teaching. In V. Gitirana et al. (Eds.), *Proceedings of the Re(s) sources 2018 international conference* (pp. 39–42). Lyon: ENS de Lyon.

Bachimont, B., & Crozat, S. (2004). Instrumentation numérique des documents: pour une séparation fonds/forme. *Revue I3, 4*(1), 95-104.

Barlet, R. (1999). L'espace épistémologique et didactique de la chimie. *Bulletin de l'Union des Physiciens, 93*(817), 1423–1448.

Baştürk-Şahín, B. N., & Tapan-Broutin, M. S. (2018a). Analysing teacher candidates' evolution into teachers through documentational approach. In V. Gitirana et al. (Eds.), *Proceedings of the Re(s)sources 2018 international conference* (pp. 43–47). ENS de Lyon.

Baştürk-Şahín, B. N., & Tapan-Broutin, M. S. (2018b). Analysis of primary mathematics teachers' lesson document preparation processes. In V. Gitirana et al. (Eds.), *Proceedings of the Re(s) sources 2018 international conference* (pp. 48–52). ENS de Lyon.

Besnier, S. (2016). *Le travail documentaire des professeurs à l'épreuve des ressources technologiques. Le cas de l'enseignement du nombre à l'école maternelle.* Thèse de doctorat. Renne: Université de Bretagne Occidentale. https://tel.archives-ouvertes.fr/tel-01326826v2/ document

Bosch, M. (2010). L'écologie des parcours d'étude et de recherche au secondaire. Diffuser les mathématiques (et les autres savoirs) comme outils de connaissance et d'actions. In *Actes du 2° Colloque International sur la théorie anthropologique du didactique.* Montpellier: IUFM.

Brousseau, G. (1986). La relation didactique: le milieu. In *Actes de la 4e école d'été de didactique des mathématiques* (pp. 54–68). IREM de Paris 7.

Brousseau, G. (1997). *Theory of didactical situations in mathematics.* Dordrecht: Kluwer Academic Publishers.

Caillot, M. (1994). Des objectifs aux compétences dans l'enseignement scientifique : une évolution de vingt ans. In F. Ropé & L. Tanguy (dir.), *Savoirs et compétences. De l'usage de ces notions dans l'école et dans l'entreprise* (pp. 95–117). Paris: L'Harmattan.

Chevallard, Y. (1982). Pourquoi la transposition didactique ? In *Actes du Séminaire de didactique et de pédagogie des mathématiques de l'IMAG* (pp. 167–194). Grenoble: Université Joseph Fourier. http://yves.chevallard.free.fr/spip/spip/IMG/pdf/Pourquoi_la_transposition_didactique.pdf.

9 Teachers' Resource Systems: Their Constitution, Structure and Evolution 253

Chevallard, Y. (1998). Analyse des pratiques enseignantes et didactique des mathématiques : l'approche anthropologique. In *Actes de l'université d'été Analyse des pratiques enseignantes et didactique des mathématiques* (pp. 91–120). IREM de Clermont-Ferrand.

Chevallard, Y. (1999). L'analyse des pratiques enseignantes en Théorie Anthropologie Didactique. *Recherches en Didactiques des Mathématiques, 19*(2), 221–266.

Chevallard, Y. (2002). Organiser l'étude. 3. Ecologie & régulation. In *Actes de la XIe école d'été de didactique des mathématiques* (pp. 41–56). Grenoble: La Pensée Sauvage.

Choppin, A. (2005). L'édition scolaire française et ses contraintes : Une perspective historique. In E. Bruillard (Ed.), *Manuels scolaires, regards croisés* (pp. 39–53). Caen: CRDP de Basse-Normandie.

Clandinin, D. J., & Connelly, F. M. (1990). Stories of experience and narrative inquiry. *Educational Researcher, 19*(5), 2–14.

Contamines, J., George, S., & Hotte, R. (2003). Approche instrumentale des banques de ressources éducatives. *Revue Sciences et Techniques Éducatives, 10*, 157–178. http://halshs.archives-ouvertes.fr/hal-00298189/.

Daele, A., & Charlier, B. (2006). *Comprendre les communautés virtuelles d'enseignants*. Paris: L'Harmattan.

de Araújo, AJ. (2009). *O ensino de álgebra no Brasil e na França: estudo sobre o ensino de equações do 1° grau à luz da teoria antropológica do didático*. Doctoral dissertation. Recife-PE: Universidade Federal de Pernambuco. https://repositorio.ufpe.br/bitstream/123456789/3947/1/arquivo3433_1.pdf

de Araújo, A. J, & Santos (2010). Equações do primeiro grau: Estudo comparativo dos programas de ensino da França e Brasil. In A. P. de Avelar Brito Lima et al. (Eds.), *Pesquisas em Fenômenos Didáticos: Alguns Cenários* (Vol. 1, pp. 33-49). Recife-PE: EDIGORA DA UFPE.

Engeström, Y. (1987). *Learning by expanding: An activity-theoretical approach to developmental research*. Helsinki: Orienta-Konsultit.

Espindola, E., & Trgalová, J. (2018). The documentational work in the initial formation of a mathematics undergraduate in training for the teaching of first degree equation. In V. Gitirana et al. (Eds.), *Proceedings of the Re(s)sources 2018 international conference* (pp. 57–60). Lyon: ENS de Lyon.

Espindola, E., Ketully, R., & Trgalová, J. (2018). Resources and didactic decisions of a teacher in the teaching of combinatorial analysis. In V. Gitirana et al. (Eds.), *Proceedings of the re(s) sources 2018 international conference* (pp. 1127–1128). Lyon: ENS de Lyon.

Essonnier, N., & Trgalová, J. (2018). Collaborative design of digital resources: role of designers' resource systems and professional knowledge. In V. Gitirana et al. (Eds.), *Proceedings of the Re(s)sources 2018 international conference* (pp. 57–60). Lyon: ENS de Lyon.

Fofana, O. B., & Sokhna, M. (2018). Analyse des écarts entre les prescriptions institutionnelles et les systèmes de ressources des enseignants : le cas de l'enseignement des limites de fonctions. In V. Gitirana et al. (Eds.), *Proceedings of the re(s)sources 2018 international conference* (pp. 61–64). Lyon: ENS de Lyon.

Goigoux, R., & Vergnaud, G. (2005). Schèmes professionnels. In J.-P. Bernié, & R. Goigoux (Ed.), *Dossier: Les gestes professionnels, La lettre de l'AiRDF n°36* (pp. 7–10).

Gueudet, G. (2013). Les professeurs de mathématiques et leurs ressources professionnelles. In M. Gandit et al. (Eds.), *Actes du Colloque CORFEM 2013*. Grenoble: Université Joseph Fourier. https://hal.archives-ouvertes.fr/hal-01144526/document.

Gueudet, G., & Trouche, L. (2008). Du travail documentaire des enseignants: genèses, collectifs, communautés. *Le cas des mathématiques. Education & Didactique, 2*, 7–33.

Gueudet, G., & Trouche, L. (2009). Towards new documentation systems for mathematics teachers? *Educational Studies in Mathematics, 71*(3), 199–218.

Gueudet, G., & Trouche, L. (2010). Des ressources aux documents, travail du professeur et genèses documentaires. In G. Gueudet, & L. Trouche (dir.), *Ressources vives. Le travail documentaire des professeurs en mathématiques* (pp. 57-74). Rennes: Presses Universitaires de Rennes et INRP.

Gueudet, G., & Trouche, L. (2012). Teachers' work with resources: Documentation geneses and professional geneses. In G. Gueudet, B. Pepin, & L. Trouche (Eds.), *From text to 'lived' resources: Mathematics curriculum materials and teacher development* (pp. 23–41). Dordrecht: Springer.

Gueudet, G., Pepin, B., & Trouche, L. (2013). Collective work with resources: an essential dimension for teacher documentation. *ZDM – Mathematics Education, 45*(7), 1003–1016.

Guin, D., & Trouche, L. (Eds.). (2002). *Calculatrices symboliques, faire d'un outil un instrument du travail mathématique, un problème didactique.* Grenoble: La Pensée Sauvage.

Hache, C., Proulx, J., & Moussa, S. (2009). Formation mathématique des enseignants : contenus et pratiques. Compte-rendu du Groupe de Travail n°1– EMF2009. In A. Kuzniak, & M. Sokhna (Eds.) *Actes du colloque Espace Mathématique Francophone EMF2009, Enseignement des mathématiques et développement : enjeux de société et de formation* (pp. 34–39). Dakar: Université Cheikh Anta Diop. http://fastef.ucad.sn/EMF2009

Hammoud, R. (2012). *Le travail collectif des professeurs en chimie comme levier pour la mise en œuvre de démarche d'investigation et le développement des connaissances professionnelles. Contribution au développement de l'approche documentaire du didactique.* Thèse de doctorat. Université Lyon 1 et Université Libanaise.

Hammoud, R. (2018). Participation in a virtual community as a lever for the evolution of chemistry teachers' resource system. In V. Gitirana et al. (Eds.), *Proceedings of the Re(s)sources 2018 international conference* (pp. 69–73). Lyon: ENS de Lyon.

Hammoud, R., & Alturkmani, M. D. (2018). Teachers' resource systems and documentation work: the case of two physics-chemistry teachers in France and two chemistry teachers in Lebanon. In V. Gitirana et al. (Eds.), *Proceedings of the re(s)sources 2018 international conference* (pp. 74–78). Lyon: ENS de Lyon.

Houart, M. (2009). *Etude de la communication pédagogique à l'université à travers les notes et les acquis des étudiants à l'issue du cours magistral de chimie.* Thèse de doctorat. Namur: Université de Namur.

Jameau, A., & Le Hénaff, C. (2018). Resources for science teaching in a foreign language. In V. Gitirana et al. (Eds.), *Proceedings of the re(s)sources 2018 international conference* (pp. 79–82). Lyon: ENS de Lyon.

Johnstone, A. H. (1993). The development of chemistry teaching: a changing response to changing demand. *Journal of Chemical Education, 70,* 701–705.

Justi, R., & Van Driel, J. (2005). The development of science teachers' knowledge on models and modelling: promoting, characterizing, and understanding the process. *International Journal of Science Education, 27*(5), 549–573.

Kermen, I. (2007). *Prévoir et expliquer l'évolution des systèmes chimiques.* Thèse de doctorat. Paris: Université Paris Diderot-Paris 7.

Le Maréchal, J. F. (1999). Modeling student's cognitive activity during the resolution of problems based on experimental facts in chemical Education. In J. Leach & A. Paulsen (Eds.), *Practical work in science education* (pp. 195–209). Dordrecht: Kluwer Academic Publishers.

Lima, I. (2018). The textbook for field public schools in Brazil – PNLD field. In V. Gitirana et al. (Eds.), *Proceedings of the re(s)sources 2018 international conference* (pp. 129–131). Lyon: ENS de Lyon.

Machado, R. N. S. J., Espindola, E., Trgalová, J., & Luberiaga, E. (2018). Abordagem documental do didático e o ensino de equação do 1° grau na educação de jovens e adultos-ensino médio. *Revista Paranaense de Educação Matemática, 7*(13), 270–294.

Margolinas, C. (2004). *Points de vue de l'élève et du professeur. Essai de développement de la théorie des situations didactiques.* Mémoire HDR. Mareille: Université de Provence – Aix-Marseille I. https://tel.archives-ouvertes.fr/tel-00429580v2/document

Martinand, J. L. (1992). *Enseignement et apprentissage de la modélisation en sciences.* Paris: INRP.

Messaoui, A. (2018). The complex process of classifying resources, an essential component of documentation expertise. In V. Gitirana et al. (Eds.), *Proceedings of the re(s)sources 2018 international conference* (pp. 83–87). Lyon: ENS de Lyon.

Pernambuco (2012a). *Parâmetros curriculares de Matemática. Ensino fundamental e médio.* Recife-PE: Secretaria de Educação.

Pernambuco (2012b). *Parâmetros curriculares de Matemática. Educação de jovens e adultos.* Recife-PE: Secretaria de Educação.

Quentin, I. (2012). *Fonctionnements et trajectoires des réseaux en ligne d'enseignants.* Thèse de doctorat. Paris: ENS Cachan.

Rabardel, P. (1999a). Eléments pour une approche instrumentale en didactique des mathématiques. In M. Bailleul (Ed.), *Actes de la Xe Ecole d'été de didactique des mathématiques* (pp. 202–213). Caen: IUFM.

Rabardel, P. (1999b). Le langage comme instrument ? Éléments pour une théorie instrumentale étendue. In Y. Clot (Ed.), *Avec Vygotski* (pp. 241-265). Paris : La Dispute.

Rabardel, P. (2002). *People and technology – A cognitive approach to contemporary instruments.* Paris: Université Paris 8. https://hal-univ-paris8.archives-ouvertes.fr/file/index/docid/1020705/filename/people_and_technology.

Remillard, J., & Heck, D. J. (2014). Conceptualizing the curriculum enactment process in mathematics education. *ZDM Mathematics Education, 46*(5), 705–718.

Robert, C., & Treiner, J. (2004). Une double émergence. *Bulletin de l'Union des Physiciens, 98*(867), 1385–1397.

Rocha, K. (2018). Uses of online resources and documentational trajectories: the case of Sésamath. In L. Fan, L. Trouche, S. Rezat, C. Qi, & J. Visnovska (Eds.), *Research on mathematics textbooks and teachers' resources: Advances and issues* (pp. 235–258). Cham: Springer.

Rocha, K., & Trouche, L. (2017). Documentational trajectory: a tool for analyzing the genesis of a teacher's resource system across her collective work. In T. Dooley & G. Gueudet (Eds.), *Proceedings of the tenth congress of the European Society for Research in Mathematics Education (CERME10)* (pp. 3732–3739). Dublin: DCU Institute of Education and ERME.

Ruthven, K. (2007). Teachers, technologies and the structures of schooling. In D. Pitta-Pantazi, & G. Philippou (Eds.), *Proceedings of the fifth congress of the European Society for Research in Mathematics Education* (pp. 52–67). Larnaca: Department of Education – University of Cyprus.

Salinas-Hernandez, U., Sacristan, A. I., & Trouche, L. (2018). Technology integration into mathematics classrooms: case study of a high-school teacher's use of GeoGebra. In V. Gitirana et al. (Eds.), *Proceedings of the Re(s)sources 2018 international conference* (pp. 88–91). Lyon: ENS de Lyon.

Sayac, N. (2018). What resources and assessment logic to design tests in mathematics at primary school in France? In V. Gitirana et al. (Eds.), *Proceedings of the re(s)sources 2018 international conference* (pp. 96–99). Lyon: ENS de Lyon.

Sayah, K. (2018a). Analyse de la structure d'un système de ressources, articulation entre aspect dynamique et aspect statique: cas d'une enseignante des mathématiques. In V. Gitirana et al. (Eds.), *Proceedings of the re(s)sources 2018 international conference* (pp. 100–103). Lyon: ENS de Lyon.

Sayah, K. (2018b). *L'intégration des ressources de Sésamath au collège : un moteur pour le développement du travail collectif des enseignants de mathématiques en Algérie.* Thèse de doctorat. Lyon: Université Claude Bernard Lyon 1.

Sokhna, M. (2006). *Formation continue à distance des professeurs de mathématiques du Sénégal: genèse instrumentale de ressources pédagogiques.* Thèse de doctorat. Montpellier: Université Montpellier II.

Sokhna, M. (2018). Systèmes de ressources et intégration des TICE : quels critères de sélection ? In V. Gitirana et al. (Eds.), *Proceedings of the re(s)sources 2018 international conference* (pp. 109–112). Lyon: ENS de Lyon.

Sokhna, M., & Trouche, L. (2015). Formation mathématique des enseignants: quelles médiations documentaires? In L. Theis (Ed.), *Pluralités culturelles et universalité des mathématiques : enjeux et perspectives pour leur enseignement et leur apprentissage. Actes Espace mathématique francophone* (EMF 2015) (pp. 624–639). Alger: Université des Sciences et de la Technologie Houari Boumediene.

Tiberghien, A. (2000). Designing teaching situations in the secondary school. In R. Millar, J. Leach, & J. Osborne (Eds.), *Improving science education: The contribution of research* (pp. 27–47). Buckingham: Open University Press.

Trouche, L., Trgalová, J., Loisy, C., & Alturkmani, M. (2018). *Ressources vivantes pour l'enseignement et l'apprentissage* (Rapport scientifique des composantes IFE et S2HEP). Lyon: Ens de Lyon. https://hal.archives-ouvertes.fr/hal-01743212v2

Van Steenbrugge, H., Remillard, J., Krzywacki, H., Hemmi, K., Koljonen, T., & Machalow, R. (2018). Understanding teachers' use of instructional resources from a cross-cultural perspective: the cases of Sweden and Flanders. In V. Gitirana et al. (Eds.), *Proceedings of the re(s) sources 2018 international conference* (pp. 117–121). Lyon: ENS de Lyon.

Vergnaud, G. (1991). La théorie des champs conceptuels. *Recherches en Didactique des Mathématiques, 10*(2), 133–170.

Vergnaud, G. (1993). Teoria dos campos conceituais. In L. Nasser (Ed.), *Anais do 1° Seminario Internacional de Educaçao Matemática do Rio de Janeiro* (pp. 1–26). Rio de Janeiro: UFRJ Projeto Fundão, Instituto de Matemática.

Vergnaud, G. (2009). Le concept d'algorithme en psychologie: *entretien réalisé par Nicolas Paratore*. http://paratore-nicolas.com/articles/concept_algo-3.pdf

Vermersch, P. (1994). *L'entretien d'explicitation*. Issy-les-Moulineaux: ESF éditeur.

Wang, C. (2018). Mathematics teachers' expertise in resources work and its development in collectives. A French and a Chinese cases. In L. Fan, L. Trouche, S. Rezat, C. Qi, & J. Visnovska (Eds.), *Research on mathematics textbooks and teachers' resources: Advances and issues* (pp. 193–213). Cham: Springer.

Wenger, E. (1998). *Communities of practice: Learning, meaning, and identity*. Cambridge, MA: Cambridge University Press.

Chapter 10
Analyzing Teachers' Work with Resources: Methodological Issues

Catherine Loisy, Hussein Sabra, Scott A. Courtney, Katiane Rocha, Dubravka Glasnović Gracin, Gilles Aldon, Mathias Front, Marie-Line Gardes, Eugenia Taranto, Ferdinando Arzarello, and Ornella Robutti

Abstract Studying teachers' work with resources leads to wide-ranging research questions requiring diverse theoretical frameworks and, consequently, various methodologies. Characterizing the dialectical relation between theoretical and methodological choices is critical. Teachers' work with resources and professional development appear intertwined, opening new avenues for research and methodological developments. After developing the main methodological issues raised in Re(s)sources International Conference, four texts illustrate research that challenge these issues. Rocha studies the long-term evolution of interactions between teachers and resources. She proposes two new notions—documentational trajectory and documentational experience—and develops methodologies adapted to their study. Glasnović Gracin and Courtney present contrasting studies on teachers' work with resources, concerning lesson planning from two distinct countries (Croatia and the USA). They develop a methodology aimed at expounding on what occurs within teachers' resource systems in different environments. Aldon, Front, and Gardes study proximity between teacher's intentions and those of

---

C. Loisy (✉) · K. Rocha · G. Aldon
École normale supérieure de Lyon, Lyon, France
e-mail: Catherine.Loisy@ens-lyon.fr

H. Sabra
University of Reims Champagne-Ardenne, Grand Est, France

S. A. Courtney
Kent State University, Kent, OH, USA

D. Glasnović Gracin
University of Zagreb, Zagreb, Croatia

M. Front · M.-L. Gardes
University of Lyon, Lyon, France

E. Taranto · F. Arzarello · O. Robutti
University of Turin, Turin, Italy

© Springer Nature Switzerland AG 2019
L. Trouche et al. (eds.), *The 'Resource' Approach to Mathematics Education*,
Advances in Mathematics Education,
https://doi.org/10.1007/978-3-030-20393-1_10

resource designers. They present a method of collaborative design and define an indicator of convergence to analyze the conjunction between intentions of the resources' authors and teacher's classroom achievement. Taranto, Arzarello, and Robutti examine teachers' professional learning in Massive Open Online Courses (MOOCs). They elaborate a theoretical framework, MOOC-MDT, which allows for analysis of the interactive nature of MOOCs and their influence on teachers' professional learning.

Keywords Content knowledge · Genesis · Methodologies · Reflective investigation · Resources · Teachers' practices · Teaching level · Trajectories studying

10.1 Introduction

The aim of Working Group 2 (WG2) was to raise methodological challenges related to research focused on teacher-resource interactions. This chapter begins with a general introduction to methodological issues that were proposed to study teachers' work with/on resources.

The analysis of teachers' interactions with resources requires considering teachers' work "as a whole." We explore the methodological issues by:

- Characterizing the dialectical relation between theoretical choices and methodological choices and the development of these relations.
- Discussing the methodology of data collection and methods of analysis that allow us to understand the forms of teachers' professional learning by their work on resources.
- Discussing the affordances of various methodologies in relation to diverse research issues and considering resources from various points of view (e.g., researcher-designer of resources, researcher-outsider, and researcher involved in collective work of resource design).
- Identifying methodological springboards that support the study of teachers' work on resources, related to the evolution of resources in a digital era.

In this chapter, we detail possible ways forward to address some of these challenges. Four contributions reported from WG2 develop and help discuss several of these issues:

- Discussing the methodology of data collection and methods of analysis that allow us to understand the forms of teachers' professional learning by their work on resources is addressed by the contribution of Katiane Rocha (see Sect. 10.3) through the analysis of teacher interactions with resources "as a whole" and by the contribution of Dubravka Glasnović Gracin and Scott A. Courtney (see Sect. 10.4) through analysis of the structure of the resource system
- Discussing the affordances of various methodologies in relation to diverse research issues and considering resources from various points of view is

addressed by the contribution of Gilles Aldon, Mathias Front, and Marie-Line Gardes (see Sect. 10.5) through analysis of teacher-resource interactions that take shape according to teaching contents and levels

- Identifying methodological springboards that support the study of teachers' work on resources related to the evolution of resources in a digital era is addressed by the contribution of Eugenia Taranto, Ferdinando Arzarello, and Ornella Robutti (see Sect. 10.6) through study, in the long term, of the evolution of teacher-resource interactions

Each contribution addresses methodological elements organized according to their main purpose. The chapter and four WG2 contributions also provide descriptions of methodologies and methodological choices that present opportunities for further research. Doing so required contributing authors to integrate and develop novel or network theories, frameworks, or methodologies that are complementary across studies.

10.2 Teacher-Resource Interactions: Some Methodological Advances and Looking Ahead

Catherine Loisy, Hussein Sabra, and Scott A. Courtney

10.2.1 Introduction

The study of teachers' work with/on resources is a fast-growing field. It leads to an abundance of research questions, requiring diverse theoretical frameworks to address them and, consequently, a diversity of methodologies.

Teachers' interactions with resources occur in a variety of settings—in and out of the classroom, at home, in lab rooms, in computer rooms, online, and so forth. Teachers' interactions with resources are also related to each teacher's idiosyncratic professional experiences. A teacher interacts with her resources from previous years, as well as with resources she has shared with peers, resources peers have shared with her, online resources, curriculum resources, and so on. She interacts with resources to address a variety of goals and teaching objectives and through her involvement over time in different collective work. Didactical approaches consider that a teacher's interactions with resources influence and are influenced by (1) her teaching experiences, (2) her teaching beliefs, and (3) the content and its presentation.

The institutional context, particularly the level of teaching (i.e., primary, secondary, post-secondary), is also crucial. The "versatility" of primary teachers, linked to the large number of disciplines they teach, has the potential to impact their interactions with resources in different ways. Regarding secondary teachers, there is an issue of content specialization, which can generate several forms of tension between didactical knowledge and disciplinary knowledge. At the tertiary level, teachers are usually researchers (i.e., specialists in a field) and are evaluated on their research activity rather than their teaching. Finally, the institutional context, as viewed on the scale of educational system and accompanying curriculum materials and resources, also has the potential to impact teaching choices and a teacher's design of her lessons.

In this chapter, we principally raise the issue of methodological developments to study teacher-resource interactions, particularly from the point of view of the relationship between theoretical choices and methodologies In addition, many of the studies discussed challenge the question of teachers' professional learning.

This first part of this chapter is structured around four points, allowing for the discussion of methodological challenges from several facets, which take into account and value the contributions of WG2. The dialectic relation between theoretical choices and methodological issues (Sect. 10.2.2) is approached with respect to three topics: (1) affordances of theoretical concepts and approaches, (2) networking theories and associated methodological developments, and (3) theoretical approaches, marking out methodological needs and developments. In addition, the progressive development of models and methodologies deployed to analyze teacher-resource interactions "as a whole" is exposed (Sect. 10.2.3). As a final point, the development of teacher-resource interactions is discussed with a focus on content and level of teaching (Sect. 10.2.4).

10.2.2 Dialectic Relation Between Theoretical Choices and Methodological Issues

The focus of this section is on methodological developments to study teacher-resource interactions, especially in relation to theoretical choices. Throughout this section, we distinguish between two forms of researchers' involvement in the field of study: the researcher that takes part in the design of the resources and the researcher as "outsider" who observes the interaction of a teacher (or a group of teachers) with resources. The teacher-resource interactions we consider are those in- and outside of the classroom. We will focus on some examples of theoretical and methodological advances encountered during WG2 of the Re(s)sources 2018 International Conference.

10.2.2.1 Affordances of Theoretical Concepts and Approaches

Over the past two decades, research into mathematics teachers' practices has increased its focus on resources and the nature of the interactions between teachers and resources (e.g., Adler 2000; Gueudet and Trouche 2009; Remillard 2005;

Ruthven 2008). Pepin et al. (2017, p. 258) present teachers' resources as "the curriculum/text, material and personal resources that teachers use and develop in their daily practice, in and for their teaching." For Gueudet and Trouche (2009, pp. 200–201), resources include "everything likely to intervene in teachers' documentation work: discussions between teachers, orally or online; students' worksheets, etc." Furthermore, a resource is never isolated, but belongs to a set of resources (Gueudet and Trouche 2009, p. 205). Pepin et al. (2017, p. 261) coined the term *teacher's resource system* for the "whole set of resources with which a teacher works [...] meaning that this set is a structured entity, aligned with mathematics teachers' practices."

The documentational approach to didactics (DAD) (Gueudet et al. 2012) is often used to study the interactions between a teacher, or a group of teachers, and resources. Studies that adopt the documentational approach consider teachers' interactions with resources and the manner resources influence teachers' knowledge and practices. Indeed, the researcher in these cases aims to be an outsider. Studying the documentational genesis leads to considering *teacher documents* as: "Document = Resources + Scheme of Utilization" (Gueudet and Trouche 2009, p. 205). The notion of scheme is defined here in the sense of Vergnaud (1998). Schemes are challenging to infer (see Chap. 2 by Ghislaine Gueudet). One source of complexity of the scheme concept is the component "operational invariant," which is invisible and not always conscious to the teacher. From a methodological point of view, it is a matter of inferring schemes by cross-referencing data from different tools and sources: interviews, observations of teachers, and so forth (Gueudet and Trouche 2009). There is, here, an affordance of the concept "operational invariant" determined by both the definition of the concept and the target of the researcher—to understand the teacher-resource interactions for a specific teaching aim.

Recent research has undertaken developments in the case of interviews, to identify schemes of resource use. Gueudet (2017) used the documentational approach in the case of teachers in higher education. She developed a methodology for analyzing interviews: *document table methodology* (see contribution of Sabra and El Hage in Chap. 11). Gonzàles-Martín et al. (2018) relied on Gueudet's (2017) methodology in their study of five higher education teachers that used the same textbook. Gonzàles-Martín et al. (2018) refined the document table methodology to consider the conditions that allow them to infer operational invariants.

Some research issues involve theoretical choices that promote experimenting with existing theories and frameworks, as well as methodological developments. For instance, taking into account the impacts of curriculum resources on the design capacity of teachers, Glasnović Gracin and Jukić Matić (2018) used Brown's (2009) Design Capacity for Enactment Framework (DCE) to investigate the interrelationship between teachers and the mobilization of textbooks and teacher guides. Brown's (2009) framework represents the idea that both the curriculum and a teacher's personal resources affect the design and enactment of instruction.

10.2.2.2 Networking Theories and Associated Methodological Developments

Very recently, there has been increased interest in innovative forms in teaching that requires theoretical and methodological developments. For instance, in the case of design of resources in the digital era, many didactical studies contribute to questioning the theoretical approaches and their networking (Abar 2018; Taranto et al. Sect. 10.6; Umameh 2018).

Assuming the potential of DAD to study the new model of teaching offered by the digital evolution, Abar (2018) analyzed the documentation work of teachers involved in a flipped classroom instructional approach. Her research reveals that the didactic decisions made to produce and transform the resources into documents are strongly influenced by the teachers' knowledge: mathematical knowledge, didactic knowledge, and technological knowledge.

MOOCs are an "iconic" example in the development methodology on resources required in the digital era. The issue of designing a MOOC to promote teachers' professional learning necessitated a joint theoretical and methodological development. The work by Taranto et al. (Sect. 10.6) examined the facilities offered by new technologies, specifically MOOCs to enhance mathematics teachers' professional learning. During each MOOC, teachers worked with, read about, implemented activities associated with, and shared thoughts and reflections about resources aligned to a mathematical topic. Taranto et al. (Sect. 10.6) developed a hybrid MOOC-Meta-Didactical Transposition (MDT) framework to analyze and describe the evolution of both researchers' and teachers' activities over time. The theoretical choices made are closely related to the characteristics of the MOOC; they are of different types: development of new concepts, adaptation, and extension of existing concepts and articulations between several theoretical frameworks. Taranto et al. (Sect. 10.6) is an example where a strong dialectic must exist between theoretical development and methodological development, in order to ensure a certain operability of theoretical concepts.

Some studies, in particular, design-based research, consider constant interactions between researchers and users of resources. The contribution of Aldon et al. (Sect. 10.5) is inscribed in this kind of study where the methodology of design is driven by theory (or a network of theories). In this case, the researcher was also a designer of resources, a situation that required collaborative work with teachers. The challenge focused on the development of a methodology for the analysis of the convergence or divergence between researcher projects and teacher projects. The methodological choice necessitated the introduction of a new theoretical concept, the "coherence of a resource" (Aldon et al. Sect. 10.5). In design-based research, there is convergence between theoretical choices and methodology at two moments. First, the theoretical choice leads to the methodology of resource design. For example, didactical engineering has been used to study the differences between the intentions of the designer of a resource and the teacher's achievement in the classroom. Second, the appropriate framework to define an indicator of convergence leads to the emergence of a new concept (i.e., the concept of coherence of a resource) and an associated methodology.

10.2.2.3 Theoretical Approaches, Marking Out Methodological Needs, and Developments

When we aim to study *genesis*, documentational genesis, or instrumental genesis (Gueudet et al. 2014), there is a challenge for researchers: investigating the interactions between teachers and resources in the long term and in various spaces. The meaning of the genesis concepts determines the characteristics of the methodology to be taken into account: in the continuum as much as possible; in the long term, to determine invariants in the forms of interactions with the resources; and in many spaces—in the classroom, at home, online, and so forth. In this context, the methodological choices are often linked to two criteria: (1) the choice of relevant spaces to collect data and (2) the choice of critical moments for observation and analysis of teacher-resource interactions.

The existence of *private spaces* (e.g., teacher's home), which a researcher cannot easily access, demonstrates the need to establish a collaborative research commitment between teachers and researchers. Two types of data can be considered: natural data (e.g., teachers' resources) and data collected by methodological tools (e.g., what a teacher says about her resources). Based on the concept of didactical contract (Brousseau 1997), the concept of "methodological contract" is defined by Sabra (2016) as a type of proposal made to clarify the roles of teacher and researcher in research activity.

The didactical contract (Brousseau 1997) is introduced in didactics of mathematics to situate the responsibilities of the teacher and the students in the mathematics classroom sessions. Sabra (2016) uses an analogy with the didactical contract to define the methodological contract. Brousseau (1997) defines the didactical contract as the set of behaviors of the teacher that are expected by the student and the set of behaviors of the student that are expected by the teacher. The didactical contract determines explicitly, but especially implicitly, what each contractor will have to manage and which he will be accountable to the other. The methodological contract is the formalization of a set of mutual expectations between the researcher and the teacher (or group of teachers), usually implicit, about an activity, individual or collective, related to the teaching of mathematics. In the methodological contract, the stakeholders are, on the one hand, the researcher and, on the other hand, the teacher(s). The main issue for stakeholders is the activity (individual and collective) of the teacher, as well as the resources produced by this activity. The methodological contract must make it possible to formalize part of the relationship between researcher and teachers, where the researcher is to be, as much as possible, an outsider. The methodological contract attempts to define the roles and responsibilities of each (researcher and teacher/or group of teachers). It appears as an indispensable instrument in research involving teachers' reflectivity about their resources (Alturkmani et al. 2019). The methodological contract also depends on the categories of methodological tools: (1) face-to-face follow-up, to capture the teachers preparing or implementing their lesson; (2) distance follow-up, for capturing the moments of pre- and post-lesson planning that researchers do not observe; and (3) reflective follow-up, interviewing teachers (see Rocha, Sect. 10.3).

A means for understanding teachers' interactions with resources over time and in several spaces is to study *documentational trajectories*, as proposed by Rocha (Sect. 10.3). Rocha and Trouche (2017) define a teacher's documentational trajectory as the interplay over time between events and resources. This interplay happens in schools or collectives. As such, a teacher's documentational trajectory is a "way to analyze *when*, *where*, *why*, *how* and *which* resources are created" (Rocha and Trouche 2017, p. 3734). Rocha (Sect. 10.3) distinguishes between reflective mapping (made by the teacher herself) and inferred mapping (made by the researcher) of both a teacher's resource system and her documentational trajectory. Tools for a teacher's reflective mapping of her documentational trajectory can capture a continuous timeline with events that were remarkable—from the teacher's point of view—to her documentation work. Similarly, tools for a teacher's mapping of her resource system can capture the evolution of her documentation work at various periods in her documentational trajectory (Rocha 2018, p. 165). Researchers can then analyze teacher's reflective mappings, along with other items from the data corpus (e.g., teacher interviews) to help reveal which events change and nourish documentational experience and, thus, support long-term examination of the evolution of teacher-resource interactions.

Both cases (i.e., "understanding trajectories" and "following-up genesis") take into account the predicated time (of substantial length) and spaces (all spaces of interaction with resources). Nevertheless, in terms of methodological requirements, there are differences between these cases. In the "understanding trajectories" case, methodology to "dig" into the past is developed; there is more emphasis on reflectivity on time and the evolution of interaction with resources from the teachers' point of view. In the "following-up genesis" case, methodology is developed to investigate the evolution "in going" over time and to encourage the reflectivity on the structuration of resources, their design, and their use; there is more emphasis on reflectivity on spaces. Time, in the "following-up genesis" case, is a "landmark" for the researcher (following-up on time).

10.2.3 Analyses of Teacher-Resource Interactions "as a Whole"

Studies involving teacher-resource interactions typically focus on a *snapshot* of a teacher's career path and the interactions that occur between the teacher and her resource system within this snapshot. Such brief or transitory impressions are frequently limited to static "for this lesson," "over this sequence of lessons," or "over the duration of the project" temporal units that may be compared with impressions derived from other teachers along similar units. What passes for "long term" in mathematics education research is comprised of multi-year studies, typically 1–5 years, where changes in a teacher's resource system and/or involving teacher–resource interactions are examined pre and post some form of intervention.

10 Analyzing Teachers' Work with Resources: Methodological Issues

Examinations of the evolution of teacher-resource interactions in a genuine long-term sense—over 5, 10, 15, 20, or more years— are rare indeed.

One of the issues that emerged from WG2 is that of teacher interactions with resources "as a whole." One rationale for such a focus is the link between teacher's professional identity and resource system (Bifano 2018). Based on a case study of a teacher of mathematics, Bifano (2018) questioned the relation between professional identity traits and a teacher's work around institutional resources. Bifano's (2018) research leads to the emergence of the notion of "documentational identity." After evoking what is understood by *wholeness*, related methodological questions are exposed. Then, methodologies attempting to capture wholeness are presented.

Teachers have always developed, at least in part, their own resources for their professional activities (Webb 2008). Ruthven (2008) suggests that these resources are organized in a system particular to a given teacher, a system of her own. This "personal" resource system and the teacher's professional development appear to be intertwined (Remillard 2005) and might include resources coming from students' work. For instance, exploring the formative assessment practices of a mathematics teacher, Umameh (2018) showed that a teacher's use of a set of digital resources allowed the teacher to teach, collate, and analyze student work, and provide feedback in real time by utilizing digital tools. These practices informed the teacher's "emergent lesson planning." Thus, the structure evolves with time: "geneses are deeply interconnected with the teacher's professional development" (Gueudet and Trouche 2008, p. 201), and light has to be shed on resources as a whole. This wholeness includes all sorts of resources and, at the same time, teacher's professional development (Gueudet and Trouche 2009). Only a *holistic research approach* is appropriate to apprehend the wholeness of teachers' practices (Monaghan 2004), the wholeness of use of resources (Gueudet and Trouche 2008), the wholeness of the system, and, more generally, the wholeness of resources intertwined with development.

The wholeness of the system of resources refers to the structure of the resource system. Indeed, a resource is never isolated, but belongs to a set of resources (Gueudet and Trouche 2009). The question of teachers' resource systems is focused in a specific chapter of this book (see Trgalová et al., Sect. 9.3, Chap. 9). Analyzing the structure of the resource system is a complex question that challenges developing a meaning for "structure" (physical or material structure, presentational structure, both).

As mentioned, in order to seize the action of a teacher in her spatio-temporal unit, Gueudet and Trouche (2009) suggest collecting data anytime, and anywhere. To achieve this, they met secondary mathematics teachers at home, because it was there that, according to these researchers, most activities involving resources of French secondary teachers take place. The interview protocol they designed takes place in three stages. Firstly, the teacher makes a presentation of the resources she used during a school year for preparing and conducting student learning. Secondly, a guided tour is conducted on three documents the teacher considers the most important for the current year. Finally, the teacher is asked to take a look at the past and the future. As this is a first step, the authors emphasized that they only collected teachers' statements (Gueudet and Trouche 2008).

Concerning the changes in development, Gueudet and Trouche (2009) consider that teachers' documentation work is at the core of their professional activity and professional development. The kinds of professional changes that Gueudet and Trouche (2009) study are change of practice and change of professional knowledge or beliefs. A teacher develops a documentation system, a "structured set of documents" (Gueudet et al. 2016, p. 190), which evolves conjointly with her professional practice. For Gueudet and Trouche (2009), observation and analysis of the documentation system allow "a better understanding of the teacher's professional development" (2009, p. 211). Is it an increase in learning or a real development? A suggestion of anchoring in Vygotsky's theory has to be done.

Affording to the *reflective investigation* proposed by DAD, Rocha (Sect. 10.3) developed a method that allows for close examination of the development of resource systems related to teachers' professional learning. In order to model teacher's history with resources, she proposed a new concept, documentational trajectory, and a specific methodology for studying the evolution of the interactions between teachers and resources in the long term (Rocha, 2018). Rocha et al. (2017) define development as an experience acquired during interactions with resources, at the interplay between events that a teacher meets and her resources. This interplay, which takes place over time, is socially situated. In order to highlight the connections between interactions with resources and events on a life-long span, she crosses different methodologies: reflective mapping of a teacher's resource system, her documentational trajectory, and her description of her own documentational experience (see Rocha, Sect. 10.3).

The question of teachers' professional learning arises at the very beginning of teacher training—e.g., with trainee or "pre-service" teachers. To bring answers to this question, Georget (2018) developed a methodology based on designing a documentation system for primary teachers embodied in a system of training activities likely to trigger dynamic processes of professional development at short, mid-, or long term. For Georget, a primary documentation system designed with:

> tools of the theory of communities of practice, with ergonomic characteristics (e.g. utility, usability, accessibility), and supported by a specific system of training activities, can help... trigger [teachers'] interest in resources, internal or external to this primary documentation system. (Georget 2018, p. 155)

This section highlighted the methodological richness that results from the idea of analyzing teacher-resource interactions "as a whole." A variety of studies attempt to capture wholeness of teacher-resource interactions, resulting in the emergence of two main ideas: resources are organized in a system proper to a given teacher, and there is a link between this system and teacher's professional development, both evolving over time. As a result, only holistic research seems to be appropriate to apprehend this wholeness. Methodological questions are concerned with how to seize spatio-temporal unit of development despite the development over time and in different places.

10.2.4 Examining the Development of Teacher-Resource Interactions with a Focus on Content and Level of Teaching

In this section, we highlight teacher-resource interactions through the teaching level lens, that is, in terms of content and in terms of institutions. From an institutional perspective (Chevallard 2006), we consider that mathematics, as enacted by teachers through instruction, is shaped by the institution where the mathematics is enacted. As such, the use of resources depends on teachers' activities that take place in institutions.

Prior research conducted at various pre-tertiary school levels indicates that teachers in their work in and out-of-class are not passive users of resources, but active designers of their own teaching resources (Gueudet et al. 2013). Similar phenomena take place at the university level (Gueudet 2017). There are several characteristics to take into consideration regarding such research related to the level of institution under examination: kindergarten and elementary school, secondary school, and higher education.

For instance, the "versatility" of elementary school teachers warrants questions about teachers' interactions with resources in different ways. The study of the structure of elementary school teachers' resource systems should take into consideration interactions between many disciplines (e.g., mathematics, history), the interaction with curriculum resources, and the beliefs of teachers about the knowledge to be taught. The methodological challenge at the elementary school level consists in application of methodologies that allow researchers to study how teachers make connections between content deriving from several disciplines. In the USA, some research suggests methodology based on the design of animations by pre-service elementary teachers (Earnest and Amador 2017), which requires simulating classroom experiences through animations. These animations illustrate pre-service teachers' beliefs through the process of translating curriculum resources into designed enactment. Earnest and Amador (2017) analyzed animations designed by pre-service teachers to address a practical concern (i.e., launch an activity to hypothetical, representative students) and respect research goals (identify both mathematical and professional beliefs).

At the secondary school level, the specialization of teachers reduces some aspects of complexity that occurs in the case of elementary teachers—secondary school teachers focus mostly on one discipline and its associated didactical knowledge. Furthermore, the collective resource design between teachers appears more frequently in secondary school (Gueudet et al. 2016) than in elementary school, offering many opportunities for professional development over a teacher's professional trajectory. In this context, we raise a main methodological issue in articulating between individual resources and collective resources. This articulation can take the form of tension or symbiosis (Gueudet et al. 2016). In addition, a long-term study is warranted to analyze the professional trajectory in terms of a teacher's interaction with resources (see Rocha, Sect. 10.3).

There are similarities in many aspects of the practices of secondary and university teachers: preparation of courses and tutorials, design of instruction, conceptions of teacher evaluations, classroom management, and interactions with students. However, the practices of university teachers overcome specificities from an institutional point of view, given their training and academic background. For example, university teachers have some freedom in the design of their courses and the choice of content to be taught. Although textbook dependence at the university level is not universal across countries (e.g., France), in many countries, the textbook is a crucial resource for both secondary and university teachers (Hora and Ferrare 2013; Mesa and Griffiths 2012). As described earlier (see Sect. 10.2.2), in an exploratory study in Canada, Gonzàles-Martín et al. (2018) focused on five university teachers' use of a specific, but commonly used, textbook to teach the topic of series in mathematics. The study identified how teachers' view on this topic interacted with their use of this textbook. Gonzàles-Martín et al. (2018) concluded that not all five teachers shared the same operational invariants that guided their actions; rather, the teachers resorted to different rules of action. Gonzàles-Martín et al. (2018) highlighted the need for methodologies to take into account the personal relationships teachers have with the content to understand deeply the use of a resource (the textbook in this case) by university teachers.

Regarding university level, most teachers are teacher-researchers. In a topical survey focusing on research at the tertiary level, Biza et al. (2016) highlighted the emerging interest in taking into consideration resources in university teaching. In particular, Biza et al. (2016) focused on interactions with resources for mathematics education and their impact on teachers' professional development. Biza et al. (2016) also pointed to the need for further research on the possible impact of their research activity on their own teaching practices. In terms of teacher-resource interactions, the kind of research described by Biza et al. (2016) suggests new methodological developments to consider, for instance, methodologies for studying research resources, teaching resources, and their interactions.

10.3 Documentational Trajectory as a Means for Understanding Teachers' Interactions with Resources Over Time: The Case of a French Mathematics Teacher

Katiane Rocha

10.3.1 Background of the Study

In their daily work, teachers face several professional problems that lead them to develop knowledge and create their own strategies to improve their teaching. In this context, we focus specifically on understanding how teachers' interactions with resources benefit their professional development over time. Next, we discuss the issue: *How to study the long-term evolution of interactions between teachers and resources?* Finally, we introduce, in the documentational approach to didactics (Gueudet and Trouche 2008; Gueudet Chap. 2), two concepts that help us analyze the evolution of teachers' documentation work: *documentational trajectory and documentational experience.* Trouche (Chap. 13) presented ten propositions of research programs to explore, with the aim of improving the documentational approach to didactics (DAD). The current study focuses on the intersection of at least three of these research programs: (a) "deepening the dialectics of schemes/situations of documentation work (associated with principle/program, P3)," (b) "deepening the analysis of conditions/effects of teachers' collective documentation work (P4)," and (c) "understanding the short vs. long episodes of teachers' documentation work (P5)." In order to achieve our research objective, we situate our study within the case of a middle school mathematics teacher and organize the report into four sections. Firstly, we introduce our theoretical framework. Secondly, we discuss some methodological choices inspired by reflective investigation. Thirdly, we present the preliminary results of our analysis. Finally, we present some considerations based on our partial analysis.

10.3.2 *Theoretical Framework*

In this section, we articulate the four components of our theoretical approach. First, we present some elements of DAD, which is the base of our work. Second, we present our perspective on professional development inspired by professional didactics, especially the notion of experience that underpins the notion of documentational experience developed in this work. Third, we focus on the notion of *scheme* proposed by Vergnaud (2009) that is at the intersection of DAD and professional didactics. Finally, we develop the notion of documentational trajectory mobilizing Fleck's framework (1981) to highlight the collective dimension in teachers' documentation work over time.

Our research is based on, and in return aims to contribute to, the development of DAD proposed by Gueudet and Trouche (2008). This approach considers that teachers are responsible for designing their resources. Gueudet and Trouche (2008) defined *documentation work* as every activity done by teachers in collecting, organizing, selecting, adapting, and designing resources. In this chapter, we use the concepts of *resources, document, documentation work, documentational genesis,* and *resource system* introduced in Chap. 2 by Gueudet.

Our analysis of teacher's professional development focuses on teachers' documentation work, following Pastré in the framework of professional didactics: "centered on the importance of the cognitive dimension present in the activity, particularly in the form of conceptualization in action[1]" (2011, p. 48). In this context,

---

[1] Our translation.

the subject (i.e., teacher) is considered as someone who adapts over time by facing several situations. Moreover, development is understood "as [the] construction of the self, as appropriation of all the events experienced by a subject to give them meaning for herself[2]" (Pastré 2011, p. 118). These events will constitute the subject's (i.e., teacher's) experience, which is defined as the accumulation and appropriation of the past by herself (Pastré 2011). In our work, we are interested in the teacher's experience acquired during her interactions with resources, and we name it *documentational experience*.

This experience is built in the context of various situations that teachers face and in which they develop their professional knowledge. The analysis of conceptualization in action—proposed by Pastré (2011) and Gueudet and Trouche (2008)—is based on the frame of Vergnaud (2009). As such, the analysis of conceptualization in action highlights that teachers' professional knowledge is developed in a process of adaptation and creation of *Schemes*. A scheme is defined as "an invariant organization of conduct for a given class of situations" (Vergnaud 2009, p. 88). We highlight in Vergnaud's studies (2009) the importance of the dialectical relationship between scheme and situation, one does not exist without the other. It is precisely the notion of situation that offers great complexity for the analysis of the action of the subject. Indeed, the term situation will be considered in a very broad sense, not as a simple task. A situation contains various objects, different types of relationships, and several concepts. Moreover, a scheme is not linked to a single situation, but to a class of situations. This class of situations is formed by neighboring situations in which the subject organizes her activity following a similar pattern.

Schemes contain structural components: (1) a *goal* or several goals (that can be decomposed into sub-goals and anticipation), related to functionality; (2) *rules of action, information gathering, and control* that govern actions controlling their variations and conditions; (3) *operational invariants*, which are the cognitive part whose "main function is to pick up and select the relevant information and infer goals and rules from it" (Vergnaud 2009, p. 88); and, finally, (4) *possibilities of inference* in situations, which make it possible to manage the singularities of certain situations that belong to the same class. Pastré (2011, p. 89) characterizes schemes as "brokers between knowledge and action,[3]" of interest for analyzing to better understand adults' professional development, in our case, teachers.

Schemes are developed over time as teachers face given classes of situations, such as lesson preparation and lesson implementation, among others, as proposed in the third Proposition (P3) that Trouche presents in Chap. 13. However, there are many events taking place in teachers' professional lives that will affect their documentation work and contribute to their documentational experiences. We name *documentational trajectory* the set of *professional events*, both of individuals and of collectives that ground teachers' documentational experiences. This definition leads us to at least three considerations about the documentational trajectory:

---

[2] Our translation.

[3] Our translation.

- First, professional events are considered in a broad sense. They can consist of a meeting with someone, or an encounter with a resource, training, a new institutional constraint, and so forth. They can be planned or unplanned by the teacher. In the documentational trajectory, each event has an effect on the teacher's documentation work, making it possible to identify some resources in the teacher's resource system associated with this event.
- Second, events and resources are historical, because they are determined by the period in which teachers' documentation work takes place. For example, in 2016, a new curriculum was implemented in France. Curriculum was designed over a 3-year cycle, instead of 1 year, and involved interdisciplinary work and new content to be taught in mathematics (e.g., programming). Such changes required curriculum designers and teachers to design new resources. These and similar events could have a strong impact on teachers' documentation work.
- Third, documentational trajectories are socially situated, because teachers' work is strongly influenced by their schools, students, institutional constraints, and other such factors. Also, documentational trajectories are strongly affected by collectives in which teachers participate, a process Fleck describes as "someone recognizes something […] as part of a given cultural context […] in a certain style of thinking, in the thought collective" (1981, p.76). In this perspective, we mobilize the broad notion of *thought collective* proposed by Fleck (1981, p. 44) which comes into play as soon as "two or more people are exchanging thoughts." A thought collective leads participants to develop a *thought style*, "characterized by standard features in the problems of interest to a thought collective, by the judgment which the thought collective considers evident, and by the methods which it applies as a means of cognition" (Fleck 1981, p. 99).

In the following section, we present some methodological choices inspired by reflective investigation, improving and proposing some methodological tools.

10.3.3 *Methodological Choices and Tools*

Our methodological choices are guided by five principles of reflective investigation proposed by Trouche et al. (2018, p. 7): (1) "long-term follow-up," allowing for the identification of stability and changes in teachers' documentation work, as proposed in the program in the fifth Proposition (P5) that Trouche presents in Chap. 13; (2) "in- and out-of-class follow-up," covering many moments when teachers' documentation work happens; (3) "reflective follow-up," leading teachers to explain and reflect about their experiences; (4) "broad collection of the material resources," keeping a record of materials designed and used by teachers; and (5) "permanent confronting the teacher' views on her documentation work, and the materiality of this work." Our methodological tools are classified into three categories: (1) face-to-face follow-up, to capture the teachers preparing or implementing their lesson; (2) distance follow-up, for capturing the moments when we are not with them; and (3) reflective follow-up, based on teacher interviews.

To analyze teachers' documentational trajectory, we needed to create new tools to attempt to parse more information about teachers' past documentation work. As in past studies, in the reflective investigation, we utilized *schematic representation of resource system (SRRS)*, because this representation shows important aspects of teachers' documentation work. However, we attempted to improve and extend this tool for our work. Indeed, instead of schematic representation, we prefer to use the expression "mapping" because it (a) points out some particular aspects about this representation like "a picture or chart that shows the different parts of something[4]" and, mostly, (b) denotes the dynamic and active process of representing something, giving means for exploring an unknown territory.

We also proposed two types of mappings: inferred and reflective. Inferred mapping is made by researchers using one or various kinds of data: researchers either create a new map or complete a map made by the teacher. This kind of data is a result of a researchers' analysis of teachers' work. Reflective mapping is made by the teacher and occurs when she reflects about her work either by creating a map or by analyzing a map made by the researcher. We asked teachers to map their resource system at several moments (e.g., at the start of their career, at the time of the study). Although these two kinds of mapping are complementary in the analysis of teachers' documentation work, reflective mapping is sometimes a base for building an inferred map. We thus divided the *SRRS* into two types: inferred mapping of the teacher's resource system (IMRS) and reflective mapping of the teacher's resource system (RMRS).

Two new tools were created based on the ideas of SRRS: reflective and inferred mapping of a teacher's Documentational Trajectory (RMDT and IMDT, respectively). These maps are very important, because they contain essential events and the associated resources. The RMDT is created by the teacher during an interview. We asked teachers to construct a continuous timeline displaying noteworthy events that influenced their documentation work. The RMDT is a door to access teachers' past documentation work. We explored this data in different ways: (1) creating our inferred maps cross-referenced with other data and (2) identifying one point to explore with teachers what serves as their "entrance" into the documentational trajectory linked with one key event or resource. We believe that this methodological tool is promising for analyzing teachers' experiences and can be used in different forms (not all of which are explored in this study): (1) thematic, for example, to follow only events about teaching algebra; (2) specific, to rebuild the trajectory of one resource; and (3) collective, to represent trajectories of one collective or of teachers that work together, among other possibilities. Moreover, the analysis of a documentational trajectory leads us to work with teachers' past professional lives, where our data are based on teachers' memories about their actions. In this context, our methodological choices lead teachers to verbalize their action and create an atmosphere in which they can reflect on their past actions (Vermersch 1994).

It is important to emphasize that the RMDT is not the only tool to analyze teachers' documentational trajectory. Indeed, we combine several tools. In this contribu-

---

[4] https://www.merriam-webster.com/dictionary/map

tion, we present the coordination between RMRS, RMDT, and teachers' lesson preparation to analyze teachers' documentational experiences and trajectory. We present three reflective mappings of resource system (RMRS) created by the same teacher. In one of them, the teacher represented the resources used during the first 5 years of her career. In the second one, she presented the resources she was currently using, in 2017. And in the third one, she presented all the resources she considered important to prepare her lessons to teach algorithms.

We took into account five criteria for choosing the two middle school mathematics teachers that we followed, Anna (followed since 2015) and Viviane (followed since 2016). First, we looked for two middle school teachers who worked in different schools, to have different contexts. Second, we sought for teachers with contrasting profiles in terms of documentational experiences. For this purpose, we chose one teacher who was participating intensively in collectives outside of her school and another one participating in collectives only within her school. Third, we wanted teachers who used the same textbook in their classrooms, in order to analyze how the same resource can nourish different documentation works. Fourth, we chose teachers having more than 15 years of experience, since we were looking for long trajectories. Finally, we chose teachers who collaborated with a colleague in their school. Wang (2018, p.198) named such a colleague a documentation-working mate that "could be a colleague with similar working experiences in her school, or someone from a totally different working context as university or research institute etc."

This last criterion is very helpful for analyzing teachers' documentation work, because when teachers produce resources together, we often have access to a rich dialogue between them. This dialogue gives us additional information about the sources of their documentation work. Here, we explore data collected from the middle school teacher, Anna, who has been followed since 2015, because our analysis of her case study has progressed further (than that of Viviane). For the preliminary analysis presented here, we established the following criteria:

- For analyzing RMDT, we first categorized the types of events which were present, looking for similarities and differences between them. Next, we focused on an event that seemed to have had a more important role in terms of Anna's documentation work. Finally, we identified how the collective work fits into this trajectory.
- For analyzing RMRS, we observed the uses of institutional and digital resources. Institutional resources are important because during the last 15 years, mathematics teaching in France has undergone tremendous change. Digital resources are chosen in accordance with French policies to integrate them in mathematics teaching. We also noted the influences of collective work on the resources system; this is related to our understanding of teaching as a social activity.
- For analyzing Anna's work with her respective documentation workmates, we employed the concept of thought style, identifying the *methods* and *common judgments* in use to design resources, as proposed in the program in the fourth Proposition (P4) that Trouche presents in Chap. 13.

In the following section, we present some preliminary results of our analysis.

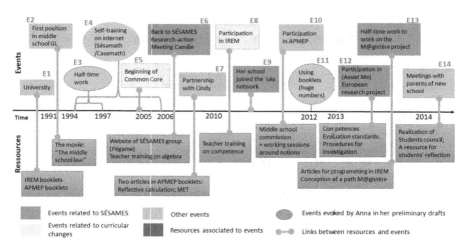

Fig. 10.1 Anna's RMDT made on 26 February 2016

10.3.4 Preliminary Results

We present here preliminary results of our analysis of one middle school mathematics teacher, Anna, in three parts. First, we study Anna's documentational trajectory (DT) using her reflective map (RMDT) and propose an inferred map (IMDT) from our perspective. Second, we study her DT using Anna's reflective map of her resource system in two moments of her career—at the start (i.e., beginning of career) and at the time of the study. Finally, we present some aspects of her collective lesson preparation and individual implementation of algorithm teaching. In this part, we identify one scheme that guides Anna's lesson preparation.

10.3.4.1 Studying Anna's Documentational Trajectory

In Fig. 10.1, we present a digital transposition of Anna's RMDT by addressing three points.[5]

---

[5] We present here more details about five acronyms (see more in Rocha 2018, p. 245): (1) The collective APMEP (Association des Professeurs de Mathématiques de l'Enseignement Public, https://www.apmep.fr/) "where teachers teaching mathematics from pre-primary schools to University and promoting teacher's training"; (2) The collective IREM (Institut de Recherche sur l'Enseignement des Mathématiques, http://www.univ-irem.fr/) in which members "articulated work between research and practice looking for diffusing research results and promoting teacher's training"; (3) Sésames (Science Education: Modeling Activities, Assessment, Simulation (Sésames, Situations d'Enseignement Scientifique: Activités de Modélisation, d'Évaluation, de Simulation)) teachers and researchers thinking about resources for teaching Algebra and promoting teacher's training; (4) IFÉ (Institut français d'éducation, http://ife.ens-lyon.fr/ife) responsible by promote research and training in France; (5) the network LéA (Lieux d'éducation associés à l'IFÉ—Associated educational Places at the French Institute for Education, http://ife.ens-lyon.fr/lea/lea-english-version) putting together researchers and teachers in a network of schools linked to IFÉ to improve teaching.

10 Analyzing Teachers' Work with Resources: Methodological Issues 275

First, among all the 14 events identified by Anna, 7 are related to collective work outside of the school (E6, E8, E9, E10, E11, E12, E13); 2 are related to collective work in her school (E7, E14); 4 are linked to institutional changes (E1, E2, E4, E5); 1 is personal and we categorize it as "other" (E3). We highlight here that her documentational trajectory is strongly affected by her collective work outside and within her school (see below). The importance of the collective work is very clearly articulated in her interview: *"I cannot work alone, [...] because I cannot be sure of myself, if nobody gives me any advices. I need the opinions of others to do something"*. Anna participates in two groups which are institutionally recognized in the field of mathematics education in France: APMEP and IREM. Anna highlights the difference in her work in the two groups as follows:

> Anna: "At IREM we see each other much more often. But at the same time, it is something that is institutional, there are mission statements, etc. The APMEP is more friends you know, we have the same vision of teaching,-- because IREM [...] it has not much renewed-- we are still largely on the same wavelength, but it is not forced. It's people who want to discuss something, so APMEP is still people who are in the same teaching philosophy. We have the same idea of what we want to do and how we want to do it. And the sharing is done, but it's more associative, you know. It's not all the same thing".

Sésames had a big impact on Anna's collective work. We can see her engagement with Sésames produced other events in her documentational trajectory. Indeed, she joined another research (Assist me), created an online training, and led her school to benefit from the advantages of the network of LéA. Sésames offered Anna the opportunity for a new partnership with a colleague, Camille. Such partnership helped Anna understand the competencies emphasized in the new French curriculum, leading to the design of a teacher training path at IREM, resulting in a chance to join IREM.

Sésames has two sets of *principles* guiding Anna's documentation work (cf. the Sésames website, Pégame: http://pegame.ens-lyon.fr/), mirroring the thought style of Sésames. The first set is composed of three principles for teaching algebra: (1) justifying computation by making explicit algebraic rules; (2) proposing proof activities; and (3) exploiting formulas to introduce the concept of function. The second set is composed of four principles for teaching mathematics: (1) providing students with sufficiently rich and open problems; (2) giving students a chance to explore; (3) giving students a chance to conjecture, and (4) giving concrete meaning to mathematics concepts. In the next section, we describe how Anna's resource system is structured to support this collective work.

10.3.5 Studying Anna's Resource System

We analyze Anna's documentational trajectory combining her interview with her reflective mappings of her own documentational trajectory and of her own resource system (Figs. 10.2 and 10.3). In Fig. 10.2, we highlight four points. First, the position of textbooks indicates their centrality in Anna's lesson preparations (courses and exercises), especially the official textbook adopted by her school (P1). Second,

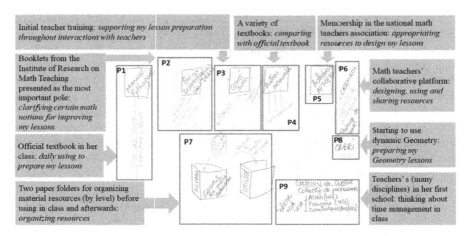

Fig. 10.2 Anna's RMRS of the first 5 years of her career (orange rectangles: researcher's analysis)

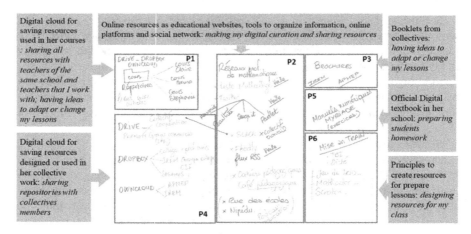

Fig. 10.3 Anna's RMRS representing resources used in 2017 (orange rectangles: researcher's analysis)

resources from formal professional collectives in France are very important for her (P2 and P5). Third, working in collectives provides Anna with opportunities to reflect on teaching (P3 and P9). Fourth, digital resources start to be integrated into her resource system (P6 and P8).

A set of resources which was important to Anna during this period was a collection of IREM booklets. These resources remained in her documentation work for a long time. She explained that these resources "took up some notions, explained them to [students] and gave examples of how they could be taught." These resources helped Anna learn about teaching mathematics, giving her mathematical didactic advice. In the mapping of her documentational trajectory, Anna explained that she had found these resources during her university studies.

In Fig. 10.3, we observe some changes in the same four points as in Fig. 10.2. Firstly, the place of textbooks has changed (P5); they are now used only to provide exercises to students. Moreover, this change is very clear for Anna, as she explained: "I need to understand why we chose this exercise instead of another, and the principle of textbooks as catalogs of exercises without any analysis does not suit me."

Secondly, resources from formal professional collectives in France were still being used as a source of new teaching ideas (P3). However, Anna is more than a user: now, she proposes resources in these booklets (P4). This is a result of one important event in Anna's trajectory—her participation in the Sésames group. Sésames is a collective that develops resources for teaching algebra. Through her experiences with Sésames, Anna learnt more about teaching algebra in middle school and developed new resources and new pedagogical practices (P6, see more details in Rocha 2018). Regarding the third point, we observed that Anna engaged in many collectives inside and outside of her school. These collectives are now her sources for additional resources. For example, she always prepares her lessons with her colleague, Cindy. Anna participates in IREM and APMEP. Collective work is very important to her documentation work. As a last point, digital resources have now a structuring role in her documentation work (P2). Therefore, digital resources serve (at least) two functions: (1) Anna has a shared space with her colleagues, where she can share her own and access others' resources. Such a shared resource space is important to her documentation work, because she can turn to others' resources for new ideas when she is not satisfied with her lesson. (2) Anna creates a system to monitor new digital resources related to mathematics teaching. For example, she follows many colleagues on Twitter (https://twitter.com/), and, once she finds interesting resources, she saves them as her "favorites." These resources give her ideas that she can then attempt to implement in her class.

10.3.5.1 Collective Lesson Preparation and Individual Implementation of Algorithm Teaching

Next, we examine Anna's lesson preparation and implementation of one lesson involving algorithms and programming in the sixth and seventh grade. Anna prepared her lesson with her documentation-working mate, Cindy. We observed (1) the first lesson preparation in 2016; (2) Anna's lesson implementation in 2016 in a sixth grade class; (3) Anna and Cindy's collaborative re-preparation in 2017; and (4) Anna's lesson implementation in 2017 in a fifth grade class. In addition, we conducted interviews before and after the last session. More precisely, we observed the 2017 session in which Anna worked on the task called *crépier psychorigide.*[6] The objectives of this resource are to *introduce algorithm thinking and to work with*

---

[6] http://www-irem.ujf-grenoble.fr/spip/IMG/pdf/fiche_prof_crepier_psychorigide.pdf

algorithmic writing. The *crépier psychorigide* resource was proposed by a team from IREM-Grenoble and offers many didactical recommendations that Anna seriously takes into account. We infer here some elements of the Anna-Cindy's (documentation-working mate's) thought style (based on areas of agreement between Anna and Cindy during lesson preparation):

- *Methods*: Anna and Cindy tended to make all decisions together; they did not like to propose tasks from textbooks, but preferred resources with didactic advice; they accumulated potential tasks for 1 year before implementing curricular changes (through digital preservation, management, and collective work, in Anna's case).
- *Judgments* about teaching algorithms and programming: Anna and Cindy did not want to use software or applications; they wanted to treat this content with short lessons throughout the year, but not as a module; they wanted to propose research problems to work on algorithmic thinking.

The Anna-Cindy (documentation-working mate) thought style strongly influenced Anna's choices. Although our analysis took these aspects into consideration, we were mainly interested in Anna's documentation work. In this context, we asked Anna to map resources that, in her opinion, nourished her thinking about lesson preparation and implementation. We note in Fig. 10.4 three aspects: a strong influence of the collective work (P2 and P3); digital curation to collect resources (P4); and institutional resources guiding her lesson preparation (P1).

We identified some elements of the scheme relating to the following situation: "choosing tasks to introduce algorithmic thinking and programming in 2016 and in 2017." Teaching algorithmic thinking and programming in middle school is a new topic creating a new situation for teaching. However, this situation is related to the broader set of situations to "choose one (or more) task(s) to introduce content to students." Facing this set of situations, we identified elements of the "scheme of

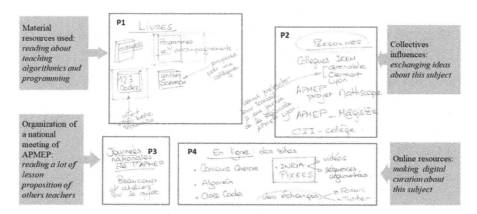

Fig. 10.4 Anna's RMRS to teach algorithmic thinking, 30 June 2017 (orange rectangles, researcher's analysis)

10 Analyzing Teachers' Work with Resources: Methodological Issues

Table 10.1 Modeling one of Anna's schemes

Goal: choosing tasks to work with students	
Rules of action	She searches for tasks that are not around computational programming She looks for tasks that allow students to do research She looks for open tasks She takes into consideration students' previous knowledge
Inferences	1° lesson preparation, she projected expectations for students' work 2° lesson preparation, she reevaluates tasks based on students' feedback After 2° lesson implementation, she said that some aspects have been adapted because of the co-animation technology teacher
Operational invariants	Putting students in a research situation is more meaningful for their learning Algorithmic thinking is a thought to be used to solve problems The work with algorithm can favor research situations It is important to use differentiated learning, because canal students can move forward at their own pace The writing of algorithms allows students to build the notion of loop Pay attention to the introduction of the concept of variable in the teaching of algorithmic thinking, because it is not the same as in mathematics. Computational thinking is a form of thought that is used to solve problems

choice of an open task to put students in a research situation to learn algorithmic thinking and programming." In Table 10.1, we model the scheme.

This scheme presents some elements of Anna's knowledge related to teaching algorithmic thinking and programming. This knowledge has guided Anna's resource design and task design. Indeed, the task *"crépier psychorigide"* was found on the Pixees[7] site, which proposes tasks for student research and gives didactic advice to teachers. This preliminary analysis provides a few elements to help us explore answers to the questions that we originally proposed.

10.3.6 Final Considerations

We come back to our initial issue: *How to study the long-term evolution of the interactions between teachers and resources?* We presented some ideas and evidence to initiate a discussion of this question, and will append three points that our work tries to contribute to this ongoing discussion.

Firstly, reflecting about our theoretical choices, the documentational approach to didactics (DAD) is a lens to view teachers' professional development through their resource design. This approach supports our thinking about the complex universe of teachers' practices. Our articulation of the relationship between DAD and professional didactics seems very powerful, because both are complementary: DAD focuses on how teachers learn to design resources; professional didactics relates to how professionals learn through their work experience. Both frameworks utilize the

---

[7] https://pixees.fr/

concept of *scheme* (Vergnaud 2009) to analyze conceptualization in action. This concept is very complex and different researchers analyzing the same action can see different elements of scheme. However, the point of identifying schemes is not to find a perfect description of subjects' actions, but rather to find some elements that are key to understanding *what they are doing* and *why they are doing it in this way*. Understanding this helps us think about how one can help teachers improve their practices in the future. However, in Vergnaud (2009), we feel the collective dimension of human activity is not brought adequately into focus. Fleck (1981) helps us consider this important dimension of learning and teaching, because teachers learn with and to teach other people.

Secondly, thinking about our theoretical proposals, the concept of teachers' documentational trajectory allows us to see more element of teacher's whole professional life in which she interacts with various resources. We are able to observe which events change and nourish her documentational experience. In the case of Anna, we were able to identify links between specific events and the evolution of her resource system, for example, abandoning textbooks and the intensive design of resources in collectives. In addition, we were able to identify professional strategies for facing new professional problems. For example, we saw Anna engaged in digital curation 1 year prior to making her curricular changes and saw her getting new ideas and discussing these ideas in her various collectives. Also, in analyzing Anna's lesson preparation, we identified some elements of scheme that related to her participation in the Sésames collective, further demonstrating how Anna's documentational trajectory helped us understand her practice.

Thirdly, in relation to our methodological choices, the principles of reflective investigation help us analyze teachers' documentation work over time. Our tools were conceived to lead teachers to reflect about their practice. In this sense, reflective mapping turned out to be a powerful tool to analyze the evolution of teachers' documentational trajectories, because these maps can show how some resources change in status and how new resource functions emerge. Our mapping tools are somewhat constrained: they try to capture part of a dynamic resource system, but offer only a static view of it. If one asks a teacher to represent the same system in two different moments, the map might be very different. As a reconstruction by teachers of how they see their work, these maps represent only the tip of the iceberg of subjects' knowledge and will always be incomplete. However, in order to create such maps, teachers need to reflect on their work and summarize important aspects of their practice. These then become a rich data set through which to understand teachers' documentation work; they help us work with teachers' memories of their documentation work over time.

In the future, we plan to further develop these tools and provide additional examples of their use in our work to analyze teachers' documentational trajectory. We hope that our analysis of teachers' professional development can improve our understanding of the complex work that teachers do, which, at some later stage of our research, might help guide the design of teacher training and the development of new government policies.

10.4 The Role of Resources in Lesson Planning: Institutional and Methodological Issues

Dubravka Glasnović Gracin and Scott A. Courtney

10.4.1 Background of the Study

Planning for a lesson has long been recognized as a primary factor impacting the efficacy of instruction (e.g., Schoenfeld 2011; Smith et al. 2008). In mathematics, focused lesson planning has been shown to support teacher enactment of cognitively demanding tasks, help teachers anticipate students' cognitive challenges, and support the generation of questions teachers can ask that promote and elicit student thinking (e.g., Smith et al. 2008). Smith et al. (2008, p. 133) assert, "One way to both control teaching with high-level tasks and promote success is through detailed planning prior to the lesson."

As introduced by Morine-Dershimer (1977) and described by Schoenfeld (2011), a teacher's lesson image is "the teacher's envisioning of how a lesson will play out" (p. 233) and can include how the teacher expects students will engage with activities, what students might find simple or challenging, potential student responses, and how the teacher anticipates dealing with these responses. Significant to teachers' lesson images are the resources used "which shape the mathematical content presented to, and used by, pupils in their mathematics learning" (Pepin et al. 2013, p. 929). For Adler, school mathematics resources "extend beyond basic material and human resources to include a range of other human and material resources, as well as mathematical, cultural, and social resources" (Adler 2000, p. 210). Such resources include teacher's knowledge-base, collegiality, communication, class period duration, manipulatives, etc. (Adler 2000). Furthermore, teachers' work with resources includes "selecting, modifying, and creating new resources, in-class and out-of-class" (Gueudet et al. 2013, p. 1004). The teacher's resource system, as defined by Pepin et al. (2017), plays important roles during lesson preparation (e.g., Sherin and Drake 2009) and classroom enactment (e.g., Remillard and Heck 2014).

Within the teacher's resource system, the textbook is particularly emphasized and used in lesson preparation and enactment. International studies, such as TIMSS 2011 (Mullis et al. 2012, p. 391), report that textbooks are "the most frequent basis of mathematics instruction at the eighth grade, used with 77% of the students internationally, on average." Therefore, frameworks employed to examine the resources teachers utilize to prepare for and implement mathematics curriculum must recognize the important role textbooks play during both lesson preparation and instruction. One such framework is that developed by Valverde et al. (2002)—a framework grounded in the International Association for the Evaluation of Educational Achievement (IEA) Tripartite Curriculum Model comprised of the intended, implemented, and attained curriculum. The intended curriculum refers to intentions, aims, and system goals; the implemented curriculum involves instruction and practice activities; and the attained curriculum refers to students' knowledge and achievement. In Valverde et al.'s (2002, p. 9) framework, "textbooks play a key role... [as] the mediators between *intention* and *implementation*," because they translate educational policy into pedagogy. As a result, Valverde et al. (2002) embed their modified IEA curriculum model with a fourth component—the *potentially implemented curriculum*—as a link between the intended and implemented curriculum. For Valverde et al. (2002), the potentially implemented curriculum is constituted primarily by textbooks. Textbooks have a major influence on teachers' practices and students' mathematics opportunities, because textbooks are considered to be one of the most important and powerful curriculum resources in mathematics education (Mullis et al. 2012; Valverde et al. 2002). Textbooks are not only widely used throughout a teacher's preparation for a lesson, but textbook content, pedagogy, and structure also strongly impact a lesson's enactment (Pepin and Haggarty 2001; Valverde et al. 2002).

Although significant, textbooks are just one of the several tools in a teacher's resource system that impact instruction. According to TIMSS 2011 (Mullis et al. 2012 p. 394), at the eighth grade, workbooks or worksheets were reported as a basis for instruction and as a supplement of instruction by 34% and 62% of students, respectively. In addition, recommendations for supporting high professional practices from the Teaching and Learning International Survey (TALIS) 2013 (Organisation for Economic Cooperation and Development 2016, p. 34) include peer collaboration and encouraging teachers to participate in "networks of information exchange." These findings raise the question of the interplay between the textbook as a main resource and other resources (e.g., workbooks, colleagues) within the resource system during lesson preparation in different environments.

Analyses of teachers' resource systems show wide variation in how resources are utilized during lesson planning (e.g., Ahl et al. 2015). For example, in some countries (or regions), teachers use textbooks and teacher guides to a large degree, while colleagues in other countries (or regions) use them less or in different ways (Lepik et al. 2015). Such results raise the question of the reasons for such differences. Important rationales surely include cultural, political, and educational traditions of each particular country or region (Pepin and Haggarty 2001).

To meaningfully explore the grounds for such variation in teachers' resource systems requires both quantitative and qualitative research methods. Quantitative methods have the potential to address the question as to *what extent* a particular resource is used (e.g., Valverde et al. 2002), while a qualitative approach has the potential to address *how* and *why* a particular resource is used (e.g., Ahl et al. 2015). Therefore, a propitious combination of quantitative and qualitative approaches may support a more nuanced conceptualization of teachers' use of resources. In the work presented here, the methodological emphasis is placed on contrasting these two complementary approaches with the aim of expounding on what occurs within teachers' resource systems.

The goal of the current study was to examine the influence and intermingling of the following three educational components on teachers as they prepare for instruction: (a) textbooks and other resources in teachers' resource systems; (b) national, regional, political, and institutional requirements and mandates; and (c) teachers' views of and perspectives on required or mandated organized resource material. As such, the study addressed the following research questions: (1) Which combinations of resources are utilized most frequently by teachers when planning for instruction? (2) Why do teachers choose to utilize certain resources over other resource options when planning for instruction and how are those resource options utilized?

In order to examine the variability (or stability) of elements within resource systems in different environments, the study analyzed existing data from the USA and Croatia. These two countries differ greatly in size and educational systems. Croatia represents a small country (130th largest population; about four million people) with a centralized education system and textbooks that must comply with standards provided by the Ministry of Science and Education (MZO). The USA represents a large country (third largest population; about 327 million people) with a decentralized education system and textbooks that are not selected, directed, or authorized by the US Department of Education. Such contrasting environments supported the authors' goal to reflect on the impact of cultural, political, and educational elements on teachers' resource systems at a global (rather than local) level.

10.4.2 Education in Croatia and the USA

Compulsory education in Croatia lasts for 8 years (age 6–15 years) and is divided into two levels: grades 1–4 and grades 5–8. All students in compulsory education follow the same national curriculum. After completing the eighth grade, students can continue their education at 4-year non-compulsory secondary schools based on their grades in elementary school. In the USA, education is compulsory over ages ranging from 5–16 years to 8–18 years depending on state laws. In most US schools, compulsory education is divided into three levels: grades K-5, grades 6–8, and grades 9–12. Unlike Croatia, the USA does not have a national curriculum, and curricula can vary broadly from state to state.

Every 4 years in Croatia, the Ministry of Science and Education (MZO) publishes a catalogue of approved textbooks for primary schools and high schools, and teachers have the freedom to choose textbooks provided they appear on the approved ministry list (Buljan Culej 2016). Student textbooks are always "accompanied by a teacher's manual . . . [and may] come . . . with a workbook, exercise book, or other tools of instruction" (Buljan Culej 2016, p. 8). Conversely, in the USA, "[t]here are no national policies governing the use of instructional materials, [and] equipment . . . although state and national organizations and the federal government provide some guidance" (Malley et al. 2016, p. 13). According to Malley et al. (2016, pp. 13–14), "The majority of states allow school districts or schools to choose the textbooks they will use. However, many states (19 in 2015) either select or recommend what textbooks can be used by all districts." In addition, some schools in the

USA have moved to online textbook formats or one-to-one classrooms, where each student is provided with her own laptop, netbook, or tablet computer—allowing students to access the mathematics textbook from school or home via the Internet (Zheng et al. 2016).

10.4.3 Theoretical Framework

The study employed Remillard and Heck's (2014) curriculum policy, design, and enactment framework, which incorporates aspects of Valverde et al.'s (2002) modified IEA model and distinguishes between the official and operational curriculum. The official curriculum involves officially sanctioned curricular elements (i.e., authorized by governing bodies), whereas the operational curriculum is operationalized through practice (i.e., what actually occurs). Although Remillard and Heck's (2014) framework conceptualizes the enacted curriculum, Pepin (2014, p. 840) describes the model as "'all-encompassing' [with links to]... the 'official' curriculum policy level; the design level; and the enactment level."

Rather than focusing on enactment, the study presented here focused on the planning phase of the system and on the triad identified by *Designated Curriculum-Teacher-Intended Curriculum-Instructional Materials* (Fig. 10.5).

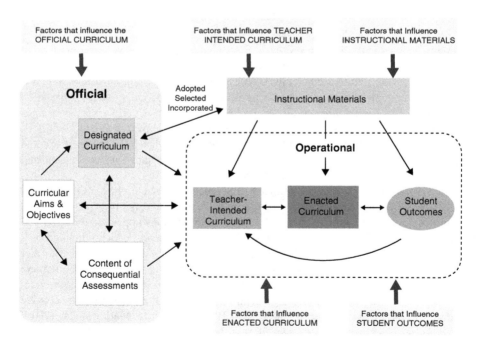

Fig. 10.5 Model of the curriculum policy, design, and enactment system (Remillard and Heck 2014, p. 709)

Designated curriculum refers to "the set of instructional plans specified by an authorized, governing body" (Remillard and Heck 2014, p. 710), such as textbooks and other official resources available to the teacher. Instructional materials refer to other used materials that are outside the official curriculum. Teacher-intended curriculum includes decisions teachers make in designing the instruction, such as lesson plans. Therefore, Remillard and Heck's (2014) framework supported the examination of official and operational components that influence teachers' intended curriculum and the resources used during lesson planning. Specifically, Remillard and Heck's (2014) framework supported reflection on methodological issues, such as the utility of quantitative and qualitative approaches to investigating the component parts of the *Designated Curriculum-Teacher-Intended Curriculum-Instructional Materials* triad (Fig. 10.5).

10.4.4 Methods

Working Group 2 (WG2) provided opportunities for future collaboration between group members. The quantitative research presented by Courtney (2018) and qualitative research presented by Glasnović Gracin and Jukić Matić (2018) prompted one such collaboration, allowing Courtney and Glasnović Gracin to address questions utilizing their existing data that were novel to each researcher's study. The conjoined study utilized "secondary analyses of existing data," as characterized by Cheng and Phillips (2014). According to Cheng and Phillips, "primary data analysis" is limited to the "analysis of data by members of the research team that collected the data, which are conducted to answer the original hypotheses proposed in the study" (2014, pp. 371–372). As such, all other analyses of "data collected for specific research studies or analyses of data collected for other purposes… are considered 'secondary analyses of existing data', whether or not the persons conducting the analyses participated in the collection of the data" (Cheng and Phillips 2014, p. 372).

The current study involved existing data from three independent country-specific projects. The first two projects focused on the Designated Curriculum and Instructional Materials from Remillard and Heck's (2014) framework (Fig. 10.5), addressed the first research question, and employed quantitative methods. In the USA, data were generated from a survey on lesson preparation and lesson plans and focused on responses to the question: "What resources do you use when preparing lessons or writing formal (or informal) lesson plans? Please explain" (Courtney 2018, p. 152). Study participants ($n = 154$) were comprised of grades 6–12 mathematics teachers, purposely sampled by state and school district. Potential respondents were chosen throughout the USA, rather than a specific district, set of districts, or state, in order to attempt to minimize redundancy in teachers' use of specific (state) standards, textbooks, and curricula.

Data collection in Croatia involved a survey (Glasnović Gracin 2011), observations, and interviews (Glasnović Gracin and Jukić Matić 2018). The Croatian project involved a survey of 987 grades 5–8 mathematics teachers from all parts of Croatia—representing 45% of the total number of Croatian grades 5–8 mathematics teachers (Glasnović Gracin 2011). This large-scale project used quantitative methods to help address the first research question by answering "to what extent" textbooks and other resources were used by survey respondents.

The third project involved a qualitative approach (case study) and aimed to address the second research question. In addition, the third project aimed to examine more in-depth the Teacher-Intended Curriculum from Remillard and Heck's (2014) framework (Fig. 10.5), i.e., how teachers use resources and the interplay among resources in lesson planning (Glasnović Gracin and Jukić Matić 2016, 2018). This small-scale project involved 12 mathematics teachers from lower secondary education in Croatia (grades 5–8). Due to limitations of space, the authors will only focus on two specific participants. These two participants were chosen due to their teaching experience (approximately 20 years each) and their participation in the previous large-scale survey (Glasnović Gracin 2011) and because they had articulated different opinions regarding the resources they used during lesson preparation. In particular, one teacher (Beth) was satisfied with the textbook, while the other (Debbie) was dissatisfied with the textbooks' content and pedagogical objectives. The case study (of all 12 teachers) included content analysis, on-site observations of participants' teaching (four lessons in each teacher's classroom) and semi-structured interviews. Content analysis included the lesson plans for the observed lessons and activities provided in teacher guides, which were compared to textbook content and to teachers' observed actions in the classroom.

Analysis involved both "research question-driven" and "data-driven" approaches, as characterized by Cheng and Phillips (2014). A data-driven approach was utilized by examining the authors' (i.e., Courtney 2018 and Glasnović Gracin and Jukić Matić 2018) existing individual datasets and deciding what kinds of questions could be addressed by integrating the available data (Cheng and Phillips 2014, p. 373). A research question-driven approach was utilized by having an "a priori hypothesis or a question in mind and then look[ing] for suitable datasets to address the question" (Cheng and Phillips 2014, p. 373)—i.e., the Glasnović Gracin (2011) and Glasnović Gracin and Jukić Matić (2016) datasets.

10.4.5   Results

Results indicated that the *Designated Curriculum-Teacher-Intended Curriculum-Instructional Materials* triad, a component of Remillard and Heck's (2014) framework, constitutes a significant part of teachers' resource systems. Analysis of the Croatian and US educational systems indicates where a resource resides in the *Designated Curriculum-Teacher-Intended Curriculum-Instructional Materials* triad is dependent on institutional and educational conditions. Similar to results from other studies (Mullis et al. 2012), the textbook was identified as the most utilized resource for lesson preparation in both the USA (indicated by 70.1% of survey respondents) and Croatia (97% of survey respondents indicated they use it "very often" or "always"). Due to the centralization of the Croatian educational system, the textbook is part of the Designated Curriculum in Remillard and Heck's (2014) framework, whereas the teacher guide and other resources are part of Instructional Material. In the USA, the textbook may be considered part of the Designated Curriculum for some US schools and school districts, but in general, the textbook, Internet, teacher guides, and other resources are all Instructional Material teachers utilize as part of the Teacher-Intended Curriculum.

The first research question required authors to examine which resources were combined most frequently *with* textbooks in the teachers' resource systems. In Croatia, participants identified the teacher guide (indicated by 77% of respondents), alternative or supplemental textbooks (67% of respondents), and "other resources" (68% respondents) as resources combined most frequently with the textbook when preparing for instruction. As stated earlier, these "secondary" resources all belong to Instructional Materials (Fig. 10.5).

In the USA, after the course textbook, the Internet (64.9%), mathematics colleagues (33.1%), and prior experience (31.2%) were the resources most utilized by teachers when preparing lessons. Only 25.3% of teachers indicated teacher (or curriculum) guides as a lesson planning resource (Courtney 2018). Since textbooks are not regulated in the USA as they are in Croatia, exploring those resources utilized most frequently in combination helped identify which resource combinations teachers believed were most productive during lesson preparation. The average number of resources US participants utilized was 2.6, with the most frequent combinations being (1) textbook and Internet (7.1% of teachers); (2) textbook, Internet, and colleagues (6.5%); and (3) textbook and prior experience (6.5%). Therefore, the textbook, even though not regulated in the USA, nevertheless, appeared in each of the most frequent resource combinations.

Results indicated significant differences in the number of resources utilized between years of experience, $X^2(5, N = 154) = 11.87$, $p = 0.037$, for teachers with 10 years or less and those with more than 10 years of mathematics teaching experience. The average number of resources utilized for teachers with 10 or less years of mathematics teaching experience was 2.5, with 41.9% of teachers utilizing three resources and 10.8% utilizing four resources. Conversely, the average number of resources utilized for teachers with more than 10 years of experience was 2.7, with 23.8% of teachers utilizing three resources, 16.3% four resources, 6.3% five resources, and 2.5% six resources. Furthermore, teachers who utilized the textbook typically also used the Internet; specifically, 63.5% of teachers who utilized the textbook as a resource when preparing lessons also used the Internet.

These results demonstrate that, despite differences in cultural, political, and educational traditions between Croatia and the USA, textbooks nonetheless play a significant role in lesson planning. Furthermore, variation occurs in terms of which resources—*in addition to* the textbook—are utilized and the degree to which such resources are employed. Such variation may simply be the result of the education systems involved—centralized vs. decentralized, national vs. no national curriculum, and regulated vs. nonregulated textbooks. It is interesting to note that curriculum objectives were not mentioned as a significant resource for lesson planning by participants of either country in the two projects. Furthermore, these results do not reveal *why* particular resources were utilized more than others. Therefore, a more productive way to both potentially grasp teachers' intentions and explore the Teacher-Intended Curriculum was through a qualitative approach.

Since the textbook is the central resource for lesson planning, but other resources are used as well, it seemed reasonable to investigate the Teacher-Intended Curriculum, and more in-depth, *how* and the reasons *why* teachers combine textbooks and other resources during lesson preparation. The small-scale Croatian project (Glasnović Gracin and Jukić Matić 2018) examined the dynamic interactions between teachers, the textbook, and teacher guide because the textbook and teacher guide are the two mostly used curriculum resources in Croatia for lesson planning (Glasnović Gracin 2011).

Participating teachers first consulted their textbook (Designated Curriculum) and then explored other resources for activities and ideas (Instructional Materials). After examining other resources, teachers returned again to the textbook to finalize their lesson planning (Teacher-Intended Curriculum) (Fig. 10.6). Results of qualitative analysis suggest the process of teachers' lesson planning cannot be described as linear, but rather as a dynamic and complex process between Designated Curriculum resources, such as textbooks and other resources, which may be Instructional Materials or additional Designated Curriculum, interacting with the Teacher-Intended Curriculum—a process that aligns with developing a lesson image, which Schoenfeld (2011, p. 233) asserts "is often much more rich than the lesson plan to which it corresponds."

The analysis of textbook content, lesson plans provided in the teacher guide, teachers' lesson plans of the observed lessons, and the classroom observations showed a strong relationship between Teacher-Intended and Enacted Curriculum. Participating teachers' lesson plans were influenced not only by the content of the textbook and teacher guide but also by other resources, such as supplemental textbooks and Internet resources. Classroom observations showed the planned resource tasks (Teacher-Intended Curriculum) were indeed used in the classroom with the aim of accomplishing the lesson objectives (Enacted Curriculum). One participant, Beth, explained that since the textbook was approved by the Croatian state board, this provided warrant to the textbook to be used in her classroom as the

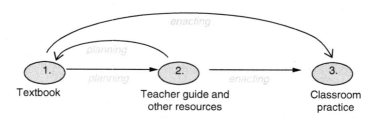

Fig. 10.6 Steps of using resources in participants' lesson planning

10 Analyzing Teachers' Work with Resources: Methodological Issues

main resource. The other resource Beth frequently used was the teacher guide. Beth's rationale for her choices is illustrated in the excerpt below.

Beth: "When I decide to use the textbook for almost the entire lesson, I consult the lesson plans in the teacher guide. I believe [the authors] suggest the best way of using the textbook. I mean [...] [the textbook and teacher guide] are both written by the same people".

Therefore, Beth preferred using Instructional Material closely aligned to the Designated Curriculum in her lesson preparation, because such resources reduced her responsibility and guaranteed the mathematics knowledge and pedagogy (Love and Pimm 1996). In addition, the lesson plans Beth utilized (Teacher-Intended Curriculum) were either copied from or directly influenced by outlines from the teacher guide (Instructional Material).

Although the second participant (Debbie) also consulted the textbook every time she prepared lessons, the textbook content and its aims did not fit her goals. Rather than relying on the textbook, Debbie used other curriculum and non-curriculum resources, such as alternative or supplemental textbooks and teacher guides, journals, and the Internet (Instructional Materials). Debbie's lesson planning process is described in the excerpt below.

Debbie: "First, I look at the textbook to see what I can use, what suits me. And then I look at other resources [...] I use [other] textbooks, as much as I have at home. They all are potential sources. Year by year, I collected a lot of materials [...] If I find something interesting that I can use, I take that [...] I use Internet".

For Debbie, the textbook was just one of many potential resources, but because it was an authoritative part of the Designated Curriculum in Croatia, she consulted the textbook first. Debbie typically only used the practice exercises from the textbook in her lessons. After examining the textbook, Debbie explored other resources resulting in lessons (Teacher-Intended Curriculum) that were developed with a combination of Instructional Materials. Debbie considered her experience to be the most powerful reason why she combined various resources (Glasnović Gracin and Jukić Matić 2018); recall that 31.2% of teachers in the US survey identified "prior experience" as a resource they utilized when planning instruction. Debbie characterized this rationale in the following excerpt.

Debbie: So... based on my experience, I know what will be important to students in the next grade, and there are some things, which I would consider important, which are not in the textbook.

Finally, Debbie consulted the Designated Curriculum above the grade level she taught as another resource for her lesson preparation. Therefore, although Debbie initially focused on the textbook (Designated Curriculum), particularly for content above grade level, she preferred using more Instructional Materials in her lesson preparation, because her experience (Instructional Materials) with the textbook (Designated Curriculum) and teacher guide (Instructional Materials) helped her identify areas of weakness requiring modification and supplementation in her lesson plan (Teacher-Intended Curriculum).

10.4.6 Discussion

Resources from the Designated Curriculum differed *between* the two countries due to the regulated (Croatia) vs. nonregulated (USA) nature of textbooks, which accompany (de)centralized education systems. Resources in Instructional Materials (teacher guide, Internet, prior experience) varied *within* the two countries, depending on individual teacher's perspectives and experiences. In Croatia, the resources teachers utilized most frequently in combination with the textbook were alternative or supplemental textbooks and the teacher guide, which are closely connected with official textbooks. In the USA, where the textbook is not regulated, participants frequently combined the Internet, colleagues, and prior experience with the textbook as important resources for lesson planning.

The three different projects employed in this report revealed some advances and limitations to both the design of the study and the methodologies employed. To address questions regarding resources teachers utilized during lesson planning, and in what combinations, required utilizing data collected from participants in countries or regions representing diverse educational systems and employing quantitative methods. Unfortunately, such data and methods did little to address *why* and *how* such resources were selected and their connections to the Designated Curriculum and Teacher-Intended Curriculum in Remillard and Heck's (2014) framework. A case study design, employing qualitative methods, allowed for these latter questions to be addressed. Although such targeted participants provided data that allowed for detailed descriptions of teachers use of resources during lesson planning, this design, and methods were unable to provide generalizations about the use of resources in a particular country or region. Therefore, the practice of combining distinct projects, each employing particular methodologies, and utilizing both the research question-driven and data-driven approaches for analyzing existing data, as presented here, shows considerable promise.

The results also reveal the nonlinear and dynamic nature of the lesson planning process in which various resources interact and influence teachers' choices. Resources of the Designated Curriculum—the textbook as the main resource in both the USA and Croatia—combine and intermingle with Instructional Materials (e.g., Internet, teacher guide, and supplemental textbooks) making the Teacher-Intended Curriculum. Although Instructional Materials in Remillard and Heck's framework (2014) refers to physical and digital curriculum resources, the results presented here show that this framework can be extended to include human and cultural resources (e.g., colleagues, teacher's prior experiences) as described by Adler (2000) as an important part of teachers' resource systems.

The process of combining resources from the Designated Curriculum and Teacher-Intended Curriculum is influenced by institutional environments of a particular country or region. The centralized curriculum and regulated textbook policies resulted in much greater textbook use in Croatia than in the USA. Conversely, the decentralized education system in the USA allowed for a variety of textbook choices and use by teachers and the potential for teachers to develop lessons utilizing a wide range of different resources. The affordances and constraints such systems provide to student learning and teacher professionalism are issues to be studied through future research.

10.5 Between Design and Use, How to Address the Question of Coherence of a Resource?

Gilles Aldon, Mathias Front, and Marie-Line Gardes

10.5.1 Background of the Study

Reflection on resources, their creation, uses, and quality is not new and becomes more and more important when the diversity of the offer and the modification of the supports impose choices. In this contribution, we are interested in the enrichment of a teacher's resource system on those occasions when she integrates a resource, and in the relationship between the intentions of the resource's authors and the way a teacher uses it. We rely on the hypothesis that a resource is designed by an author with intentions that can be interpreted by the users of the resource. By resource system, we consider all the resources a teacher uses in the preparation of her lessons. The concept of coherence, as often defined in educational contexts (Boning 2007; Mangiante-Orsola 2012; Newmann et al. 2001; Schmidt et al. 2005), concerns a global logic, in the sense of how the elements are linked together within a curriculum or in teachers' practices. Such interpretation does not allow for the conceptualization of relationships existing between a resource, or a set of resources, necessarily created by authors with particular intentions, and their actual uses—specifically, uses by someone else than one of the resource authors. From this perspective, we define the *coherence of a resource in situation* to identify fundamental elements for the analysis of the relationships between the use of a resource and its design. To model this coherence, we rely on the theory of didactic situations (Brousseau 1997), and more particularly, on the concept of *milieu* in its internal organization—the so-called structuring of milieux (Bloch and Gibel 2011; Margolinas 2004). This paper aims to illustrate the complete methodological process, from the design of a resource in a design-based research paradigm (DBR Collective 2003; Swan 2014)—theoretically driven by epistemological considerations and didactic principles—to the experience of a teacher managing the resource and using it to prepare a classroom session. We observed the practice and interviewed a teacher through the theoretical construct of the concept of coherence of a resource in situation. We present the context, the design methodology of a particular resource, and the theoretical construct tested in a case study.

10.5.2 Theoretical Framework from Design to Use of a Resource

10.5.2.1 Epistemological Considerations

EXPRIME is a CD-ROM resource (Aldon et al. 2010) that proposes a set of theoretical texts, problem-solving situations, proposals for their implementation, student productions, and didactical analyses. EXPRIME is part of a theme "research problems" for the class, notably "open problems" (Arsac and Mante 2007; Arsac et al. 1988) that has been explored for many years by the IREM of Lyon. Here, the word "open" means that students confronted with the problem do not know either the solution or the mathematical approach. In this context, it seemed necessary to add a reflection on the relationship with mathematical objects by affirming their central position for the construction of knowledge. We agree with Arsac and Mante (2007) on the potential for modifications of perceptions of mathematics, and we take up the implementation characteristics of "open problems" and changes considered as positive in terms of their impact on the learning process. Assuming that each student builds her own knowledge in a social group led us to produce situations where the objective environment is such that the student can engage herself in a process that potentially leads to knowledge construction (i.e., to the structured integration of new knowledge in a living system of thinking). For us, the major and necessary role of social interactions in the elaboration of knowledge requires that the proposed situations integrate phases of individual research and phases of exchanges, oppositions, and debates—which forge and enrich mathematical constructions. We rely on the "open problem" scenario, which contains (a) phases of individual and group research and intragroup debates, (b) phases of the presentation of results and intergroup debates, and, finally, (c) a phase of institutionalization, which is fundamental for students to know what they have learned from their research. Although this scenario has proven its worth in the evolution of students' relationships with mathematics, other students, and the teacher, we wondered if it genuinely allowed for the construction of knowledge. To understand the potentialities of the scenario from this point of view, it is necessary to question the mathematics itself present in the locution "relation to mathematics." Therefore, we first questioned the research activity in class, the relation to mathematical objects that is induced, and the potential mathematical constructions. We refer to Polya (1945/2004), Lakatos (1963/2015), and Schoenfeld (1985) to attempt to identify invariants of an individual's research activity. With regard to classroom research activity, we also refer to Arsac and Mante (2007) and Perrin (2007), who put forward approach called "experimental method," described as follows:

> It includes several steps to be repeated as necessary: experiment, observation of the experiment, formulation of the conjectures, attempts at proof, counter-experience, possible production of counter-examples, formulation of new conjecture, new attempt at proof, etc. (Perrin 2007, p. 5)

This modeling approach has allowed some analyses and proposals for didactic devices, but we wondered to what extent it could be abstracted from a critical examination of the objects of experiments. In our opinion, we cannot do without questioning the relationship to the objects at stake if we want to be sure of the mathematical nature of the products of a research activity. The place of objects is particularly central from the point of view of an experimental dimension, defined by Durand-Guerrier as:

> [...] the back and forth between working with the objects that one is trying to define and delimit and elaborating and/or placing to the test of a theory, most often local, aiming to account for the properties of these objects (Durand-Guerrier 2006, p. 17)

We consider, on the one hand, that mathematical activity is based on a field of experience, consisting of a set of objects, familiar enough to allow an exploration, and, on the other hand, the relevance of the objects produced in the activity as judged by the quality of the feedback they produce on the "real." Thus, trials, formulations of conjectures, and attempts at proof can only appear meaningful when the student, acting on mathematical objects or some of its representations, produces new knowledge, allowing for new understanding of the mathematical situation.

Thus, didactical situations should be considered more as environments conducive to mathematical questioning than as paths leading inevitably either to the expected result or possibly to a barrier only the teacher can overcome. We specify that didactical situations must allow for rich mathematical activity and, particularly in its experimental dimension, that they are at times resistant, at the crossroads of diverse fields of knowledge, and of easy devolution (Gardes 2018). We add that these situations allow for confrontations with mathematical objects and the capacity to weave around an object to explore a web of relationships and meanings (Front 2012).

These epistemological considerations were at the core of the construction of the EXPRIME resource. The method used regarding the effective construction of the EXPRIME resource was based on a design-based research methodology (DBR Collective 2003; Swan 2014), that is, to say, a method allowing the gap to be bridged between research and praxis, by combining the design of an educational artifact and research on its impact in an educational community. The design of the EXPRIME resource project involved a team of teachers, educational researchers, mathematics researchers, and teacher trainers.

10.5.2.2 Design-Based Research

> Design-Based Research is a formative approach to research, in which a product or process (or "tool") is envisaged, designed, developed, and refined through cycles of enactment, observation, analysis, and redesign, with systematic feedback from end users. (Swan 2014, p. 148)

Design-based research is also characterized by a theory-driven methodology. In particular, the *cycles of enactment, observation, analysis, and redesign* quoted by

Swan are always connected to a theoretical framework. In this sense, design-based research is both a methodology allowing for collaborative work between different communities having a common goal and a framework allowing analyses to be based on theoretical foundations.

Like Cobb and Gravemeijer (2008), we distinguish cycles of three phases of a design experiment: (1) preparing for experiment, (2) experimenting in classroom to support students' learning, and (3) conducting retrospective analyses. The initial phase is both a mathematical analysis of the mathematical situation and a didactic analysis (a priori analysis), ensuring the feasibility in a given class of didactic situations built on the mathematical situation. This phase involves common work done both by teachers and researchers, who each bring their own competencies regarding the analysis. For example, the mathematical analysis prompts mathematicians to consider the outcomes and new questions the mathematical situation allows. Teachers consider the mathematical objects under consideration that students are familiar with, and educational researchers anticipate possible behaviors of students confronted with the situation. Addressing these different points of view, a didactic situation is proposed and experimented with in the second phase of the work. The goal of this second phase is to ensure that the envisioned trajectory allows students to encounter mathematical objects and knowledge. The third phase allows to complete the analysis and revise the didactic situation, by taking into account both the teacher's advice and the results of observation. The iterative process, characteristic of the design-based research, thus cycles through to a new iteration of the three phases. The design methodology of EXPRIME was grounded on these theoretical considerations and led to a common work between mathematicians, mathematics education researchers, and teachers. The mathematical outcomes of a situation can initially be external to teachers in a manner aligned with how the restrictive use of mathematical objects to solve the problem is external to mathematicians. The process of internalization (Arzarello et al. 2014) enriches the teachers' set of resources, in particular, illustrating the potentiality of the mathematical situation, as well as allowing researchers to better understand the learning. Accordingly, we jointly designed the resource as a teaching proposal to enable teachers to develop classroom resources based on the epistemological and mathematical considerations described above. After numerous experiments, the mathematical richness of seven situations was confirmed and led to the creation of a digital resource. This digital resource was designed to be studied along a variety of paths. From the beginning, it was possible to browse theoretical texts concerning the experimental dimension in mathematics (Dias and Durand-Guerrier 2005) and presentations made in symposia and conferences. It was also possible to grasp the spirit of the resource by going through a general presentation. Finally, the situations were presented following a common structure:

- Mathematical problem, which is the basis of the situation, for example, "study of consecutive nonnegative integers".

- Mathematical objects that can be used, which correspond to the mathematical objects involved in the mathematical problem, classified following the grade level, form, or year.
- Learning situations, which propose the didactical situations that were tested and that are accompanied with observations reports.
- References, linked to the mathematical problem or teaching and learning situations related to the theme
- Synthesis, which constitutes a ten-page summary of the content.
- Related situations, which are all the possible outcomes of the mathematical problem the authors envisaged.

The tests and observations were made in classes of teachers who were members of the design team, and thus well aware of the authors' intentions. To observe proximity between the resource authors' intentions and those of the teachers using the resource in a general context, a new tool had to be built. In the following sections, we define the concept of *coherence of a resource in situation* and test the theoretical construction and coherence in situation of the EXPRIME resource through a case study.

10.5.3 The Concept of Coherence in Situation in Relation to the Theory of Didactical Situations

The structure of the *milieu* which has been proposed by Brousseau (1986) and extended and clarified by Margolinas (2004) and Bloch and Gibel (2011) provide a framework for analyzing both a teacher's and her students' work. The teacher plays a fundamental role in different positions: a) designer when she develops her didactic project; b) observer when students are working in an a-didactic situation; and c) teacher when organizing the devolution of the situation and, later, the institutionalization of knowledge. The study of a didactic situation thus leads us to consider the entire environment of the learner, the teacher being one of the elements of this environment. In our work, we consider the point of view of the teacher and use the structure of the *milieux* within a "decreasing analysis." That is, we use an analysis starting from the *noospherian teacher*—a teacher who thinks very generally about teaching, or about teaching mathematics, confronted to designing a milieu in a situation not yet finalized. Table 10.2 is a representation of this structure, taking into account that the milieu of a situation n is the situation $n-1$, which means that the different levels are nested. Therefore, it is possible to see the lower or upper levels from a certain level. The metaphor of an onion skin has been used to show this possible view from one level to the others, as well as indicating a more important difficulty in seeing the levels from a point of view away from (or different from) the actual situation of the student or teacher. Table 10.2 must be considered in a dynamic way, actors moving from one level to another, and not necessarily in a linear progression.

Table 10.2 Structuring of the milieux (Margolinas 2004)

Level	Student	Teacher	Situation	Milieux
M + 3 design	–	T + 3: Noospherian	S + 3: Noospherian situation	Upper didactic levels
M + 2: Project	–	T + 2 developer	S + 2: Design situation	
M + 1: Didactic	St + 1: Reflective	T + 1: Projector	S + 1: Project situation	
M0: Learning	St0: Student	T0: Teacher	S0: Didactic situation	Didactic level
M-1: Reference	St-1: Learner	T-1: Observer	S-1: Learning situation	Lower didactic levels
M-2: Objective	St-2: Acting	–	S-2: Reference situation	
M-3: Material	St-3: Objective	–	S-3: Objective situation	

Margolinas (2004) proposes the concept of *didactic bifurcation*. When a teacher designs a situation for the students, she projects her intentions of teaching, that is, her willingness to change the students' knowledge system. The teacher then constructs a didactic situation based on a milieu. In their position, the students are unaware of the teacher's intentions, but they can imagine them and in turn project their own a-didactic situation by relying on the material environment the teacher has built in an objective situation. There is a bifurcation when, confronted with this material environment, students grasp a situation different from that envisaged in the intentions of the teacher. In this case, it can happen that students can only use naturalized knowledge and act in the reference to the objective situation, but never reach a learning situation where experiences are interpreted and analyzed to reach the targeted knowledge. For example, students were asked to solve the following problem: Is it possible to find two different non-negative integers a and b such that $1/a + 1/b = 1$[8]? A group of four students tried to solve this problem algebraically without success. They wrote:

$1/a + 1/b = 1 \rightarrow (a + b)/ab = 1 \rightarrow a = b/(b - 1)$ and $b = a/(a - 1)$ which leads to the tautology $a = a$ and $b = b$

The students showed they were able to calculate correctly, but by remaining at that level, they were not able to overcome the difficulty. They stayed in the two lowest levels without encountering new knowledge, because, in this case, the material milieu did not prevent this calculation from being made and the objective milieu let them calculate without any chance of reaching a solution. The students continued their calculation without being in contradiction with the didactical contract (Sect. 10.2). We employ the notion of didactical contract following Brousseau and Warfield:

---

[8] This problem comes from the more general mathematical situation: obtaining 1 in the sum of Egyptian fractions that is to say fractions with numerator 1. This situation is one of the EXPRIME situations.

the set of reciprocal obligations and 'sanctions' which each partner in the *didactical situation* imposes or believes himself to have imposed, explicitly or implicitly, on the others, or are imposed, or he believes to have been imposed, on him with respect to the knowledge in question (Brousseau and Warfield 1999, p.7).

The students invested the algebraic aspects of the problem without ever seeing that the problem was an arithmetic one. Indeed, the problem could be overcome using arithmetic reasoning:

$a = b/(b - 1)$ but b and $b - 1$ are relatively prime because of the Bezout relation: $b + (-1)(b - 1) = 1$. Hence $b - 1$ divides b if and only if $b = 2$. Then, $a = 2$, which proves that it is not possible to find two *different* non-negative numbers such that $1/a + 1/b = 1$.

The model of the structuring of the milieu was not built to take into account the resource's authors. Yet, in the process of constructing resources, the authors are part of the set of potential didactic situations that can be built on this resource. We propose to add to the model of the structure of the milieu an additional point of view, that of the author in interaction with the structure of the milieu of didactic situations. We then define the concept of coherence of a resource in situation. The teacher, in the situation of construction, confronts herself to the resource and instrumentalizes it to build her own document, and the support of a didactic situation. She then interprets the resource as a musician interprets a musical work, translating the intentions of the resource for her own project. In a noospherian situation, the teacher interacts with the design milieu, including her set of resources. In particular, the teacher interprets the intentions of the author of a resource through the interactions with the resource. Following a process similar to that of didactic bifurcations explained in the previous paragraph, the design situation may carry intentions distinct from those of the resource leading to a different didactic situation among the didactic situations potentially carried by the resource. In this case, we will speak of a *bifurcation of construction. The coherence of a resource in situation is then judged by the non-bifurcation of construction.*

To test this concept, we experimented with a methodology of didactic engineering with a teacher. We used the concept of didactic engineering (Artigue 1988) as a method based on didactic realization, validated by a confrontation of an a priori analysis and an a posteriori analysis. The a priori analysis is built around the analysis of the resource and a collection of the author's intentions. The a posteriori analysis is built on the observation and analysis of the implemented situation. Comparing these two analyses allows us to conclude whether there is a bifurcation or not that is to say to the non-coherence or the coherence of the resource in the considered situation.

After defining the concept of coherence of a resource in situation and proposing the method, we will examine a particular case study involving the EXPRIME resource (Aldon et al. 2010) as an example. This will allow us to study both the coherence of this resource and the consistency of the concept.

10.5.4 Case Study for an Application of the Concept of Coherence in Situation

In order to consider the coherence of the resource in situation, we analyze how a teacher includes it in his set of resources and how he uses it in the design of a didactic situation. In the following paragraph, we confront the intentions of the authors with the actual construction of a didactic situation by JFC, the teacher who agreed to implement a problem-solving situation by relying on the resource EXPRIME. In terms of methodology, we gave JFC the EXPRIME resource and allowed him to work alone, interviewed him about the choices he made and the way he made them, observed his class lesson, and collected his impressions through an on-the-spot interview just after the class. The institutional constraints that JFC perceived (as does every teacher in a particular institution) prevented him from trying new pedagogical approaches:

> JFC: "I did things, ah, some problems that were a bit open, I will say, with a class organization that is not a group work, but a classical organization..."

JFC clearly stated his difficulty in considering the progression of the prescribed curriculum under this teaching practice:

> JFC: "I think this kind of attitude comes with experience on this kind of problem ah so to do it again, I think it should be good, if I have time but I will try to do it again once, but I believe I cannot do more for time issues".

In the project situation, JFC used the resource to plan the didactic organization of the session, based on the problem chosen and on the sessions already proposed:

> JFC: "I showed them an open problem that of the two straight lines that cut off the sheet and I told them, well this is an example of an open problem, they'd love to, they have searched a bit, we talked about it again, I proposed a solution and it was fine because we had just learnt the homothety with complex numbers so it was dead on time".

In this project situation, JFC put himself in the position of the students to see what they could do; the resource appeared to help complete the analysis of the mathematical situation. JFC used the resource to refine his skills to organize a research situation in the classroom. In the didactic situation, JFC presented his situation to students by following a scenario proposed in the resource. He added, in accordance with his particular noospherian position, a reflection on meta-cognition. JFC, in the didactic situation, quickly placed his students in an "upper-didactic situation" by anticipating a priori a reflective return on their "cognitive adventure." During the phase of research in the classroom, the teacher (JFC), as an observer of the situation, measured the distance between his intentions in terms of the progress of didactic time and the actual work of the students, but maintained a willingness to start from his students' proposals. All the dialogues and observations showed the tension between the desire to propose to students defined parameters in order to solve the problem algebraically and the desire to let students explore the tracks they wish to explore:

JFC: I was a bit surprised that it was so long to start and I was also surprised, [...] that they do not set the problem faster. Uh well it's a good awareness... I'll know it's true that we are distorted by what we're used to do and so I did not imagine they would have, they need a helping hand like that to setup uh".

However, one can think the teacher enlarged his repertoire of didactic answers in such a situation and completes his resource system even if the resource did not prevent this possible difficulty of students not making more progress on the problem. In the implementation of the situation, JFC resolutely placed himself in a potential situation proposed by the resource and orchestrated a research situation that joined the expectations of the author. In terms of methodology, the theoretical construct of the concept of coherence of a resource in situation come both from the methodological process of the resource design, taking into account both the didactic point of view, the feasibility in an ordinary classroom, and the theoretical and epistemological considerations. As illustrated in the above case study (with JFC), the concept of coherence of a resource in situation allowed us to reach conclusions regarding the relationships between the EXPRIME authors' intentions and the actual didactic situations constructed by JFC.

10.5.5 Discussion

The first part of the contribution presented the methodology leading to the design of the resource EXPRIME, whereas the second part highlighted the theoretical construct of the concept of coherence of a resource in situation. The dialectic between design and use has been a force engine of the methodological choices leaning on the specific theoretical framework of the Theory of Didactical Situations. The concept of didactic bifurcation, initially defined in the lower levels of the structuring milieu, was extended to the upper levels. This extension seems to have a theoretical scope that should be explored in different contexts. The purpose of this study comes from the legitimate question as to how the author can address the "life" of her resource and the way by which users adapt a resource for their own purposes. This leads us to address the question of a theoretical founding in order to define precisely the concept of coherence of a resource. The theoretical framework constituted of the Design-Based Research (Swan 2014) and the theory of didactic situations supported a definition of the *coherence of a resource in situation*. We consider the design methodology, and particularly the collaborative work within a design-based research—including different categories of actors—to help account for the obstacles to the dissemination of the authors' intentions and, in this way, favors the coherence of the resource. This study allows us to implement this concept under these conditions, and, also, makes it possible to envisage its use in wider fields. Beyond the specific didactic engineering, the concept of coherence will have to be tested in other contexts and with other resources. Particularly, another field of experimentation that we can explore will have to deal with contexts of ordinary class and with "ordinary" resources, such as school textbooks. It is for this reason that we developed a second circle of engagement for teachers, interested in the role of problems in the teaching of mathematics, but outside the design team. It is in this context that we can, through the study of the coherence of a resource in situation, consider expanding the subject to the study of the dissemination of resources and their impact on mathematics education.

10.6 MOOC-MDT: A Theoretical Framework to Analyze the Interactive Nature of a MOOC and Its Influence on Teachers' Professional Learning

Eugenia Taranto, Ferdinando Arzarello, and Ornella Robutti

10.6.1 Background of the Study

A Massive Open Online Course (MOOC) is an online course aimed at unlimited participation and open access via the web (Kaplan and Haenlein 2016). MOOCs are a recent and widely researched development in distance education. First introduced in 2008, MOOCs emerged as a popular mode of learning by 2012 (Pappano 2012). Early MOOCs were based on open licensing of content, structure, and learning goals and often emphasized open-access features to promote the reuse and remixing of resources. Some later MOOCs, despite the fact that they maintained free access for students, used closed licenses for course materials (Cheverie n.d.). In addition to traditional course materials, such as filmed lectures, readings, and problem sets, many MOOCs provide interactive user forums to support community interactions among students, professors, and teaching assistants (Adamopoulos 2013; Panero et al. 2017; Taranto et al. 2017b). Therefore, a MOOC can be considered as a digital resource with many other digital resources inside (Taranto et al. 2018).

Despite their success, the emergence and use of MOOCs for teacher professional learning (PL) is still uncommon, especially in mathematics. Moreover, the specific intersection of MOOCs and teachers' PL is insufficiently researched. On the contrary, there exists a wide literature base exploring ways teachers can experience PL in traditional, face-to-face courses, particularly for themes concerning the relationship between education and technology (Robutti et al. 2016). It is worth noting that, in a panorama where MOOCs for teachers are rare, our initiative to provide MOOCs for mathematics teacher education was the first such example in Italy—it has continued, annually, since 2015, inside the so-called *Math MOOC UniTo* project. Furthermore, the strength of our initiative is that the MOOCs are used for teacher education; therefore, they are deeply embedded into the Italian institutional framework. Moreover, the MOOCs are studied from the point of view of the researcher, so they are objects of research. Based on this, Taranto (2018) developed a theoretical framework, the *MOOC-MDT*, which aims to understand the complexities of the learning trajectories of participants in a MOOC. MOOC participants are comprised of in-service mathematics secondary school teachers (henceforth referred to as MOOC-teachers) and mathematics teacher educators (MTEs). MTEs are researchers and expert teachers[9] involved in the MOOC design and delivery. By "learning trajectory,"[10] Taranto (2018) means how these participants interact online, both with the platform and with each other, in particular, *if* and *how* these interactions change participants' knowledge and beliefs and generate perception of change in their practices. In our project, we have collected and analyzed data coming from MOOC-teachers' posts from the communication message boards, questionnaires, interviews with a sample of MOOC-teachers, and resources that teachers designed and uploaded to the MOOC platform. In this contribution, we illustrate data from the forum, because our purpose is to show the theoretical framework elaborated and corresponding methodology, addressing the following research question: How can we analyze the interactive nature of a MOOC and its influence on teachers' professional learning?

10.6.2 A Glimpse on the Existing Literature

Taranto (2018) revised the *Meta-Didactical Transposition* model (MDT) (Arzarello et al. 2014) and re-elaborated it from a framework apt to describe face-to-face teachers' PL to a new one, suitable for describing PL dynamics within a MOOC environment. To achieve this, Taranto integrated MDT through a *hybridization process*[11] (Arzarello 2016) with the *Instrumental Approach* (IA) (Verillon and Rabardel 1995) and the *Connectivism* (Siemens 2005), obtaining what she termed the MOOC-MDT. Here, we briefly recall the key points considered in these three theoretical frameworks. In the following section, we show the result of their combination, namely, the MOOC-MDT.

---

[9] With this expression, we mean in-service teachers who have long teaching experience and who have obtained a 2-year master's degree to become trainers in mathematics education.

[10] The choice of this term to refer to teachers' education programs is in tune with Simon definition of Learning Trajectory: "The Hypothetical learning trajectory consists of the goal for the students' learning, the mathematical tasks that will be used to promote students' learning and hypothesis about the process of the students' learning" (Simon 1995).

[11] *Hybridization* is a very specific type of *networking of theories* (Bikner-Ahsbahs and Prediger 2014). In networking of theories, researchers use different theories (generally from mathematics education) to study the same problem, possibly producing different levels of combination/ integration of the different theories. We have a *hybridization of a theory* T_0 when a more or less extensive fragment of another theory T_1 (possibly also from a different theoretical field) is introduced *coherently*, *operatively*, and *productively* into the theory T_0 but only partially altering its principles and methodology. Typically, researchers hybridize a theory when they realize that their working theory gives only a partially satisfactory answer to the research question they are facing; so, they introduce some new theoretical fragments, coherent with the starting frame, in order to develop a more satisfactory analysis.

The MDT (Arzarello et al. 2014) pays attention to the *community of the researchers* and the community *of the teachers* involved in a face-to-face educational program. This theoretical approach is based on the notion of didactical praxeology (Chevallard 1999) and offers an analytical tool to describe the possible evolution of teachers' and researchers' meta-didactical praxeologies during the educational process and within the institutional context (Robutti 2018). The researchers-teachers interaction along the program may support this evolution toward shared praxeologies.

While in a face-to-face course, teachers and researchers can discuss the materials and content that are presented from time to time, so that they can reflect on these possible evolutions of the didactical praxeologies, in a MOOC such discussion and reflection is unlikely to happen. First, because the materials and contents must all be prepared and defined prior to the start of the MOOC. Second, the MTEs and MOOC-teachers do not have opportunities for discussion. Everything happens online, more in an asynchronous than a synchronous manner. In fact, the MTEs do not know when or what a MOOC-teacher actually viewed in the MOOC. In addition, MTEs do not know if the MOOC-teachers have deeply understood the proposed materials. There are materials, where everything (e.g., suggestions, clarifications) is explained. However, it cannot be taken for granted that these materials are read by everyone. Although there are spaces for online communication, where MOOC-teachers can compare and contrast mostly with each other, not all teachers are on this space at the same time. Therefore, the usual contexts of face-to-face teacher education are not present: a community consisting of MTEs and MOOC-teachers does not tend to be formed, because of issues of distance and time. For those reasons, we analyze the interactions in a MOOC and their impact on teachers using the MDT model, but expanded according to the specific affordances of a MOOC.

The *instrumental genesis*, from the IA framework (Verillon and Rabardel 1995), describes the transition from an artifact as an object to its evolution as an instrument that incorporates some knowledge because of the aimed-directed actions of a subject with it. It is based on two dual intertwined processes:

- *Instrumentation* (from the artifact to the subject): it leads to the development or appropriation of utilization schemes which progressively constitute into techniques which allow humans to solve given tasks efficiently.
- *Instrumentalization* (from the subject to the artifact): it progressively transforms the artifact for specific uses with the related utilization schemes. So, it is the adaptation of the artifact to human cognitive structures.

From the Connectivism framework, we consider the notions of *personal knowledge* and *learning*. *Personal knowledge* is a particular kind of network. Nodes in personal knowledge are any entity that can be connected to another node (e.g., information, data, images, ideas), while an arc is a connection, a relationship, and a link between two nodes (Siemens 2005). *Learning* is a continual process of building, developing, self-organizing knowledge understood as a network (Siemens 2005). Therefore, learning not only adds new nodes but also connects existing nodes and makes sense of these connections. Personal knowledge can be understood as an evolving network: the knowledge at a given moment corresponds to a timely conformation of the network, while the act of learning, of increasing knowledge, corresponds to the process by which the structure and complexity of the network expands.

It might seem that there is an "abuse" of language with respect to the use of the term "learning" for teachers. In fact, it is not the learning process that typically takes place in a classroom with students. Learning is understood in a connectivist sense. It is not only a "literal" learning of new things; rather it means to be able to see differently concepts that were already known: reflecting, thinking again, integrating them under a different perspective (Taranto 2018), and in this way, improving professional competences. Teachers' learning is therefore *an expansion of network of knowledge*, which is possible through the sharing of practices and didactical theories. This is in line with what was observed in the MDT. In fact, the expansion of the network of knowledge corresponds to the researchers and teachers' praxeologies that can evolve. Protagonists are the MTEs, the MOOC-teachers, and the MOOC, each with its own network of knowledge. According to Siemens (2005, p. 5) "knowledge may reside in non-human appliances." Therefore, we can say that the nodes of the MOOC's network of knowledge are all the mathematical activities and technological resources that are uploaded. A MOOC participant (i.e., MTEs and MOOC-teachers) network of knowledge evolves because of new connections within it that emerge when the individual uses the MOOC and technology inserted in it. A MOOC participant's network of knowledge also evolves when she acts in a specific context (the MOOC and her daily environment). Furthermore, the factors supporting the genesis of new connections within the MOOC's networks are the MOOC participants' interactions within it. Therefore, a focus on the interactions that take place within a MOOC is an area of interest.

10.6.3 MOOC-MDT: A New Theoretical Framework

Taranto (2018) made a hybridization of the *instrumental genesis* from the IA and the *network of knowledge* from Connectivism with the MDT, obtaining the MOOC-MDT, which is illustrated below.

In the design phase, the MOOC is a world inhabited by the MTEs who propose resources to be included in it. At this stage, a MOOC can be considered as an *artifact,* that is, a static set of materials. The *MOOC-artifact* has its own network of knowledge: its nodes are the content, ideas, images, and videos used in the MOOC; the connections are the links between node pairs. When the MOOC is ready, it is opened in order to accommodate the entry of MOOC-teachers. So, when a MOOC module is activated, it dynamically generates a complex structure that we call an *ecosystem*: "all the relations (exchange of materials, experiences and personal ideas/points of view) put in place by participants of an online community thanks to the technological tools through which they interact with each other, establishing connections within the given context" (Taranto et al. 2017b, p. 2481).

Learning within a MOOC happens in a connectivist modality: each MOOC-teacher is part of a community, with which she comes into contact and has the opportunity to share her own views, self-organize information, create new connections, and question existing ones. Moreover, what is shown in the MOOC should encourage MOOC-teachers to experiment in their classrooms. In fact, during the implementation of the MOOC-artifact network of knowledge, the MTEs foster its ecosystem nature, sharing tools and posing appropriate key questions. Moreover, since the tasks are designed by the MTEs, this more or less explicitly suggests to MOOC-teachers that they should use the proposed material in their classes. In this way, the MOOC is enriched with reports about MOOC-teachers' teaching experiences: this process produces an organic cycle that encourages other MOOC-teachers to experience the same materials.

The community of MOOC-teachers is made of subjects who are involved in the MOOC-ecosystem and who transform it into an instrument. As in many social platforms, every participant develops her/his own way through the system, but within the affordances that the system itself supports. The MOOC-teacher has to solve tasks, through techniques, properly justified. In fact, she must look at the proposed material, share her thoughts through sharing tools, and experience the MOOC activities. These tasks are not predetermined; they depend on the time, approach, and depth with which each MOOC-teacher addresses them. The techniques are the ways in which the MOOC-teacher extends and modifies her network of knowledge, drawing on the ecosystem and influencing it in turn, thus, impacting all other MOOC-teachers. Therefore, the *MOOC-ecosystem* network of knowledge is dynamic: it evolves as the MOOC-artifact network, thanks to each participant's contribution. Also, each MOOC participant's network of knowledge evolves as a personal self-organization (Siemens 2005, p. 4) of the ecosystem. The process of transformation from artifact to instrument (Verillon and Rabardel 1995) is here reinterpreted by the evolution from artifact to ecosystem/instrument—a process Taranto et al. (2017b, p. 2482) called the "*double learning process.*" The double learning process has the following components, intertwined and self-feeding each other:

- **Instrumentation/self-organization** (from the ecosystem to the individual = E $\rightarrow$ I): process by which the MOOC-ecosystem network of knowledge expands the individual's network of knowledge. In particular, the *instrumentation* is the phase by which the chaos (Siemens 2005, p. 4) of the ecosystem network reaches the individual. The many novelties of views and experiences make sure that the individual compares herself with new utilization schemes (USs). A phase of *self-organization* of the MOOC information follows: when the individual selects which USs proposed by the MOOC are valuable and which are not.
- **Instrumentalization/sharing** (from the individual to the ecosystem = E $\leftarrow$ I): process by which the individual's network of knowledge expands the MOOC-ecosystem network of knowledge. The *instrumentalization* is the phase by which the individual, with her renewed network of knowledge, independently builds new connections. The individual is stimulated by a task requested by the MOOC

and she caters to the ecosystem to turn it according to her own (new) USs. The individual wants to integrate it with her own cognitive structures. *Sharing* is the phase by which the MOOC welcomes the contribution of the individual and makes it available to all: information goes toward (is available to) all members.

Since the number of MOOC participants is massive, the process is iterative: a phase of sharing is followed by a new instrumentation; a self-organization by an instrumentalization. It should be emphasized that the two processes are "intertwined"—there is no moment in which one ends and the next one begins.

10.6.4 The Math MOOC UniTo Project

The *Math MOOC UniTo* project started in spring 2015 at the Department of Mathematics "G. Peano," University of Turin. It is focused on designing and delivering MOOCs for mathematics teachers, mainly from secondary schools. The project aimed to increase teachers' professional competencies and improve their classroom practices. Four MOOCs were designed, one for each of the main topics in the official Italian programs for secondary school: Geometry, Arithmetic and Algebra, Change and Relations, Uncertainty and Data. The MOOCs were designed to be offered one per year, starting in 2015.[12] These MOOCs are open, free, and available online for teachers through the department teacher professional development Moodle platform (http://difima.i-learn.unito.it/). Each 10-week MOOC is subdivided into modules lasting one or two weeks.

The MTEs team is composed of the contributing authors (two university professors and a Ph.D. student), along with ten expert secondary school teachers. The entire MTE team is involved in each MOOC design, their delivery, and in monitoring their evolution in terms of interaction among participants. In particular, the expert teachers proposed the topics to be discussed in each MOOC and then developed the initial materials. These materials were subsequently revised by university researchers and then included in the MOOCs. Digital resources replace the MTEs' voice and explanations that are usually done in face-to-face courses; therefore, MOOC-teachers interact with videos, images, interactive texts, software, etc. In this way, the MTEs are able to communicate their training intentions at a distance and share research results, methodologies, and teaching strategies that MOOC-teachers can then use in their own classes with students. These digital resources are prepared and defined before the MOOC begins, and with care, to encourage the subsequent MOOC-teachers' instrumentation/self-organization phase. In addition, the MTEs help MOOC-teachers solve technical problems

---

[12] So far, the first three have been delivered and the fourth one is a work in progress. They are called, respectively, MOOC Geometria (based on geometry contents, from October 2015 to January 2016), MOOC Numeri (based on arithmetic and algebra contents, from November 2016 to February 2017), and MOOC Relazioni e Funzioni (based on changes and relations concepts, from January 2018 to April 2018).

(sending personal e-mail or uploading tutorials uploaded to the platform) and recall the tasks to be done week by week with weekly emails.

Each week, MOOC-teachers worked individually to become familiar with different approaches. In our MOOCs, these activities included watching videos where an expert introduced the mathematical topic of the week or reading about mathematical activities drawing on a laboratory methodology based on inquiry (Harlen and Léna 2013), explicitly suggested by the Italian curriculum, and, optionally,[13] experimenting with these in their classroom. The MOOC-teachers were invited to share thoughts and comments about the activities and their contextualization within their personal experience, using specific communication message boards (CMBs). In each activity, MTEs inserted a specific question to be answered or a title that served as talking point.

On the one hand, choosing resources that support interactions (e.g., the CMBs) that increase the birth of new connections and/or nodes in the MOOC-teachers' network of knowledge is a methodological choice that fosters the development of the instrumentation/self-organization phase. On the other hand, inserting specific stimulus questions or titles in the CMBs, or inviting MOOC-teachers to experiment with the activities with their own students is a methodological choice that promotes and increases the interactions among MOOC-teachers, hence the development of the instrumentalization/sharing phase. Moreover, the MTEs chose to limit their own interventions in the CMBs to a minimum in order to support the birth of a "MOOC-teachers only" online community. In fact, our MOOCs methodology aims to create collaborative contexts for teachers' work, where MOOC-teachers can learn from these kinds of practices.

In the following, we concentrate our analysis on MOOC Geometria, the first delivered MOOC. There were 424 in-service mathematics secondary school teachers from all Italian regions who participated in MOOC Geometria.

10.6.5 MOOC Materials and MOOC-Teachers' Interactions

At the design level, the MOOC-artifact is a repository of materials rich in innovative teaching methods and specific technological tools from which teachers can draw inspiration (Taranto et al. 2017a). MOOC Geometria contains five modules, each with contents and teaching suggestions, such as the mathematics laboratory (Anichini et al. 2004), group work, mathematical discussion (Bussi et al. 1995), use of technology (especially GeoGebra with guided examples of constructions), and use of materials, such as cardboard and string. Each module lasts from 1 to 2 weeks. In the following, we examine an example of an activity, along with feedback from the MOOC-teachers. Then we illustrate how these elements of the MOOC-artifact have given rise to specific learning processes implemented by the MOOC-teachers in the MOOC-ecosystem/instrument.

---

[13] If the MOOC-teachers liked them; if MOOC-teachers were explaining at that time topics close to those proposed in their own classes

Module 1 of MOOC Geometria is focused on the concept of distance between a point and a line (connected to other concepts, including perpendicular and height). The proposed activities are directed to avoid or overcome student misconceptions related to these concepts. One activity is "the mainmast" for lower secondary school students (grades 6–8) and is developed from a concrete situation: the teacher gives each student a white circular sheet with a sketch of a boat on a sea wave. School students are asked to draw, on a round sheet (to avoid references), the mainmast of a boat: they have to concentrate on the perpendicular. The activity continues with observations of the various drawings and with discussions of the various solutions. The teacher can intervene directly with the request: "Explain why?" This activity should ground the discussion around the two concepts: (i) *vertical* (physical concept linked to the gravitational field) and (ii) *perpendicular* (geometric concept linked to the right angle).

The communication message board (CMB) embedded into Module 1 was the forum. In the forum, the MTEs have inserted an assignment to stimulate discussion among the MOOC-teachers: "*Share your ideas and/or teaching experiences related to the topics of the mainmast activity.*" The forum collected 24 discussions,[14] each containing from 0 to 62 response replicas, for 207 posts in total. The forum also keeps track of the date and time each post was published. It is interesting to note that MOOC-teachers responded *asynchronously* on the forum at all times of the day and night, ranging from 05:51 (5:51 a.m., early in the morning) to 01:48 (1:48 a.m., midnight).

To make a qualitative analysis of MOOC-teachers' posts in the CMBs, in the light of the double learning process, we base on the linguistics analysis of *lexical contrast* (Mohammad et al. 2013). Namely, in the sentences of MOOC-teachers' posts, we identify word pairs (specifically, verb tenses, adjectives) that have some degree of contrast in meaning each other and mark the reference either to instrumentation/self-organization or to instrumentalization/sharing:

- For **instrumentation/self-organization** (E → I), the verbs are in the future tense (e.g., I *will* do it, I *will* re-propose, I *will* test it, I *will* use it) or the MOOC-teacher uses verbs or adjectives to express their own judgment (e.g., I *have* noticed, I *really* appreciated, *nice* idea).
- For **instrumentalization/sharing** (E ← I), the verbs refer to own self when one is creating new connection stimulated by the MOOC-ecosystem (e.g., I reflect, I know, I thought), while the verbs are in the present tense when one shares her didactical praxeologies (e.g., I *do* this, I *use* that).

These criteria are used for distinguishing the phases of the double learning process throughout data analysis. In the following, all the interventions are written in normal type, whereas bold type is inserted by the authors to accomplish the analysis.

---

[14] In the terminology of the Moodle forum, a discussion is defined as the set of posts that are grouped in response to an original post, which opened the topic of the discussion.

Table 10.3 MOOC-teachers' asynchronous discussion on the forum in Module 1

Discussion (started by X; on dd/mm/yy; at hh:mm)	Reply (by X; on dd/mm/yy; at hh:mm)	Intervention	Double learning process
ON THE HEIGHTS OF THE TRIANGLE (by A.P.; 26/10/15; 18:22)	…		
	E.L.I; 26/10/15; 20:08	Hi, […] I do not teach in any school at the moment […] but I have experience of tutoring. Speaking of heights and perpendicular lines […] to make a fourteen-year-old pupil understand how to draw the height of one side of a triangle, whatever nature it had, **I invite to** stretch out thumb and index finger of one hand (usually the left) so as to position the index finger on the side in question: The position of the thumb, once intercepted the vertex opposite the side in question, identified the desired height.	E ← I
	A.A.; 29/10/15; 12:47	**Genial,** the set square always at your fingertips! **I will immediately adopt** your suggestion	E → I
	E.G.; 31/10/15; 16:02	Dear, **I also use** this strategy ("natural" set square) for lower secondary school boys, and **I realized that** it works very well, even after some time.	E → I

We chose to report an example that emblematically illustrates how the general affordances of the MOOC-instrument can intertwine with the personal contribution of the participants. The example, in fact, shows how the hybridized theory is particularly useful for analyzing the specificity of such phenomena (Table 10.3).

E.L.I, despite being a novice teacher, suggested a strategy (instrumentalization/sharing) that she uses with students to whom she teaches privately. E.L.I's post has a double meaning. On the one hand, she already self-organized the MOOC information on the proposed activities to overcome the student's misconceptions about height, namely, she compared her USs with those proposed by the MOOC.[15] On the other hand, she develops an instrumentalization phase: she realized that in her network, not only were similar nodes already present (concept of height and difficulty encountered by the students on it during her tutoring), but also that there was a node that seemed not present in the MOOC-ecosystem network: the manual set square, one of her teaching strategies. E.L.I then decided to implement the sharing phase, adding this node to the ecosystem network. Two other MOOC-teachers responded (process of instrumentation/self-organization), connecting their network of knowledge to this node (the manual set square). In particular, it is noted that while for A.A., the manual set square is a new node that adds to her network, for E.G., it recalls an already present node. So, the awareness of an existing connection emerges

---

[15] Note, moreover, E.L.I posts in a discussion already started: see in Table 10.3 the presence of ellipsis before the E.L.I line. This also denotes that E.L.I has carried out an information self-organization.

in E.G. and her articulation of it demonstrates ownership (as with E.L.I), confirming the manual set square as an effective strategy for student learning.

10.6.6 Some Remarks on MOOC-MDT

Hybridization takes place by considering two components: one from IA (the instrumental genesis), the other from Connectivism (the network of knowledge). These are implanted in the MDT, which is thus adapted to MOOC own dynamics. The community of participants becomes subject and object of a new, more complex kind of instrumental genesis: the double learning process. In fact, it maintains the structure of the instrumental genesis, with directions from the subject to the object and vice versa. It is also enriched with the point of view of Connectivism. In the MDT, the researchers shape their proposal according to the practices they think appropriate and are able to know how teachers interpreted the proposal. On the contrary, inside the MOOC-MDT the process appears to be more difficult to control. The MTEs do not know "what" the MOOC-teachers have actually looked at among the available materials, nor can they know how MOOC-teachers interpreted these materials. At the same time, the MOOC-teachers benefit from material provided, not only by MTEs but also by other MOOC-teachers that share their ideas using the online communication space. The process evolves stochastically: a determining role is played by individual MOOC-teachers and whether they feel part of a community with whom to collaborate, to inspire, and to share results. Considering the interactions that took place in the forum, teachers exhibited confidence in exchanging ideas and experiences. The forum tool was accepted and managed on the basis of a growth of knowledge of the MOOC-teachers, namely in terms of expanding their own network of knowledge, adding the nodes proposed by other forum participants (provided the MOOC-teacher considered such nodes valuable). Actually, adding a node to one's own network means expanding it. That is what it means to learn in a connective connotation. From this point of view, all those who have intervened have certainly given proof of successful learning, or an expansion of their own network of knowledge. Moreover, a partial sharing of the meta-didactical praxeology that MTEs wanted to transpose to the MOOC-teachers emerges. Specifically, the one linked to overcoming misconceptions related to the concept of height. Of course, we cannot talk about shared praxeology for MDT. In fact, sharing (in the sense of the double learning process) does not take place for everyone or even between everyone concurrently, but a partial sharing begins to take shape—at least among those who intervened in the forum. The MOOC-artifact can be considered simultaneously an individual and a collective instrument. From the one side, each participant transforms the artifact into their own instrument; however, this process happens within the asynchronous interactions trough the affordances allowed by the artifact itself. Hence, the final result is a sort of hybrid instrument where the researcher finds personal and shared components created within the ecosystem. The theoretical lens of the double learning process showed to be suitable for analyzing this new instrument in its peculiar novelties. MOOCs for mathematics teacher education offer a promising area for research. This contribution begins the discussion of what such a framework might entail and hopefully motivates further research into MOOCs for mathematics teachers' professional learning.

10.7 Discussion

Catherine Loisy, Hussein Sabra, and Scott A. Courtney

Three fundamental points ground the methodological questions that were proposed in Sect. 10.2: (1) the dialectic relation between theoretical choices and methodological issues, (2) the need to study teacher-resource interactions "as a whole," and (3) the need to take into account content and level of teaching in developing methodologies. We discuss these three questions, based on the four contributions (Aldon et al. Sect. 10.5; Glasnović Gracin and Courtney, Sect. 10.4; Rocha, Sect. 10.3; Taranto et al., Sect. 10.6), each of which placed an emphasis on different aspects. Then, we broaden the discussion on methodological issues by inserting into the discourse a perspective not present in the four contribution—the Vygotskian approach—and the question of what constitutes "sufficient" length in long-term studies. Lastly, we propose an opening to debate for further work on the methodological issue.

10.7.1 Discussion on the Three Issues

10.7.1.1 Dialectic Relation Between Theoretical Choices and Methodological Issues

The question of dialectic relation between theoretical choices and methodological issues is addressed in three ways: (1) affordances of theoretical concepts and approaches, (2) specific case of networking theories, and (3) methodological contract.

Regarding affordances of theoretical concepts and approaches, there is a necessity to further operationalize the development of analytical tools, such as: schemes, genesis, and trajectories. The theoretical approaches designed and utilized to study teacher-resource interactions establish new methodological issues: the length of long-term studies, the issue of trajectories, and the issue of genesis (some aspects remain open questions for further work). In addition, such theoretical approaches generate issues around developments that take into account the articulation between quantitative and qualitative data, as well as the articulation between natural data (e.g., teachers' resources)—where some are offered by digital tool, and data collected by methodological tools.

The digital era opens new ways to access quantitative data and natural data. Although a networking theories approach (e.g., coordinating, combining, synthesizing, or integrating strategies) offers unique theoretical solutions, methodological issues remain a challenge for further work. The methodological contract supports collaboration by formalizing a set of mutual expectations between the researcher and teacher (or group of teachers) about an activity, individual, or collective, related to mathematics teaching. As such, methodological contracts can help to mind the gap between the designers' intention and the teacher's achievement in the classroom.

10.7.1.2 Discussion on the Analyses of Teacher-Resource Interactions "As a Whole"

Specific questions arise from the postulate of an organization of resources in a system intertwined with the teacher's professional development. Some questions refer to how it is developed by a teacher in (inter)-relation with others, as well as with the resources that are available in her environment. Others questions concern the organization of this system, the personal form it takes for a given teacher at one moment in her development. Therefore, special methodologies have to be developed in order to catch the organization of the structure and the way it is built, without losing sight of the teacher's professional evolution. At that juncture, catching and analyzing the resource system of a given teacher and its evolution over time will possibly provide access to her professional development. At the same time, the structure of resources cannot be understood without taking into account her state of development.

10.7.1.3 Discussion on Content and Level of Teaching

Research on/with methodologies that focus on content is a work in progress. The issue of coherence of resources in terms of content opens new opportunities for research that simultaneously takes into account the actors (designers, users of resources) and the epistemological and didactical characteristics of content.

Further research is needed that takes into account the epistemological and cognitive specificities of content and its organization in resources, particularly with the opportunities that provide for digital affordances (interactions between users, dynamic representation of content, etc.). Some research aligned with the documentational approach develop new analytical frameworks to study, i.e., in the case of e-textbooks, the connectivity in terms of content, as well as in terms of potential of linking between users and resources (Gueudet et al. 2018). The connectivity of the concept of 'resource content' offers new possibilities to for account the content and its specificities, even beyond the particular case of the textbooks.

Research on resources at the university level, particularly methodological issues, is a field that has not been sufficiently explored to date. Biza et al. (2016), in an

ICMI study, highlight that the body of research on university professors' practices is growing, where the issue of teacher-resource interactions is crucial. Areas that necessitate further development include the issue of relationships between research activity and teaching practices—although some current research is in progress (Tabchi 2018)—and the issue of collective work of design of resources in higher education.

10.7.2 How Methodological Issues Could Be Enlightened in the Light of the Theory of Vygotsky

Vygotsky's approach is not present in the approaches of researchers who contributed to this chapter. In order to fill this gap and broaden the lens for theoretical discourse, it will be useful to highlight these studies through the Vygotskian approach to development—a theory that could also open new qualitative methodological perspectives. Studying internal and external variables is requisite to understanding teacher-resource interactions. External variables are approached from the point of view of contextual elements, such as the level of education, the content to be taught, and the social interactions involved. Internal variables are approached from the point of view of the wholeness of the teacher's resource system.

10.7.2.1 A Continual Process of Development that Could Contribute to Clarify the Question of Contextual Elements

Vygotsky's historical-cultural theory considers development as a continual process, a *self-propulsion* (Schneuwly 1994) moved by internal contradiction. This process results from the appropriation of the realizations of humans, which are cumulatively reified in objects and language over the history of humanity. Human's higher psychological functions constitute an inter-functional system that is always acting. Contradictions are overcome in a process of intrapsychic reorganization. The system is called "personality," a word used not with its present-day signification, but chosen to designate *cultural development* and to emphasize the *inter-functional links* between functions (Vygotsky 1931/1997). During childhood, developmental process creates new higher psychological functions in reorganizing lower ones. In adulthood, psychic processes are already controlled and oriented consciously and voluntarily, however, cultural learning still has an effect (Yvon 2012). Adults' thinking continues to increase and their conceptual structure changes, but the interrelations between cultural learning and development could be different. It is important to emphasize that the Vygotskian approach leads us to consider professional development as *a process interrelated to the characteristics of the environments* in which the person acts (Loisy 2018), and not as the application of a "professional development" program.

In Vygotsky's historical-cultural theory, the concept of *zone of proximal development* separates and connects social learning and individual development. The actual zone of development is independent from any problem solving, and the proximal development is determined by *collaboration* with more capable persons (Cole 1985). Now, teachers' interactions with resources are a social process—social in the sense that the teacher "is social," or interacts, with others (e.g., other teachers, students) and because resources are social artifacts. In both cases, internal *contradictions*, the source of development, can occur. The work done with other teachers is also a social situation with persons who are potentially more capable in one or another domain. Therefore, this situation could potentially create a zone of proximal development and create a perspective for studying teachers' social learnings. Digital environments, such as MOOCs, can be designed to support social interactions around activities and experiences. In such spaces, participants are encouraged to contrast their productions with other participants. These comparisons may produce internal contradictions, sources of self-propulsions (Schneuwly 1994) for the participants. As a consequence, MOOCs could be analyzed as potential development situations (Mayen 1999).

Teacher-resource interaction is a learning process that produces documents. A document is the result of a process that mobilizes and adjusts schemes and resources. Reflective investigation method (Gueudet and Trouche 2012) is a methodology that allows for observations of the underlying process, the dimension of preparation activities, including at home or any time the teacher prepares for instruction. Documents produced by a teacher are probably reflecting the *interrelations* between the subject (the teacher) and her environment (her social milieu of work). As a consequence, documents are a candidate for studying *lived experience*, the subject-environment interrelation (Loisy 2018). Studying teacher-resource interactions in the long-term of a career reveals the professional learnings allowed by diverse interactions and should reveal characteristics of contexts that favor professional learnings. Furthermore, such studies could help in understanding *intrapsychic reorganization processes*, in other words, development.

10.7.2.2 Vygotsky's Theory and the Question of Wholeness

Teacher interactions with resources are not isolated. Such interactions appear to take shape according to scientific, didactical and pedagogical knowledge, teacher's preferences, interpretation of teaching contents, and contexts of action, including: teaching levels, social interactions in the work space, individual space where teachers finalize their preparation, and governmental and administrative requirements and mandates. Teacher interactions with resources are a long-term, evolving process of a teacher's trajectory and can be studied "as a whole". For all these reasons, the theory of Vygotsky (1931/2014) appears to constitute a base (a) *to better understand the phenomena at work* and (b) *to enrich methodologies*, allowing for understanding this important part of teachers' work in the perspective of their development.

According to Vygotsky's historical-cultural theory, it is congruent to consider teacher-resource interaction as a factor of development. Interrelation *between* the subject and her environment is the determinant factor of development, rather than the environment per se or the subject alone, as defended by Vygotsky (1931–1934/2018). Subject-environment interrelation must be considered; resulting in the need to address the question: According to Vygotsky's theory, what sense of agency is to be given to the resource itself? Therefore, teacher-resource interaction must be considered. Teacher-resource interactions are a social activity that potentially contributes to learning—the potential not only to learn to produce resources but also to learn to teach. As a consequence, teacher-resource interaction can be considered as a social situation potentially allowing development. As such, it would be instructive to study the potential development granted by teacher-resource interactions through the lens of Vygotsky's theory.

In research focusing on teachers learning and development, researcher–teacher interaction can also be promoted as a social situation for potential development (Loisy 2018). Involving teachers in the comprehension of processes, as suggested by the reflective investigation methodology (Gueudet and Trouche 2012), is a methodological proposition congruent with this idea. Reflective mapping is another methodological perspective congruent with this idea. Obviously, it is a way of collecting data on non-tangible dimensions of work on resources (see Bifano 2018; Rocha, Sect. 10.3), and also a semiotic activity that allows one to become aware of the lived experience. As a consequence, this is a social situation for potential development (Loisy 2018).

10.7.3 Genuine Long-Term Studies in Mathematics Education as a New Perspective

As described earlier (Sect. 10.2.4), studies involving teacher-resource interactions typically focus on snapshots of teachers' career paths and the interactions that occur between teachers and their resource systems within these snapshots. Examinations of the evolution of teacher-resource interactions in a genuine long-term sense (e.g., 5 or more years) are scarce. In some sense, mathematics education is looking to explore teacher-resource interactions in a manner aligned with the documentary *Up Series* (Apted 2013), which has been following the lives of 14 British children on a septennial basis since 1964. As of 2012, the series has had eight episodes spanning 49 years—one episode every 7 years since the children were 7 years old. Similar documentary series include the *Jordbro* suite (Hartleb 1973) and *Die Kinder von Golzow* (Junge 2007). Constraints to such long-term research on teachers work include teacher availability and willingness to participate in recurring data gathering episodes, teacher retention and mobility, administrative consistency in the allowance of teacher participation over time, extended or

10 Analyzing Teachers' Work with Resources: Methodological Issues

periodic project funding, and researcher continuity. Furthermore, any examination of the evolution of teacher-resource interactions can overburden both researchers and participants and requires complex methodologies or distinct methodological choices. Such methodologies and methodological choices were discussed in WG2 and articulated by some of the contributions presented in this chapter (see Rocha, Sect. 10.3; Taranto, et al., Sect. 10.6).

10.7.4 In Order to Open the Debate

In this chapter, we provided an overview of methodologies utilized to study teachers' work with/on resources and the documentation system. We identified three fundamental points around the methodological question: (1) the dialectic relation between theoretical choices and methodological issues, (2) the need to study teacher-resource interactions "as a whole," and (3) the need to take into account content and level of teaching in developing methodologies. Four representative examples of the diversity in ways to manage these methodological challenges were presented. As this chapter deals with methodological issues, the theoretical frameworks constructed by the four contributions present variations that we accept because this is not the main purpose. Built upon the general introduction of these questions and the four contributions of this chapter, these three questions were discussed and some perspectives opened.

References

Abar, C. (2018). The documentary approach to didactics in a flipped classroom proposal. In V. Gitirana, T. Miyakawa, M. Rafalska, S. Soury-Lavergne, & L. Trouche (Eds.), *Proceedings of the re(s)source 2018 international conference* (pp. 139–142). Lyon: ENS de Lyon.

Adamopoulos, P. (2013). What makes a great MOOC? An interdisciplinary analysis of student retention in online courses. In *Proceedings of the 34th International Conference on Information Systems (ICIS 2013)* (pp. 1–21). Milan: Association for Information Systems Electronic Library (AISeL).

Adler, J. (2000). Conceptualising resources as a theme for teacher education. *Journal of Mathematics Teacher Education, 3*, 205–224.

Ahl, L., Gunnarsdóttir, G. H., Koljonen, T., & Pálsdóttir, G. (2015). How teachers interact and use teacher guides in mathematics – Cases from Sweden and Iceland. *Nordic Studies in Mathematics Education, 20*(3–4), 179–197.

Aldon, G., Cahuet P.-Y., Durand-Guerrier, V., Front, M., Krieger D., Mizony M., & Tardy, C. (2010). *Expérimenter des problèmes de recherche innovants en mathématiques à l'école.* Lyon: Cédérom INRP.

Alturkmani, M.-D., Daubias, P., Loisy, C., Messaoui, A., & Trouche, L. (2019). Instrumenter les recherches sur le travail documentaire des enseignants : le projet AnA.doc. *Éducation & Didactique, 13*(2).

Anichini, G., Arzarello, F., Ciarrapico, L., Robutti, O., & Statale, L. S. (2004). *Matematica 2003. La matematica per il cittadino.* Lucca: Matteoni Stampatore.

Apted, M. (Ed.). (2013). *Up series* [TV documentary]. United Kingdom: First Run Pictures.

Arsac, G., & Mante, M. (2007). *Les pratiques du problème ouvert*. Lyon: Scéren CRDP de Lyon.

Arsac, G., Germain, G., & Mante, M. (1988). *Problème ouvert et Situation-problème*. Lyon: IREM de Lyon, Université Claude-Bernard Lyon 1.

Artigue, M. (1988). Ingénierie didactique. *Recherches en didactique des mathématiques, 9*(3), 281–208.

Arzarello, F. (2016). Le phénomène de l'hybridation dans les théories en didactique des mathématiques et ses conséquences méthodologiques, *Conférence au Xème séminaire des jeunes chercheurs de l'ARDM*, Lyon, May 7–8.

Arzarello, F., Robutti, O., Sabena, C., Cusi, A., Garuti, R., Malara, N. A., & Martignone, F. (2014). Meta-didactical transposition: A theoretical model for teacher education programs. In A. Clark-Wilson, O. Robutti, & N. Sinclair (Eds.), *The mathematics teacher in the digital era: An international perspective on technology focused professional development* (Vol. 2, pp. 347–372). Dordrecht: Springer.

Bifano, F. (2018). Institutional resources at university admission: Emerging documentational identity for the analysis of the professor's work. In V. Gitirana, T. Miyakawa, M. Rafalska, S. Soury-Lavergne, & L. Trouche (Eds.), *Proceedings of the re(s)source 2018 international conference* (pp. 147–150). Lyon: ENS de Lyon.

Bikner-Ahsbahs, A., & Prediger, S. (2014). *Networking of theories as a research practice in mathematics education*. Berlin: Springer.

Biza, I., Giraldo, V., Hochmuth, R., Khakbaz, A., & Rasmussen, C. (2016). Research on teaching and learning mathematics. *ICME-13 Tropical surveys*. Hamburg: Springer.

Bloch, I., & Gibel, P. (2011). Un modèle d'analyse des raisonnements dans les situations didactiques. Étude des niveaux de preuves dans une situation d'enseignement de la notion de limite. *Recherches en didactique des mathématiques, 31*(2), 191–228.

Boning, K. (2007). Coherence in general education: A historical look. *Journal of General Education, 56*(1), 1–16.

Brousseau, G. (1986). *Théorisation des phénomènes d'enseignement des mathématiques*. Thèse de doctorat. Bordeaux: Université de Bordeaux 1.

Brousseau, G. (1997). *Theory of didactical situations in mathematics 1970–1990*. Dordrecht: Kluwer Academic Publishers.

Brousseau, G., & Warfield, V. M. (1999). The case of Gaël. *The Journal of Mathematical Behavior, 18*(1), 7–52.

Brown, M. (2009). The teacher-tool relationship: Theorizing the design and use of curriculum materials. In J. T. Remillard, B. A. Herbel-Eisenmann, & G. M. Lloyd (Eds.), *Mathematics teachers at work: Connecting curriculum materials and classroom instruction* (pp. 17–36). New York: Routledge.

Buljan Culej, J. (2016). Croatia. In I. V. S. Mullis, M. O. Martin, S. Goh, & K. Cotter (Eds.), *TIMSS 2015 encyclopedia: Education policy and curriculum in mathematics and science*. Chestnut Hill: TIMSS & PIRLS International Study Center, Lynch School of Education, Boston College.

Bussi, M. G. B., Boni, M., & Ferri, F. (1995). *Interazione sociale e conoscenza a scuola: la discussione matematica*. Modena: Centro Documentazione Educativa.

Cheng, H. G., & Phillips, M. R. (2014). Secondary analysis of existing data: Opportunities and implementation. *Shanghai Archives of Psychiatry, 26*(6), 371–375.

Chevallard, Y. (1999). L'analyse des pratiques enseignantes en théorie anthropologique du didactique. *Recherches en didactique des mathématiques, 19*(2), 221–265.

Chevallard, Y. (2006). Steps towards a new epistemology in mathematics education. In M. Bosch (Ed.), *Proceedings of the fourth congress of the European Society for Research in Mathematics Education* (pp. 21–30). Barcelona: FUNDEMI-1QS.

Cheverie, J. (n.d.). *MOOCs an intellectual property: Ownership and use rights*. https://er.educause.edu/blogs/2013/4/moocs-and-intellectual-property-ownership-and-use-rights. Accessed 18 Apr 2017.

10 Analyzing Teachers' Work with Resources: Methodological Issues

Cobb, P., & Gravemeijer, K. (2008). Experimenting to support and understand learning processes. In A. E. Kelly, R. A. Lesh, & J. Y. Baek (Eds.), *Handbook of design research methods in education* (pp. 68–95). New York: Routledge.

Cole, M. (1985). The zone of proximal development: Where culture and cognition create each other. In J. V. Wertsch (Ed.), *Culture, communication, and cognition: Vygotskian perspectives* (pp. 146–161). Cambridge, MA: Cambridge University Press.

Courtney, S. A. (2018). Preparing to teach mathematics: Results from a survey on mathematics teacher resources in the United States. In V. Gitirana, T. Miyakawa, M. Rafalska, S. Soury-Lavergne, & L. Trouche (Eds.), *Proceedings of the re(s)source 2018 international conference* (pp. 151–154). Lyon: ENS de Lyon.

Design Based Research Collective. (2003). Design-based research: An emerging paradigm for educational inquiry. *Educational Researcher, 32*(1), 5–8.

Dias, T., & Durand-Guerrier, V. (2005). Expérimenter pour apprendre en mathématiques. *Repères IREM, 60,* 61–78.

Durand-Guerrier, V. (2006). La résolution de problèmes, d'un point de vue didactique et épistémologique. In L. Trouche, V. Durand-Guerrier, C. Margolinas, & A. Mercier (Eds.), *Actes des journées mathématiques de l'INRP* (pp. 17–23). Lyon: INRP.

Earnest, D., & Amador, J. (2017, online first). Lesson planimation: Preservice elementary teachers' interactions with mathematics curricula. *Journal of Mathematics Teacher Education.*

Fleck, L. (1981). *Genesis and development of a scientific fact.* Chicago: University of Chicago Press (original edition, 1934).

Front, M. (2012). Pavages semi-réguliers du plan : une exploration favorable aux élaborations mathématiques. *Repères IREM, 89,* 5–37.

Gardes, M.-L. (2018). Démarches d'investigation et recherche de problèmes. In G. Aldon (Ed.), *Le Rallye mathématique, un jeu très sérieux !* (pp. 73–96). Poitiers: Canopé Editions.

Georget, J.-P. (2018). A primary documentation system embodied in a system of training activities for trainee teachers of mathematics. In V. Gitirana, T. Miyakawa, M. Rafalska, S. Soury-Lavergne, & L. Trouche (Eds.), *Proceedings of the re(s)source 2018 international conference* (pp. 155–158). Lyon: ENS de Lyon.

Glasnović Gracin, D. (2011). *Requirements in mathematics textbooks and PISA assessment.* Doctoral dissertation. University of Klagenfurt. Klagenfurt: University of Klagenfurt.

Glasnović Gracin, D., & Jukić Matić, L. (2016). The role of mathematics textbooks in lower secondary education in Croatia: An empirical study. *The Mathematics Educator, 16*(2), 31–58.

Glasnović Gracin, D., & Jukić Matić, L. (2018). The dynamic interactions between teacher and resources in the use of the textbook and teacher guide. In V. Gitirana, T. Miyakawa, M. Rafalska, S. Soury-Lavergne, & L. Trouche (Eds.), *Proceedings of the re(s)source 2018 international conference* (pp. 159–162). ENS de Lyon: Lyon.

Gonzàles-Martín, A., Nardi, E., & Biza, I. (2018). From resource to document: Scaffolding content and organising student learning in teachers' documentation work on the teaching of series. *Educational Studies in Mathematics, 98*(3), 231–252.

Gueudet, G. (2017). University teachers' resources systems and documents. *International Journal of Research in Undergraduate Mathematics Education, 3,* 198–224.

Gueudet, G., & Trouche, L. (2008). Du travail documentaire des enseignants : genèses, collectifs, communautés. Le cas des mathématiques. *Éducation & didactique, 2*(3), 7–33. http://educationdidactique.revues.org/342.

Gueudet, G., & Trouche, L. (2009). Towards new documentation systems for mathematics teachers? *Educational Studies in Mathematics, 71*(3), 199–218.

Gueudet, G., & Trouche, L. (2012). Teachers' work with resources: Documentational geneses and professional geneses. In G. Gueudet, B. Pepin, & L. Trouche (Eds.), *From text to 'lived' resources: Mathematics curriculum materials and teacher development* (pp. 23–41). New York: Springer.

Gueudet, G., Pepin, B., & Trouche, L. (Eds.). (2012). *From textbooks to 'lived' resources: Mathematics curriculum materials and teacher development.* New York: Springer.

Gueudet, G., Pepin, B., & Trouche, L. (2013). Collective work with resources: An essential dimension for teacher documentation. *ZDM – Mathematics Education, 45*(7), 1003–1016.

Gueudet, G., Buteau, C., Mesa, V., & Misfeldt, M. (2014). Instrumental and documentational approaches: From technology use to documentation systems in university mathematics education. *Research in Mathematics Education, 16*(2), 139–155.

Gueudet, G., Pepin, B., Sabra, H., & Trouche, L. (2016). Collective design of an e-textbook: Teachers' collective documentation. *Journal of Mathematics Teacher Education, 19*(2–3), 187–203.

Gueudet, G., Pepin, B., Restrepo, A., Sabra, H., & Trouche, L. (2018). E-textbooks and connectivity: Proposing an analytical framework. *International Journal of Science and Mathematics Education, 16*, 539–558.

Harlen, W., & Léna, P. (2013). The legacy of the Fibonacci project to Science and Mathematics, 19–53. https://www.fondation-lamap.org/sites/default/files/upload/media/minisites/international/Fibonacci_Book.pdf. Accessed 27 Oct 2018.

Hartleb, R. (Ed.). (1973). *Från en barndomsvärld* [TV documentary]. Sweden: Olympia Filmproduktion HB.

Hora, M. T., & Ferrare, J. J. (2013). Instructional systems of practice: A multidimensional analysis of math and science undergraduate course planning and classroom teaching. *The Journal of the Learning Sciences, 22*(2), 212–257.

Junge, W. (Ed.). (2007). *Die Kinder von Golzow* [TV documentary]. East Germany: Deutsche Film-Aktiengesellschaft (DEFA), Germany: ARD.

Kaplan, A. M., & Haenlein, M. (2016). Higher education and the digital revolution: About MOOCs, SPOCs, social media, and the cookie monster. *Business Horizons, 59*, 441–450.

Lakatos, I. (1963/2015). Proofs and refutations: The logic of mathematical discovery. Cambridge: Cambridge University Press.

Lepik, M., Grevholm, B., & Viholainen, A. (2015). Using textbooks in the mathematics classroom – The teachers' view. *Nordisk matematikkdidaktik, 20*(3–4), 129–156.

Loisy, C. (2018). *Le développement professionnel des enseignants à l'heure du numérique. Le cas du supérieur. Propositions théoriques et méthodologiques.* Mémoire d'habilitation à diriger des recherches. Lyon: ENS de Lyon.

Love, E., & Pimm, D. (1996). "This is so": A text on texts. In A. J. Bishop, K. Clements, C. Keitel, J. Kilpatrick, & C. Laborde (Eds.), *International handbook of mathematics education* (Vol. 1, pp. 371–409). Dordrecht: Kluwer Academic Publisher.

Malley, L, Neidorf, T., Arora, A., & Kroeger, T. (2016). United States. In I. V. S. Mullis, M. O. Martin, S. Goh, & K. Cotter (Eds.), TIMSS 2015 encyclopedia: Education policy and curriculum in mathematics and science. Chestnut Hill: TIMSS & PIRLS International Study Center, Lynch School of Education, Boston College. http://timssandpirls.bc.edu/timss2015/encyclopedia/download-center/. Accessed 15 Jan 2019.

Mangiante-Orsola, C. (2012). Une étude de la cohérence en germe dans les pratiques de professeurs des écoles en formation initiale puis débutants. *Recherches en Didactique des Mathématiques, 32*(3), 289–331.

Margolinas, C. (2004). *Points de vue de l'élève et du professeur. Essai de développement de la théorie des situations didactiques.* Mémoire d'habilitation à diriger des recherches. Marseille: Université de Provence-Aix Marseille I.

Mayen, P. (1999). Des situations potentielles de développement. *Éducation Permanente, 139*, 65–86.

Mesa, V., & Griffiths, B. (2012). Textbook mediation of teaching: An example from tertiary mathematics instructors. *Educational Studies in Mathematics, 79*(1), 85–107.

Mohammad, S., Dorr, B. J., Hirst, G., & Turney, P. (2013). Computing lexical contrast. *Computational Linguistics, 39*(3), 555–590.

Monaghan, J. (2004). Teachers' activities in technology-based mathematics. *International Journal of Computers for Mathematical Learning, 9*(3), 327–357.

10 Analyzing Teachers' Work with Resources: Methodological Issues

Morine-Dershimer, G. (1977, April 4–8). What's a plan? Stated and unstated plans for lessons. *Annual meeting of the American Educational Research Association*, New York, NY.

Mullis, I. V. S., Martin, M. O., Foy, P., & Arora, A. (2012). *TIMSS 2011 international results in mathematics*. Chestnut Hill: TIMSS & PIRLS International Study Center, Lynch School of Education, Boston College.

Newmann, F.-M., Smith, B., Allensworth, E., & Bryk, A.-S. (2001). Instructional program coherence: What it is and why it should guide school improvement policy. *Educational Evaluation and Policy Analysis, 23*(4), 297–321.

Organisation for Economic Co-operation and Development (OECD) (2016). *Supporting Teacher Professionalism: Insights from TALIS* 2013. Paris: TALIS, OECD Publishing.

Panero, M., Aldon, G., Trgalová, J., & Trouche, L. (2017). Analysing MOOCs in terms of teacher collaboration potential and issues: The French experience. In T. Dooley & G. Gueudet (Eds.), *Proceedings of the tenth congress of the European Society for Research in mathematics education (CERME 10)* (pp. 2446–2453). Dublin: DCU Institute of Education and ERME.

Pappano, L. (2012, November 2). The year of the MOOC. *The New York Times*, pp. 26–32.

Pastré, P. (2011). *La didactique professionnelle. Approche anthropologique du développement chez les adultes*. Paris: Presses universitaires de France.

Pepin, B. (2014). Re-sourcing curriculum materials: In search of appropriate frameworks for researching the enacted mathematics curriculum. *ZDM – Mathematics Education, 46*(5), 837–842.

Pepin, B., & Haggarty, L. (2001). Mathematics textbooks and their use in English, French and German classrooms: A way to understand teaching and learning cultures. *ZDM – Mathematics Education, 33*(5), 158–175.

Pepin, B., Gueudet, L., & Trouche, L. (2013). Re-sourcing teachers' work and interactions: A collective perspective on resources, their use and transformation. *ZDM – Mathematics Education, 45*, 929–943.

Pepin, B., Xu, B., Trouche, L., & Wang, C. (2017). Developing a deeper understanding of mathematics teaching expertise: An examination of three Chinese mathematics teachers' resources systems as windows into their work and expertise. *Educational Studies in Mathematics, 94*(3), 257–274.

Perrin, D. (2007). L'expérimentation en mathématiques. *Petit x, 73*, 6–34.

Polya, G. (1945/2004). How to solve it: A new aspect of mathematical method. Princeton, Princeton University Press.

Remillard, J. T. (2005). Examining key concepts in research on teachers' use of mathematics curricula. *Review of Educational Research, 75*(2), 211–246.

Remillard, J. T., & Heck, D. J. (2014). Conceptualizing the curriculum enactment process in mathematics education. *ZDM – Mathematics Education, 46*(5), 705–718.

Robutti, O. (2018). Meta-didactical transposition. In S. Lerman (Ed.), *Encyclopedia of mathematics education*. Heidelberg: Springer.

Robutti, O., Cusi, A., Clark-Wilson, A., Jaworski, B., Chapman, O., Esteley, C., & Joubert, M. (2016). ICME international survey on teachers working and learning through collaboration: June 2016. *ZDM – Mathematics Education, 48*(5), 651–690.

Rocha, K., (2018). Uses of online resources and documentational trajectories: The case of Sésamath. In L. Fan, L. Trouche, S. Rezat, C. Qi, & J. Visnovska (Eds.), *Research on mathematics textbooks and teachers' resources: Advances and issues* (pp. 235–258). Cham: Springer.

Rocha, K., & Trouche, L. (2017). Documentational trajectory: A tool for analyzing the genesis of a teacher's resources system across her collective work. In T. Dooley & G. Gueudet (Eds.), *Proceedings of the tenth congress of the European Society for Research in Mathematics Education* (pp. 3732–3739). Dublin: DCU Institute of Education & ERME.

Rocha, K., Trouche, L., & Gueudet, G. (2017). Documentational trajectories as a means for understanding teachers' engagement with resources: The case of French teachers facing a new curriculum. In G. Schubring, L. Fan, & V. Geraldo (Eds.), *Proceedings of the second international conference on mathematics textbook research and development* (pp. 400–409). Rio de Janeiro:

Instituto de Matemática, Universidade Federal do Rio de Janeiro, consulté à l'adresse http://www.sbembrasil.org.br/files/ICMT2017_.pdf

Ruthven, K. (2008). Teachers, technologies and the structures of schooling. In D. Pitta-Pantazi & G. Philippou (Eds.), *Proceedings of the fifth congress of the European Society for Research in Mathematics Education (CERME 5)* (pp. 52–67). Larnaca: Cyprus.

Sabra, H. (2016). L'étude des rapports entre documentations individuelle et collective: Incidents, connaissances et ressources mathématiques. *Recherches en Didactique des Mathématiques, 36*(1), 49–95.

Schmidt, W.-H., Hsing, C. W., & McKnight, C. C. (2005). Curriculum coherence: An examination of US mathematics and science content standards from an international perspective. *Journal of Curriculum Studies, 37*(5), 525–559.

Schneuwly, B. (1994). Contradiction and development: Vygotsky and paedology. *European Journal of Psychology of Education, 9*(4), special issue. Learning and development: Contributions from Vygotsky, 281–291.

Schoenfeld, A. H. (1985). *Mathematical problem solving*. Orlando, FL: Academic Press.

Schoenfeld, A. H. (2011). *How we think: A theory of goal-oriented decision making and its educational applications*. New York: Routledge.

Sherin, M. G., & Drake, C. (2009). Curriculum strategy framework: Investigating patterns in teachers' use of a reform-based elementary mathematics curriculum. *Journal of Curriculum Studies, 41*(4), 467–500.

Siemens, G. (2005). Connectivism: A learning theory for the digital age. International Journal of Instructional Technology and Distance Learning, 2(1), 3–10. http://www.itdl.org/Journal/Jan_05/article01.htm. Accessed 28 Sept 2017.

Smith, M. S., Bill, B., & Hughes, E. K. (2008). Thinking through a lesson: Successfully implementing high-level tasks. *Mathematics Teaching in the Middle School, 14*(3), 132–138.

Simon, M. (1995). Reconstructing mathematics pedagogy from a constructivist perspective. *Journal for Research in Mathematics Education, 26*, 114–145.

Swan, M. (2014). *Design based research, encyclopedia of mathematics education*. New York: Springer.

Tabchi, T. (2018). University teachers-researchers' practices: The case of teaching discrete mathematics. In V. Durand-Guerrier, R. Hochmuth, S. Goodchild, & N. M. Hogstad (Eds.), *Proceedings of the second conference of the International Network for Didactic Research in University Mathematics (INDRUM 2018, 5 April–7 April 2018)* (pp. 432–441). Kristiansand: University of Agder and INDRUM.

Taranto, E. (2018). *MOOC's Zone Theory: creating a MOOC environment for professional learning in mathematics teaching education*. PhD dissertation. Turin University.

Taranto, E., Arzarello, F., & Robutti, O. (2017a). *MOOC: repository di strategie e metodologie didattiche in matematica, Annali online della Didattica e della Formazione Docente 14* (pp. 257–279).

Taranto, E., Arzarello, F., Robutti, O., Alberti, V., Labasin, S., & Gaido, S. (2017b). Analyzing MOOCs in terms of their potential for teacher collaboration: The Italian experience. In T. Dooley & G. Gueudet (Eds.), *Proceedings of the tenth congress of European Society for Research in Mathematics Education (CERME10)* (pp. 2478–2485). Dublin: DCU Institute of Education and ERME.

Taranto, E., Arzarello, F., & Robutti, O. (2018). MOOC as a resource for teachers' collaboration in educational program. In V. Gitirana, T. Miyakawa, M. Rafalska, S. Soury-Lavergne, & L. Trouche (Eds.), *Proceedings of the re(s)sources 2018 international conference* (pp. 167–170). Lyon: ENS de Lyon.

Trouche, L., Gueudet, G., & Pepin, B. (2018). Documentational approach to didactics. In S. Lerman (Ed.), *Encyclopedia of mathematics education*. New York: Springer.

Umameh, M. A. (2018). A mathematics teacher's use of digital resources for formative assessment. In V. Gitirana, T. Miyakawa, M. Rafalska, S. Soury-Lavergne, & L. Trouche (Eds.),

10 Analyzing Teachers' Work with Resources: Methodological Issues

Proceedings of the re(s)source 2018 international conference (pp. 171–174). Lyon: ENS de Lyon.

Valverde, G. A., Bianchi, L. J., Wolfe, R. G., Schmidt, W. H., & Houang, R. T. (2002). *According to the book: Using TIMSS to investigate the translation of policy into practice through the world of textbooks*. Dordrecht: Kluwer academic publisher.

Vergnaud, G. (1998). Towards a cognitive theory of practice. In K. Jeremy & A. Sfard (Eds.), *Mathematics education as a research domain: A search for identity* (pp. 227–241). Dordrecht: Kluwer academic publisher.

Vergnaud, G. (2009). The theory of conceptual fields. *Human Development, 52*(2), 83–94.

Verillon, P., & Rabardel, P. (1995). Cognition and artifacts: A contribution to the study of thought in relation to instrumented activity. *European Journal of Psychology of Education, 10*(1), 77–101.

Vermersch, P. (1994). *L'entretien d'explicitation en formation continue et initiale*. Paris: ESF.

Vygotsky, L.S. (1931/1997). The history of the development of the higher mental functions. In R.W. Rieber (Ed.), *The collected works of Vygotsky, 4* (pp. 1–251). New York: Plenum Press [1st ed. 1931].

Vygotski, L.S. (1931/2014). *Histoire du développement des fonctions psychiques supérieures* (Trad. F. Sève). Paris: La Dispute [1st ed. 1931].

Vygotski, L.S. (1931–1934/2018) *La science du développement de l'enfant. Textes pédologiques 1931–1934* (Trad. I. Leopoldoff). Berne: Peter Lang.

Wang, C. (2018). Mathematics teachers' expertise in resources work and its development in collectives. A French and a Chinese cases. In L. Fan, L. Trouche, S. Rezat, C. Qi, & J. Visnovska (Eds.), *Research on mathematics textbooks and teachers' resources: Advances and issues* (pp. 193–214). Cham: Springer.

Webb, M. E. (2008). Impact of IT on science education. In J. Voogt & G. Knezek (Eds.), *International handbook of information Technology in Primary and Secondary Education* (pp. 133–148). London: King's College London.

Yvon, F. (2012). Penser la formation professionnelle avec Vygotski. In F. Yvon, & Y. Zinchenko, *Vygotski, une théorie du développement et de l'éducation* (pp. 381–398). Moscou et Montréal: Université d'État de Moscou Lomonossov et Université de Montréal.

Zheng, B., Warschauer, M., Lin, C. H., & Chang, C. (2016). Learning in one-to-one laptop environments: A meta-analysis and research synthesis. *Review of Educational Research, 86*(4), 1052–1084.

Chapter 11
Documentation Work, Design Capacity, and Teachers' Expertise in Designing Instruction

Sebastian Rezat, Carole Le Hénaff, Jana Visnovska, Ok-Kyeong Kim, Laurence Leroyer, Hussein Sabra, Suzane El Hage, and Chongyang Wang

Abstract Teachers use resources in order to support their teaching, to support student learning, and to advance their own pedagogical and content knowledge. Using resources is intrinsically linked to particular knowledge and skills. These are conceptualized within different theoretical frames as competencies, aspects of design capacity, teacher expertise, professional knowledge, or utilization schemes within the instrumentation process. We discuss four different conceptualizations of teachers' work with resources, problems they aim to address, and exemplars of empirical studies in which such conceptualizations are used. We then discuss the affordances, constraints, and blind spots of these frameworks and indicate how they overlap and complement each other.

Keywords Teachers' professional work · Design capacity · Documentation work · Use of resources

---

S. Rezat (✉)
Paderborn University, Paderborn, Germany
e-mail: srezat@math.upb.de

C. Le Hénaff
University of Western Brittany, Brest, France

J. Visnovska
The University of Queensland, Brisbane, Australia

O.-K. Kim
Western Michigan University, Kalamazoo, MI, USA

L. Leroyer
Normandie University, Unicaen, CIRNEF, Caen, France

H. Sabra · S. El Hage
University of Reims Champagne Ardenne, Grand Est, France

C. Wang
École Normale Supérieure de Lyon, Lyon, France

© Springer Nature Switzerland AG 2019
L. Trouche et al. (eds.), *The 'Resource' Approach to Mathematics Education*,
Advances in Mathematics Education,
https://doi.org/10.1007/978-3-030-20393-1_11

11.1 Introduction

This chapter was developed from the key issues discussed in Working Group 3 during the Re(s)sources 2018 conference in Lyon. The aim of Working Group 3 was to develop a deeper understanding of different theoretical approaches and of how they contribute to insights into teachers' work with resources in empirical studies. This chapter gives a general introduction to four influential frameworks that have been proposed to conceptualize teachers' work with resources, namely, the documentation approach to didactics (Gueudet and Trouche 2009), the framework of components of the teacher–curriculum relationship (Remillard 2005), the design capacity for enactment framework (Brown 2002, 2009), and the socio-didactical tetrahedron (Rezat and Sträßer 2012). To illustrate both, how some of these frameworks are used in conducting empirical research and how such use leads to postulation of new theoretical and analytical constructs, we include and discuss four selected contributions that were submitted to Working Group 3 at the Re(s)sources 2018 conference in Lyon.

11.2 Conceptualizing Teachers' Work with Curriculum Materials and Resources

Sebastian Rezat, Carole Le Henaff, and Jana Visnovska

In their daily work, teachers use resources in order to prepare their lessons, support their teaching, support students' learning, and advance their own pedagogical and content knowledge. A research interest in this particular aspect of teachers' professional work arose in relation to two types of phenomena: 1) implementation of curricular reforms (Remillard 2005) and 2) an ever-increasing offer and diversification of curriculum materials and other teaching resources (Gueudet and Trouche 2009), particularly digital resources[1]. Both are intrinsically linked to change: changes in students' opportunities to learn, in teachers' instructional practices that generate these opportunities, and in the conditions of teachers' daily work and professional development. Following many failed attempts to promote change of students' mathematical learning and/or instructional practice solely through curriculum materials (Keitel et al. 1980; Ball and Cohen 1996; Remillard 2005), teachers' *use* of these materials and their *professional work and development* have become the focus of research attention.

The efforts to understand teacher's use of curriculum materials and other resources, both in the moment and over time, have led to a refined view of teacher's professional work. It is no longer viable to conceptualize teachers as transmitters or

---

[1] Issues related to digital resources are further developed in Chap. 12 by Drijvers, Gitirana, Monaghan, and Okumus.

mediators of the content and aims of curriculum materials, as a variety of ways in which teachers contribute to designing the opportunities to learn have been documented (Brown 2002). The teachers' design work is usually based on and triggered by their use of multiple resources and has often been described in terms of crafting instruction. Mathematics teachers' planning decisions have been linked to their knowledge and beliefs about mathematics and mathematics education and to the teachers' perceptions of their learners' needs (e.g., Shulman 1986; Yang and Leung 2015).

Various theoretical frames and tools have been developed to conceptualize teacher's work with resources in order to craft instruction (see, for instance, Chap. 5 by Artigue). In the first part of this chapter, we give a short overview of four approaches that are currently used, often concurrently, to conceptualize teachers' work with resources in empirical studies: The documentational approach to didactics (Gueudet and Trouche 2009), the framework of components of the teacher–curriculum relationship (Remillard 2005), the design capacity for enactment framework (Brown 2002, 2009), and the socio-didactical tetrahedron (Rezat and Sträßer 2012). We will compare the different frameworks in terms of the purposes they were developed to advance, and their affordances and constraints with respect to those purposes. Among other issues, we will attend to how these approaches allow for considerations of proactively supporting teachers' professional development. Given the pragmatic importance of change to the work of teaching, different conceptualizations—in our case of relationships of teachers and resources—should not only be explored based on how they allow us to capture teachers' work and document change. It is crucial to also explore to what extent they currently provide tools to proactively inform change.

The four frameworks presented in this section relate differently to notions that have long been present in describing the phenomena of teacher learning, including teachers' knowledge, beliefs, practices, perspectives, and expertise. Furthermore, they highlight different phases or levels of the curriculum (e.g., written curriculum, planned curriculum, enacted curriculum, attained curriculum) resulting from teachers' use of curriculum materials and resources.

In describing the different frameworks, we will relate the notions and concepts used in the frameworks to the more general notions of teachers' practices, knowledge, beliefs, and expertise as well as clarify their relation to the level of curriculum considered.

11.2.1 Documentational Approach to Didactics

In their seminal article, Gueudet and Trouche (2009) introduce the documentational approach to didactics (DAD) as a theoretical approach, which aims at understanding teachers' professional development through the lens of their professional use of resources. The object of study is *teachers' documentation work*, which Gueudet and Trouche (2009) generally describe as "looking for resources, selecting/designing mathematical tasks, planning their succession and the associated time management, etc." (p. 199). Thus, teachers' documentation work is associated with teacher's design of the planned curriculum. Gueudet further elaborates this notion in Chap. 2.

Although the development of the approach was initiated by the growing availability of digital resources, the very notion of resources within DAD comprises traditional print and digital resources as well as material and nonmaterial resources, such as discussions with colleagues (cf. Adler 2000), when these are used by teachers to re-source their work. However, studies that aim at a better understanding of teachers' adoption of new (and especially digital) resources into their set of previously used resources remain prominent within DAD. This is because adoption process generates conditions under which teachers' documentation work can become more accessible to be studied. In addition, understanding interrelation and interaction of various "new" and "old" resources during adoption is pragmatically significant to supporting teacher change.

According to Gueudet and Trouche (2009), the main premises of the DAD include that (a) changes in teachers' use of resources reflect an important aspect of teachers' professional development, (b) understanding teachers' work with resources at any point in time entails understanding an important aspect of teachers' expertise, and (c) change of professional practice and change of professional knowledge or beliefs are connected.

The DAD builds on the instrumental approach according to Rabardel (2002). At the heart of the instrumental approach lies the distinction between the artifact[2] and the instrument. While an artifact is a material or symbolic object, the instrument is a "composite [psychological] entity made up of an artifact component (an artifact, a fraction of an artifact or a set of artifacts) and a scheme component (one or more utilization schemes, often linked to more general action schemes)" (Rabardel 2002, p. 86). Thus, the instrument links the artifact to individual cognitive representations related to the use of the artifact for a restricted class of situations, referred to as utilization schemes.

The DAD draws a parallel distinction between resources and documents. By replacing the term "artifact" with the plural term "resources," the DAD underlines the importance of understanding the use of a resource in the wider context of a set of resources. While this dimension is inherent in the instrumental approach itself (Rabardel's notion of the instrument also relates to a set of artifacts), DAD proponents viewed it as particularly important to highlight the multiplicity of resources in teachers' work. Just like the instrument, a document then consists of a set of resources and related utilization schemes for a particular class of situations.

Teachers' knowledge is incorporated in the notion of scheme, conceptualized within DAD according to Vergnaud (1998). Vergnaud describes operational invariants as the essential components of schemes, because they represent the knowledge incorporated in schemes. While Vergnaud conceptualizes mathematical knowledge with theorems- and concepts-in-action, Rezat (2011) suggested the notion

---

[2] From the two synonymous spellings artifact and artefact, we regularly use artifact. The only exception is if the other spelling is used in direct quote.

beliefs-in-action when referring to the knowledge incorporated in schemes related to the use of resources.

The terminological choice of "resources" and "documents" aimed to more seamlessly align with teachers' intuitive interpretations than the original terminology of artifacts and instruments. Nevertheless, it would be unwise to rely on the words alone for their meaning: "documents" are not necessarily material (as the term would suggest), but are instead a psychological entity—like the instrument in the sense of Rabardel. The processes, in which documents are developed, are referred to as documentational genesis.

In addition to these processes, DAD provides means to capture the processes of teachers' collective work with resources (Pepin et al. 2013). Building on Wenger's (1998) notion of communities of practice, DAD conceptualizes teachers' collective work with resources as comprising changes both in teachers' participation in collective practices of the group (community genesis) and in teachers' views, production, and uses of various resources (community documentational genesis), highlighting the duality between teachers' participation and documentation (Gueudet and Trouche 2012a).

Within the instrumental approach, the social dimension was inherent in the notion of utilization schemes. DAD similarly attends to social dimension of teachers' professional development and brings to the center of attention the immediate social circumstances in which teachers' work with relevant artifacts takes place. Including social and human resources, and acknowledging their fluid nature, motivates DAD to explicitly study the process of community genesis. Through this, social and human resources are seen to generate the very conditions within which the instrumental genesis, conceived here as collective documentational genesis, takes place.

Since the first introduction of DAD, a variety of analytical notions focusing on particular aspects of teachers' work with resources have been proposed. Documentational experience, documentational trajectory, documentation-working mate, and documentational expertise are but a few examples (Rezat et al. 2018). In Sect. 11.5, Wang characterizes documentation expertise in detail and demarcates this notion from other kindred notions such as pedagogical design capacity (Brown 2002) and teacher design capacity (Pepin et al. 2017). These analytical notions in the realm of DAD enrich its core by drawing particular attention to the development of documents over time and also adding the dimension of quality in terms of expertise. While such additions are consistent with DAD's aim of providing a comprehensive framework for analyzing teachers' work with resources, they also suggest that it is yet not clear which analytical tools are likely to become the most relevant or consequential for the endeavors of meaningfully understanding and supporting teachers' work.

11.2.2 Components of Teacher–Curriculum Relationship

Based on an extensive literature review, Remillard (2005) synthesized key constructs of the teacher–curriculum relationship, proposing a framework for characterizing and studying teachers' interactions with curriculum materials. Part of the goal was to understand the impact that the different conceptualizations of constructs such as "curriculum use" had on knowledge in the field and on classroom teaching and learning.

The main constructs of the framework are the teacher, the designed (or written) curriculum, the participatory relationship between teacher and curriculum, the resulting curriculum planned by the teacher, and the curriculum enacted in the classroom. For the teacher, Remillard (2005) highlights resources, perspectives, and stances that the teacher brings to the participatory relationship. These include pedagogical content knowledge, subject matter knowledge, beliefs/goals/experience, pedagogical design capacity, perception of and stance toward curriculum, perceptions of students, tolerance for discomfort, and identity. She also points out that teacher's perception of and stance towards curriculum materials and the teacher's professional identity may critically shape teachers' interactions with curriculum materials and still need to be further investigated.

Related to the designed (written) curriculum, Remillard distinguishes aspects of the objectively given structure (e.g., representations of concepts, material objects and representations, representations of tasks, structures, voice, look) and how these are perceived by the user in terms of subjective schemes.

This framework shares a number of considerations with those of the DAD. While the designed curriculum is conceived as a resource in the sense of DAD, the participatory teacher–curriculum relationship is consistent with the dialectic process of documentational genesis, in that both the teacher and the resource are changed in the process of their interactions. On the other hand, planned and enacted curricula are documents (rather than resources) in sense of DAD, as these terms capture resources in use. However, while Remillard acknowledges that the planned and the enacted curriculum needs to be distinguished due to different contextual factors, DAD does not differentiate between documents on different levels of curriculum use.

The differences in the two frameworks are due to, primarily, differences in their purpose. While DAD aims to understand teachers' work and growth via understanding changes in their resource systems, Remillard's framework is motivated by exploring teachers' interactions with specific resources across different stages of the instructional process. Given the smaller grain of analysis, this framework might be better suited to informing back the resource design or deriving means for teacher support when they are learning to work with new designed resources.

11.2.3 Design Capacity for Enactment

Like Remillard, Brown (2002, 2009) offers a theoretical framework for considering the relationship between curriculum materials and teacher practice. However, his design capacity for enactment framework (DCE-framework) "is rooted in the notion that all teaching involves a process of design in which teachers use curriculum materials in unique ways as they craft instructional episodes" (Brown 2009, p. 18). Similar to the instrumental approach (and as distinct from the DAD), curriculum materials are conceptualized as artifacts (and not resources) within an activity theory (Vygotsky 1978; Wertsch 1998) perspective. Accordingly, they are viewed as mediational means, which afford and constrain human activity.

The aim of the framework is to understand "how the features of the materials interact with the capacities that teachers bring to the interaction" (Brown 2009, p. 26). Brown considers several features of the curriculum materials to be a resource in teacher–tool interactions, including (a) physical objects and representations of physical objects, (b) representations of tasks (procedures), and (c) representations of concepts (domain representations). The resources that the teacher brings into these interactions include teacher's knowledge (subject matter knowledge, pedagogical content knowledge), skills, goals, and beliefs.

According to Brown, these factors are a starting point for identifying and situating the aspects that influence the teacher–tool relationship, but are not exhaustive. In particular, Brown points to the fact that the teachers' abilities to use curriculum materials in productive ways in order to craft instruction are not only a matter of the resources that the teacher and the tool bring to the interaction, but in addition a matter of an ability to perceive "the affordances of the materials and making decisions about how to use them to craft instructional episodes that achieve her goals" (Brown 2009, p. 29). Therefore, he introduces his widely referenced notion of *pedagogical design capacity* (PDC), "defined as a teacher's capacity to perceive and mobilize existing resources in order to craft instructional episodes" (Brown 2009, p. 29). The design capacity for enactment framework and the notion of pedagogical design capacity are mutually related. According to Brown (2002) the DCE-framework describes the resources and, thus, the *what* that influences teachers' interaction with curriculum materials, while PDC accounts for the *how* these resources are used. As he points out, this differentiation is crucial, because he documented that teachers with similar resources can possess very different capacities to mobilize these resources in order to design instruction.

11.2.4 Socio-Didactical Tetrahedron

Rezat and Sträßer (2012) introduce the didactical tetrahedron as a model of the didactical situation as a whole. They take the classical didactical triangle, which models the relation between teacher, student, and the (mathematical) object, as a starting point. Adopting an activity theoretical perspective, they argue that artifacts need to be considered as a fourth constituent of the didactical situation, because of their ability to afford and constrain activity and thus have structuring effects on the whole system. Each face of the resulting tetrahedron, except the classical didactical triangle, can be regarded as an individual activity system in which artifacts serve as mediational means. However, the model draws particular attention to the interaction and interrelatedness of these activity systems and the need to view the didactical situation as a systemic whole.

By referring to the didactical triangle, the authors consider the didactical situation in the classroom in the first place. Nonetheless, Rezat (2009) argues that the model is also applicable to the preparation work of the teacher. In this case, students are part of the system as the (imagined) subject the teacher's activity is directed at.

In order to include social and institutional influences on teaching and learning mathematics and classroom interaction, Rezat and Sträßer (2012) expanded the didactical tetrahedron based on Engeström's model of the activity system (Engeström 1987). The resulting *socio-didactical tetrahedron* includes the societal and institutional dimensions of *rules, communities*, and *division of labor* for both teachers and students. The students belong to the community of their peers, their family, and maybe their tutors. The teacher's community in the narrow sense is constituted by his/her colleagues and—in a wider sense—by the *noosphere*, which Chevallard describes as "the 'sphere' of those who 'think' about teaching. Crudely put, it consists of all those persons who share an interest in the teaching system, and who 'act out' their impulses in some way or another" (Chevallard 1992, p. 216).

The members of the institution, e.g., the school principal, shape the community shared by students and teachers (and they also shape mathematics instruction). The system of rules of the students and of the teacher, respectively, is constituted by rules and norms about being a teacher and teaching or about being a student and learning, respectively. The division of labor within the model relates to the relevance of mathematics in society and the public image of mathematics.

In activity theory, the social, societal, and institutional dimension is mirrored or apparent in the interaction of the user and the artifact and thus can be conceived as resources in the sense of DAD. The socio-didactical tetrahedron (SDT) draws particular attention to their influence on the activity. It provides a structure for some of the societal and structural resources, which influence activity, and thus allows for a more differentiated view on the interaction of these resources within the activity.

11.2.5 Frameworks in Empirical Studies

The remainder of this chapter presents three empirical studies by Sabra and El Hage, Leroyer, and Kim, and a conceptual piece by Wang. What brings the four contributions together is the attempt to characterize, through different theoretical and methodological frameworks, and by exploring various study objects, teachers' work with resources, and in particular the development of their expertise through their practice as designers, whether they work alone or in groups. They exemplify the wide range of applications of the previously described frameworks and were particularly chosen, because they also propose or exemplify refinements or new analytical tools to the frameworks used.

In the first contribution (Sect. 11.3), Leroyer discusses a framework for analyzing teachers' professional postures produced in the process of documentational genesis and reports on the initial test of this framework in a case study with one French primary teacher. The postures refer to the factors that condition the teacher preparation activity in which interactions between teacher and teaching resources take place. Leroyer has developed a model in which teacher postures and learning supports are linked. The model aims to bring to attention different types of learning goals for students that teachers may prioritize during their preparation work and how these become visible in the products of that work.

In the second contribution (Sect. 11.4), Sabra and El Hage adopt the DAD to address a subject of study that has yet to be explored: how research and teaching interacts in the documentation work of instructors in higher education settings, particularly at a French university. The authors explore how the perceptions of instructors in mathematics and physics, of their research resources, shaped the relation that they maintained between their research activity and their teaching practices. Sabra and El Hage explore broadening the scope of applications of DAD to tertiary settings. They indicate that the collective design of resources in both teaching and research institutions constitutes an important direction for future research which could "elucidate the complex forms of relation between research and teaching in the practices of university teachers."

In the third contribution (Sect. 11.5), Wang elaborates the concept of *documentational expertise* (as an aspect of the DAD) based on a literature review and a series of studies with Chinese high school mathematics teachers. She demarcates this concept from other teacher capacities in the literature and uses it to characterize (1) how teachers develop within collectives, (2) understandings of the knowledge to be taught, (3) how it can be taught, and (4) how teachers' practice can be improved.

Finally, Kim (Sect. 11.6) grounds her work in PDC but also contextualizes it within DAD. She outlines five dimensions of a teacher capacity different from PDC for productive use of existing resources and thus tackles the issue of quality in resource use. Drawing on analyses of elementary teachers' work in the United States, she documents how teachers may not always identify or make use of mathematical affordances present in their resources. In doing so, she argues for the need of nurturing conceptions for productive resource use in teacher education and professional development, and the role of resources in increasing teacher capacity.

Including the following four sections as self-standing contributions allows us to offer additional insights into how different researchers combine and reconcile in their work some of the frameworks that we introduced. We conclude by discussing the use of these frameworks and their affordances and constraints.

11.3 Approaching Knowledge Transmission via Learning Supports: A Conceptual Model[3]

Laurence Leroyer

Teaching can be regarded as a design activity. Pepin et al. (2017) write "we concur with Brown (2009), as we understand his notion of design, to regard 'design' as the practice of designing for teaching, as in lesson preparation (that is design before enactment), as well as in teaching, what we labelled as 'design-in-use' that happens during enactment of the resources /materials" (p. 801).

To prepare the activity supports that will then be introduced to the pupils, the teachers interact with resources as they design for classroom use. They select resources, modify them, and use them. This documentation work "is central to teachers' professional activity" and includes "processes where design and enacting are intertwined" (Gueudet and Trouche 2012b, p. 24).

Faced with a multitude and diversity of resources, it is the teachers' duty to judge the quality of these resources. In a research on teachers' professionalization in initial training, we noticed that students' interest in critically exploring teaching resources keeps decreasing (Leroyer and Bailleul 2017). The question of adequacy of teaching resources is no longer integrated into a didactic reflection that is itself part of the teaching activity. This is even more worrying when we know that learning supports contribute to students' knowledge development. For this reason, it might be important to support teachers to view teaching and particularly documentation work as a design activity and thus engage them in considering quality of resources and developing their design skills.

With Georget (Leroyer and Georget 2017), we have designed a model that allows approaching the teacher trainers' documentation work with a specific focus. This model was used as a tool in trainers' training to develop their design skills and specifically their capacity to think of a training-support approach to knowledge development.

A question arises then: Can this model be adapted for teachers' documentation work? If so, its use could help teachers raise awareness of this work. When incorporated to teachers' training program, it could be used as a tool to strengthen their reflection and question the effects of learning supports they design.

I first overview the origins and theoretical framework of the model developed with Georget. I then specify the research question and present successively the methodology, the results, and the concluding discussion.

---

[3] Acknowledgment: The author of this section would like to thank Jean-Philippe Georget, co-designer of the model in a training context.

11.3.1 A Model Based on an Exploratory Study on the Documentation Work of Teacher Trainers

In 2016, I conducted an exploratory study on the teachers' trainers and their design practice with resources (Leroyer in press). The documentational approach to didactics (Gueudet and Trouche 2012b) provided a framework for this exploratory study. In training preparation, a teacher trainer utilizes and transforms existing resources and designs new resources (recombined resources). Four questions structured this study in which trainers' interactions with material resources (textbook, curriculum, scientific paper, video recording of a lesson, etc.) were considered:

- What are the resources used by the trainers when they design training?
- How do the trainers access these resources?
- What are the training supports designed by the trainers from these resources?
- What are the intended uses of the training supports designed?

- In line with the instrumental approach (Rabardel 2002), I considered a training support to be a material artifact made up of a medium (e.g., paper, digital, video) and a content. For example, a texts corpus, a worksheet, and a slideshow are training supports. I distinguished training supports from supports intended for the trainer only, such as preparation worksheet, or reading notes. A learning support becomes an instrument when the trainer uses it. Rabardel (2002) wrote "the instrument is a composite entity made up of an artifact component … and a scheme component … An instrument therefore consists of two types of entities: a material or symbolic artifact produced by the subject or others; one or more associated utilization schemes" (p. 86). Referring to the DAD, a learning support contains "recombined resources," which, associated with "schemes of utilization," correspond to a "document." The DAD considers the document as the result of the subject's activity, which captures subject's interactions with resources. Therefore, the subject develops his/her own resources and uses.

In my exploratory study, I documented that the trainers relied on different training supports and differed in their intended uses. It appeared that the trainers' perspectives on knowledge, trainees, and training seemed to influence their documentation work. For example, in one of his training sessions, one trainer planned to present specific theoretical knowledge by means of a slideshow. The trainees were then expected to use this knowledge to analyze textbooks. For this trainer, theoretical knowledge was very important for teaching. Another trainer planned to engage teachers in an activity designed for pupils' learning. The trainees were given the pupils' materials and a worksheet to note the possible pupils' difficulties. For this trainer, it was important to propose concrete situations that could emerge in teachers' classrooms and in this way allow for her trainees' learning by doing.

In their paper entitled *Training engineering: formalization of teacher training experiences*[4], Bailleul and Thémines (2013) distinguish four trainers' postures[5]—epistemologist, guide, engineer, and didactician—referring, respectively, to the relationship to science, to the others, to time and organization, and to tools. For them, the trainer is led to ask himself several questions in training preparation. These questions are organized along two axes. The first axis focuses on the knowledge to be studied and transmitted and the logic of its presentation. The second axis concerns the place given to individual in training and the activities offered to them. The authors identify tensions between these axes and thus highlight four trainers' postures. They formalize the axes, tensions, and postures in a model.

With Georget, we have adopted this model and sought to identify how these postures are "reflected" in the training supports. We then developed and tested a model in which trainers' postures and training supports are linked.

11.3.2 The Model to Transfer: A Model in Which the Training Support Crystallizes and Materializes the Trainer Postures

For the trainers' postures, we relied on Bailleul and Thémines (2013) model with several modifications presented in Leroyer and Georget (2017). The modified model includes two axes of questions that the trainer is led to ask himself during his/her planning, and the four training dimensions related to these axes. These training dimensions are professional knowledge, organization/operationalization (which includes spatial, material, temporal organization), trainees, and tasks. Between these dimensions, four pairs of tensions are identified: continuity/rupture, involvement/application, transmission/construction, and theorization/pragmatism (see Fig. 11.1).

- From the point of view of trainees' place regarding knowledge: if trainees are taken into account (what they know and what they need), continuity is privileged; if they are not, rupture is privileged.
- From the point of view of the role of knowledge regarding trainee's task: if knowledge is an end in itself, theorization is privileged; if knowledge is an answer to a professional problem, pragmatism is privileged.
- From the point of view of trainees' place regarding the organization: if the organization allows interaction with trainees, the trainees are involved (involvement); if it is not the case, application is privileged.
- From the point of view of the logic on which the organization and tasks are based: if the aim of the organization and task is to get trainees to build the knowledge themselves, the construction of knowledge is privileged and put into the

---

[4] Translated from the French by the author of this contribution.

[5] A closer definition of this term is provided in the following section.

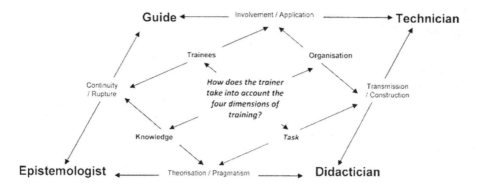

Fig. 11.1 The four trainers' postures

hands of trainees; if organization and task aim at the transmission of knowledge to trainees, transmission is privileged.

Among these tensions, we can identify four trainers' postures: s/he can be regarded as a guide, as an epistemologist, as a didactician and as a technician (see Fig. 11.1). To clarify the term posture, we refer to Bucheton and Soulé (2009) who define a posture as a pre-constructed scheme of "think-say-do" that the individual summons in response to a given school situation or task. This posture is constructed in the social, personal, and scholarly history of the individual. And, these individuals may change posture in the course of the task according to the new meaning they attribute to it. The posture is both on the side of the individual in a given context and on the side of the object and the situation. These postures are:

- The *epistemologist* refers to the knowledge presented/constructed without taking learners into account—knowledge is an end in itself.
- The *didactician* refers to knowledge-construction tasks given to the trainees in a pragmatic concern, where knowledge is an answer to a professional problem.
- The *technician* refers to the knowledge used by trainees that can only be transmitted and not reconstructed—this posture also refers to the control of the training process.
- The *guide* refers to the consideration of trainees' needs in a search for continuity and involvement.

From this work and from the result of the exploratory study, we thought that the learning supports that have been designed by the trainers crystallize and materialize trainers' postures. We thus included a dimension related to each identified posture in our model of training supports that the teacher trainers design:

- The epistemological dimension related to the epistemologist posture
- The didactic dimension related to the didactician posture
- The technical dimension related to the technician posture
- The relational dimension related to the guide posture

We defined each training support dimension based on what the support tool aims to develop:

- Related to the epistemological dimension, it aims at developing knowledge. It brings explicit professional knowledge.
- Related to the didactic dimension, it aims at developing actions/elaborations. It generates actions that sustain the elaboration of knowledge by the trainees.
- Related to the technical dimension, it aims at developing specific way of working. It leads trainees to comply with the trainer's plan.
- Related to the relational dimension, the training support aims at developing interactions between participants in teacher training. It generates relationships between trainees.

In adapting this model to a classroom teaching context, I suggest several changes. I substitute "trainees" with "pupils" and "professional knowledge" with "academic knowledge." The tensions remain the same as well as the postures. I present below the model adapted to a classroom teaching context (see Fig. 11.2). The research question can be clarified: do the trainers' postures and the training supports dimensions apply to the teachers' postures and the learning supports?

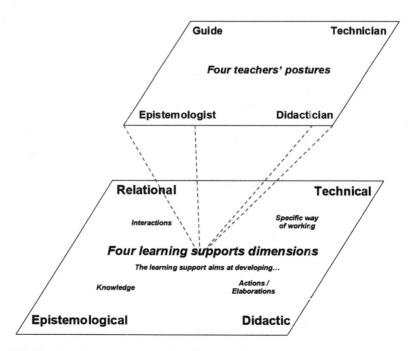

Fig. 11.2 How learning supports crystallize the teacher's postures

11.3.3 Methodology

To test the model in a classroom teaching context, I used case study methodology. Results reported here come from the first case study conducted with a male primary school teacher. Further case studies will be conducted to test and refine the model.

11.3.3.1 Data Collection

The case study is based on a semi-structured interview that addressed the following themes:

- The teacher characteristics and contextual factors (teacher's course of study, professional background, mathematical knowledge for teaching, and teaching contexts). The aim was to contextualize the teacher's point of view.
- The presentation and explanation of one of the teacher's lesson plans in mathematics. To do this, the teacher relied on his preparation and his learning supports. After the interview, the preparation and learning supports were kept by the interviewer and constitute data for purposes of the analysis.

- The teacher's understanding of knowledge, teaching, learners, and learning were investigated. At the end of the interview, I asked this question: In your opinion, how did what you are and what you think about mathematics knowledge, mathematics teaching, and pupils, influence your designed session? The aim was to access:
- The teacher's intentions both in the learning support design and in its intended use, which may remain implicit in his teaching preparation worksheet
- The teacher's relationships with each teaching dimension

The case study was conducted with a French teacher, Matthew, who was in his 13th year of primary school teaching. For the last 2 years, he taught special-needs children with cognitive function disorders. Some of his pupils had difficulties processing information, memorizing the tasks to be performed, planning their work, verbalizing, etc.

Matthew's university education background is in English studies. During the semi-structured interview, he chose to present a geometry session designed for a group of three pupils, even though he never received training on geometry as part of his in-service teacher training. The objective of Matthew's geometry lesson was "reproducing geometric figures on a grid." During the interview, he presented his third classroom session. To contextualize this session, he provided an overview of the two previous sessions.

During the first session, the pupils were asked to reproduce a complex geometric figure that corresponded to tangram pieces on a grid. In view of the difficulties experienced by his pupils, the teacher simplified the task for the second session, where the pupils were asked to reproduce a simple geometric figure on the grid: a square. During the third session, Matthew wanted the pupils to compare their produced square to the model square. The goal for the pupils was to identify how well they could use instruments to trace a figure and compare/discuss the techniques to correctly reproduce the figure on the grid.

11.3.3.2 Data Analysis

I adopted a three-stage analysis. Step 1: I identified each dimension of the learning supports and of the lesson plan. I listed, in a table, the learning supports and their function within the tasks given to the pupils introduced in the lesson plan. In Matthew's lesson plan, I identified eight learning supports (see column 1, Table 11.1). For each learning support, I indicated the pupils' task. This made it possible to deduce a function for each of them. For example, the enlargement of pupils' worksheets handed out by the teacher allowed me to understand that the learning support aimed to both highlight the mathematical content in the performed task and remind the learners what they needed to compare (see line 3, Table 11.1).

I took note of whether the learning supports relied on interactions, knowledge, specific way of working, or actions/elaborations. In the previous example, I identified two predominant dimensions in the learning support, a relational dimension because it supported exchanges about the meaning of the elements contained and an organizational dimension because the display of this learning support allowed pupils to remember what they needed to compare (see columns 4–7, line 3, Table 11.1).

To quantify whether some of the dimensions prevailed, I noted the timeframe needed for each of these dimensions. This timeframe refers to the time of the phase in which the learning support is used. This analysis relies on the lesson plan containing chronological indications. When a learning support contained several dimensions, I indicated the same timeframe for each dimension.

Step 2: I identified the teacher's postures based on the lesson plan and on the interview. I list the learning supports and the tasks given to the pupils. I added the teacher's comments on each task and learning support, and his general comments, based on the interviews (see excerpts in Table 11.2). I used this to infer the teacher's relationship to knowledge, pupils, tasks, and organization.

Step 3: I compared the dimensions of the learning supports with that of the teacher's postures to check their adequacy.

The model will be considered transferable to a teaching context if, for subsequent cases studied, I find an adequate relationship between the teachers' postures and the dimensions of the learning supports.

Table 11.1 Determination and quantification of the dimensions in Matthew's learning supports

Learning support (*) displayed or (**) handed out by the teacher	Function of the learning support It allows to …	Task given to the pupil	Learning support aims at developing…			
			Interactions	Knowledge	Specific way of working	Actions elaborations
Geometric figures drawn by the pupils in previous sessions (*)	- make it easier to recall and verbalize what has been done in the last sessions.	Listen to the teacher (recall the project activity and previous tasks) Acknowledge one's own production and make personal remarks			X 2 min	
Enlargement (A3) of pupils' worksheet (*) (one square correctly drawn—identified by a tick—and three squares (A, B, C) not correctly drawn—identified by a cross).	- understand the content of the support to perform the task. - keep in mind what has to be compared.	Observe and discuss the meaning of the elements of the worksheet	X 3 min		X 3 min	
Poster (with the title: "To succeed in drawing a figure, I must …: ") (*)	- anticipate what is expected.	Listen to the aims of the activity (look for mistakes and list the elements needed to correctly draw a square on the grid).			X 1 min	
Pupil's worksheet (A4), same as enlarged pupil worksheet (A3). (**)	- compare the figures.	In pairs, look for what is wrong on figures A B C / Find the differences between figures A B C and the square that has been correctly drawn.	X 7 min		X 7 min	X 7 min
Tracing paper showing a square correctly drawn (**) Magnifying glass (**)	Easily make comparisons.					
Enlargement of pupil's worksheet (*)	- establish landmarks during the collective exchange. - make interactions easier and thus progress in the subject. - highlight all mistakes so that all pupils can see and explain them.	Watching the squares (A, B, C) in succession, point out the mistakes identified in each figure and express them in a sentence. Reword sentences using appropriate vocabulary.	X 15 min	X 15 min	X 15 min	X 15 min
Poster (*)	- keep a written record of what has been said.	Tell how to correctly draw a square on a grid (pupils' sentences are written down on the poster)				
Enlargement of pupil's worksheet with the mistakes being circled. Poster completed (*)	- make it easier to recall and verbalize	Answer the question: "What have we done today?"		X 2 min		
			25 min	17 min	30 min	22 min

340   S. Rezat et al.

Table 11.2 Extracts from Matthew's interview

1	"I noticed that my pupils had … needs in terms of drawing and dealing with a grid … They like to manipulate this kind of things (tangrams) and to reproduce the figures … They can gather ideas and see if they have any ideas in common with the other group."
2	"I want them to start from an observation that comes in their minds … that their reproductions are not precise enough … and that they can find out what their own needs are. That is for me the key element of the sequence."
3	[Regarding the order in which the figures are presented] "The mistakes are sorted in an ascending order … Here in figure (A), there are only few mistakes, here in figure (B), we also have new mistakes and here in figure (C) once again, there are many more new mistakes. I didn't want to start directly with figure C that shows several things."
4	"It suits me fine because this is a learning project that we can build together; it's important that everyone gets awareness that they need to progress because their current level does not allow them to do what they are told; they also need to know that I'm going to help them, and finally, that we will all help each other, that together we will find ways to progress and succeed in reaching our goal."
5	"The goal was to deal with the needs that pupils would have to correctly draw a geometric figure on a grid; those needs can be identified through a comparison process between the wrong reproductions and a model."

11.3.4   Initial Findings

The analysis as presented in Table 11.1 and, more specifically, its last four columns related to the dimensions of Matthew's learning supports, highlights the predominance of three dimensions: the technical, relational, and didactical dimensions. The epistemological dimension remains present but to a lower extent.

In three of Matthew's learning supports, several dimensions dominate. I will take the example of the pupils' worksheet that Matthew designed to allow pupils to compare their own square with the expected one.

The worksheet showed four squares drawn on a grid. The first row of two squares showed a square accompanied by a tick and a second square, with the letter A inside, accompanied by a cross. The second row showed two squares, marked as B and C, each accompanied by a cross. The squares A, B, and C reproduced the drawings made by some of the pupils during the previous session. The tick meant that the trace was correct and the cross meant that the trace was incorrect. This pupils' worksheet included a technical dimension. The symbols and the letters were there to guide the pupils in their allocated task. The letters involved a comparison between the incorrect squares and the correct one in a specific order. This worksheet also included group work. As such, this learning support also had a relational dimension. Moreover, it made it possible for the pupils to identify their mistakes, which can be regarded as a didactic dimension.

Other learning supports presented a single dimension, such as a tracing paper showing a square correctly drawn, which could be overlapped with the produced squares to help identify mistakes. At the end of the session, the poster indicating the "rules" to avoid mistakes represented the epistemological dimension.

11 Documentation Work, Design Capacity, and Teachers' Expertise

Matthew's comments highlighted several postures. Taking into account the needs of pupils and what they were used to rely on, Matthew demonstrated a guide posture. For him, it was important that pupils interacted with each other (see Table 11.2, extract 1). The didactician posture appeared in Matthew's intentions for the pupils to develop their own sense of knowledge by getting fully involved in the activity (see Table 11.2, extract 2). The order in which the figures were presented was meant to guide the content of the progression emerging from collective interactions (see Table 11.2, extract 3), suggesting the technician posture. Matthew's ideas of learners, learning, and teaching were reflected in the postures identified (Table 11.2, extract 4). Matthew did not explicitly address pupils' mathematical knowledge during the interview. He instead focused on his teaching approach (Table 11.2, extract 5).

The analysis of Matthew's interview makes it possible to identify three dominant postures (a guide, a didactician, and a technician postures). In his learning supports, three dimensions dominate (technical, relational, and didactician dimensions). These dimensions correspond to the predominant postures. Therefore, there is an adequate relationship between teacher postures and the learning support dimensions: the learning supports crystallize the teacher's postures. In this case, the use of model in a teaching context is conclusive.

11.3.5 Discussion of the Theoretical and Methodological Aspects of the Contribution

In the DAD, when a teacher interacts with resources, for a given class of situations, instrumentalization and instrumentation processes take place. During this documentational genesis, teacher and resource characteristics both influence the processes that contribute to the development of a document. The reflective investigation of the teachers' documentation work—a methodology developed at the origin of the DAD—takes into account the history of the teacher and the context in which he/she evolves. Thus, in the data collection system, a questionnaire provides information about "the teacher's career" and "current working environment" but also of his/her "professional and personal history" (Gueudet and Trouche 2012b).

The model presented above intends to contribute to this very point—to elaborate how the DAD approach can usefully clarify the teacher's characteristics. The four teacher's postures refer to the teacher's professional and personal history and to his/her relationship to knowledge, pupils, tools, and organization of learning. Theorizing that the teacher's postures influence how this teacher designs the learning supports for his/her pupils, these supports can then be seen as crystallizing the elements of these postures.

From a methodological point of view, we can analyze what teachers tell us about their documentation work when they design their teaching and learning supports and consider these teachers' claims as traces of the documentational genesis process.

The additional collection and analysis of the teacher-designed learning supports, as described in the presented model, provides access to elements that do not necessarily appear in interview analysis alone. In this way, the collection and analysis of learning supports, and the links postulated by the presented model between learning supports and the underlying teacher postures, present an investigative tool that enriches substantially the analysis of the comments collected during teacher interviews.

11.3.6 Perspectives

In the presented model, the dimensions of the learning supports are based on their effects on pupils. Introducing a third level, "the pupils' level," could further enrich the model and allow analyzing both the design and implementation of teaching. The interactions between learning supports and pupils could be clarified by focusing on pupils' postures. It could also be interesting to integrate into the model the contextual elements such as the pupils' characteristics, the aims of teaching expected by society, or the contingencies of the profession.

The use of this model in training could be used to develop teachers' reflection on their documentation work based on a critical analysis of their learning supports and postures, thus contributing to teacher professional development. Finally, it would be interesting to understand the effects of the use of this model in teacher professional development on the teachers' documentation work and evolution, requiring longitudinal study designs and data collection.

11.4 Forms of Relation between Teaching and Research at University

Hussein Sabra and Suzane El Hage

The professional activity of an academic often involves teaching and research. We aim to study the relation between teaching and research activities and uncover the disciplinary specificities in this relation. In the present study, we consider particularly the disciplines of physics and mathematics. In France, academics categorized as "teachers–researchers" are responsible for both research and teaching at different program levels (i.e., tertiary level and master's degree programs). They typically do not have the luxury to choose which courses they teach. Some university teachers consider the introductory courses that address the basics of classical physics or mathematics as important, general and necessary for students, but too basic regarding their expertise in their field of research. In contrast, teaching at master's level enables researchers to teach scientific ideas of their research interest to a classroom of their potential research assistants.

We present an exploratory study and aim to contribute to the understanding of teaching practices at university and the factors underpinning it. We study the research activity of university teachers through the lens of the interactions with resources. Following Adler (2000), we give to the "resource" here, a meaning related to the verb "re-source," to source again or differently. Our study is closely related to those considering resources for teaching at university level (Gueudet et al. 2014; Gueudet 2017; Gonzàlez-Martin et al. 2018). We particularly focus on the place of *research resources* and their impact on the design and use of *resources in and for teaching*.

Some researches in science education attempted to find evidence of positive or negative correlations between academics' research and teaching without taking into account a specific discipline (Elton 1986; Neumann 1992). For instance, some tried to characterize the relation that may occur between teaching activity and research activity (symbiosis, conflict, tension, etc.). Neumann (1992) presented three aspects of what he called "nexus" that can exist between teaching and research: (1) the tangible aspects, generally link to an articulation between content transfer of knowledge from research in teaching; (2) intangible aspects, which relate to the actions of the researcher in the teaching activity and vice versa; and (3) the global aspect, which relates to nexus between teaching institution and research institution. In a more recent study, Elton (2001) examined the reasons behind the presence or absence of the relation between teaching and research in the practice of university teachers. In a perspective of transformation of practice, he suggested ways that could reinforce "positive" articulations between the two kinds of activities.

The question of the correlations between the two activities of a university teacher has been studied recently in relation to the discipline involved. As an example, Madsen and Winsløw (2009) emphasized that the relation between research and teaching in the case of mathematics significantly differs from the physical geography discipline. In their comparative study between teachers in geography and mathematics, they emphasized the fact that the forms of relation between teaching and research strongly depended on the disciplinary specificities (institutional and epistemological characteristics of the discipline). They also stressed that the relation that can take place between both teaching and research activities depended on the perceptions the university teachers had of the specificities of their disciplines.

We aim to understand the relation between teaching and research within the mathematics and physics disciplines through the lens of interaction with resources. They can take place at different moments of teaching practices: in the design of the classroom sessions, the choice of the contents, the implementation of resources in the classroom, and in the evaluation of learning. In addition, university teachers could use the same resources in their teaching practices and in their research activities (Broley 2016). Indeed, our general research question is: when and how do the resources coming from research activity enrich the teacher's capacity to re-design them for his/her teaching work?

To address this question, we use the documentational approach to didactics (DAD; Gueudet et al. 2012). We will discuss the scope of DAD to consider the university teachers' interactions with resources in mathematics and physics across teaching and research institutions.

11.4.1 Documentational Work in Research and Teaching Institutions

The DAD proposes a holistic point of view on teachers' work, considering the activity of the teacher as a continuous process. In the DAD, there is a distinction between resources and documents. We define here resources as all the things that could re-source a university teacher activity (research and teaching). The interaction with the resources generates a document, which is the association of resources and a scheme of use of these resources. We can assume that in the case of university teachers the research resources re-source particularly the research activity. However, this dimension is not investigated here. We are interested in how research resources influence the design of resources for teaching.

A scheme is used here as defined by Vergnaud (1998), as the invariant organization of conduct for a set of situations having the same aim. According to Vergnaud (1998), a scheme is a dynamic structure that has four interacting components: aim, rules of actions, operational invariants, and possibilities of inferences. A class of situations includes all the situations having the same aim.

A university teacher develops a professional experience by interacting with the teaching institution and the research institution simultaneously (Madsen and Winsløw 2009). The interactions with resources in each of the institutions are related on the one hand to the specific classes of situations (research classes of situations, teaching classes of situations) and, on the other hand, to the specificities of the discipline. The relation between research and teaching could take place as a migration and adaptation of the resources between institutions, or also like a dissemination by a university teacher of the professional knowledge and mode of teaching (the "operational invariants"—component of scheme of resource use, Gueudet and Trouche 2009).

We distinguish between (1) the teaching document (aims related to the class of situations of teaching, resources for teaching, rules of action, and operational invariants) in the meaning of Gueudet (2017) and (2) the research document (aims related to the class of situations of research, resources for research, rules of action, and operational invariants). Each kind of document is considered in its institution with corresponding conditions and constraints. Gueudet (2017) notes that university teachers develop a resource system for research in the research institution and a resource system for teaching in the teaching institution. The study of both resource systems and their interaction is not our aim here. We are interested in the process of interaction between both systems from the point of view of "pivotal" resources in research activities of the university teacher.

The concept of *pivotal resources* is characterized in previous studies using DAD as resources that intervene in several classes of situations (Gueudet 2017, see also Gueudet, Chap. 2). In these studies, the pivotal resource is considered in documentation work related to teaching. In our contribution, we define a pivotal resource as a resource that contributes for a given teacher to the development of many research documents. We consider that a pivotal resource is used in several classes of research situations. Frequent use of a pivotal resource could influence a part of the research activity. We assume that if there are relations between research and teaching activities, these will take place in terms of the classes of situations where pivotal resources from research are mobilized. We hypothesized that there is at least one pivotal resource in the research work of a given mathematician or a given physicist. It could be a software for numerical computation, a foundational book in his/her field of research, or others. Consequently, our research questions were:

Q1: How do pivotal research resources inform us about the teaching practices at university?

Q2: How do the pivotal resources coming from the research institution enrich the teacher's capacity to re-design and use them for his/her teaching work?

11.4.2 Context and Methodology of the Study

11.4.2.1 Data Collection

This study is based on six interviews with French university teachers: three mathematicians and three physicists (see Table 11.3). To keep the anonymity of the university teachers interviewed, we will call them M1, M2, and M3 for the mathematicians and P1, P2, and P3 for the physicists. We note that every university teacher conducts research in a specific area of their discipline; however, this is not the case for their teaching. A university teacher teaches a variety of what is called "teaching units" in the French system in each semester. He/she must teach at different levels, a variety of subjects and topics ranging from the basic level in a discipline to very specialized courses in his/her field of research.

We constructed the interview guidelines in two distinct parts: the research activity part and the teaching activity part. We did not ask direct questions about resources so that the interviewee could express him/herself freely about research and teaching activities. This choice allowed us to identify the resources quoted in their answers to be considered as a pivotal resource. The semi-structured interviews lasted between 60 and 90 minutes and took place in the office of the university teacher. All the interviews were audio recorded and conducted in French.

Table 11.3 Profiles of the six university teachers

	Gender	Research experience	Research domain	Teaching experience	Teaching level
M1	Male	16 years	Mathematical modeling of physical phenomena	16 years	Undergraduate degree (mathematics and computer sciences) and master's degree (applied mathematics)
M2	Male	6 years	Mathematical modeling of scientific phenomena	6 years	Undergraduate degree (mathematics)
M3	Male	17 years	Mathematician (number theory)	17 years	Undergraduate (mathematics) and master's degree (pure mathematics)
P1	Female	19 years	Nuclear physics	19 years	Undergraduate degree (chemistry)
P2	Male	11 years	Nuclear physics	11 years	Undergraduate degree (chemistry) and master's degrees (nuclear material and aging of nuclear materials)
P3	Male	25 years	Electronic microscopy	25 years	Undergraduate degree (physics) and master's degree (scientific instrumentation and bioimaging)

Table 11.4 The research document table and the teaching document table

Research document table			
Research aims	Resources	Rules of action	Operational invariants
Teaching document table			
Teaching aims	Resources	Rules of action	Operational invariants

11.4.2.2 Analyzing the Data

The transcripts of the interviews were coded according to the theoretical framework and our adaptation in order to build two tables for each interview. The teaching documents table corresponds to the teaching activity, and the research documents table corresponds to the research activity (see Table 11.4). The tables allowed us to consider the list of documents in the two institutions: research institution and teaching institution.

To build the teaching documents tables, we proceeded in the same way as Gueudet (2017). Specifically, in the transcript of the teaching part of each interview, we tracked the given answer for the aim of the teaching activity (e.g., "preparing tutorial project"). For each aim, we added the resources explicitly mentioned in the transcribed declaration. Then, we identified stable elements in the way these resources were used (rules of actions). Concerning stability, we relied on the teacher's declarations (e.g., "for preparing tutorial project, we always start by elaborating

11 Documentation Work, Design Capacity, and Teachers' Expertise

Table 11.5 Identifying pivotal resource (Resource 1) in this research documents table. Resource 1 appears also in the teaching documents table

Research documents table			
Aims (Ai)	Resources	Rules of actions (RA)	Operational invariants (OI)
A1	Resource 1	RA1	OI1
A2	Resource 2	RA2	OI2
A3	Resource 3, Resource 1	RA3	OI3
…	…	…	…
An	Resource 4, Resource 1	RAn	OIn
Teaching documents table			
Aims (Ai)	Resources	Rules of actions (RA)	Operational invariants (OI)
A1	Resource 1	RA1	OI1
A2	Resource 5	RA2	OI2
A3	Resource 6, Resource 1	RA3	OI3
…	…	…	…
An	Resource 7, Resource 8	RAn	OIn

many projects simultaneously"). Finally, we noted the operational invariants. This corresponded to statements in the interview such as "I do it this way … because I think that …"

We proceeded in the same way for the research part of the interview in order to build the research documents table. First, we defined a research aim (e.g., "improve the absorption of sunlight by cells"). Then we added resources (e.g., "Coating material," "bibliographical references") and identified rules of actions in the declaration (e.g., "doing a literature review," "Have a hypothesis"). Finally, we noted the operational invariants (e.g., "hypothesis based on the bibliography").

Once both tables were built, we first identified the pivotal resources in the research documents table (see Table 11.5).

We proceeded to check whether the pivotal resource in the research documents table (Resource 1 in Table 11.5) was mentioned or not in the teaching documents table. When this was the case, we considered the teaching document where this resource appears (the table line corresponding to the document). If not, we tried to understand the reason behind the lack of this resource regarding the operational invariant in research institution and/or the consideration and constraints in the teaching institution.

This methodology enabled us to question the resource mobilization process from research institutions to teaching institutions, by considering a horizontal analysis of each document in each institution.

11.4.3 Forms of Relation Between Research and Teaching in Terms of Resources

We now present our analysis of the cases and the corresponding results. We identified two forms of relation between research and teaching in terms of resources in both disciplines (physics and mathematics). We characterize those forms, and we present forms of relation that appear in the case of one discipline.

11.4.3.1 First Form: Research Resource in Instantiation Processes

In the case of P2, we identified five research aims in the research institution. The resource *nuclear material* was the pivotal resource in his research activity (it appeared in four out of the five identified aims). P2's research activity of using nuclear material entailed carrying out experiments. The results of those experiments had different features depending on the research aims (develop a coherent protocol, develop a simulation, compare empirical results with theoretical mathematical results). In the teaching institution, we identified two teaching documents where P2 mentioned explicitly the resource "nuclear material." Let us develop the case of one of the two teaching documents. While P2 planed the courses with his colleagues, he taught the content of the unit entitled *Diffusion and crystallography applied to nuclear material* alone. The unit aimed to sensitize students to some parameters (specifically two or three characteristics) related to the nuclear material (see Table 11.6).

In the case of M1, we identified seven research aims in the research institution. The resource *software* (Matlab, Maple, etc.) was the pivotal resource in numerical modeling research (it appeared in six out of the seven aims). M1 used the software to generate conjectures and to validate a conjecture or a modeling method. The software occupied the central place in his research approach. In the teaching institution, we identified two teaching documents where the software was used. M1 used the software with the master's degree students in order to sensitize students to the characteristics of the software in the activity of mathematical modeling (see Table 11.6).

In Table 11.6, we present two teaching documents corresponding to P2 and M1, respectively. The two teaching documents can be subsumed under the more general aim "sensitizing students to the characteristics of a resource from research."

In both cases (Table 11.6), we qualify the use of pivotal research resources in the teaching institution as an action of instantiation of it. The instantiation of this resource consists of the mobilization of the research resource from the research institution in the teaching institution in, as far as possible, the similar situations and in the similar role but in a more restricted domain of validity.

Table 11.6 Two teaching documents related to the same general aim of "sensitizing students to the characteristics of a resource from research"

	P2—teaching document	M1—teaching document
Aims	Sensitizing students to two to three specific parameters (characteristics) related to the *nuclear material*	Sensitizing students to the characteristics of *software* in the activity of mathematical modeling
Resources	Resources from previous teaching years of the same module (diffusion and crystallography applied to *nuclear material*). Colleagues	*Software* for numerical computing Resources from previous teaching years that contain problems to solve
Rules of action (way to use the resources)	Discussions with colleagues Collaboratively choosing the two or three parameters to teach	Choosing *software* used in the research Choosing and adapting a problem so that the selected software would provide an interface for manipulation, observation, or experimentation
Operational invariants (reasons for using them this way)	The *nuclear material* is such a wide domain. There are many parameters to take into account in an experiment. We have to raise awareness on two or three specific parameters.	The modeling activity in mathematics is exploratory and experimental

11.4.3.2 Second Form: Research Resource as a Scaffold for the Learning of Disciplinary Content

In the case of P3, we identified three research aims in the research institution. The resource *electronic microscope* was the pivotal resource. It was explicitly mentioned in two out of the three identified research documents. In his research activities, P3 used the electronic microscope to observe and study objects that ranged in millimeters. In the teaching institution, the resource *electronic microscope* was mentioned explicitly in three teaching aims out of the four we identified. We present and develop only one teaching document here (see Table 11.7). The aim of P3's teaching was the students' understanding of theoretical ideas related to the design and the use of the electronic microscope. P3 explained that his priority was to teach "strong scientific bases," because students needed to consider many parameters which were interrelated and depended on each other. P3 taught what he called "basic theoretical knowledge" that he saw as useful in understanding how the electronic microscope works. In his teaching, he did not include examples of how he uses the microscope in his research.

In the case of M2, we identified six aims related to his research activities. In three of these, *software* (Matlab, Maple, Scilab, etc.) was the pivotal resource for numerical computation and graphical simulations. M2's research activity using a

Table 11.7 Two teaching documents related to the same general aim of "supporting the use of specific resources by students"

	P3—teaching document	M2—teaching document
Aims	Co-development and co-implementation of M2 level courses (nano-characterization module)	Designing sessions to experiment and discover mathematical properties with software
Resources	Colleagues *Electronic microscope*	Software for numerical computation Resources corresponding to the course in question
Rules of action (way to use the resources)	Elaborate the content of the module with my colleague	Select a phenomenon of stability of differential equation Show the stability by using a graphical representation Offer the possibility to vary values and parameters in order to lead a discussion about hidden properties.
Operational invariants (reasons for using them this way)	We must teach the theoretical bases of how the two devices work: scanning electron microscopy and transmission electron microscopy We do not have time to handle all electronic microscope devices	Software is a tool that gives the results in a visual way and hides the properties We have to stimulate the spirit of imagination to make links between representations and mathematical properties that underpin these.

software particularly consisted of analyzing, modeling biological phenomena, validating the experimental results, and communicating results to the biologists he worked with. In the teaching institution, the software for numerical simulations appeared in two teaching documents. One of them corresponded to the aim "designing sessions to experiment and discover mathematical properties with software" (see Table 11.7).

In Table 11.7, we present two teaching documents corresponding to P3 and M2, respectively. These can be subsumed under the more general aim "supporting the use of specific resources by students."

M2 assigns the same role to the software in the construction of knowledge in both institutions (research and teaching), while the operational invariants show that M2 uses software in the teaching institution to scaffold disciplinary content related to the design of the resource as well as to its use.

In both cases (Table 11.7), the university teachers use the pivotal research resource to scaffold the disciplinary content for teaching. The scaffolding takes place during the designing process and the implementation of the disciplinary content.

11 Documentation Work, Design Capacity, and Teachers' Expertise

11.4.3.3 Other Forms That Appeared in One Case

In the case of P1, we identified five research aims in the research institution. According to the research documents table, the *bibliographic references* (which include searching for references and reading them) were the pivotal resources. They appeared in two research aims. P1's research activities that used bibliographic references consisted of (a) knowing not only what has already been done in the field about the topic but also what has not been done yet and (b) being able to have a valid idea/hypothesis based on references. In the teaching documents table, we identified two teaching documents where the resource *bibliographic references* was mentioned explicitly in the column "resources." We noticed that in the two teaching documents, *bibliographic references* were used to put students in a research situation (one of the two teaching documents is presented in Table 11.8). We highlight that when P1 talked about "students actually doing research" she meant that students were involved in a process based on scientific methods. It was not research as such because the open problem that students worked on has already been solved (P1 knew the answer). Therefore, bibliographic references mobilized in the teaching institution were not the same as those that P1 mobilizes in her research. However, we can describe the relation in terms of development of the research process attitude: students were learning how to build a relevant bibliography on a subject and how to read it.

We qualify the interactions between research and teaching institutions as an action of spreading scientific attitude (research process) in the teaching task. P1 seems to give an importance to the functions of the bibliographical references. She encourages the students to do a systematic literature review and read articles and is spreading her scientific attitude in learning situations.

In the case of M3, there is a pivotal resource in the research documents table; however, it is not mentioned in the teaching documents table. This result is strengthened by the words of M3 during the interview acknowledging that there is a gap between mathematics research activity and mathematics teaching activity. From his

Table 11.8 One teaching document where *bibliographic references* is a key resource

	P1—teaching document
Aims	Follow tutored project
Resources	Ceramic and Pigment subjects *Bibliographic references*
Rules of action (way to use the resources)	Elaborate the contents of many tutored projects Ask students to work in groups of 6 after choosing a project Ask students to do a bibliography research and to carry out experiments Support students when they ask for help (answer the questions; change the orientation of students during research processes) Ask students to give an oral presentation related to the tutored projects
Operational invariants (reasons for using them this way)	Students have to be active, have to work by themselves, and have to feel responsible from A to Z

point of view, if there is a link, it will be in the way of teaching (operational invariant). M3 teaches the proof following the same process as in his research: he makes hypotheses, and then he determines the properties to be mobilized. There are no resources in common between teaching institution and research institution. He has a perception of a "separation" between the two institutions. He does not place his students in research situations. According to him, to be able to learn, the whole community of the class does not have to know how to solve tasks. This case shows that the relations that can exist might not always be tangible (Neumann 1992, see Sect. 11.4.1). The relations between the way of teaching and research could be captured as "when you teach, follow the same approach as in your research" in the treatment of a proof.

In both cases reported in this section, there is a relation between teaching and research which could be seen through the process of using the resources in the classroom and not only as a process of migration of resources from the research institution to the teaching institution.

11.4.4 Findings, Discussion, and Perspectives

It appears that the relation maintained between research and teaching depends closely on the university teachers' perceptions of his/her research resources. We remind the reader that our methodological choice requires identification of the pivotal research resources of university teachers and then study of their use in teaching. The results support our hypothesis that the pivotal resources from research tend to be mobilized in classes of teaching situations. We identified two forms of relation between research and teaching that appear in both mathematics and physics cases: (1) adapting a research resource to teaching through instantiation processes, and (2) using a research resource to scaffold disciplinary content.

As a result of our study, we can conclude that the DAD helps to determine some aspects of relation between research activity and teaching practices at university. The DAD offers a possibility to characterize a tangible nexus (Neumann 1992) between research and teaching (via the kind of interaction with resources) but also an intangible nexus (Neumann 1992) related to the interaction links to the specific professional knowledge of the university teachers; the operational invariants resulting from the research activity partly determine teaching practices.

We have extended the use of the DAD to consider the interactions with the resources in the research institution. In terms of their use, there are many differences concerning the teaching interactions with them. In this proposed extension, an important notion could construct a direction for a new perspective, which is "research aim" or "research interests." In fact, researchers do not know precisely what they are aiming at.

The study of the relation between the research resource system and the teaching resource system deserves further—possibly a long-term—study that would also comprise observations. We assume that a teacher may show both identified forms of relation between teaching and research depending on the teaching aims (indeed, the associate class of situation). This is a field to explore in order to understand the interactions between the teaching resources system and the research resources system. Lastly, designing resources collectively, with peers, in both teaching and research institutions constitutes an important direction for future research. It can elucidate the complex forms of relation between research and teaching in the practices of university teachers.

11.5 Toward a Conceptual Model of Documentation Expertise

Chongyang Wang

In a time of information technologies, teachers' resource work is getting more convenient but not necessarily more efficient. The resources for users are richer; the possibility of working with/as resource designers in potential communities is rising due to the emergence of new technologies (Pepin et al. 2015). At the same time, richness comes along with the problem of "resource quality" (Pepin et al. 2013) and the importance of users' resource appropriation (Trouche et al. 2013). Important questions are as follows: How to work more productively with resources (Kim, Sect. 11.6)? How to better transmit the knowledge with learning supports (Leroyer, Sect. 11.3)? How to be qualified for multiple working roles when working as both a researcher and a teacher (Sabra and El Hage, Sect. 11.4)?

Facing an immensity of potentially suitable resources, teachers need some relevant expertise allowing their successful resource integration (Ruthven 2014). This section aims at exploring this expertise aspect of teachers' documentation work, which is termed as documentation expertise (DE; Wang 2018) for distinguishing it from the related concepts. To propose a conceptual model of DE, efforts are made in two steps: a first model of DE is proposed based on a literature review and reflections on a pilot study in China (Pepin et al. 2016); a refined model through two contrasting cases studies. This section presents the preliminary results for the first DE model in four sections: firstly, a discussion on the key issues for proposing the notion of DE; secondly, some reflections on the Chinese pilot study; thirdly, the conceptual DE model; and finally, a conclusion.

11.5.1 Three Key Issues Drawn for DE

This section concerns three issues: (1) the necessity to propose the notion of DE from the perspective of terminology choice; (2) the specificity of DE compared with the related concepts; and (3) the links between DE and DAD through the notions of resource system and scheme.

11.5.1.1 Documentation and Expertise: Terminology Choice

The notion of DE is proposed based on two considerations: the origin of the term *documentation* in DAD, and the match of expertise with the nature of teacher's work and resources.

Firstly, the term "documentation" in DAD was drawn from the French word "ingénierie documentaire" (Gueudet et al. 2012, p. ix), referring to the terminology of "document management research" (Gueudet and Trouche 2009, p. 205). The roots of this term reveal a potential aspect of documentation work: there could exist specific knowledge or expertise (as engineering), with systematic and operational principles (as management).

Secondly, the term "expertise" matches the nature of resource and teacher's work. On the one hand, teaching is described as inherently a cultural activity (Stigler and Hiebert 1999) and as culturally shaped (Bishop 2002). Resources also bear some cultural and contextual imprints, such as in Adler's (2000) socio-cultural resources or in Brown's (2002) conception of resources as cultural artifacts (cultural tools). On the other hand, expertise is often considered as "highly contextualized" (Berliner 1988, p. 6), "culture-bound" (Schoenfeld 2011, p. 328), and needs to be understood in terms of socio-cultural contexts and education systems (Li and Kaiser 2011). Thus, to study teachers' expertise in their resource work, the cultural and institutional contexts need to be considered, and empirical research with contrasting case studies is especially relevant.

11.5.1.2 Distinguishing DE from Teacher Design Capacity and Pedagogical Design Capacity

Concepts related to capacity in teachers' resource work have been developed, such as pedagogical design capacity (PDC; Brown 2002) and teacher design capacity (TDC; Pepin et al. 2017). The specificity of DE is claimed through a demarcation with the two capacities.

PDC was proposed as a capacity that individual teachers exhibit to "craft" episodes to achieve their instructional goals (Brown 2002), through perceiving and mobilizing the existing resources. Perceiving refers to the ability to notice and recognize potential resources, while "mobilize" was claimed to be the fundamental term of PDC (Remillard 2005). It was further pointed out by Leshota and Adler

(2018) that PDC "is not what a teacher 'has', like knowledge" (p. 92), and that each teacher's PDC has its own specificity, reflecting his/her preferences, contexts and own understandings of different features of the resources. The work in PDC emphasized design but also included "perceiving affordances, making decisions and following through plans" (Brown 2009, p. 29).

TDC (Pepin et al. 2013) was proposed based on the notion of design by Brown, regarding the practice of designing in both phases of lesson preparation and teaching (design-in-use). It was initially dedicated to (digital) curriculum resources use, with three essential components: goal(s) of the design activity, a set of principles (robustness and flexibility), and reflection-in-action (Pepin et al. 2017).

DE is distinguished from the other two capacities by three aspects. Firstly, as the expertise of documentation work, DE is evidenced in all teacher–resources interactions inside and outside of the classroom. It covers more than the phases of designing resources (perceiving and mobilizing) and design-in-use, and also includes management of the resources. Secondly, DE concerns teachers' views of resources, which makes the resources (both the scale and category) diverse and extends the resources beyond instructional resources (Brown 2002), curriculum materials (Remillard 2005) or digital curriculum resources (Pepin et al. 2017). Thirdly, DE is linked with the individual teachers' multiple work roles at school, with the value of expertise in their cultural/institutional contexts.

Along with PDC and TDC, DE is not a uniform standard or ideal state for teachers to achieve, but a framework for reflecting on teachers' expertise as they make use of resources, for understanding their resources, resource systems, and the diverse schemes they develop for fulfilling their tasks and adapting resources to their working contexts.

11.5.1.3 Two Concepts for Constructing the DE Model: Resource System and Scheme

Resource system and scheme are considered as two key concepts in DAD (Trouche, Chap. 13). To propose and explore the DE model (with its structure and components), this section presents the two concepts and how they support in framing the DE model.

A resource system is "the set of resources accumulated and organized (over time) by a teacher in line with his/her regular teaching activity" (Trouche et al. 2018). It is not merely a collection of resources, but a functional entity and a coherent system (Ruthven 2009). "The word 'system' is purposefully chosen to emphasize that this system is highly structured, the structure being linked, more or less explicitly, to teacher activity" (Gueudet et al. 2013, p. 1004). For Ruthven (Chap. 3), the resource system expands both the notion of textbook (into a systematic curriculum scheme combining diverse resources into a coherent program), and the notion of library (into a resource repository organized systematically to make contents readily searchable and usable). These statements emphasize three aspects of resource system: it is a structured, systematical, and functioning repository of resources; it is formed and organized with personal preferences of the teachers; and it is dynamically developed along with teacher's documentation work and professional development. The documentation work can be viewed as a process of interaction between the outside world and teachers' resource system: the teacher adapts resources and schemes to the resource system while organizing, maintaining, and managing it.

Scheme, the second key concept, was defined by Vergnaud (2009) as "the invariant organization of activity for a certain class of situations" (p. 88) with four components: (1) goal/sub-goals, which is connected to the target of specific situations; (2) rules of action, for transforming reality, searching information and controlling the results; (3) operational invariants, the conceptual basis for selecting the appropriate information and identifying the most appropriate rules of action; and (4) possibilities of inferences, which allow the subject to think and compute the activities in different situations. For Vergnaud (1998), "competences are composed of schemes aimed at facing situations" (p. 230); and schemes are the operational side of knowledge (knowledge in action). This makes schemes analyzable and enables to see teacher expertise through the lens of schemes.

Schemes can be named and classified by situations: Schemes get developed by being adapted to situations, while situations work as a key to understand and analyze schemes, they are so intricate that we can use an expression concerning situations to refer to a scheme, or an expression concerning schemes to refer to a situation (Vergnaud 2009). Situation was considered as the problem to be dealt with (Vergnaud 1998) and categorized into two classes (Vergnaud 1990): one is familiar for the subject, and the necessary treatments and competences are ready in his/her repertoire, and the other is new to/for the subject and requires the subject to reflect and explore. A scheme can be expressed in a form of scheme/sub-schemes along with goal/sub-goals of the situation.

In this way, DE is characterized through two dimensions: a static dimension evidenced from the structure and elements of the resource system; a dynamic dimension evidenced from the process of integrating resources, including (1) the systematic management of the resource system; and (2) the appropriation and transformation of the resources for specific documentation work, such as selecting, modifying and creating new resources, by individuals or by a group of teachers working together, in-class and out-of-class (Gueudet and Trouche 2012b). The concrete potential components of each dimension will be presented after the reflections on a pilot study in the following section.

11.5.2 A Reflection on Methodology and DE Model with a Chinese Pilot Study

In 2014, a pilot study of teacher expertise through resource system analysis was conducted, which involved two in-depth interviews with three Chinese mathematics teachers (Pepin et al. 2016). The process and results provoke some reflections on the potential components for formulating the DE model and for the methodological tools.

The three teacher participants in the pilot study were colleagues with whom I worked in a high school for more than 6 months in the same office. After a long-term observation of their office work and classroom teaching, two rounds of in-depth interviews were conducted: a first interview was about their resource work including the resources used in their daily work. Each of them was invited to draw a *schematic representation of the resource system* (SRRS; Gueudet et al. 2012) to represent the structure of the resources they mentioned in a specific lesson preparation/implementation activity. The second interview was about their perceptions of teacher expertise and suggestions for novice teachers about how to get it developed.

The results showed the diverse structures and components of their resource systems, even though they worked in the same physical space with a lot of shared resources and frequent exchanges: (1) In order to categorize the resources in their resource systems, some referred to the location (at home/office or in computer/notebooks), or to the source (from colleagues or self-purchased), or to the function (for preparing exams or for homework); (2) in order to organize their resource systems, some centered their resources on printed curriculum materials and kept paper-and-pencil notes, while others focused on digital resources and on linking the resources through cloud drives; and (3) in order to denote the resource elements in their resource systems, some considered only material resources like textbooks, while others also referred to the collective discussion with colleagues, social communications, and cooperative projects.

There were also some strategies in developing expertise revealed from their self-descriptions of specific lesson preparation activities. One teacher valued the openness of the resource system, and the spirit of sharing and exchanging resources/experiences with others. Another teacher stressed that combining teaching practices with the contemporary educational theories was important. Yet another suggested that it was essential to keep up with the requirements and trends of the curriculum program and high school entrance exams.

The pilot study yielded reflections on the DE model. When studying an individual teacher's resource system, three aspects are worth considering: (1) the collective aspect, especially those with cultural and institutional characters, such as the Chinese Teaching Research Group (Wang 2018); (2) the student aspect, which was emphasized by a Chinese teacher in the pilot study as important to get teaching effects feedbacks for better adjusting their following lessons; (3) the design aspect, which reflects to what extent the resources were proceeded, forming teachers' personal resources. DE could differ in terms of these aspects for different teachers.

In addition, the pilot study inspired some methodological considerations. Schoenfeld (2011) pointed out that one needs to be careful about researchers' own orientations on expertise when studying teacher expertise. This echoes the principle of "confronting teachers' view" (Trouche et al. 2018) in DAD. To see the difference between the teacher's view and the researcher's view on the structure and elements of the teacher's resource system, the tool of SRRS is expanded into *inferred mapping of resource system* (IMRS)" (created by the researcher based on the observations of and interviews with the teachers about their resource work) and *reflective mapping of resource system* (RMRS) (created by the teachers based on their own reflection) (Wang 2018). In this way, the tools of IMRS and RMRS could bring more information for a more precise description of SRRS. These mappings need to be adapted in several times for obtaining different descriptions of resource system from the teachers and for catching the changes in the mappings caused by teachers' better understanding of their resource system or by its development. Considering the flexibility, the order in which IMRS and RMRS are constructed can be different: a RMRS can be developed through a further interview based on the previous IMRS, and vice versa. Besides, for better understanding of teacher's collective aspect of documentation work, the notion of documentation-working mate (Wang 2018) was proposed as someone who has close interactions in documentation work with the targeted teacher therefore forming his/her smallest collective. The documentation-working mate is chosen by the targeted teacher and followed in the same way.

A conceptual DE model will be presented next based on the literature review and the pilot study.

11.5.3 A First Conceptual Model of DE

This section contains three parts: a discussion on the nature of DE, followed by a description of the static dimension of DE comprising six views of the resource system, and the description of the dynamic dimension of DE encompassing five schemes.

11.5.3.1 Some Ideas on the Nature of DE

This section presents some ideas about the nature of DE:

- Unnormalized and off standard. DE is neither a standard nor a universal stereotype for all mathematics teachers, but a framework to be verified and enriched through more contrasting cases.
- Contextually diverse. DE contains a contextual and culture-bound character in different contexts. It does not only inherit the culture-bound nature of expertise, but also echoes the cultural aspect of resources, which makes DE diverse in different cultural and institutional contexts.
- Bi-directionality of adapting and self-adaptiveness. As the expertise aspect of documentation work, DE should be evidenced in both the process of adapting resources (instrumentalization) and self-adapting to resources (instrumentation).
- Multidimensional framework. DE could be analyzed in terms of two dimensions: the static dimension, i.e., the structure and elements of resource system, and the dynamic dimension, i.e., schemes related to teachers' specific documentation

activities, including how they manage their resource systems. The resource system develops dynamically along with teacher professional development, but it can be analyzed as a dynamic process composed of static moments, like making screenshots from a video.

11.5.3.2 A Static Dimension of the Structure and Elements of Resource System

A resource system is dynamically developed along with teachers' documentation work and professional development. It can be studied in specific moments, which is referred to as a *static dimension*, relating to the structure and elements of teachers' resource system. It contains six views (see in Fig. 11.3). A "view" could be understood as a lens used by the researcher to study the resource system and its structure/elements from a particular perspective. Three of them (collective, student, and design), as discussed before, were inspired by the pilot study. The other three were chosen concerning the keywords of the research field: mathematics and didactic (Gueudet and Trouche 2009, p. 214), and curriculum (Pepin et al. 2017). There could be more views included if it is necessary for other research interests.

The horizontal axis denotes that DE is developing continuously along with time, but it does not mean that an advanced or expert teacher must be strong within each view. Besides, the evaluation of DE is not discussed in this study. On the vertical axis, there is no hierarchical order among these six views. One resource can be seen from multiple views. For instance, inside a teacher's resource system, a curriculum program could be considered through both the views of didactic and curriculum.

(1) The mathematics view allows the teachers to gather mathematical information and make logical considerations from the perspective of mathematics. For example, when teaching the notion of algorithm, the teacher might reflect on its different definitions in mathematics and in informatics, where this concept orig-

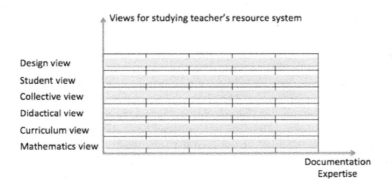

Fig. 11.3 The six views for studying teachers' resource system

inated and how it was developed, and the links with other mathematics knowledge.

(2) The curriculum view assists the teacher to catch the ideas and requirements from the curriculum program or the textbooks. The teacher might consider the curriculum expectations, the suggestions for teachers, and the available interpretative resources.

(3) The didactical view distinguishes teaching as a profession (Berliner 1988), providing the principles to guide teachers' practice and choice of resources related to their teaching and school settings.

(4) The student view allows teachers to arrange their resource design in terms of the students' needs/interests, and take their feedbacks as important references to adjust their subsequent teaching.

(5) The collective view refers mainly to professional collectives, allowing teachers to benefit from collective interactions, enriching their resource system with new resources, or learning new schemes of working with resources.

(6) The design view is closely linked to teachers' personal documentation work habits and preferences. For example, to what extent and how are the resources advanced and designed?

For studying the specific elements of the resource system, three indicators are considered: (1) Content: What is the resource and its function? (2) Structure: What is the position of it in the resource system? Which view does it belong to? What are its links with other resources, inside its view, and across other views? (3) Activeness: Are the resources often used? How are they managed and where are they stored?

The six views and three indicators are proposed for exploring the structure and elements of the resource system through the tools of IMRS and RMRS, which is considered as a static dimension. The management of the resource system will be considered as part of the dynamic dimension in the next section.

11.5.3.3 A Dynamic Dimension of the Schemes in Documentation Work

In DAD, the use of resources and corresponding schemes of usage constitute teacher's documentation work. As a kind of "knowledge in action" (Vergnaud 1998), a scheme is considered here as the basic unit in characterizing the *dynamic dimension* of DE, including how to manage the resource system and how to integrate the available resources to confront situations.

As discussed earlier (in Sect. 11.5.1), schemes (and their four components) are inseparably linked to situations. The situations are either familiar or unfamiliar to teachers. Thus, I assume that no matter if the necessary competences or resources are ready or not for the situations, the schemes can be decomposed into sub-schemes and named based on the goal/sub-goals of the situations.

Similar to what Shulman (1987) proposed in his model of pedagogical reasoning and action, the six activities (comprehension, transformation, instruction, evaluation, reflection, and a new comprehension) form a cycle of teacher's pedagogical reasoning. Inspired by this, five phases were selected based on the definition of documentation work (Gueudet et al. 2012): searching and selecting (from teacher's resource system, or resources outside), modifying and adapting in the situation, accumulating resources back to the resource system, and reflecting through the whole documentation work (see in Fig. 11.4). They do not necessarily occur in a sequential order. Since documentation work is a continuous process, DE could be evidenced in more than five phases if further studies subdivide the process in depth.

Figure 11.4 shows a process of teacher's documentation work and how a resource system is developed: In front of a given situation either familiar or not, a teacher could search for resources either in (the gray circle filled with stars) or out (the white square filled with black dots) of their resource system. The four-point and five-point gray stars mixed in the resource system refer to different types and functions of resources. For example, a teacher selects resources from his/her resource system (four-point stars in the blue square), adapts and modifies them according to the needs of situation (from four-point stars in the white square to five-point stars in the gray square), and, in the end, accumulates it back to his/her resource system. He/she could also look for resources that are not familiar for him/her (black dots in the white square), make modifications in order to adapt these resources to the situation (from gray dot in the white square to four-point stars in the gray square), and then accumulate them to the resource system. The changes of the colors and shapes refer to the transformation on the resources. Reflecting accompanies the whole documentation work.

The five schemes involved in the current conceptual model are not presented in detail with all of the four components of scheme but based on the third component of operational invariants, namely, the conceptual basis for choosing the most appro-

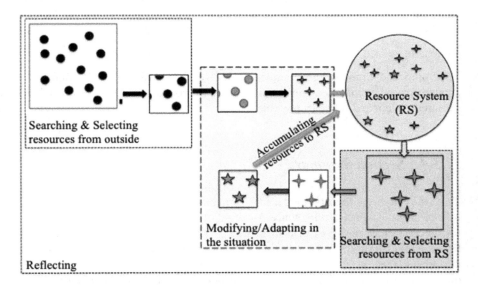

Fig. 11.4 The dynamic process with five phases for evidencing DE

priate rules of action. The specific contents of the five schemes, as well as the remaining three components (goals, rules of action, and inferences), will be illustrated in specific situations of the contrasting cases.

– Scheme related to searching for resources

Searching for resources includes the integration of available resources and experiences. Generally, the expert teachers bring richer and more personal resources to the problem that they are trying to solve (Berliner 2001), draw on their previous teaching experiences as well as the reflections thereon (Borko and Livingston 1989), or use planning materials from previous years as cues (Livingston and Borko 1989).

– Scheme related to selecting resources

Selecting resources is a process of identifying the useful resources by referring to factors like teaching objects, students' learning conditions, requirements from the curriculum program, and teachers' own understanding about what should be taught.

– Scheme related to adapting resources

Adapting resources comprises a process of transforming the resources into a form ready to be used, or familiar for the teacher. Experienced teachers can balance content-centered and student-centered instruction (Borko and Livingston 1989) and adjust syllabus guidelines and institutional expectations with their own educational beliefs and ideologies (Calderhead 1984).

– Scheme related to accumulating resources

Accumulating resources belongs to the management of the resource system. Experienced teachers have the consciousness to include, share off, and store the resources in a structured way. Since accumulating resources depends on the personal working habits, it could differ among different teachers.

– Scheme related to reflecting on the documentation work.

"Doing and thinking are complementary" (Schön 1983, p. 280). Reflection appears in the whole documentation work and makes the development of the resource system and schemes possible.

11.5.4 Section Summary

This study presents the first model of DE mainly based on a literature review and reflections on a Chinese pilot study. As a kind of expertise shown and evidenced in documentation work, DE inherits the nature of both teacher expertise and documentation work: culturally influenced and evaluated, continuously and dynamically developed, shaping and shaped by resources, able to be evidenced from a static dimension (structure and elements of the resource system) and dynamic dimension (schemes of managing a resource system and of the documentation work in specific situations). To study the static dimension of a resource system, the new tools of RMRS and IMRS were expanded to differentiate the views from teachers and researchers. The new concept of documentation-working mate was proposed to study the collective aspect of documentation work. The model of DE is thus presented from a static dimension in terms of the structure and elements of a resource system (with six views and three indicators), and a dynamic dimension with five basic schemes as part of documentation work. The aim of the DE model is not to formulate an ideal stereotype with a list of standards, but a framework to see the diverse preferences of teachers from different contexts. This model of DE is only a preliminary result. To propose a richer and more elaborated model of DE, a second step of verifying it by specific case studies (in China and in France) will be conducted in my following work.

11.6 Teacher Capacity for Productive Use of Existing Resources[6]

Ok-Kyeong Kim

Mathematics teachers use a variety of resources to design instruction. How they use, adapt, and transform the resources to teach mathematics influences the quality of instruction, and teachers are required to have the capacity for using them productively. Focusing on curriculum resources that teachers use for daily instruction, this section describes teacher capacity needed for using existing curriculum resources productively. For that purpose, a set of analyses are drawn from the Curriculum Use for Better Teaching (ICUBiT) project, whose goals were (1) to identify components of the capacity that Brown (2009) calls *pedagogical design capacity* (PDC, i.e., a teacher's ability to perceive and mobilize existing curricular resources in order to design instruction) and (2) to develop tools to measure PDC. As such, to investigate the capacity for using existing resources productively, I drew on Brown's (2009) notion of PDC. However, exploring the capacity for productive use of existing resources through the analyses in this section can be one way to study PDC, and I do not intend to equate the capacity elaborated here with PDC. I instead attempt to answer to the following question: What are the components of teacher capacity needed for productive use of existing resources?

The ICUBiT project gathered data from elementary teachers in the United States who were using five different curriculum programs (each program included resources for students and teachers for daily lessons), ranging from commercially developed to reform-oriented. The five curriculum programs were analyzed to

---

[6] Acknowledgment: This section is based on work supported by the National Science Foundation under grants No. 0918141 and No. 0918126. Any opinions, findings, conclusions, or recommendations expressed in this section are those of the author and do not necessarily reflect the views of the National Science Foundation.

account for the kinds of content and pedagogical support for teachers and ways in which such support was provided. Also, classroom data were analyzed from various perspectives to examine ways in which teachers used their curriculum program to teach everyday lessons. These analyses of curriculum programs and teachers' use of curriculum resources shed light on specific aspects of teacher capacity needed for effective use of existing resources. I describe some significant aspects of the teacher capacity along with examples from the ICUBiT project and related literature.

11.6.1 Theoretical Background

Although Brown's notion of PDC is drawn on initially, investigating teacher capacity for using existing resources productively is situated in a broad research context. First, this capacity seems critical in teachers' documentation work (Gueudet and Trouche 2009) in that one important aspect of the documentation work relates to how teachers use existing resources and how this affects their documentation work. According to Gueudet and Trouche (2009), teachers are engaged in documentation work, such as looking for resources and selecting tasks. Gueudet et al. distinguish between resources and documents. Resources are a range of artifacts for teaching, such as textbooks, software, and discussions with a peer teacher, whereas documents are evolving products of teachers' documentation work, which include resources, usage (action rules), and operational invariants (cognitive structure guiding resource use). How teachers use the resources is observable; in contrast, operational invariants are often invisible but can be interpreted from ways in which teachers use the resources. In the analyses to explore teacher capacity for productive resource use, I mainly focused on artifacts for teaching, especially existing curriculum resources for everyday teaching, i.e., student texts and teacher manuals. However, I attended to teachers' usage, i.e., how teachers read, adapt, and use existing resources to teach mathematics lessons. Also, I inferred teachers' operational invariants to make sense of the ways in which they used the resources. Examining teachers' use of resources along with their operational invariants supports the inquiry into teacher capacity needed for resource use.

I consider teacher decision making around using existing resources as pedagogical reasoning and action (Shulman 1987) and using knowledge in teaching practice as elaborated in knowledge quartet by Rowland and his colleagues (e.g., Rowland et al. 2005). When making decisions in planning and teaching mathematics lessons, teachers use their own personal resources, such as their experiences with and knowledge of mathematics content, curriculum (resources), and students. They also transform the resources they use in a way that fit their instructional goal and their students' need. The notion of contingency in the knowledge quartet by Rowland et al. (2005) highlights teachers' design of instruction beyond the plans they have made and the resources they use. This is similar to what Remillard (1999) calls improvisation, or "on-the-spot curriculum construction" (p. 331), which indicates teacher moves that are not specified in the written lessons (i.e., individual lessons outlined for teaching in the existing resources). Examining teachers' decisions on how to use resources to design instruction and their improvisations is eventually digging deeper into teachers' reasoning and knowledge in use, which helps explore teacher capacity for productive resource use.

The productivity of using existing resources depends on the opportunity for students to learn during instruction. When the resources are used productively, enacted lessons must create opportunities for students to learn the mathematical points of the lessons with sufficient cognitive demand on the students (Kim 2018). Students need to explore, reason about, and understand the target mathematics of the lessons. Therefore, teacher capacity for productive resource use should be examined in terms of whether the resource use supports students' learning of the mathematical points of the lessons, and what aspects of resource use support or do not support student learning and how. Mathematical points have dual aspects: conceptual foundation and procedural competence. Each lesson contains both aspects even when it places more emphasis on one aspect than the other (Kim 2018, 2019). Generating opportunities for students to engage in the dual aspects of the mathematical points is fundamental for student learning.

Finally, I insist that exploring teacher capacity of productive resource use is based on the participatory relationship between teachers and resources (Remillard 2005). Using notions of instrumentation and instrumentalization, Gueudet and Trouche (2009) also illustrate the mutual interaction between a teacher and resources in documentation work. Teacher capacity needed for using resources productively is grounded in such bilateral influences that shape both parties. This relationship generates the research context that examines not only the components of the teacher capacity needed for using resources productively but also the role of the resources in supporting teachers to develop such a capacity.

11.6.2 Data Sources

In order to explore the capacity needed for productive use of existing resources, I drew on data gathered from 25 teachers in grades 3–5 in the ICUBiT project in the United States. These teachers were using five different curriculum programs, each of which contained resources for teachers and students, such as the teacher's guide for everyday teaching, student materials, and the implementation guide (five teachers per curriculum program), ranging from reform-oriented to commercially developed. The teachers were (1) asked to keep a Curriculum Reading Log (i.e., on a copy of written lessons they indicated parts they read, parts they planned for instruction, and parts influenced their planning), (2) observed in three consecutive lessons in each of two rounds, and (3) interviewed after each round of observations. All observations were videotaped, and all interviews were audiotaped. Then, both video- and audio-taped data were transcribed for analysis. Scrutinizing teacher capacity for productive resource use, this section draws on a range of analyses on various aspects of resource use by the teachers, such as sequencing lessons, using intervention resources, and deciding whether to follow the guidance in the written lessons (e.g., Kim 2015, 2018, 2019). I documented patterns of the teachers' resource use within each analysis (e.g., using, omitting, or changing a significant component in the written lesson), their effectiveness in terms of the mathematical points of the lessons, and teachers' rationale for their decisions. The mathematical points of individual lessons were determined based on a careful reading of objectives, directions for teachers and students, tasks and problems, and other descriptions about the lessons. Then, for every significant teacher move, it was determined whether it supported or hindered the mathematical points of each lesson. Searching for patterns of use and their productivity in these analyses revealed critical components of the capacity for productive resource use. I also drew on literature related to teacher capacity and resource use to compare the patterns that surfaced in the analyses. For more details about how the data were analyzed in each investigation, see the papers cited.

11.6.3 Teacher Capacity

The teachers in the ICUBiT project made various decisions regarding how to use their curriculum program. Some decisions impacted enacted lessons positively toward students' learning of the mathematics of the lessons; others did not. Although a range of support features were provided in the written lessons, it was evident that teacher improvisations occurred quite often regardless of programs used (Kim 2019). Various teacher decisions on resource use, kinds of improvisations, and teachers' reasoning behind their decisions revealed different aspects of resource use and teacher capacity needed. Below, five specific aspects of teacher capacity for productive resource use are described along with brief examples from the data in the ICUBiT project. Although described individually, I view these as interrelated components of teacher capacity, which are not mutually exclusive.

11.6.3.1 Articulating Mathematical Points of the Lessons

Using existing resources to teach mathematics, teachers first read and make sense of the written lessons. In doing so, they need to identify the mathematical points of the lessons and evaluate how well the lesson activities, tasks, and problems support students' learning of the mathematical points (Remillard and Kim 2017; Sleep 2012). Then, they need to organize lesson activities toward the mathematical points in instruction (Brown et al. 2009; Sleep 2012). Failing to identify the mathematical points of the lessons, teachers orchestrate lesson activities away from the mathematical points (Kim 2015, 2018, 2019).

One third-grade teacher in the ICUBiT project considered identifying and using keywords as the goal of the lessons on creating and solving multiplication and division story problems, and emphasized keywords instead of the meaning of the two operations in instruction (Kim 2015, 2019). The mathematical points of the written lessons she used were (1) understanding the meaning of multiplication and division, and their relationship, and (2) using them to solve and create multiplication and division story problems. Placing greater emphasis on keywords in place of the meaning of the two operations, the teacher said, "The keywords for recognizing what multiplication and division are, and how to pull those out of a story problem and use them to advantage for the kids. ... it was definitely valuable." The teacher thought keywords were important to highlight although using them was not suggested in the teacher's guide.

With keywords as the goal of the lessons in her mind, the teacher altered or omitted important lesson components that had a great potential to support students' understanding of multiplication and division. For example, there was a lesson component that asked students in pairs to come up with story problems for two related expressions (i.e., 6 × 3 and 18 ÷ 3) so that students could see the differences between multiplication and division contexts. Instead of this task, the teacher asked students to generate a list of keywords for each of the two operations. The teacher made comments, as students offered some expressions as keywords, whether each suggested word would be acceptable for each operation. In doing so, she lost an opportunity to highlight characteristics of multiplication and division in relation to each other. The loss of meaning continued in the following lesson when students were creating multiplication and division story problems. The teacher often said, "If it says 'in each', it's gonna be a division problem." Or, "Now remind me, what are our multiplication keywords? If it's a multiplication story problem it's gonna have what key words in it?" While focusing on keywords, such as "in all," and "share equally," the teacher did not use the important terms, such as number of groups, number in each group, and equal groups, to explain the characteristics of and differences between multiplication and division. As a result, after spending 2 days on generating multiplication and division story problems, still more than half of her students were not able to complete the task. On the third day of classroom observations, there was a range of student-generated story problems. Some students had stories but no questions; some students did not have multiplication or division contexts (addition or subtraction instead); and some students had only one type of story problems (all multiplication or all division)

11.6.3.2 Steering Lessons Toward the Mathematical Points

Sometimes teachers identified the mathematical points of the lessons properly and yet had hard time steering instruction toward these points. This was observable when they were challenged by students' difficulty in understanding the mathematical idea, when they did not use proper resources available in the written lesson, or when the written lesson did not provide sufficient resources for the mathematical points (Kim 2018, 2019). An example of the last case is one teacher using a commercially developed program who taught a lesson on mean. The written lesson indicated the meaning of a mean in different places for teachers as follows (Charles et al. 2008);

Like the median and the mode, the mean tells what is typical of the numbers in a set of data. The mean is sometimes called the average (p. 404). Explain that an average levels off or evens out the numbers in the data set so that all the numbers are the same (p. 404). Averaging involves distributing numerical data evenly across a set of numbers and provides a single number to describe what is typical in that set of numbers (p. 404A)

The lesson also included a picture of cube towers in the case of 7, 4, and 4 (see Fig. 11.5) to illustrate what the mean of a set of numbers means. The mathematical points of the lesson were (1) understanding what the mean of a set of numbers means and the procedure to find the mean and (2) finding the mean of a set of numbers. The explanations above and the picture of cube towers made the teacher think hard about the concept of the lesson and set that as an important goal for the lesson. She said, "I liked the idea of how it levels out. So that's what conceptually I was thinking in my head." She also related this meaning with the procedure to find the mean of a set of numbers. She said, "They've got a whole bunch of chips. This person only has three chips. But when you combine everything and then divide it evenly, how it levels out. ... division is dividing up as evenly as you can, the leveling out part." She also recognized the importance of the term, "typical" as the meaning of the mean of a data set.

However, steering the lesson toward the mathematical points identified was very challenging for this teacher, especially without sufficient resources in the written lesson. Other than the explanations provided for teachers and the picture of the cube towers, the lesson was mostly about the procedure to find the mean of a set of numbers, namely, "adding all and dividing the sum by the number of data." Different sets of numbers were given to students, who were asked to calculate mean. The teacher attempted to incorporate the idea of "leveling out" by using cubes. She put students in groups, distributed cubes to each student, and asked them to count how many each had, and then "combine all in the center and share them evenly." Unfortunately, this activity of using cubes, and the teachers' directions and additional comments did not create an opportunity for students to make sense of what the mean of a data set means, let alone how the procedure to find the mean of a data set works. During the follow-up interview, she confessed, "I probably didn't articulate it well to my students," although it made sense to her.

Fig. 11.5 Representing the meaning of the mean of 7, 4, and 4

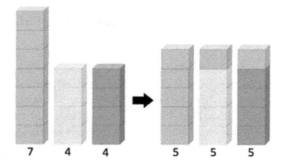

Articulating mathematical points and steering lessons toward the mathematical points are aspects of teacher capacity that are not limited to individual lessons. Teachers need to articulate mathematical points of a series of lessons (an entire unit or a set of consecutive lessons) and teach students through a proper mathematical pathway so that the students can understand the connections and relationships in the mathematical points and develop a coherent mathematical storyline, or "a deliberate progression of mathematical ideas" (Sleep 2012, p. 954) across lessons. Teachers need to envision how mathematical ideas are intended to develop over a series of lessons, and sequence tasks and lessons according to this progression. Otherwise, students may have difficulty develop a proper understanding of the complete ideas across lessons. For example, sequencing tasks and lessons in a way that eased up on the first 2 days and then enacted a series of important explorations all on one single day, a fifth-grade teacher rushed students to make sense of common fractions (specifically 1/4, 3/4, 1/8, 3/8, 1/3, 2/3, 1/6, etc.) and their percent equivalents (Kim 2018). Although the teacher was aware of the mathematical goals of the lessons, this way of steering a series of lessons significantly hindered the students' engagement in the mathematical points of the lessons: (1) understanding relationships between percent and fractions, and (2) using these relationships, known equivalents, and representations to determine fraction equivalents of common fractions.

11.6.3.3 Recognizing Affordances and Constraints of the Resource in Use

As teachers read and make sense of the resources and identify the mathematical points of the lessons/activities/tasks, they also recognize what aspects/components/features of the lessons/activities/tasks support or do not support students' learning of the mathematical points. In order to use existing resources productively, teachers need to recognize such affordances and constraints of the resources they use, with respect to their students' learning of the mathematical points (Atanga 2014; Brown 2009; Choppin 2011; Kim 2015, 2018, 2019; Kim and Son 2017). Teachers who were not able to recognize the affordances may not use them in instruction. Also, teachers who do not recognize the constraints hardly try to make up the limitations. Depending on their evaluation of the affordances and constraints along with their students' need, teachers can decide whether they use, change, or omit components of lessons/activities/tasks, or add new elements to enact lessons (Kim 2019). Therefore, recognizing affordances and constraints is critical for using the existing resources productively.

For example, even when one third-grade teacher identified the mathematical points of the lessons, she did not recognize that visual representations (fraction circles or pictures, bars, and number line) provided in the resources were useful to promote students' understanding. Not seeing the usefulness of those representations for the procedure of subtracting a fraction from a whole number, the teacher dismissed the need for using the representations in supporting students' conceptual understanding of the procedure for subtracting a fraction from a whole number (Kim 2018). Even when students suggested to use a representation, the teacher refused to do so. Mentioning that the representations were too simplified and tended to confuse students, the teacher did not recognize the affordances of the representations in supporting students' conceptual understanding of the procedure. On the contrary, she saw those representations as constraints and avoided them in all the lessons observed. After three days of listening to the teachers' explanations and using the procedure, the students in this class still had hard time making sense of what they did.

The third-grade teacher using keywords also did not see the affordances of several activities and representations. Whereas the teacher emphasizing keywords did not identify the mathematical points of the lessons accurately, the teacher above was able to clearly identify the mathematical points of the lessons she taught. In fact, she was trying to steer instruction in order to support students to (1) understand the relationship between improper fractions and mixed numbers and (2) use the relationship to add fractions to get a mixed number or subtract a fraction from a whole number. Yet, not seeing the usefulness of the representations provided in the written lessons, the teacher dismissed them entirely while orchestrating classroom activities.

11.6.3.4 Using Affordances

Recognizing the affordances of existing resources is important; so is using those affordances in instruction. Brown's (2009) definition of PDC includes both "perceive and mobilize" the existing resources. In particular, using those resources together as a coherent set seems critical in using the existing resources well (Atanga 2014). Various components of the resources are designed to support students' learning of the mathematical points. Resources as a set rather than separate elements indicate the synergy that they can generate in supporting teachers to steer instruction toward the mathematical points. In the ICUBiT project, when using resources productively to teach lessons, teachers were using a range of elements provided in the resources toward the mathematical points of the lessons. Otherwise, as seen in the earlier example of the teacher focusing on keywords, teachers altered or omitted useful, important resources (e.g., representations and tasks). Sometimes they added new elements which were not productive in place of critical resources suggested. In other cases, teachers used the affordances unproductively.

The fifth-grade teacher mentioned earlier recognized the usefulness of 10×10 grids to relate fractions and their percent equivalences (e.g., 3/4 = 75%). But, the teacher used the grids not very effectively in the second observed lesson, by asking students to shade their own grids and write the fraction and the percent that each of their grids represented. Students shaded their grids randomly and wrote a fraction and percent pair mainly by counting the number of squares shaded (e.g., 79 squares shaded, so the grid represents 79/100 and 79%) without much attention given to the relationship between fractions and percent, especially percent equivalents of target common fractions, such as halves, tenths, fourths, eighths, thirds, and sixths. This was problematic because the mathematical point of the lessons was not about determining fraction-percent pairs of 10 × 10 grids shaded randomly. The written lessons were deliberately focusing on using the grids to relate common fractions and their percent equivalents, moving from easy fractions (e.g., 1/2 = 50%) to harder fractions (e.g., 1/4 = 25%) and finally to more complex fractions (e.g., 1/3 = 33%). As explained earlier, the teacher identified the mathematical points of the lessons, but her instructional moves led away from the learning pathway carefully laid out across the lessons. The biggest step away from the pathway was misusing the 10 × 10 grid in the second lesson.

11.6.3.5 Filling in Gaps and Holes

Recognizing constraints of the existing resources does not necessarily lead to productive ways of overcoming them, which is another important aspect of the capacity needed for effective use of existing resources. In the ICUBiT project, teachers tended to add new elements to the written lessons to enact them (Kim 2019). Some elements were intentionally added as planned; others were improvised in response to students. Whether these new elements are planned in advance or improvised during instruction, they have to support students' learning of the mathematical points of the lesson. Especially, those intended to overcome the constraints of the written lessons or improve the written lessons must be prepared carefully to increase the opportunity for students to learn the mathematical points of the lessons.

One teacher used a curriculum program whose individual lessons were designed for multiple class periods so that students could explore related mathematical ideas in depth over 2–3 days (Kim and Atanga 2013, Kim 2019). In a lesson written for 3 estimated days, students were asked to use base-ten pieces (i.e., pieces for ones, longs for tens, and flats for hundreds) to measure the area of a coat, and compare and order large numbers. This lesson was designed for geometrical and numerical explorations combined. The conceptual aspect of the mathematical point of the lesson was understanding how to measure an irregular shape and place value; the procedural aspect was using base-ten pieces to measure the area of an irregular shape, and ordering, comparing, and adding four-digit numbers. The students were using the concept of symmetry to efficiently measure the area of a coat (i.e., only measuring a half of the area and doubling the number found) and making sense of the large numbers as the resulting areas would be thousands of single pieces. As the lesson was complex in nature, detailed guidance was provided for instruction in the teacher's guide. However, there was still room for additional elements and improvisations as the teacher enacted the lesson. Noticing that her students needed a review on symmetry before starting a task of finding the area of a coat, the teacher asked students questions about area and symmetry, which effectively supported students' understanding of the nature of measuring the area of a shape like a coat and their work on the task. In fact, the teacher identified the mathematical points accurately, and noticed the affordances of the task and how the task could fall apart because of its nature. From these recognitions, she not only used the task and resources as suggested in the written lesson but also included additional steps to support students to use the base-ten pieces appropriately to measure the area of a coat. All of these aspects enabled the teacher to orchestrate her instruction toward the mathematical points effectively.

The fourth-grade teacher described earlier, who used blocks in a lesson on mean, recognized that the task for students in the written lesson mainly focused on the procedure to find the mean of a set of numbers and also recognized that the cube towers in Fig. 11.5 could be used to highlight the conceptual foundation for students' understanding of mean. In order to support students to make sense what the mean of a set of numbers means and why the procedure to find the mean works, the teacher asked students to use cubes to determine the mean of four different numbers before moving to the main student task. As described earlier, however, this was not productive because her use of cubes was not supporting students to understand what the mean really means or how the procedure works. Basically, showing the procedure of "add/combine them all and divide by four" with the cubes, the teacher intended, but was not able to highlight the conceptual nature of the mean—what the mean of the four numbers really represents, i.e., levelling out or evening out across the numbers.

There are no perfect curriculum resources that fit in any classroom situation; proper change, omission, or addition is needed as teachers are engaged in documentation work. Yet, the way teachers fill in the gaps and holes in the existing resources should be determined toward students' engagement in the mathematical points of the lessons.

11.6.4 Discussion

It was evident in the ICUBiT project data that different components of the capacity are interrelated. For example, identifying the mathematical points of a lesson was critical in making further decisions and using existing resources. Without accurate mathematical points identified, teachers can hardly steer instruction toward these mathematical points. Moreover, they can seldom recognize the affordances and constraints of the resources in use. The teacher emphasizing keywords had a number of missed opportunities to support students to think about the meaning of multiplication and division to solve and create story problems. Also, not seeing the importance of comparing multiplication and division in contexts and related problems, the teacher eliminated those components from her instruction, which, in fact, would have been good for students' understanding of the meaning of the two operations and their differences. In this sense, helping teachers articulate mathematical points of lessons seems to be a reasonable starting point to support them to develop the capacity for productive resource use.

The data used for this section also revealed that the teachers in the ICUBiT project had certain operational invariants, the notion that Gueudet and Trouche (2009) use to indicate cognitive structure guiding resource use. Unproductive use of existing resources is often rooted in operational invariants or conceptions that are not appropriate (Kim 2019). For example, the teacher emphasizing keywords in multiplication and division story problems believed keywords helped students' learning of operations and solving story problems. She said, "I know without those key pieces of information these kids can't be successful at finding the answers to story problems." Also, the teacher, not using representations in the lessons on operations with fractions, believed that representations were not helpful but instead were confusing students' thinking. Therefore, in order to support teachers to develop the capacity needed for productive use of existing resources, teacher education (i.e., teacher preparation and professional development) needs to support teachers to examine their own conceptions and generate such opportunities in their resource use.

Teacher knowledge is a critical element in teacher capacity for productive resource use, and developing the teacher capacity draws on different kinds of knowledge and skills. In particular, the knowledge of content and curriculum in mathematical knowledge for teaching [MKT] (Ball et al. 2008) and knowledge of curriculum embedded mathematics [KCEM] (Remillard and Kim 2017) seem very important for all five aspects of the teacher capacity for productive resource use. One approach to building the capacity is increasing teacher knowledge; another is working on the capacity (i.e., learning to make proper decisions in using resources) and cultivating the knowledge needed at the same time. The latter seems more promising. In this way, inappropriate conceptions can also be assessed against specific decisions and their productivity, and revised toward a higher capacity. In fact, increasing knowledge in building the capacity can help develop proper conceptions for the capacity. For example, the teacher using keywords extensively can become aware of her improper use of keywords and make better decisions toward the meaning of multiplication and division next time, by increasing knowledge needed through, for example, (1) unpacking the meaning of multiplication and division carefully, (2) looking into how different problem contexts embed this meaning and how these contexts can support students' thinking and learning of the operations, and (3) examining the actual impact of her use of keywords on students' understanding and thinking. All of these opportunities can help not only develop knowledge needed for the capacity for productive resource use, but also amend any inappropriate conceptions, such as the one on keywords.

11.7   Discussion and Perspectives

Sebastian Rezat, Carole Le Henaff, and Jana Visnovska

All four frameworks that are presented in Sect. 11.2 and are applied in Sects. 11.3, 11.4, 11.5 and 11.6 conceptualize teachers' work with resources. Since they are focusing on the same object, they share some commonalities, but they also put different emphasis on particular aspects of teacher documentation work. This is partly visible in the empirical studies and the theoretical contribution in Sects. 11.3, 11.4,

11.5, and 11.6. While Leroyer (Sect. 11.3) and Sabra and El Hage (Sect. 11.4) only draw on DAD, Wang (Sect. 11.5) explicitly demarcates her notion of DE from PDC and teacher design capacity (Pepin et al. 2017), and Kim (Sect. 11.6) contextualizes her study in both, PDC and DAD.

In light of the four study examples, we now discuss commonalities and differences of the four frameworks presented in Sect. 11.2, highlight some of their affordances, and point out some constraints. In particular, we discuss how the frameworks approach the focused activity and mediational means, the role of students, the role of institutional aspects, issues related to intentions, collective work, the quality of resource use, and the potential of the frameworks to inform change.

11.7.1 Focused Activity and Mediational Means

The four presented frameworks conceptualizing teachers' work with resources are grounded in activity theory. Therefore, they share the focus on mediational means and their capacity to afford and constrain human activity in a participatory relationship with mutual impacts. However, the mediational means are called and conceptualized differently in the four frameworks: artifacts, curriculum materials, or resources.

While artifacts can be both material and nonmaterial objects such as signs, the scope of the artifacts that are considered in the different theories varies. DAD refers to Adler's (2000) wide notion of resources including nonmaterial resources. By referring to resources instead of artifacts, DAD even goes beyond the notion of artifacts in activity theory. The main difference between artifacts in activity theory and resources in DAD is that artifacts are designed by humans with an intention, while a resource neither needs to be designed by humans nor does it need to be designed with a particular intention. DAD focuses on the interplay of these resources in the instrumentalization by and instrumentation of the teacher in the construction of the document. Both Remillard's (2005) framework of components of the teacher–curriculum relationship and Brown's (2002) design capacity for enactment framework in principle focus on material curriculum resources. However, both of them include a number of resources such as subject matter knowledge and pedagogical content knowledge, skills, beliefs, and perceptions of curriculum materials and students, which influence teachers' use of material curriculum resources. While in Remillard's and Brown's frameworks the role and the interplay of all these resources are open and subject to empirical studies, this interplay is partly structured in DAD by the notions of instrumentalization and instrumentation and the related notion of scheme.

The wide notion of resources in DAD may at times create difficulties in identifying the resources that are relevant for a specific purpose and limiting the scope of resources that are included in studies of teacher's documentation work. This becomes particularly apparent in Kim's contribution (Sect. 11.6), in which she conceptualizes teacher's capacity for productive use of resources. The five components of teacher's productive use of resources she identifies are (1) articulating the mathematical points of the lessons, (2) steering lessons toward the mathematical points of the lessons, (3) recognizing affordances and constraints of the resource in use, (4) using affordances, and (5) filling in gaps and holes. Looking at these components from the perspective of DAD, it would be interesting to go a step further and identify the resources that a teacher must possess or access in order to demonstrate productive use of teaching resources, and thus the capacity Kim outlines.

The frameworks also differ in the activity that is in focus. Studies based on DAD often operationalize the teachers' documentation work by analyzing teachers' reflections and planning activities that take place outside the classroom. In other words, a notion of document constructed in those ways shares similarities with the planned curriculum. According to the definition of documentational work, the document could be understood as the utilization of resources in order to develop the planned curriculum in particular situations. Prior experiences from enacting the planned curriculum, including insights into students' work, are considered to be a resource in the documentation work.

As opposed to the focus of DAD, SDT focuses on the activity inside the classroom, in which teachers and students interact with shared artifacts. Thus, SDT affords the analysis of interactions of teachers and students through artifacts. Consequently, artifacts that are solely used by teachers (or by students) are not the primary focus of SDT. A focus on the artifacts that are only used by the teacher would mean to focus only on one triangle side of the SDT. In such case, the students would become the (imagined) subject at which the teacher's activity is directed.

In comparison, Remillard's (2005) framework aims to represent design-stages of a curriculum resource that include before, during and after classroom practice. She distinguishes written, planned, and enacted curriculum and thus acknowledges that the enacted curriculum might differ significantly from both the planned curriculum (because it is co-constructed by teacher and students) and the written one (if the designers' and teachers' goals differ). Besides their role as co-constructors of the enacted curriculum, students play a role in the resources that the teacher brings to the participatory relationship with curriculum materials as teachers' perception of students.

Brown's (2002, 2009) metaphor of "teaching as design" seems to relate to both teachers' planning activities and the design of instruction in class. Therefore, it comprises the planned and the enacted curriculum.

The role of the attained curriculum, that is, students' actual performance and learning achievements, remains opaque in all four frameworks. The attained curriculum is not mentioned explicitly in any of the frameworks, and therefore, its role within the frameworks is open to suspicion. It could be conceived of as part of teachers' perception of students in Remillard's (2005) framework or as such become a resource in the DAD. Teachers' perceptions of students' attained curriculum might also lead to an adjustment of the learning goals and thus influence teachers' interaction with resources.

11.7.2 The Role of Students

In DAD, PDC, and the framework of the teacher–curriculum relationship, students play a minor role. In DAD the student is not explicitly mentioned. However, in her model of documentational expertise, which is closely related to DAD, Wang (Sect. 11.5) mentions the "student view" as one possible view to study and understand teachers' resource systems. If a teacher's resource system is studied from this perspective, the selection and adjustments of resources with regard to students' needs and feedback are the matter of interest.

In Remillard's (2005) and Brown's (2002) frameworks, students appear in terms of teachers' perception of students and in terms of teachers' knowledge about students' behavior. Siedel and Stylianides (2018) find that many teachers' selection of resources is "student driven," that is, "driven by consideration of their students' [perceived] needs" (p. 132, our insertion). The authors exemplify that the teachers' consideration of students' needs does not only have implications for the selection of resources, but also regarding their use.

In Kim's conceptualization of teacher's capacity for productive resource use (Sect. 11.6), students appear related to each of the five components of teachers' productive resource use. Students' learning processes appear as the objective at which the teacher's productive resource use is directed. A reason might be that these components are partly derived from observing teachers' activities in the classroom with students. It is possible that this is an implicit assumption within DAD, the design capacity for enactment framework, and the framework of components of the teacher–curriculum relationship. Namely, that the goal of teachers' design activities is always to provide students with resources that will best support their learning progress. However, given the competing agendas to which teachers routinely have to attend, is an implicit assumption like this sufficient when we theorize their work with resources?

Several contributions that use the DAD, design-capacity-for-enactment framework, or the framework of components of teacher–curriculum relationship have underlined the effects of the use of resources on students' learning and the search for innovative resources to support students' learning (Argaud et al. 2018; Barbosa and Vale 2018; Leroyer 2018; Rodrigues et al. 2018). However, in these cases, the intentions attributed to the teacher together with the selection and use of resources based on these intentions, are projected on the potential learning that students will carry out on the basis of the used resources. The underlying hypothesis is that the better the teacher knows his/her students, the more expertise he/she develops in his/her design capacity related to the goal of supporting the students' learning in the best possible way. And, in the same way, the more he/she knows about the subject he/she teaches, the more expertise he/she gains. Nevertheless, these assumptions remain to be empirically tested.

Unlike previous frameworks, the socio-didactical tetrahedron (SDT) accounts explicitly for the student as a user of curriculum materials and resources. This is related to the different focus of the framework, which is to model the overall didactical situation in the classroom focusing on the artifacts that both teachers and students use.

Consequently, with exception of SDT, the frameworks give a relatively minor consideration to students. While SDT acknowledges the student as a coequal user of artifacts, the other frameworks regard students as influences on the written and enacted curriculum, and include them indirectly in terms of teachers' perception of how students influence the next cycle of the planned curriculum. This difference might arise from the different foci of the frameworks: while SDT models the use of artifacts in the classroom, the other frameworks focus on teachers' interaction with curriculum materials during their planning and teaching activities.

11.7.3   The Role of Institutions

It is key to consider what place is occupied by the institution in the frameworks used for studying teachers' work with resources in the instrumentation process. The meaning of institution here is twofold. In the more usual sense of the term (Douglas 1987), the institution is understood as that which organizes, structures, even prescribes, and controls the activity of teachers. But Douglas (1987) also develops a new conception of institutions as "legitimate social groups." For example, Wang (Sect. 11.5), relying on this definition, called groups of teachers who regularly work collectively on a regular basis an institution. The place occupied by the institution, in the second sense of the term, is indeed crucial in the development of teachers' competencies related to the use of resources.

Martinez et al. (2018) problematize the role played by institutional prescriptions in the selection and modification of teachers' resources. The resources provided by the institution are linked to particular intentions and goals. However, teachers have to make use of these resources, or in other words, attribute their individual functions to them (instrumentalization), perceive their affordances and constraints, and incorporate them into the resource system. Thus, they are not released of the problems of selecting "good" materials for teaching mathematics and incorporating these materials in their teaching practice.

Sabra and El Hage use the DAD to investigate the use of resources in a university context. Referring to Madsen and Winsløw (2009), Sabra and El Hage (Sect. 11.4) differentiate between the teaching institution and the research institution of university teachers. Analyzing the use of a pivotal resource, they are able to better understand the relation of the research institution and the teaching institution through the lens of DAD. Thus, they use DAD to understand the use of resources in different institutions and the mutual relationships. Wang (Sect. 11.5) also acknowledges the role of the institution in the notion of DE and stresses the dependency of DE on institutional contexts.

It appears that DAD enables to grasp and better understand institutional aspects in professional work in different contexts through the lens of resource use. Due to their roots in activity theory, it is likely that this is also the case for the other frameworks, since the main assumption there is that the whole activity with its cultural and historical heritage is crystallized in the use of the artifact.

11.7.4 Intentions

The decisive aspect of institutional prescriptions largely forms the basis of the relationship between teachers and their practice, and therefore, the development of teachers' competencies related to their use of resources. This aspect also crosses teaching subjects, as Gruson et al. (2018) have shown, by comparing the design capacity of English and mathematics teachers: "Firstly, they both trust and use consistently 'officially approved' resources. The need to be in line with the official curriculum is an operational invariant (Vergnaud 1998) shared by both teachers."

The design of a resource therefore seems closely linked to the "patterns of intention" (Baxandall 1985) underlying the teachers' use of resources. The initial didactic intention (Margolinas and Wozniak 2010), conceptualized by Sensevy (2011) as "strategic rules," can be readjusted at any time.

When studying use of resources, it seems therefore necessary not to try to study a "reconstituted historical state of mind, (…) but a relation between the object and its circumstances" (Baxandall 1985, p. 42). Sensevy (2011, p. 192) adds that such intentions do not only apply to persons, but also to resources. For instance, developers have specific intentions which they aim to communicate via the designed resources. Similarly, teachers develop and refine their didactic intentions, while they conceive the resources, and while they use them in their class. We can suppose that the intentions resulting from planning and teaching activities are closely related to teachers' documentational expertise (Sect. 11.5) and their usual postures (Sect. 11.3) but could also be shaped by the intentions communicated by the resource itself. For example, students' work with a resource can incite teachers to re-organize their didactic intentions, as well as the use of the resource, in the course of action. In addition, some resources are devoid of initial didactic intentions when teachers select them.

As all discussed frameworks are grounded in activity theory or sociocultural perspectives, they allow for the analysis of this tension of intentions. Resources as mediational means are inherently situated culturally, institutionally, and historically (Wertsch 1998). An analysis of mediated action from a sociocultural or activity theoretical perspective can thus provide insights into the relationship of the intentions inherent in the mediational means and those of the user.

11.7.5 Collective Work and Design Capacity

The place of collective work is a crucial point to question in the study of teachers' use of resources but also of teachers' expertise. Indeed, the work of a teacher is part of both a report, and a path, which are specific to him/her, and which are linked to his/her academic training, as well as to his/her experience in teaching a certain type of knowledge. But design capacity, in a general way, and the development of expertise, is not limited to these aspects, as Wang notably shows it in her section (Sect. 11.5).

Indeed, it is important to take into account, when studying the documentation genesis of a teacher, how he/she fits into a collective, and what this collective brings to him/her in the development of competencies that are related to the use of resources. Wang (2018), Quéré (2018), and Ratnayake and Thomas (2018) also describe that exchanges within a group of teachers, or with other education professionals, have important effects on teachers' didactic reflections. For example, Quéré has shown that teachers who work collectively with the same teaching object, and with the same resource, are led to develop their conception of the knowledge at stake in these resources, but also their conception of the design and use of these resources.

This aspect also echoes the lesson studies (Miyakawa and Winsløw 2009) and their contribution to the development of teachers' competencies that are related to the use of their resources. Indeed, as Scardamalia (2002) put it, "creating a shared intellectual resource and a rallying point for community work helps to provide an alternative to tasks, lessons, projects and other expert-designed motivators of work, replacing them with a system of interactions around ideas that leads to the continual improvement of these ideas" (2002, p. 9). Wang (Sect. 11.5) also highlights the determining aspect that collective work brings to the development of teachers' competencies. She argues that teachers' individual resource systems may be studied and understood in terms of how collectives influence them and how they are used.

We rarely find studies of teachers' collective work with resources based on other frameworks than DAD. This might be due to the very wide notion of resources that is at the heart of DAD as opposed to the other frameworks. In the view of DAD, the collective might become a resource for the individual teacher in his/her documentational work.

The SDT also has the potential to contribute to the understanding of the role of communities and collectives in the use of artifacts, since it includes different communities on a social level. The frameworks by Brown (2002) and Remillard (2005) share their focus on the single teacher and his/her individual resources that he/she brings to the participatory relationship with curriculum materials. Therefore, communities and collectives play a subordinate role so far in the studies using these frameworks.

11.7.6 The Quality of Resource Use

The frameworks presented in Sect. 11.2 provide a language to describe resource use and to understand it from the perspective of activity theory. However, they do not account for the quality of the outcomes of the use of resources. The frameworks are not used to evaluate whether or not a document, the use of a curriculum material, or a "crafted instructional episode" is appropriate for the instructional goal, or whether or not it supports learning in a desired way. Their main intention is to better understand the interaction between the teacher and the (curriculum) resource.

Brown's notion of PDC seems to be a partial exception, because he explains PDC as a relation between teachers' perception of the affordances of the resource and a goal to be achieved by a designer-intended use of the resource. Therefore, this framework appears best suited for adaptations that would aim at evaluating the quality of resource use by different teachers.

Males et al. (2018) and Cooper et al. (2018) suggest two different methodological approaches to teacher's perception of the affordances and constraints of resources. Males et al. (2018) differentiate three interrelated phases of teachers interacting with a resource while reading: (1) curricular attending, (2) curricular interpreting, and (3) curricular responding. In order to grasp precisely what teachers attend to in a curricular resource, they suggest to use an eye-tracking methodology, which records eye movement in between and fixation time on particular locations on the page. While the methodology produces highly detailed data, the interpretation of this data requires further theoretical foundation. In particular, it remains unclear whether or how could long or short fixations of gaze and different patterns of eye-movement across the page contribute to informing us about teacher perceptions of the affordances and constraints of used materials.

Cooper et al. (2018) developed a tagging tool for digital resources. While the main intention is to provide a tool in order to support teachers as co-designers of curriculum, the tool enables the researchers to represent and analyze teachers' perceptions of the curriculum materials, the choices they make, and sequences of the enacted curriculum.

The concern with quality of resource use is also apparent in Kim's notion of teacher's capacity of productive resources use (Sect. 11.6). Based on her analysis of teachers' use of primary curriculum programs, Kim explores the components of teacher's capacity to use resources productively. Her main criterion for productive resource use is that enacted lessons create opportunities to learn the mathematical core of the enacted materials with an appropriate cognitive demand.

11.7.7 Potential of the Frameworks to Inform Change

When researching aspects of (mathematics) teachers' work and professional development, documenting and understanding the change is often the primary aim. This has several reasons. First—like in any profession—an individual teacher's practice and rationales that underpin his/her decisions are expected to undergo changes with time and teaching experience. Second, institutional expectations for what the job of teaching (mathematics) has to entail, including the tools that teachers are expected to use in their work, also change with time, and teachers are expected to make adaptations to their practices and rationales that would reflect this ever-renewing stream of changing expectations. Third, the most important, it is generally recognized that improvements to what mathematics students get to learn in schools, which students get to learn this mathematics, and how well will they understand it, cannot occur without changes in instructional practices that generate conditions for student learning.

The frameworks discussed in this chapter are currently used—in presented example studies and beyond—to capture and describe teacher's work with resources. We are proposing that in increasing the level of detail in these descriptions, the field might also need to take steps to investigate to what extent the new distinctions could be more broadly useful to inform change, and in particular provide better guidance about how teacher professional development can be supported. This direction is generally of interest to DAD research community, as illustrated by Leroyer (Sect. 11.3) who is anticipating and proposing to study how her framework of teachers' postures can be used for purposes of teacher professional development.

Notably, all discussed frameworks point out the multitude of personal resources that teachers bring to documentation work. Irrespective of the labels used for naming them, these personal resources are considered to be the result of the teacher's history of participation in the profession of teaching. They are assembled through the teacher's responses to opportunities, expectations, and problem situations, and stabilize those responses that prove to be the most reasonable from within this teacher's point of view.

Some of these resources can be explicit and some implicit for the teacher, and researchers often postulate these, based on empirical data, as being assumptions held by teachers about what kind of mathematics is the key for students to learn, what to look for in a curricular/instructional resource, how and when student learning happens, what might be the reasons for students' struggle, or how should teachers organize classroom events to effectively support the learning process. Research strongly suggests that changing curricular or instructional resources rarely fundamentally challenges teachers' assumptions. This was the case even in situations when new resources were produced with the explicit intent to change teachers' focus and rebuild their practices (e.g., NSF-funded curriculum materials in the United States) and where external guidance was provided to teachers (Simon et al. 2000). Indeed, successful cases of supporting productive shifts in some of these assumptions are rare and appear unduly resource-intensive (e.g., Carpenter et al. 1989; Visnovska and Cobb 2019).

However, it appears that to make mathematics learning meaningful for more students, we would benefit from supporting many more mathematics teachers in rethinking and rebuilding their assumptions, and changing their instructional practices. It is our opinion that frameworks that conceptualize teacher–resource interactions and relationships are uniquely positioned to support such work. It would also appear that improvements are possible in this respect.

Let us take DAD as an example. A number of studies conducted within this approach document teachers' resource systems, and explore how these change in response to introduction of a new (often digital) resource (see, for instance, Chap. 12 by Drijvers, Gitirana, et al.). From a design research perspective, insights generated in such studies of change could contribute to design theories of teacher learning. However, it is important to clarify that analyses conducted within DAD do not establish how teachers usually work with resources under unspecified conditions. Their activity theory roots position teacher learning as situated and the findings speak to design theories about teacher learning under particular conditions of support.

Within design research, means of supporting learning are theorized, designed for intentionally, and treated as an inherent aspect of any learning theory. In contrast, DAD subsumes the means of proactively supporting teacher learning within the rather broad notion of resources (which include material, human, and social-cultural). This does not appear problematic when creating point-in-a-time accounts of teachers' resource systems (see, e.g., Sect. 11.6), or retrospective accounts of their development. However, when design of a proactive support for specific changes in teachers' resource systems is the goal (such as changes in teachers' assumptions about nature of students' mathematical learning), the lack of theoretical differentiation between teachers' starting point situation and the required means of support, provision of which would have to be designed for, becomes problematic.

It is equally problematic that when theorizing all elements present within teachers' situation as 'resources', the responsibility to derive support (e.g., gather and select resources) appears to rest primarily—and possibly solely—with the teachers. While variability in teachers' access to resources explains why very different uses of the same classroom instructional resource are the result, this insight (and the theory guiding it) does not seem to distribute the responsibility for the result sufficiently among the players who substantially contributed to it (e.g., designers, school and system instructional leaders). It is our opinion that these kinds of consequences of theoretical tools we produce need to be continuously examined and addressed.

11.8 Conclusions

In this chapter, we provided an overview of four influential frameworks that conceptualize teachers' use of (curriculum) materials in paper or digital format including relevant resources in the interaction with the materials. Additionally, four empirical studies exemplify the application of these frameworks to a wide range of settings and contribute to their further theoretical development and elaboration. Based on the general introduction of the frameworks and the four example studies, we discussed the affordances and constraints of these frameworks.

While all frameworks are grounded in activity theory and thus share their focus on the mediational role of artifacts within activity, they vary in the scope of artifacts and resources and the activity in focus. Due to these differences, they afford or constrain the particular focus on different phases or levels of curriculum (e.g., designed, planned, enacted, attained) and the investigation of the role of communities and collectives, institutions, and students.

The scientific interest in understanding teacher's work with curriculum materials and resources grew out of the desire to promote change in teaching and learning mathematics accompanied by the experience that it does not suffice to provide reform-oriented curriculum materials. The frameworks discussed in this chapter contribute to an understanding of the complex relationship and interaction between the curriculum materials and the resources of the teachers. Furthermore, there is a growing interest to account for a quality aspect in teachers' use of resources. This tendency is mirrored in the contributions by Wang (Sect. 11.5) and her notion of DE and Kim (Sect. 11.6) and her aim to investigate teachers' capacity for productive use of resources. However, we argue that the insights in teachers' use of resources need to be used to further exploit the potential of the frameworks in order to proactively support specific changes in teachers' resource systems and their use in order to promote change in mathematics teaching and learning.

References

Adler, J. (2000). Conceptualizing resources as a theme for teacher education. *Journal of Mathematics Teacher Education, 3*(3), 205–224.

Argaud, H.-C., Douaire, J., & Emprin, F. (2018). The evolution of a resource stemming from research. In V. Gitirana, T. Miyakawa, M. Rafalska, S. Soury-Lavergne, & L. Trouche (Eds.), *Proceedings of the re(s)sources 2018 international conference* (pp. 179–182). Lyon: ENS de Lyon.

Atanga, N. A. (2014). *Elementary school teachers' use of curricular resources for lesson design and enactment.* Unpublished dissertation in Western Michigan University.

Bailleul, M., & Thémines, J. F. (2013). L'ingénierie de formation: formalisation d'expériences en formation d'enseignants. In A. Vergnioux (Ed.), *Traité d'ingénierie de la formation, L'Harmattan* (pp. 85–112). Paris.

Ball, D. L., & Cohen, D. K. (1996). Reform by the book: what is – Or might be – The role of curriculum materials in teacher learning and instructional reform? *Educational Researcher, 25*(9), 6–8,14.

Ball, D. L., Thames, M. H., & Phelps, G. (2008). Content knowledge for teaching: What makes it special? *Journal of Teacher Education, 59*(5), 389–407.

Barbosa, A., & Vale, I. (2018). Math trails: a resource for teaching and learning. In V. Gitirana, T. Miyakawa, M. Rafalska, S. Soury-Lavergne, & L. Trouche (Eds.), *Proceedings of the re(s) sources 2018 international conference* (pp. 183–186). Lyon: ENS de Lyon.

Baxandall, M. (1985). *Patterns of intention: on the historical explanation of pictures.* New Haven: Yale University Press.

Berliner, D. C. (1988). *The development of expertise in pedagogy. Charles W. Hunt Memorial Lecture presented at the annual meeting of the American Association of Colleges for Teacher Education.* New Orleans, Louisiana.

Berliner, D. C. (2001). Learning about and learning from expert teachers. *International Journal of Educational Research, 35*(5), 463–482.

Bishop, A. J. (2002). Critical challenges in researching cultural issues in mathematics education. *Journal of Intercultural Studies, 23*(2), 119–131.

Borko, H., & Livingston, C. (1989). Cognition and improvisation: differences in mathematics instruction by expert and novice teachers. *American Educational Research Journal, 26*(4), 473–498.

Broley, L. (2016). The place of computer programming in (undergraduate) mathematical practices. In E. Nardi, C. Winsløw, & T. Hausberger (Eds.), *Proceedings of INDRUM 2016 first conference of the International Network for the Didactic Research in University Mathematics* (pp. 360–369). Montpellier: University of Montpellier and INDRUM.

Brown, M. (2002). *Teaching by design: understanding the intersection between teacher practice and the design of curricular innovations* Doctoral thesis. Evanston: Northwestern University.

Brown, M. W. (2009). The teacher-tool relationship: theorizing the design and use of curriculum materials. In J. T. Remillard, B. A. Herbel-Eisenmann, & G. M. Lloyd (Eds.), *Mathematics teachers at work: connecting curriculum materials and classroom instruction* (pp. 17–36). New York: Routledge.

Brown, S. A., Pitvorec, K., Ditto, C., & Kelso, C. R. (2009). Reconceiving fidelity of implementation: an investigation of elementary whole-number lessons. *Journal for Research in Mathematics Education, 40*(4), 363–395.

Bucheton, D., & Soulé, Y. (2009). Les gestes professionnels et le jeu des postures de l'enseignant dans la classe: un multi-agenda de préoccupations enchâssées. *Éducation & Didactique, 3*(3), 29–48.

Calderhead, J. (1984). *Teachers' classroom decision-making.* London: Holt, Rinehart and Winston.

Carpenter, T. P., Fennema, E., Peterson, P. L., Chiang, C.-P., & Loef, M. (1989). Using knowledge of children's mathematics thinking in classroom teaching: An experimental study. *American Educational Research Journal, 26,* 499–531.

Charles, R. I., Crown, W., Fennell, F., et al. (2008). *Scott Foresman–Addison Wesley mathematics.* Glenview: Pearson.

Chevallard, Y. (1992). A theoretical approach to curricula. *Journal für Mathematikdidaktik, 13*(2/3), 215–230.

Choppin, J. (2011). The role of local theories: Teacher knowledge and its impact on engaging students with challenging tasks. *Mathematics Education Research Journal, 23,* 5–25.

Cooper, J. Olsher, S., & Yerushalmy, M. (2018). Reflecting on didactic metadata of learning sequences. In V. Gitirana, T. Miyakawa, M. Rafalska, S. Soury-Lavergne, & L. Trouche (Eds.), *Proceedings of the re(s)sources 2018 international conference* (pp 191–194). Lyon: ENS de Lyon.

Douglas, M. (1987). *How institutions think.* London: Routledge.

Elton, L. (1986). Research and teaching: symbiosis or conflict. *Higher Education, 15,* 299–304.

Elton, L. (2001). Research and teaching: conditions for a positive link. *Teaching in Higher Education, 6,* 43–56.

Engeström, Y. (1987). *Learning by expanding. An activity-theoretical approach to developmental research.* Helsinki: Orienta-Konsultit Oy.

Gonzàles-Martín, A., Nardi, E., & Biza, I. (2018). From resource to document: Scaffolding content and organising student learning in teachers' documentation work on the teaching of series. *Educational Studies in Mathematics, 98*(3), 231–252.

Gruson, B., Gueudet, G., Le Hénaff, C., & Lebaud, M.-P. (2018). Investigating teachers' work with digital resources. A comparison between teaching of mathematics and English. *Revue Suisse des Sciences de l'Éducation, 40*(2).

Gueudet, G. (2017). University teachers' resources systems and documents. *International Journal of Research in Undergraduate Mathematics Education, 3*(1), 198–224.

Gueudet, G., & Trouche, L. (2009). Towards new documentation systems for mathematics teachers? *Educational Studies in Mathematics, 71*(3), 199–218.

Gueudet, G., & Trouche, L. (2012a). Communities, documents and professional geneses: Interrelated stories. In G. Gueudet, B. Pepin, & L. Trouche (Eds.), *From text to 'lived' resources: Mathematics curriculum materials and teacher development* (pp. 305–322). New York: Springer.

11 Documentation Work, Design Capacity, and Teachers' Expertise

Gueudet, G., & Trouche, L. (2012b). Teachers' work with resources: documentational geneses and professional geneses. In G. Gueudet, B. Pepin, & L. Trouche (Eds.), *From text to 'lived' resources: Mathematics curriculum materials and teacher development* (pp. 23–41). New York: Springer.

Gueudet, G., Pepin, B., & Trouche, L. (Eds.). (2012). *From text to 'lived' resources: Mathematics curriculum materials and teacher development*. New York: Springer.

Gueudet, G., Pepin, B., & Trouche, L. (2013). Collective work with resources: An essential dimension for teacher documentation. *ZDM Mathematics Education, 45*(7), 1003–1016.

Gueudet, G., Buteau, C., Mesa, V., & Misfeldt, M. (2014). Instrumental and documentational approaches: From technology use to documentation systems in university mathematics education. *Research in Mathematics Education, 16*(2), 139–155.

Keitel, C., Otte, M., & Seeger, F. (1980). *Text Wissen Tätigkeit*. Königstein: Scriptor.

Kim, O. K. (2015). The nature of interventions in written and enacted lessons. In Beswick, J., Muir, T., & Wells, J. (Eds.), *Proceedings of 39th psychology of mathematics education conference* (Vol. 3, pp. 153–160). Hobart: PME.

Kim, O. K. (2018). Teacher decisions on lesson sequence and their impact on opportunities for students to learn. In L. Fan, L. Trouche, C. Qi, S. Rezat, & J. Visnovska (Eds.), *Research on mathematics textbooks and teachers' resources. Advances and issues* (pp. 315–339). Springer.

Kim, O. K. (2019). *Teacher fidelity decisions and the quality of enacted lessons*. Manuscript submitted for publication.

Kim, O. K., & Atanga, N. A. (2013). Teachers' decisions on task enactment and opportunities for students to learn. In *Proceedings of the 35th annual meeting of the North American Chapter of the International Group for the Psychology of Mathematics Education* (pp. 66–73). Chicago: University of Illinois at Chicago.

Kim, O. K., & Son, J. (2017). Preservice teachers' recognition of affordances and limitations of curriculum resources. In *Proceedings of 41st psychology of mathematics education conference* (Vol. 3, pp. 57–64). Singapore: PME.

Leroyer, L. (2018). The capacity to think of transmission of knowledge from learning supports: A proposition of a conceptual model. In V. Gitirana, T. Miyakawa, M. Rafalska, S. Soury-Lavergne, & L. Trouche (Eds.), *Proceedings of the re(s)sources 2018 international conference* (pp. 203–207). Lyon: ENS de Lyon.

Leroyer, L. (in press) La question des ressources dans le travail de conception des formateurs d'enseignants: cadres théoriques et perspectives de recherche. In I. Verscheure, M. Ducrey-Monnier & L. Pelissier (Eds.), *Enseignement et Formation: éclairage de la didactique comparée*. Toulouse: Presses universitaires du Midi.

Leroyer, L., & Bailleul, M. (2017), Les supports d'enseignements dans la représentation du métier chez des professeurs d'école débutants. In R. Gras & J. C. Régnier (Eds.), *L'analyse statistique implicative: des sciences dures aux sciences humaines et sociales* (pp. 411–421). Toulouse: Cépadues.

Leroyer, L., & Georget, J. P. (2017). De l'analyse du travail des formateurs à l'élaboration d'une modélisation, outil pour la formation de formateurs. Communication présentée au 4e colloque international de Didactique Professionnelle, Lille, France, juin.

Leshota, M., & Adler, J. (2018). Disaggregating a Mathematics Teacher's Pedagogical design capacity. In L. Fan, L. Trouche, S. Rezat, C. Qi, & J. Visnovska (Eds.), *Research on mathematics textbooks and teachers' resources. Advances and issues* (pp. 89–117). Cham: Springer.

Li, Y., & Kaiser, G. (2011). Expertise in mathematics instruction: advancing research and practice from an international perspective. In Y. Li & G. Kaiser (Eds.), *Expertise in mathematics instruction: An international perspective* (pp. 3–15). New York: Springer.

Livingston, C., & Borko, H. (1989). Expert-novice differences in teaching: a cognitive analysis and implications for teacher education. *Journal of Teacher Education, 40*(4), 36–42.

Madsen, L. M., & Winsløw, C. (2009). Relations between teaching and research in physical geography and mathematics at research-intensive universities. *International Journal of Science and Mathematics Education, 7*, 741–763.

Males, L., Setniker, A., & Dietiker, L. (2018). What do teachers attend to in curriculum materials? In V. Gitirana, T. Miyakawa, M. Rafalska, S. Soury-Lavergne, & L. Trouche (Eds.), *Proceedings of the re(s)sources 2018 international conference* (pp. 207–210). Lyon: ENS de Lyon.

Margolinas, C., & Wozniak, F. (2010). Rôle de la documentation scolaire dans la situation du professeur: le cas de l'enseignement des mathématiques à l'école élémentaire. In G. Gueudet & L. Trouche (Eds.), *Ressources vives. Le travail documentaire des professeurs en mathématiques* (pp. 233–249). Rennes: PUR.

Martinez, M., Cruz, R., & Soberanes, A. (2018). The mathematical teacher: a case study of instrumental genesis in the UAEM. In V. Gitirana, T. Miyakawa, M. Rafalska, S. Soury-Lavergne, & L. Trouche (Eds.), *Proceedings of the re(s)sources 2018 international conference* (pp. 211–214). Lyon: ENS de Lyon.

Miyakawa, T., & Winsløw, C. (2009). Un dispositif japonais pour le travail en équipe d'enseignants: étude collective d'une leçon. *Éducation & Didactique, 3*(1), 77–90.

Neumann, R. (1992). Perceptions of the teaching-research nexus: A framework for analysis. *Higher Education, 23*, 159–171.

Pepin, B., Gueudet, G., & Trouche, L. (2013). Re-sourcing teachers' work and interactions: A collective perspective on resources, their use and transformation. *ZDM – Mathematics Education, 45*(7), 929–943.

Pepin, B., Gueudet, G., Yerushalmy, M., Trouche, L., & Chazan, D. (2015). E-textbooks in/for teaching and learning mathematics: A disruptive and potentially transformative educational technology. In L. English & D. Kirshner (Eds.), *Handbook of international research in mathematics education* (3rd ed., pp. 636–661). New York: Taylor & Francis.

Pepin, B., Xu, B., Trouche, L., & Wang, C. (2016). Chinese expert teachers' resource systems: A window into their work and expertise. *Educational Studies in Mathematics, 94*(3), 257–274.

Pepin, B., Gueudet, G., & Trouche, L. (2017). Refining teacher design capacity: Mathematics teachers' interactions with digital curriculum resources. *ZDM - Mathematics Education, 49*(5), 799–812.

Quéré, N. (2018). Collective designing of open educational resources: What effects on teachers' design capacity? In V. Gitirana, T. Miyakawa, M. Rafalska, S. Soury-Lavergne, & L. Trouche (Eds.), *Proceedings of the re(s)sources 2018 international conference* (pp. 215–218). Lyon: ENS de Lyon.

Rabardel, P. (2002). *People and technology: A cognitive approach to contemporary instruments.* Retrieved from https://halshs.archives-ouvertes.fr/file/index/docid/1020705/filename/people_and_technology.pdf

Ratanayake, I., & Thomas, M. (2018). Documentational genesis during teacher collaborative development of tasks incorporating digital technology. In V. Gitirana, T. Miyakawa, M. Rafalska, S. Soury-Lavergne, & L. Trouche (Eds.), *Proceedings of the re(s)sources 2018 international conference* (pp. 219–222). Lyon: ENS de Lyon.

Remillard, J. T. (1999). Curriculum materials in mathematics education reform: a framework for examining teachers' curriculum development. *Curriculum Inquiry, 29*, 315–342.

Remillard, J. T. (2005). Examining key concepts in research on teachers' use of mathematics curricula. *Review of Educational Research, 75*(2), 211–246.

Remillard, J. T., & Kim, O. K. (2017). Knowledge of curriculum embedded mathematics: Exploring a critical domain of teaching. *Educational Studies in Mathematics, 96*(1), 65–81.

Rezat, S. (2009). *Das Mathematikbuch als Instrument des Schülers. Eine Studie zur Schulbuchnutzung in den Sekundarstufen.* Wiesbaden: Vieweg+Teubner.

Rezat, S. (2011). Interactions of teachers' and students' use of mathematics textbooks. In G. Gueudet, B. Pepin, & L. Trouche (Eds.), *From text to 'lived' resources. Mathematics curriculum materials and teacher development* (pp. 231–246). New York: Springer.

Rezat, S., & Sträßer, R. (2012). From the didactical triangle to the socio-didactical tetrahedron: artifacts as fundamental constituents of the didactical situation. *ZDM Mathematics Education, 44*(5), 641–651.

Rezat, S., Visnovska, J., Trouche, L., Qi, C., & Fan, L. (2018). Present research on mathematics textbooks and teachers' resources in ICME-13: Conclusions and perspectives. In L. Fan, L. Trouche, C. Qi, S. Rezat, & J. Visnovska (Eds.), *Research on mathematics textbooks and teachers' resources. Advances and issues* (pp. 343–358). Cham: Springer.

Rodrigues, A., Baltar, P. & Bellemain, F. (2018). Analysis of a task in three environments: paper and pencils, manipulative materials and Apprenti Géomètre. In V. Gitirana, T. Miyakawa, M. Rafalska, S. Soury-Lavergne, & L. Trouche (Eds.), *Proceedings of the re(s)sources 2018 international conference* (pp. 223–226). Lyon: ENS de Lyon.

Rowland, T., Huckstep, P., & Thwaites, A. (2005). Elementary teachers' mathematics subject knowledge: The knowledge quartet and the case of Naomi. *Journal of Mathematics Teacher Education, 8,* 255–281.

Ruthven, K. (2009). Towards a naturalistic conceptualisation of technology integration in classroom practice: The example of school mathematics. *Education & Didactique, 3*(1), 131–159.

Ruthven, K. (2014). Frameworks for analysing the expertise that underpins successful integration of digital technologies into everyday teaching practice. In A. Clark-Wilson, O. Robutti, & N. Sinclair (Eds.), *The mathematics teacher in the digital era* (pp. 373–393). Dordrecht: Springer.

Scardamalia, M. (2002). Collective cognitive responsibility for the advancement of knowledge. In B. Smith (Ed.), *Liberal education in a knowledge society* (pp. 67–98). Chicago: Open Court.

Schoenfeld, A. H. (2011). Reflections on teacher expertise. In Y. Li & G. Kaiser (Eds.), *Expertise in mathematics instruction.* Boston: Springer.

Schön, D. (1983). *The reflective practitioner.* New York: Basic Books.

Sensevy, G. (2011). *Le sens du savoir. Éléments pour une théorie de l'action conjointe en didactique.* Bruxelles: De Boeck.

Shulman, L. S. (1986). Those who understand: Knowledge Growth in Teaching. *Educational Researcher, 15*(2), 4–14.

Shulman, L. S. (1987). Knowledge and teaching: Foundations of the new reform. *Harvard Educational Review, 57*(1), 1–22.

Siedel, H., & Stylianides, A. J. (2018). Teachers' selection of resources in an era of plenty: An interview study with secondary mathematics teachers in England. In L. Fan, L. Trouche, C. Qi, S. Rezat, & J. Visnovska (Eds.), *Research on mathematics textbooks and teachers' resources. Advances and issues* (pp. 119–144). Cham: Springer.

Simon, M. A., Tzur, R., Heinz, K., Kinzel, M., & Smith, M. S. (2000). Characterizing a perspective underlying the practice of mathematics teachers in transition. *Journal for Research in Mathematics Education, 31*(5), 579–601.

Sleep, L. (2012). The work of steering instruction toward the mathematical point: A decomposition of teaching practice. *American Education Research Journal, 49*(5), 935–970.

Stigler, J. W., & Hiebert, J. W. (1999). *The teaching gap: Best ideas from the world's teachers for improving education in the classroom.* New York: Free Press.

Trouche, L., Drijvers, P., Gueudet, G., & Sacristan, A. I. (2013). Technology-driven developments and policy implications for mathematics education. In A. J. Bishop, M. A. Clements, C. Keitel, J. Kilpatrick, & F. K. S. Leung (Eds.), *Third international handbook of mathematics education* (pp. 753–790). New York: Springer.

Trouche, L., Gueudet, G., & Pepin, B. (2018). The documentational approach to didactics. In S. Lerman (Ed.), *Encyclopedia of mathematics education.* New York: Springer. doi:https://doi.org/10.1007/978-3-319-77487-9_100011-1

Vergnaud, G. (1990). La théorie des champs conceptuels. *Recherches en Didactique des Mathématiques, 10*(2-3), 133–170.

Vergnaud, G. (1998). Toward a cognitive theory of practice. In A. Sierpinska & J. Kilpatrick (Eds.), *Mathematics education as a research domain: A search for identity* (pp. 227–241). Dordrecht: Kluwer.

Vergnaud, G. (2009). The theory of conceptual fields. *Human Development, 52,* 83–94.

Visnovska, J., & Cobb, P. (2019). Supporting shifts in teachers' views of a classroom statistical activity: Problem context in teaching statistics. *Mathematical Thinking and Learning* doi: https://doi.org/10.1080/10986065.2019.1576003

Vygotsky, L. (1978). *Mind in society: The development of higher psychological processes.* Cambridge: Harvard University Press.

Wang, C. (2018). Mathematics teachers' expertise in resources work and its development in collectives. A French and a Chinese cases. In L. Fan, L. Trouche, C. Qi, S. Rezat, & J. Visnovska (Eds.), *Research on mathematics textbooks and teachers' resources. Advances and issues* (pp. 193–213). Cham: Springer.

Wenger, E. (1998). *Communities of practice: Learning, meaning, and identity.* Cambridge: Cambridge University.

Wertsch, J. V. (1998). *Mind as action.* New York: Oxford University Press.

Yang, X., & Leung, F. K. S. (2015). The relationships among pre-service mathematics teachers' beliefs about mathematics, mathematics teaching, and use of technology in China. *EURASIA Journal of Mathematics, Science and Technology Education, 11*(6), 1363–1378.

Chapter 12
Transitions Toward Digital Resources: Change, Invariance, and Orchestration

Paul Drijvers, Verônica Gitirana, John Monaghan, Samet Okumus, Sylvaine Besnier, Cerenus Pfeiffer, Christian Mercat, Amanda Thomas, Danilo Christo, Franck Bellemain, Eleonora Faggiano, José Orozco-Santiago, Mdutshekelwa Ndlovu, Marianne van Dijke-Droogers, Rogério da Silva Ignácio, Osama Swidan, Pedro Lealdino Filho, Rafael Marinho de Albuquerque, Said Hadjerrouit, Tuğçe Kozaklı Ülger, Anders Støle Fidje, Elisabete Cunha, Freddy Yesid Villamizar Araque, Gael Nongni, Sonia Igliori, Elena Naftaliev, Giorgos Psycharis, Tiphaine Carton, Charlotte Krog Skott, Jorge Gaona, Rosilângela Lucena, José Vieira do Nascimento Júnior, Ricardo Tibúrcio, and Anderson Rodrigues

Abstract This chapter reports on the work of Working Group 4 and focuses on the integration of digital resources into mathematics teaching and learning practices. There are five central sections, focusing on, instrumental genesis, instrumental orchestration, the documentational approach to didactics, digital resources and teacher education, and the design of learning environments with the use of digital resources. A range of constructs and theoretical approaches are covered in these five

P. Drijvers · M. van Dijke-Droogers
Freudenthal Institute, Utrecht University, Utrecht, The Netherlands

V. Gitirana (✉) · R. Lucena
CAA - Núcleo de Formação Docente, Federal University of Pernambuco, Caruaru, PE, Brazil
e-mail: veronica.gitirana@gmail.com

J. Monaghan
Agder University, Kristiansand, Norway

University of Leeds, Leeds, UK

S. Okumus
Recep Tayyip Erdogan University, Rize, Turkey

S. Besnier
CREAD: Center of Research on Education, Learning and Didactic, University Rennes 2, Rennes, France

C. Pfeiffer
Cerenus Pfeiffer, Stellenbosch University, Stellenbosch, South Africa

C. Mercat · P. Lealdino Filho
S2HEP (EA4148), IREM, Claude Bernard Lyon 1 University, Lyon, France

© Springer Nature Switzerland AG 2019
L. Trouche et al. (eds.), *The 'Resource' Approach to Mathematics Education*,
Advances in Mathematics Education,
https://doi.org/10.1007/978-3-030-20393-1_12

sections, and the opening section comments on construct validity and issues in "networking" theoretical frameworks. The chapter can be viewed as a literature review which surveys past and present (at the time of writing) scholarship with an eye to possible future research. The chapter is extensive in several dimensions: a large range of digital resources and applications are considered; the subjects using digital resources are not just teachers but also students, student teachers and student teacher

---

A. Thomas
University of Nebraska-Lincoln, Lincoln, NE, USA

D. Christo · S. Igliori
PUC/SP – Pontifíce Catholic University of São Paulo, São Paulo, Brazil

F. Bellemain · R. da Silva Ignácio · R. Marinho de Albuquerque · R. Tibúrcio · A. Rodrigues
Federal University of Pernambuco, Recife, Brazil

E. Faggiano
University of Bari Aldo Moro, Bari, Italy

J. Orozco-Santiago · F. Yesid Villamizar Araque
Cinvestav-IPN, Centre for Research and Advanced Studies, Mexico City, Mexico

M. Ndlovu
University of Johannesburg, Johannesburg, South Africa

O. Swidan
Ben-Gurion University of the Negev, Beer Sheva, Israel

S. Hadjerrouit · A. S. Fidje
Agder University, Kristiansand, Norway

T. Kozaklı Ülger
Bursa Uludağ University, Bursa, Turkey

E. Cunha
Instituto Politécnico de Viana do Castelo, Viana do castelo, Portugal

G. Nongni
University of Laval, Quebec City, Canada

E. Naftaliev
Achva Academic College, Arugot, Israel

G. Psycharis
National and Kapodistrian University of Athens, Athens, Greece

T. Carton
Paris 8 University, Saint-Denis, France

C. Krog Skott
University College Copenhagen, Copenhagen, Denmark

J. Gaona
Universidad Academia Humanismo Cristiano, Santiago, Chile

J. Vieira do Nascimento Júnior
State University of Feira de Santana, Feira de Santana, Brazil

educators. Issues raised in the sections include individual and collective use of resources, the adaptation of these resources for specific learning goals and to prepare (pre- and in-service) teachers for the use of digital resources.

Keywords Digital resources · instrumental genesis · instrumental orchestration · documentational approach to didactics · teacher education · design of learning environments

12.1 Introduction

Paul Drijvers, Verônica Gitirana, John Monaghan and Samet Okumus

This chapter reports on the work of Working Group 4 (WG4), which had the title of this chapter. This introduction to the chapter describes the original remit of WG4, outlines the range of papers accepted, describes and comments on the formation of five thematic subgroups formed during the conference, and comments on constructs and theoretical frameworks referred to in these thematic sub-groups.

> Digital resources have become an important part of teachers' and students' resource systems. the integration of digital resources into teaching and learning practices, however, raises many questions to teachers and educators.
> How to choose appropriate resources from the myriad of available options?
> How to adapt these resources to the specific learning goals at stake?
> How to orchestrate the students' use of the digital resources?
> What do student resource systems look like?
> How to prepare pre- and in-service teachers for these challenging tasks?
> Which role can digital resources play in assessment?
> Which opportunities do they offer for new learning formats, such as blended learning and flipped classrooms?
> How do classroom experiences inform the (re)design of a digital resource?
> What are the options for personalized learning in adaptive environments?

The remit of WG4:

In this working group, some of these issues will be addressed from theoretical perspectives, including instrumental genesis, instrumental orchestration and documentational genesis.

WG4 was the only Working Group to focus on digital resources and the only one to include a focus on students' use of the digital resources; it is hardly surprising, then, that it was the biggest Working Group – 25 papers and 2 posters. The papers can be found in the conference proceedings. The titles, below, give a flavor of the issues discussed in WG4 at the conference:

- A proposal of instrumental orchestration to integrate the teaching of physics and mathematics.
- Instrumental meta-orchestration for teacher education.
- Orchestrations at kindergarten: articulation between manipulatives and digital resources.
- Orchestrating the use of student-produced videos in mathematics teaching.
- Pre-service mathematics teachers' investigation of the constraints of mathematical tools.
- Transition from a paper–pencil to a technology-enriched teaching environment: A teacher use of technology and resource selection.
- An examination of teacher-generated definitions of digital instructional materials in mathematics.
- Teachers' intervention to foster inquiry-based learning in a dynamic technological environment.
- TPACK addressed by trainee teacher educators' documentation work.
- The birth of the documentary system of mathematics pre-service teachers in a supervised internship with the creation of a digital textbook chapter.
- Planning of the teaching of the standard deviation using digital documentary resources.
- LEMATEC Studium: A support resource for teaching mathematics.
- Using an app to collect data on students' use of resources for learning mathematics.
- Analysis of the use of resources on internet by pre-service mathematics teachers.
- From sample to population: A hypothetical learning trajectory for informal statistical inference.
- Teaching and learning of function transformations in a GeoGebra-focused learning environment.
- Creation of innovative teaching situation through instrumental genesis to maximize teaching specific content: Acid–base chemical balance.
- A proposal of instrumental orchestration to introduce eigenvalues and eigenvectors in a first course of linear algebra for engineering students.
- Teaching computational thinking in class: A case for unplugged scenario.
- A computational support for the documentational work mathematics teachers documentational work in EFII.
- From digital "bricolage" to the start of collective work: What influences do secondary teachers non-formal digital practices have on their documentation work?
- Digital resources: Origami folding instructions as lever to mobilize geometric concepts to solve problems.
- Exploring teachers' design processes with different curriculum programs.
- Prospective teachers' interactions with interactive diagrams: Semiotic tools, challenges and new paths.
- Instructors' decision-making when designing resources: The case of online assessments.

The Working Groups met in three 2-hour sessions over the conference. At first, it was difficult to see themes through the diversity of approaches and foci, but five themes appeared: instrumental genesis, instrumental orchestration, the documentational approach to didactics, teacher education, and design. We (the WG4 organizers) suggested these themes to the WG4 members and a collective discussion endorsed the themes as representative. Members were asked to pick their theme-group by going to different areas of a large room – everyone went to an area without fuss (a form of "embodied validity" for the five themes). The theme-groups then started discussing their theme: initially how their paper fitted into the theme and then structuring ideas and constructs around the theme. These five theme groups liaised after the conference and produced the next five sections of this chapter. We now move on to constructs and theoretical frameworks.

We first comment on what we mean by "constructs" and "theoretical frameworks." We use the word "construct" for a mental image and name of a phenomenon. "Instrumental genesis" and "instrumental orchestration" are examples of constructs. Zbiek et al. (2007) use constructs "that have specific applications to mathematics, that have an empirical basis, and that help one understand relationships among tool, activity, students, teacher, a curriculum content" (p. 1172). Also, academics may use constructs to talk about general properties of "things" in the real world. Academics should, of course, ensure that the constructs they use are clearly tied to the real world and accurately describe the phenomenon under examination – this is called "construct validity." A "theoretical framework" (or "theory" or "theoretical approach") is a perspective for interpreting reality that usually includes a number of constructs specific to the theory. There are "grand" and "local" theoretical frameworks: Piaget's (1955) genetic epistemology is a grand theory and radical constructivism, and the theory of didactical situations includes local theories that are aligned with Piaget's grand theory (see Lester 2005). The *documentational approach to didactics* is a local theory, but what, if any, is the grand theory to which it is aligned? "Networking" theoretical frameworks (using a bit of one in another) has occupied the attention of mathematics education academics for several decades (see Kidron et al. 2018); the state of the art with networking theoretical frameworks is that it is often possible (at some level) but must be done with careful attention to detail. We now comment on constructs and theoretical frameworks referred to in these thematic sub-groups.

The principal construct of Sect. 12.2 is instrumental genesis. It is aligned with Rabardel's instrumentation theory and constructs from Vergnaud's (2011) Piagetian approach (e.g., operational invariants). The authors utilize Gibson's construct of affordances in their discussion of instrumental genesis. The principal construct of Sect. 12.3 is instrumental orchestration (IO) (which makes essential use of instrumental genesis). Central constructs of IO are "didactical configurations" and "exploitation modes" and, in later formulations, "didactical performances." There is mention of possible networking with Koehler and Mishra's (2009) *Technological, Pedagogical and Content Knowledge* (TPACK) framework teachers' professional knowledge and Ruthven's (2014) model of *Structuring features of classroom practice*. Besnier and Gueudet's (2016) construct of "chaining orchestrations" (which itself arose from networking IO with *the Anthropological theory of didactics*) is also used. The section ends by employing ideas from Lakoff and Núñez's (2000) embodied cognition perspective. The focus of Sect. 12.4 is the local theory *documentational approach to didactics (DAD)*, which links, obviously, to IO. The section explicitly discusses networking DAD to other theoretical frameworks, for example, *Activity Theory*, the *Joint action theory in didactics* and TPACK (and a variant, the model *Mathematical pedagogical technological knowledge*). A host of emerging construct is considered, for example, "documentational trajectory" and "resource system metamorphosis," among others. Section 12.5 employs constructs introduced in earlier sections but implicitly introduces new theoretical frameworks because this section is essentially concerned with teacher education and how one views teachers, and teaching depends very much on one's theoretical perspective. There was no room in that section to consider possible tensions in some of these perspectives, but we take the opportunity here to mention that Teresa Assude's approach is informed by *the Anthropological theory of didactics* and Kathleen Heid's by *constructivism* and that networking these approaches is problematic. Section 12.6 is concerned with the design of learning environments. As with other sections, it considers various theoretical approaches and employs a number of specialized constructs, but an added element of complexity is that the design of learning environments is not just a meeting of approaches, it is a meeting place of disciplines – computer science and didactics (with ideas and approaches from engineering).

We make these comments on constructs and theoretical frameworks partly as an advanced warning to the reader but partly to remind ourselves to be aware of the importance of construct validity and the difficulty of networking theoretical approaches.

12.2 Instrumental Genesis: A Theoretical Lens to Study Mathematical Activities with Digital Tools

Cerenus Pfeiffer, Danilo Christo, Mdutshekelwa Ndlovu, Said Hadjerrouit and Sonia Igliori

This section focuses on instrumental genesis.[1] For this, we will seek to investigate, in a synthetic way, what instrumental genesis means. One answer to this question was presented by Gueudet (Chap. 2) when she took up the foundation elements of this theory, the distinction between an artifact (a digital artifact for the purpose of this section), a product of human activity designed for human activity and directed by objectives, and an instrument developed by a given subject (Rabardel 1995); the notion of instrument as an artifact + utilization scheme; the notion of scheme with

---

[1] This section also mentions "documentational genesis." Sect. 12.4 below considers the Documentational Approach to Didactics. The processes governing instrumental genesis and documentational genesis are similar, although the underlying artifacts these processes work on differ.

its four components, the objective of the activity, rules of action, operational invariants, and inferences (Vergnaud 1996); and highlighted two processes behind instrumental genesis – instrumentation and instrumentalization.

12.2.1 Theoretical Approaches to Instrumental Genesis

Drijvers and Trouche (2008) view instrumentalization as the process by which subjects shape the instrument and its use, and instrumentation is the process by which the artifact influences the activity and the thinking of the subjects. Both aspects influence and are influenced by the pedagogical design of the teachers, which gives rise to this genesis. Ratnayake and Thomas (2018) argue that teachers have to adapt digital resources and appropriate them to their practices by shaping and transforming them (instrumentalization and instrumentation). Lagrange and Monaghan (2009) argue that the availability of technology challenges the stability of teaching practices; techniques that are used in "traditional" settings can no longer be applied in a routine-like manner when technology is available. In order to help teachers to benefit from technological resources in everyday mathematics teaching, it is therefore important to have more knowledge about the new teaching techniques that emerge in the technology-rich classroom and how these relate to teachers' views on mathematics education and the role of technology as a teaching resource therein (Drijvers et al. 2010). Drijvers et al. (2013a) also contend that a deep understanding of students' learning processes is a core challenge of research in mathematics education.

The theory of instrumental genesis (TIG) ascribes a major role to artifacts that mediate human activity in carrying out a task (Drijvers et al. 2013a). When the artifact is used to carry out a task, it becomes an instrument (Drijvers and Trouche 2008). Ndlovu et al. (2011) also view instrumentation as the process by which the user of the artifact is mastered by his or her tools or by which the artifact influences the user by allowing him or her to develop activity or utilization schemes within some boundaries. Such limits include constraints, which assist the user in one way and impede in another; enablements, which effectively make the user able to do something; and potentialities, which open up possibilities and affordances that favor particular gestures or movement sequences (see also Noss and Hoyles 1996; Trouche 2004).

The notion of "affordance" is particularly important to the theory of instrumental genesis. The notion was originally proposed by E & J Gibson in the 1950s. Gibson (1977) is an authoritative account and refers to action possibilities, that is, what the user can do with an object. Norman (1988) applied the notion of affordances to digital tools. In this context, affordances refer to the perceived and actual properties of the tool, primarily those fundamental properties that determine just how the tool could possibly be used. Kirchner et al. (2004) developed three levels of affordances for digital tools. Firstly, technological affordances are properties of digital tools that are linked to usability issues. Secondly, educational or pedagogical affordances are properties of tools that act as facilitators of teaching and learning, and, finally, social affordances are properties of tools that act as social facilitators.

Given these considerations, we argue that, within the context of instrumental genesis, the affordances of digital tools are actualized at the technological, didactical/pedagogical and social levels. Technological affordances provide opportunities that facilitate the learning of mathematics, such as ease-of-use, ease-of navigation, accurate and quick completion of mathematical activities, drawing of graphs and functions, etc. Didactical/pedagogical affordances help in building and transforming mathematical expressions that support conceptual understanding of mathematics, such as collecting real data and creating a mathematical model; using a slider to vary a parameter or drag the vertex points of a triangle in geometry software; moving between symbolic, numerical, and graphical representations; simulating mathematical concepts; or exploring regularity, change, etc. Finally, social affordances facilitate group work and discussion, collaborative learning, and students taking greater control over their own learning (see Hadjerrouit 2017).

12.2.2 Papers Presented at the Conference

Taranto et al. (2018) treat a Massive Open Online Course (MOOC) as an artifact, that is, a static set of materials. They claim that when a MOOC module is activated, it dynamically generates a complex structure that is called an ecosystem. The researchers add that the process of transforming an artifact into an instrument is replaced here by the evolution, artifact – ecosystem/instrument.

In a similar vein, Ratnayake and Thomas (2018) analyze the process of designing tasks using the structure of documentational genesis and identify a series of items in the set of resources employed by the research communities of teachers. These include artifacts such as the criteria for designing rich tasks, the three-point framework for lesson planning, delivery and review and an exemplary task, GeoGebra, students' worksheet, and an A-level syllabus. The tasks before and after an intervention were evaluated using the Rich Task Framework, which comprises 12 factors including the appropriateness of the tasks for the instrumental genesis of the student. They claim that groups that freely shared ideas were more flexible in their use of digital technology than others, seeking and incorporating appropriate digital technology techniques into the tasks to help students understand mathematical concepts. This, they claim, allowed them to improve their personal instrumental genesis by learning new techniques and follow-up schemes; this evidences a development in professional instrumental genesis. Overall, this research suggests that there is merit in encouraging teachers to design digital technology tasks by working collaboratively in small groups provided specific support is given to the professional development of teachers to assist them. In turn, there may be beneficial effects in the broader documentary and instrumental geneses.

In Lucena et al. (2018), the notion of instrumental genesis appears in the scope of IO, when metaphorically they say that an orchestra in general can be recognized as an instrumental grouping comprising a conductor and instrumentalists, their instruments and scores, all well arranged in a space for the purpose of performing a piece of music. This concept of IO aims to model the practice of the teacher to sustain the instrumental genesis of students in rich mathematical learning. They cite Rabardel (1995) to argue that instrumental genesis is a transformation of an artifact by the action of someone, transforming it into an instrument while the subject goes through the process of instrumentation integrating it into their practice. The transformation of the artifact into an instrument is not characteristic of the structure of the tool but of the schemes that the subject develops to integrate it. They go on to say that, from their perspective of students' instrumental genesis, two concepts are fundamental for the orchestrating teacher: the concept of scheme and the concept of situation (that does not assume here the meaning of didactic situation but the meaning of task). The idea here is that any complex situation can be analyzed as a combination of tasks, each with its own nature, and difficulties are important to know.

Orozco et al. (2018) inform us that the integration and the use of new technologies in mathematics education have had an impact, but in many cases, this impact is anarchic; the digital age induces change to the access of information and construction of knowledge, among other actions by human beings. It is a fact that these new and sophisticated tools do not immediately become efficient instruments of teaching-learning. The instrumental approach (Guin and Trouche 1999) is a structure that allows one to take into account the role of technology in learning and teaching mathematics, in which the role of the teacher in this structure is fundamental, since s/he is responsible for the instrumental genesis of students, carried out by means of orchestrations (Drijvers et al. 2010).

In the paper by Igliori and Almeida (2018), instrumental genesis is implicit, since it is present in the production of the teacher's documentation. The paper presents a web tool, built for the purpose of providing digital resources, which favor the instrumentalization of the user teacher. The construction steps, from the digital objects to the teaching of mathematics at the elementary school level, can still be used as support in the work of the instrumentalization of its students. The process of instrumentalization is the first step of instrumental genesis.

Pfeiffer and Ndlovu (2018) describe their research carried out with students in a bridging program at a South African university participating in a qualitative study with TIG as a theoretical framework. This exploratory study investigates which instrumentation processes are dominant in a GeoGebra-enhanced mathematics learning environment to support students to develop an understanding of concepts in function transformations and circle geometry. The instrumentation process in this study was thus how GeoGebra shaped the thinking of the students and how it helped them to understand concepts. The instrumentalization process, in turn, was how the students used GeoGebra on their own as a tool, for example, to validate their answers and test their conjectures. During in-depth and focus-group interviews in Pfeiffer's (2017) study, students were asked if GeoGebra had helped them with certain concepts. Most of them affirmed that GeoGebra use had indeed helped them to better understand function transformation and circle geometry. The following responses concern perceived affordances of GeoGebra.

- "I knew from last year that if you reflected a graph about the y-axis, the x-values change sign (from positive to negative or negative to positive). We were just doing it mechanically, but with GeoGebra, this year, I could see what is going on (visual affordance) and it made sense."
- "I could see the signs. I understand now better why the sign changes if g(x) is reflected in x-axis ..... then I know the negative sign has to stand in front of g(x) and it also meant that the new graph is h(x)."
- "With all the different circle geometry theorems, you could see which angles are equal to each other or different segments. I could see them."
- "It helped. Specially to see them visually (visual affordances). Like the chords, the angle subtended by the same chord to show that they are equal."

These responses suggest that the students acquired "physical and logico-mathematical" knowledge of function transformations. GeoGebra use also afforded the students an opportunity to link visual graphic representations to the algebraic representations of the same concepts.

The visual affordances of GeoGebra identified by students are as follows:

- GeoGebra acted as a tool to visualize the transformations, the utilization scheme of changing sliders, and gave them an enactive sense of what the parameter in the equations mean: that the change in the equation transforms the original function; the instrumented action scheme of typing the transformation notation gave them visual understanding of how the horizontal translation, reflection in x- and y-axis, occurs; and that the reflection in the $y = x$ means the inverse graph of a function.
- The utilization scheme of changing the colors of the different resultant graphs helped students compare them to the original graph, resulting in better understanding the nature of the "shifts."
- GeoGebra use gave students a better understanding of sketching the inverse graph of an exponential function because they came to know it as a mirror image of the exponential graph. It enabled them to use the instrumented action scheme of sketching the graph by using critical points.
- GeoGebra use also helped with the understanding (instrumental genesis) of theorems in circle geometry – for example, showing which angles are equal and which angles are subtended by the same chord or arcs. Responses showed how GeoGebra shaped the thinking of the students and how it helped them to understand and visualize theorems.

With regard to the instrumentalization process, responses of the students showed how GeoGebra was independently utilized as a tool to validate their answers and test their conjectures. Observations showed how the students discussed and analyzed the properties of a GeoGebra applet and conjectured what the transformation of the function should be. They tested and validated their conjectures by dragging sliders in the applet. The students, therefore, had an opportunity to make and validate conclusions about the type of transformation on the basis of intuition or experi-

12 Transitions Toward Digital Resources: Change, Invariance, and Orchestration

ence obtained through GeoGebra. Observations also showed how students acquired or discovered physical knowledge of function transformations and circle geometry.

We now turn to visualization, the ability to use and reflect upon pictures, graphs, animations, images, and diagrams on paper or with digital tools with the purpose of communicating information, thinking about and advancing understandings (Arcavi 2003). Visualization tools are becoming important in mathematics education.

Two papers emphasize the role of visualization tools for teaching and learning mathematics. Barbosa and Vale (2018) highlight the potential of visual solutions and strategies to promote mathematical learning. Even though the term "instrumental genesis" is not explicitly mentioned in the article, there are clear indications of instrumentation and instrumentalization processes. The authors present two examples of tasks and their visual solutions. The first one is related to the area of the area of rhombus using a visual figure with colors (a square) as an artifact with four midpoints of each side of the square. In the process of instrumentation, the students shaped the artifact using their own mathematical knowledge to find a visual solution to the problem, while the artifact enabled the students to produce the solutions within its constraints (instrumentalization). The second example involved the manipulation of rational numbers, equations, and proportionality. The students produced many solutions including a solution obtained by visualization. Similar to the rhombus task, instrumentation and instrumentalization processes were at work in this case, too. The paper points to the affordances of visualizations to achieve more efficient solutions, since these provide additional strategies. The social affordances of the tool are also emphasized, since it allowed students to discuss their strategies.

The second paper on visualization tools, Martinez et al. (2018), describes a case of instrumental genesis at a Mexican university, where teachers use digital technology to give feedback on their teaching practice in order to move from instrumentation to instrumentalization and orchestration processes. The intention is to establish the importance of the digital tools as supports for didactical activities and mediators of mathematical knowledge in classrooms. This can be characterized as the teacher's instrumental genesis, where the processes of instrumentation and instrumentalization are intertwined, involving the planning of the class session, selection, distribution, and management of the artifacts with their affordances and constraints; giving rise to a scheme of use by identifying the features of the artifacts, the subjects of the activity, and their knowledge; and thus providing a form of IO.

The final paper we consider in this section demonstrating the usefulness of the theory of instrumental genesis is the paper on teaching computational thinking (CT) in classroom environments (Lealdino Filho and Mercat 2018). Even though the process of instrumental genesis is not explicitly mentioned in this article, there are clear indications of instrumentation and instrumentalization processes, affordances, and constraints of the artifacts as well. As an example of CT, the article presents a binary magic trick using five cards with numbers. The task consists of asking the student to choose a secret number between 1 and 31, showing her/him each card one after another to decide whether the card contains the secret number. In terms of instrumentation, the work consists of understanding the binary magic trick and writing an algorithm which performs it. The algorithm is the artifact that is shaped by the student using his/her knowledge of CT and mathematics. The algorithm itself has its own rules with affordances and constraints that must be followed by the students in order to return the same result independently of who performs the steps. This is the instrumentalization process. The article shows the possibility of using CT to design an algorithm without the use of digital tools. Implementing the algorithm on a computer follows basically the same logic, but it requires understanding the programming language in order to create an algorithm for the computer to yield the solution to be achieved. In addition, instrumental geneses that use programming languages as artifacts that mediate between the student and the task have an element of creativity in order to solve the problem. Programming is an iterative process where it is common for a program not to work as expected and thus cannot yield the correct answer the first time it is performed, in contrast to conventional digital tools such as GeoGebra, for example. The search for a better or more efficient solution can be achieved in various ways such as testing the program with different data and strategies, discussions with fellow students and the teacher, or conducting a search on the Web for alternative solutions, etc. The programming process provides affordances and constraints at the technological, pedagogical/didactical, and social level and creates interactions that facilitate the emergence of varied utilization schemes for the students. The combination of technological, pedagogical, and social elements, in addition to the creativity element of the programming process has huge impact on students' instrumental genesis and the schemes they develop when using CT and mathematics.

We conclude this section by noting that although much has been built on the notion of instrumental genesis (e.g., instrumental orchestration and documentational genesis), there is still much to learn about instrumental genesis itself.

12.3 Revisiting Instrumental Orchestration: Past Findings and Future Perspectives

Paul Drijvers, Sylvaine Besnier, José Orozco-Santiago, Tuğçe Kozaklı Ülger and Freddy Yesid Villamizar Araque

Soon after instrumental genesis was recognized as a key process in exploiting the potential of digital technology in mathematics education, it was acknowledged that teachers play a crucial role in enhancing this process. Instrumental orchestration arose an answer to the question of how to foster students' instrumental genesis. Even though the focus may have shifted toward teachers practices in terms of the DAD since then, this chapter revisits IO and identifies five future perspectives of this notion, to further extend its value for mathematics educations, and for teacher training in particular: (1) a shift toward student-centered orchestrations, (2) extending the repertoire of orchestrations, (3) chaining orchestrations, (4) didactical performance, and (5) teachers' and students' gestures.

12.3.1 Past Findings

As shown in Sect. 12.2, the notion of instrumental genesis was an important step ahead in research on the use of digital tools in mathematics education. It acknowledged the subtlety and the complexity of turning artifacts into (parts of) instruments through the joint development of techniques for using a particular tool for a particular task, and the corresponding insights to understand the mathematics involved. Soon, the crucial role of teachers in this process was recognized. The question was what teachers can do to foster this co-emergence of techniques and schemes, i.e., to create appropriate environments to make instrumental genesis happen. This is where the notion of IO came into play.

An instrumental orchestration was defined by Trouche (2004) as the teacher's intentional and systematic organization and use of the various artifacts available in a learning environment in a given mathematical task situation to guide students' instrumental genesis. An IO consists of two layers, a didactical configuration and an exploitation mode. A didactical configuration is an arrangement of artifacts in the environment or, in other words, a configuration of the teaching setting and the artifacts involved in it. Through the didactical configuration, the teacher "sets the scene" for instrumental genesis. An exploitation mode is the way the teacher wants to exploit a didactical configuration for the benefit of the didactical intentions. It is the expected way in which the didactical configuration can be exploited for the targeted instrumental genesis. As a paradigmatic example of an IO, Trouche (2004) presented the "Sherpa orchestration," in which a student uses an artifact in front of the class, thus allowing the teacher to guide the use, the students to react to that and the Sherpa student (and, through her/him, the class) to get feedback on the techniques *in use*.

This notion of IO soon received attention. Assude (2007) introduced the notion of instrumental integration, including initiation, exploration, reinforcement, and symbiosis (see also Hollebrands and Okumus 2018). Also, it was pointed out that, in spite of the somewhat formal word "orchestration," the teacher in this model should not be considered a conductor of a symphony orchestra but, rather, a jazz band leader who prepares a global partition but also is open to improvisation and interpretation (Drijvers and Trouche 2008; Trouche and Drijvers 2010).

To do justice to the multiple *ad hoc* decisions that teachers take in split seconds while teaching, the IO model was expanded with a third layer called didactical performance (Drijvers et al. 2010). The didactical performance refers to all (bounded) choices made on the fly with respect to how to actually perform in the chosen didactical configuration and exploitation mode: what question to pose now, how to do justice to (or to set aside) any particular student input, how to deal with an unexpected aspect of the mathematical task or the technological tool, or other emerging goals. Figure 12.1 depicts the three IO layers.

Since its early years, the notion of IO has widened its scope. Its relationships with other models for teacher behavior and teacher knowledge have been investigated. For example, Tabach (2011, 2013) and Drijvers et al. (2013b) combined and contrasted the IO approach with the TPACK model on teachers' professional knowledge. The

Fig. 12.1 The three-layer model of an IO

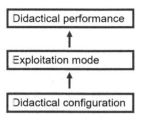

two lenses showed to be complementary and together provided a richer view on teachers' practices in ICT-rich classrooms. Also, the relationships with Ruthven's model of Structuring features of classroom practice (SFCP) framework have been explored (Bozkurt and Ruthven 2017; Ruthven 2014). In particular, the instrumental orchestration shows resemblance with the Activity Structure notion in the SFCP framework. To explore another connection, Trouche and Drijvers (2014) investigated the relation between instrumental orchestration and the notion of webbing. Whereas webbing focuses on the construction of a web of connected mathematical ideas, instrumental orchestration stresses the situation that invites this process. A further focus on teachers' practices with respect to designing, using and arranging resources has been developed under the name of the documentational approach to didactics, which is elaborated in Sect. 12.4. As far as student level and age are concerned, the work on instrumental orchestration originally focused on the upper secondary level, but since then, it has been widened, as far as kindergarten level (Besnier 2018; Carlsen et al. 2016).

If we look back at these developments, how well did IO do over the previous 15 years? It did lead to the acknowledgement that the way in which teachers foster instrumental genesis is a key issue. In addition to this, some orchestration types have been identified. In spite of the widening scope described above, however, we wonder if IO really had the impact that it might have had. Our view is that its potential has not yet been fully exploited, if we take into account the limited number of publications on this topic on the one hand, and the increasing role of digital tools in mathematics education on the other. The agenda for this section, therefore, is to revitalize the notion of IO. To do so, we outline five future perspectives that we consider promising and address below: (1) a shift toward student-centered orchestrations, (2) extending the repertoire of orchestrations, (3) chaining orchestrations, (4) didactical performance, and (5) teachers' and students' gestures.

12.3.2 Future Perspectives

12.3.2.1 A Shift Toward Student-Centered Orchestrations

When digital technology became more common in mathematics education, it was hoped that it would offer opportunities for students' ownership of their learning and that it would provide a "context where the learner is consciously engaged in constructing a public entity, whether it's a sand castle on the beach or a theory of the universe" (Papert and Harel 1991, p. 1). In line with this view, one might be tempted to expect new types of student-centered orchestrations to emerge, which invite students engage in mathematics through creating mathematical objects.

Findings so far, however, seem to show a dominance of teacher-centered orchestrations. Drijvers et al. (2010) quote teachers privileging teacher-centered orchestrations such as Technical demo because they feel more in control of the situation, compared to student-centered orchestrations. This reminds of the experiences in the UK, where the large-scale introduction of interactive whiteboards in the UK led to traditional teacher-centered teaching practices: "the mere introduction of such technologies is insufficient to promote greater interactivity in the classroom, and indeed, that use may have had detrimental effects" (Rudd 2007, p. 2).

As another example of teachers preferring teacher-centered orchestrations, Kozaklı Ülger and Tapan Broutin (2018) described a study on one mathematics teacher's integration of technology in her course. Compared to her lessons, which usually were traditional, new orchestrations were observed in her technology-enriched lessons, and she implemented various orchestration types in the teaching process: Explain-the-screen, Discuss-the-screen, Link-screen-board and Not-use-tech (Drijvers et al. 2010). However, this did not prevent the teaching process from being teacher-centered. In spite of tablets with GeoGebra being available, the teacher hardly used them and stuck to whole-class teaching. This preference for teacher-centered orchestrations may have different reasons. The first reason is that students lack the skills of using software, in this study GeoGebra and that the teacher does not want to spend precious teaching time to make them more experienced. The second reason is the lack of technological-pedagogical knowledge and experience by the teacher. Consequently, she might feel losing control if much is left to the students' initiative. For example, students might come up with solutions, strategies and questions that are beyond the teacher's knowledge and experience.

To make students take full benefit of the potential digital technology offers, it might be good to use more student-oriented orchestrations. To be capable of doing so, teachers should feel the confidence on their own technical skills, trust their student learning capacities with respect to using digital tools, and dare to be out of control and to deal with unexpected situations. How pre- and in-service mathematics teachers can acquire these skills and how they can make a shift toward student-centered orchestrations is a research question that deserves more attention.

12.3.2.2 Extending the Repertoire of Orchestrations

In the literature, a small number of orchestrations have been identified. After Trouche's (2004) paradigmatic Sherpa orchestration, the collection of IOs remained very limited until the publications by Drijvers et al. (2010, 2013b). This resulted in the identification of classes of whole-class and individual orchestrations, ranging from being more teacher-centered to more student-centered (see Fig. 12.2). Since then, other researchers used this typology as a point of departure to identify additional IOs or describe variations (Tabach 2011, 2013).

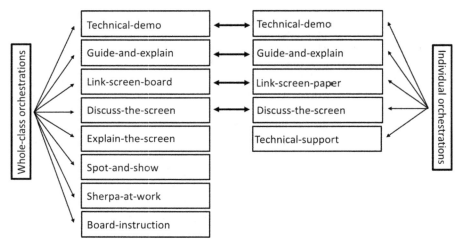

Fig. 12.2 Whole-class and individual orchestrations. (From Drijvers et al. 2013b, p. 998)

The question is, however, how context specific this limited repertoire is, how general are the orchestration types, and how do they depend on the digital tools *in use*, the mathematical topic, the teachers' views on teaching, and other possible factors? Also, we expect the repertoire to need further extension, for example, in the light of the increasing diversity of digital tools that came into play, such as MOOCs, flipped classroom tools, etc. For example, Orozco et al. (2018) study instrumental orchestrations in the case of university-level courses in linear algebra and the topic of eigenvalues and eigenvectors in particular. Digital tools include computer algebra systems and dynamic geometry software, and the results might shed light on possibly new orchestrations in this context.

In short, many questions on the repertoire of IOs are waiting to be answered. How general is the set of IOs identified so far? Do we need a more comprehensive taxonomy of orchestrations? How exactly is the relationship between the IO and the targeted instrumentation schemes? These questions are high on the future research agenda in our field.

12.3.2.3 Chaining Orchestrations

So far, the focus within IO research has been on isolated orchestrations. Hardly any attention is paid to integrating them into instructional sequences. How can teachers sequence orchestrations into productive chains? Are there specific chains that form natural sequences, like IO trajectories? Even if this idea was present in the early years of instrumental orchestration (e.g., see Trouche 2004), it has not been further elaborated so far.

In addressing these questions, an interesting approach could be to first identify the teachers' goals while setting up a classroom organization. To characterize such an organization, Besnier (2016) developed a link between moments of study (Chevallard 2002) and the notion of orchestration. Chevallard considered that "whatever the concrete path of the study, certain types of situations are almost necessarily present during the study" (Chevallard 2002, p. 11).[2] These types of situations are called moments of study. Chevallard identified four types of moments, described by Besnier (2016) as follows: designing and implementing introduction and discovery moments; designing and implementing learning and training moments; designing and implementing synthesis moments; and designing and implementing evaluation moments. While studying IO in Kindergarten, Besnier (2018) observed an orchestration linked to the design and implementation of a moment of synthesis, to support discussions between pupils about the procedures they used for solving a mathematical task. This orchestration was called "the manipulatives and software duo" and was considered a variant of the "link screen board" orchestration already identified in secondary school (Drijvers et al. 2010). We consider these two orchestrations as a part of a continuum, which starts with prior orchestrations that give the students the opportunity to experience moments of introduction and discovery and to experiment moments of learning and training.

Besnier and Gueudet (2016) identified specific chains of orchestrations within the same lesson. Orchestrations took place successively but also simultaneously. With regard to successive orchestrations, the authors observed, in a moment of introduction and discovery, a chain of three types of orchestrations, "discuss the screen," "explain the screen," and "Sherpa at work," and note teachers combining teacher-centered and student-centered orchestrations for the same goal. In this chain, the teacher leaves more or less room for the students' experience or actions. When should students be given more control? When should the teacher take over? In connection with these questions, this manipulation of orchestration chains, by the teacher and for the benefit of students' learning, seems to require dexterity and expertise from the teacher.

As for the simultaneous orchestrations, we observed orchestrations such as "accompanied use" and "peer work" carried out simultaneously during learning and training moments. The teacher's expertise in choosing a particular orchestration targeted at specific students and simultaneously managing several orchestrations seemed crucial here, to do justice to the differences between students.

In spite of this example, much remains unknown about the ways in which IOs may be chained and connected. This is an important topic to investigate in more detail and to address in pre-service and in-service teacher training.

12.3.2.4 Didactical Performance

As shown in Fig. 12.1, the IO model distinguishes three levels: a didactical configuration (the setting), an exploitation mode (the way in which the teacher intends to use this setting), and a didactical performance (the way in which the teacher actually

---

[2] Our translation.

carries out the teaching, including unforeseen events and follow-up decisions). So far, research has mainly focused on the didactical configurations and exploitation modes. It has hardly addressed the latter phase of didactical performance, which in the end might be decisive in the IO's effect. How do teachers take their decisions, and how can they be empowered to do so in a fruitful way?

Villamizar et al. (2018) studied the teacher's didactical performance in a high school course that integrated mathematics, physics and digital technology using the Cuvima model (Cuevas et al. 2017). The objective was to promote insight into both sciences based on the modeling of a physical phenomenon. One of the didactical configurations included printed guides, a projection room and tablets, with an app for video analysis and dynamic geometry. In groups of three, the students investigated the physical phenomenon of conservation of energy in the free fall of a ball.

The teacher's exploitation mode was guided by the four phases of the Cuvima model: experimentation of a physical phenomenon (use of guides and tablets), modeling by digital device (use of apps in the tablets), and conceptual analysis in physics and mathematics (use of didactic guides, projector, and blackboard), in which the teacher used Link-screen-board and Discuss-the-screen orchestrations (Drijvers et al. 2010). The teacher's didactical performance was evident during the discussion of the results, in which the teacher pointed out that the experimental data were imprecise. To improve data collection, a student proposed to add new artifacts as pointers to the tablet (USB, On-The-Go and mouse); in response to this, the teacher assigned this student the role of *Sherpa-student* (Trouche 2004). This decision clearly illustrates the importance of the didactical performance.

To summarize, the "proof of the pudding" of an IO to an important extent depends on the teacher's didactical performance. Consequently, it is highly relevant to know more about effective didactical performance and about the ways in which pre- and in-service teachers can further develop their skills on this point.

12.3.2.5 Teachers' and Students' Gestures

As part of the didactical performance, teachers use gestures while teaching. Students gesture as well while using digital tools. What is the relationship between the type of gestures and the techniques invited in the IO? Is there a relationship between the gestures, seen from an embodied perspective, and the techniques in use?

Notions on embodiment (Lakoff and Núñez 2000) stress that cognition, even in the domain of mathematics, is rooted in bodily experiences, which take place in interaction with the world. Sensori-motor schemes, in this view, might form a foundation for instrumentation schemes that are formed through instrumental genesis. However, research on IO seems to have neglected the embodiment and gesture perspective, and, in fact, one might wonder how to incorporate this view in the integration of digital tools in mathematics education. For example, Kozaklı Ülger and Tapan Broutin (2018) showed that even in technology-enriched lessons, teachers may prefer typical teacher gestures, such as tracing out a curve in the air, to using technological resources.

In short, further research is needed to investigate how IOs can take into account the bodily experiences in which mathematical experiences are rooted. How can we use digital technology to overcome the limitation of just neglecting embodiment? What is the relationship between mathematical concepts, body and the material activity with instruments? Recent developments in this field suggest promising relationships between the use of digital tools, gesture, and embodiment (e.g., see Ferrara and Sinclair 2016), but much is to be explored in more detail in this field.

12.3.3 Conclusion

This reflection on the past and the future of the notion of IO, on the one hand, shows its potential: it is widely acknowledged that teachers play a crucial role in enhancing the process of instrumental genesis, and that appropriate support to students is a subtle matter. The three-layer IO model may help teachers become aware of this subtlety and to develop their skills in exploiting the affordances of digital technology in their mathematics classes. For example, the notion of didactical performance highlights the flexibility that IOs need, to allow on-the-fly adaptations by the teacher. As such, the notion of IO is considered an answer to the question of how to foster students' instrumental genesis.

On the other hand, the increasing role of digital technology in mathematics education and the wide variety of digital tools makes us feel the IO model has not yet been fully exploited. We recommend further research in the five directions outlined above, to further develop IO as both a theoretical and a practical framework but also to better align it with current trends in mathematics education, including foci on student-centered learning and on the importance of gestures and embodiment as foundations of mathematical knowledge.

12.4 Perspectives of the Documentational Approach to Didactics with Regard to Transitions Toward Digital Resources

Sylvaine Besnier, Verônica Gitirana, Rogério da Silva Ignácio, Rafael Marinho de Albuquerque, Gael Nongni, Giorgos Psycharis, Charlotte Krog Skott and José Vieira do Nascimento Júnior

The roots of the DAD (Gueudet and Trouche 2008) are interrelated with a transition of research interest from resources used by teachers and/or teacher educators to digital resources. The increasing development of the DAD (Trouche et al. 2018), however, points to its potential to obtain deeper understanding of teachers' practice with resources, digital or not. A basic assumption of DAD is that the multiplicity of the digital resources (including applets and e-textbooks) offers increased opportunities for teachers to design their lessons and modify teaching approaches traditionally adopted in the classroom. At the same time, new digital means such as e-textbooks, offering new potential structures to the teacher and new interactions with the users, influences teachers' work at the level of both design and professional development. Also, the study of collective design work taking place in diverse contexts and communities raises the question of collective documentational genesis.

As in the evolution of other theoretical approaches, its use as a framework implies the identification of gaps that lead to new developments within its own theoretical construction. These advances are often strongly demarcated by characteristics of the object or context analyzed. For example, Rocha (2018) introduces the notions of "documentational experience" and "documentational trajectory" as theoretical and methodological tools to analyze teachers' documentation processes over long periods of time.

In this section, we discuss some perspectives of DAD appearing in research on the transition toward digital resources. We address two main questions in this chapter:

- What are the perspectives under which DAD has been used to study to support teachers'/teacher educators' effective transition toward digital resources?
- How is DAD influenced by (and how does DAD influence) these perspectives in terms of networking, extensions, and new areas of research?

This section is structured in the six subsections: DAD, connections with IO, networking of DAD and other theories in the transition toward digital resources, individual and collective documentation work in the transition toward digital resources, the development of DAD in relation to pre-service teachers, using the reflective methodology of DAD to support teachers' meta-cognitive reflections on their practices, and DAD and the design of digital resources. The section closes with final remarks.

12.4.1 DAD, Connections with Instrumental Orchestration

As discussed in the previous section, the framework of IO (Trouche 2004) was created to allow exploration of the ways by which teachers create systematic and intentional arrangements of artifacts and persons at the classroom to facilitate learners' instrumental genesis. Trouche (2005) and Drijvers and Trouche (2008) argue that it is not enough to adapt classical mathematical situations, but teachers must design new situations considering the affordances and constraints of the technologies. Designing new situations partly based on digital resources requires the development of specific skills and knowledge of the teacher.[3] Several research studies that are

---

[3] Concerning the question of knowledge and skills mobilized in a broader perspective of resource use (not only with digital resources), reference can be made to the work of Working Group 3:

based on DAD explore the complexity of teachers' practices in relation to the use of digital resources. To understand this complex work, these studies focus on the skills, knowledge, and expertise of teachers in the context of the design and implementation of situations involving digital resources (e.g., Psycharis and Kalogeria 2018; Ratnayake and Thomas 2018). This work also looks at the (bounded) choices made by teachers and factors that may explain these (bounded) choices. To take these issues into account, we note that explicit links between DAD and IO have been developed as part of research that considers teachers' practice toward the integration of digital technology.

Kozaklı Ülger and Tapan Broutin (2018) use DAD to understand teachers' (bounded) choices in classroom planning in rich digital environments, using DAD and IO in a complementary way. To understand teachers' practice in a technological environment, it considers IO to analyze teachers' actions in a technologically enriched environment, and DAD to determine teachers' (bounded) choices of resource and changes in this process. This case study looks at the practices of a teacher for whom designing and implementing instruction in a technological environment is new. The study highlights an important aspect of this work as "weaving" (Billington 2009) as a common occurrence in observations. They observed teachers' movement with the available tools. Three tools were used: board, computer + screen, and body movements. During the lesson, digital tools were intentionally used, while in spontaneous situations, teachers used wooden boards or gestures.

The complementarity of the two frameworks is also explored in Besnier (2018), who uses DAD to study aspects of teachers' documentation of their process of orchestrating classroom lessons for teaching numbers at kindergarten (4- and 5-year-old pupils) with digital and analogic materials. The research focus is on the teachers' adaptations of resources as well as on their classroom orchestrations. For Besnier, orchestration is considered as part of the document developed by the teacher. Orchestration corresponds to the recombined resources, and the action rules part of the document. In this context orchestrations are the emergent part of the scheme. In this research, Besnier identified a variant of the "link-screen-board orchestration" (Drijvers et al. 2010), called "the manipulatives and software duo" orchestration. This orchestration and its implementation are linked in the case of the teacher to professional knowledge related to importance of verbalization and peer exchanges. To allow pupils to discover the procedures, they must experiment in the technological environment and discuss this experimentation with each other. Besnier argues that it is necessary for the teacher to create a new resource and to implement an orchestration and to make a link between manipulatives and software. The changes in orchestrations observable in classrooms are then considered as the mark of changes in the teachers' resource systems. They reflect on changes in teachers' knowledge.

Considering the importance of IO within teacher documentation, Lucena (2018) and Lucena et al. (2018) propose the notion of "instrumental meta-orchestration" to

---

"Instrumentation, skills, design capacity, expertise"; see Chap. 4 of this book, "Documentation Work, Design Capacity, and Teachers' Expertise in Designing Instruction."

promote teacher reflection about IO with regard to their documentational genesis in integrating digital resources. They work within a composition of IO, sometimes sequenced, sometimes overlapping, focusing on meta-situations, which allow teachers to reflect on the notion of IO.

12.4.2 Networking of DAD and Other Theories in the Transition Toward Digital Resources

The assumptions and challenges, reinforced with existing research work based on DAD over the last decade, suggest advantages of using additional theoretical lens to study phenomena related to teachers' and/or teacher educators' (TEs) documentation work (DW) including the use of digital resources. We now consider attempts to connect DAD with other theoretical frameworks and constructs. One strand of this research targets elaboration and refinement of theoretical terms traditionally used to describe mathematics teachers' work inside and outside the classroom such as "mathematics teacher design" and "mathematics teacher design capacity." Networking of DAD with Brown's (2009) theory of "teachers as designers" is based on the common perception of teacher interaction with curriculum resources by the two theories as a participatory two-way process of mutual adaptation (Pepin et al. 2017). This research is anchored in the French Sésamath association for the design of a grade 10 e-textbook and a European funded project targeting inquiry-based learning in mathematics and science (PRIMAS). The study leads to a new definition of "teacher design capacity" as comprising (1) an orientation or goal, (2) a set of design principles (called robust principles) that are evidence-informed (e.g., from own practice) and supported by justification for their (bounded) choices, and (3) "Reflection-in-action" type of implicit understanding developed in the course of instruction ("design-in-use"). This definition is used to investigate design capacity development stemming from teachers' transformation of digital curriculum resources to (re-)design instruction and work with/in collectives.

Another case of networking, between DAD and Cultural-Historical Activity Theory (CHAT), was triggered by the need to investigate design processes in teacher collectives working on the development of e-textbooks (Gueudet et al. 2016). The authors study the activity system of a community of teachers working in the context of a teacher association (Sésamath) for about 4 years to design/redesign a chapter (functions) of an e-textbook. At the micro-level, DAD allowed the researchers to capture the evolution of resources and rules shared by the community. At the macro-level, CHAT helps them to understand different types of collective geneses that result from tensions in the system indicating a change of the object of the activity at different moments: from designing a "toolkit" for mathematics teachers to interactive exercises and, finally, to a more "classical e-textbook." However, the authors do not provide a theoretical explanation of the term collective geneses. Similarly, Essonnier and Trgalová (2018) connect DAD with Engeström's (1987) activity theory and Fischer's (2001) concept of community-of-interest, as described later in this chapter.

Another strand of studies concerns networking of DAD to theoretical frameworks focusing on aspects of teachers'/TEs' knowledge. Psycharis and Kalogeria (2018) network DAD and the TPACK framework (Mishra and Koehler 2006) to study trainee TEs' DW in technology enhanced mathematics. They investigate which TPACK forms of knowledge targeted by trainee TEs in their documents and which operational invariants are related to these forms of knowledge. The analysis reveals one type of documents emphasizing the T aspect of TPACK (instructive) and two types of documents emphasizing the P aspect of TPACK (explanatory, facilitative). Operational invariants underlying trainee TEs' DW are directly linked to the trainees' teaching practice as well as to their epistemologies concerning the role of technology in the teaching and learning of mathematics and the ways they conceive trainee teachers ("as students"/"of students"). Ratnayake and Thomas (2018) connect the DAD with the theoretical model of *Mathematical Pedagogical Technology Knowledge* (MPTK) (Thomas and Hong 2005) to study what factors influence secondary mathematics teachers' development and implementation of digital technology algebra tasks. Although knowledge is not explicitly considered as a resource in DAD, MPTK includes an extension of the concept of resources to embrace aspects of Schoenfeld's (2010) decision-making theory which includes teacher's knowledge as a primary resource.

Another aspect of networking concerns connections between DAD and frameworks used to study teachers' DW in different subject fields. For instance, Messaoui (2018) connects DAD and *Personal Information Management* (Jones 2007) to study the operational invariants underlying the scheme of how a teacher classifies a new resource in her/his resource system. The analysis, based on the observation of teachers' classification of resources in using computers, reveals operational invariants related to didactic knowledge (e.g., type of activity, teaching grade) as well as knowledge linked to digital literacy (e.g., create a file, drag and drop a folder). Another example is the study of Jameau and Le Hénaff (2018) who combine DAD and the *Joint action theory in didactics* (Sensevy 2011) to explore how a science teacher uses digital resources (e.g., videos) for her *Content and Language Integrated Learning* lessons to support language and science learning.

12.4.3 Individual and Collective Documentation Work in the Transition Toward Digital Resources

In their seminal article introducing DAD, Gueudet and Trouche (2009a) emphasize teachers' involvement in professional collectives as one out of three fundamental factors of the theory. Despite this early emphasis on the collective dimension, they do not theoretically detail it further. Rather, they describe teachers' DW as highly personal, as it results from their professional, social, and personal background. It is thus interesting to see how this distinction or interplay between collective and individual DW is treated in the ongoing development of DAD.

The need for further development of this interplay is spurred by the evolution of digital technologies offering both new opportunities for learning formats for teachers, teacher educators, etc., and new forms of collaboration (e.g., e-mail communication, designing and sharing of resources on platforms, and noninstitutional digital spaces). Such new formats and forms are the primary focus in our selection of papers from both inside and outside the *Re(s)source 2018 International Conference*.

Gueudet and Trouche (2011) and Gueudet et al. (2012) investigate an innovative, online teacher-training program in France (Pairform@nce) designed to sustain ICT integration but from two different perspectives, teachers and online teacher educators. Both papers focus on the teachers' collective DW and provide empirical evidence of professional development in terms of documentational genesis. However, in this early stage in the development of DAD, the conception of the interplay between the individual and collective in DW is rather vague. In recognition of this, Gueudet and Trouche (2011) suggest further developments of this interplay: "What is the 'common part' of the individual documents generated by a collective work? To what extent is it possible to speak of a common knowledge coming from a community documentation genesis?" (p. 410).

More recently, Carton (2018a) and Essonnier and Trgalová (2018) investigate entirely new digital forms of teacher collaboration. Carton (2018a) studies how teachers use non-institutional digital spaces to enrich their DW using an early definition of "the social" by Gueudet and Trouche (2008). The paper provides empirical evidence that these spaces offer favorable settings for collective work. Essonnier and Trgalová (2018) study the influence of designers' resource systems and knowledge on their (bounded) choices when collaboratively designing a c-book (c for creative) in the MC^2-project (Mathematical Creativity Squared Project – http://mc2-project.eu/) by supplementing DAD with activity theory (Engeström 1987) and the concept of Community-of-interest (Fischer 2001). Networking DAD with other approaches, the authors argue, provides a more coherent theoretical conceptualization of the collaborative design, where they foreground the designers' joint enterprise and social interactions by viewing the collaborative design "as a collective DG (documentational genesis), starting from a resource or a set of resources contributed to the joint enterprise by the designers and resulting in a c-book resource" (Essonnier and Trgalová 2018, p. 62).

The work of other professionals rather than teachers also inspired and promoted developments of DAD. For example, Kieran et al. (2013) extend the framework to the collective activity of design researchers (i.e., the authors), contributing convincing analytical interpretations of the interplay between individual and collective documentational genesis. Focusing on "the team's documentational genesis" (p. 1048), they analyze what they call a "taken-as-shared genesis" by using a dual perspective. An individual perspective: "a document relates directly to the cognitive structures of those who have been involved in its design" (p. 1047), combined with a social perspective: "Each round of the process (of genesis) encouraged the sharing of individual IOs (Operational invariants) (and associated ARs (action rules)), so that eventually the final version of the (...) document came to be based on a shared set of IOs" (p. 1049). However, the authors do not theoretically elaborate these concepts and processes to provide a coherent taken-as-shared approach.

Hence, in recent developments of DAD, we see promising theoretical and analytical proposals of how to interpret the interplay between individual and collective DW in the transition to digital resources, either by linking DAD to other theoretical approaches or by extending the framework beyond primary and lower secondary teachers' work. Despite this, there is a need for further theoretical elaboration of the interplay to provide more accurate answers to the requests mentioned by Gueudet and Trouche (2011).

12.4.4 The Development of DAD in Relation to Pre-service Teachers Exploiting Digital Resources

In the first publications introducing DAD (Gueudet and Trouche 2008, 2009a, b, 2010), and even in more recent ones (Besnier 2016), the research considers teachers in the middle of their careers. Prieur (2016) includes teachers at the beginning of their careers in his investigations of teachers' documentational genesis (the heart of DAD). Nonetheless, further studies of teachers' documentational genesis are needed. Indeed, the elements of a scheme's development often take place during initial teacher training.

Nongni and DeBlois (2018) discuss documentational genesis in the transition of pre-service teachers to becoming teachers and their "epistemological stances" when planning lessons. Leroyer (2018) investigates the influence of these stances (Bailleul and Thémines 2013) on the interactions between teachers and their resources. According to them, the teacher can adopt three epistemological stances: the ancient pupil, the university student, and the teacher (DeBlois 2012). Nongni and DeBlois (2018) observe the influence of these epistemological stances on the documentational genesis, in part on the use patterns and arrangement variables. They also observe the influence of pre-service teacher's documentational genesis on epistemological stances, in particular how documentational genesis allows the transition of pre-service teachers to becoming teachers and their epistemological stances when they are interested in students' understanding. Nongni and DeBlois (2017, 2018) also orient the documentational genesis toward the arrangement variables, artifacts and didactic variables, when studying how the pre-service teachers exploit digital resources. They posit a reciprocal influence among these variables that could provide a framework for understanding the documentational genesis of pre-service teachers with regard to digital resources, by observing these epistemological stances (DeBlois 2012). The epistemological stances adopted by the pre-service teachers can then be used to understand pre-service teachers' development in their anticipation of activities while planning their teaching.

Assis et al. (2018) also investigate pre-service teachers' activities, within a *documentational trajectory* (Rocha 2018), and go toward the understanding of what they call a *resource metamorphosis*, from the "resource to study" toward the "resource to teach." When studying an early-career teacher's resource system, they analyze the pre-service mathematics teacher training to consider how they structure their resource systems. The concept of *resource system metamorphosis* helps them understand the transition from a system of study-oriented resources to a teaching-oriented resource system. Their study presents the activities of two teachers who transpose between two classes of different situations: one structured to perform mathematical tasks using Dynamic Geometry and another to create tasks for students to learn mathematics using Dynamic Geometry. The results suggest that pre-service teachers rely on their study-oriented resources, including textbooks to develop their *teaching-oriented resource system*, which includes dynamic geometry tasks.

Ignácio et al. (2018) focus on a pre-service teacher who is developing a supervised internship project that involves two cycles of the production and use of a digital textbook chapter on the role teaching. The analysis of the production of this material shows that, in addition to the visible adaptations of printed textbook parts for the digital medium, the pre-service teacher mobilized a vast system of resources previously developed. The analysis provides evidence that the pre-service teacher has developed professional knowledge related to the development and use of digital resources for the teaching of functions.

12.4.5 Using a Reflective Methodology of DAD to Support Teachers' Metacognitive Reflections on Their Practices

The term "reflective investigation methodology" was introduced in the context of DAD to study teachers' DW (Pepin et al. 2013). Enlarging the term beyond methods of data collection and analysis, Ignácio et al. (2018) use it to organize a teacher education program for pre-service teachers involving design, use, reflection and validation of an e-textbook chapter.

Reflecting about one's own documentation process also appeared as an important tool for action research. Nascimento Jr. et al. (2018) use DAD, networked to other theories, to analyze and modify their own actions while designing and experimenting with innovative lessons integrating digital technology for university science teaching and learning. Among other aspects, their own documentational genesis was analyzed considering the analysis of students' instrumentation. Conventional and innovative digital resources interacted and played relevant roles in the process. Drawing attention to their own experiences, they acknowledge how little they can control the outcomes of such interactions.

DAD research which involves a self-reflective methodology allows the subject to focus on his/her own documentation, documentational genesis, systems of document, and documentation work, in particular, on how one creates his/her own "individual schemes of use" (Gueudet and Trouche 2009a, p. 204). For example, Nascimento Jr. et al. (2018) argue that an attempt to adapt multiple materials (including traditional textbooks, e-books, online familiar and unfamiliar materials making use of large databases) demands that teachers require not only design capacity to prepare lessons, but also expertise and decision-making skills. DAD can help teacher educators to be aware of these needs, as is discussed in (Males et al. 2018, p. 207) with regard to emerging methodology "What do teachers attend to in curriculum materials?"

Thomas and Edson (2018) also focus on the need to consider meta-cognitive processes when analyzing teachers' documentation work. They examine teachers' conceptions of digital instructional resource as a way to understand how digital resources impact on teachers' work. They contrast teachers' definition of theoretical terms. As regards DAD, they consider resource and document from the teachers' perspective (i.e., who designs, selects, and implements resources). They show that while defining the term, the teachers "tended not to distinguish between the resource and the genesis through which it becomes a document" (p. 343). Thus, they argue, teachers' DW may also occur in the meta-cognitive process of defining "what counts" as digital instructional materials in a more general sense.

12.4.6 DAD and the Design of Digital Resources

DAD has been used to analyze not only teachers' work but also the work of other professionals (researchers, software designers, artists, etc.) involved in the process of designing digital resources. It has also been used to interpret, mainly for classifying, actions and principles related to the design of digital resources, as well as to design curricular digital resource for their effective use by teachers.

Essonnier and Trgalová (2018) consider the DAD as a tool to identify the designer's resource system and its influence in choosing digital resources, which is consonance with the motivation of Bellemain et al. (2018), for using the DAD to identify and establish requirements for a web environment to support teachers' DW and the design of digital resources. Indeed, they develop the idea of a web document, based on the DAD concept of a document: software composed of other software programs or digital components, that is, a set of digital resources and utilization schemes designed by a teacher for a specific teaching aim. They propose a classification for such resources (static, dynamic and active) depending on the kind of content displayed and/or interaction made possible with these digital documents. For them, an activity is interpreted as a web document activity, since teachers organize both the activity to be done by students and students' actions in the activity, generating a new document. Design issues are considered further in Sect. 12.6.

12.4.7 Final Remarks

DAD has its origins within the digital resources integration problem, and its evolution within digital scenarios brings into the approach new needs and new concepts such as *documentational expertise, documentational trajectory*, and *metamorphosis of the resource system*. These new concepts and tools now comprise part of the framework. In its origin, the networking of theories, sometimes articulated and sometimes contrasted, has led to new networks that bring new issues into DAD discourse, especially within teachers' transition toward digital resource systems.

The potential of networking between IO and DAD is especially important in research. It sheds light on how to support teachers' use of digital resources and, at the same time, the effects on their documentation as well as the correlation between teachers' documentation and teachers' choice of resources. This dialectic leads us to consider both frameworks for understanding teachers' effective use of digital resources and also goes toward an extension of IO into an instrumental meta-orchestration framework to teachers' education toward using IO as a support to design this use. The use of DAD in teacher education goes even further, with extensions of DAD examining the beginning of the documentation process within initial teacher training, as well as extending the idea of resource systems to pre-service teachers; a reflective methodology is important in dealing with teachers' initial education. This elicitation of the characteristics of teachers' documentation can also be used to improve one's own practice in action research. Characteristics of teachers' work on the web also lead to perspectives of analyzing collective documentation and individual documentation within the collective work. The research considered in this section suggests the need for more investigations and greater precision regarding the collective documentation approach. The continuous evolution of research using DAD to support teachers' effective transition toward digital resource also leads to the emergence of new concepts and research tools for improving DAD.

12.5 Digital Resources and Teacher Education

Samet Okumus, Amanda Thomas, Eleonora Faggiano, Osama Swidan, Elisabete Cunha, Elena Naftaliev and Rosilângela Lucena

Mathematics teachers are the principal actors who are responsible for planning and enacting school mathematical activity; and their enactment of technology into the mathematics classroom is influenced by a wide range of factors (Assude et al. 2010; Zbiek and Hollebrands 2008). The factors of technology integration are like a jigsaw puzzle in that each component must be supported and merged into another for a successful implementation of technology into practice. A missing, or weakly connected, piece in this jigsaw puzzle may impede or impoverish the use of technology.

One factor that influences the enactment of technology in mathematics classrooms is teachers' knowledge. For instance, the TPACK framework (Koehler and Mishra 2009) describes aspects of teacher knowledge that interact to influence how teachers integrate technology for the teaching of content (i.e., mathematics). Assude et al. (2010) categorize some of the factors that influence mathematics teachers' utilization of technology into four components: "the social, political, economic, and cultural level, the mathematical and epistemological level, the school and institutional level, the classroom and didactical level" (p. 406). Heid (2008) stresses the importance of how teachers use technology and how their educational beliefs affect educational settings and student learning with technology, since students are likely to use technology in the way that their teacher designed curriculum. She draws from research studies to highlight that teachers who have constructivist teaching beliefs are more likely to integrate technology into curriculum and allow students to be explorers through the use of technology.

12.5.1 Teaching Activity Prior to a Mathematics Lesson

Artzt et al. (2015) characterize mathematics teaching activity in three stages: decisions teachers make before, during, and after a lesson. Teachers' activity prior to a mathematics lesson includes lesson planning and considering the affordances and constraints of tools and resources to be integrated in the lesson. During the lesson, teachers' work focuses on monitoring and regulating. Evaluating and revising are the main mathematics teaching activities after a lesson.

12.5.1.1 Lesson Planning

Artigue (2002) identifies four key dimensions in technology-enhanced mathematics learning: the mathematics, the teacher, the learner, and the tool. These dimensions also apply to the documentation work in which teachers engage prior to teaching a lesson (Gueudet and Trouche 2009a). Along with the four key dimensions, Zbiek and Hollebrands (2008) identify external factors that must be considered when planning for technology-enhanced mathematics teaching, including ready access to technology and support staff, technology training and professional development, time constraints, logistical constraints, technology and device availability, and the availability of curriculum materials that capitalize on technology. The relationship between curriculum materials and technology resources is particularly salient to consider as teachers engage in documentation work prior to teaching mathematics lessons because the nature of this work requires teachers to select and integrate curriculum materials with technology and other resources.

With respect to the epistemological stance of curriculum materials, Choppin (2018) finds that teachers who engage in lesson design work with new types of curriculum materials tend to exhibit practices aligned with the curriculum programs to which they are most accustomed. Thus, when teachers plan lessons that integrate emerging technology resources with existing curriculum materials, prior practices and habituation to curriculum resource should be considered. Teachers' documentation work during the planning phase of lessons also includes the identification of potential resources that could enhance the mathematical and didactical goals of the lesson. In defining what constitutes digital instructional materials, findings from Thomas and Edson (2018) suggest that teachers consider not only the resource itself but how, where, and by whom it might be used. That is, teachers consider resources in relation to the context and learners, as well as their potential use for the lesson.

Zbiek and Hollebrands (2008) note that "teachers' conceptions, beliefs, knowledge, and use of technology seemed to influence the activities they created for their students who were using technology to learn mathematics" (p. 310). According to Farrell's (1996) findings, technology affects teachers' selections of tasks and activity types in mathematics curriculum. Based on her research study, Farrell (1996) observes that teachers are more likely to prefer using activities that require investigation and group work when they use technology. In addition, with the use of technology, teachers adopt tasks requiring more problem solving and higher level thinking (Farrell 1996). Such preferences could be considered as a result of shifts of teachers' and students' roles when technology is integrated. When planning to teach mathematics with technology, teachers should consider the resources available to them, the affordances and constraints associated with those resources (Kennewell 2001) and, more importantly, how those resources relate to the lesson's mathematical and didactical goals (Artigue 2002).

12.5.1.2 Affordances and Constraints of Tools

In recent years, digital tools and online resources have become increasingly accessible for teachers. When teachers incorporate technologies into mathematics lessons, "they may also utilize activities and examples from curricula that use technology. Finally, they include representations and strategies specific to technology" (Hollebrands et al. 2016, p. 273). However, as Dick and Burrill (2016) emphasize, "realizing the unique benefits of dynamic interactive mathematics technologies to enhance students' conceptual learning of mathematics depends heavily on teachers having the skills and knowledge necessary to make sound judgments in choosing and using these technologies in the classroom" (p. 43).

Mathematical tools have different affordances and constraints for mathematical learning. An affordance is considered by means of what an environment offers the agent who uses the tool (Gibson 1977) and "a constraint of an environment is related to affordance in as much as it specifies what the environment does not afford" (Monaghan 2016, p. 168). Okumus and Ipek (2018) emphasize that teachers should be able to identify not only the affordances but also constraints of the tools. In Okumus and Ipek's (2018) study, pre-service mathematics teachers work out the Triangle Inequality Theorem with hands-on manipulatives and digital tools, and identify tools that do not "stay true to the mathematics" (Dick and Burrill 2016,

p. 29). Tools may give rise to misconceptions or obstacles for students, and teachers have important roles in identifying them (Okumus and Ipek 2018).

Dick and Burrill (2016) use design principles that may assist teachers in choosing digital tools. For example, according to the *Sandbox Principle*, "technology-based environments should be constrained to minimize the change that students inadvertently escape or get lost in irrelevant aspects of the technology" (p. 29). A constraint in the design of a digital tool may also give an opportunity for mathematical learning, rescuing students from irrelevant aspects of the technology (Dick and Burrill 2016; Naftaliev and Yerushalmy 2017).

Naftaliev and Yerushalmy (2017) design interactive diagrams that are "relatively small unit(s) of interactive text in e-textbooks or another materials" (p. 154) with built-in constraints. Students generate different representations using the tool and attempt to overcome the built-in constraints of interactive diagrams by modifying the given representations or constructing new ones. According to the researchers, constraints of interactive diagrams play an important role in mathematical investigation. In this sense, Naftaliev and Yerushalmy's (2017) use of constraints of interactive diagrams seems to align with Kennewell's (2001) perspective who asserted:

> The affordances are the attributes of the setting which provide potential for action; the constraints are the conditions and relationships amongst attributes which provide structure and guidance for the course of actions… Constraints are not the opposite of affordances; they are complementary, and equally necessary for activity to take place (p. 106).

Dick and Burrill (2016) claim that constraints of digital tools are helpful in directing students to think mathematically and "serve to support student attention and focus on the mathematical implications of the actions they take on the mathematical objects in the environment" (p. 30). Some researchers argue that constraints of digital tools can give students more opportunities for mathematical learning than hands-on manipulatives (Dick and Burrill 2016; Kaput 1995). According to Kaput (1995), "most physical actions on physical manipulatives do not leave a trace sufficiently complete to reconstitute the actions that produced them" (Kaput 1995, p. 167). Dick and Burrill (2016) claim that hands-on manipulatives do not have any constraints and "can be arranged in ways that are mathematically nonsensical" (p. 30). On the other hand, digital tools can be constrained, which allow for removing irrelevant aspects of the technology. The built-in constraints can assist students with focusing on relevant aspects of technology that are linked to mathematics.

In recent years, several researchers have used duos of artifacts: pairs of hands-on manipulatives and digital tools that support one another (Faggiano et al. 2016; Maschietto and Soury-Lavergne 2013; Voltolini 2018). In Cunha's (2018) study, students follow written directions and fold papers during the origami activities. Then, they are asked to reproduce the required construction steps using a dynamic geometry program. The researcher states that the activity enables students to explore the mathematical relationships between hands-on manipulatives and the digital tool and stimulates students to produce representations to accomplish the origami task.

In Maschietto and Soury-Lavergne's (2013) research study, primary school students produce turning gestures using a gear train of five wheels (Pascaline) to perform arithmetic operations. Based on the feedback from the pascaline students used, Maschietto and Soury-Lavergne design a new artifact (e-pascaline) that is the pascaline digital counterpart. The design of the e-pascaline is influenced by student-produced signs that emerge during the use of the pascaline, and the semiotic potential of the e-pascaline is promoted by the continuity (similar usages) and discontinuity (different usages) between the two artifacts. Design decisions for the duo of the artifacts are made with regard to didactic goals, so that using one artifact adds value to the other. The researchers stressed "that the pascaline also has added value compared with the e-pascaline, which explains why one cannot be substituted for the other" (Maschietto and Soury-Lavergne 2013, p. 969).

In this line, Voltolini (2018) proposes a duo, combining digital and pen-and-paper environments, through triangle-construction tasks, taking into attention the links between the two, highlighting the continuity and discontinuities of the duo of artifacts to promote "the evolution of pupil knowledge" (p. 87). Also, Faggiano et al. (2016) investigate the synergic use of manipulative and digital artifacts (passing from one to the other) to construct and conceptualize axial symmetry and its properties, trying to understand how this synergic action is developed so that each task improves the learning of the others.

12.5.2 Teaching Activity During a Mathematics Lesson

According to Artzt et al. (2015), the main tasks of mathematics teachers during lesson implementation are *monitoring* and *regulating*. When the teacher monitors students, he or she "observes, listens to, and elicits participation of students on an ongoing basis to assess student learning and disposition toward mathematics" (p. 87). Regulation refers to in-the-moment lesson adjustments, "teachers must be flexible and able to modify their lessons based on their formative assessment of the students" (p. 75).

12.5.2.1 Monitoring

Researchers have characterized teachers' utilization of digital tools in technology-enhanced mathematics learning with a focus on how they position technology with regard to mathematics and students. For example, Drijvers et al. (2010) observe three teachers' dynamic algebra java applets integration into the mathematics classroom with a focus on how they orchestrate the whole-class discussions. The results indicate that each teacher's focus differs. The first teacher, who focuses on students' learning using technology, utilizes student-centered orchestrations. On the other hand, the second teacher, who focuses on conventional representations of mathematics, associates technology with representations. The third teacher, whose focus is technology, gives technology directions and utilizes teacher-centered orchestrations.

12 Transitions Toward Digital Resources: Change, Invariance, and Orchestration

Swidan et al. (2018) identify the orchestration processes of teachers who aim to promote inquiry-based learning in a classroom setting where students collaborate in small groups and use digital resources. The researchers pay special attention to the ways the teachers use the digital resources to boost inquiry-based learning. While teachers are monitoring students, they stand beside students without intervening for a while. This passive teacher action is noted as necessary but insufficient to boost the inquiry processes of students. After a short passive intervention, observing what students are doing, asking students about their exploration processes and requiring them to provide a short summary of their reasoning are found to be helpful in focusing the teachers' attention on the learning objects.

Erfjord (2011) examines three mathematics teachers' utilization of a dynamic geometry program and how teachers organize conditions for instrumental genesis (e.g., organization of students' work, central focus of lessons, etc.). Classroom activities include drawing, constructing geometric figures, and working on parallel and perpendicular mathematical objects using technological and non-technological tools. Two of the teachers focus on technical aspects of the technology and instrumentalization-related tasks (e.g., making constructions that did not mess up). On the other hand, the teacher whose focus is instrumentation (e.g., have students discuss different methods of constructions) utilizes student-centered orchestrations. Tabach (2011) associates a mathematics teacher's orchestration of digital tools with her technological pedagogical knowledge. The researcher reports that the mathematics teacher utilizes more student-centered utilizations over time as her technological pedagogical content knowledge changes.

12.5.2.2 Regulating

Research indicates that teachers regulate their instruction by making *ad hoc* decisions due to feedback from students and factors such as time shortages (Artzt et al. 2015; Cayton et al. 2017; Drijvers et al. 2010). Stockero and Van Zoest (2013) emphasize *pivotal teaching moments* that may prompt teachers to regulate their lessons. They define pivotal teaching moments as "instance(s) in a classroom lesson in which an interruption in the flow of the lesson provides the teacher an opportunity to modify instruction in order to extend or change the nature of students' mathematical understanding" (Stockero and Van Zoest 2013, p. 127). Cayton et al. (2017) identify pivotal teaching moments in technology-rich geometry classrooms. They find that a teacher who utilizes student-centered approaches pursues students' thinking and extends their mathematical thinking by asking follow-up questions in response to pivotal teaching moments. Leung and Bolite-Frant (2015) emphasize mathematics teachers' regulating of instruction as opening a *pedagogical space* when they use a digital tool with *discrepancy potential*. According to the researchers:

> The discrepancy potential of a tool is a pedagogical space generated by (i) feedback due to the nature of the tool or design of the task that possibly deviates from the intended mathe-

matical concept or (ii) uncertainty created due to the nature of the tool or design of the task that requires the tool users to make decisions (p. 212).

On the other hand, teachers may not manage to capitalize on the discrepancy potential of tools. For example, Ruthven et al. (2008) find that one mathematics teacher conceals anomalous situations of dynamic geometry software and makes changes to the lesson on the fly. However, teachers' mathematical knowledge and familiarity with the technology is an important factor for such *ad hoc* decisions.

12.5.3 Teaching Activity After a Lesson

According to Artzt et al. (2015), as a post-active stage of teaching, teachers should be able to evaluate and revise their lessons using "information from evaluations of student learning and instructional practices" (p. 88) that should develop students' mathematical thinking better than their earlier plans. Self-reflectivity may contribute in capturing the important changes that digital resources bring to the teachers' practice. In this line of thought, researchers emphasize that pre-service and in-service teachers should be supported in building up reflective competencies or in becoming *reflective practitioners* (Atkinson 2012; Jaworski 2014).

12.5.3.1 Evaluating

Self-reflectivity is not usually a spontaneous practice and requires motivation. The impact of teachers' beliefs about the role of digital resources in teaching and learning of mathematics plays an important role in technology integration, and "the greatest challenge for professional development aimed at effectively using dynamic interactive mathematics technologies: moving the teachers' tool perspective to one supporting *student* investigation and exploration" (Dick and Burrill 2016, p. 46). Analysis and design of mathematics tasks, the exploration of overarching ideas linked to mathematical contents and the analysis of videotaped classroom situations may enhance teachers' instruction (e.g., Scherrer and Stein 2013). However, as Barth-Cohen et al. (2018) point out, videotaping of classroom discourse remains a challenging and understudied tool.

Lucena et al. (2018) use IO to develop teacher capabilities in integrating digital resource in classroom and propose a new framework, *instrumental meta-orchestration*, that embraces theory and practice. According to the researchers, "an instrumental meta-orchestration is a systematic and intentional design of artifacts and human beings, in an environment of formation by an agent, to execute a meta-situation of formation which aims to guide teachers in their instrumental genesis about the theoretical model of instrumental orchestration" (Lucena et al. 2018, p. 300). A sequence of orchestrations is integrated, sequenced and imbricated to enable theoretical reflection on the practice of IO. Instrumental meta-orchestration requires active involvement in observation, analysis of discourse using a theoretical lens, and also promotes reflection on different aspects (e.g., content, theory, and practice), particularly when a digital tool integration is utilized.

12.5.3.2 Revising

Several researchers have developed frameworks to assist teachers, teacher educators or curriculum writers in evaluating, creating and refining tasks that support students' thinking (Naftaliev 2018; Scherrer and Stein 2013; Sherman et al. 2017; Trocki and Hollebrands 2018). These frameworks bring theories into practices as teachers revise and (re)create their tasks/lessons embracing a critical lens. For example, Sherman et al. (2017) combine two fine-grained frameworks for pre-service teachers: cognitive demands of tasks (high-level vs low-level) (Stein and Smith 1998) and the roles of technology in using these tasks (amplifier vs. reorganizer) (Pea 1985). The researchers find that pre-service teachers most often create high-level tasks that may support students' thinking. Furthermore, they most often use technology as a reorganizer in which "technology has the capability to transform students' activity, supporting a shift in students' mathematical thinking to something that would be difficult or impossible to achieve without it" (Sherman and Cayton 2015, p. 307).

Naftaliev (2018) examines pre-service teachers' interactions with interactive curriculum materials. The study uses a semiotic framework for analyzing the pedagogical functionality of interactive materials (Naftaliev and Yerushalmy 2017). Naftaliev's (2018) study includes five interaction stages. Pre-service teachers first develop intended curriculum with interactive materials, then analyze classroom scenarios where interactive materials are enacted. In the third stage, pre-service teachers build upon their experiences to develop comic representations of scenarios about classes engaged with the interactive materials. The comics are developed in LessonSketch (Herbst et al. 2011), a media-rich environment that "allows creating experiences around classroom scenarios performed with cartoon characters in the form of a slide show" (Naftaliev 2018, p. 305). During the fourth stage, teachers engage in learning mathematics units with interactive materials and reflect on their own processes of learning. In the last stage, the pre-service teachers design their own unit for mathematics teaching and learning with interactive materials and presented an episode of a classroom scenario in which the class is engaged with the units. The semiotic framework for pedagogical functionality of interactive materials and the five-stage procedure enable facilitating the pre-service teachers' design processes, to share, to discuss, and to modify their decisions.

12.5.4 Concluding Remarks

Adequately incorporating technology in the mathematics classroom may be a battle many teachers encounter. Some may only use it sparingly, while others do not use it at all. This, almost certainly, stems from the traditional nature in which teachers have learned and subsequently teach. With the use of technology, teachers may find an increase in classroom discourse as a positive outcome. Applets, computer software, calculators, and other forms of technology may allow students to think more conceptually while offering multiple representations quickly. As a result, students may be able to have more focused discussion about why or how something works, rather than just accept one way of doing something. With technology use, questioning strategies may also change (Zbiek and Hollebrands 2008). The use of technology can increase the questions that can be asked about a given situation and even heighten the demand of questions. However, "technology itself is not a panacea that will remedy students' difficulties as they learn mathematics. Rather, it is teachers' decisions about how, when, and where to use technology that determine whether its use will enhance or hinder students' understandings of mathematics" (Hollebrands and Zbiek 2004, p. 259).

12.6 The Design of Learning Environments with the Use of Digital Resources

Christian Mercat, Franck Bellemain, Marianne van Dijke-Droogers,
Pedro Lealdino Filho, Anders Støle Fidje, Tiphaine Carton, Jorge Gaona,
Ricardo Tibúrcio and Anderson Rodrigues

The use of digital resources in learning environments, designed and used in a wide variety of ways, is growing. In this context, the discussion of the effectiveness of a designed resource for stimulating learning is an important debate, requiring research in this design process. In this chapter, we will discuss two approaches to gain more information about how to design digital resources: (1) design *for use* and (2) design *in use*. After explaining this difference, we describe how this distinction can shed light on different approaches to digital resources design for learning. Digital resources used in any given didactic situation may range over many different types of resources, and encompassing this complexity in a single theoretical framework is challenging. Hypothetical Learning Trajectories (HLT) (Simon 1995; Simon and Tzur 2004) is a means that can help structure the context and use of a design. IO and the DAD can function as pivotal theoretical constructs to observe teachers' designs. These two approaches can guide the two forms of designs, we have introduced, involving their collective aspects in the life-cycle of a resource, going through diverse disseminations, appropriations, uses and redesigns. These redesigns, ultimately addressed to the students, happen in a variety of contexts ranging from horizontal (socially creative and collaborative group work) to more vertical situations in a one-to-many dissemination from a "guru" to her followers or informal numerical spaces such as blogs or social media.

12.6.1 Design for and in Use

There are various approaches to design, with regard to the use and design of (digital) resources. In this part of the text, we elaborate on "design *for use*" (1) and "design *in use*" (2).

By design *for use*, we refer to studies where a theoretically based design includes conjectures and hypotheses about the way (digital) resources can be used to promote learning in practice: we look at studies that focus on the design of learning environments based on theories, sometimes in combination with teaching skills. In this approach, we focus on the teacher's system of resources and on ways to structure all elements involved in the implementation, such as the necessary and specific educational software engineering, the role of various actors, and the role of instrumentation and instrumentalization.

By "design *in use*," we refer to studies that focus on the way in which learning environments with digital resources are used, particularly through the orchestration of the use, although envisioned a priori by the designers but put into practice by teachers and students. Investigating how this is actually done in practice is a rich source about what works and how it works for further agile design loops, rapidly taking into account actual use. Based on these two approaches, linked in a dialectic way, we can enrich the knowledge about the design of stimulating learning environments with digital resources. Of course, the line between design *for use* and design *in use* is not so clear because the learning environment design already anticipates usage, and the actual use by teachers implies in return adaptations, additions, modifications or in-depth changes of these environments. This ambiguity is related to the teacher's own work, which, for the orchestration of an environment rich in technology, finally develops an activity close to that of an engineer and assistants rather than the usual metaphor of the orchestral conductor where each musician should master his/her own instrument. The difficulty of clearly distinguishing the two designs *for use* and *in use* is also relative to the vocabulary. The verbs we use when talking about the actions of either a computer engineer or a teacher are more or less the same: they both *conceive, design, elaborate, develop*, and *create* resources, but the level of actions is usually different, leading to the design of technical resource for the first and pedagogical resource for the second, all addressed ultimately to the final user, the student. To use a concrete example in order to try to explicit the difference, let us take the case of the use of videos as pedagogical resource. It is a commonly used type of resource, and for the needs of its didactic exploitation, many adjustments can be useful: indexation, selection of extracts, insertion of subtitles and comments, incrustation, etc. The development of interfaces that allow such adjustments is typically a design *for use* issue and their use by the teacher is design *in use*.

The dialectic between design *for use* and design *in use* translates into an articulation between two engineering process with a certain tension between them, on the one hand, the design, founded by theoretical principles, of resources and supports, structures and bindings, for the teacher to use, and, on the other hand, the need for support structuring his actual orchestration, offering some flexibility and documenting the needed adjustments and revisions.

To better highlight this dialectic between design *for use* and design *in use*, and the articulation that it assumes between production-engineering and use-engineering, we can use the elements of IO and associate at some point the design *for use* with a didactical configuration, its elaboration by the engineer and its configuration by the teacher and the design *in use* when the exploitation mode and didactical performance are the primary concerns.

12.6.2 Tackling Complexity

Designing and developing resources and their supports for teachers and their pupils to use are an extremely broad and complex problem; thus even if we limit the study to digital resources, there are many kinds of resources and many ways to use them. A first step to reduce this complexity is suggested by Adler (2000) who proposes a classification of resources as *object* and *action*. In other words, inspired by the IO and the DAD, the classification of resources is based on their own characteristics and their utilization schemes:

– Developed by the teacher for the instrumentation and instrumentalization of these resources.
– Developed by learners when these resources are involved in activities.

Silva (2018) develops this theoretical framework to provide a basis for specifications of a digital system that allows teachers to describe and store resources by integrating them into his/her resource system according to their specific characteristics and utilization schemes. We regard the creation of such systems, for the organization and articulation of existing resources, as having potential to enrich the range of object-action-activity of the teacher.

12.6.3 Designing New Resources for Use

The engineering processes underlying the creation of these resources and supports are various and depend on the kind of resource conceived. Indeed, Tchounikine (2011) argues that we do not implement the same theoretical and methodological

12 Transitions Toward Digital Resources: Change, Invariance, and Orchestration

principles in, for example, designing a microworld[4] or a supporting environment for collaborative learning.

In the context of design *for use* of digital resources, an important line of research and development is interested in the conception of artifacts that effectively enable the teacher to offer mathematical activities to the learners in a computational environment. Typically, microworlds, simulations or games are considered useful in activities designed to foster mathematical thinking. Common software of choice in school mathematics is dynamic geometry systems, but we are interested as well in more general microworlds and simulations, offering tools which may be:

– Used by the teacher for the orchestration of didactical situations.
– Used by the learner for the exploration and the resolution of problems related to specific mathematical content.

Many other parameters have to be taken into account: the context of design; individual or group use (and, in the latter case, collaborative or cooperative); the context of use; whether *for use* in the presence of the teacher, collectively in synchronized distance learning or individually in asynchronous learning. We focus here on the contexts of a few examples.

Designing a new resource *for use* may be approached from a multidisciplinary, even transdisciplinary, perspective. The design *for use* of new resources can be analyzed with regard to the "transposition informatique" (Balacheff 1994) supported by a prior analysis of the epistemological, cognitive, didactic, and informatic dimensions. *Didactical Informatic Engineering* (Tiburcio and Bellemain 2018), a rereading of the didactic engineering (Artigue 1990) considering the Information Technology (IT) dimension, proposes a systematic, operational and anchored approach in the didactics of the mathematics of the "transposition informatique."

By integrating the IT dimension to the didactic engineering, it is a matter of carefully analyzing the actual contributions of IT to support the mathematical activity of the learners. Thanks to the interfaces and operational capabilities of the computer, Siqueira and Bellemain (2018) are particularly interested in the contribution of dynamic representations and articulations between these representations. Such a resource can create an interactive object that provides feedback on abstract notions it represents. The theoretical and methodological principles used in didactical informatic engineering and the specification (design) of these digital resources are rooted in epistemology, the theory of semiotic registers of representation (Duval 1993), the theory of didactical situations (Brousseau 1997) and the Anthropological Theory of Didactics (Chevallard 2002).

As an example of an implementation of this specific didactic informatic engineering model, we consider the LEMATEC project (www.lematec.net.br), in which design of artifacts allows for the dynamic articulation of various representations of mathematical objects. The mathematical contents addressed by these resources are the notion of function (Function Studium, Bellemain et al. 2016), the conics (Conic Studium, Siqueira and Bellemain 2018), and area and perimeter (Magnitude

---

[4] See Hoyles & Noss (1992) for an explication of this term.

Studium, Rodrigues et al. 2018). In the context of teaching, the "designing-a-new-resource" open question can become the guiding thread of the teaching of various disciplinary contents with varying focus depending on the specific content approach. In the study of Lealdino Filho and Mercat (2018) on teaching computational thinking in classroom environments, unplugged resources can be used to promote computational thinking, and this activity leads the students to *design* digital resources. Material resources are therefore designed *for use* and digital resources are not the initial teaching resource but the *product* of the activity. This study, in the Computer-Science unplugged framework, elaborates computational thinking competences through implementing a design without an a priori use of computers. An initial step in the convergent thinking phase (Mercat et al. 2017) is describing impressions, beliefs about what is experienced, here a magical trick but generative art and optical illusions in other works. In order to express them, thinking and expressing takes place, iteratively replacing an abstract and subjective construct, by a concrete, objective, and meaningful method which makes any information-processing agent return the expected result. Solving the task of writing an algorithm to perform the magical trick and to solve this particular problem did not need the use of any digital resource. Implementing it on a computer requires further work in order to translate the phenomena into a programming language. Implementing the activity requires versatility and flexibility on the side of the teacher. The possibility exists, of course, to restrict the tools made available to the students and conduct a thorough a priori analysis of the possible implementations that might emerge.

12.6.4 From Resource for Use to Resource in Use

In the perspective of "design *in use*," these artifacts have to be increased with tools that, when used by the teacher, allow their orchestration in her teaching, with minute tweaking and documentation process (Gueudet and Trouche 2008). To continue with the example of dynamic geometry, in addition to tools for editing and manipulation of figures, we find functions for the configuration of menus, the elaboration of a statement, the sharing of a figure at a distance, etc.

The implementation of learning activities using (digital) resources requires a system in which all elements involved in the design and implementation of learning activities are structured and organized. On the designer side, to make this instrumentalization and organization possible requires developing interfaces, supports, guides to instrumentation, as well as, on the teacher's side, robust resources systems, in an IO or in a documentation process. Investigating the design *for use* by the teacher of digital resources is the best way to gather information of how teachers build and use resources and systems of resources.

Brown (2009) investigates how the teacher works as a designer and regulates his/her Pedagogical Design Capacity (PDC). He proposed to draw a parallel between design and teaching, showing that these two activities share common procedures: "Teachers must perceive and interpret existing resources, evaluate the constraints of the classroom setting, balance tradeoffs and devise strategies – all in the pursuit of their instructional goals." Stating that we should consider "teaching as design," he developed the concept of PDC in order to describe how teachers would interpret and use curriculum materials. Using the example of a middle school science teacher trying to set up a science lab in her class, he defined PDC as a "skill in perceiving the affordances of the materials and making decisions about how to use them to craft instructional episodes that achieve her goals." Pepin et al. (2017) also argued that design could be considered, when applied to teachers, as "designing for teaching." We could therefore say that there is a strong link between teachers' design activities and their DW.

In a design *for use*, HLT (Simon 1995; Simon and Tzur 2004) can structure a priori information on both sides, of the teacher and of the expected users, helping the designers to shape the resources *for use*. During a teaching experiment, an HLT is implemented and tested, gathering data on the use of the resources, leading to a revision of the design. For example, in the study by van Dijke-Droogers et al. (2018), a HLT was designed and a teaching experiment (in the Netherlands) was conducted to evaluate and revise this HLT. The challenge was to invite ninth grade students, inexperienced with sampling, to making informal statistical inferences without the knowledge of the formal probability theory. As educational materials that focus on the development of informal statistical inferences for grade 9 in the Netherlands hardly exist, the materials had to be designed. In the HLT, the students were expected to proceed from a first experience with sampling physical objects, through an understanding of sampling variation and resampling, to reasoning with the simulated empirical sampling distribution. Design guidelines were identified through a literature review, and the possibilities of (digital) resources were explored. The designed eight-step HLT included information about the theoretical background, the learning steps, teaching approach, lesson activities, tools and materials, practical guidelines, expected student behavior, and data collection. For example, in step 6, students investigated what happened if the sample size increased. The hypothesis in this step was that students would understand that the characteristics (e.g., the mean) and the shape of the distribution of a larger sample usually better resemble the underlying population. To conceptualize this idea, students used TinkerPlots (Konold and Miller 2005) to easily and quickly simulate samples of different sizes. A learning activity based on growing samples (Bakker 2004) and the use of TinkerPlots was expected to help students develop aspects of informal inference and argumentative reasoning (Ben-Zvi 2006). Next, the students were asked in step 6 to compare similarities and differences between their simulated sample results and during a whole-class session, to the underlying population. Embedding students' findings in a classroom discussion was expected to enhance their statistical reasoning (Bakker 2004). This HLT was, as a next step, tested in a teaching experiment. The teaching experiment comprised a ten 45-minute lesson series and was piloted in one class with 20 students. The data analysis consisted of verifying whether the designed hypotheses actually occurred. To this end, for each step of the design, the formulated hypotheses were translated into visible student behavior.

12.6.5 Design in Use

When designing *in use*, the investigation can focus on the *instrumentation* of specific resources to enrich and refine the schemes used by the teachers in this instrumentation. There are many ways to observe *orchestration*, that is, to say the way the teacher appropriates these available resources and rely on them to conduct the activity of the students.

For example, Fidje (2018) in his study investigates the way teachers use student-produced video in mathematics teaching. This research aimed to identify and characterize different orchestrations used by a teacher in a mathematical discussion with regard to student-produced videos. Open coding was used to propose a framework adopted from Brown's (2009) degrees of artifact appropriation: offloading (use as is), adapting the resource, and improvising (disregard the resource and enact without specific guidance from the presentation). The findings show that the teacher orchestrated the use of videos in distinctly different ways, capitalizing on the affordances and working around the constraints of the medium. The teacher applied what appeared as a quite fixed framework for every mathematical problem presented in the discussion, first, with a presentation of the problem, followed by an elaboration through a back-and-forth discussion, and ending with a conclusion and connecting the current problem with the succeeding problems. This fixed framework was evident throughout the lesson; a new problem was never presented without a conclusion to the former. Within this framework, a number of orchestrations related to the student-produced videos emerged. Firstly, there were *offloading* orchestrations where the teacher used the videos as they were. The most notable examples of offloading were when the teacher used the videos as an introduction to a problem or as the conclusion to the problem. Secondly, the teacher used *adaptation* orchestration, as he chose to adapt most of the student-produced videos in some way or another. For example, the teacher started the video, paused it, and directed a question to the presenters in the video. Thirdly, the teacher used *hybrid* orchestrations, where students were asked to present something from their video. The teacher used this orchestration to improve the video or to elaborate on the problem addressed. Fourthly, the teacher gradually improved orchestrations. The improving orchestrations were all prompted by the presentations in the videos, even though they were not used to present or elaborate the questions. This study showed how the teacher identified perceived affordances in the different use of the resource in his lesson design, while planning the lesson, culminating in utilization schemes for the set of resources used.

12.6.6 Collaboration as a Way to Optimize Design

Gueudet et al. (2013) reflected upon conditions which were necessary for collective work to happen. They defined this collective work as "teachers working with 'other participants', that is, teachers working with and in teams, communities and networks." They proposed the following criteria: a common working room, "official" working hours, and possibly the intervention of institutions linked to school. After analyzing the DW of two mathematic teachers, their representations and practice of collective work, they came to the conclusion that collective lesson or task preparation was very important for teachers' DW. Nevertheless, they argued that the simple fact of being colleagues – working with the same students or in the same schools were not accurate sufficient criteria to guarantee satisfactory collective work. According to them, collective work and design could develop owing to conditions very similar to that of "communities of practice" (Wenger 1998) – groups of teachers who share a "joint enterprise, a mutual commitment, and a resource repertoire" (Pepin et al. 2013): a "mutual endeavor," that is to say, agreeing to work on resources according to similar objectives; "minding the system," that is to say agreeing on norms of participation and pedagogical actions; and "common forms of addressing and making sense of resources," in other words, allowing shared resources to become collective resources appropriated by the group. Therefore, these conditions are complex to gather as material settings (getting specific time and space, e.g., a common room to work together) are not sufficient for satisfactory collective design to happen. It requires both a sharing of values about teaching and teachers' subject-matter and a sharing of resources. It also requires a particular attention to boundary crossing allowed by brokers, bringing new acceptable techniques and ideas into a community. They enrich the community without disrupting it, allowing for social creativity in the realm of technology enhanced learning, as Essonnier (2018) shows in her PhD thesis.

Carton (2018a) showed that indirect collaboration on non-formal digital shared spaces could foster teachers' Pedagogical Design Capacity, but also that non-formal digital common spaces could offer favorable settings for collective work even though it might lead to individual design. The analysis she carried out showed that networks and platforms that were not originally dedicated to education or linked to school institutions could offer favorable settings for collective work, for instance, small groups of teachers connected through apps (Google Drive, Dropbox, WhatsApp), e-mail correspondence or social media (Facebook groups or pages which are not institutional but linked to subject matters or groups dealing with teachers' professional identity and experiences). These groups appeared to be either defined by precise circumstances (teachers who met during their internship year during their teacher education and wanted to stay in touch), or by teachers who already knew each other personally or professionally or who already met or built an online relation because they shared affinities or a similar status.

Different degrees of collaboration seemed to happen in these non-formal digital spaces: first, each teacher interviewed admitted they consulted, were inspired by, copied, printed, or used colleagues resources available on the Internet, through personal spaces like blogs, websites, social media like Facebook pages, or subject-matter dedicated groups, in order to "see what others do" and to "inspire" oneself, most of the time "without saying thank you." This pedagogical monitoring activity seemed to trigger a documentational genesis (Gueudet and Trouche 2008), starting with a selection of the initial resources owing to a follow-up of the colleagues' work, even if there was no communication between the teachers.

Then, teachers seemed to value these non-formal groups because they felt they could express themselves or ask questions about didactical practices or resources without fear of judgment or assessment, which could be considered as an indirect way of getting feedback about one's resources. Expression of shared trust and good-will seemed to be two essential criteria to reach the first step of collective work: not only getting teachers to upload their resources but also getting them to express their own "voice" (Remillard 2010, p. 206) or affordances about their resources or their practices. Other connections between participants of these non-formal groups were 1) their desire to develop their resource system alongside their didactical practices in order to avoid routines and to adapt to their students; 2) a feeling of loneliness regarding these interrogations or due to their interest in digital resources among their school team.

Although every teacher who engaged (either actively or indirectly) in digital groups admitted these spaces were a melting pot which fostered their documentary work, they almost never mentioned that actual collective design happened directly within the space where they found the resources. The feedback around posted activities or documents seemed more frequent than the actual reposting of transformed resources. Digital spaces, which constituted small groups bound by close ties (WhatsApp, Dropbox, email correspondence, private mailbox on apps), seemed to be more favorable for collective feedback on resources, as modified resources were exchanged and commented upon, while in bigger groups, especially on social media (Facebook and Twitter) dialogue and interactivity seemed to serve each participant's professional development more than collective work.

In the MC^2 project (Essonnier 2018; Essonnier et al. 2018), a platform, named CoICode, was designed for capturing some of the social interactions regarding the path of an idea, documenting its diverse sources and influences until the final first cycle of a pedagogical resource. The analysis of the produced traces allowed for the characterization of traits in a community that promote social creativity. Of course, the TPACK of its members have to be compatible and complement each other. The context and atmosphere have to be free and trustful enough to allow for a fruitful divergent phase but professional enough to succeed in producing something usable as the conclusion of a convergent phase.

Teachers' collective work is also shaped by and for students, mainly through non-formal interactions. Carton's (2018b) analysis of 24 semi-structured interviews around secondary teachers' creativity showed that teachers described their DW as if it was a kind of "addressed creativity," in the first place addressed to their students. Participants of the study seemed to consider students both as an "audience" and as feedback providers, offering the most direct and genuine assessment teachers could get, which turned into a strong motivation for documentational genesis (Gueudet and Trouche 2009b), or design.

Lastly, the analysis also revealed that most teachers felt that their PDC and skills in crafting pedagogical episodes were mostly underestimated by school institutions. Therefore, some of the interviewees chose to turn to companies (either publishing houses or edtech players) that would "publish" their work – either through textbooks or instructional kits. They seemed to expect a symbolical, financial and professional recognition of their expertise from these partnerships, even though they admitted the deals did not often offer them satisfactory conditions, most of all from a financial point of view. Interestingly, some of the interviewees seemed to implement design habits born from their DW into paid projects, for instance, lessons presented as sheets which were used as models for an instructional kit. A hypothesis which needs further research would be to consider that teachers accept these kinds of partnerships because they throw light upon their PDC and therefore serve their professional development.

12.6.7 From Design in Use to Design for Use

The discussion presented in this chapter shows the richness of the theoretical constructs such as IO and DAD to observe, analyze, systematize and anticipate the activity, individual or collective, of the teacher using digital resources and systems, and this from multiple insights. The first contribution of the works presented is obviously relative to the models by allowing their validation, refinements and evolutions. A second contribution is relative to the conception and development of digital resources, interfaces, supports and systems, which scaffold the engineering-teaching activity undertaken by the teacher.

The realization of resources and platforms founded on theoretical and theoretical reflections is useful for several reasons. The first is that engineering questions theories because it requires tangible operational answers, which can be programed and computed, and this in turn promotes the evolution of the theories. The second is that produced artifacts and platforms provide ways of validating the answers provided by theories. We can consider a theoretical validation by the evaluation of the adequacy between the realization and its specifications. The adequacy in a semi-theoretical setup in laboratory with technologically experienced teachers might differ from practical experimentation by ordinary teachers. The third is that the designed artifacts and platforms are products that enrich teachers' resource systems, participating in their professional development, and infusing theoretical research into society.

A first focus of the research presented concerns on resources and their characterization by their own specificities, by the utilization scheme implemented by the teachers, and by the instrumental geneses implemented by the students. From this first insight, Adler's (2000) systematization of resources (object-action-activity) helps us to better analyze the choice and use of teachers' resources, and provides theoretical and methodological principles to produce the specifications for computer supports for these choices and uses.

A second focus is on the activity of the teacher as an engineer observing and analyzing his activity of preparing his teaching and producing material from digital resources. In particular, the teacher's PDC or HLT can be evaluated.

Although we focus on the conception and implementation of supports for didactic material production for the teacher, many possible orchestrations and articulations of resources can be built since the produced didactic material can be a didactic situation based on problem solving, a list of training exercises, a multimedia presentation of a specific content, a digital textbook, etc. For each of these possible resource orchestrations, specific supports can be provided. Generally, conceiving and implementing supports for the "design *in use*" of resources needs a wide variety of investigations, mostly built on the IO and DAD to understand the way teachers and researchers are selecting, taking decisions, combining and articulating resources, freely or with the support/constraint of platforms, individually or collectively. It has the purpose of several works presented during the Re(s)sources 2018 international conference.

12.7 Conclusion: What Has and Has Not Been Addressed

Paul Drijvers, Verônica Gitirana, John Monaghan and Samet Okumus

The questions in the original remit of WG4 have been unevenly addressed in the Working Group papers and, consequently, in this chapter. Neither the question regarding opportunities for new learning formats, such as blended learning and flipped classrooms, nor the question on what student resource systems look like have been addressed. There has also been little consideration of the role that digital resources play in assessment. The questions on how to choose appropriate resources and how to adapt them to specific learning goals, as well as the question regarding options for personalized learning, have been considered, among other things, in Sects. 12.3 and 12.4. The question on how to prepare pre- and in-service teachers has been addressed in Sect. 12.5.

New foci (or, at least, new takes on existing foci) have been introduced. The relationship between instrumental genesis and affordances is considered in some depth in Sect. 12.2 (and mentioned elsewhere). This is, we feel, an important focus for further work and could link with issues in the design of resources for teaching and for learning. Section 12.3 considers five areas (student-centered orchestrations; extending the repertoire of orchestrations; chaining orchestrations; didactical performance; and gestures) where the model of IO is not fully exploited. This section could/should be used as a springboard for further work in these areas. Section 12.4 raises and partially addresses a number of questions regarding networking the DAD to other theoretical framework, but as we noted in our Introduction, further work needs to be done here. Section 12.5 considers many conceptions of teaching (with digital resources) and advances knowledge in doing so, but further advancement requires networking these conceptions. Section 12.6 helps us appreciate that how learning environments are designed and used in practice and what works (and how it works). Further work in this area includes not just networking theoretical frameworks but networking fields of study (designers and didacticians).

References

Adler, J. (2000). Conceptualising resources as a theme for teacher education. *Journal of Mathematics Teacher Education, 3*(3), 205–224.

Arcavi, A. (2003). The role of visual representations in the learning of mathematics. *Educational Studies in Mathematics, 52*(3), 215–241.

Artigue, M. (1990). Ingénierie didactique. *Recherches en didactique des mathématiques, 9*(3), 281–307.

Artigue, M. (2002). Learning mathematics in a CAS environment: The genesis of a reflection about instrumentation and the dialectics between technical and conceptual work. *International Journal of Computers for Mathematical Learning, 7*, 245–274.

Artzt, A. F., Armour-Thomas, E., Curcio, C., & Gurl, T. J. (2015). *Becoming a reflective mathematics teacher: A guide for observations and self-assessment* (3rd ed.). New York: Routledge.

Assis, C., Gitirana, V., & Trouche, L. (2018). The metamorphosis of resource systems of prospective teacher: From studying to teaching. In V. Gitirana, T. Miyakawa, M. Rafalska, S. Soury-Lavergne, & L. Trouche (Eds.), Proceedings of the re(s)sources 2018 international conference (pp. 39–42). Lyon: ENS de Lyon, Retrieved on November 8th, 2018, at https://hal.archives-ouvertes.fr/hal-01764563

Assude, T. (2007). Teacher's practices and degree of ICT integration. In D. Pitta-Pantazi, & G. Philippou (Eds.), *Proceedings of the Fifth Congress of the European Society for Research in Mathematics Education* (pp. 1339–1348). Larnaca: University of Cyprus and ERME.

Assude, T., Buteau, C., & Forgasz, H. (2010). Factors influencing implementation of technology-rich mathematics curriculum and practices. In C. Hoyles & J.-B. Lagrange (Eds.), *Mathematics education and technology – Rethinking the terrain. The 17th ICMI study* (pp. 405–419). New York: Springer.

Atkinson, B. (2012). Rethinking reflection: Teachers' critiques. *The Teacher Educator, 47*, 175–194.

Bailleul, M., & Thémines, J. F. (2013). L'ingénierie de formation : formalisation d'expériences en formation d'enseignants. In A. Vergnioux (Ed.),. *Traité d'ingénierie de la formation L'Harmattan* (pp. 85–112). Paris.

Bakker, A. (2004). *Design research in statistics education: On symbolizing and computer tools.* Utrecht: CD Beta Press.

Balacheff, N. (1994). La transposition informatique. Note sur un nouveau problème pour la didactique. In M. Artigue, R. Gras, C. Laborde, & P. Tavignot (Eds.), *Vingt ans de Didactique des Mathématiques en France* (pp. 364–370). Grenoble: La Pensée Sauvage.

Barbosa, A., & Vale, I. (2018). Math trails: A resource for teaching and learning. In V. Gitirana, T. Miyakawa, M. Rafalska, S. Soury-Lavergne, & L. Trouche (Eds.), *Proceedings of the re(s) sources 2018 international conference* (pp. 183–186). Lyon: ENS de Lyon. Retrieved on November 8th, 2018, at https://hal.archives-ouvertes.fr/hal-01764563.

Barth-Cohen, L. A., Little, A. J., & Abrahamson, D. (2018). Building reflective practices in a pre-service math and science teacher education course that focuses on qualitative video analysis. *Journal of Science Teacher Education, 29*(2), 83–101.

Bellemain, F., Tiburcio, R., Silva, C., & Gitirana, V. (2016). *Function Studium software.* Recife-PE: LEMATEC Research Group.

Bellemain, F., Rodrigues, A., & Rodrigues, A. D. (2018). LEMATEC Studium: A support resource for teaching mathematics. In V. Gitirana, T. Miyakawa, M. Rafalska, S. Soury-Lavergne, & L. Trouche (Eds.), *Proceedings of the re(s)sources 2018 international conference* (pp. 255–258). Lyon: ENS de Lyon. Retrieved on November 8th, 2018, at https://hal.archives-ouvertes.fr/hal-01764563.

Ben-Zvi, D. (2006). Scaffolding students' informal inference and argumentation. In A. Rossman & B. Chance (Eds.), *Proceedings of the Seventh International Conference on Teaching Statistics (CD-ROM).* Voorburg: International Statistical Institute.

Besnier, S. (2016). *Le travail documentaire des professeurs à l'épreuve des ressources technologiques : Le cas de l'enseignement du nombre à l'école maternelle*. PhD. Brest: Université de Bretagne Occidentale, https://tel.archives-ouvertes.fr/tel-01397586/document

Besnier, S. (2018). Orchestrations at kindergarten: Articulation between manipulatives and digital resources. In V. Gitirana, T. Miyakawa, M. Rafalska, S. Soury-Lavergne, & L. Trouche (Eds.), *Proceedings of the re(s)sources 2018 international conference* (pp. 259–262). Lyon: ENS de Lyon. Retrieved on November 8th, 2018, at https://hal.archives-ouvertes.fr/hal-01764563.

Besnier, S., & Gueudet, G. (2016). Usages de ressources numériques pour l'enseignement des mathématiques en maternelle : orchestrations et documents. *Perspectivas em Educação Matemática, 9*(21), 978–1003.

Billington, M. (2009). Establishing didactical praxeologies: teachers using digital tools in upper secondary mathematics classrooms. In V. Durand-Guerrier, S. Soury-Lavergne & F. Arzarello (Eds.), *Proceedings of the Sixth Congress of European Research in Mathematics Education* (pp. 1330–1339). Lyon, France: ENS de Lyon.

Bozkurt, G., & Ruthven, K. (2017). Classroom-based professional expertise: A mathematics teacher's practice with technology. *Educational Studies in Mathematics, 94*(3), 309–328.

Brousseau, G. (1997). *Theory of didactical situations in mathematics. Didactique des mathématiques, 1970–1990 (edited and translated by N. Balacheff, M. Cooper, R. Sutherland, & V. Warfield). Dordrecht, NL*. Kluwer Academic Publishers.

Brown, M. W. (2009). The teacher-tool relationship: Theorizing the design and use of curriculum materials. In J. T. Remillard, B. A. Herbel-Eisenmann, & G. M. Lloyd (Eds.), *Mathematics teachers at work: Connecting curriculum materials and classroom instruction* (pp. 17–36). New York: Routledge.

Carlsen, M., Erfjord, I., Hundeland, P. S., & Monaghan, J. (2016). Kindergarten teachers' orchestration of mathematical activities afforded by technology: Agency and mediation. *Educational Studies in Mathematics, 93*(1), 1–17.

Carton, T. (2018a). From digital "bricolage" to the start of collective work – What influences do secondary teachers non-formal digital practices have on their documentation work? In V. Gitirana, T. Miyakawa, M. Rafalska, S. Soury-Lavergne, & L. Trouche (Eds.), *Proceedings of the re(s)sources 2018 international conference* (pp. 263–266). Lyon: ENS de Lyon. Retrieved on November 8th, 2018, at https://hal.archives-ouvertes.fr/hal-01764563.

Carton, T. (2018b). *Case study: How teachers' everyday creativity can be associated with an edtech player's strategies*. Présenté au XXIe Congrès de la SFSIC – Création, créativité et médiations, Saint-Denis, 13-15 juin 2018.

Cayton, C., Hollebrands, K., Okumuş, S., & Boehm, E. (2017). Pivotal teaching moments in technology-intensive secondary geometry classrooms. *Journal of Mathematics Teacher Education, 20*(1), 75–100.

Chevallard, Y. (2002). *Organiser l'étude. 1. Structures & fonctions. Actes de la XIe école d'été de didactique des mathématiques* (pp. 3–32). La Pensée Sauvage : Grenoble. http://yves.chevallard.free.fr/spip/spip/IMG/pdf/Organiser_l_etude_1.pdf

Choppin, J. (2018). Exploring teachers' design processes with different curriculum programs. In V. Gitirana, T. Miyakawa, M. Rafalska, S. Soury-Lavergne, & L. Trouche (Eds.), *Proceeedings of the re(s)sources 2018 international conference* (pp. 267–270). Lyon: ENS de Lyon. Retrieved on November 8th, 2018, at https://hal.archives-ouvertes.fr/hal-01764563.

Cuevas, C. A., Villamizar, F. Y., & Martínez, A. (2017). Aplicaciones de la tecnología digital para activiDADes didácticas que promuevan una mejor comprensión del tono como cualiDAD del sonido para cursos tradicionales de física en el nivel básico. *Enseñanza de las Ciencias, 35*(3), 129–150.

Cunha, E. (2018). Digital resources: Origami folding instructions as lever to mobilize geometric concepts to solve problems. In V. Gitirana, T. Miyakawa, M. Rafalska, S. Soury-Lavergne, & L. Trouche (Ed.), *Proceeedings of the Re(s)sources 2018 International Conference* (pp. 271–274). Lyon: ENS de Lyon. Retrieved on November 8th, 2018, at https://hal.archives-ouvertes.fr/hal-01764563

Deblois, L. (2012). De l'ancien élève à l'enseignant. Quel parecours. In J. Proulx, C. Corriveau, & H. Squalli (Eds.), *Formation mathématique pour l'enseignement des mathématiques* (pp. 313–320). Québec: Presses de l'Université du Québec.

Dick, T., & Burrill, G. (2016). Design and implementation principles for dynamic interactive mathematics technologies. In M. Niess, S. Driskell, & K. Hollebrands (Eds.), *Handbook of research on transforming mathematics teacher education in the digital age* (pp. 23–52). Hershey: IGI Global Publishers.

Drijvers, P., & Trouche, L. (2008). From artifacts to instruments: A theoretical framework behind the orchestra metaphor. In G. W. Blume & M. K. Heid (Eds.), *Research on technology and the teaching and learning of mathematics. Cases and perspectives* (Vol. 2, pp. 363–392). Charlotte: Information Age.

Drijvers, P., Doorman, M., Boon, P., Reed, H., & Gravemeijer, K. P. (2010). The teacher and the tool: Instrumental orchestrations in the technology-rich mathematics classroom. *Educational Studies in Mathematics, 75*(2), 213–234.

Drijvers, P., Godino, J. D., Font, V., & Trouche, L. (2013a). One episode, two lenses. *Educational Studies in Mathematics, 82*(1), 23–49.

Drijvers, P., Tacoma, S., Besamusca, A., Doorman, M., & Boon, P. (2013b). Digital resources inviting changes in mid-adopting teachers' practices and orchestrations. *ZDM – Mathematics Education, 45*(7), 987–1001.

Duval, R. (1993). Registres de représentation sémiotique et fonctionnement cognitif de la pensée. *Annales de didactique et de sciences cognitives, 5*(1), 37–65.

Engeström, Y. (1987). *Learning by expanding: An activity-theoretical approach to developmental research*. Helsinki: Orienta-Konsultit.

Erfjord, I. (2011). Teachers' initial orchestration of students' dynamic geometry software use: Consequences for students' opportunities to learn mathematics. *Technology, Knowledge and Learning, 16*(1), 35–54.

Essonnier, N. K. (2018). *Étude de la conception collaborative de ressources numériques mathématiques au sein d'une communauté d'intérêt*. PhD. Lyon: Université de Lyon, https://tel.archives-ouvertes.fr/tel-01868226/document

Essonnier, N., & Trgalová, J. (2018). Collaborative design of digital resources: Role of designers' resource systems and professional knowledge. In V. Gitirana, T. Miyakawa, M. Rafalska, S. Soury-Lavergne, & L. Trouche (Eds.), *Proceeedings of the re(s)sources 2018 international conference* (pp. 61–64). Lyon: ENS de Lyon. Retrieved on November 8th, 2018, at https://hal.archives-ouvertes.fr/hal-01764563.

Essonnier, N., Kynigos, C., Trgalová, J., & Daskolia, M. (2018). Role of context in social creativity for the design of digital resources. In L. Fan, L. Trouche, S. Rezat, C. Qi, & J. Visnovska (Eds.), *Research on mathematics textbooks and Teachers' resources: Advances and issues* (pp. 215–233). Cham: Springer.

Faggiano, E., Montone, A., & Mariotti, M. A. (2016). Creating a synergy between manipulatives and virtual artefacts to conceptualize axial symmetry at Primary School. In C. Csíkos, A. Rausch, & J. Szitányi (Eds.), *Proceedigns of the 40th conference of the international group for the Psychology of Mathematics Education: PME 40* (Vol. 2, pp. 235–242). Szeged: International Group for the Psychology of Mathematics Education.

Farrell, A. (1996). Roles and behaviors in technology-integrated precalculus classrooms. *Journal of Mathematical Behavior, 15*(1), 35–53.

Ferrara, F., & Sinclair, N. (2016). An early algebra approach to pattern generalisation: Actualising the virtual through words, gestures and toilet paper. *Educational Studies in Mathematics, 92*(1), 1–19.

Fidje, A. S. (2018). Orchestrating the use of student-produced videos in mathematics teaching. In V. Gitirana, T. Miyakawa, M. Rafalska, S. Soury-Lavergne, & L. Trouche (Eds.), *Proceedings of the re(s)sources 2018 international conference* (pp. 275–278). Lyon: ENS de Lyon. In *Retrieved on November 8th, 2018, at* https://hal.archives-ouvertes.fr/hal-01764563.

Fischer, G. (2001). Communities of interest: Learning through the interaction of multiple knowledge systems. In S. Bjørnestad, R. Moe, A. Mørch, & A. Opdahl (Eds.), *Proceedings of the 24th Information Systems Research Seminar in Scandinavia* (pp. 1–14). Bergen: The University of Bergen

Gibson, J. J. (1977). *The ecological approach to visual perception.* Boston: Houghton Mifflin.

Gueudet, G., & Trouche, L. (2008). Du travail documentaire des enseignants?: Genèses, collectifs, communautés. Le cas des mathématiques. *Education & Didactique, 2*(3), 7–33.

Gueudet, G., & Trouche, L. (2009a). Towards new documentational systems for mathematics teachers? *Educational Studies in Mathematics, 71*(3), 199–218.

Gueudet, G., & Trouche, L. (2009b). Vers de nouveaux systèmes documentaires des professeurs de mathématiques?). In I. Bloch & F. Conne (Eds.), *Nouvelles perspectives en didactique des mathématiques. Cours de la XIVe école d'été de didactique des mathématiques* (pp. 109–133). Paris: La Pensée Sauvage.

Gueudet, G., & Trouche, L. (2010). Des ressources aux documents, travail du professeur et genèses documentaires. In G. Gueudet & L. Trouche (Eds). *Ressources vives: le travail documentaire des professeurs en mathématiques* (pp. 57–74). Paideia, Rennes: Presses Universitaires de Rennes & INRP.

Gueudet, G., & Trouche, L. (2011). Mathematics teacher education advanced methods: An example in dynamic geometry. *ZDM – Mathematics Education, 43*(3), 399–411.

Gueudet, G., Sacristan, A., Soury-Lavergne, S., & Trouche, L. (2012). Online paths in mathematics teacher training: New resources and new skills for teacher educators. *ZDM – Mathematics Education, 44*(6), 717–731.

Gueudet, G., Pepin, B., & Trouche, L. (2013). Collective work with resources: An essential dimension for teacher documentation. *ZDM – Mathematics Education, 45*(7), 1003–1016.

Gueudet, G., Pepin, B., Sabra, H., & Trouche, L. (2016). Collective design of an e-textbook: Teachers' collective documentation. *Journal of Mathematics Teacher Education, 19*(2), 187–203.

Guin, D., & Trouche, L. (1999). The complex process of converting tools into mathematical instruments: The case of calculators. *International Journal of Computers for Mathematical Learning, 3*(3), 195–227.

Hadjerrouit, S. (2017). Assessing the affordances of SimReal+ and their applicability to support the learning of mathematics in teacher education. *Issues in Informing Science and Information Technology Education, 14*, 121–138.

Heid, M., K. (2008). Calculator and computer technology in the K-12 curriculum some observations from a US perspective. In Z. Ususkin, & E. Willmore (Eds.), Mathematics curriculum in Pacific rim countries-China, Japan, Korea, and Singapore: Proceedings of a conference (pp. 293–304). Charlotte, Information Age Publishing.

Herbst, P., Chazan, D., Chen, C., Chieu, V. M., & Weiss, M. (2011). Using comics-based representations of teaching, and technology, to bring practice to teacher education courses. *ZDM – Mathematics Education, 43*(1), 91–103.

Hollebrands, K., & Okumus, S. (2018). Secondary mathematics teachers' instrumental integration in technology-rich geometry classrooms. *Journal of Mathematical Behavior, 49*(1), 82–94.

Hollebrands, K., & Zbiek, R. (2004). Teaching mathematics with technology: An evidence-based road map for the Journey. In R. Rubenstein & G. Bright (Eds.), *Perspectives on the teaching of mathematics: Sixty-sixth yearbook* (pp. 259–270). Reston: National Council of Teachers of Mathematics.

Hollebrands, K., McCulloch, A. W., & Lee, H. S. (2016). Prospective teachers; incorporation of technology in mathematics lesson plans. In M. Niess, S. Driskell, & K. Hollebrands (Eds.), *Handbook of research on transforming mathematics teacher education in the digital age* (pp. 272–292). Hershey: IGI Global.

Hoyles, C., & Noss, R. (1992). A pedagogy for mathematical microworlds. *Educational Studies in Mathematics, 23*(1), 31–57.

Igliori, S. B. C., & Almeida, M. V. (2018). Un support numérique pour le travail de documentation des enseignants de mathématiques de l'EFII (Collège, en France). In V. Gitirana, T. Miyakawa, M. Rafalska, S. Soury-Lavergne, & L. Trouche (Eds.), *Proceeedings of the re(s)sources 2018 international conference* (pp. 288–291). Lyon: ENS de Lyon. Retrieved on November 8th, 2018, at https://hal.archives-ouvertes.fr/hal-01764563.

Ignácio, R., Lima, R., & Gitirana, V. (2018). The birth of the documentary system of mathematics pre-service teachers in a supervised internship with the creation of a digital textbook chapter. In V. Gitirana, T. Miyakawa, M. Rafalska, S. Soury-Lavergne, & L. Trouche (Eds.), *Proceeedings of the re(s)sources 2018 international conference* (pp. 292–295). Lyon: ENS de Lyon. retrieved on November 8th 2018 at https://hal.archives-ouvertes.fr/hal-01764563.

Jameau, A., & Le Hénaff, C. (2018). Resources for science teaching in a foreign language. In V. Gitirana, T. Miyakawa, M. Rafalska, S. Soury-Lavergne, & L. Trouche (Eds.), *Proceeedings of the re(s)sources 2018 international conference* (pp. 79–82). Lyon: ENS de Lyon. retrieved on November 8th 2018 at https://hal.archives-ouvertes.fr/hal-01764563.

Jaworski, B. (2014). Reflective practicioner in mathematics education. In S. Lerman (Ed.), *Encyclopedia in mathematics education* (pp. 529–532). Dordrecht: Springer.

Jones, W. (2007). Personal information management. *Annual Review of Information Science and Technology, 41*(1), 453–504.

Kaput, J. J. (1995). Overcoming physicality and the eternal present: Cybernetic manipulatives. In R. Sutherland & J. Mason (Eds.), *Exploiting mental imagery with computers in mathematics education* (pp. 161–177). Berlin: Springer.

Kennewell, S. (2001). Using affordances and constraints to evaluate the use of information and communications technology in teaching and learning. *Journal of Information Technology for Teacher Education, 10*(1–2), 101–116.

Kidron, I., Bosch, M., Monaghan, J., & Palmér, H. (2018). Theoretical perspectives and approaches in mathematics education research. In T. Dreyfus, M. Artigue, D. Potari, S. Prediger, & K. Ruthven, (Eds.), *Developing Research in Mathematics Education*: Twenty years of communication, cooperation and collaboration in Europe. London: Routledge.

Kieran, C., Boileau, A., Tanguay, D., & Drijvers, P. (2013). Design researchers' documentational genesis in a study on equivalence of algebraic expressions. *ZDM – Mathematics Education, 45*(7), 1045–1056.

Kirchner, P., Strijbos, J.-W., Kreijns, K., & Beers, B. J. (2004). Designing electronic collaborative learning environments. *Educational Technology Research and Development, 52*(3), 47–66.

Koehler, M. J., & Mishra, P. (2009). What is technological pedagogical content knowledge? *Contemporary Issues in Technology and Teacher education, 9*(1), 60–70.

Konold, C., & Miller, C. D. (2005). *TinkerPlots: Dynamic data exploration (computer software, Version 1.0)*. Emeryville: Key Curriculum Press.

Kozaklı Ülger, T., & Tapan Broutin, M. S. (2018). Transition from a paper-pencil to a technology enriched environment: A teacher's use of technology and resource selection. In V. Gitirana, T. Miyakawa, M. Rafalska, S. Soury-Lavergne, & L. Trouche (Eds.), *Proceedings of the re(s) sources 2018 international conference* (pp. 344–347). Lyon: ENS de Lyon. Retrieved on November 8th, 2018, at https://hal.archives-ouvertes.fr/hal-01764563.

Lagrange, J. B., & Monaghan, J. (2009). On the adoption of a model to interpret teachers' use of technology in mathematics lessons. In V. Durand-Guerrier, S. Soury-Lavergne & F. Arzarello (Eds.). *Proceedings of the Sixth Congress of European Research in Mathematics Education* (pp. 1605–1614). Lyon: ENS de Lyon.

Lakoff, G., & Núñez, R. E. (2000). *Where mathematics comes from: How the embodied mind brings mathematics into being*. New York: Basic Books.

Lealdino Filho, P., & Mercat, C. (2018). Teaching computational thinking in classroom environments: A case for unplugged scenario. In V. Gitirana, T. Miyakawa, M. Rafalska, S. Soury-Lavergne, & L. Trouche (Eds.), *Proceedings of the re(s)sources 2018 international conference* (pp. 296–299). Lyon: ENS de Lyon. Retrieved on November 8th, 2018, at https://hal.archives-ouvertes.fr/hal-01764563.

Leroyer, L. (2018). The capacity to think of transmission of knowledge from learning supports: A proposition of a conceptual model. In V. Gitirana, T. Miyakawa, M. Rafalska, S. Soury-Lavergne, & L. Trouche (Eds.), *Proceeedings of the re(s)sources 2018 international conference* (pp. 203–206). Lyon: ENS de Lyon. Retrieved on November 8th, 2018, at https://hal.archives-ouvertes.fr/hal-01764563.

Lester, F. K. (2005). On the theoretical, conceptual, and philosophical foundations for research in mathematics education. *ZDM – Mathematics Education, 37*(6), 457–467.

Leung, A., & Bolite-Frant, J. (2015). Designing mathematics tasks: The role of tools. In A. Watson & M. Ohtani (Eds.), *Task design in mathematics education:. The 22nd ICMI study* (pp. 191–225). Cham: Springer.

Lucena, R. (2018). *Metaorquestração Instrumental: um modelo para repensar a formação teórico-prática de professores de matemática.* Doctoral thesis. Mathematics and Technological Education Pos-graduation Program. Recife-Brazil: UFPE.

Lucena, R., Gitirana, V., & Trouche, L. (2018). Instrumental meta-orchestration for teacher education. In V. Gitirana, T. Miyakawa, M. Rafalska, S. Soury-Lavergne, & L. Trouche (Eds.), *Proceedings of the re(s)sources 2018 international conference* (pp. 300–303). Lyon: ENS de Lyon. Retrieved on November 8th, 2018, at https://hal.archives-ouvertes.fr/hal-01764563.

Males, L., Setniker, A., & Dietiker, L. (2018). What do teachers attend to in curriculum materials? In V. Gitirana, T. Miyakawa, M. Rafalska, S. Soury-Lavergne, & L. Trouche (Eds.), *Proceedings of the re(s)sources 2018 international conference* (pp. 207–210). Lyon: ENS de Lyon. Retrieved on November 8th, 2018, at https://hal.archives-ouvertes.fr/hal-01764563.

Martinez, M., Cruz, R., & Soberanes, A. (2018). The mathematical teacher: A case study of instrumental genesis in the UAEM. In V. Gitirana, T. Miyakawa, M. Rafalska, S. Soury-Lavergne, & L. Trouche (Eds.), *Proceedings of the re(s)sources 2018 international conference* (pp. 211–214). Lyon: ENS de Lyon. retrieved on November 8th, 2018, at https://hal.archives-ouvertes.fr/hal-01764563.

Maschietto, M., & Soury-Lavergne, S. (2013). Designing a duo of material and digital artifacts: The pascaline and Cabri Elem e-books in primary school mathematics. *ZDM – Mathematics Education, 45*(7), 959–971.

Mercat, C., Lealdino Filho, P., & El-Demerdash, M. (2017). Creativity and technology in mathematics : From story telling to algorithmic with Op'Art. *Acta Didactica Napocensia, 10*(1), 63–70.

Messaoui, A. (2018). The complex process of classifying resources, an essential component of documentation expertise. In V. Gitirana, T. Miyakawa, M. Rafalska, S. Soury-Lavergne, & L. Trouche (Eds.), *Proceedings of the res(s)ource 2018 international conference* (pp. 83–87). Lyon: ENS de Lyon. Retrieved on November 8th, 2018, at https://hal.archives-ouvertes.fr/hal-01764563.

Mishra, P., & Koehler, M. J. (2006). Technological pedagogical content knowledge: A framework for teacher knowledge. *Teachers College Record, 108*(6), 1017–1054.

Monaghan, J. (2016). Developments relevant to the use of tools in mathematics. In J. Monaghan, L. Trouche, & J. M. Borwein (Eds.), *Tools and mathematics: Instruments for learning* (pp. 163–180). New York: Springer.

Naftaliev, E. (2018). Prospective teachers' interactions with interactive diagrams: Semiotic tools, challenges and new paths. In V. Gitirana, T. Miyakawa, M. Rafalska, S. Soury-Lavergne, & L. Trouche (Eds.), *Proceedings of the res(s)ource 2018 international conference* (pp. 304–307). Lyon: ENS de Lyon. Retrieved on November 8th, 2018, at https://hal.archives-ouvertes.fr/hal-01764563.

Naftaliev, E., & Yerushalmy, M. (2017). Design digital tasks: Interactive diagrams as resource and constraint. In A. Leung & A. Baccaglini-Frank (Eds.), *The role and potential of using digital technologies in designing mathematics education tasks* (pp. 153–173). Cham: Springer.

Nascimento, J., Jr., Carvalho, E., & Farias, L. M. (2018). Creation of innovative teaching situation through instrumental genesis to maximize teaching specific content: Acid-base chemical balance. In V. Gitirana, T. Miyakawa, M. Rafalska, S. Soury-Lavergne, & L. Trouche (Eds.),

12 Transitions Toward Digital Resources: Change, Invariance, and Orchestration 441

Proceedings of the res(s)ource 2018 international conference (pp. 308–311). Lyon: ENS de Lyon. Retrieved on November 8th, 2018, at https://hal.archives-ouvertes.fr/hal-01764563.

Ndlovu, M., Wessels, D., & De Villiers, M. (2011). An instrumental approach to modelling the derivative in sketchpad. *Pythagoras, 32*(2), 1–15.

Nongni, G, & DeBlois, L. (2017). Planification de l'enseignement de l'écart-type en utilisant les ressources documentaires. In A. Adihou, J. Giroux, A. Savard, & K.M. Huy (Eds.). *Données, variabilité et tendance vers le futur. Acte du Colloque du GDM* (pp. 205–2012). Canada, Québec: Université McGill.

Nongni, G., & DeBlois. (2018). Planning of the teaching of the standard deviation using digital documentary resources. In V. Gitirana, T. Miyakawa, M. Rafalska, S. Soury-Lavergne, & L. Trouche (Eds.), *Proceedings of the re(s)sources 2018 international conference* (pp. 312–315). Lyon: ENS de Lyon. Retrieved on November 8th, 2018, at https://hal.archives-ouvertes.fr/hal-01764563

Norman, D. A. (1988). *The psychology of everyday things*. New York: Basic Books.

Noss, R., & Hoyles, C. (1996). *Windows on mathematical meanings: Learning cultures and computers*. Dordrecht: Kluwer Academic Publishers.

Okumus, S., & Ipek, A.S. (2018). Pre-service mathematics teachers' investigation of the constraints of mathematical tools. In V. Gitirana, T. Miyakawa, M. Rafalska, S. Soury-Lavergne, & L. Trouche (Eds.), *Proceedings of the re(s)source 2018 international conference* (pp. 316–319). Lyon: ENS de Lyon, retrieved on November 8th, 2018, at https://hal.archives-ouvertes.fr/hal-01764563

Orozco, J., Cuevas, A., Madrid, H., & Trouche, L. (2018). A proposal of instrumental orchestration to introduce eigenvalues and eigenvectors in a first course of linear algebra for engineering students. In V. Gitirana, T. Miyakawa, M. Rafalska, S. Soury-Lavergne, & L. Trouche (Eds.), *Proceedings of the re(s)sources 2018 international conference* (pp. 320–323). Lyon: ENS de Lyon. Retrieved on November 8th, 2018, at https://hal.archives-ouvertes.fr/hal-01764563.

Papert, S., & Harel, I. (1991). Preface, situating constructionism. In I. Harel & S. Papert (Eds.), *Constructionism, research reports and essays, 1985–1990* (p. 1). Norwood: Ablex.

Pea, R. D. (1985). Beyond amplification: Using the computer to reorganize mental functioning. *Educational Psychologist, 20*(4), 167–182.

Pepin, B., Gueudet, G., & Trouche, L. (2013). Re-sourcing teachers' work and interactions: A collective perspective on resources, their use and transformation. *ZDM – Mathematics Education, 45*(7), 929–943.

Pepin, B., Gueudet, G., & Trouche, L. (2017). Refining teacher design capacity: Mathematics teachers' interactions with digital curriculum resources. *ZDM – Mathematics Education, 49*(5), 799–812.

Pfeiffer, C. R. (2017). *A study of the development of mathematical knowledge in a GeoGebra-focused learning environment*. Unpublished PhD dissertation. Stellenbosch: Stellenbosch University.

Pfeiffer, C. R., & Ndlovu, M. (2018). Teaching and learning of function transformations in a GeoGebra-focused learning environment. In V. Gitirana, T. Miyakawa, M. Rafalska, S. Soury-Lavergne, & L. Trouche (Eds.), *Proceedings of the re(s)sources 2018 international conference* (pp. 324–327). Lyon: ENS de Lyon. Retrieved on November 8th, 2018, at https://hal.archives-ouvertes.fr/hal-01764563.

Piaget, J. (1955). *The construction of reality in the child*. London: Routledge & Kegan Paul Limited.

Prieur, M. (2016). *La conception codisciplinaire de métaressources comme appui à l'évolution des connaissances des professeurs de sciences. Les connaissances qui guident un travail de préparation pour engager les élèves dans l'élaboration d'hypothèses ou de conjectures*. PhD. Lyon: Université de Lyon, https://hal.archives-ouvertes.fr/tel-01364778v2/document

Psycharis, G., & Kalogeria, E. (2018). TPACK addressed by trainee teacher educators' documentation work. In V. Gitirana, T. Miyakawa, M. Rafalska, S. Soury-Lavergne, & L. Trouche (Eds.),

Proceedings of the re(s)source 2018 international conference (pp. 328–331). Lyon: ENS de Lyon. Retrieved on November 8th, 2018, at https://hal.archives-ouvertes.fr/hal-01764563.

Rabardel, P. (1995). *Les hommes et les technologies: Approche cognitive des instruments contemporains.* Paris: Armand Colin.

Ratnayake, I., & Thomas, M. (2018). Documentational genesis during teacher collaborative development of tasks incorporating digital technology. In V. Gitirana, T. Miyakawa, M. Rafalska, S. Soury-Lavergne, & L. Trouche (Eds.), *Proceedings of the re(s)source 2018 international conference* (pp. 219–222). Lyon: ENS de Lyon. Retrieved on November 8th, 2018, at https://hal.archives-ouvertes.fr/hal-01764563.

Remillard, J. (2010). Modes d'engagement : comprendre les transactions des professeurs avec les ressources curriculaires en mathématiques. In G. Gueudet, & L. Trouche (Eds.), *Ressources vives: le travail documentaire des professeurs en mathématiques* (pp. 201–216). Rennes/Lyon: INRP/PUR.

Rocha, K. (2018). Uses of online resources and documentational trajectories: The case of Sésamath. In L. Fan, L. Trouche, C. Qi, S. Rezat, J. & Visnovska (Eds.), Research on mathematics textbooks and teachers' resources: Advances and issues. ICME-13 monograph (pp. 235–258). Cham: Springer.

Rodrigues, A., Baltar, P., & Bellemain, F. (2018). Analysis of a Task in three Environments: paper and pencils, manipulative materials and Apprenti Géomètre 2∗. In V. Gitirana, T. Miyakawa, M. Rafalska, S. Soury–Lavergne, & L. Trouche (Eds.), *Proceedings of the Re(s)source 2018 International Conference* (pp. 223–226). Lyon: ENS de Lyon. Retrieved on November 8th, 2018, at https://hal.archives-ouvertes.fr/hal-01764563

Rudd, T. (2007). *Interactive whiteboards in the classroom.* Bristol: Futurelab Report – IWBs.

Ruthven, K. (2014). Frameworks for analysing the expertise that underpins successful integration of digital technologies into everyday teaching practice. In A. Clark-Wilson, O. Robutti, & N. Sinclair (Eds.), *The mathematics teacher in the digital era* (pp. 373–393). Dordrecht: Springer.

Ruthven, K., Hennessy, S., & Deaney, R. (2008). Constructions of dynamic geometry: A study of the interpretative flexibility of educational software in classroom practice. *Computers and Education, 51*(1), 297–317.

Scherrer, J., & Stein, M. K. (2013). Effects of a coding intervention on what teachers learn to notice during whole–group discussion. *Journal of Mathematics Teacher Education, 16*(2), 105–124.

Schoenfeld, A. H. (2010). *How we think: A theory of goal–oriented decision making and its educational applications.* New York: Routledge.

Sensevy, G. (2011). *Le Sens du Savoir. Éléments pour une théorie de l'action conjointe en didactique.* Bruxelles: De Boeck.

Sherman, M. F., & Cayton, C. (2015). Using appropriate tools strategically for instruction. *Mathematics Teacher, 109*(4), 306–310.

Sherman, M. F., Cayton, C., & Chandler, K. (2017). Supporting PSTs in using appropriate tools strategically: A learning sequence for developing technology tasks that support students' mathematical thinking. *Mathematics Teacher Educator, 5*(2), 122–157.

Silva, A. (2018). *Concepção de um suporte para a elaboração de webdocumentos destinados ao ensino da geometria: o caso das curvas cônicas.* Dissertação do mestrado. Programa de Pós-graduação em Educação Matemática e Tecnológica. UFPE, Recife.

Simon, M. A. (1995). Reconstructing mathematics pedagogy from a constructivist perspective. *Journal for Research in Mathematics Education, 26*(2), 114–145.

Simon, M. A., & Tzur, R. (2004). Explicating the role of mathematical tasks in conceptual learning: An elaboration of the hypothetical learning trajectory. *Mathematical Thinking and Learning, 6*(2), 91–104.

Siqueira, J. E. M., & Bellemain, F. (2018). A dynamic multirepresentacional resource for conics. In V. Gitirana, T. Miyakawa, M. Rafalska, S. Soury-Lavergne, & L. Trouche (Eds.), *Proceedings of the re(s)source 2018 international conference* (pp. 359–361). Lyon: ENS de Lyon. Retrieved on November 8th, 2018, at https://hal.archives-ouvertes.fr/hal-01764563.

Stein, M. K., & Smith, M. S. (1998). Mathematical tasks as a framework for reflection: From research to practice. *Mathematics Teaching in the Middle School, 3*(4), 268–275.

Stockero, S. L., & Van Zoest, L. R. (2013). Characterizing pivotal teaching moments in beginning mathematics teachers' practice. *Journal of Mathematics Teacher Education, 16*(2), 125–147.

Swidan, O., Arzarello, F., & Sabena, C. (2018). Teachers' interventions to foster inquiry-based learning in a dynamic technological environment. In V. Gitirana, T. Miyakawa, M. Rafalska, S. Soury-Lavergne, & L. Trouche (Eds.), *Proceedings of the re(s)source 2018 international conference* (pp. 332–335). Lyon: ENS de Lyon. Retrieved on November 8th, 2018, at https://hal.archives-ouvertes.fr/hal-01764563.

Tabach, M. (2011). A mathematics teacher's practice in a technological environment: A case study analysis using two complementary theories. *Technology, Knowledge and Learning, 16*(3), 247–265.

Tabach, M. (2013). Developing a general framework for instrumental orchestration. In B. Ubuz, Ç. Haser, & M. A. Mariotti (Eds.), *Proceedings of the Eighth Congress of the European Society for Research in Mathematics Education* (pp. 2744–2753). Ankara: Middle East Technical University and ERME.

Taranto, E., Arzarello, F., & Robutti, O. (2018). MOOC as a resource for teachers' collaboration in educational program. In V. Gitirana, T. Miyakawa, M. Rafalska, S. Soury-Lavergne, & L. Trouche (Eds.), *Proceedings of the re(s)source 2018 international conference* (pp. 167–170). Lyon: ENS de Lyon. Retrieved on November 8th, 2018, at https://hal.archives-ouvertes.fr/hal-01764563.

Tchounikine, P. (2011). *Computer science and educational software design—A resource for multidisciplinary work in technology enhanced learning.* New York: Springer.

Thomas, A., & Edson, A. J. (2018). An examination of teacher-generated definitions of digital instructional materials in mathematics. In V. Gitirana, T. Miyakawa, M. Rafalska, S. Soury-Lavergne, & L. Trouche (Eds.), *Proceedings of the re(s)source 2018 international conference* (pp. 340–343). Lyon: ENS de Lyon. Retrieved on November 8th, 2018, at https://hal.archives-ouvertes.fr/hal-01764563.

Thomas, M. O. J., & Hong, Y. Y. (2005). Teacher factors in integration of graphic calculators into mathematics learning. In H. L. Chick & J. L. Vincent (Eds.), *Proceedings of the 29th conference of the International Group for the Psychology of mathematics education* (Vol. 4, pp. 257–264). Melbourne: University of Melbourne.

Tiburcio, R., & Bellemain, F. (2018). Computational engineering, didactical, educational software, software engineering. In V. Gitirana, T. Miyakawa, M. Rafalska, S. Soury-Lavergne, & L. Trouche (Eds.), *Proceedings of the re(s)source 2018 international conference* (pp. 262–264). Lyon: ENS de Lyon. Retrieved on November 8th, 2018, at https://hal.archives-ouvertes.fr/hal-01764563.

Trocki, A., & Hollebrands, K. (2018). The development of a framework for assessing dynamic geometry task quality. *Digital Experiences in Mathematics Education, 4*(2–3), 110–138.

Trouche, L. (2004). Managing the complexity of human/machine interactions in computerized learning environment: Guiding students' command process through instrumental orchestrations. *International Journal of Computers for Mathematics Learning, 9*(3), 281–307.

Trouche, L. (2005). Construction et conduite des instruments dans les apprentissages mathématiques : Nécessité des orchestrations. *Recherches en Didactique des Mathématiques, 25*, 91–138.

Trouche, L., & Drijvers, P. (2010). Handheld technology: Flashback into the future. *ZDM – Mathematics Education, 42*(7), 667–681.

Trouche, L., & Drijvers, P. (2014). Webbing and orchestration; two interrelated views on digital tools in mathematics education. *Teaching Mathematics and its Applications, 33*(3), 193–209.

Trouche, L., Gueudet, G., & Pepin, B. (2018, Online First). Documentational approach to didactics. In S. Lerman (Ed.), *Encyclopedia of mathematics education.* New York: Springer. doi:https://doi.org/10.1007/978-3-319-77487-9_100011-1.

van Dijke-Droogers, M., Drijvers, P., & Bakker, A. (2018). From sample to population: A hypothetical learning trajectory for informal statistical inference. In V. Gitirana, T. Miyakawa, M. Rafalska, S. Soury-Lavergne, & L. Trouche (Eds.), *Proceedings of the re(s)source 2018 international conference* (pp. 348–351). Lyon: ENS de Lyon. Retrieved on November 8th, 2018, at https://hal.archives-ouvertes.fr/hal-01764563.

Vergnaud, G. (1996). *The theory of conceptual fields. In. L.P. Steffe, P.Nesher, P. cobb, G.a. Goldin, & B. Greer (Eds.), Theories of Mathematical Learning* (pp. 210–239). Mahwah: Laurence Erilbaum.

Vergnaud, G. (2011). Au fond de l'action, la conceptualisation. In J. M. Barbier (Ed.), *Savoirs théoriques et savoirs d'action* (pp. 275–292). Paris: Presses Universitaires de France.

Villamizar, F., Cuevas, C., & Martinez, M. (2018). A proposal of instrumental orchestration to integrate the teaching of physics and mathematics. In V. Gitirana, T. Miyakawa, M. Rafalska, S. Soury-Lavergne, & L. Trouche (Eds.), *Proceedings of the re(s)source 2018 international conference* (pp. 352–355). Lyon: ENS de Lyon. Retrieved on November 8th, 2018, at https://hal.archives-ouvertes.fr/hal-01764563.

Voltolini, A. (2018). Duo of digital and material artefacts dedicated to the learning of geometry at primary school. In L. Ball, P. Drijvers, S. Ladel, H. Siller, M. Tabach, & C. Vale (Eds.), *Uses of technology in primary and secondary mathematics education* (pp. 83–99). Cham: Springer.

Wenger, E. (1998). *Communities of practice: Learning, meaning, and identity.* Cambridge: Cambridge University Press.

Zbiek, R.M., & Hollebrands, K. (2008). A research-informed view of the process of incorporating mathematics technology into classroom practice by inservice and prospective teachers. In M. K. Heid & G. Blume (Eds.), *Research on technology in the learning and teaching of mathematics: Syntheses and perspectives.* Charlotte: Information Age Publishers.

Zbiek, R. M., Heid, M. K., Blume, G. W., & Dick, T. P. (2007). Research on technology in mathematics education: A perspective of constructs. In F. K. Lester (Ed.), *Second handbook of research on mathematics teaching and learning* (Vol. 2, pp. 1169–1207). Charlotte: Information Age.

Part IV
Conclusions

Chapter 13
Evidencing Missing Resources of the Documentational Approach to Didactics. Toward Ten Programs of Research/Development for Enriching This Approach

Luc Trouche

Abstract This chapter proposes a view from inside the documentational approach to didactics (DAD), starting from determining some essential resources missing of DAD, to proposing ten programs of research/development for developing it. It could be considered as a follow-up of Chap. 1, where Ghislaine Gueudet situates the current state of DAD in looking back to its origin: This chapter proposes a possible future of this approach in analyzing its current state. It determines the missing resources of DAD in questioning current and past PhD students who have anchored their research in DAD. What did/do they learn in using DAD as a main theoretical resource; to which extent did/do they estimate that they have enriched DAD by their own work? Which are, according to them, the still missing resources of DAD? Which of these resources should be developed by DAD from itself and/or in co-working with other theoretical frameworks? From this inquiry, this chapter proposes ten perspectives of research, aiming to develop theoretical blind points of DAD, or to develop methodological tools, or to deepen the cultural/social aspects of DAD in questioning the naming systems used by teachers when interacting with resources. This chapter echoes actually different perspectives of research already present, as promising germs, in previous chapters of the book.

Keywords Documentational approach to didactics · Missing resources · Research program · Resource system · Theoretical networking

---

This chapter originates from a lecture given to the Re(s)sources 2018 International Conference. Video in English, with French subtitles, available at http://video.ens-lyon.fr/ife/2018/2018-05-30_009_Ressources2018_Luc_Trouche_v1.mp4

L. Trouche (✉)
French Institute of Education, ENS de Lyon, France
e-mail: luc.trouche@ens-lyon.fr

© Springer Nature Switzerland AG 2019
L. Trouche et al. (eds.), *The 'Resource' Approach to Mathematics Education*,
Advances in Mathematics Education,
https://doi.org/10.1007/978-3-030-20393-1_13

447

13.1 Introduction

This chapter is dedicated to the future of the documentational approach to didactics (DAD). Looking toward the future usually starts with "looking back," and questions such as the following arise: where do we come from, which was the path we followed for arriving here, which issues did we have to face, and which were the "missing" resources in our view that we need to advance DAD?

My first book (Trouche et al. 1998) was written with my 37 students, while I was still teaching mathematics in a secondary school: *Experiencing and proving. Experimenting mathematics in schools with symbolic calculators, 38 variations on a given topic.* It was a great experience, for me, to learn from my students regarding my own teaching, the potential of the mathematical problems we had faced together, and the "missing" resources in the mathematical environment of the classroom. Twenty years later, I will situate my talk in the same spirit, drawing from interactions with students and young researchers having used DAD, for retrospective and prospective reflections.

These reflections result from ten programs of research, the number 10 resonating with the 10 years of DAD. Actually, I wished for a reasonable number, and 10 appeared as a good compromise between a too small number of huge programs and a too big number of scattered programs. Nevertheless, I was thinking of these programs in a kind of "free attitude" mood: I wrote this chapter shortly before retiring as professor emeritus, having in mind that I will not be in charge of coordinating these programs (but hoping to participate in some of them!). Also, I was thinking of these programs more in terms of necessity, than in terms of feasibility, in an essential perspective of transmission to the community that I have tried to contribute to during the previous 10 years. When, in the following, I use the "we," it will designate this community, i.e., people studying teachers' work with resources under, at least partially, the umbrella of DAD.

After this introduction, this chapter is structured in seven sections: after this introductory section, in Sect. 13.2, I present the way of investigation I have used for detecting DAD existing and missing resources and inferring the corresponding research programs; Sect. 13.3 evidences some main DAD resources; Sect. 13.4 focuses on some missing *theoretical* resources; Sect. 13.5 on some missing *methodological* ones; Sect. 13.6 questions the necessity of an extension/expansion of the theory; Sect. 13.7 turns back to what is grounding each theory in terms of history, culture, and, finally, words; and Sect. 13.8 discusses the processes to be continued, carried on, or engaged.

13 Evidencing Missing Resources of the Documentational Approach to Didactics 449

13.2 Learning from Those Who Have Appropriated and Developed DAD

In this section, I briefly situate the roots of my experience as a researcher, then I present the way I have gathered the data for designing this chapter.

13.2.1 Rooting a Personal Experience

My personal teaching experience started when I was a mathematics teacher in secondary schools, using and designing resources for this purpose. I have already cited the work done with my secondary school students. As a researcher, I have already tried to describe my own intellectual trajectory (Trouche 2009), made of encounters with teachers, teacher educators, and researchers; projects of research; contrasted cultural situations; and students.

Tracing the encounters with researchers is often easy, as these encounters usually produce scientific resources (papers or books): developing an instrumental approach to didactics, with Dominique Guin (Guin and Trouche 1998), then with Kenneth Ruthven (Guin et al. 2005); developing the notion of instrumental orchestration with Paul Drijvers (Drijvers and Trouche 2008); developing the documentational approach to didactics with Ghislaine Gueudet (Gueudet and Trouche 2009), associating then Birgit Pepin (Gueudet et al. 2012); and developing a wider reflection on tools and mathematics with John Monaghan (Monaghan et al. 2016). Besides, some of the publications mentioned before were collective books; acting as an editor provided me the opportunity to meet the authors participating in the present book.

Tracing the encounters with the diversity of actors of mathematics education, teachers, teacher educators, researchers, students, engineers, is, generally, not so easy, because these encounters occurred in a variety of organizations and contexts. I keep mainly in mind my experience as the director of the Institute of Research on Mathematics Teaching of Montpellier (Trouche 2005a), as the president of the French Commission on Mathematics Teaching (Trouche 2017), and as a member of the EducTice Team of the French Institute of Education. Three research projects had also a major role in developing DAD and crossing it with other approaches: a regional project, PREMaTT[1]; a national project, ReVEA[2]; and a European project, MC2.[3]

I also learnt a lot from my experiences in scientific stays abroad: In Brazil (UFPE, Recife), where I deepened the idea of *webdocuments* (Bellemain and Trouche 2016); in China (ECNU, Shanghai), where I better understood the importance of

---

[1] PREMaTT: Thinking the resources of mathematics teachers in a time of transitions (http://ife.ens-lyon.fr/ife/recherche/groupes-de-travail/prematt)

[2] ReVEA: Living resources for learning and teaching (https://www.anr-revea.fr)

[3] MC2: Mathematical creativity squared (http://www.mc2-project.eu/)

teachers' collective work (Wang et al. 2018); in Mexico (Cinvestav, Mexico DF), where I better understood the importance of socio-cultural approaches (Radford 2008); and in Senegal, where I discovered the missing teaching resources of developing countries (Sokhna and Trouche 2016). A symposium, co-organized with Janine Remillard et al. in the frame of the second International Conference on Mathematics Textbooks (2017), *Teacher-Resource Use around the World*, offered a good opportunity for crossing these experiences.

Finally, I believe that my main learning sources were the PhD students themselves, appropriating, using, and developing DAD. We really know indeed what we try to appropriate, what we use, what we experience, what we develop in a creative way. What is true for any artefact is all the more true for a theoretical framework. Till now, ten students have defended their PhD, considering DAD as part of their theoretical framework.[4] About ten PhDs are in progress in the same frame. And a number of PhDs and post-doc students are more or less exposed to DAD through scientific stays or research projects. Obviously, the different elements rooting my own experience are not isolated: PhD, research projects, and international collaboration are linked, for example, via PhDs' co-supervision. But my choice, for conceiving this chapter, was to privilege the direct feedback of students, keeping in mind the fundamental dialectic between learning and teaching. I like, in this perspective, the Chinese translation of "Teaching," which is 教学 (Jiàoxué: a concatenation of two characters meaning, respectively, "teaching" and "learning").

13.2.2 Method for Gathering Data Grounding This Chapter

I collected students' feedback by two means: a seminar and a questionnaire.

The monthly "Resources seminar" was organized in the French Institute of Education, from September 2017 to June 2018, gathering about 15 PhD and post-doc students.[5] Each session of this seminar gave the opportunity to two students for presenting and connecting their work. It allowed for questioning the main concepts of DAD and for surfacing evidence of some missing resources.

The questionnaire was launched in December 2017, the answers being expected for March 2018. It was sent to students or young researchers using, or having used, DAD in their PhDs. I did not aim to reach all the people filling these conditions, but only the students and young researchers that I knew closely enough, with respect to their general research work. I got 29 answers from the 32 people solicited (see the corresponding names in the final acknowledgements, see "Acknowledgements"). In the letter accompanying the questionnaire, I motivated it by the necessity, for me, to prepare a lecture for the Re(s)sources International Conference and by my intention to base my lecture on their reflective view of DAD, for benefiting the development

---

[4] See the list of the corresponding PhD here: https://ens-lyon.academia.edu/enslyonacademiaedu/PhD

[5] http://eductice.ens-lyon.fr/EducTice/seminaires/ressource-2017-2018

13 Evidencing Missing Resources of the Documentational Approach to Didactics

of the research community itself. Then I asked a limited number of questions and left it up to people to more or less develop their answers.

The questions are:

1. You have used instrumental approach (IAD) and/or documentational approach to didactics (DAD). To what extent did these frames support your research?
2. In using DAD, did you feel that there were resources missing? In which circumstances? What new resources (theoretical as well as methodological) should this approach develop?
3. For designing these missing resources, which theoretical networking should be developed? Which new research programs to be launched?

The first question mentions the instrumental approach to didactics, taking into account that some students finished their PhD before the introduction of DAD (e.g., Sokhna 2006); for them, DAD appeared as a natural follow-up of their previous research. Some other students (e.g., Lucena et al. 2016) are using the notion of instrumental orchestration, situating themselves somewhere in between IAD and DAD. Actually, IAD acted as an incubator of DAD (see Gueudet, Chap. 2).

I started my writing from the answers given to these questions and from the interactions having occurred in the monthly Resources seminar. I have tried of course to take into account the whole set of answers. Then I crossed, gathered, and structured them according to my own experience (Sect. 13.2.1). Doing this, I was aware of some limitations coming from the methodology itself: some students may have thought that their difficulties come from their own lack, and not from the theoretical framework itself. This is the reason why the formal and informal interactions with these students were important for complementing some points in the students' answers. This work gave matter to ten programs of research and/or development.

13.3 The Productive and Constructive Aspects of a Theoretical Framework

In this section, I present essentially the answers to the first question, distinguishing three parts: (1) the way DAD supports the research, (2) the resources already developed for/by this approach, and (3) the main missing resource.

13.3.1 To What Extent Does DAD Support Your Research?

The contributions of the DAD could be classified into three main categories, *understanding*, *designing*, and *rethinking*.

Understanding concerns mainly the resources in their *diversity* and their *complexity*, and their *potential* for resourcing teachers' work, but also as critical *inter-*

faces between teachers and students or between *individual* and *collective* work or between designers and users and as markers or *witnesses* of teachers' professional development.

Understanding concerns then:

- The *potential* of various things for resourcing teachers' work;
- The *complexity* of the integration processes;
- The *interactions* between teachers and *students*;
- The interactions between *individual* and *collective* teachers' work;
- The gap between designers' *expectations* and teachers' *uses*;
- The metamorphosis from *prospective teachers* to *teachers at work*;
- Teachers' professional development over a *long period*.

Designing concerns mainly a didactical engineering dimension of the research work, focusing on the role of digital resources for renewing tasks and supports to teachers' work.

Designing concerns then:

- Tasks integrating *digital resources*;
- *Digital supports* for helping teachers to design their own resources.

Rethinking concerns teacher education and the nature itself of "what is teaching, what is a teacher," with a double component of designers and collective-reflective practitioners.

Rethinking concerns then:

- *Pre-service as well as in-service teacher education.*
- Teachers themselves as resource *designers* and *collective-reflective practitioners*.

What I retain from these answers is the central role of the notion of "resources" in the emergence of DAD and, more specifically, the role of digital resources and the double potential of the approach for its practical component (supporting design) and its conceptual component (rethinking teaching and teacher education). This could be compared to the emergence of the instrumental approach to didactics (e.g., Guin and Trouche 1998), but the issue was, at this time, mainly the integration of one new artifact (in this case, symbolic calculators). DAD proposes a holistic approach to teachers' work, taking into account the new universe of resources offered to teacher use, design, and re-design.

13.3.2 The New Resources Developed by/for DAD over the Past 10 years

What appears clearly during these last 10 years, and that is always the case when a new approach is proposed, is the flourishing process of creating concepts and names: first of all about the resources themselves but also about the events occurring over the time of designing and using, about the knowledge guiding the process of design and use, about the collective sheltering of these processes, and about the methodology of research, quite complex, to be constructed due to the diversity of times and places where the issues of teaching resources are addressed.

The answers to the questionnaire mention this creative process: being supported by a given frame goes on with contributing to the development of this frame, in the dynamics of each PhD:

- About resources: mother and daughter resources, complemented by the notions of structuring mother resources and oriented daughter resources; pivotal resources; meta-resources; proper, recycled, and intermediary resources; block of resources; cycle of life of a given resource; resource systems for learning (resp. for teaching).
- About events: documentational incidents; didactical incident.
- About knowledge: didactical affinity, documentational identity; documentational expertise; information competencies, documentational experience, and documentational trajectory.
- About collectives: mother, daughter collective, and hub collective (ReVEA project), documentation-working mate.
- About methodological design: methodological contract, reflective, and inferred mapping of a resource system.

Of course, other conceptual developments occurred during the past 10 years (see Gueudet, Chap. 2), I just mention here the contributions evoked over the questionnaire answers. The awareness of this conceptual diversity leads naturally to the need for a map allowing us to circulate into this new field.

13.3.3 Research Program n°1: Designing a DAD Living Multi-language Glossary

The need for a tool allowing one to master the conceptual field of DAD appears in a number of answers. Actually, a seed of such a tool had been developed at the emergence of the approach, by Ghislaine Gueudet, Rim Hammoud, and Hussein Sabra (the two first PhD students situating their work in DAD) and me, on a website, mainly in French, dedicated to DAD (http://educmath.ens-lyon.fr/Educmath/recherche/approche_documentaire) and offering a glossary presenting a definition of 21

Curriculum support: Resource elaborated for a teaching purpose (see the notion of *curriculum material*, Remillard 2005).
Remillard, J.T. (2005). Examining key concepts in research on teachers' use of mathematics curricula. *Review of Educational Research 75*(2), 211-246.

Fig. 13.1 An example (our translation) from the glossary developed at the emergence of DAD

Situations side of AnA.doc
Situation: Sophie (a middle school mathematics teacher), evokes her professional experience with resources
Editor: Rocha, April 2016
Description: In a one-hour interview, in her school, we asked Sophie about the events over time that influenced her interactions with her **resources** for teaching. Due to her different roles (member of a teacher association, teacher educator…), the events linked to her **collective work** are particularly underlined.
From the information she gave, we tried to infer her **resource system** and her **documentational trajectory**.
Glossary side of AnA.doc
Documentational trajectory: this concept is currently developed in the frame of the Rocha's PhD. For now, a documentational trajectory is constituted by all the events influencing over time, the teacher documentation work, i.e. both her resource system and the associated knowledge (Rocha, 2016)

Fig. 13.2 An extract of the AnA.doc platform (our translation): each expression in bold (in the situations side) has a corresponding definition in the glossary side

critical terms grounding DAD, supported by the first papers written in this period (see Fig. 13.1).

But this seed was not developed further, as it is always difficult to combine the development of a field and the development of a map allowing us to explore this expending field.

A new initiative was more recently launched, in the frame of the ReVEA project: The AnA.doc platform (Alturkmani et al. 2019) gave access to a set of *situations* of teacher documentation work (see also Sect. 13.5.4) and to a glossary integrating definitions of the main concepts used in the analyses (see Fig. 13.2). Then the glossary evolves with the analyses of the situations themselves: new concepts appear, and the meaning of each of them could also evolve, according to the evolution of the theory itself. The problem, here, is that the AnA.doc platform was developed in the frame of a given project, in French, and it works like a prototype, for a rather small community.[6]

---

[6] AnA.doc is available at https://www.anr-revea.fr/anadoc. A password is needed for accessing it, to be asked to the author of this chapter.

A twofold discussion: - What could be a Chinese explanation, and, if possible, translation, of critical terms of DAD such as *instrumentation* or *instrumentalisation*? - What could be an English explanation, and, if possible translation, of critical terms used for describing teachers' documentation work, such as 磨课 (Mó kè)? This explanation needed (see picture right side) actually a lot of words and gestures[105]?	

Fig. 13.3 An episode of a master class, in ECNU (Shanghai): discussing the concepts and their translation

Drawing from my experience of teaching in different contexts, I think that we need to combine the design of a glossary and the reflection of its instantiation in different languages. I realized the interest of such work in teaching, in English, in China (Fig. 13.3): explaining a definition in a very different language provides opportunities to deepen the corresponding concept, to give examples and counter-examples. The process of *denominating concepts* is essential for the development of each scientific field (Rousseau and Morvan 2000).

Such work has existed in other emergent fields, for example, in the field of TEL (technology-enhanced learning), with two meta-projects, intending to create an intellectual platform to support the conceptual and theoretical integration in this research area: a TEL Thesaurus and a TEL Dictionary. "Both tools are fully interdisciplinary, multilingual and takes into account the multicultural and epistemological roots of research on learning" (https://www.tel-thesaurus.net). Far from hiding the difficulty arising from translation processes, this platform profits from these issues for enriching the concepts at stake. For each language taken into account by the platform, a list of terms is proposed. An editor is in charge of each of them, and proposes for it: a definition, comments on its history, related terms, the translation issues, the disciplinary issues, and some key references. The editor is also in charge of accepting and managing the contributions proposing complementary or alternative views on each aspect of the "identity card" of this term in a given language.

It leads to my first potential program of research/development: developing a DAD living and multi-language glossary.

For me, it is really a condition for developing a scientific community, its concepts, and methods. It is also a condition for each researcher to express his/her analyses and write papers in his/her own language, necessary for both the dissemination of a new theoretical frame and its enrichment in encountering other cultures of teaching and of research.

13.4 Back to Basics, Deepening the Model of DAD Itself, Through Four Research Programs

I address in this section some theoretical issues related to DAD. Starting by the missing resources pointed out by the answers to the questionnaire, I propose afterward four potential programs of research aiming to take into account these theoretical needs.

13.4.1 The Missing Theoretical Resources

Ten years is a quite short period for the genesis of a theoretical frame, crossing different scientific fields (see Gueudet, Chap. 2). In this initial phase, some fuzzy aspects could appear. In his answer, one PhD student pointed out some wavering, for example about the notion of document, often presented with an equation (different languages used, our translation in English):

- In Gueudet and Trouche (2010): a document = recombined resources + a scheme of utilization;
- In Trouche (2016): a document = combined resources + schemes of utilization;
- In Bellemain and Trouche (2016): a document = resources + a scheme of instrumented action;
- In Pepin et al. (2017): a document = the joint resources + their usages + knowledge guiding their usages.

Is there one or several schemes developing with a given document? What means "utilization" in the expression "scheme of utilization" (and what is the balance between using and designing)? Are usages only *guided* by teacher's knowledge (and what about usages *producing* new knowledge?). This conceptual wavering reveals the underlying complexity of the processes at stake. I have classified answers to the questionnaire into four categories, that could be related to different sensitive points of the theoretical model:

- A category for *resources and resource systems*: what could be considered as a resource (gestures, languages, artefacts…)? What are the resource systems components? What about students' resource systems and their interactions with teachers' resource systems?
- A category for the dialectic *schemes/situations*: how could they be simultaneously analyzed in their joint evolution?
- A category for the dialectic *between individual vs. collective documentation work of teachers*, their context and effects.
- A category for *the length of teachers' professional development* (dialectic between short vs. long geneses).

13 Evidencing Missing Resources of the Documentational Approach to Didactics

Drawing from these categories, I propose the following four potential research programs.

13.4.2 Research Program n°2: Modeling the Structure and the Evolution of Teachers' Resource Systems

This program takes into account the first category of students' propositions (Sect. 13.4.1), answering the questionnaire, about *resources* and *resource systems* (issues already addressed in Chaps. 2, 3, and 9).

About the notion of resource, from the beginning of DAD, we rely on Adler's productive metaphor: "I also argued for the verbalization of resource as 're-source'" (2012, p. 4). Doing this, we cultivated a kind of ambiguity, using the term resource sometimes for something having the *potential* to re-source teachers' activity, and sometimes for something already integrated in teachers' activity. The following quotation (Trouche et al. 2018a, b Online First) is interesting from this point of view:

> Retaining [Adler's] point of view, DAD took into consideration a wide spectrum of 'resources' that have the potential to resource teacher activity (e.g., textbooks, digital resources, emails exchanged with colleagues, students' sheets), resources speaking to the teacher (Remillard 2005) and supporting her/his engagement.

This quotation is interesting, because it begins with the notion of "resource as a potential," then it goes on with the notion of a "resource interacting with a teacher," and finally it ends by the notion of a "resource supporting a teacher."

Actually, when we use the expression "curriculum resources," we use it in a first meaning of "potential resources"; when we use the expression "a teacher's resource," we use it in the second meaning of a resource already *adopted* (which often means *adapted*, as a result of the instrumentalization processes) by him/her. Finally, we have to make clear that this second meaning is the one that DAD is retaining. This choice is coherent with the whole sentence of Adler:

> I also argued for the verbalization of resource as 're-source'. In line with 'take-up', I posited that this discursive move shifts attention off resources per se and refocuses it on teachers working with resources, on teachers re-sourcing their practice (2012, p. 4).

It was also what we said in the seminal paper introducing this approach (my translation): "What the activity of a teacher encompasses, it is a set of resources" (Gueudet and Trouche 2008, p. 7). With this idea, comes a direct consequence: "A resource is never isolated; it belongs to a set of resources" (Gueudet and Trouche 2009, p. 205). This essential distinction between resource per se and resources integrated into the activity of a given teacher opens a wide space for issues:

- If we consider the resources per se, how could we analyze their potential (epistemic, didactical), their variability, and their quality?

458   L. Trouche

- If we consider the resources *of a given teacher*, how could we capture and analyze their diversity, from gestures to artifacts (Salinas and Trouche 2018) and their role all along his/her documentation work?
- How could we capture and analyze the process from potential resources to resources integrated into teachers' practices? Hammoud (2012) has introduced the notions of *mother resources* and *daughter resources*, Alturkmani et al. (2018) the notions of *structuring mother resources*, and *oriented daughter resources*: some first steps for analyzing the dialectic between *potential and actual resources*.

About the notion of resource system. Considering a teacher's resource leads then to consider the set of resources it belongs to, that is, *their resource system.* The choice of the expression resource *system* constitutes a strong statement, meaning that the set of resources that a teacher had appropriated is not messy, but is organized according to a given structure. Besides, from the beginning of DAD, a teacher's resource system is defined in an indirect manner: "The resource system of the teacher constitutes the 'resource' part of her documentation system (i.e., without the scheme part of the documents)" (Gueudet and Trouche 2012a, p. 27). This definition leads to what I call a top-down perspective, starting from the analysis of a part of the documentation system (i.e., a document developed for a given purpose), for inferring the resources involved in this genesis. I plead for a more balanced point of view, combining this top-down perspective, and a bottom-up perspective (from the resource system to the documentation system). Considering the set of a teacher's resources as a *system* opens also a wide space of questions:

- From which point of view could we analyze this structure (from a location point of view, from the mathematics knowledge point of view, from a curricular point of view, from a didactical point of view…), and how can we articulate these different points of view?
- How could we characterize such a system? As an open dynamic system, or…? And which consequence should have such a characterization?
- Analyzing a given system leads to analyze specific points and specific links. Some works have already (see Gueudet, Chap. 2) pointed out typical resources as pivotal, or meta, resources; we need certainly to deepen this classification.
- Could this analysis lead to evidence, for a given teacher, missing resources (and from which point of view?), as Chevallard and Cirade (2010) did, considering not the resources of a given teacher but the resources of the profession itself?
- For a given teacher, we could distinguish different resource systems intersecting his/her own resource system: the classroom resource system (see Ruthven, Chap. 3), his/her students' resource systems, and the resource systems of various collectives she/he participates in. Analyzing the *interfaces* (Trouche et al. 2019) between these resource systems could shed some light on the teacher's own resource system.

There are many ways of addressing the issues related to resource systems (e.g., analyzing their links to documentation systems), but the joint study of the resources themselves and the system structuring them seems to be promising and corresponds to the first set of answers to the questionnaire. Therefore, my second potential research program will be: **Modeling the structure and the evolution of teachers' resource systems.**

13.4.3 Research Program n°3: Deepening the Dialectics of Schemes/Situations of Documentation Work

This program takes into account the second category of students' propositions (Sect. 13.4.1), answering the questionnaire, about the dialectic schemes/classes of situations. These propositions question the model grounding DAD (Fig. 13.4), asking for further developments at three levels: the notion of scheme, the notion of situation, and the structure of documentation work (issues already addressed in Chap. 11).

The first level of reflection is related to the notion of scheme, which is certainly complex (Vergnaud 2009). But the notion of *utilization scheme* should be particularly questioned. If we go back to the instrumental approach to didactics, I had distinguished (Trouche 2005b, p. 150) *usage schemes and instrumented action scheme*, following Rabardel's distinction:

- *Usage sche*mes related to "secondary tasks." These can be located at the level of elementary schemes (meaning they cannot be broken down into smaller units liable to meet an identifiable sub-goal), but it is by no means necessary: they can themselves be constituted as wholes articulating a set of elementary schemes. Their distinctive feature is that they are orientated toward secondary tasks corresponding to the specific actions and activities directly related to the artifact.
- *Instrument-mediated action schemes* which consist of wholes deriving their meaning from the global action which aims at operating transformations on the object of activity. These schemes incorporate usage schemes as constituents. Their distinctive feature is their relation to "primary tasks." They make up what Vygotsky called "instrumental acts," which, due to the introduction of the

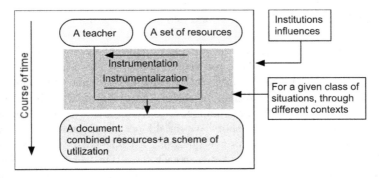

Fig. 13.4 A representation of a documentational genesis. (See Gueudet, Chap. 2)

instrument, involve a restructuring of the activity directed toward the subject's main goal [...]. Usage schemes constitute specialized modules, which, in coordination with one another and also with other schemes, assimilate and mutually adapt in order to constitute instrument-mediated action scheme (Rabardel 2002, p. 83).

A scheme is developed in order to accomplish a given task, then associating the development of a document to a scheme of utilization is certainly reduced. Some works (e.g., Messaoui 2018) have begun to address this issue. I think that we could distinguish *usage scheme* (e.g., storing a new resource in his/her own resource system) and *document action scheme*, oriented "toward the subject's main goal" (e.g., preparing a given lesson). It opens new questions, in the context of documentation work, toward a typology of usage schemes, and the possible decomposition of documentation action scheme in different usage schemes.

The second level of reflection is related to the DAD model (Fig. 13.4) itself. It was very productive, allowing a lot of deep analyses of teachers' documentation work over the last 10 years. Pointing out the dialectical processes of instrumentation and instrumentalization allowed, on one side, to study the effects of resources on teacher's activity and on the other side to study the creative effects of the teacher on the resources she/he mobilized. The weaker aspect of the model is to consider the class of situations, and, finally, the situation themselves, as given once for ever. But situations never repeat.... Following Bernstein (1996), "a situation is always a repetition without repetition." Vergnaud (2009), in his theory, situates as essential the pair scheme/class of situations, evidencing their joint *evolution* as a key condition of each cognitive process:

> The function of schemes, in the present theory, is both to describe ordinary ways of doing, for situations already mastered, and give hints on how to tackle new situations. Schemes are adaptable resources: they assimilate new situations by accommodating to them. Therefore the definition of schemes must contain ready-made rules, tricks and procedures that have been shaped by already mastered situations; but these components should also offer the possibility to adapt to new situations. On the one hand, a scheme is the invariant organization of activity for a certain class of situations; on the other hand, its analytic definition must contain open concepts and possibilities of inference (Vergnaud 2009, p. 88).

This adaptive aspect of schemes opens then a new question, aiming to rethink the DAD initial model (Fig. 13.4) for taking into account the joint evolution scheme/class of situations.

The third level of reflection is related to the *structure* of the documentation work. During the past 10 years, we have focused on operational invariants, for inferring teacher's knowledge in action. I think that we should give more importance to the rules of action, of gathering information, and of control, as well as to the inferences, that Vergnaud considers as other components of a scheme. We used to look at a resource system as a structured entity; we should look at a documentation work as a structured entity as well. It opens new questions, as: what are the successive stages of such a work; what are the links between each stage (the events/issues triggering the passage from one stage to another stage); is there a model of documentation work characterizing a teacher's profile, or/and a class of situations, or/and a discipline? What about the model of documentation work of two (or more) teachers working together?

Such a reflection has begun in some works, for example, Trouche et al. (2019). Studying the preparation of a new lesson by two teachers, a "DAD-driven" analysis points out successive stages of their documentation work (analyzing the curriculum, visiting resources from their own resource systems, comparing-selecting some of them, writing a first version of a lesson plan based on the combination of these resources, trying to integrate this lesson plan in a global progression, evidencing some missing resources and looking for them out of their resource systems but in their "resource confident zone"…). This paper (ibid.) evidences also that the structure of a teacher's documentation work resulting from a given analysis, even if it follows a common model (Fig. 13.5), is strongly sensitive to the theoretical lens grounding this analysis; in this case, three different lenses are used, DAD, Cultural and Historical Activity Theory (Engeström 2014), and Anthropological Theory of the Didactic (Chevallard 1999). Such a structural analysis of teachers' documentation seems to be promising and should be continued.

To me, these three levels (the level of scheme, of situation, and of documentation work) are strongly interrelated, and they motivate my third potential research program: **Deepening the dialectics of schemes/situations of documentation work.**

13.4.4 Research Program n°4: Deepening the Analysis of Conditions/Effects of Teachers' Collective Documentation Work

This program takes into account the second category of students' propositions (Sect. 13.4.1), answering the questionnaire, about the dialectic *between individual vs. collective documentation work of teachers*, their context and effects. In this section, we trace the history of this dialectic in the genesis of DAD, before formulating a new research program.

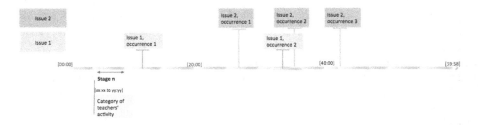

Fig. 13.5 A model for supporting analyses of teachers' documentation work (Trouche et al. 2019), proposing to cut into successive stages the work of a teacher interacting with resources

From its beginning (Chap. 2 of this book; Gueudet and Trouche 2008, p. 17), DAD has situated each documentation work as taken in a *bundle of institutional determinations* (from school to society). Thus, among the nine main teachers' families of activity that Gueudet and Trouche (2010) distinguished, two are mainly concerned with collectives:

- Participating in school collective activities (accompanying students for a journey, participating to the school board, monitoring teachers' training)
- Participating in professional collectives out of school (teachers associations, trade unions…) (p. 68, our translation).

The choice was made, at this starting point, to focus on collectives presenting the strong features of *communities of practice* (Wenger 1998), i.e., a shared commitment, a participation in a shared project, and the existence of a reification process, i.e., producing "things" recognized as a common wealth). The argument was (Gueudet and Trouche 2008, our translation):

> We retain, in our work, the frame of the communities of practice, because it appears to suit the collectives we want to study, but also because the dialectic participation/reification seems particularly relevant for studying the documentation work. Indeed, it allows to understand the interplay between the commitment in a community and the production of resources (p. 19).

This choice was indeed productive, allowing us to develop concepts such as *community documentation genesis*, or *community documentation* (Gueudet and Trouche 2008). However, the issue was that most of the collectives where teachers meet, sometimes occasionally, and in an informal manner, are not real communities of practice. This was probably the reason why further studies enlarge the scope of the collectives taken into account, calling out other theoretical frames as Hammoud (2012) using the *Cultural and Historical Activity Theory* of Engeström (2014), Rocha (2018a, b) using the theory of *Thought collectives* (Fleck 1934/1981), or Sabra (2011) using the theory of the *Common worlds* (Béguin 2004).

A special issue of ZDM (Pepin et al. 2013a), dedicated to *Re-Sourcing Teacher Work and Interaction*, confirmed the large vision of teachers' collective work, proposing a holistic perspective on collaborative design, (ICT) resources, and professional development. It raised new issues of *coherence* and *quality*, coming from teachers sharing resources outside institutional settings. Besides, in this special issue, Gueudet et al. (2013) maintained a focus on communities of practice, retaining three conditions for the development of such communities (p. 1014): a *mutual endeavor, minding the system*, and *common forms of addressing and making sense of resources.*

From 2014, new collaboration with China (via the links between ENS de Lyon and East China Normal University) opened a new field of inquiry, giving access to collective work as a regular part of teacher documentation and an essential mean of professional development (Pepin et al. 2016). Wang's PhD, between France and China, gave means for contrasting the collective documentation work in the two sides (Wang 2018). Chap. 7, in this book, contrasts the collective documentation work between China and Japan.

From 2015 to 2017, a European project, MC2 (see footnote 4), analyzed the creative aspect, for mathematics teachers' documentation work, of combining design processes occurring in community of practices and community of interest (i.e., communities gathering very different people, just sharing the interest for developing creative resources for mathematics teaching). The cross-fertilizing of these different communities appeared very productive (Essonnier et al. 2018). In the French PREMaTT project (see footnote 2), the objective was to stimulate the design process in a network of schools, considered as "small factories," supported by researchers and a monthly meeting in a "laboratory for innovative design": then the teachers are exposed to a variety of collectives, in regular as well as in artificial settings.

Finally, in the recent period, a focus has been made on "micro-collective." Wang (2018) developed the idea of "documentation-working mates," standing for a pair of teachers working together regularly. This smallest collective appears to be a good frame for deepening the analysis of the collective documentation work, the interactions between the two teachers evidencing some aspects of their schemes (Trouche et al. 2019).

Then it seems that we have accumulated, in the recent years, a rich experience about teachers' collective documentation work. This diversity of collectives, as well as the diversity of theoretical frameworks mobilized, opens new questions, aiming to rethink the DAD initial model (Fig. 13.6) conceived in the case of a Community of Practice. To what extent is it possible to speak of a "shared repertoire"? Of a collective resource system? To what extent is it possible to speak of common components of scheme? Of shared knowledge? What about teachers belonging to different collectives? How is it possible to take into account the diversity of a collective a given teacher belongs to?

This set of questions motivates a fourth potential research program: **Deepening the analysis of conditions/effects of teachers' collective documentation work, toward an updated model.**

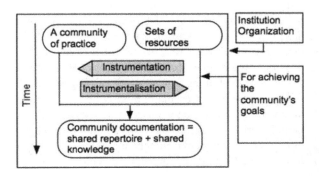

Fig. 13.6 Model of a collective documentation work in the case of a community. (Gueudet and Trouche 2012b, p. 308)

13.4.5 Research Program n°5: Modeling Teachers' Working with Resource Trajectories and Professional Development over Time

This program takes into account the fourth category of students' propositions (Sect. 13.4.1), answering the questionnaire, about *the length of teachers' professional development* (dialectic between short vs. long geneses). Deepening teachers' documentation work needs to have a large spatial view (all the contexts where this work happens, it is the purpose of the two previous potential programs) and a large time view; it is the purpose of this program. As stated by Pastré (2005, our translation): "There are two main poles of human activity, the first one is structured around the couple scheme – situation [...] the second one around the experience acquired, and constantly transformed by the actors" (p. 231). We address in the following discussion: this general issue of time, as an essential component of documentational geneses; the different perspectives allowing us to take into account the short vs. the long periods of time; and, finally, the need for a model of teacher professional development when interacting with resources.

For Vergnaud (2009), time is an essential component of conceptualization: "For instance the analysis of additive structures shows that the concepts of addition and subtraction develop over a long period of time, through situations calling for theorems of very different levels" (p. 89). Adapting this sentence, we could say that teachers' documentation schemes develop over long periods of time, through situations calling for operational invariants of very different levels. The issue is that, constrained by the duration of a PhD (about 4 years) and research projects (most of the time maximum 4 years), we do not have case studies exceeding this length of time. Unfortunately, starting the construction of DAD, we did not plan a follow-up of a collection of case studies; otherwise we would have today some 10-year long case studies. Finally, the only 10-year documentation cases that we have are…ourselves, as researchers interacting with resources.

We have then a number of cases studying the evolution of teachers' documentation work over a short period of time, this period being generally carefully chosen for its hypothetical potential for provoking changes in teachers' documentation work or/and for revealing the strongest invariants allowing the teachers to face the issues at stake: for instances, a period of curricular change (Rocha, Chap. 10), a period of *documentational incident* (Sabra 2016), or a period of *professional metamorphosis* (Assis, Chap. 9, studying the passage from pre-service to in-service teachers). The French ReVEA program (footnote 3) also allowed to analyze, over 4 years, some deep evolutions (Trouche et al. 2018a, b), due, in mathematics, to the curriculum evolutions (introduction of programming and algorithmics, needing to integrate new resources and to modify her/his relationship to the ready-made calculation tools), to the new means for storing and sharing information (Dropbox, Google Drive…), and to the development of e-textbooks. Indeed, the rapid evolution of the teaching environment and of the schooling form itself (e.g., flipped classrooms) could lead to the idea that "it is enough to consider short periods of time for capturing major evolutions." The long history of integration of tools in education (see, e.g., the integration of Interactive White Boards, Karsenti 2016) makes us aware of the necessity to distinguish between superficial and quick teaching changes on one side, deep and slow ones on the other sides. It is the reason why we need to combine short- and long-term follow-up of teachers' documentation work.

The ReVEA program aimed to propose, at a national level, and for a set of contrasted disciplines, an institutional observatory for following, over a long period of time, the evolution of teachers' interactions with resources. Unfortunately, this project did not happen. For taking into account the long period of time, we have actually two main perspectives: firstly, organizing a long-time follow-up and collecting data live during the whole period (difficult for the reasons evoked above; technically possible in using new tools for data collection, see Sect. 13.5.3) and, secondly, resting on teachers' "documentation memory." Some in-progress projects are following this last perspective: Rocha (2018a, Chapter 10), introducing the concepts of *documentational experience* and *documentational trajectory*; Loisy (Chap. 10), introducing the concept of *professional trajectory*; or Santacruz and Sacristan (2018), introducing the concept of *reflective documentational path*. The operationalization of these concepts lies on a double re-construction, a reflective re-construction, by the teacher him/herself from his/her own experience, drawing on the resources she/he used and designed, the events she/he crossed, and the collectives she/he participated in, and a re-construction by the researcher, using the teacher's reflective view, the effective traces of his/her experiences, and the interactions with the teacher, allowing to dig into these traces. This operationalization often results in a complex drawing (Fig. 13.7). Zooming in over a long-time trajectory to consider shorter periods could give the impression of a fractal structure, to be investigated further.

The analyses of *teachers' trajectory* (we keep this expression for designating the various concepts introduced above) are necessarily linked to a point of view on teachers' professional development in interacting with resources. This professional development has been thought under different models as *Mathematics teaching expertise* (Pepin et al. 2016), *teaching design capacity* (Pepin et al. 2017), *pedagogical design capacity* (Brown 2009), *information competencies* (Messaoui, to be

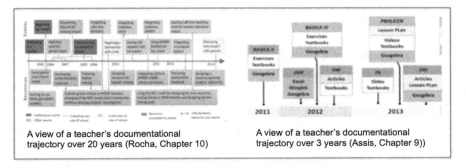

Fig. 13.7 Zooming in and zooming out of a teacher's documentational trajectory, determined by a sequence of critical events, critical resources used/designed, and critical collectives: an appearance of fractal structure

published), or *documentational expertise* (Wang, Chap. 11). This diversity opens a set of questions: how could we collect data allowing us to study teachers' interactions with resources over a long period? Focusing on sensitive periods (as beginning teachers, or changing position)? Which concepts to be introduced for charting the evolution of teachers' experience over this time? How could we combine the study of different trajectories (in various collectives, in various institutions…)? Finally, how can we model teachers' professional development in interaction with resources? (or to what extent does the diversity of concepts used call up for a multidimensional model of teachers' professional development?)

This set of questions motivates my fifth potential research program: **Modeling teachers' working with resources' trajectories and professional development over time.**

I reviewed in this section, from the missing resources pointed out by the answers to the questionnaire, four potential research programs (numbered 2, 3, 4, and 5). Not surprisingly, concerning a developing theoretical frame, these programs mainly concern concepts and models. I will come back to these programs in a synthetic way later, in the discussion section (Sect. 13.6, Fig. 13.15). In the following section, I address some methodological issues.

13.5   Issues of Methodological Design

I address in this section some methodological issues related to DAD. Starting from the missing resources pointed out by the answers to the questionnaire, I propose then three potential programs of research aiming to take into account these methodological needs.

13.5.1   DAD as an Incubator of Methodology for Analyzing Teachers' Work with Resources

Gueudet (Chap. 2) points out the importance of the development of a specific methodology, called *reflective investigation methodology*, for deepening DAD. I have already evidenced in this chapter (Sect. 13.3.2), from the answers to the questionnaire, to what extent the development of new methodological tools appeared both as a result and a need of/for DAD. Indeed, the need for analyzing very heterogeneous resources leads to a very diverse collection of data (see, for instance, Fig. 13.8).

This methodology evolves, as each methodology represents a living theoretical framework. For example, Gueudet, in Chap. 2 (Sect. 13.3.2), distinguishes, in her retrospective view of the beginning of DAD, four principles grounding the reflective investigation methodology. Trouche et al. (2018b Online First) add a fifth one: *The principle of permanently confronting the teacher's views on her documentation*

13 Evidencing Missing Resources of the Documentational Approach to Didactics 467

work and the materiality of this work (materiality coming, e.g., from the collection of material resources, from the teacher's practices in her classrooms), evidencing the need to respect the reflective view of the teacher and the analysis of the researcher.

Chapter 10 in this book, dedicated to methodological issues, evidences both the convergence of the DAD methodological discussions, due to the principles grounding these shared principles, and their diversity, due to the variety of contexts and research questions. This diversity also reveals the underlying complexity of the processes at stake. I have classified answers to the questionnaire into three categories, that could be related to different sensitive points of the methodological model:

- A category on *reflectivity*. How to support and to stimulate it? How to collect and analyze informal data coming from teacher's self productions?
- A category on *tracing resources*. How to trace teachers' interactions? How to study evolving resources? How to manage large-scale studies? How to develop quantitative analysis? Which kind of algorithms could be developed for structuring data analysis?

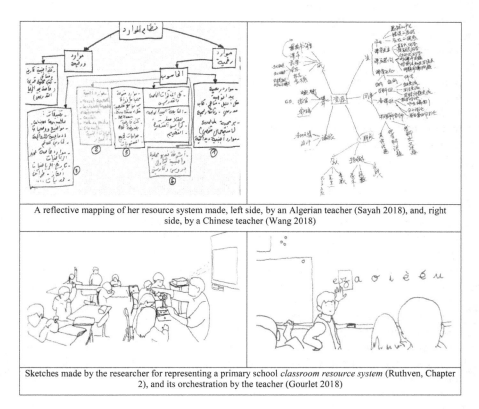

| A reflective mapping of her resource system made, left side, by an Algerian teacher (Sayah 2018), and, right side, by a Chinese teacher (Wang 2018) |

| Sketches made by the researcher for representing a primary school *classroom resource system* (Ruthven, Chapter 2), and its orchestration by the teacher (Gourlet 2018) |

Fig. 13.8 Drawings representing resource systems, by the teachers themselves, or by the researcher

- A category on *representing data*. How could data and data analyses be stored and presented, particularly in the case of collectives? Which kinds of hybrid support could be developed, for sharing the data and discussing the related analyzes, in combining images and sounds, via webdocuments?

Drawing from these categories, I propose the following three potential research programs.

13.5.2 Research Program n°6: Looking for Methodological Models for Stimulating Reflectivity – Storing and Analyzing Related Data

This program takes into account the first category of students' propositions (Sect. 13.5.1), answering the questionnaire, about *stimulating teachers' reflectivity*. Reflectivity is a structural component of the reflective investigation methodology for at least two essential reasons: getting information on teachers' documentation work as a *continuous* process (the need to know what happens between two meetings with the researcher) and getting information on documentational geneses as *long* processes (the need to know what happened a long time before). Working on reflectivity raises two issues, not fully addressed until now: how to stimulate reflectivity and how to analyze the very diverse data resulting from the expression of teacher's reflectivity?

The first issue is to take into account the reflectivity, that has been done until now mainly through three means: through a *contract* specifying the role of the teacher; through specific *collective settings* for making the teacher confident; through specific situations aiming to stimulate teacher's self investigation. Sabra (2016) has defined what he calls a *methodological contract* as a "system of *mutual expectations* between the teacher and the researcher": the teacher will describe his/her documentation work, knowing that the researcher is not here for a judgment, or an assessment, but for better understanding "teachers interacting with resources," producing then new knowledge that could benefit further the whole profession. Wang (2018) followed two "documentation-working mates," i.e., teachers preparing regularly their lessons together, and she benefited in this situation of natural reflectivity, each teacher "speaking to the researcher through her documentation working mate." Gueudet and Trouche (2010) used a situation proposed by Oddone et al. (1981), the "Instruction to the double": they asked the teacher to imagine that she/he will be replaced in his/her classroom by another teacher, looking exactly as himself/herself, and that she/he has to transmit his/her own resources and instructions, so that the students would see no difference with their usual teacher and his/her double. These three means (methodological contract, collective settings, instruction to the double) have not been investigated in a systematic way.

I think that we should indeed develop a more systematic "reflection on reflectivity," its conditions and effects. Vermersch (2012) gives a general frame for rethinking a methodology aiming at the explicitation, by a subject, of his/her action. His book presents the historical, epistemological, and practical coherence of the technique of explicitation, as a general issue that had addressed the philosophy over a long time. Drawing from the philosopher Husserl, he evidences the deep links between consciousness, passive memory, and attention. We should draw ourselves from this general frame for rethinking the way we stimulate, and use, teacher's reflectivity about his/her interactions with resources, ancient as well as current.

The second issue to address is the analysis of data produced by the "reflective teacher," particularly the various representations, or mappings, that a teacher is asked to design, or design for himself/herself. Caraës and Marchand-Zanartu (2011) have evidenced the dynamics of such "images of thought." Fig. 13.9 shows the case of Alfred H. Barr mapping his field of interest, reconsidering regularly his view, deepening at each time his knowledge of the field. It gives also an idea of the complexity of the work of transposition – inference, for going from a handmade drawing to a "proper" printed version. The analysis of such drawings raises a lot of difficulties, which have not been addressed by the diverse case studies developed under the umbrella of DAD. Hammoud (2012, p. 216) has begun to propose a method, drawing from methods coming from the field of cognitive mapping (Cossette 1994, 2003), which allows to infer some information from teachers' drawings or sketches.

These issues open a wide field of questions, that are, to me, interrelated: Which settings or tools should be thought for stimulating teachers' reflectivity? How to combine, and make profit of, individual, and collective, reflectivity? Which kind of

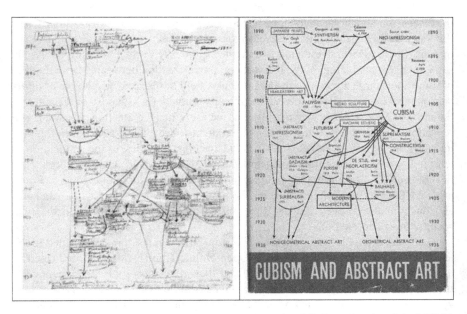

Fig. 13.9 Left, one of the mappings of modern art drawn by A.H. Barr, founder of the MOMA (Caraës and Marchand-Zanartu 2011, p. 86), and right side, a transposition of these mappings for printing a MOMA poster

expressions of teacher's reflectivity should we privilege? Which analyses should be developed for understanding the traces of these expressions? And finally, should we look for a single model for stimulating, tracing, analyzing teachers' reflectivity?

This set of questions motivates my sixth potential research program: **Looking for methodological model(s) for stimulating reflectivity; storing and analyzing related data.**

13.5.3 Research Program n°7: Developing Models Combining Quantitative and Qualitative Studies of Interactions Between Teachers and Resources

This program takes into account the second category of students' propositions (Sect. 13.5.1), answering the questionnaire, about *tracing teachers' resources*. There is, indeed, a contrast between the abundance of data provided by teachers using (individually as well collectively) digital resources and the frequent "artisanal" character of methods used by researchers for investigating these data. In this section, I firstly point out some emerging tools for addressing the "big data" coming from teachers' documentation work; secondly, I evidence the remaining complexity, suggesting a new research program.

Sabra analyzed the emails exchanged by a group of 30 teachers, members of the association Sabra (2011, p. 200), designing an online textbook. Just at the time of the discussion about one chapter, he had to take into account about 1000 emails, and this huge number leads him to develop specific methods for analyzing discussion threads. Such quantitative methods remained quite rare in the DAD corpus. At the same time, for analyzing, in the Internet era, the interaction between a large number of users and a large number of resources, a new field of research developed, as *information architecture* (Pedauque 2006, already quoted by Gueudet in Chapter 2; Salaün 2012); *learning analytics*, for the measurement, collection, analysis, and reporting of data about learners and their contexts (already used for education policy purposes, see Ferguson et al. 2016); and teaching analytics, as the application of learning analytics techniques to understand teaching and learning processes. Teaching analytics is used, for example, for analyzing classroom interactions (Prieto et al. 2016) or for analyzing online teachers' interactions when they search and create educational resources (Xu and Reker 2012), and developing, in this perspective, specific tools and methods.

Such analytic tools are in progress. Salaün (2016), in a seminar dedicated to the analysis of interactions in a Massive Open Online Course (MOOC) dedicated to mathematics teacher education, recognized that: "We miss tools for dynamically following up the documentation work of a given community" (Fig. 13.10). Moreover, we need to be aware that it is impossible to totally understand teachers' documentation work by large quantitative studies. Jansen (2018), comparing the efficiency of modeling in experimental and human sciences, underlines that there are four essential factors that make the simulations of society qualitatively more difficult than those of matter: the heterogeneity of humans; the lack of stability of anything; the many relationships to be considered both temporally and spatially; the reflexivity of the humans who react to the models that one makes of their activity.

These issues open a set of questions: which interactions could be developed with the field of teaching analytics for modeling teachers' interactions with resources? How to articulate quantitative studies and qualitative case studies? These questions motivate my seventh potential research program: **Developing models combining quantitative and qualitative studies of interactions between teachers and resources.**

13.5.4 Research Program n°8: Thinking Reflective and Collaborative Supports for Capturing, Analyzing, and Sharing Data Related to Teachers' Documentation Work

This program takes into account the third category of students' propositions (Sect. 13.5.1), answering the questionnaire, about *representing data*. The diversity of interrelated data to be collected when following teachers' documentation work calls up for specific support. In this section, we firstly evoke several attempts aiming to address this issue, then we evidence some main questions needing further research.

A first attempt was the *documentation valise*, described by Gueudet (Chap. 2, Sect. 13.4.2). A documentation valise gathers a set of data concerning a teacher's

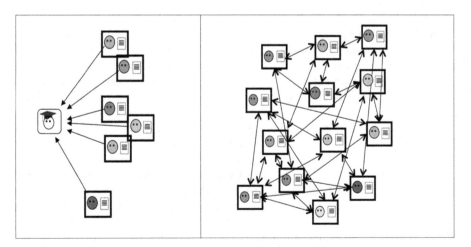

Fig. 13.10 From a teacher-centered setting (each student interacting with a teacher) to a collaborative work setting (each learner interacting with each learner), a leap in complexity. (Salaün 2016)

case study: the ambition is to make understandable, by a researcher from outside (i.e., not involved in this study), the case and its study. Only one case, Vera's case, is presented on the website dedicated, at its beginning, to DAD.[7] The case focuses on a *lesson cycle*, following four steps (preparing the lesson, implementing it, debriefing throughout assessing students' work, and reflecting the whole process). The interface provides general information on the case's context (curriculum, school, teacher) and on the research context (objectives, methodology). It provides also specific information on the lesson cycle: the videos of each step, the video scripts made by the researcher, and the resources used/produced by the teacher. It gives no means to the reader for commenting on the data or proposing an alternative analysis of what happened. Due to this limitation, and as no specific interface was developed for supporting the design of such documentation valises, this methodological perspective was rarely used for studying teachers' documentation work and presented to the community (see Pepin et al. 2015). Finally, the documentation valise remained a metaphor of the documentation work as a journey, needing, as each journey to gather and transport personal resources, and producing new resources (as travelogues).

After this first attempt, I had the chance to work, in 2015, for 2 months, with a research team in Brazil, Lematec,[8] interested in developing interactive online supports in the context of teacher training, and, from this stay, emerged this idea of *webdocument* or webdoc (as an abbreviation of "web documentary") defined by Wikipedia (https://en.wikipedia.org/wiki/Web_documentary) as "a unique medium to create non-linear productions that combine photography, text, audio, video, animation, and infographics based on real time content. This way the publications progresses over several weeks [...] the viewer acquires control of navigation, in a way becoming the author or creator of its own personalized documentary." First examples of such webdocuments were developed in the context of this scientific stay (see Lucena and Assis 2015, including English, French, and Portuguese versions), allowing to store both data related to a teacher's documentation work and a preliminary analysis of these data according to a given research question. Compared to the documentation valise, it constitutes a real improvement, constituting a passage from a metaphor to its operationalization. Bellemain and Trouche (2016) describe (French and English versions) the development of this interface and of the associated reflection.

Following this dynamic, a third attempt occurred in the context of the French ReVEA project, with the AnA.doc platform (Alturkmani et al. 2019). In addition to a glossary (introduced in this Chapter, Sect. 13.3.3), AnA.doc distinguished two essential levels (Fig. 13.11): a level of situations, for *storing* data, and a level of webdoc, for *analyzing* them. Compared to the Brazilian webdocuments, it could be considered as an improvement, for two points of views: distinguishing these two levels of storage analysis; giving tools for grounding the analysis on excerpts of date (e.g., a 1-minute video and not the whole video), leading to more accurate statements.

---

[7] http://educmath.ens-lyon.fr/Educmath/recherche/approche_documentaire/documentation-valise

[8] http://lematec.net.br/lematecNEW/

13 Evidencing Missing Resources of the Documentational Approach to Didactics 473

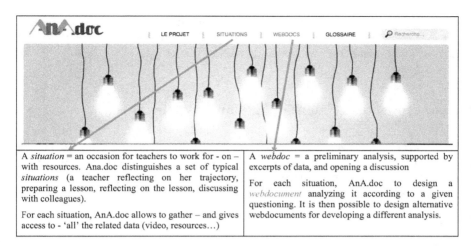

A *situation* = an occasion for teachers to work for - on – with resources. Ana.doc distinguishes a set of typical *situations* (a teacher reflecting on her trajectory, preparing a lesson, reflecting on the lesson, discussing with colleagues). For each situation, AnA.doc allows to gather – and gives access to - 'all' the related data (video, resources…)	A *webdoc* = a preliminary analysis, supported by excerpts of data, and opening a discussion For each situation, AnA.doc to design a *webdocument* analyzing it according to a given questioning. It is then possible to design alternative webdocuments for developing a different analysis.

Fig. 13.11 The AnA.doc platform, articulating two essential levels (situations vs. webdocs) for analyzing teachers' documentation work

A webdoc could be considered then as a preliminary analysis, a short text with a small number of short excerpts, allowing a quite easy appropriation in order to facilitate the discussion of these preliminary results. Ana.doc is thought as a tool for developing analyses of teachers' documentation work within a community of research. Several communications in scientific conferences were then supported by AnA.doc (Messaoui 2018; Rocha 2018b).

A fourth attempt is an ongoing project, PREMaTT (Sect. 13.4.4), aiming to develop a twin AnA.doc platform, dedicated to both researchers and teachers, crossing the reflective, collaborative, and research analysis of situations of documentation work.

These developments were studied in the frame of the young researchers' workshop of the International Re(s)source conference.[9] Further developments could be then be expected. The design of such a platform opens actually a set of questions: how could we develop flexible platforms for storing and analyzing data coming from teachers' documentation work that could be used both by small communities and at a large scale? Could we combine the development of such a platform and the combination of individual teachers' travelogues? How could we think travelogues jointly designed and used by teachers and researchers? This set of questions motivates my eighth potential research program: **Thinking reflective and collaborative supports for capturing, analyzing, and sharing data related to teachers' documentation work.**

This section was dedicated to the missing resources of DAD, from a methodological point of view, proposing three potential research programs (see Sect. 13.7, discussion section, Fig. 13.15, for a synthetic presentation). The methodological developments, of course, could not happen from a reflection restricted to DAD, but

---

[9] See session C at https://resources-2018.sciencesconf.org/resource/page/id/10

have the benefit of the interactions with other theoretical frameworks. In the following section, we deepen an issue already addressed in this chapter, the conditions and interest for crossing DAD with other theoretical frameworks.

13.6 Toward an Extension/Expansion of the Theory

In this section, I go back to the questionnaire answers regarding the link to be built between DAD and other theoretical frames. Then I examine this question from a general point of view. Drawing from these considerations, I propose finally a ninth potential research program.

13.6.1 Back to the Questionnaire

The third point of the questionnaire was (Sect. 13.2): *For designing missing resources, which are the possible theoretical crossings? Which new research programs are to be launched?*

In the following, we consider firstly answers questioning the theoretical crossing itself, then we consider the theoretical crossings that are proposed, and, finally, we analyze the current intertwining between DAD and other theoretical frameworks.

There is always, when looking for some theoretical missing resources, a choice to be made between developing the frame housing your research and looking outside this frame for getting these resources. Some answers to the questionnaire privilege the first choice, proposing, for example, to deepen the concept of mediation in introducing the concept of *documentational mediation* (Sokhna 2018), or to deepen the theory of instrumental orchestration by introducing the concept of *meta-orchestration* (Lucena et al. 2016).

Most of the answers to the questionnaire suggest theoretical crossings: first of all with theories in didactics (didactics of mathematics, joint action in didactics, or professional didactics); secondly, with theories speaking of resources and technology (information and communication sciences, theory of variations, boundary objects, or TPACK); thirdly, with theories speaking of collective, history, and culture (lesson studies, cultural and historical activity theory, models of Wartofsky, anthropological approach to didactics, or sociology); and, fourthly, with theories speaking of computation (computer sciences, constructionism, and computational thinking).

The need for theoretical means for taking into account the social and cultural aspect is reinforced by answers underlining the necessity to study teachers' work with resources in rural, or poor schools, or specific communities, and the necessity to address the issues of equity and access to resources.

These answers reflect not only the intended crossings with other theoretical frameworks, but existing connections, from the origin of DAD (see Gueudet,

Chap. 2; Artigue, Chap. 5; and in this chapter Sects. 13.4.3 and 13.4.4, for the frames mobilized for studying collective aspects of teachers' documentation work). Going further, we could analyze the *resources* produced by the researchers using DAD – their scientific papers – and extract the theoretical references used, for evaluating the degree of connection of DAD with other fields. Tools for making such an analysis exist (Fig. 13.12). We could identify the papers using DAD at an international level and apply these tools to this set of papers.

We could develop also this analysis from another point of view: choosing the most "popular" paper presenting DAD, that is, the paper written by Gueudet and Trouche (2009) published by Educational Studies in Mathematics, quoted, according to Google Scholar (on January 11, 2019), 287 times, and studying the theoretical frames of the articles quoting this paper.

Beyond these statistical considerations, how could we analyze the interest of connecting DAD with other frames? This is the purpose of the following sub-section.

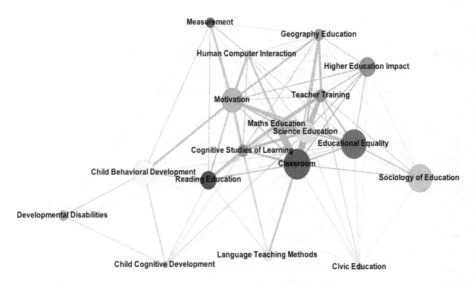

Fig. 13.12 Clusters of educational research, from the references used by 22,000 papers written between 2000 and 2004 in journals recognized by the French Ministry of Higher Education. (Trouche 2014, p. 2)

13.6.2 Theorizing the Interactions of DAD with Other Scientific Frames

Artigue (Chap. 5) proposes a view of a theoretical frame as a *research praxeology*: "The basic idea is to consider that the model of praxeologies that ATD uses to model human practices might be useful to approach the issue of connection between theories, by making clear that theories emerge from research practices and condition these in return, and that connection between theories involves thus necessarily much more than the theories themselves. They cannot be productively established by just looking for connections between theoretical discourses."

This approach enables her to analyze the development of DAD as a *full research praxeology*, but not a *complete* one, as it continuously extends and diversifies research problématiques, and, in this dynamic, reinforces and diversifies its theoretical connections. It is the case, for example, of a recent paper (Trouche et al. 2019, already presented Sect. 13.4.3), using three theoretical lenses for analyzing the work of two teachers preparing together a lesson. This paper is written for a special issue *Curriculum ergonomics* of the International Journal of Educational Research (Choppin et al. 2018). The issue editors define this new field as "exploring the interaction between the design and use of curriculum materials." Participating in this special issue constitutes indeed on occasion, in facing a new research problématique, to cross DAD with other theoretical frames. To which objectives? To deepen and strengthen DAD as a theoretical construct? To reinforce and diversify its theoretical connections? Or to extend or expand DAD? I try to address these issues in the following sub-section.

13.6.3 Research Program n°9: Thinking DAD as a Theoretical Frame Interacting with Other Frames and as a Component of a Wider Field of Research

The recent history of DAD is a history of expanding its borders (see Gueudet, Chapter 2): from mathematics to other disciplines, from secondary schools to pre-primary schools and higher education, and to a variety of contexts (social, cultural, formal/informal), from teachers to a variety of actors of education (including students).

It is perhaps the time, 10 years after its emergence, to question the "raison d'être" of this frame. Taking advantage of the acronym DAD as a palindrome, we could translate it either as *documentational approach to didactics* or as *didactical approach to documentation*. This second "translation" of the acronym is perhaps more consistent with the research praxeology of DAD, its tasks and techniques, technology, and theory. And if DAD defines itself as a didactical approach to documentation, it means of course that there are other approaches to documentation (psychological, sociological...). This is conceptualized in the introduction of the book, proposing the new acronym RAME, standing for "'Resource' Approach to Mathematics Education," and embracing DAD more largely as a field of research.

Following this thread, for addressing the whole set of disciplines to be taught, I have in mind that we could also introduce the expression *documentational studies*, as a way of developing *a new multidisciplinary academic field embracing the complexity* (Monteil and Romerio 2017) of "teachers interacting with resources." We could have in mind the example of *environmental studies* as a "multidisciplinary academic field, which systematically studies human interaction with the environment in the interests of solving complex problems" (Wikipedia).

It opens a set of questions: how could we analyze the position and evolution of DAD with respect to different communities of research, throughout the papers produced by researchers referring to this theoretical frame? How could we define a new research praxeology aiming to study, according to different lenses, the interactions between teachers and resources? This set of questions motivates my ninth potential research program: **Thinking of DAD both as a theoretical frame interacting with other frames and as a component of a wider field of research.**

From theoretical to social and cultural diversity: the following section tackles this last issue, related to the naming systems used, by teachers, in different contexts.

13.7 Crossing Teachers' Languages for Puzzling out Names, Meanings, and Resource Systems' Structure

In this section, I tackle the issue of taking into account the social and cultural diversity of teachers' documentation work: firstly, from the analysis of curriculum, resources, and interactions with resources; secondly, from the analysis of the naming systems designed-used by teachers over their documentation work; and, thirdly, for proposing a last potential research program.

13.7.1 Contrasting Teachers' Documentation Work Across Cultural and Social Boundaries

The need for developing comparative studies is mentioned in the answers to the questionnaire. Actually, as soon as we consider teaching resources across the national boundaries, their role in the *"figured world"* of classroom resource systems (Pepin 2009, in the case of England, France and Germany) or as *crucial interfaces between culture, policy, and teacher curricular practice* (Pepin et al. 2013b, in the case of France and Norway) appears clearly. Remillard et al. (2014), contrasting the case of Flanders, USA, and Sweden, speak of *the voice of curricular material.* Comparative studies seem to be as interesting when the countries are close (see

478 L. Trouche

Miyakawa and Xu, Chap. 7 for the cases of China and Japan) as when the countries are far away (Wang 2018 for the cases of China and France). Pepin et al. (Chap. 6) evidence the interest of large comparative studies for deepening the work of teachers as designers. But, till now, the issue of the *words* used by teachers when working with resources has not really been addressed.

13.7.2 Teachers' Naming Systems as Revealing the Springs of Their Documentation Work

The issue here is essentially different from that addressed in Sect. 13.3.3 (giving birth to our first potential research program): there it was the issue of denominating/ translating concepts of an emerging scientific field. Here we are speaking of words used by teachers in their daily documentation work, words conceived not as isolated entities but as *systems* revealing the deep structure of *thought-languages* (Jullien 2015).

I realized the interest of studying these naming systems when teaching in Shanghai a master class, working on interviews of teachers conducted by students themselves (Fig. 13.13). The richness of words showed, for instance, the importance to distinguish the resources designed for oneself, and the resources designed for the school community. Actually, it was impossible to translate from Chinese to English word by word: the only possibility was to analyze the Chinese system of words for inferring the structure of their documentation work, what we did for writing a paper on Chinese teachers' resource system (Pepin et al. 2016).

This study of teachers' naming systems has been already engaged in the frame of the *Lexicon* project (Artigue, Chap. 5; Clarke et al. 2017), supported at an international level by a number of researchers. It aims to "document the naming systems

Category: *The resources designed by the teacher*

- 人格化的材料 the materials processed by the teacher with a strong sense of herself
- 从专业眼光提炼过的材料 materials selected and adapted from a common professional community preference
- 经过教师自己重新理解后的材料 materials re-explained by the teacher
- 转化/活化的材料 transformed / lived materials: the seemingly irrelevant materials developed into academic materials

Category: *Teaching through the way of...*

- 言说 speech, lecture, presentation
- 表演 performance (acting, showing)
- 夸张的肢体动作 exaggerating gestures
- 模拟声响 imitating voices

Fig. 13.13 Analyzing the interview of a teacher (educational philosophy in higher education) by the student who made the interview. (Personal source, master class on educational research, ECNU, Shanghai 2016)

> **Календарно-тематичний план/ Calendar thematic plan**
>
> - A document made by teacher for every grade before every academic year according to the curriculum.
> - Identifies the order of themes and lessons to be taught according to the numbers of hours for teaching of the themes specified in the curriculum, numbers of the lessons per week and school schedule.
> - Allowed differences with the curriculum up to 10%
> - Mandatory document
> - Should be examined by the methodical association of teachers of the school, agreed with Vice-director in teaching and upbringing work and approved by Director of the school before the 30th of August.

Fig. 13.14 Explicating word naming, a critical teacher resource in Ukraine (Gitirana et al. 2018)

(lexicons) employed by different communities speaking different languages to describe the phenomena of the mathematics classroom."

The phenomena of the mathematics classroom are far from recovering the whole teachers' documentation work. Studying naming systems employed by different communities speaking different languages to describe the phenomena of their documentation work, essentially, remains to be done.

13.7.3 Research Program n°10: Contrasting Naming Systems Used by Teachers in Describing Their Documentation Work, Toward a Deeper Analysis of Teachers' Resource Systems

This study was at the center of the Young Researcher Workshop (session D),[10] following the International Conference Re(s)sources 2018. The session has analyzed data gathered beforehand in different languages and cultural contexts (Arabic, Brazilian, Chinese, Dutch, French, Mexican, Turkish, and Ukrainian). The data had been collected from interviews, focusing on the preparation of a lesson and on teachers' resource systems. For each of these questions, the teachers have been asked to name their resources, describe their classification and the steps of their documentation work. Preliminary work has been done, describing in English the reality to which these terms refer, and proposing examples and counter-examples. The session allowed a cross-presentation and analysis of these data (see, e.g., Fig. 13.14 for a Ukrainian case). Understanding a given name needs to study its institutional definition, but also its meaning in a given culture (in Ukraine, the meaning of a "plan," a "methodical association"...), for a given teacher, and the

---

[10] https://resources-2018.sciencesconf.org/resource/page/id/10

place of the corresponding resource in the teacher's documentation work (the position of this particular name in a global naming system). It leads to an anthropological approach to teachers' resources, taking into account linguistic, cultural, social, and historical backgrounds.

This is the beginning of a process: thinking of teachers' resource through the lens of the naming system they develop and use. This process opens a set of questions: Which methodology for gathering relevant data gives access to teachers' naming systems? Which interaction with the Lexicon project? How to differentiate institutional naming systems and teachers' personal naming systems? How contrasting naming systems come from a same culture vs. crossing different cultures (see Wang et al. 2019 for contrasting a Chinese and a Mexican case)? This set of questions motivates my tenth potential research program: **Contrasting naming systems used by teachers in describing their resources and documentation work, toward a deeper analysis of teachers' resource systems.**

This research program closes the short list of ten potential research programs coming from the answers to my questionnaire... and from my own interpretation and construction.

13.8   Discussion

In this section, I propose firstly a retrospective and critical view on the ten potential research programs; then I review some ongoing works, which could be related to these programs; and finally, I propose a metaphor aiming to capture the complexity of teachers' documentation work.

13.8.1   A Global View on Ten Research Programs, as Ten Interconnected Perspectives of Research and Development

My ambition was not, of course, to determine all the resources that the development of DAD requires and to infer research programs aiming to design all these resources. I drew these missing resources only from answers I received to the questionnaires, and these answers came from new research problématiques creating new theoretical or methodological needs. The ten research programs built from these missing resources reflect my own point of view and my "orchestrating experience." After the lecture given at the International Re(s)sources conference, when writing this chapter of this book, I also tried to integrate some inputs of the previous chapters. Even now, I am aware of the incomplete character of this investigation. The search for missing resources looks like a "mise an abîme," each collection of missing resources appealing for "finding resources missing in the missing resources that have been

1. Conceiving a DAD living multi-language glossary	6. Looking for methodological model(s) for stimulating reflectivity; storing and analyzing related data
2. Modeling the structure and the development of teachers' resource systems	7. Developing models combining quantitative and qualitative studies of interactions between teachers and resources
3. Deepening the dialectics of schemes / situations of documentation work	8. Thinking reflective and collaborative supports for capturing, analyzing and sharing data related to teachers' documentation work.
4. Deepening the analysis of conditions / effects of teachers collective documentation work, towards an updated model	9. Thinking DAD both as a theoretical frame interacting with other frames, and as a component of a wider field of research
5. Modeling 'teachers working with resources' trajectories and professional development over the time.	10. Contrasting naming systems used by teachers in describing their resources and documentation work, towards a deeper analysis of teachers' resource systems

Fig. 13.15 A kaleidoscope of ten perspectives of research

found." Then we could say that it is an imperfect work by nature: impossible to determine a complete missing resource system…

Actually, these ten "research programs" constitute rather *perspectives* of research and development, as their construction, as programs, remain to be done. Of course, these perspectives are not independent: e.g., Program 1 (about a DAD multi-language glossary) is linked with Program 2 (about the structure of teachers' resource systems) and with Program 3 (about documentation schemes). When I look at these ten perspectives of research, I consider finally them as a *kaleidoscope* of perspectives (see Fig. 13.15): according to the point of view that the reader will adopt, when moving around these perspectives, she/he will discover a new panorama of the research to be thought for developing the scientific field.

At this stage of the development of DAD, from these ten perspectives of research, what stands out is mainly a matter of *names* (names of concepts as well as names used by teachers) and a matter of *models*, that is, in my opinion, the symptoms of a construct coming out of the first experimentations, needing both well-defined material and well-defined plans for going further. From solid findings (see Gueudet, Chap. 2) to solid foundings…

A last remark on these perspectives. When formulating them, I focused on teachers: *teachers'* resource systems, interactions between *teachers* and resources… Considering the extension of the theory, I think we should consider more widely, beyond the teachers, students, educators… and, finally, each actor involved in a learning/teaching process, these two processes being strongly connected (Sect. 13.2.1).

13.8.2 Ongoing Programs, Taking into Account Some of These Perspectives of Research

These perspectives are not proposed in a vacuum. Chap. 2 as well as the current chapter have shown the variety of works already addressing at least a part of these research perspectives. We could consider the ongoing and future PhDs, the conferences to come, and the research projects.

There are about ten ongoing PhDs having chosen the main frame of DAD. I hope that this book, and the research perspectives that it proposes, will inspire other PhDs.

The Re(s)sources 2018 International Conference (Gitirana et al. 2018) had witnessed the vitality of the research in this area. In this book, Chaps. 9, 10, 11 and 12 evidence the reflection spurred by the conference working groups. The Young Researchers Workshop[11] following the conference have opened also several research sites. Among them, the reflection and development on didactic metadata for tagging teachers' resources (coordinated by Yerushalmy and Cooper), on webdocuments (coordinated by Bellemain, Alturkmani, and Gitirana), and on the naming systems used by teachers in a variety of cultural contexts (coordinated by Rafalska and me) seem to be particularly active.

The next international conference will take into account these issues, for example the CERME conference (https://cerme11.org/), February 2019, with several thematic working groups mentioning the resources in their titles: Curricular resources and task design in mathematics education; teaching mathematics with technology and other resources; and teaching mathematics with technology and other resources.[12] Finally, let us quote the ICMT3 (https://tagung.math.uni-paderborn.de/event/1/), September 2019, dedicated to research and developments on textbooks.

Regarding the research to come, I am sure that a number of them will attend the sensitive points that we have underlined, as the issue of collective work: for example, at an international level, the next ICMI study[13] to be launched will be dedicated to mathematics teachers working and learning in collaborative groups.

Then… A number of improvements are hoped for during the years to come.

---

[11] https://resources-2018.sciencesconf.org/resource/page/id/10

[12] However, as we develop in Sect. 13.7, the reflection on resources is not restricted to the research groups whose title includes the word "resources." Taking into account the matter of teachers' work, their *resources*, is certainly a major feature of the current research in educational research.

[13] The ICMI studies are launched by the International Commission on Mathematica Instruction: https://www.mathunion.org/icmi/conferences/icmi-study-conferences. The next study will be the 25th one.

Fig. 13.16 The cover of the first book presenting, in French, DAD. (Gueudet and Trouche 2010)

13.8.3 A Fruitful Metaphor

I would like to close this chapter by a metaphor. Editing our first book in French (Gueudet and Trouche 2010), for presenting DAD, we had chosen, on the front page, a Calder's mobile (Fig. 13.16).

We had motivated this choice with this short text (p. 371, our translation):

> A mobile combines dynamics and stability, invariance and movement, like the geneses at the heart of this book; reminds us that "the most profound tendency of all human activity is the march toward equilibrium" (Piaget 1964). This mobile is part of Calder's series of "gongs", sound mobiles, thanks to collisions between metallic elements produced during their movement; visual and auditory development, visible and invisible resources. It speaks about the individual, interaction, collective … the necessary commitment of each for a common work.

Some years later, at this stage of development of DAD, and after reading the book of Wohlleben (2017 for the French version) about the secret life of trees, I would choose another metaphor for thinking of teachers' resource systems, as well as for teachers' collective in action: the metaphor of a forest.

Trees learn, support, interact within a complex, highly interconnected ecosystem, where diversity is an asset, and experience a valued richness. A symbiosis is formed, underground, between tree roots and mycorrhizal fungi. Through this network, carbon, phosphorus, nitrogen or hydrogen, circulate from one tree to another. After cutting a tree, the subterranean relationships between the tree's roots and neighboring trees intensify for a whole period of time, as if to capture the experience of the cut-off tree.

Rogerio Ignacio and Cibelle Assis, from Brazil, who were in the French Institute of Education for preparing the Re(s)sources International Conference, proposed to push this metaphor further, in evoking a specific Brazilian tree: the anacardier of Pirangi. Its main feature is to develop a whole forest from one tree, its roots diving in, and emerging from, the earth for developing new trees. This is certainly a fruitful metaphor, as it invited to consider, for understanding the development of a given resource, the whole set of roots feeding it, and linking it to a complex resource system.

Living and supportive resources…

Acknowledgements To the PhD, post-doc students, and young researchers having, via their answers, given the essential matter to this chapter: Gilles Aldon, Mohammad Alturkmani, Cibelle Assis, Franck Bellemain, Sylvaine Besnier, Fernando Bifano, Elisangela Espindola, Nataly Essonnier, Verônica Gitirana, Rim Hammoud, Sonia Igliori, Rogerio Igniacio, Carole Le Henaff, Rosilangela Lucena, Anita Messaoui, Katiane Rocha, Jose Orozco, Michèle Prieur, Nolwenn Quéré, Hussein Sabra, Ana Isabel Sacristian, Ulises Salinas, Marisol Santacruz, Karima Sayah, Moustapha Sokhna, Chantal Tuffery, Michael Umameh, Chongyang Wang, Luxizi Zhang, and Mingyu Shao.

To the reviewers of this chapter, for their inspiring comments, Ghislaine Gueudet, John Monaghan, Birgit Pepin, and Janine Remillard.

References

Adler, J. (2012). Knowledge resources in and for school mathematics teaching. In G. Gueudet, B. Pepin, & L. Trouche (Eds.), *From text to 'lived' resources: Mathematics curriculum materials and teacher development* (pp. 3–22). New York: Springer.

Alturkmani, M., Daubias, P., Loisy, C., Messaoui, A., & Trouche, L. (2019). Instrumenter les recherches sur le travail enseignant: le projet AnA.doc. *Education & didactique, 13*(2).

Alturkmani, M. D., Trouche, L., & Morge, L. (2018). Étude des liens entre affinités disciplinaire et didactique, et travail de l'enseignant: le cas d'un enseignant de physique-chimie en France. *Recherches en didactique des sciences et des technologies, 17*, 129–157.

Béguin, P. (2004). Monde, version des mondes et monde commun. *Bulletin de Psychologie., 469*(57), 45–48.

Bellemain, F., & Trouche, L. (2016). *Comprendre le travail des professeurs avec les ressources de leur enseignement, un questionnement didactique et informatique*, invited lecture, I Simpósio Latinoamericano de Didática da Matemática, 01 a 06 de novembro de 2016, Bonito – Mato Grosso do Sul – Brasil. Retrieved at https://drive.google.com/file/d/0B6OphkgfrkD3ZFRtTDJ2anRfSWM/view

13 Evidencing Missing Resources of the Documentational Approach to Didactics 485

Bernstein, N. A. (1996). On dexterity and its development. In M. L. Latash & M. T. Turvey (Eds.), *Dexterity and its development* (pp. 3–245). New York: Psychology Press.

Brown, M. (2009). The teacher-tool relationship: Theorizing the design and use of curriculum materials. In J. T. Remillard, B. A. Herbel-Eisenmann, & G. M. Lloyd (Eds.), *Mathematics teachers at work: Connecting curriculum materials and classroom instruction* (pp. 17–36). New York: Routledge.

Caraës, M.-H., & Marchand-Zanartu, N. (2011). *Images de pensées*. Paris: Editions de la Réunion des musées nationaux.

Chevallard, Y. (1999). L'analyse des pratiques enseignantes en théorie anthropologique du didactique. *Recherches en Didactique des Mathématiques, 19*(2), 221–266.

Chevallard, Y., & Cirade, G. (2010). Les ressources manquantes comme problem professionnel. In G. Gueudet & L. Trouche (Eds.), *Ressources vives. Le travail documentaire des professeurs en mathématiques* (pp. 41–55). Lyon: Paideia, PUR et INRP.

Choppin, J., Roth McDuffie, A., Drake, C., & Davis, J. (2018). Curriculum ergonomics: Conceptualizing the interactions between curriculum design and use. *International Journal of Educational Research* 92, 75–85. Retreived February 21, at https://doi.org/10.1016/j.ijer.2018.09.015.

Clarke, D., Mesiti, C., Cao, Y., & Novotna, J. (2017). The lexicon project: Examining the consequences for international comparative research of pedagogical naming systems from different cultures. In T. Dooley & G. Gueudet (Eds.), *Proceedings of the tenth congress of the European society for research in mathematics education* (CERME10, February 1–5, 2017) (pp. 1610–1617). Dublin: DCU Institute of Education and ERME.

Cossette, P. (1994). Les cartes cognitives au service de l'étude des organisations. In P. Cossette (dir.), *Cartes cognitives et organisations* (pp. 3–12). Québec: Presses de l'Université Laval et Paris: Editions Eska.

Cossette, P. (2003). Méthode systématique d'aide à la formulation de la vision stratégique: Lllustration auprès d'un propriétaire-dirigeant. *Revue de l'Entreprenariat, 2*(1), 17.

Drijvers, P., & Trouche, L. (2008). From artifacts to instruments: A theoretical framework behind the orchestra metaphor. In K. Heid & G. Blume (Eds.), *Research on technology and the teaching and learning of mathematics, Vol.2, cases and perspectives* (pp. 363–392). Charlotte: Information Age.

Engeström, Y. (2014). *Learning by expanding*. Cambridge: Cambridge University Press.

Essonnier, N., Kynigos, C., Trgalová, J., & Daskolia, M. (2018). Role of the context in social creativity for the design of digital resources. In L. Fan, L. Trouche, S. Rezat, C. Qi, & J. Visnovska (Eds.), *Research on mathematics textbooks and teachers' resources: Advances and issues* (ICME-13 monograph) (pp. 215–234). Cham: Springer.

Ferguson, R., Bracher, A., Clow, D., Cooper, A., Hillaire, G., Mittelmeier, J., Rienties, B., Ullmann, T., Vuorikari, R., & Castano Munoz, J. (2016). *Research evidence on the use of learning analytics: Implications for education policy*. Bruxelles: Publications Office of the European Union. https://doi.org/10.2791/955210.

Fleck, L. (1981). *Genesis and development of a scientific fact*. Chicago: University of Chicago Press (original edition, 1934).

Gitirana, V., Miyakawa, T., Rafalska, M., Soury-Lavergne, S., & Trouche, L. (Eds.) (2018). Proceedings of the Re(s)sources 2018 International Conference. *ENS de Lyon*, https://hal.archives-ouvertes.fr/hal-01764563v3/document

Gourlet, P. (2018). *Montrer le faire, construire l'agir. Une approche développementale de la conception mise en œuvre à l'école primaire*. PhD, Paris: Université Paris 8.

Gueudet, G., Pepin, B., & Trouche, L. (Eds.). (2012). *From text to 'lived' resources: Mathematics curriculum materials and teacher development*. New York: Springer.

Gueudet, G., Pepin, B., & Trouche, L. (2013). Collective work with resources: An essential dimension for teacher documentation. *ZDM – Mathematics Education, 45*(7), 1003–1016.

Gueudet, G., & Trouche, L. (2008). Du travail documentaire des enseignants : genèses, collectifs, communautés. *Le cas des mathématiques. Education et didactique, 2*(3), 7–33.

Gueudet, G., & Trouche, L. (2009). Towards new documentation systems for mathematics teachers? *Educational Studies in Mathematics, 71*(3), 199–218.

Gueudet, G., & Trouche, L. (2010). Des ressources aux documents, travail du professeur et genèses documentaires. In G. Gueudet, & L. Trouche (Eds.), *Ressources vives. La documentation des professeurs en mathématiques* (pp. 7–74). INRP et PUR.

Gueudet, G., & Trouche, L. (2012a). Teachers' work with resources: documentation geneses and professional geneses. In G. Gueudet, B. Pepin, & L. Trouche (Eds.), *From text to 'lived' resources: Mathematics curriculum materials and teacher development* (pp. 23–41). New York: Springer.

Gueudet, G., & Trouche, L. (2012b). Communities, documents and professional geneses: Interrelated stories. In G. Gueudet, B. Pepin, & L. Trouche (Eds.), *From text to 'lived' resources: Mathematics curriculum materials and teacher development* (pp. 305–322). New York: Springer.

Guin, D., Ruthven, K., & Trouche, L. (Eds.). (2005). *The didactical challenge of symbolic calculators: Turning a computational device into a mathematical instrument.* New York: Springer.

Guin, D., & Trouche, L. (1998). The complex process of converting tools into mathematical instruments. The case of calculators. *The International Journal of Computers for Mathematical Learning, 3*(3), 195–227.

Hammoud, R. (2012). *Le travail collectif des professeurs en chimie comme levier pour la mise en oeuvre de démarches d'investigation et le développement des connaissances professionnelles. Contribution au développement de l'approche documentaire du didactique.* PhD, Lyon: Université Lyon 1. https://tel.archives-ouvertes.fr/tel-00762964/document

Jansen, P. (2018). *Pourquoi la société ne se laisse-t-elle pas mettre en equations?* Paris: Le Seuil, Coll. Science ouverte.

Jullien, F. (2015). *De l'être au vivre. Lexique euro-chinois de la pensée.* Paris: Gallimard.

Karsenti, T. (2016). *The interactive whiteboard (IWB): Uses, benefits, and challenges. A survey of 11683 students and 1131 teachers.* Montreal: CRIFPE.

Lucena, R., & Assis, C. (2015). *Webdoc Sistema de Recursos e o Trabalho Coletivo do Professor: Uma Via de Mão Dupla.* Recife (Brazil): LEMATEC (UFPE). Retrieved at http://lematec.net.br/webdocs/webdoc2/. Access codes to be asked to the authors.

Lucena, R., Gitirana, V., & Trouche, L. (2016). Teoria da orquestração instrumenta: um olhar para formação docente. *I Simpósio Latinoamericano de Didática da Matemática*, 01 a 06 de novembro de 2016, Bonito – Mato Grosso do Sul – Brasil.

Messaoui, A. (2018). Concevoir des ressources pour enseigner, un levier pour le développement des compétences informationnelles des professeurs? In *Objets, supports, instruments : regards croisés sur la diversité des ressources mobilisées en interaction. SHS Web of Conferences, 52, 02003.* Retreived at https://doi.org/10.1051/shsconf/20185202003

Monaghan, J., Trouche, L., & Borwein, J. (2016). *Tools and mathematics: Instruments for learning.* New York: Springer.

Monteil, L., & Romerio, A. (2017). Des disciplines aux studies. Savoirs, trajectoires, politiques. *Revue d'anthropologie des connaissances, 11*(3), 231–244.

Oddone, I., Re, A., & Briante, G. (1981). *Redécouvrir l'expérience ouvrière: vers une autre psychologie du travail?* Paris: Editions sociales.

Pastré, P. (2005). Genèse et identité. In P. Rabardel, & P. Pastré (Dir.), *Modèles du sujet pour la conception* (pp. 231–260). Toulouse: Octarès.

Pédauque, R. T.. coll.(2006). *Le document à la lumière du numérique.* Caen: C & F éditions.

Pepin, B. (2009). The role of textbooks in the 'figured world' of English, French and German classrooms – A comparative perspective. In L. Black, H. Mendick, & Y. Solomon (Eds.), *Mathematical relationships: Identities and participation* (pp. 107–118). London: Routledge.

Pepin, B., Gueudet, G., & Trouche, L. (2013a). Re-sourcing teachers' work and interactions: A collective perspective on resources, their use and transformation. *ZDM – Mathematics Education, 45*(7), 929–944.

Pepin, B., Gueudet, G., & Trouche, L. (2013b). Investigating textbooks as crucial interfaces between culture, policy and teacher curricular practice: Two contrasted case studies in France and Norway. *ZDM – Mathematics Education, 45*(5), 685–698.

Pepin, B., Gueudet, G., & Trouche, L. (2015). Comfortable or lost in paradise? – Affordances and constraints of mathematics e-textbooks in/for curriculum enactment, communication to the symposium *Mathematics curriculum contingencies: From authoring to enactment via curriculum resources*, chaired by D. Clarke, K. Ruthven and M.K. Stein, in the frame of the AERA 2015 meeting, Chicago, 16–20 April.

Pepin, B., Gueudet, G., & Trouche, L. (2017). Refining teacher design capacity: Mathematics teachers' interactions with digital curriculum resources. *ZDM – Mathematics Education, 49*(5), 799–812.

Pepin, B., Xu, B., Trouche, L., & Wang, C. (2016). Developing a deeper understanding of *mathematics teaching expertise:* Chinese mathematics teachers' resource systems as windows into their work and expertise. *Educational Studies in Mathematics, 94*(3), 257–274. http://rdcu.be/koXk.

Piaget, J. (1964). *Six études de psychologie*. Genève: Edition Gonthier.

Prieto, L. P., Sharma, K., Dillenbourg, P., & Jesús, M. (2016). Teaching analytics: Towards automatic extraction of orchestration graphs using wearable sensors. In *Proceedings of the sixth international conference on Learning Analytics & Knowledge (LAK '16)* (pp. 148–157). New York: ACM. https://doi.org/10.1145/2883851.2883927.

Rabardel, P. (2002). *People and technology: A cognitive approach to contemporary instruments*. Paris: Université Paris 8. Retreived at https://hal.archives-ouvertes.fr/hal-01020705

Radford, L. (2008). The ethics of being and knowing: Towards a cultural theory of learning. In L. Radford, G. Schubring, & F. Seeger (Eds.), *Semiotics in mathematics education: Epistemology, history, classroom, and culture* (pp. 215–234). Rotterdam: Sense Publishers.

Remillard, J. T. (2005). Examining key concepts in research on teachers' use of mathematics curricula. *Revue of Educational Research, 75*(2), 211–246.

Remillard, J.T., Van Steenbrugge, H., & Bergqvist, T. (2014). A cross-cultural analysis of the voice of curriculum materials. In K. Jones, C. Bokhove, G. Howson, & L. Fan (Eds.), *Proceedings of the first International Conference on Mathematics Textbook Research and Development* (ICMT-2014) (pp. 395–400). Southampton: University of Southampton.

Remillard, J. T., Van Steenbrugge, H., & Trouche, L. (2017). Teacher-resource use around the world. In G. Schubring, L. Fan, & V. Giraldo (Eds.), *Proceeding of the second international conference on mathematics textbooks, research and development* (pp. 129–132). Rio de Janeiro: Instituto de Matemática, Universidade Federal do Rio de Janeiro. http://www.sbembrasil.org.br/files/ICMT2017.pdf.

Rocha, K. (2018a). Uses of online resources and documentational Trajectories: The case of Sésamath. In L. Fan, L. Trouche, S. Rezat, C. Qi, & J. Visnovska (Eds.), *Research on mathematics textbooks and teachers' resources: Advances and issues* (ICME-13 monograph) (pp. 235–259). Cham: Springer.

Rocha, K. (2018b). Les trajectoires documentaires, une proposition de modèle pour analyser les interactions des enseignants avec les ressources au fil du temps: la plateforme AnA.doc, un outil d'instrumentation de cette analyse. In *Objets, supports, instruments : regards croisés sur la diversité des ressources mobilisées en interaction. SHS Web of Conferences, 52*, 02004. Retreived at https://doi.org/10.1051/shsconf/20185202004.

Rousseau, D., & Morvan, M. (2000). *La dénomination*. Paris: Odile Jacob.

Sabra, H. (2011). *Contribution à l'étude du travail documentaire des enseignants de mathématiques: les incidents comme révélateurs des rapports entre documentations individuelle et communautaire*. PhD, Lyon: Université Lyon 1. https://tel.archives-ouvertes.fr/tel-00768508/document

Sabra, H. (2016). L'étude des rapports entre documentations individuelle et collective: Incidents, connaissances et ressources mathématiques. *Recherches en Didactique des Mathématiques, 36*(1), 49–95.

Salaün, J.-M. (2012). *Vu, lu, su. Les architectes de l'information face à l'oligopole du Web*. Paris: La Découverte.

Salaün, J.-M. (2016). Quelques leçons du MOOC Archinfo sur la collaboration et l'évaluation par les pairs. Séminaire du projet MORCEF. ENS de Lyon.

Salinas, U., & Trouche, L. (2018). Uso de gestos –como recurso-mediador– por un profesor de bachillerato para enfrentar un desafío didáctico no previsto por él. *Unión. Revista iberoamericana de educación matemática, 54,* 6–24. http://asenmacformacion.com/ojs/index.php/union/article/view/369.

Santacruz, M., & Sacristan, A.-I. (2018). Reflecting on the paths for selecting digital resources for (geometry) teaching: The case of a first grade teacher. In V. Gitirana, T. Miyakawa, M. Rafalska, S. Soury-Lavergne, & L. Trouche (Eds.) *Proceedings of the Re(s)sources conference* (pp. 92–95). Lyon: ENS de Lyon. Retrieved November 8, 2018, at https://hal.archives-ouvertes.fr/hal-01764563

Sayah, K. (2018). *L'intégration des ressources de Sésamath au collège: un moteur pour le développement du travail collectif des enseignants de mathématiques en Algérie*. PhD, Université Lyon 1.

Sokhna, M. (2006). *Formation à distance des professeurs de mathématiques au Sénégal, genèse instrumentale de ressources pédagogiques*. PhD, Université Lyon 1. Retreived at https://tel.archives-ouvertes.fr/tel-00917620

Sokhna, M. (2018). Systèmes de ressources et intégration des TICE: quels critères de sélection ? In V. Gitirana, T. Miyakawa, M. Rafalska, S. Soury-Lavergne, & L. Trouche (Eds.), *Proceedings of the Re(s)sources conference* (pp. 109–112). Lyon: ENS de Lyon. Retrieved November 8, 2018, at https://hal.archives-ouvertes.fr/hal-01764563

Sokhna, M., & Trouche, L. (2016). Repenser la formation des enseignants en France et au Sénégal: une source d'interactions fécondes. In M. Artigue (coord.), La tradition didactique française au delà des frontières. Exemples de collaborations avec l'Afrique, l'Amérique latine et l'Asie (pp. 27–38). *Présentation de la communauté didactique française à ICME 13*, Hambourg. http://www.cfem.asso.fr/cfem/Collaborationsdidactiquesfrancaises.pdf

Trouche, L. (2005a). Les IREM: des raisons des réseaux. *Plot 11,* 2–7, consulté le 17 mai 2016 à. http://www.apmep.fr/IMG/pdf/IREM.pdf

Trouche, L. (2005b). An instrumental approach to mathematics learning in symbolic calculators environments. In D. Guin, K. Ruthven, & L. Trouche (Eds.), *The didactical challenge of symbolic calculators: Turning a computational device into a mathematical instrument* (pp. 137–162). New York: Springer.

Trouche, L. (2009). Penser la gestion didactique des artefacts pour faire et faire faire des mathématiques: histoire d'un cheminement intellectuel. *L'Educateur, 3,* 35–38.

Trouche, L. (dir.) (2014). *EducMap, pour une cartographie dynamique des recherches en éducation*. Research report CNRS-Université de Lyon. https://hal.archives-ouvertes.fr/hal-01546661

Trouche, L. (2016). Prendre en compte les métamorphoses du Numérique. *Union, 45,* 7–23.

Trouche, L. (2017). L'enseignement des mathématiques, un point de vue international centré sur les ressources des professeurs. *La lettre de Grema, 17,* 2–6.

Trouche, L., et al. (1998). *Expérimenter et prouver. Faire des mathématiques au lycée avec des calculatrices symboliques. 38 variations sur un thème imposé*. Montpellier: IREM, Université Montpellier 2.

Trouche, L., Gitirana, V., Miyakawa, T., Pepin, B., & Wang, C. (2019). Studying mathematics teachers interactions with curriculum materials through different lenses: Towards a deeper understanding of the processes at stake. *International Journal of Educational Research 93,* 53–67. Retreived February 21, at https://doi.org/10.1016/j.ijer.2018.09.002.

Trouche, L., Gueudet, G., & Pepin, B. (2018a, Online First). The documentational approach to didactics. In S. Lerman (Ed.), *Encyclopedia of mathematics education*. New York: Springer.

Trouche, L., Trgalová, J., Loisy, C., & Alturkmani, M. (2018b). *Ressources vivantes pour l'enseignement et l'apprentissage. Contribution des composantes IFÉ et S2HEP de l'ANR ReVEA*. ENS de Lyon. https://hal.archives-ouvertes.fr/hal-01743212

Vergnaud, G. (2009). The theory of conceptual fields. *Human Development, 52*, 83–94. https://doi.org/10.1159/000202727.

Vermersch, P. (2012). *Explicitation et phénoménologie*. Paris: PUF.

Wang, C. (2018). Mathematics teachers' expertise in resources work and its development in collectives: A French and a Chinese cases. In L. Fan, L. Trouche, S. Rezat, C. Qi, & J. Visnovska (Eds.), *Research on mathematics textbooks and teachers' resources: Advances and issues* (ICME-13 monograph) (pp. 193–213). Cham: Springer.

Wang, C., Salinas, U., & Trouche, L. (2019). From teachers' naming systems of resources to teachers' resource systems: Contrasting a Chinese and a Mexican case. In U. T. Jankvist, M. van den Heuvel-Panhuizen, & M. Veldhuis (Eds.), *Proceedings of the eleventh congress of the European society for research in mathematics education* (pp. xxxx–yyyy). Utrecht: Freudenthal Group & Freudenthal Institute, Utrecht University and ERME.

Wang, C., Trouche, L., & Pepin, B. (2018). An investigation of Chinese mathematics teachers' resources work and their professional development in collectives. In G. Schubring, L. Fan, & V. Giraldo (Eds.), *Proceeding of the second international conference on mathematics textbooks, research and development* (pp. 144–157). Rio de Janeiro: Instituto de Matemática, Universidade Federal do Rio de Janeiro. http://www.sbembrasil.org.br/files/ICMT2017.pdf.

Wenger, E. (1998). *Communities of practice. Learning, meaning, identity*. Cambridge: Cambridge University Press.

Wohlleben, P. (2017). *La vie secrete des arbres. Ce qu'ils ressentent. Comment ils communiquent. Un monde inconnu s'ouvre à nous*. Paris: Editions des Arènes.

Xu, B., & Recker, M. (2012). Teaching analytics: A clustering and triangulation study of digital library user data. *Educational Technology & Society, 15*(3), 103–115.

Chapter 14
Afterword: Reflections on the Documentational Approach to Didactics

Jeffrey Choppin

Abstract In this afterword, I briefly summarize the documentational approach to didactics (DAD) since a number of authors have already comprehensively done so earlier in this volume. The 2018 Re(s)sources International Conference demonstrated the breadth, promise, and growth of DAD and how it allows the field to productively problematize the interactions between curriculum resources and those who use them. As a friendly outsider, I have explored DAD and grown increasingly familiar with it. Below, I explore key contributions of DAD and the strengths of its theoretical underpinnings. I then provide challenges and limitations of DAD before connecting it to my recent work in curriculum ergonomics.

Keywords Curriculum resources · Curriculum use · Mediated action · Ergonomics

The 2018 Re(s)sources International Conference, related to the theme of this book, *The "Resource" Approach to Mathematics Education*, demonstrated the breadth, promise, and growth of the documentational approach to didactics (DAD). I will only briefly summarize DAD here, as a number of authors have already comprehensively done so earlier in this volume. This afterword is written from the perspective of a "friendly outsider," someone whose work is associated with the educational problems explored by DAD and who has grown increasingly familiar with DAD over the last several years, but who was not instrumental in developing it and has only recently taken it up in his work. Similar to the objects of study in DAD, my work has focused on how teachers take up and transform curriculum resources as they plan and enact lessons, how teachers learn from designing lessons using curriculum resources, and how the characteristics of curriculum resources shape teachers' practices. More recently, I studied how the characteristics of digital curriculum resources shape their potential uses. Furthermore, I recently co-edited a special issue on *curriculum ergonomics*, for which DAD serves as a theoretical foundation.

J. Choppin (✉)
Warner School of Education, University of Rochester, New York, USA
e-mail: jchoppin@warner.rochester.edu

© Springer Nature Switzerland AG 2019
L. Trouche et al. (eds.), *The 'Resource' Approach to Mathematics Education*,
Advances in Mathematics Education,
https://doi.org/10.1007/978-3-030-20393-1_14

14.1 Opening Thoughts

I start this section with a brief summary of my interpretation of DAD and then explain the perspective from which I write this afterword. In Choppin, Roth McDuffie, Drake, and Davis (2018), we summarize DAD in the following way:

> [DAD] explores the teacher-tool relationship, the role of activity systems and collectives, collections of resources and patterns of use of those resources, and the transformational process for both teachers and resources in the documentation process. The documentational approach articulates an iterative process by which teachers appropriate and transform curriculum resources... As teachers develop understanding of the characteristics of artifacts and appropriate them for their own use, they transform them into resources that fit within their schemes of use. Schemes of use are stable practices established by the teachers' prior experiences and the institutional and political contexts in which teachers operate. The use of the transformed artifact, now considered a resource, in the design and enactment of lessons is the process of design in use. (p. 79)

This interpretation aligns well with key descriptions of DAD supplied by Gueudet in the volume. She states that the "instrumental approach distinguishes between an artefact, product of the human activity, designed for a goal-directed human activity, and an instrument developed by a subject using the artefact" (p. 20). Furthermore, she states that a scheme "comprises several components: the aim of the activity; rules of action, of control and rules for taking information; operational invariants and possibilities of inferences" (p. 20). Finally, she describes documents as the "set of recombined resources and a scheme of use of these resources" and documentational genesis as "the process of development of a document" (p. 22). Thus, the documentation approach explores how users draw from and design curriculum resources, while focusing on the individual and institutional contexts and rules of action in which this activity takes place.

DAD derives from a number of concepts and theoretical approaches. As noted by Gueudet (this volume), DAD builds from the following concepts and approaches: the instrumental approach (Rabardel 1995) and instrument systems (Rabardel and Bourmaud 2005); instrumental orchestration (Trouche 2004); scheme of use (Vergnaud 1998); document management (Baron et al. 2007); curriculum script (Ruthven 2007); and resources in use (Adler 2000). In addition, Trouche (2004) points to the role of cognitive ergonomics as a foundation as well. More recently, there has been an attempt to connect DAD to sociocultural theories, such as communities of practice (Wenger 1998), activity systems (Engeström 1999), and, more broadly, situated and mediated cognition (Wertsch and Toma 1995; Wertsch 1991). These theoretical connections, highlighted by Artigue at the Re(s)sources conference and in this volume, paint a rich intellectual foundation for DAD and its continued growth.

Being a friendly outsider allows me to play the roles of both fan and critic. These roles, plus the connections to the work on curriculum ergonomics, frame the organization of this afterword. First, I begin by discussing the contributions and strengths of DAD, as evidenced by the presentations at the conference and the chapters in this book. Second, I identify what I see as potential limitations and challenges that should be addressed by researchers interested in expanding the reach and impact of

14 Afterword: Reflections on the Documentational Approach to Didactics

DAD. Third, I connect DAD to the field of curriculum ergonomics to highlight the overlap and differences and to further frame the role and impact of DAD.

As an introductory caveat, in this afterword I intentionally avoid using DAD terminology in favor of plain language, to highlight the phenomena explored by DAD. In doing so, I most likely miss some nuances and theoretical meaning. Furthermore, given the comprehensive and complex nature of DAD and the way it is applied by an increasingly large and diverse group of researchers, as evidenced at the Re(s) sources conference, it is likely that I will not capture the full breadth and depth of current iterations of DAD. For these likely oversights, I apologize in advance.

14.2 Contributions of DAD

In this section, I explore five ways that DAD has contributed to an increased theorization and understanding of the ways teachers understand and transform curriculum resources. The five major contributions I name are that DAD:

- Problematizes the relationship between teachers and curriculum resources.
- Provides nuance to the notion of resources and resource use.
- Explores teacher learning from engaging in curriculum design.
- Considers teachers as agents in their own learning.
- Connects design and use, especially in the era of the use of digital curriculum resources.

I explain these in turn below.

14.2.1 DAD Problematizes the Relationship Between Teachers and Curriculum Resources

DAD provides important nuance and theoretical understanding to the relationship between teachers and curriculum resources. Much of work prior to DAD, and to the similar work of Remillard (2005), presented a static view of this relationship, with a major focus on the extent that teachers enacted curricula with *fidelity*. The construct of fidelity poses a narrow view of the role and agency of teachers, who are viewed as following or not following the materials according to the designers' intentions. Furthermore, the role of designer was limited to specialists or experts who were distant from classrooms. DAD hypothesizes a much more active and meaningful role for teachers as designers by theorizing how teachers develop an understanding of characteristics of curriculum resources and then transform those characteristics over iterations of use. Connecting teachers' understanding and use of curriculum resources to theories of instruments, documents, and artifacts provides insights into the complexity and understanding entailed when design and use interact. Given the increasing interplay between design and use in the digital era, DAD brings timely focus and sophistication to this research.

14.2.2 DAD Provides Nuance to the Notion of Resources and Resource Use

The second contribution is that DAD provides nuance to the notion of resources and resource use. As Trouche (this volume) states, resources are not just materials, they are *materials in systems*. That is, materials are always part of a larger system that teachers access when designing curriculum. The system implies two things: one, a larger set of resources teachers consider when selecting and modifying resources to fit their needs; and two, the national and institutional contexts in which teachers operate as they make decisions about what resources to use and how to use them. Situating teachers' work within these larger systems is crucial to understanding the actions and professional growth of teachers. Furthermore, complexifying the notion of resource by considering the historical, cultural, and political dynamic around their use and transformation enhances our understanding of the factors (including systems and cultures) that influence teachers' work with resources.

14.2.3 DAD Explores Teacher Learning from Engaging in Curriculum Design

The third contribution is the notion that teachers learn from their interactions with curriculum resources. As teachers understand and transform curriculum resources in the documentation process, they develop professional knowledge and capabilities. Over time, as a result of understanding and transforming curriculum resources (e.g., documentational genesis), teachers develop more complex and sophisticated resource systems and use them more productively in their design processes. In short, teachers grow and learn as they understand, transform, and use resources. This emphasis is consistent with findings from my own work, in which teachers developed *local theories of instruction* (Choppin 2011a) to situate the resources within broader instructional sequences and conjectures about student learning with respect to those sequences. This knowledge leads to *learned adaptations* (Choppin 2011b) in which teachers' transformation of resources was informed by their local theory of instruction. Similarly, in DAD, teachers learn over successive iterations how to transform resources to best fit their pedagogical needs, changing themselves and the resources along the way.

14.2.4 DAD Considers Teachers as Agents in Their Own Learning

A fourth important insight from DAD is that teachers exercise agency with respect to their own actions and professional learning. This includes both individual and collective agency in terms of the choices teachers make as they select, design, and implement curriculum. Thus, the professional development of teachers is not externally determined by policy decisions or allocations of resources; their learning is influenced by the choices they make in their professional practice and their reflections on the consequences of those choices.

14.2.5 DAD Connects Design and Use in the Era of the Use of Digital Curriculum Resources

The fifth major contribution of DAD is the connection between design and use, something that is increasingly relevant in an era that is marked by a profusion of digital resources. The conflation between design and use takes place in multiple domains. First, teachers select digital resources from the myriad choices available to them to create curriculum sequences. Second, teachers revise resources they find on the internet. Third, in some cases they play a collective role in creating and revising digital resources, as in the case of Sesamath (2009). This work is important for two reasons. First, DAD recognizes and provides insights into the complex roles teachers take on and teacher learning from engaging in design and redesign of digital resources. Second, teachers and schools increasingly are turning to digital resources as the basis of curriculum design; this leads to questions of capacity to engage in the work and the coherence of the resulting curriculum. DAD may provide insights into both of these educational problems just as policy makers begin contemplating them. An example of the urgency of this work is the recent turn to open resources, whose quality is uneven and which rarely constitute coherent sequences of instructional activities.

14.3 Strengths of DAD: Theoretical Underpinnings and Connections

The documentational approach builds from foundations that give it breadth and depth. First, DAD is a holistic theory, encompassing a wide range of teacher practices and learning in relation to the design and redesign of curriculum resources. Second, DAD initially was based on several important theories mentioned earlier and has expanded its connections to include such theories as mediated action, cultural–historical activity theory (CHAT), and communities of practices, as noted by Gueudet and Artigue in this volume. Below, I briefly explore each of these strengths.

14.3.1 DAD Is a Holistic Theory

Researchers use DAD as a theoretical framework to explore a variety of phenomena, including teachers' design practices (see Pepin, et al. Chap. 6), the role of the instructional context (see Miyakawa and Xu's Chap. 7), the role of both individual and collective design work, the role of systems and resource systems, the affordances and use of pedagogical tools (e.g., Drijvers et al. 2010), and so on, as noted by Trouche in this volume. The breadth of the topics addressed by DAD was evident at the Re(s)sources conference as well as in this volume, which points to a strength but also leads to some cautions regarding overreach and lack of rigorous uses of the theory.

14.3.2 DAD Has Robust Connections to Other Theories

There have been recent efforts to connect DAD to a range of other theories, as noted by Gueudet and Artigue in this volume. The focus on the role of artifacts, communities of practice, and activity systems have led DAD theorists to look closely at the work of Engeström, Lave and Wenger, Vygotsky, and Wertsch. These theorists, all situated within the sociocultural theoretical domain, postulate various forms of culturally and socially situated cognition. DAD considers the dialectical relationship between tool and user (Wertsch and Toma 1995, Wertsch 1991), the mediated interaction between artifact and user (Vygotsky 1978; Wertsch and Toma 1995), the role of collective practices in the work and learning of individuals (Lave and Wenger 1991; Wenger 1998), and the activity system in which teachers operate. The activity systems include division of labor, rules, and goal-focused behaviors to the foci already mentioned (Engeström 1999). Thus, these theories have the potential to add more theoretical grounding to DAD, to provide additional nuance and explanation to DAD, and to connect to broader empirical work outside of curriculum resources. Furthermore, DAD can inform the continual evolution of these theories by providing a new context to expand the work.

These theories add to the existing foundational work described by Artigue, Gueudet, and Trouche in this volume. In addition, DAD researchers have connected to more contemporary work on the relationship between teachers and curriculum resources in the US context, with respect to the work of Remillard (2005). Making explicit these connections enhances the accessibility and theoretical basis of DAD, clarifying and elaborating the phenomena under study and decreasing the potentially insular and opaque nature of the terminology used in DAD.

14 Afterword: Reflections on the Documentational Approach to Didactics

14.4 Potential Limitations and Challenges of DAD

While DAD has made substantial contributions and build from considerable theoretical foundations and affordances as noted above, there are some potential limitations and challenges to the theory and its future evolution and use.

14.4.1 Need for More Empirical Work

First, there is a need for more sustained and intensive empirical work that illustrates the tenets of DAD in practice (what does it look like, how can DAD be used to see actions and practices in a particular way). The empirical work is needed to further validate the theory and force adherents to refine the theory to take into account the contingencies of the complex contexts in which it is applied. In my view, the main value of a theory is its explanatory power with respect to the phenomena under study. At times, DAD-related work lacks empirical examples and rigorous operationalization of concepts in data analysis, leaving me to wonder what the authors meant by key terms. Theory for theory sake limits the audience to a small group of academics, most of whom have a stake in the theory. There is a cost to applying theory in contexts when conducting empirical studies, as the articulation of ideas in a theory is immediately tested when applied to the dynamic contexts of teachers' professional lives. The benefit is that the theory gains validity and explanatory power. I consider much of the work of DAD to be well conceived and theoretically grounded but weak in operationalizing terms in data analysis.

14.4.2 Issues with Use of Specialized Terminology

Second, the heavy use of specialized terminology in the application of DAD is a two-edged sword. On the one hand, the terminology carries meaning imbued by the theories on which DAD is based; on the other hand, the use of specialized terminology requires the reader to seek clarification by going back to the foundational theories or DAD literature that defines those terms. This is cumbersome and discouraging to the reader. The terminology is rarely operationalized with empirical examples or analytic categories, making it difficult for an outsider, even a friendly one, to fully understand the phenomena being described. There is not necessarily an easy solution to this: using plain language in lieu of specialized terminology has its own drawbacks, especially with respect to the lack of explicit theoretical connections in such language, and it can be too specific, lacking the ability to apply to multiple contexts. There is no easy solution to this problem, just a tension that needs to be recognized and balanced more evenly than what is current in the DAD literature.

14.4.3 Questioning Assumptions Behind Research Methods

Third, the methods require additional testing and refinement. There has been an expansion of the methodology, especially with regard to two recent methods: *reflective investigation* and *schematic representation of a resource system* (SRRS). These methods speak directly to increasingly systematized data collection and analysis in DAD. However, there are some assumptions underlying these methods that need to be tested. The first assumption is that teachers are fully aware of the resources they draw upon and how they draw upon them; there needs to be a recognition that any method that claims to fully account for what resources teachers use and how they use them has inherent flaws. People cannot articulate every thought that pops into their head, and much of what people think is tacit, below the level of awareness. Consequently, real-time observation of planning entails inferences on the part of the researcher or incomplete accounts of participants. If a researcher chooses a retrospective methodology, there is the danger of incomplete reports from the teacher due to an increase in mediating factors in retrospective accounts (Ericsson and Simon 1980). Thus, any SRRS map is inherently incomplete and skewed.

A second assumption is that curriculum contexts and resource systems are stable; in many contexts, at least in the US, teachers' curriculum contexts are not stable from year to year for many reasons (change in grade level, change in curriculum policy, or change in curriculum materials). This affects the researcher's ability to make claims regarding teacher learning and, more generally, documentation, if teachers are forced to continually change the resources on which they draw.

A third assumption is that resource use is a fairly unambiguous process that can be clearly documented and described. As someone who has conducted intensive naturalistic longitudinal studies of teachers using curriculum resources, I can attest to the methodological complexities in terms of documenting both use and learning from that use. I found it challenging to generate well-defined accounts of teachers' understanding of resources, the teachers' transformation of those resources over time, and what teachers learned from using and transforming resources. The data collection and analysis were onerous, messy, and time-consuming. I studied 12 teachers teaching instructional sequences of six to ten instructional sessions; for some teachers, I studied them teaching multiple instructional sequences over multiple years. My data corpus consisted of several hundred hours of video, numerous interviews with teachers, and collections of curriculum artifacts. Collecting and analyzing these data required a tremendous amount of field time and years of work. The chief method I used, video-stimulated recall, entailed creating video cases of teachers for each instructional unit they taught, allowing teachers to view the video cases, and then interviewing them using a semi-structured protocol. This method is similar in purpose and function to reflective investigation. I asked the teachers about their understanding of the materials, how students engaged with the materials, changes the teachers made to the resources, and justifications for those changes. In the reported DAD methodology, there is little indication of the methodological messiness or ambiguity entailed in this kind of data collection and analysis.

A fourth assumption is that teachers inherently learn from or are purposeful about the use of curriculum resources. While this is sometimes the case, it is also possible that teachers, many if not most, are often overloaded and are instrumental with respect to their actions around curriculum resources. That is, teachers pick what is convenient and efficient, and are mainly concerned with whether students are able to quickly and accurately complete mathematical tasks; they are less concerned with more complex and meaningful engagement and learning. These teachers transform resources to make it easier for students to successfully and efficiently complete tasks. While this is a type of learning from the use of curriculum materials, it is not necessarily a desirable capacity in the eyes of many mathematics educators and researchers. Other teachers use curriculum resources as scripts and undertake little purposeful transformation of the materials. How does DAD theorize *the extent to which* such teachers engage in the documentation process and learn from it?

14.4.4 Connecting DAD Findings to Instructional Outcomes

Perhaps the most notable limitation in current DAD research is the connection of empirical findings of teachers' documentational processes to instructional outcomes, such as classroom discursive practices, use of challenging and complex tasks, conceptual learning, and so forth. In my research, most of the teachers were unremarkable in the way they talked about curriculum design. They could talk extensively about the mathematical content and progression, what students were required to do in tasks, and what errors cropped up during enactment, but they did not have nuanced ways of describing student thinking with respect to tasks. Furthermore, the instrumental uses of curriculum described above were often associated with direct teaching, in which they explained and modeled tasks in ways that reduced ambiguity and opportunity for students to engage in productive struggle. Their teaching was procedurally focused, whereas the teachers who could articulate how tasks were associated with student thinking employed practices that were more conceptually oriented and had greater and more substantial student participation in the classroom discourse. Connecting research to instructional outcomes will enhance the explanatory power and impact of DAD.

14.5 Connecting to Curriculum Ergonomics

Recently, I co-edited an issue in the International Journal of Educational Research on *curriculum ergonomics*. We defined curriculum ergonomics as the study of the interactions between design and use of curriculum resources, with a focus on the *fit* or alignment between design and use, designer and user (Choppin et al. 2018). Making explicit connections between curriculum ergonomics, DAD, and the design and participatory approaches to the use of curriculum resources, we made the following assumptions:

- Teachers engage in active design work as they draw from curriculum resources to plan and enact lessons;
- Teachers work within systems (instructional contexts that are culturally based and historically situated) that influence their practices;
- Teachers' belief systems and prior curriculum experiences influence how they perceive and use curriculum resources; and.
- Teachers' professional growth is influenced by their use of curriculum resources. (p. 79).

Furthermore, similar to DAD, we built from research in cognitive ergonomics, noting four themes from that research that are applicable to the study of curriculum design and use: decision making in complex environments; effect of cognitive load on decision making; the complexity of environments that involve both human and machine interactions; and the ability of creativity support tools or environments to expand the capabilities of users. We concluded that the "research on cognitive ergonomics describes the demands on people operating in complex and dynamic environments, including the challenges of responding to real-time information while simultaneously interacting with people to attain an ambitious goal" (p. 78). We discussed how these findings related to characteristics of digital curriculum resources, stating that while digital resources may enhance teachers' creative design efforts, they may also add to the cognitive complexity of teaching, with potential impacts on teachers' ability to handle the cognitive load. I hope that DAD will provide insights into this dilemma.

The design and participatory approaches we discuss in Choppin et al. (2018) imply that both teachers and curriculum resources have agency with respect to how resources are understood and taken up. Referencing the work of Remillard (2005), we stated that the "teacher-tool relationship implies that the curriculum resources afford and constrain teachers' use of curriculum resources, while simultaneously the characteristics of the teacher and the context influence the use of the curriculum resources" (p. 80). This perspective has similarities to DAD in that teachers exercise agency, resources have the dual role of possessing design attributes while also being the object of ongoing design, context of use plays a role, and teachers are transformed from re-sourcing curriculum resources. On the other hand, we argue that the design and participatory approaches depart from DAD in their explicit attention to the agency of resources, particularly resources that push teachers to engage in new forms of instruction. On this latter point, DAD has been agnostic. I expect that as DAD continues to evolve and to build extensively from large-scale empirical work, the potentially transformative role of resources will be more evident.

We identified five themes related to curriculum ergonomics that resonate with DAD: teachers' relationship with and capacity to use curriculum resources; alignment between design intentions and patterns of curriculum use; ways in which curriculum resources influence instruction; ways in which curriculum features are purposefully designed to achieve a certain purpose (e.g., an educative purpose); and dissolution of boundaries between design and use. Most of these themes are extensively elaborated in DAD framework and research, so they merit no further discussion here. However, we see curriculum ergonomics as exploring more strongly than DAD the alignment between teachers' use of curriculum resources and the designers' intentions for the use of those resources. We problematize this notion of alignment, stating:

> The designer and user may not share the same goals due to a range of reasons related to teachers' histories, perspectives, capabilities, and factors in the instructional context. There are two complications in considering alignment between design and use. The first is that the intentions of the designers may not be transparent, as the design is distinct from their intentions; similarly, one must consider the intentions of the users or their interpretation of the design as separate from actual use. (Choppin et al. 2018, p. 80)

Thus, the ways teachers understand and use curriculum resources are influenced by intentions as well as design features, and there are tensions between intentions of designers and users, between intentions and actual design, and between design and actual use. Thus, curriculum ergonomics emphasizes the alignment between goals and uses in ways that extend what DAD has explored.

14.6 Final Thoughts

The chapters in this volume and the presentations at the conference provide a comprehensive accounting of the richness, flexibility, and vigor of DAD, demonstrating both a rich, if brief, tradition and a promising future. DAD has brought necessary attention to the dynamics and issues related to curriculum design and use at a time when digital resources – with their promise and shortcomings – are becoming ubiquitous. As researchers extend the theoretical connections and empirical base of DAD, the theory will face tensions between becoming more comprehensive and simultaneously more diffuse. It will be important to continue to gather the community of researchers who rely on DAD to develop common understandings, to address the dilemmas raised here and others that emerge, and to reduce the drift of individual users of the theory.

References

Adler, J. (2000). Conceptualizing resources as a theme for teacher education. *Journal of Mathematics Teacher Education, 3*(3), 205–224.

Artigue, M. (this volume). Reflecting on a theoretical approach from a networking perspective: The case of the documentational approach to didactics. In L. Trouche, G. Gueudet, & B. Pepin (Eds.), *The 'resource' approach to mathematics education*. Cham: Springer.

Baron, M., Guin, D., & Trouche, L. (2007). *Environnements informatisés et ressources numériques pour l'apprentissage: conception et usages, regards croisés*. Paris: Hermès.

Choppin, J. (2011a). Learned adaptations: Teachers' understanding and use of curriculum resources. *Journal of Mathematics Teacher Education, 14*, 331–353. https://doi.org/10.1007/s10857-011-9170-3.

Choppin, J. (2011b). The role of local theories: Teacher knowledge and its impact on engaging students with challenging tasks. *Mathematics Education Research Journal, 23*(1), 5–25. https://doi.org/10.1007/s13394-011-0001-8.

Choppin, J., Roth McDuffie, A., Drake, C., & Davis, J. (2018). Curriculum ergonomics: Conceptualizing the interactions between curriculum design and use. *International Journal of Educational Research, 92*, 75–85.

Drijvers, P., Doorman, M., Boon, P., Reed, H., & Gravemeijer, K. (2010). The teacher and the tool: Instrumental orchestrations in the technology-rich mathematics classroom. *Educational Studies in Mathematics, 75*(2), 213–234. https://doi.org/10.1007/s10649-010-9254-5.

Engeström, Y. (1999). Activity theory and individual and social transformation. In Y. Engeström, R. Miettennen, & R.-L. Punamaki (Eds.), *Perspectives on activity theory* (pp. 19–38). New York: Cambridge University Press.

Ericsson, K. A., & Simon, H. A. (1980). Verbal reports as data. *Psychological Review, 87*, 215–251.

Gueudet, G. (this volume). Studying teachers' documentation work Emergence of a theoretical approach. In L. Trouche, G. Gueudet, & B. Pepin (Eds.), *The 'resource' approach to mathematics education*. Cham: Springer.

Lave, J., & Wenger, E. (1991). *Situated learning: Legitimate peripheral participation*. New York: Cambridge University Press.

Rabardel, P. (1995). *Les hommes et les technologies, approche cognitive des instruments contemporains*. Paris: Armand Colin.

Rabardel, P., & Bourmaud, G. (2005). Instruments et systèmes d'instruments. In P. Rabardel & P. Pastré (Eds.), *Modèles du sujet pour la conception. Dialectiques activités développement* (pp. 211–229). Octarès: Toulouse.

Remillard, J. T. (2005). Examining key concepts in research on teachers' use of mathematics curricula. *Review of Educational Research, 75*(2), 211–246.

Ruthven, K. (2007). Teachers, technologies and the structures of schooling. In D. Pitta-Pantazi & G. Philippou (Eds.), *Proceedings of the fifth congress of the European Society for Research in mathematics education* (pp. 52–67). Larnaca: University of Cyprus and ERME.

Sésamath. (2009). *Le manuel Sésamath 6e* (Génération 5 ed.). Chambéry: Sésamath.

Trouche, L. (2004). Managing complexity of human/machine interactions in computerized learning environments: Guiding students' command process through instrumental orchestrations. *International Journal of Computers for Mathematical Learning, 9*, 281–307.

Trouche, L. (this volume). Evidencing the missing resources of the documentational approach to didactics, towards new programs of research. In L. Trouche, G. Gueudet, & B. Pepin (Eds.), *The 'resource' approach to mathematics education*. Cham: Springer.

Vergnaud, G. (1998). Toward a cognitive theory of practice. In A. Sierpinska & J. Kilpatrick (Eds.), *Mathematics education as a research domain: A search for identity* (pp. 227–241). Dordrecht: Kluwer Academic Publisher.

Vygotsky, L. S. (1978). *Mind in society*. Cambridge, MA: Harvard University Press.

Wenger, E. (1998). *Communities of practice: Learning, meaning, and identity*. Cambridge: Cambridge University Press.

Wertsch, J. V. (1991). *Voices of the mind: A sociocultural approach to mediated action*. Cambridge, MA: Harvard University Press.

Wertsch, J. V., & Toma, C. (1995). Discourse and learning in the classroom: A sociocultural approach. In L. Steffe & J. Gale (Eds.), *Constructivism in education* (pp. 159–174). Hillsdale. Lawrence Erlbaum Associates, Inc.

References

Abar, C. (2018). The documentary approach to didactics in a flipped classroom proposal. In V. Gitirana, T. Miyakawa, M. Rafalska, S. Soury-Lavergne, & L. Trouche (Eds.), *Proceedings of the re(s)source 2018 international conference* (pp. 139–142). Lyon: ENS de Lyon.

Abboud-Blanchard, M., & Vandebrouck, F. (2014). Geneses of technology uses: A theoretical model to study the development of teachers' practices in technology environments. In B. Ubuz, Ç. Haser, & M. A. Mariotti (Eds.), *Proceedings of the eighth congress of the European society for research in mathematics education* (pp. 2504–2514). Ankara: Middle East Technical University and ERME.

Abboud-Blanchard, M., Caron, F., Dorier, J.-L., & Sokhna, M. (2015). Ressources dans l'espace mathématique francophone. In L. Theis (Ed.), *Pluralités culturelles et universalité des mathématiques : enjeux et perspectives pour leur enseignement et leur apprentissage – Actes du colloque EMF2015 – Plénières* (pp. 40–66). Alger: Université des Sciences et de la Technologie Houari Boumediene.

Adamopoulos, P. (2013). What makes a great MOOC? An interdisciplinary analysis of student retention in online courses. In *Proceedings of the 34th international conference on information systems (ICIS 2013)* (pp. 1–21). Milan: Association for Information Systems Electronic Library (AISeL).

Adler, J. (2000). Conceptualizing resources as a theme for teacher education. *Journal of Mathematics Teacher Education, 3*(3), 205–224.

Adler, J. (2012). Knowledge resources in and for school mathematics teaching. In G. Gueudet, B. Pepin, & L. Trouche (Eds.), *From text to 'lived' resources: Mathematics curriculum materials and teacher development* (pp. 3–22). New York: Springer.

Ahl, L., Gunnarsdóttir, G. H., Koljonen, T., & Pálsdóttir, G. (2015). How teachers interact and use teacher guides in mathematics – Cases from Sweden and Iceland. *Nordic Studies in Mathematics Education, 20*(3–4), 179–197.

Aldon, G. (2011). *Interactions didactiques dans la classe de mathématiques en environnement numérique: construction et mise à l'épreuve d'un cadre d'analyse exploitant la notion d'incident*. PhD. Lyon, France: Université Lyon 1, https://tel.archives-ouvertes.fr/tel-00679121v2/document

Aldon, G., Cahuet, P.-Y., Durand-Guerrier, V., Front, M., Krieger, D., Mizony, M., & Tardy, C. (2010). *Expérimenter des problèmes de recherche innovants en mathématiques à l'école*. Lyon: Cédérom INRP.

Aldon, G., Hitt, F., Bazzini, L., & Gellert, U. (Eds.). (2017). *Mathematics and Technology: A C.I.E.A.E.M. Sourcebook*. New York: Springer International Publishing.

© Springer Nature Switzerland AG 2019
L. Trouche et al. (eds.), *The 'Resource' Approach to Mathematics Education*,
Advances in Mathematics Education,
https://doi.org/10.1007/978-3-030-20393-1

504 References

Alturkmani, M. D. (2015). *Genèse des affinités disciplinaire et didactique et genèse documentaire : le cas des professeurs de physique-chimie en France.* Thèse de doctorat. Lyon: École Normale Supérieure de Lyon.

Alturkmani, M. D., Trouche, L., & Morge, L. (2018). Étude des liens entre affinités disciplinaire et didactique, et travail de l'enseignant : le cas d'un enseignant de physique-chimie en France. *Recherches en Didactique des Sciences et des Technologies, 17,* 129–157.

Alturkmani, M.-D., Daubias, P., Loisy, C., Messaoui, A., & Trouche, L. (2019a). Instrumenter les recherches sur le travail documentaire des enseignants : le projet AnA.doc. *Éducation & Didactique, 13*(2).

Alturkmani, M., Daubias, P., Loisy, C., Messaoui, A., & Trouche, L. (2019b). Instrumenter les recherches sur le travail enseignant: le projet AnA.doc. *Education & didactique, 13*(2).

Alturkmani, M.-D., Daubias, P., Loisy, C., Messaoui, A., & Trouche, L. (in press). Instrumenter les recherches sur le travail documentaire des enseignants : le projet AnA.doc. *Éducation & didactique.*

Andrews, P. (2007). Negotiating meaning in cross-national studies of mathematics teaching: Kissing frogs to find princes. *Comparative Education, 43*(4), 489–509.

Anichini, G., Arzarello, F., Ciarrapico, L., Robutti, O., & Statale, L. S. (2004). *Matematica 2003. La matematica per il cittadino.* Lucca: Matteoni Stampatore.

Apted, M. (Ed.). (2013). *Up series* [TV documentary]. United Kingdom: First Run Pictures.

Arcavi, A. (2003). The role of visual representations in the learning of mathematics. *Educational Studies in Mathematics, 52*(3), 215–241.

Argaud, H.-C., Douaire, J., & Emprin, F. (2018). The evolution of a resource stemming from research. In V. Gitirana, T. Miyakawa, M. Rafalska, S. Soury-Lavergne, & L. Trouche (Eds.), *Proceedings of the re(s)sources 2018 international conference* (pp. 179–182). Lyon: ENS de Lyon.

Arsac, G., & Mante, M. (2007). *Les pratiques du problème ouvert.* Lyon: Scéren CRDP de Lyon.

Arsac, G., Germain, G., & Mante, M. (1988). *Problème ouvert et Situation-problème.* Lyon: IREM de Lyon, Université Claude-Bernard Lyon 1.

Artigue, M. (1988). Ingénierie didactique. *Recherches en didactique des mathématiques, 9*(3), 281–208.

Artigue, M. (1990). Ingénierie didactique. *Recherches en didactique des mathématiques, 9*(3), 281–307.

Artigue, M. (2002). Learning mathematics in a CAS environment: The genesis of a reflection about instrumentation and the dialectics between technical and conceptual work. *International Journal of Computers for Mathematical Learning, 7,* 245–274.

Artigue, M. (Ed.). (2009). Connecting approaches to technology enhanced learning in mathematics: The TELMA experience. *International Journal of Computers for Mathematical Learning, 14*(3).

Artigue, M. (2015). Perspective on design research: The case of didactical engineering. In A. A. Bikner, K. Knipping, & N. Presmeg (Eds.), *Approaches to qualitative research in mathematics education* (pp. 467–496). Dordrecht: Springer.

Artigue, M. (this volume). Reflecting on a theoretical approach from a networking perspective: The case of the documentational approach to didactics. In L. Trouche, G. Gueudet, & B. Pepin (Eds.), *The 'resource' approach to mathematics education.* Cham: Springer.

Artigue, M., & Bosch, M. (2014). Reflection on networking through the praxeological lens. In A. Bikner-Ahsbahs & S. Prediger (Eds.), *Networking of theories as a research practice in mathematics education* (pp. 249–266). New York: Springer.

Artigue, M., Bosch, M., & Gascón, J. (2011a). La TAD face au problème de l'interaction entre cadres théoriques en didactique des mathématiques. In M. Bosch, J. Gascón, A. Ruiz Olarría, M. Artaud, A. Bronner, Y. Chevallard, G. Cirade, C. Ladage, & M. Larguier (Eds.), *Un panorama de la TAD. Actes du troisième congrès de la TAD* (pp. 33–56). Centre de Recerca Matemàtica: Barcelona.

References

Artigue, M., Bosch, M., & Gascón, J. (2011b). La TAD face au problème de l'interaction entre cadres théoriques en didactique des mathématiques. In M. Bosch et al. (Eds.), *Un panorama de la TAD. Actes du troisième congrès de la TAD* (pp. 33–56). Centre de Recerca Matemàtica: Barcelona.

Artigue, M., Novotná, J., Grugeon-Allys, B., Horoks, J., Hospesová, A., Moraová, H., Pilet, J., & Žlábková, I. (2017). Comparing the professional lexicons of Czech and French mathematics teachers. In B. Kaur, W. K. Ho, T. L. Toh, & B. H. Choy (Eds.), *Proceedings of PME 41* (Vol. 2, pp. 113–120). Singapore: PME.

Artzt, A. F., Armour-Thomas, E., Curcio, C., & Gurl, T. J. (2015). *Becoming a reflective mathematics teacher: A guide for observations and self-assessment* (3rd ed.). New York: Routledge.

Arzarello, F. (2016). Le phénomène de l'hybridation dans les théories en didactique des mathématiques et ses conséquences méthodologiques, *Conférence au Xème séminaire des jeunes chercheurs de l'ARDM*, Lyon, May 7–8.

Arzarello, F., Robutti, O., Sabena, C., Cusi, A., Garuti, R., Malara, N. A., & Martignone, F. (2014). Meta-didactical transposition: A theoretical model for teacher education programs. In A. Clark-Wilson, O. Robutti, & N. Sinclair (Eds.), *The mathematics teacher in the digital era: An international perspective on technology focused professional development* (Vol. 2, pp. 347–372). Dordrecht: Springer.

Assis, C., & Gitirana, V. (2017). An analysis of the engagement of preservice teachers with curriculum resources in Brazil. In G. Schubring, L. Fan, & V. Giraldo (Eds.), *Proceedings of the second international conference on mathematics textbook research and development* (ICMT2). Rio de Janeiro-RJ: Universidade Federal do Rio de Janeiro.

Assis, C., Gitirana, V., & Trouche, L. (2018). The metamorphosis of resource systems of prospective teacher: From studying to teaching. In V. Gitirana, T. Miyakawa, M. Rafalska, S. Soury-Lavergne, & L. Trouche (Eds.), *Proceedings of the re(s)sources 2018 international conference* (pp. 39–42). Lyon: ENS de Lyon. Retrieved on November 8th, 2018, at https://hal.archives-ouvertes.fr/hal-01764563.

Assude, T. (2007). Teacher's practices and degree of ICT integration. In D. Pitta-Pantazi & G. Philippou (Eds.), *Proceedings of the fifth congress of the European society for research in mathematics education* (pp. 1339–1348). Larnaca: University of Cyprus and ERME.

Assude, T., Buteau, C., & Forgasz, H. (2010). Factors influencing implementation of technology-rich mathematics curriculum and practices. In C. Hoyles & J.-B. Lagrange (Eds.), *Mathematics education and technology – Rethinking the terrain. The 17th ICMI study* (pp. 405–419). New York: Springer.

Atanga, N. A. (2014). *Elementary school teachers' use of curricular resources for lesson design and enactment*. Unpublished dissertation in Western Michigan University.

Atkinson, B. (2012). Rethinking reflection: Teachers' critiques. *The Teacher Educator, 47*, 175–194.

Bachimont, B. (2010). Le numérique comme support de la connaissance: entre matérialisation et interprétation. In G. Gueudet & L. Trouche (Eds.), *Ressources vives. Le travail documentaire des professeurs en mathématiques* (pp. 75–90). Rennes/Lyon: Presses Universitaires de Rennes et INRP.

Bachimont, B., & Crozat, S. (2004). Instrumentation numérique des documents: pour une séparation fonds/forme. *Revue I3, 4*(1), 95–104.

Bailleul, M., & Thémines, J. F. (2013). L'ingénierie de formation: formalisation d'expériences en formation d'enseignants. In A. Vergnioux (Ed.), *Traité d'ingénierie de la formation, L'Harmattan* (pp. 85–112). Paris.

Bakker, A. (2004). *Design research in statistics education: On symbolizing and computer tools*. Utrecht: CD Beta Press.

Balacheff, N. (1994). La transposition informatique. Note sur un nouveau problème pour la didactique. In M. Artigue, R. Gras, C. Laborde, & P. Tavignot (Eds.), *Vingt ans de Didactique des Mathématiques en France* (pp. 364–370). Grenoble: La Pensée Sauvage.

506   References

Balacheff, N. (1995). *Conception, Connaissance et Concept. Didactique et technologies cognitives en mathématiques. Séminaires 1994–95* (pp. 219–244). Grenoble: Université Joseph Fourier.

Balacheff, N., & Margolinas, C. (2005). cK¢ Modèle de connaissances pour le calcul de situations didactiques. In A. Mercier & C. Margolinas (Eds.), *Balises en Didactique des Mathématiques* (pp. 75–106). Grenoble: La Pensée Sauvage éditions.

Ball, D. L., & Cohen, D. K. (1996a). Reform by the book: What is-or might be-the role of curriculum materials in teacher learning and instructional reform? *Educational Researcher, 25*(9), 6–8. 14.

Ball, D. L., & Cohen, D. K. (1996b). Reform by the book: what is – Or might be – The role of curriculum materials in teacher learning and instructional reform? *Educational Researcher, 25*(9), 6–8,14.

Ball, D. L., Hill, H. C., & Bass, H. (2005). Knowing mathematics for teaching. Who knows mathematics well enough to teach third grade, and how can we decide? *American Educator, 30*(3), 14–46.

Ball, D. L., Thames, M., & Phelps, G. (2008). Content knowledge for teaching: What makes it special? *Journal of Teacher Education, 59*(5), 389–407.

Barbosa, A., & Vale, I. (2018). Math trails: A resource for teaching and learning. In V. Gitirana, T. Miyakawa, M. Rafalska, S. Soury-Lavergne, & L. Trouche (Eds.), *Proceedings of the re(s) sources 2018 international conference* (pp. 183–186). Lyon: ENS de Lyon. Retrieved on November 8th, 2018, at https://hal.archives-ouvertes.fr/hal-01764563.

Barlet, R. (1999). L'espace épistémologique et didactique de la chimie. *Bulletin de l'Union des Physiciens, 93*(817), 1423–1448.

Baron, M., Guin, D., & Trouche, L. (dir.) (2007). *Environnements informatisés et ressources numériques pour l'apprentissage: conception et usages, regards croisés.* Paris: Hermès.

Barrow-Green, J. (2006). Much necessary for all sortes of men': 450 years of Euclid's *Elements* in English. *BSHM Bulletin: Journal of the British Society for the History of Mathematics, 21*(1), 2–25.

Barth-Cohen, L. A., Little, A. J., & Abrahamson, D. (2018). Building reflective practices in a preservice math and science teacher education course that focuses on qualitative video analysis. *Journal of Science Teacher Education, 29*(2), 83–101.

Bartolini Bussi, M., & Mariotti, M. A. (2008). Semiotic mediation in the mathematics classroom: Artefacts and signs after a Vygotskian perspective. In L. English et al. (Eds.), *Handbook of international research in mathematics education* (pp. 750–787). New York: LEA.

Baştürk-Şahín, B. N., & Tapan-Broutin, M. S. (2018a). Analysing teacher candidates' evolution into teachers through documentational approach. In V. Gitirana et al. (Eds.), *Proceedings of the Re(s)sources 2018 international conference* (pp. 43–47). ENS de Lyon.

Baştürk-Şahín, B. N., & Tapan-Broutin, M. S. (2018b). Analysis of primary mathematics teachers' lesson document preparation processes. In V. Gitirana et al. (Eds.), *Proceedings of the Re(s) sources 2018 international conference* (pp. 48–52). ENS de Lyon.

Baxandall, M. (1985). *Patterns of intention: on the historical explanation of pictures.* New Haven: Yale University Press.

Becker, J. P., Silver, E. A., Kantowski, M. G., Travers, K. J., & Wilson, J. W. (1990). Some observations of mathematics teaching in Japanese elementary and junior high schools. *Arithmetic Teacher, 38*(2), 12–21.

Béguin, P. (2004). Monde, version des mondes et monde commun. *Bulletin de Psychologie., 469*(57), 45–48.

Bellemain, F., & Trouche, L. (2016). *Comprendre le travail des professeurs avec les ressources de leur enseignement, un questionnement didactique et informatique*, invited lecture, I Simpósio Latinoamericano de Didática da Matemática, 01 a 06 de novembro de 2016, Bonito – Mato Grosso do Sul – Brasil. Retrieved at https://drive.google.com/file/d/0B6OphkgfrkD3ZFRtTDJ2anRfSWM/view

Bellemain, F., Tiburcio, R., Silva, C., & Gitirana, V. (2016). *Function Studium software.* Recife-PE: LEMATEC Research Group.

References

Bellemain, F., Rodrigues, A., & Rodrigues, A. (2018). LEMATEC Studium: a support resource for teaching mathematics. In V. Gitirana, T. Miyakawa, M. Rafalska, S. Soury-Lavergne, & L. Trouche (Eds.), *Proceedings of the re(s)sources 2018 international conference* (pp. 255–258). Lyon: ENS de Lyon. Retrieved on November 8th, 2018 at https://hal.archives-ouvertes.fr/hal-01764563.

Ben-Peretz, M. (1990). *The teacher-curriculum encounter: Freeing teachers from the tyranny of texts*. Albany: SUNY Press.

Ben-Zvi, D. (2006). Scaffolding students' informal inference and argumentation. In A. Rossman & B. Chance (Eds.), *Proceedings of the seventh international conference on teaching statistics (CD-ROM)*. International Statistical Institute: Voorburg.

Berliner, D. C. (1988). *The development of expertise in pedagogy. Charles W. Hunt Memorial Lecture presented at the annual meeting of the American Association of Colleges for Teacher Education*. New Orleans, Louisiana.

Berliner, D. C. (2001). Learning about and learning from expert teachers. *International Journal of Educational Research, 35*(5), 463–482.

Bernard, A., & Proust, C. (Eds.). (2014). *Scientific sources and teaching contexts throughout history: Problems and perspectives*. Dordrecht/Heidelberg/New York/London: Springer.

Bernstein, N. A. (1996). On dexterity and its development. In M. L. Latash & M. T. Turvey (Eds.), *Dexterity and its development* (pp. 3–245). New York: Psychology Press.

Besnier, S. (2016a). Usages de ressources technologiques pour l'enseignement du nombre à l'école maternelle et développement professionnel des professeurs, *Adjectif.net*. Retrieved on February 2019 at http://www.adjectif.net/spip/spip.php?article415

Besnier, S. (2016b). *Le travail documentaire des professeurs à l'épreuve des ressources technologiques. Le cas de l'enseignement du nombre à l'école maternelle*. Thèse de doctorat. Renne: Université de Bretagne Occidentale. https://tel.archives-ouvertes.fr/tel-01326826v2/document

Besnier, S. (2016c). *Le travail documentaire des professeurs à l'épreuve des ressources technologiques : Le cas de l'enseignement du nombre à l'école maternelle*. PhD. Brest: Université de Bretagne Occidentale, https://tel.archives-ouvertes.fr/tel-01397586/document

Besnier, S. (2018). Orchestrations at kindergarten: Articulation between manipulatives and digital resources. In V. Gitirana, T. Miyakawa, M. Rafalska, S. Soury-Lavergne, & L. Trouche (Eds.), *Proceedings of the re(s)sources 2018 international conference* (pp. 259–262). Lyon: ENS de Lyon. Retrieved on November 8th, 2018, at https://hal.archives-ouvertes.fr/hal-01764563.

Besnier, S., & Gueudet, G. (2016). Usages de ressources numériques pour l'enseignement des mathématiques en maternelle: orchestrations et documents. *Perspectivas em Educação Matemática, 9*(21), 978–1003. http://seer.ufms.br/index.php/pedmat/article/view/2215/2279.

Beswick, N. (1974). Library resource Centres: A developing literature. *Journal of Librarianship, 6*(1), 54–62.

Bezemer, J., & Kress, G. (2008). Writing in multimodal texts: A social semiotic account of designs for learning. *Written Communication, 25*(2), 166–194.

Bezemer, J., & Kress, G. (2016). *Multimodality, learning and communication: A social semiotic frame*. New York: Routledge.

Bidwell, J. K., & Clason, R. G. (Eds.). (1970). *Readings in the history of mathematics education*. Washington, DC: National Council of Teachers of Mathematics.

Bifano, F. (2018). Institutional resources at university admission: Emerging documentational identity for the analysis of the professor's work. In V. Gitirana, T. Miyakawa, M. Rafalska, S. Soury-Lavergne, & L. Trouche (Eds.), *Proceedings of the re(s)source 2018 international conference* (pp. 147–150). Lyon: ENS de Lyon.

Bikner-Ahsbahs, A., & Prediger, S. (2008). Networking of theories – An approach for exploiting the diversity of theoretical approaches. In B. Sriraman & L. English (Eds.), *Theories in mathematics education* (pp. 483–506). New York: Springer.

Bikner-Ahsbahs, A., & Prediger, S. (Eds.). (2014a). *Networking of theories as a research practice in mathematics education*. New York: Springer.

Bikner-Ahsbahs, A., & Prediger, S. (2014b). *Networking of theories as a research practice in mathematics education.* Berlin: Springer.

Bikner-Ahsbahs, A., Prediger, S., & Networking Theories Group (Eds.). (2014). *Networking of theories as a research practice in mathematics education.* New York: Springer International Publishing.

Billington, M. (2009). Establishing didactical praxeologies: Teachers using digital tools in upper secondary mathematics classrooms. In V. Durand-Guerrier, S. Soury-Lavergne, & F. Arzarello (Eds.), *Proceedings of the sixth congress of European research in mathematics education* (pp. 1330–1339). Lyon, France: ENS de Lyon.

Bishop, A. J. (2002). Critical challenges in researching cultural issues in mathematics education. *Journal of Intercultural Studies, 23*(2), 119–131.

Biza, I., Giraldo, V., Hochmuth, R., Khakbaz, A., & Rasmussen, C. (2016). *Research on teaching and learning mathematics* (ICME-13 Tropical surveys). Hamburg: Springer.

Bloch, I., & Gibel, P. (2011). Un modèle d'analyse des raisonnements dans les situations didactiques. Étude des niveaux de preuves dans une situation d'enseignement de la notion de limite. *Recherches en didactique des mathématiques, 31*(2), 191–228.

Boesen, J., Helenius, O., Bergqvist, E., Bergqvist, T., Lithner, J., Palm, T., & Palmberg, B. (2014). Developing mathematical competence: From the intended to the enacted curriculum. *The Journal of Mathematical Behavior, 33*, 72–87.

Boning, K. (2007). Coherence in general education: A historical look. *Journal of General Education, 56*(1), 1–16.

Borko, H. (2004). Professional development and teacher learning: Mapping the terrain. *Educational Researcher, 33*(8), 3–15.

Borko, H., & Livingston, C. (1989). Cognition and improvisation: differences in mathematics instruction by expert and novice teachers. *American Educational Research Journal, 26*(4), 473–498.

Bosch, M. (2010). L'écologie des parcours d'étude et de recherche au secondaire. Diffuser les mathématiques (et les autres savoirs) comme outils de connaissance et d'actions. In *Actes du 2° Colloque International sur la théorie anthropologique du didactique.* Montpellier: IUFM.

Bozkurt, G. (2016). *Teaching with technology: A multiple-case study of secondary teachers' practices of GeoGebra use in mathematics teaching.* Unpublished PhD thesis, University of Cambridge.

Bozkurt, G., & Ruthven, K. (2017a). Teaching with GeoGebra: Resource systems of mathematics teachers. In G. Aldon & J. Trgalová (Eds.), *Proceedings of the 13th international conference on technology in mathematics teaching [ICTMT 13]* (pp. 216–223). Lyon: École Normale Supérieure de Lyon/Université Claude Bernard Lyon 1.

Bozkurt, G., & Ruthven, K. (2017b). Classroom-based professional expertise: A mathematics teacher's practice with technology. *Educational Studies in Mathematics, 94*(3), 309–328.

Brock, W. H. (1975). Geometry and the universities: Euclid and his modem rivals 1860–1901. *History of Education, 4*(2), 21–35.

Broley, L. (2016). The place of computer programming in (undergraduate) mathematical practices. In E. Nardi, C. Winsløw, & T. Hausberger (Eds.), *Proceedings of INDRUM 2016 first conference of the International Network for the Didactic Research in University Mathematics* (pp. 360–369). Montpellier: University of Montpellier and INDRUM.

Brousseau, G. (1986a). La relation didactique: le milieu. In *Actes de la 4e école d'été de didactique des mathématiques* (pp. 54–68). IREM de Paris 7.

Brousseau, G. (1986b). *Théorisation des phénomènes d'enseignement des mathématiques. Thèse de doctorat. Bordeaux: Université de Bordeaux, 1.*

Brousseau, G. (1997a). *Theory of didactical situations in mathematics* (N. Balacheff, M. Cooper, R. Sutherland, & V. Warfield, Eds.). Dordrecht: Kluwer Academic Publisher.

Brousseau, G. (1997b). *Theory of didactical situations in mathematics.* Dordrecht: Kluwer Academic Publishers.

References

Brousseau, G. (1997c). *Theory of didactical situations in mathematics 1970–1990*. Dordrecht: Kluwer Academic Publishers.

Brousseau, G. (1997d). *Theory of didactical situations in mathematics. Didactique des mathématiques, 1970–1990* (edited and translated by N. Balacheff, M. Cooper, R. Sutherland, & V. Warfield). Dordrecht: Kluwer Academic Publishers.

Brousseau, G. (1998). *Théorie des situations didactiques*. Grenoble: La pensée sauvage.

Brousseau, G., & Warfield, V. M. (1999). The case of Gaël. *The Journal of Mathematical Behavior, 18*(1), 7–52.

Brousseau, G., Brousseau, N., & Warfield, G. (2014). *Teaching fractions through situations: A fundamental experiment*. Dordrecht: Springer.

Brown, M. (1989). Graded assessment and learning hierarchies in mathematics – An alternative view. *British Educational Research Journal, 15*(2), 121–128.

Brown, M. (2002). *Teaching by design: understanding the intersection between teacher practice and the design of curricular innovations* Doctoral thesis. Evanston: Northwestern University.

Brown, M. W. (2009a). The teacher-tool relationship: Theorizing the design and use of curriculum materials. In J. T. Remillard, B. A. Herbel-Eisenmann, & G. M. Lloyd (Eds.), *Mathematics teachers at work: Connecting curriculum materials and classroom instruction* (pp. 17–36). New York: Routledge.

Brown, M. (2009b). Toward a theory of curriculum design and use: Understanding the teacher-tool relationship. In J. T. Remillard, B. A. Herbel-Eisenmann, & G. M. Lloyd (Eds.), *Mathematics teachers at work: Connecting curriculum materials and classroom instruction* (pp. 17–36). New York: Routledge.

Brown, M., & Edelson, D. (2003). *Teaching as design: Can we better understand the ways in which teachers use materials so we can better design materials to support their changes in practice*. Evanston: Centre for Learning Technologies in Urban Schools (design brief).

Brown, S. A., Pitvorec, K., Ditto, C., & Kelso, C. R. (2009). Reconceiving fidelity of implementation: an investigation of elementary whole-number lessons. *Journal for Research in Mathematics Education, 40*(4), 363–395.

Bucheton, D., & Soulé, Y. (2009). Les gestes professionnels et le jeu des postures de l'enseignant dans la classe: un multi-agenda de préoccupations enchâssées. *Éducation & Didactique, 3*(3), 29–48.

Bueno-Ravel, L., & Gueudet, G. (2007). Online resources in mathematics: Teachers' genesis of use. In D. Pitta-Pantazi & G. Philippou (Eds.), *Proceedings of the fifth congress of the European society for research in mathematics education* (pp. 1369–1378). University of Cyprus and ERME: Larnaca.

Buljan Culej, J. (2016). Croatia. In I. V. S. Mullis, M. O. Martin, S. Goh, & K. Cotter (Eds.), *TIMSS 2015 encyclopedia: Education policy and curriculum in mathematics and science*. Chestnut Hill: TIMSS & PIRLS International Study Center, Lynch School of Education, Boston College.

Bussi, M. G. B., Boni, M., & Ferri, F. (1995). *Interazione sociale e conoscenza a scuola: la discussione matematica*. Modena: Centro Documentazione Educativa.

Caillot, M. (1994). Des objectifs aux compétences dans l'enseignement scientifique : une évolution de vingt ans. In F. Ropé & L. Tanguy (dir.), *Savoirs et compétences. De l'usage de ces notions dans l'école et dans l'entreprise* (pp. 95–117). Paris: L'Harmattan.

Cajori, F. (1910). Attempts made during the eighteenth and nineteenth centuries to reform the teaching of geometry. *American Mathematical Monthly, 17*(10), 181–201.

Calderhead, J. (1984). *Teachers' classroom decision-making*. London: Holt, Rinehart and Winston.

Cao, Z., Seah, W., & Bishop, A. (2006). A comparison of mathematical values conveyed in mathematics textbooks in China and Australia. In F. K. S. Leung et al. (Eds.), *Mathematics education in different cultural traditions: A comparative study of East Asia and the west* (pp. 483–493). New York: Springer.

Caraës, M.-H., & Marchand-Zanartu, N. (2011). *Images de pensées*. Paris: Editions de la Réunion des musées nationaux.

Carlsen, M., Erfjord, I., Hundeland, P. S., & Monaghan, J. (2016). Kindergarten teachers' orchestration of mathematical activities afforded by technology: Agency and mediation. *Educational Studies in Mathematics, 93*(1), 1–17.

Carpenter, T. P., Fennema, E., Peterson, P. L., Chiang, C.-P., & Loef, M. (1989). Using knowledge of children's mathematics thinking in classroom teaching: An experimental study. *American Educational Research Journal, 26*, 499–531.

Carton, T. (2018a). From digital "bricolage" to the start of collective work – What influences do secondary teachers non-formal digital practices have on their documentation work? In V. Gitirana, T. Miyakawa, M. Rafalska, S. Soury-Lavergne, & L. Trouche (Eds.), *Proceedings of the re(s)ources 2018 international conference* (pp. 263–266). Lyon: ENS de Lyon. Retrieved on November 8th, 2018, at https://hal.archives-ouvertes.fr/hal-01764563.

Carton, T. (2018b). *Case study: How teachers' everyday creativity can be associated with an edtech player's strategies.* Présenté au XXIe Congrès de la SFSIC – Création, créativité et médiations, Saint-Denis, 13-15 juin 2018.

Cayton, C., Hollebrands, K., Okumuş, S., & Boehm, E. (2017). Pivotal teaching moments in technology-intensive secondary geometry classrooms. *Journal of Mathematics Teacher Education, 20*(1), 75–100.

Cazes, C., Gueudet, G., Hersant, M., & Vandebrouck, F. (2007). Using e-exercise bases in mathematics: Case studies at university. *International Journal of Computers for Mathematical Learning, 11*(3), 327–350.

Cecconi, S. (2007). *Site personnel du dessinateur Serge Cecconi* (IREM de Grenoble) http://perso.orange.fr/serge.cecconi/cariboost2/index.html.

Charles, R. I., Crown, W., Fennell, F., et al. (2008). *Scott Foresman–Addison Wesley mathematics.* Glenview: Pearson.

Chemla, K. (Ed.). (2012). *The history of mathematical proof in ancient traditions.* Cambridge: Cambridge University Press.

Chemla, K., Keller, A., & Proust, C. (Eds.). (forthcoming). *Cultures of computation and quantification in the Ancient World.* New York: Springer.

Cheng, H. G., & Phillips, M. R. (2014). Secondary analysis of existing data: Opportunities and implementation. *Shanghai Archives of Psychiatry, 26*(6), 371–375.

Chevallard, Y. (1982). Pourquoi la transposition didactique ? In *Actes du Séminaire de didactique et de pédagogie des mathématiques de l'IMAG* (pp. 167–194). Grenoble: Université Joseph Fourier. http://yves.chevallard.free.fr/spip/spip/IMG/pdf/Pourquoi_la_transposition_didactique.pdf.

Chevallard, Y. (1985). *La transposition didactique.* Grenoble: La Pensée Sauvage éditions.

Chevallard, Y. (1992). A theoretical approach to curricula. *Journal für Mathematikdidaktik, 13*(2/3), 215–230.

Chevallard, Y. (1998). Analyse des pratiques enseignantes et didactique des mathématiques : l'approche anthropologique. In *Actes de l'université d'été Analyse des pratiques enseignantes et didactique des mathématiques* (pp. 91–120). IREM de Clermont-Ferrand.

Chevallard, Y. (1999). L'analyse des pratiques enseignantes en Théorie Anthropologie Didactique. *Recherches en Didactiques des Mathématiques, 19*(2), 221–266.

Chevallard, Y. (2002a). Ecologie et régulation. In J.-L. Dorier, M. Artaud, M. Artigue, R. Berthelot, & R. Floris (dir.), *Actes de la XIème Ecole d'été de didactique des mathématiques, Corps* (pp. 41–56). Grenoble: La Pensée Sauvage.

Chevallard, Y. (2002b). Organiser l'étude. In J.-L. Dorier, M. Artaud, M. Artigue, R. Berthelot, & R. Floris (Eds.), *Actes de la Xème Ecole d'été de didactique des mathématiques* (pp. 3–22, 41–56). Grenoble: La Pensée Sauvage éditions.

Chevallard, Y. (2002c). Organiser l'étude. 3. Ecologie & régulation. In *Actes de la XIe école d'été de didactique des mathématiques* (pp. 41–56). Grenoble: La Pensée Sauvage.

Chevallard, Y. (2002d). *Organiser l'étude. 1. Structures & fonctions. Actes de la XIe école d'été de didactique des mathématiques* (pp. 3–32). La Pensée Sauvage : Grenoble. http://yves.chevallard.free.fr/spip/spip/IMG/pdf/Organiser_1_etude_1.pdf

References

Chevallard, Y. (2006). Steps towards a new epistemology in mathematics education. In M. Bosch (Ed.), *Proceedings of the fourth congress of the European society for research in mathematics education* (pp. 21–30). Barcelona: FUNDEMI-1QS and ERME.

Chevallard, Y., & Cirade, G. (2010a). Les ressources manquantes comme problème professionnel. In G. Gueudet & L. Trouche (Eds.), *Ressources vives. Le travail documentaire des professeurs en mathématiques* (pp. 41–56). Rennes/Lyon: Presses Universitaires de Rennes et INRP.

Chevallard, Y., & Cirade, G. (2010b). Les ressources manquantes comme problem professionnel. In G. Gueudet & L. Trouche (Eds.), *Ressources vives. Le travail documentaire des professeurs en mathématiques* (pp. 41–55). Lyon: Paideia, PUR et INRP.

Cheverie, J. (n.d.). *MOOCs an intellectual property: Ownership and use rights.* https://er.educause.edu/blogs/2013/4/moocs-and-intellectual-property-ownership-and-use-rights. Accessed 18 Apr 2017.

Choppin, A. (2005). L'édition scolaire française et ses contraintes : Une perspective historique. In E. Bruillard (Ed.), *Manuels scolaires, regards croisés* (pp. 39–53). Caen: CRDP de Basse-Normandie.

Choppin, J. (2011a). Learned adaptations: Teachers' understanding and use of curriculum resources. *Journal of Mathematics Teacher Education, 14*, 331–353. https://doi.org/10.1007/s10857-011-9170-3.

Choppin, J. (2011b). The role of local theories: Teacher knowledge and its impact on engaging students with challenging tasks. *Mathematics Education Research Journal, 23*(1), 5–25. https://doi.org/10.1007/s13394-011-0001-8.

Choppin, J. (2018). Exploring teachers' design processes with different curriculum programs. In V. Gitirana, T. Miyakawa, M. Rafalska, S. Soury-Lavergne, & L. Trouche (Eds.), *Proceeedings of the re(s)sources 2018 international conference* (pp. 267–270). Lyon: ENS de Lyon. Retrieved on November 8th, 2018, at https://hal.archives-ouvertes.fr/hal-01764563.

Choppin, J., Carson, C., Borys, Z., Cerosaletti, C., & Gillis, R. (2014). A typology for analyzing digital curricula in mathematics education. *International Journal of Education in Mathematics, Science, and Technology, 2*(1), 11–25.

Choppin, J., Roth McDuffie, A., Drake, C., & Davis, J. (2018). Curriculum ergonomics: conceptualizing the interactions between curriculum design and use. *International Journal of Educational Research, 92*, 75–85. Retrieved on February 21st 2019 at https://doi.org/10.1016/j.ijer.2018.09.015.

Civil, M. (1985). Sur les "livres d'écoliers" à l'époque paléo-babylonienne. In J.-M. Durand & J.-R. Kupper (Eds.), *Miscellanea Babylonica, Mélanges offerts à M. Birot* (pp. 67–78). Paris: RC.

Clandinin, D. J., & Connelly, F. M. (1990). Stories of experience and narrative inquiry. *Educational Researcher, 19*(5), 2–14.

Clarke, D. (2013). *Cultural studies in mathematics education.* Paper presented at the Eighth Congress of the European Society for Research in Mathematics Education, Antalya, Turkey.

Clarke, D. J. (2017). Using cross-cultural comparison to interrogate the logic of classroom research in mathematics education. In B. Kaur, W. K. Ho, T. L. Toh, & B. H. Choy (Eds.), *Proceedings of PME 41* (Vol. 1, pp. 1–13). Singapore: PME.

Clarke, D., Mesiti, C., Cao, Y., & Novotna, J. (2017). The lexicon project: Examining the consequences for international comparative research of pedagogical naming systems from different cultures. In T. Dooley & G. Gueudet (Eds.), *Proceedings of the tenth congress of the European society for research in mathematics education* (CERME10, February 1–5, 2017) (pp. 1610–1617). Dublin: DCU Institute of Education and ERME.

Cobb, P., & Gravemeijer, K. (2008). Experimenting to support and understand learning processes. In A. E. Kelly, R. A. Lesh, & J. Y. Baek (Eds.), *Handbook of design research methods in education* (pp. 68–95). New York: Routledge.

Cobb, P., & Jackson, K. (2015). Supporting teachers' use of research-based instructional sequences. *ZDM – Mathematics Education, 47*, 1027–1038.

Cole, M. (1985). The zone of proximal development: Where culture and cognition create each other. In J. V. Wertsch (Ed.), *Culture, communication, and cognition: Vygotskian perspectives* (pp. 146–161). Cambridge, MA: Cambridge University Press.

Confrey, J., Gianopulos, G., McGowan, W., Shah, M., & Belcher, M. (2017). Scaffolding learner-centered curricular coherence using learning maps and diagnostic assessments designed around mathematics learning trajectories. *ZDM – Mathematics Education, 49*(5), 717–734.

Contamines, J., George, S., & Hotte, R. (2003). Approche instrumentale des banques de ressources éducatives. *Revue Sciences et Techniques Éducatives, 10*, 157–178. http://halshs.archives-ouvertes.fr/hal-00298189/.

Cooper, J., Olsher, S., & Yerushalmy, M. (2018). Reflecting on didactic metadata of learning sequences. In V. Gitirana, T. Miyakawa, M. Rafalska, S. Soury-Lavergne, & L. Trouche (Eds.), *Proceedings of the re(s)sources 2018 international conference* (pp. 191–194). Lyon: ENS de Lyon. Retrieved on November 8th 2018 at https://hal.archives-ouvertes.fr/hal-01764563.

Cossette, P. (1994). Les cartes cognitives au service de l'étude des organisations. In P. Cossette (dir.), *Cartes cognitives et organisations* (pp. 3–12). Québec: Presses de l'Université Laval et Paris: Editions Eska.

Cossette, P. (2003). Méthode systématique d'aide à la formulation de la vision stratégique: Lllustration auprès d'un propriétaire-dirigeant. *Revue de l'Entreprenariat, 2*(1), 17.

Courtney, S. A. (2018). Preparing to teach mathematics: Results from a survey on mathematics teacher resources in the United States. In V. Gitirana, T. Miyakawa, M. Rafalska, S. Soury-Lavergne, & L. Trouche (Eds.), *Proceedings of the re(s)source 2018 international conference* (pp. 151–154). Lyon: ENS de Lyon.

Crozat, S. (2007). Bonnes pratiques pour l'exploitation multi-usages de contenus pédagogiques: la raison du calcul est toujours la meilleure. In M. Baron, D. Guin, & L. Trouche (dir.), *Environnements informatisés et ressources numériques pour l'apprentissage: conception et usages, regards croisés* (pp. 255–286). Paris: Hermès.

Cuevas, C. A., Villamizar, F. Y., & Martínez, A. (2017). Aplicaciones de la tecnología digital para activiDADes didácticas que promuevan una mejor comprensión del tono como cualiDAD del sonido para cursos tradicionales de física en el nivel básico. *Enseñanza de las Ciencias, 35*(3), 129–150.

Cunha, E. (2018). Digital resources: Origami folding instructions as lever to mobilize geometric concepts to solve problems. In V. Gitirana, T. Miyakawa, M. Rafalska, S. Soury-Lavergne, & L. Trouche (Eds.), *Proceedings of the Re(s)sources 2018 International Conference* (pp. 271–274). Lyon: ENS de Lyon. Retrieved on November 8th, 2018, at https://hal.archives-ouvertes.fr/hal-01764563.

Cviko, A., McKenney, S., & Voogt, J. (2014). Teacher roles in designing technology-rich learning activities for early literacy: A cross-case analysis. *Computers & Education, 72*, 68–79.

Daele, A., & Charlier, B. (2006). *Comprendre les communautés virtuelles d'enseignants*. Paris: L'Harmattan.

Davis, E. A., & Krajcik, J. (2005). Designing educative curriculum materials to promote teacher learning. *Educational Researcher, 34*(3), 3–14.

de Araújo, AJ. (2009). *O ensino de álgebra no Brasil e na França: estudo sobre o ensino de equações do 1° grau à luz da teoria antropológica do didático*. Doctoral dissertation. Recife-PE: Universidade Federal de Pernambuco. https://repositorio.ufpe.br/bitstream/123456789/3947/1/arquivo3433_1.pdf

de Araújo, A. J., & Santos. (2010). Equações do primeiro grau: Estudo comparativo dos programas de ensino da França e Brasil. In A. P. de Avelar Brito Lima et al. (Eds.), *Pesquisas em Fenômenos Didáticos: Alguns Cenários* (Vol. 1, pp. 33–49). Recife-PE: EDIGORA DA UFPE.

de los Arcos, B., Farrow, R., Pitt, R., Weller, M., & McAndrew, P. (2016). Adapting the curriculum: How K-12 teachers perceive the role of open educational resources. *Journal of Online Learning Research, 2*(1), 23–40.

De Varent, C. (2018). *Pluralité des concepts liés aux unités de mesure. Liens entre histoire des sciences et didactique, le cas de l'aire du carré dans une sélection de textes anciens*. PhD. Paris: Université Paris Diderot.

References

Deblois, L. (2012). De l'ancien élève à l'enseignant. Quel parecours. In J. Proulx, C. Corriveau, & H. Squalli (Eds.), *Formation mathématique pour l'enseignement des mathématiques* (pp. 313–320). Québec: Presses de l'Université du Québec.

Delnero, P. (2010). Sumerian Extract Tablets and Scribal Education. *Journal of Cuneiform Studies, 62*, 53–69.

Delnero, P. (2012). Memorization and the transmission of sumerian literary compositions. *Journal of Near Eastern Studies, 71*, 189–208.

Design Based Research Collective. (2003). Design-based research: An emerging paradigm for educational inquiry. *Educational Researcher, 32*(1), 5–8.

Dias, T., & Durand-Guerrier, V. (2005). Expérimenter pour apprendre en mathématiques. *Repères IREM, 60*, 61–78.

Dick, T., & Burrill, G. (2016). Design and implementation principles for dynamic interactive mathematics technologies. In M. Niess, S. Driskell, & K. Hollebrands (Eds.), *Handbook of research on transforming mathematics teacher education in the digital age* (pp. 23–52). Hershey: IGI Global Publishers.

Dietiker, L., & Riling, M. (2018). Design (in)tensions in mathematics curriculum. *International Journal of Educational Research, 92*, 43–52.

Douglas, M. (1987). *How institutions think*. London: Routledge.

Drijvers, P., & Trouche, L. (2008). From artifacts to instruments: A theoretical framework behind the orchestra metaphor. In G. W. Blume & M. K. Heid (Eds.), *Research on technology and the teaching and learning of mathematics. Cases and perspectives* (Vol. 2, pp. 363–392). Charlotte: Information Age.

Drijvers, P., Doorman, M., Boon, P., Reed, H., & Gravemeijer, K. (2010). The teacher and the tool: Instrumental orchestrations in the technology-rich mathematics classroom. *Educational Studies in Mathematics, 75*(2), 213–234. https://doi.org/10.1007/s10649-010-9254-5.

Drijvers, P., Godino, J. D., Font, V., & Trouche, L. (2013a). One episode, two lenses. *Educational Studies in Mathematics, 82*(1), 23–49.

Drijvers, P., Tacoma, S., Besamusca, A., Doorman, M., & Boon, P. (2013b). Digital resources inviting changes in mid-adopting teachers' practices and orchestrations. *ZDM – Mathematics Education, 45*(7), 987–1001.

Durand-Guerrier, V. (2006). La résolution de problèmes, d'un point de vue didactique et épistémologique. In L. Trouche, V. Durand-Guerrier, C. Margolinas, & A. Mercier (Eds.), *Actes des journées mathématiques de l'INRP* (pp. 17–23). Lyon: INRP.

Durell, C. V. (1939). *A new geometry for schools*. London: Bell.

Duval, R. (1993). Registres de représentation sémiotique et fonctionnement cognitif de la pensée. *Annales de didactique et de sciences cognitives, 5*(1), 37–65.

Earnest, D., & Amador, J. (2017, online first). Lesson planimation: Preservice elementary teachers' interactions with mathematics curricula. *Journal of Mathematics Teacher Education.*

Education Committee of the EMS. (2011). "Solid findings" in mathematics education. *Newsletter of the European Mathematical Society, 81*, 46–48.

Elton, L. (1986). Research and teaching: symbiosis or conflict. *Higher Education, 15*, 299–304.

Elton, L. (2001). Research and teaching: conditions for a positive link. *Teaching in Higher Education, 6*, 43–56.

Engeström, Y. (1987). *Learning by expanding. An activity-theoretical approach to developmental research*. Helsinki: Orienta-Konsultit Oy.

Engeström, Y. (1999). Activity theory and individual and social transformation. In Y. Engeström, R. Miettennen, & R.-L. Punamaki (Eds.), *Perspectives on activity theory* (pp. 19–38). New York: Cambridge University Press.

Engeström, Y. (2001). Expansive learning at work: Toward an activity theoretical reconceptualization. *Journal of Education, 14*(1), 133–156.

Engeström, Y. (2014). *Learning by expanding*. Cambridge: Cambridge University Press.

Erfjord, I. (2011). Teachers' initial orchestration of students' dynamic geometry software use: Consequences for students' opportunities to learn mathematics. *Technology, Knowledge and Learning, 16*(1), 35–54.

Ericsson, K. A., & Simon, H. A. (1980). Verbal reports as data. *Psychological Review, 87*, 215–251.

Espindola, E., & Trgalová, J. (2018). The documentational work in the initial formation of a mathematics undergraduate in training for the teaching of first degree equation. In V. Gitirana et al. (Eds.), *Proceedings of the re(s)sources 2018 international conference* (pp. 57–60). Lyon: ENS de Lyon.

Espindola, E., Ketully, R., & Trgalová, J. (2018). Resources and didactic decisions of a teacher in the teaching of combinatorial analysis. In V. Gitirana et al. (Eds.), *Proceedings of the re(s) sources 2018 international conference* (pp. 1127–1128). Lyon: ENS de Lyon.

Essonnier, N. K. (2018). *Étude de la conception collaborative de ressources numériques mathématiques au sein d'une communauté d'intérêt*. PhD. Lyon: Université de Lyon, https://tel.archives-ouvertes.fr/tel-01868226/document

Essonnier, N., & Trgalová, J. (2018a). Collaborative design of digital resources: role of designers' resource systems and professional knowledge. In V. Gitirana et al. (Eds.), *Proceedings of the re(s)sources 2018 international conference* (pp. 57–60). Lyon: ENS de Lyon.

Essonnier, N., & Trgalová, J. (2018b). Collaborative design of digital resources: Role of designers' resource systems and professional knowledge. In V. Gitirana, T. Miyakawa, M. Rafalska, S. Soury-Lavergne, & L. Trouche (Eds.), *Proceeedings of the re(s)sources 2018 international conference* (pp. 61–64). Lyon: ENS de Lyon. Retrieved on November 8th, 2018, at https://hal.archives-ouvertes.fr/hal-01764563.

Essonnier, N., Kynigos, C., Trgalová, J., & Daskolia, M. (2018). Role of the context in social creativity for the design of digital resources. In L. Fan, L. Trouche, S. Rezat, C. Qi, & J. Visnovska (Eds.), *Research on mathematics textbooks and Teachers' resources: Advances and issues (ICME-13 monograph)* (pp. 215–233). Cham: Springer.

Faggiano, E., Montone, A., & Mariotti, M. A. (2016). Creating a synergy between manipulatives and virtual artefacts to conceptualize axial symmetry at Primary School. In C. Csíkos, A. Rausch, & J. Szitányi (Eds.), *Proceedigns of the 40th conference of the international group for the Psychology of Mathematics Education: PME 40* (Vol. 2, pp. 235–242). Szeged: International Group for the Psychology of Mathematics Education.

Fan, L., Zhu, Y., & Miao, Z. (2013). Textbook research in mathematics education: Development status and directions. *ZDM – Mathematics Education, 45*(5), 633–646.

Fan, L., Miao, Z., & Mok, A. (2015). How Chinese teachers teach mathematics and pursue professional development: Perspectives from contemporary international research. In L. Fan et al. (Eds.), *How Chinese teach mathematics. Perspectives from insiders* (pp. 43–72). Singapore: World Scientific.

Fan, L., Trouche, L., Qi, C., Rezat, S., & Vinovska, J. (2017). Topic study group no. 38. Research on resources (textbooks, learning materials, etc.). In G. Kaiser (Ed.), *Proceedings of the 13th international congress on mathematical education* (pp. 561–564). New York: Springer.

Fan, L., Trouche, L., Qi, C., Rezat, S., & Vinovska, J. (Eds.). (2018). *Research on mathematics textbooks and teachers' resources. Advances and issues* (ICME-13 Monograph). Cham: Springer.

Farrell, A. (1996). Roles and behaviors in technology-integrated precalculus classrooms. *Journal of Mathematical Behavior, 15*(1), 35–53.

Ferguson, R., Bracher, A., Clow, D., Cooper, A., Hillaire, G., Mittelmeier, J., Rienties, B., Ullmann, T., Vuorikari, R., & Castano Munoz, J. (2016). *Research evidence on the use of learning analytics: Implications for education policy*. Bruxelles: Publications Office of the European Union. https://doi.org/10.2791/955210.

Fernandez, C., & Yoshida, M. (2004). *Lesson study – A Japanese approach to improving mathematics teaching and learning*. Mahwah: Lawrence Erlbaum.

Ferrara, F., & Sinclair, N. (2016). An early algebra approach to pattern generalisation: Actualising the virtual through words, gestures and toilet paper. *Educational Studies in Mathematics, 92*(1), 1–19.

References 515

Fidje, A. S. (2018). Orchestrating the use of student-produced videos in mathematics teaching. In V. Gitirana, T. Miyakawa, M. Rafalska, S. Soury-Lavergne, & L. Trouche (Eds.), *Proceedings of the re(s)sources 2018 international conference* (pp. 275–278). Lyon: ENS de Lyon. In *Retrieved on November 8th, 2018, at* https://hal.archives-ouvertes.fr/hal-01764563.

Fischer, G. (2001). Communities of interest: Learning through the interaction of multiple knowledge systems. In S. Bjørnestad, R. Moe, A. Mørch, & A. Opdahl (Eds.), *Proceedings of the 24th information systems research seminar in Scandinavia* (pp. 1–14). Bergen: The University of Bergen.

Fleck, L. (1981). *Genesis and development of a scientific fact.* Chicago: University of Chicago Press (original edition, 1934).

Fleck, L. (2005). Genèse et développement d'un fait scientifique. In *Les Belles-lettres.* Paris.

Fofana, O. B., & Sokhna, M. (2018). Analyse des écarts entre les prescriptions institutionnelles et les systèmes de ressources des enseignants : le cas de l'enseignement des limites de fonctions. In V. Gitirana et al. (Eds.), *Proceedings of the re(s)sources 2018 international conference* (pp. 61–64). Lyon: ENS de Lyon.

Folcher, V. (2005). De la conception pour l'usage au développement de ressources pour l'activité. In P. Rabardel, & P. Pastré (dir.) *Modèles du sujet pour la conception* (pp. 189–210). Toulouse: Octarès.

Friberg, J. (2007). *A remarkable collection of babylonian mathematical texts* (Vol. I). New York: Springer.

Front, M. (2012). Pavages semi-réguliers du plan : une exploration favorable aux élaborations mathématiques. *Repères IREM, 89,* 5–37.

Fujii, T. (2015). The critical role of task design in lesson study. In A. Watson & M. Ohtani (Eds.), *Task design in mathematics education* (pp. 273–286). Cham: Springer.

Gardes, M.-L. (2018). Démarches d'investigation et recherche de problèmes. In G. Aldon (Ed.), *Le Rallye mathématique, un jeu très sérieux !* (pp. 73–96). Poitiers: Canopé Editions.

Georget, J.-P. (2018). A primary documentation system embodied in a system of training activities for trainee teachers of mathematics. In V. Gitirana, T. Miyakawa, M. Rafalska, S. Soury-Lavergne, & L. Trouche (Eds.), *Proceedings of the re(s)source 2018 international conference* (pp. 155–158). Lyon: ENS de Lyon.

Gibbons, R. (1975). An account of the Secondary Mathematics Individualized Learning Experiment. *Mathematics in School, 4*(6), 14–16.

Gibson, J. J. (1977). *The ecological approach to visual perception.* Boston: Houghton Mifflin.

Gillespie, R. J., & Humphreys, D. A. (1970). The application of a learning resource system in teaching undergraduate chemistry. *Pure and Applied Chemistry, 22*(1-2), 111–116.

Gitirana, V., Teles, R., Bellemain, P.B., Castro, A., Andrade, Y., Lima, P., & Bellemain, F. (2013). *Jogos com sucata na Educação Matemática.* Recife-NEMAT: Editora Universitária da UFPE.

Gitirana, V., Miyakawa, T., Rafalska, M., Soury-Lavergne, S., & Trouche, L. (2018a). *Proceedings of the re(s)sources 2018 international conference.* Lyon: ENS de Lyon. Retrieved on November 8th 2018 at https://hal.archives-ouvertes.fr/hal-01764563.

Gitirana, V., Miyakawa, T., Rafalska, M., Soury-Lavergne, S., & Trouche, L. (Eds.) (2018b). Proceedings of the re(s)sources 2018 international conference. *ENS de Lyon,* https://hal.archives-ouvertes.fr/hal-01764563v3/document

Glasnović Gracin, D. (2011). *Requirements in mathematics textbooks and PISA assessment.* Doctoral dissertation. University of Klagenfurt. Klagenfurt: University of Klagenfurt.

Glasnović Gracin, D., & Jukić Matić, L. (2016). The role of mathematics textbooks in lower secondary education in Croatia: An empirical study. *The Mathematics Educator, 16*(2), 31–58.

Glasnović Gracin, D., & Jukić Matić, L. (2018). The dynamic interactions between teacher and resources in the use of the textbook and teacher guide. In V. Gitirana, T. Miyakawa, M. Rafalska, S. Soury-Lavergne, & L. Trouche (Eds.), *Proceedings of the re(s)source 2018 international conference* (pp. 159–162). ENS de Lyon: Lyon.

Goigoux, R., & Vergnaud, G. (2005). Schèmes professionnels. In J.-P. Bernié, & R. Goigoux (Ed.), *Dossier: Les gestes professionnels, La lettre de l'AiRDF n°36* (pp. 7–10).

516 References

Gonzàles-Martín, A., Nardi, E., & Biza, I. (2018). From resource to document: Scaffolding content and organising student learning in teachers' documentation work on the teaching of series. *Educational Studies in Mathematics, 98*(3), 231–252.

Goodlad, J. I. (1979). *Curriculum inquiry. The study of curriculum practice*. New York: McGraw-Hill.

Goos, M. (2014). Communities of practice in mathematics teacher education. In S. Lerman (Ed.), *Encyclopedia of mathematics education* (pp. 82–84). Dordrecht: Springer.

Goujon, C. (2016). *Didactisation de pratiques de savoir scientifiques, transactions avec des publics scolaires et non scolaires. Des scientifiques, de leur laboratoire à la Fête de la science.* PhD. Rennes, France: Université de Bretagne Occidentale. https://hal.archives-ouvertes.fr/tel-01692314/document

Gourlet, P. (2018). *Montrer le faire, construire l'agir. Une approche développementale de la conception mise en œuvre à l'école primaire*. PhD, Paris: Université Paris 8.

Graystone, J. A. (1978). The role of the teacher in resource based learning: Towards a conceptual framework. *British Educational Research Journal, 4*(1), 27–35.

Gruson, B., Gueudet, G., Le Hénaff, C., & Lebaud, M.-P. (2018). Investigating teachers' work with digital resources. A comparison between the teaching of mathematics and English. *Revue Suisse des Sciences de l'Education, 40*(2), 485–501.

Gu, L. Y., & Wang, J. (2003). Teachers' professional development in action education. *Curriculum-Textbook-Pedagogy, 1*(2), 2–10.

Gueudet, G. (2008). Learning mathematics in class with online resources. In C. Hoyles, J.-B. Lagrange, L. Hung Son, & N. Sinclair (Eds.), *Proceedings of the 17th ICMI study conference "Technology revisited"* (pp. 205–212). Hanoi: Hanoi University of Technology.

Gueudet, G. (2013a). Digital resources and mathematics teacher development at university. In B. Ubuz, Ç. Haser, & M. A. Mariotti (Eds.), *Proceedings of the eighth congress of the European society for research in mathematics education* (pp. 2336–2345). Ankara: Middle East Technical University and ERME.

Gueudet, G. (2013b). Les professeurs de mathématiques et leurs ressources professionnelles. In M. Gandit et al. (Eds.), *Actes du Colloque CORFEM 2013*. Grenoble: Université Joseph Fourier. https://hal.archives-ouvertes.fr/hal-01144526/document.

Gueudet, G. (2017). University teachers' resources systems and documents. *International Journal of Research in Undergraduate Mathematics Education, 3*(1), 198–224.

Gueudet, G. (this volume). Studying teachers' documentation work: Emergence of a theoretical approach. In L. Trouche, G. Gueudet, & B. Pepin (Eds.), *The 'resource' approach to mathematics education*. Cham: Springer.

Gueudet, G., & Lebaud, M.-P. (2016). Comment les enseignants de mathématiques choisissent les manuels ? Étude sur le cas des manuels de seconde, édition 2014. *Repères IREM, 102*, 85–97.

Gueudet, G., & Pepin, B. (2018). Didactic contract at university: A focus on resources and their use. *International Journal of Research in Undergraduate Mathematics Education, 4*(1), 56–73.

Gueudet, G., & Trouche, L. (2008a). Du travail documentaire des enseignants: Genèses, collectifs, communautés. Le cas des mathématiques. *Education & Didactique, 2*(3), 7–33. http://educationdidactique.revues.org/342.

Gueudet, G., & Trouche, L. (2008b). Du travail documentaire des enseignants: genèses, collectifs, communautés. Le cas des mathématiques. *Education & Didactique, 2*(3), 7–34.

Gueudet, G., & Trouche, L. (2009a). Towards new documentation systems for mathematics teachers? *Educational Studies in Mathematics, 71*(3), 199–218.

Gueudet, G., & Trouche, L. (2009b). Vers de nouveaux systèmes documentaires des professeurs de mathématiques? In I. Bloch & F. Connes (Eds.), *Nouvelles perspectives en didactique des mathématiques. Cours de la XIVe école d'été de didactique des mathématiques* (pp. 109–133). La Pensée Sauvage éditions: Grenoble.

Gueudet, G., & Trouche, L. (2009c). Vers de nouveaux systèmes documentaires des professeurs de mathématiques? In I. Bloch & F. Conne (Eds.), *Nouvelles perspectives en didactique des mathématiques. Cours de la XIVe école d'été de didactique des mathématiques* (pp. 109–133). Paris: La Pensée Sauvage.

References

Gueudet, G., & Trouche, L. (Eds.). (2010a). *Ressources vives. Le travail documentaire des professeurs en mathématiques*. Rennes/Lyon: Presses Universitaires de Rennes/INRP.

Gueudet, G., & Trouche, L. (2010b). Des ressources aux documents, travail du professeur et genèses documentaires. In G. Gueudet & L. Trouche (Eds.), *Ressources vives: le travail documentaire des professeurs en mathématiques* (pp. 57–74). Paideia, Rennes: Presses Universitaires de Rennes & INRP.

Gueudet, G., & Trouche, L. (2010c). Des ressources aux documents, travail du professeur et genèses documentaires. In G. Gueudet, & L. Trouche (Eds.), *Ressources vives. La documentation des professeurs en mathématiques* (pp. 7–74). INRP et PUR.

Gueudet, G., & Trouche, L. (Eds.). (2010d). *Ressources vives. Le travail documentaire des professeurs en mathématiques*. Rennes/Lyon: Presses Universitaires de Rennes et INRP.

Gueudet, G., & Trouche, L. (2010e). Des ressources aux documents, travail du professeur et genèses documentaires. In G. Gueudet & L. Trouche (Eds.), *Ressources vives. Le travail documentaire des professeurs en mathématiques* (pp. 57–74). Rennes/Lyon: Presses Universitaires de Rennes et INRP.

Gueudet, G., & Trouche, L. (2010f). Genèses communautaires, genèses documentaires: histoires en miroir. In G. Gueudet & L. Trouche (Eds.), *Ressources vives. Le travail documentaire des professeurs en mathématiques* (pp. 129–145). Rennes/Lyon: Presses Universitaires de Rennes et INRP.

Gueudet, G., & Trouche, L. (2011). Mathematics teacher education advanced methods: An example in dynamic geometry. *ZDM – Mathematics Education, 43*(3), 399–411.

Gueudet, G., & Trouche, L. (2012a). Teachers' work with resources. Documentational geneses and professional geneses. In G. Gueudet, B. Pepin, & L. Trouche (Eds.), *From text to 'Lived' resources: Mathematics curriculum materials and teacher development* (pp. 23–41). New York: Springer.

Gueudet, G., & Trouche, L. (2012b). Communities, documents and professional geneses: Interrelated stories. In G. Gueudet, B. Pepin, & L. Trouche (Eds.), *From text to 'lived' resources: Mathematics curriculum materials and teacher development* (pp. 305–322). New York: Springer.

Gueudet, G., & Vandebrouck, F. (2011). Technologie et evolution des pratiques enseignantes: études de cas et éclairages théoriques. *Recherches en Didactique des Mathématiques, 31*(3), 271–314.

Gueudet, G., Pepin, B., & Trouche, L. (Eds.). (2012a). *From textbooks to 'lived' resources: Mathematics curriculum materials and teacher documentation*. New York: Springer.

Gueudet, G., Sacristan, A., Soury-Lavergne, S., & Trouche, L. (2012b). Online paths in mathematics teacher training: New resources and new skills for teacher educators. *ZDM – Mathematics Education, 44*(6), 717–731.

Gueudet, G., Pepin, B., & Trouche, L. (2013). Collective work with resources: An essential dimension for teacher documentation. *ZDM – Mathematics Education, 45*(7), 1003–1016.

Gueudet, G., Buteau, C., Mesa, V., & Misfeldt, M. (2014). Instrumental and documentational approaches: From technology use to documentation systems in university mathematics education. *Research in Mathematics Education, 16*(2), 139–155.

Gueudet, G., Pepin, B., Sabra, H., & Trouche, L. (2016). Collective design of an e-textbook: teachers' collective documentation. *Journal of Mathematics Teacher Education, 19*(2–3), 187–203.

Gueudet, G., Pepin, B., Sabra, H., Restrepo, A., & Trouche, L. (2018). E-textbooks and connectivity: Proposing an analytical framework. *International Journal for Science and Mathematics Education, 16*(3), 539–558.

Guin, D., & Trouche, L. (1998). The complex process of converting tools into mathematical instruments. The case of calculators. *The International Journal of Computers for Mathematical Learning, 3*(3), 195–227.

Guin, D., & Trouche, L. (1999). The complex process of converting tools into mathematical instruments: The case of calculators. *International Journal of Computers for Mathematical Learning, 3*(3), 195–227.

518 References

Guin, D., & Trouche, L. (Eds.). (2002a). *L'instrumentation de calculatrices symboliques: un problème didactique*. Grenoble: La Pensée Sauvage éditions.

Guin, D., & Trouche, L. (Eds.). (2002b). *Calculatrices symboliques, faire d'un outil un instrument du travail mathématique, un problème didactique*. Grenoble: La Pensée Sauvage.

Guin, D., & Trouche, L. (2005). Distance training, a key mode to support teachers in the integration of ICT ? Towards collaborative conception of living pedagogical resources. In M. Bosch (Ed.), *Proceedings of the Fourth European conference on research on mathematics education* (pp. 1020–1029). Barcelona: FUNDEMI IQS—Universitat Ramon Llull and ERME.

Guin, D., Ruthven, K., & Trouche, L. (Eds.). (2005). *The didactical challenge of symbolic calculators: Turning a computational device into a mathematical instrument*. New York: Springer.

Hache, C., Proulx, J., & Moussa, S. (2009). Formation mathématique des enseignants : contenus et pratiques. Compte-rendu du Groupe de Travail n°1– EMF2009. In A. Kuzniak & M. Sokhna (Eds.), *Actes du colloque Espace Mathématique Francophone EMF2009, Enseignement des mathématiques et développement : enjeux de société et de formation* (pp. 34–39). Dakar: Université Cheikh Anta Diop. http://fastef.ucad.sn/EMF2009.

Hadjerrouit, S. (2017). Assessing the affordances of SimReal+ and their applicability to support the learning of mathematics in teacher education. *Issues in Informing Science and Information Technology Education, 14*, 121–138.

Haggarty, L., & Pepin, B. (2002). An investigation of mathematics textbooks and their use in English, French and German classrooms: Who gets an opportunity to learn what? *British Educational Research Journal, 28*(4), 567–590.

Hammoud, R. (2012a). *Le travail collectif des professeurs en chimie comme levier pour la mise en oeuvre de démarches d'investigation et le développement des connaissances professionnelles. Contribution au développement de l'approche documentaire du didactique*. PhD. Lyon, France: Université Lyon 1, https://tel.archives-ouvertes.fr/tel-00762964/document

Hammoud, R. (2012b). *Le travail collectif des professeurs en chimie comme levier pour la mise en œuvre de démarche d'investigation et le développement des connaissances professionnelles. Contribution au développement de l'approche documentaire du didactique*. Thèse de doctorat. Université Lyon 1 et Université Libanaise.

Hammoud, R. (2018). Participation in a virtual community as a lever for the evolution of chemistry teachers' resource system. In V. Gitirana et al. (Eds.), *Proceedings of the re(s)sources 2018 international conference* (pp. 69–73). Lyon: ENS de Lyon.

Hammoud, R., & Alturkmani, M. D. (2018). Teachers' resource systems and documentation work: the case of two physics-chemistry teachers in France and two chemistry teachers in Lebanon. In V. Gitirana et al. (Eds.), *Proceedings of the re(s)sources 2018 international conference* (pp. 74–78). Lyon: ENS de Lyon.

Harlen, W., & Léna, P. (2013). The legacy of the Fibonacci project to Science and Mathematics, 19–53. https://www.fondation-lamap.org/sites/default/files/upload/media/minisites/international/Fibonacci_Book.pdf. Accessed 27 Oct 2018.

Hart, L. C., Alston, A., & Murata, A. (Eds.). (2011). *Lesson study research and practice in mathematics education. Learning together*. Dordrecht: Springer.

Hartleb, R. (Ed.). (1973). *Från en barndomsvärld* [TV documentary]. Sweden: Olympia Filmproduktion HB.

Haspekian, M. (2008). Une genèse des pratiques enseignantes en environnement instrumenté. In Vandebrouck (Ed.), *La classe de mathématiques: activités des élèves et pratiques des enseignants* (pp. 293–318). Octares: Toulouse.

Haspekian, M. (2014). Teachers' instrumental geneses when integrating spreadsheet software. In A. Clark-Wilson, O. Robutti, & N. Sinclair (Eds.), *The mathematics teacher in the digital era* (pp. 241–275). New York: Springer.

Heath, T. L. (Ed.). (1908). *The thirteen books of Euclid's elements* Cambridge: Cambridge University Press.

Heid, M., & K. (2008). Calculator and computer technology in the K-12 curriculum some observations from a US perspective. In Z. Ususkin & E. Willmore (Eds.), *Mathematics curriculum in Pacific rim countries-China, Japan, Korea, and Singapore: Proceedings of a conference* (pp. 293–304). Information Age Publishing: Charlotte.

References

Herbst, P., Chazan, D., Chen, C., Chieu, V. M., & Weiss, M. (2011). Using comics-based representations of teaching, and technology, to bring practice to teacher education courses. *ZDM – Mathematics Education, 43*(1), 91–103.

Hilprecht, H. V. (1906). *Mathematical, metrological and chronological tablets from the temple library of Nippur*. Philadelphia: University of Pennsylvania.

Hollebrands, K., & Okumus, S. (2018). Secondary mathematics teachers' instrumental integration in technology-rich geometry classrooms. *Journal of Mathematical Behavior, 49*(1), 82–94.

Hollebrands, K., & Zbiek, R. (2004). Teaching mathematics with technology: An evidence-based road map for the journey. In R. Rubenstein & G. Bright (Eds.), *Perspectives on the teaching of mathematics: Sixty-sixth yearbook* (pp. 259–270). Reston: National Council of Teachers of Mathematics.

Hollebrands, K., McCulloch, A. W., & Lee, H. S. (2016). Prospective teachers; incorporation of technology in mathematics lesson plans. In M. Niess, S. Driskell, & K. Hollebrands (Eds.), *Handbook of research on transforming mathematics teacher education in the digital age* (pp. 272–292). Hershey: IGI Global.

Hora, M. T., & Ferrare, J. J. (2013). Instructional systems of practice: A multidimensional analysis of math and science undergraduate course planning and classroom teaching. *The Journal of the Learning Sciences, 22*(2), 212–257.

Houart, M. (2009). *Etude de la communication pédagogique à l'université à travers les notes et les acquis des étudiants à l'issue du cours magistral de chimie*. Thèse de doctorat. Namur: Université de Namur.

Howsam, L., Stray, C., Jenkins, A., Secord, J. A., & Vaninskaya, A. (2007). What the Victorians learned: Perspectives on nineteenth-century schoolbooks. *Journal of Victorian Culture, 12*(2), 262–285.

Hoyles, C., & Noss, R. (1992). A pedagogy for mathematical microworlds. *Educational Studies in Mathematics, 23*(1), 31–57.

Høyrup, J. (2000). The finer structure of the Old Babylonian mathematical corpus. Elements of classification, with some results. In J. Marzahn & H. Neumann (Eds.), *Assyriologica et Semitica. Festschrift für Joachim Oelsner anläßlich seines 65* (pp. 117–178). Ugarit Verlag: Münster.

Høyrup, J. (2002). *Lengths, widths, surfaces. A portrait of Old Babylonian Algebra and its Kin*. Berlin/Londres: Springer.

Huang, R., Takahashi, A., & da Ponte, J. P. (Eds.). (2019). *Theory and practice of lesson studies*. New York: Springer International Publishing.

Huizinga, T. (2009). *Op weg naar een instrument voor het meten van docentcompetencies voor het ontwikkelen van curricula [Towards an instrument to measure teacher competencies for the development of curricula]*. Enschede: University of Twente.

Igliori, S. B. C., & Almeida, M. V. (2018). Un support numérique pour le travail de documentation des enseignants de mathématiques de l'EFII (Collège, en France). In V. Gitirana, T. Miyakawa, M. Rafalska, S. Soury-Lavergne, & L. Trouche (Eds.), *Proceedings of the re(s)sources 2018 international conference* (pp. 288, Lyon–291). ENS de Lyon: . Retrieved on November 8th, 2018, at https://hal.archives-ouvertes.fr/hal-01764563.

Ignácio, R., Lima, R., & Gitirana, V. (2018). The birth of the documentary system of mathematics pre-service teachers in a supervised internship with the creation of a digital textbook chapter. In V. Gitirana, T. Miyakawa, M. Rafalska, S. Soury-Lavergne, & L. Trouche (Eds.), *Proceedings of the re(s)sources 2018 international conference* (pp. 292–295). Lyon: ENS de Lyon. Retrieved on November 8th 2018 at https://hal.archives-ouvertes.fr/hal-01764563.

Isoda, M., Stephens, M., Ohara, Y., & Miyakawa, T. (Eds.). (2007). *Japanese lesson study in mathematics: Its impact, diversity and potential for educational improvement*. Singapore: World Scientific Publishing.

Jackson, K., Cobb, P., Wilson, J., Webster, M., Dunlap, C., & Applegate, M. (2015). Investigating the development of mathematics leaders' capacity to support teachers' learning on a large scale. *ZDM – Mathematics Education, 47*, 93–104.

520 References

Jameau, A., & Le Hénaff, C. (2018). Resources for science teaching in a foreign language. In V. Gitirana, T. Miyakawa, M. Rafalska, S. Soury-Lavergne, & L. Trouche (Eds.), *Proceeedings of the re(s)sources 2018 international conference* (pp. 79–82). Lyon: ENS de Lyon. Retrieved on November 8th 2018 at https://hal.archives-ouvertes.fr/hal-01764563.

Jansen, P. (2018). *Pourquoi la société ne se laisse-t-elle pas mettre en equations?* Paris: Le Seuil, Coll. Science ouverte.

Jaworski, B. (2014a). Communities of inquiry in mathematics teacher education. In S. Lerman (Ed.), *Encyclopedia of mathematics education* (pp. 76–78). Dordrecht: Springer.

Jaworski, B. (2014b). Reflective practicioner in mathematics education. In S. Lerman (Ed.), *Encyclopedia in mathematics education* (pp. 529–532). Dordrecht: Springer.

Johnstone, A. H. (1993). The development of chemistry teaching: a changing response to changing demand. *Journal of Chemical Education, 70*, 701–705.

Jones, W. (2007). Personal information management. *Annual Review of Information Science and Technology, 41*(1), 453–504.

Jullien, F. (2015). *De l'être au vivre. Lexique euro-chinois de la pensée*. Paris: Gallimard.

Junge, W. (Ed.). (2007). *Die Kinder von Golzow* [TV documentary]. East Germany: Deutsche Film-Aktiengesellschaft (DEFA), Germany: ARD.

Justi, R., & Van Driel, J. (2005). The development of science teachers' knowledge on models and modelling: promoting, characterizing, and understanding the process. *International Journal of Science Education, 27*(5), 549–573.

Kaplan, A. M., & Haenlein, M. (2016). Higher education and the digital revolution: About MOOCs, SPOCs, social media, and the cookie monster. *Business Horizons, 59*, 441–450.

Kaput, J. J. (1995). Overcoming physicality and the eternal present: Cybernetic manipulatives. In R. Sutherland & J. Mason (Eds.), *Exploiting mental imagery with computers in mathematics education* (pp. 161–177). Berlin: Springer.

Karsenti, T. (2016). *The interactive whiteboard (IWB): Uses, benefits, and challenges. A survey of 11683 students and 1131 teachers*. Montreal: CRIFPE.

Keitel, C., Otte, M., & Seeger, F. (1980). *Text Wissen Tätigkeit*. Königstein: Scriptor.

Kennewell, S. (2001). Using affordances and constraints to evaluate the use of information and communications technology in teaching and learning. *Journal of Information Technology for Teacher Education, 10*(1–2), 101–116.

Kermen, I. (2007). *Prévoir et expliquer l'évolution des systèmes chimiques*. Thèse de doctorat. Paris: Université Paris Diderot-Paris 7.

Kheong, F. H., Sharpe, P., Soon, G. K., Ramakrishnan, C., Wah, B. L. P., & Choo, M. (2010). *Math in focus: The Singapore approach by Marshall Cavendish*. Boston: Houghton Mifflin Harcourt.

Kidron, I., Bosch, M., Monaghan, J., & Palmér, H. (2018). Theoretical perspectives and approaches in mathematics education research. In T. Dreyfus, M. Artigue, D. Potari, S. Prediger, & K. Ruthven (Eds.), *Developing research in mathematics education. Twenty years of communication, cooperation and collaboration in Europe* (pp. 254–275). New York/London: Routledge.

Kieran, C., Boileau, A., Tanguay, D., & Drijvers, P. (2013). Design researchers' documentational genesis in a study on equivalence of algebraic expressions. *ZDM – Mathematics Education, 45*(7), 1045–1056.

Kim, O. K. (2015). The nature of interventions in written and enacted lessons. In J. Beswick, T. Muir, & J. Wells (Eds.), *Proceedings of 39th psychology of mathematics education conference* (Vol. 3, pp. 153–160). Hobart: PME.

Kim, O. K. (2018). Teacher decisions on lesson sequence and their impact on opportunities for students to learn. In L. Fan, L. Trouche, C. Qi, S. Rezat, & J. Visnovska (Eds.), *Research on mathematics textbooks and 'teachers resources. Advances and issues* (ICME-13 monograph) (pp. 315–339). Cham: Springer.

Kim, O. K. (2019). *Teacher fidelity decisions and the quality of enacted lessons*. Manuscript submitted for publication.

Kim, O. K., & Atanga, N. A. (2013). Teachers' decisions on task enactment and opportunities for students to learn. In *Proceedings of the 35th annual meeting of the North American chapter of the international group for the psychology of mathematics education* (pp. 66–73). Chicago: University of Illinois at Chicago.

References

Kim, O. K., & Son, J. (2017). Preservice teachers' recognition of affordances and limitations of curriculum resources. In *Proceedings of 41st psychology of mathematics education conference* (Vol. 3, pp. 57–64). Singapore: PME.

Kimura, T. (2015). *Hako kara miruto* [Viewing from inside box]. Document distributed at the monthly meeting of research Association for Mathematics Teaching in Jōetsu on 5th May, 2015.

Kirchner, P., Strijbos, J.-W., Kreijns, K., & Beers, B. J. (2004). Designing electronic collaborative learning environments. *Educational Technology Research and Development, 52*(3), 47–66.

Koehler, M. J., & Mishra, P. (2005). What happens when teachers design educational technology? The development of technological pedagogical content knowledge. *Journal of Educational Computing Research, 32*(2), 131–152.

Koehler, M. J., & Mishra, P. (2009). What is technological pedagogical content knowledge? *Contemporary Issues in Technology and Teacher education, 9*(1), 60–70.

Konold, C., & Miller, C. D. (2005). *TinkerPlots: Dynamic data exploration (computer software, Version 1.0)*. Emeryville: Key Curriculum Press.

Kozaklı Ülger, T., & Tapan Broutin, M. S. (2018). Transition from a paper-pencil to a technology enriched environment: A teacher's use of technology and resource selection. In V. Gitirana, T. Miyakawa, M. Rafalska, S. Soury-Lavergne, & L. Trouche (Eds.), *Proceedings of the re(s) sources 2018 international conference* (pp. 344–347). Lyon: ENS de Lyon. Retrieved on November 8th, 2018, at https://hal.archives-ouvertes.fr/hal-01764563.

Kynigos, C., & Kolovou, A. (2018). Teachers as designers of digital educational resources for creative mathematical thinking. In L. Fan, L. Trouche, C. Qi, S. Rezat, & J. Visnovska (Eds.), *Research on mathematics textbooks and teachers' resources: Advances and issues* (ICME-13 monograph) (pp. 145–164). Cham: Springer.

Kynigos, C., & Lagrange, J.-B. (Eds.) (2014). Special issue: Representing mathematics with digital media: Working across theoretical and contextual boundaries. Educational Studies in Mathematics 85(3).

Lagrange, J.-B. (Ed.). (2013). *Les technologies numériques pour l'enseignement: usages, dispositifs et genèses*. Toulouse: Octarès.

Lagrange, J. B., & Monaghan, J. (2009). On the adoption of a model to interpret teachers' use of technology in mathematics lessons. In V. Durand-Guerrier, S. Soury-Lavergne, & F. Arzarello (Eds.), *Proceedings of the sixth congress of European research in mathematics education* (pp. 1605–1614). Lyon: ENS de Lyon.

Lakatos, I. (1963/2015). *Proofs and refutations: The logic of mathematical discovery*. Cambridge: Cambridge University Press.

Lakoff, G., & Núñez, R. E. (2000). *Where mathematics comes from: How the embodied mind brings mathematics into being*. New York: Basic Books.

Lave, J., & Wenger, E. (1991). *Situated learning: Legitimate peripheral participation*. New York: Cambridge University Press.

Le Maréchal, J. F. (1999). Modeling student's cognitive activity during the resolution of problems based on experimental facts in chemical Education. In J. Leach & A. Paulsen (Eds.), *Practical work in science education* (pp. 195–209). Dordrecht: Kluwer Academic Publishers.

Lealdino Filho, P., & Mercat, C. (2018). Teaching computational thinking in classroom environments: A case for unplugged scenario. In V. Gitirana, T. Miyakawa, M. Rafalska, S. Soury-Lavergne, & L. Trouche (Eds.), *Proceedings of the re(s)sources 2018 international conference* (pp. 296–299). Lyon: ENS de Lyon. Retrieved on November 8th, 2018, at https://hal.archives-ouvertes.fr/hal-01764563.

Leinhardt, G. (1989). Math lessons: A contrast of novice and expert competence. *Journal for Research in Mathematics Education, 20*(1), 52–75.

Lepik, M., Grevholm, B., & Viholainen, A. (2015). Using textbooks in the mathematics classroom – The teachers' view. *Nordisk matematikkdidaktik, 20*(3–4), 129–156.

Leroyer, L. (2018a). The capacity to think of transmission of knowledge from learning supports: A proposition of a conceptual model. In V. Gitirana, T. Miyakawa, M. Rafalska, S. Soury-Lavergne, & L. Trouche (Eds.), *Proceedings of the re(s)sources 2018 international conference* (pp. 203–207). Lyon: ENS de Lyon.

Leroyer, L. (2018b). The capacity to think of transmission of knowledge from learning supports: A proposition of a conceptual model. In V. Gitirana, T. Miyakawa, M. Rafalska, S. Soury-Lavergne, & L. Trouche (Eds.), *Proceeedings of the re(s)sources 2018 international conference* (pp. 203–206). Lyon: ENS de Lyon. Retrieved on November 8th, 2018, at https://hal.archives-ouvertes.fr/hal-01764563.

Leroyer, L. (in press). La question des ressources dans le travail de conception des formateurs d'enseignants: cadres théoriques et perspectives de recherche. In I. Verscheure, M. Ducrey-Monnier, & L. Pelissier (Eds.), *Enseignement et Formation: éclairage de la didactique comparée*. Toulouse: Presses universitaires du Midi.

Leroyer, L., & Bailleul, M. (2017). Les supports d'enseignements dans la représentation du métier chez des professeurs d'école débutants. In R. Gras & J. C. Régnier (Eds.), *L'analyse statistique implicative: des sciences dures aux sciences humaines et sociales* (pp. 411–421). Toulouse: Cépadues.

Leroyer, L., & Georget, J. P. (2017). De l'analyse du travail des formateurs à l'élaboration d'une modélisation, outil pour la formation de formateurs. Communication présentée au 4e colloque international de Didactique Professionnelle, Lille, France, juin.

Leshota, M., & Adler, J. (2018). Disaggregating a mathematics teacher's pedagogical design capacity. In L. Fan, L. Trouche, S. Rezat, C. Qi, & J. Visnovska (Eds.), *Research on mathematics textbooks and teachers' resources. Advances and issues* (pp. 89–117). Cham: Springer.

Lester, F. K. (2005). On the theoretical, conceptual, and philosophical foundations for research in mathematics education. *ZDM – Mathematics Education, 37*(6), 457–467.

Leung, A., & Bolite-Frant, J. (2015). Designing mathematics tasks: The role of tools. In A. Watson & M. Ohtani (Eds.), *Task design in mathematics education: The 22nd ICMI study* (pp. 191–225). Cham: Springer.

Lewis, C., & Hurd, J. (2011). *Lesson study step by step: How teacher learning communities improve instruction*. Portsmouth: Heinemann.

Li, Y. (2007). Curriculum and culture: An exploratory examination of mathematics curriculum materials in their system and cultural contexts. *The Mathematics Educator, 10*(1), 21–38.

Li, Y., & Kaiser, G. (2011). Expertise in mathematics instruction: Advancing research and practice from an international perspective. In Y. Li & G. Kaiser (Eds.), *Expertise in mathematics instruction: An international perspective* (pp. 3–15). New York: Springer.

Li, Y., & Lappan, G. (Eds.). (2014). *Mathematics curriculum in school education*. New York: Springer International Publishing.

Lima, I. (2006). *De la modélisation des connaissances des élèves aux décisions didactiques des professeurs: étude didactique dans le cas de la symétrie orthogonale*. Doctoral thesis. Université J. Fourier, Grenoble.

Lima, I. (2018). The textbook for field public schools in Brazil -PNLD field. In V. Gitirana, T. Miyakawa, M. Rafalska, S. Soury-Lavergne, & L. Trouche (Eds.), *Proceedings of the re(s) sources 2018 international conference* (pp. 129–131). Lyon: ENS de Lyon. Retrieved on November 8th, 2018 at https://hal.archives-ouvertes.fr/hal-01764563.

Livingston, C., & Borko, H. (1989). Expert-novice differences in teaching: a cognitive analysis and implications for teacher education. *Journal of Teacher Education, 40*(4), 36–42.

Loisy, C. (2018). *Le développement professionnel des enseignants à l'heure du numérique. Le cas du supérieur. Propositions théoriques et méthodologiques*. Mémoire d'habilitation à diriger des recherches. Lyon: ENS de Lyon.

Love, E., & Pimm, D. (1996). "This is so": A text on texts. In A. J. Bishop, K. Clements, C. Keitel, J. Kilpatrick, & C. Laborde (Eds.), *International handbook of mathematics education* (Vol. 1, pp. 371–409). Dordrecht: Kluwer Academic Publisher.

Lucena, R. (2018). *Metaorquestração Instrumental: um modelo para repensar a formação teórico-prática de professores de matemática*. Doctoral thesis. Mathematics and Technological Education Pos-graduation Program. Recife-Brazil: UFPE.

Lucena, R., & Assis, C. (2015). *Webdoc Sistema de Recursos e o Trabalho Coletivo do Professor: Uma Via de Mão Dupla*. Recife (Brazil): LEMATEC (UFPE). Retrieved at http://lematec.net.br/webdocs/webdoc2/. Access codes to be asked to the authors.

References

Lucena, R., Gitirana, V., & Trouche, L. (2016). Teoria da orquestração instrumenta: um olhar para formação docente. *I Simpósio Latinoamericano de Didática da Matemática*, 01 a 06 de novembro de 2016, Bonito – Mato Grosso do Sul – Brasil.

Lucena, R., Gitirana, V., & Trouche, L. (2018). Instrumental meta-orchestration for teacher education. In V. Gitirana, T. Miyakawa, M. Rafalska, S. Soury-Lavergne, & L. Trouche (Eds.), *Proceedings of the re(s)sources 2018 international conference* (pp. 300–303, ENS de Lyon). Lyon: . Retrieved on November 8th, 2018, at https://hal.archives-ouvertes.fr/hal-01764563.

Machado, R. N. S. J., Espindola, E., Trgalová, J., & Luberiaga, E. (2018). Abordagem documental do didático e o ensino de equação do 1° grau na educação de jovens e adultos-ensino médio. *Revista Paranaense de Educação Matemática, 7(13)*, 270–294.

Madsen, L. M., & Winsløw, C. (2009). Relations between teaching and research in physical geography and mathematics at research-intensive universities. *International Journal of Science and Mathematics Education, 7*, 741–763.

Males, L., Setniker, A., & Dietiker, L. (2018). What do teachers attend to in curriculum materials? In V. Gitirana, T. Miyakawa, M. Rafalska, S. Soury-Lavergne, & L. Trouche (Eds.), *Proceedings of the re(s)sources 2018 international conference* (pp. 207–210). Lyon: ENS de Lyon. Retrieved on November 8th, 2018, at https://hal.archives-ouvertes.fr/hal-01764563.

Malley, L., Neidorf, T., Arora, A., & Kroeger, T. (2016). United States. In I. V. S. Mullis, M. O. Martin, S. Goh, & K. Cotter (Eds.), *TIMSS 2015 encyclopedia: Education policy and curriculum in mathematics and science*. Chestnut Hill: TIMSS & PIRLS International Study Center, Lynch School of Education, Boston College. http://timssandpirls.bc.edu/timss2015/encyclopedia/download-center/. Accessed 15 Jan 2019.

Mangiante-Orsola, C. (2012). Une étude de la cohérence en germe dans les pratiques de professeurs des écoles en formation initiale puis débutants. *Recherches en Didactique des Mathématiques, 32*(3), 289–331.

Margolinas, C. (2002). Situations, milieu, connaissances: analyse de l'activité du professeur. In J.-L. Dorier, M. Artaud, M. Artigue, R. Berthelot, & R. Floris (Eds.), *Actes de la XIe Ecole d'été de didactique des mathématiques* (pp. 141–156). Grenoble: La Pensée Sauvage éditions.

Margolinas, C. (2004). *Points de vue de l'élève et du professeur. Essai de développement de la théorie des situations didactiques*. Mémoire d'habilitation à diriger des recherches. Marseille: Université de Provence-Aix Marseille I. https://tel.archives-ouvertes.fr/tel-00429580v2/document

Margolinas, C. (2014). *Task design in mathematics education. Proceedings of ICMI Study 22*. ICMI Study 22, Oxford, United Kingdom, 2013. 978-2-7466-6554-5. Accessed October 2018 at https://hal.archives-ouvertes.fr/hal-00834054v3/document

Margolinas, C., & Wozniak, F. (2010a). Rôle de la documentation scolaire dans la situation du professeur: le cas de l'enseignement des mathématiques à l'école élémentaire. In G. Gueudet & L. Trouche (Eds.), *Ressources vives. Le travail documentaire des professeurs en mathématiques* (pp. 223–251). Rennes/Lyon: Presses Universitaires de Rennes et INRP.

Margolinas, C., & Wozniak, F. (2010b). Rôle de la documentation scolaire dans la situation du professeur: le cas de l'enseignement des mathématiques à l'école élémentaire. In G. Gueudet & L. Trouche (Eds.), *Ressources vives. Le travail documentaire des professeurs en mathématiques* (pp. 233–249). PUR: Rennes.

Mariotti, M. A., & Maracci, M. (2010). Un artefact comme instrument de médiation sémiotique: une ressource pour le professeur. In G. Gueudet & L. Trouche (Eds.), *Ressources vives. Le travail documentaire des professeurs en mathématiques* (pp. 91–107). Rennes/Lyon: Presses Universitaires de Rennes et INRP.

Martinand, J. L. (1992). *Enseignement et apprentissage de la modélisation en sciences*. Paris: INRP.

Martinez, M., Cruz, R., & Soberanes, A. (2018). The mathematical teacher: A case study of instrumental genesis in the UAEM. In V. Gitirana, T. Miyakawa, M. Rafalska, S. Soury-Lavergne, & L. Trouche (Eds.), *Proceedings of the re(s)sources 2018 international conference* (pp. 211–214). Lyon: ENS de Lyon. Retrieved on November 8th, 2018, at https://hal.archives-ouvertes.fr/hal-01764563.

Maschietto, M., & Soury-Lavergne, S. (2013). Designing a duo of material and digital artifacts: The pascaline and Cabri Elem e-books in primary school mathematics. *ZDM – Mathematics Education, 45*(7), 959–971.

Mason, J., & Spence, M. (1999). Beyond mere knowledge of mathematics: The importance of knowing-to act in the moment. *Educational Studies in Mathematics, 38*, 135–161.

Matuk, C. F., Linn, M. C., & Eylon, B. S. (2015). Technology to support teachers using evidence from student work to customize technology-enhanced inquiry units. *Instructional Science, 43*(2), 229–257.

Mayen, P. (1999). Des situations potentielles de développement. *Éducation Permanente, 139*, 65–86.

Means, B. (2007). Technology's role in curriculum and instruction. In F. M. Connelly (Ed.), *The Sage handbook of curriculum and instruction* (pp. 123–144). London: Sage.

Mercat, C., Lealdino Filho, P., & El-Demerdash, M. (2017). Creativity and technology in mathematics : From story telling to algorithmic with Op'Art. *Acta Didactica Napocensia, 10*(1), 63–70.

Mesa, V., & Griffiths, B. (2012). Textbook mediation of teaching: An example from tertiary mathematics instructors. *Educational Studies in Mathematics, 79*(1), 85–107.

Messaoui, A. (2018a). The complex process of classifying resources, an essential component of documentation expertise. In V. Gitirana, T. Miyakawa, M. Rafalska, S. Soury-Lavergne, & L. Trouche (Eds.), *Proceedings of the res(s)ource 2018 international conference* (pp. 83–87). Lyon: ENS de Lyon. Retrieved on November 8th, 2018, at https://hal.archives-ouvertes.fr/hal-01764563.

Messaoui, A. (2018b). Concevoir des ressources pour enseigner, un levier pour le développement des compétences informationnelles des professeurs? In *Objets, supports, instruments : regards croisés sur la diversité des ressources mobilisées en interaction. SHS Web of Conferences, 52, 02003.* Retreived at https://doi.org/10.1051/shsconf/20185202003

MEXT. (2008). *Course of study: Arithmetic.* Retrieved from http://www.mext.go.jp/en/policy/education/elsec/title02/detail02/1373859.htm

Michalowski, P. (2012). Literacy, schooling and the transmission of knowledge in early mesopotamian culture. In W. S. van Egmond & W. H. van Soldt (Eds.), *Theory and practice of knowledge transfer. Studies in school education in the Ancient Near East and beyond* (pp. 39–57). PIHANS: Leiden.

Middeke-Conlin, R. (forthcoming). *The making of a scribe: Errors, mistakes, and rounding numbers in the Old Babylonian kingdom of Larsa.* New York: Springer.

Ministry of Education, People's Republic of China. (2001). *Mathematics curriculum standard for compulsory education (the trial version).* Beijing: Beijing Normal University Press.

Ministry of Education, People's Republic of China. (2003). *Mathematics curriculum standard for senior secondary schools (the trial version).* Beijing: Beijing Normal University Press.

Mishra, P., & Koehler, M. J. (2006). Technological pedagogical content knowledge: A framework for teacher knowledge. *Teachers College Record, 108*(6), 1017–1054.

Miyakawa, T. (2015). What is a good lesson in Japan? An analysis. In M. Inprasitha et al. (Eds.), *Lesson study: Challenges in mathematics education* (pp. 327–349). Singapore: World Scientific.

Miyakawa, T., & Winsløw, C. (2009a). Didactical designs for students' proportional reasoning: An "open approach" lesson and a "fundamental situation". *Educational Studies in Mathematics, 72*(2), 199–218.

Miyakawa, T., & Winsløw, C. (2009b). Un dispositif japonais pour le travail en équipe d'enseignants: étude collective d'une leçon. *Éducation & Didactique, 3*(1), 77–90.

Miyakawa, T., & Winsløw, C. (2013). Developing mathematics teacher knowledge: The paradidactic infrastructure of "open lesson" in Japan. *Journal of Mathematics Teacher Education, 16*(3), 185–209.

Miyakawa, T., & Winsløw, C. (2017, Online first). Paradidactic infrastructure for sharing and documenting mathematics teacher knowledge: A case study of "practice research" in Japan. *Journal of Mathematics Teacher Education, 22*, 281–303.

Mohammad, S., Dorr, B. J., Hirst, G., & Turney, P. (2013). Computing lexical contrast. *Computational Linguistics, 39*(3), 555–590.

Monaghan, J. (2004). Teachers' activities in technology-based mathematics. *International Journal of Computers for Mathematical Learning, 9*(3), 327–357.

Monaghan, J. (2016). Developments relevant to the use of tools in mathematics. In J. Monaghan, L. Trouche, & J. M. Borwein (Eds.), *Tools and mathematics: Instruments for learning* (pp. 163–180). New York: Springer.

Monaghan, J., Trouche, L., & Borwein, J. (2016). *Tools and mathematics: Instruments for learning*. New York: Springer.

Monteil, L., & Romerio, A. (2017). Des disciplines aux studies. Savoirs, trajectoires, politiques. *Revue d'anthropologie des connaissances, 11*(3), 231–244.

Morine-Dershimer, G. (1977, April 4–8). What's a plan? Stated and unstated plans for lessons. *Annual meeting of the American Educational Research Association*, New York, NY.

Mullis, I. V. S., Martin, M. O., Foy, P., & Arora, A. (2012a). *TIMSS 2011 international results in mathematics*. Boston: Boston College/IEA.

Mullis, I. V. S., Martin, M. O., Foy, P., & Arora, A. (2012b). *TIMSS 2011 international results in mathematics*. Chestnut Hill: TIMSS & PIRLS International Study Center, Lynch School of Education, Boston College.

Naftaliev, E. (2018). Prospective teachers' interactions with interactive diagrams: Semiotic tools, challenges and new paths. In V. Gitirana, T. Miyakawa, M. Rafalska, S. Soury-Lavergne, & L. Trouche (Eds.), *Proceedings of the res(s)ource 2018 international conference* (pp. 304–307). Lyon: ENS de Lyon. Retrieved on November 8th, 2018, at https://hal.archives-ouvertes.fr/hal-01764563.

Naftaliev, E., & Yerushalmy, M. (2017). Design digital tasks: Interactive diagrams as resource and constraint. In A. Leung & A. Baccaglini-Frank (Eds.), *The role and potential of using digital technologies in designing mathematics education tasks* (pp. 153–173). Cham: Springer.

Nascimento, J., Jr., Carvalho, E., & Farias, L. M. (2018). Creation of innovative teaching situation through instrumental genesis to maximize teaching specific content: Acid-base chemical balance. In V. Gitirana, T. Miyakawa, M. Rafalska, S. Soury-Lavergne, & L. Trouche (Eds.), *Proceedings of the res(s)ource 2018 international conference* (pp. 308–311). Lyon: ENS de Lyon. Retrieved on November 8th, 2018, at https://hal.archives-ouvertes.fr/hal-01764563.

NCTM. (1989). *Curriculum and evaluation standards for school mathematics*. Reston: Author.

Ndlovu, M., Wessels, D., & De Villiers, M. (2011). An instrumental approach to modelling the derivative in sketchpad. *Pythagoras, 32*(2), 1–15.

Neugebauer, O., & Sachs, A. J. (1945). *Mathematical cuneiform texts*. New Haven: American Oriental Series & American Schools of Oriental Research.

Neugebauer, O., & Sachs, A. J. (1984). Mathematical and metrological texts. *Journal of Cuneiform Studies, 36*, 243–251.

Neumann, R. (1992). Perceptions of the teaching-research nexus: A framework for analysis. *Higher Education, 23*, 159–171.

Newmann, F.-M., Smith, B., Allensworth, E., & Bryk, A.-S. (2001). Instructional program coherence: What it is and why it should guide school improvement policy. *Educational Evaluation and Policy Analysis, 23*(4), 297–321.

Nicolet, G. (2016). *La 'Maison aux tablettes' et l'enseignement à Mari à l'époque paléo-babylonienne* Université de Genève.

Nieveen, N., & van der Hoeven, M. (2011). Building the curricular capacity of teachers: Insights from the Netherlands. In P. Picard & L. Ria (Eds.), *Beginning teachers: Challenge for educational systems. CIDREE Yearbook 2011* (pp. 49–64). Lyon: ENS de Lyon, Institut Français de l'Éducation.

Nongni, G., & DeBlois, L. (2017). Planification de l'enseignement de l'écart-type en utilisant les ressources documentaires. In A. Adihou, J. Giroux, A. Savard, & K. M. Huy (Eds.), *Données, variabilité et tendance vers le futur. Acte du Colloque du GDM* (pp. 205–2012). Canada, Québec: Université McGill.

526 References

Nongni, G., & DeBlois, L. (2018). Planning of the teaching of the standard deviation using digital documentary resources. In V. Gitirana, T. Miyakawa, M. Rafalska, S. Soury-Lavergne, & L. Trouche (Eds.), *Proceedings of the re(s)sources 2018 international conference* (pp. 312–315). Lyon: ENS de Lyon. Retrieved on November 8th, 2018, at https://hal.archives-ouvertes.fr/hal-01764563.

Norman, D. A. (1988). *The psychology of everyday things*. New York: Basic Books.

Noss, R., & Hoyles, C. (1996). *Windows on mathematical meanings: Learning cultures and computers*. Dordrecht: Kluwer Academic Publishers.

Oddone, I., Re, A., & Briante, G. (1981). *Redécouvrir l'expérience ouvrière: vers une autre psychologie du travail?* Paris: Editions sociales.

Okumus, S., & Ipek, A. S. (2018). Pre-service mathematics teachers' investigation of the constraints of mathematical tools. In V. Gitirana, T. Miyakawa, M. Rafalska, S. Soury-Lavergne, & L. Trouche (Eds.), *Proceedings of the re(s)source 2018 international conference* (pp. 316–319). Lyon: ENS de Lyon. Retrieved on November 8th, 2018, at https://hal.archives-ouvertes.fr/hal-01764563.

Organisation for Economic Co-operation and Development (OECD). (2016). *Supporting teacher professionalism: Insights from TALIS 2013*. Paris: TALIS, OECD Publishing.

Orozco, J., Cuevas, A., Madrid, H., & Trouche, L. (2018). A proposal of instrumental orchestration to introduce eigenvalues and eigenvectors in a first course of linear algebra for engineering students. In V. Gitirana, T. Miyakawa, M. Rafalska, S. Soury-Lavergne, & L. Trouche (Eds.), *Proceedings of the re(s)sources 2018 international conference* (pp. 320–323). Lyon: ENS de Lyon. Retrieved on November 8th, 2018, at https://hal.archives-ouvertes.fr/hal-01764563.

Osborn, M. (2004). New methodologies for comparative research? Establishing 'constants' and 'contexts' in educational experience. *Oxford Review of Education, 30*(2), 265–285.

Pan, M. (2005). On core competitive power in the 21st century in China: Rational structure of "education and talent". *China Higher Education Research, 3*, 1–2.

Panero, M., Aldon, G., Trgalová, J., & Trouche, L. (2017). Analysing MOOCs in terms of teacher collaboration potential and issues: The French experience. In T. Dooley & G. Gueudet (Eds.), *Proceedings of the tenth congress of the European Society for Research in mathematics education (CERME 10)* (pp. 2446–2453). Dublin: DCU Institute of Education and ERME.

Papert, S., & Harel, I. (1991). Preface, situating constructionism. In I. Harel & S. Papert (Eds.), *Constructionism, research reports and essays, 1985–1990* (p. 1). Norwood: Ablex.

Pappano, L. (2012, November 2). The year of the MOOC. *The New York Times*, pp. 26–32.

Pastré, P. (2005). Genèse et identité. In P. Rabardel, & P. Pastré (Dir.), *Modèles du sujet pour la conception* (pp. 231–260). Toulouse: Octarès.

Pastré, P. (2011). *La didactique professionnelle. Approche anthropologique du développement chez les adultes*. Paris: Presses universitaires de France.

Pea, R. D. (1985). Beyond amplification: Using the computer to reorganize mental functioning. *Educational Psychologist, 20*(4), 167–182.

Pédauque, R. T. (coll.) (2006). *Le document à la lumière du numérique*. Caen: C & F éditions.

Pédauque, R. T. (coll.) (2007). *La redocumentarisation du monde*. Toulouse: Cépaduès éditions.

Penuel, W., Roschelle, J., & Shechtman, N. (2007). Designing formative assessment software with teachers: An analysis of the co-design process. *Research and Practice in Technology Enhanced Learning, 2*(1), 51–74.

Pepin, B. (2005). Can we compare like with like in comparative education research? – Methodological considerations in cross-cultural studies in mathematics education. In B. Hudson & J. Fragner (Eds.), *Researching teaching and learning of mathematics II* (pp. 39–54). Linz: Trauner Verlag.

Pepin, B. (2009). The role of textbooks in the 'figured world' of English, French and German classrooms – A comparative perspective. In L. Black, H. Mendick, & Y. Solomon (Eds.), *Mathematical relationships: Identities and participation* (pp. 107–118). London: Routledge.

Pepin, B. (2014). Re-sourcing curriculum materials: In search of appropriate frameworks for researching the enacted mathematics curriculum. *ZDM – Mathematics Education, 46*(5), 837–842.

References

527

Pepin, B. (2018). Enhancing teacher learning with curriculum resources. In L. Fan, L. Trouche, C. Qi, S. Rezat, & J. Visnovska (Eds.), *Research on mathematics textbooks and teachers' resources. Advances and issues* (ICME-13 monograph) (pp. 359–374). Cham: Springer.

Pepin, B., & Haggarty, L. (2001). Mathematics textbooks and their use in English, French, and German classrooms: A way to understand teaching and learning cultures. *ZDM – Mathematics Education, 33*(5), 158–175.

Pepin, B. & Jones, K. (Eds.) (2016). Mathematics teachers as partners in task design. Double Special Issue of *Journal of Mathematics Teacher Education* 19(2 &3).

Pepin, B., Gueudet, G., & Trouche, L. (Eds.). (2013a). Resourcing teacher work and interaction: New perspectives on resources design, use, and teacher collaboration. *ZDM -Mathematics Education, special issue, 7*, 45.

Pepin, B., Gueudet, G., & Trouche, L. (2013b). Investigating textbooks as crucial interfaces between culture, policy and teacher curricular practice: Two contrasted case studies in France and Norway. *ZDM - Mathematics Education, 45*(5), 685–698.

Pepin, B., Gueudet, G., & Trouche, L. (2013c). Re-sourcing teacher work and interaction: A collective perspective on resource, their use and transformation. *ZDM – Mathematics Education, 45*(7), 929–943.

Pepin, B., Gueudet, G., Yerushalmy, M., Trouche, L., & Chazan, D. (2015a). E-textbooks in/for teaching and learning mathematics: A disruptive and potentially transformative educational technology. In L. English & D. Kirshner (Eds.), *Handbook of international research in mathematics education* (3rd ed., pp. 636–661). New York: Taylor & Francis.

Pepin, B., Gueudet, G., & Trouche, L. (2015b). Comfortable or lost in paradise? – Affordances and constraints of mathematics e-textbooks in/for curriculum enactment, communication to the symposium *Mathematics curriculum contingencies: From authoring to enactment via curriculum resources*, chaired by D. Clarke, K. Ruthven and M.K. Stein, in the frame of the AERA 2015 meeting, Chicago, 16–20 April.

Pepin, B., Gueudet, G., Yerushalmy, M., Trouche, L., & Chazan, D. (2016a). E-Textbooks in/for teaching and learning mathematics: A disruptive and potentially transformative educational technology. In L. English & D. Kirshner (Eds.), *Handbook of international research in mathematics education* (pp. 636–661). New York: Taylor & Francis.

Pepin, B., Gueudet, B., Yerushalmy, M., Trouche, L., & Chazan, D. (2016b). E-textbooks in/for teaching and learning mathematics: A disruptive and potentially transformative educational technology. In L. English & D. Kirshner (Eds.), *Handbook of research in mathematics education* (3rd ed., pp. 636–661). London: Taylor & Francis.

Pepin, B., Xu, B., Trouche, L., & Wang, C. (2016c). Chinese expert teachers' resource systems: A window into their work and expertise. *Educational Studies in Mathematics, 94*(3), 257–274.

Pepin, B., Xu, B., Trouche, L., & Wang, C. (2016d). Developing a deeper understanding of *mathematics teaching expertise:* Chinese mathematics teachers' resource systems as windows into their work and expertise. *Educational Studies in Mathematics, 94*(3), 257–274. http://rdcu.be/koXk.

Pepin, B., Gueudet, G., & Trouche, L. (2017a). Refining teacher design capacity: Mathematics teachers' interactions with digital curriculum resources. *ZDM – Mathematics Education, 49*(5), 799–812.

Pepin, B., Choppin, J., Ruthven, K., & Sinclair, N. (2017b). Digital curriculum resources in mathematics education: Foundations for change. *ZDM – Mathematics Education, 49*(5), 645–661.

Pepin, B., Xu, B., Trouche, L., & Wang, C. (2017c). Developing a deeper understanding of mathematics teaching expertise: An examination of three Chinese mathematics teachers' resources systems as windows into their work and expertise. *Educational Studies in Mathematics, 94*(3), 257–274. https://doi.org/10.1007/s10649-016-9727-2.

Pepin, B., Gueudet, G., & Trouche, L. (2017d). Refining *teacher design capacity:* Mathematics teachers' interactions with digital curriculum resources. *ZDM – Mathematics Education, 49*(5), 799–812. https://doi.org/10.1007/s11858-017-0870-8; http://rdcu.be/tmXb

Pepin, B., Delaney, S., Rezat, S., & Stylianides, A. J. (2017e). Introduction to the papers of TWG22: Curricular resources and task design in mathematics education. In T. Dooley & G. Gueudet (Eds.), *Proceedings of the tenth congress of the European mathematical society for research in mathematics education* (pp. 3615–3618). Dublin: DCU Institute of Education and ERME.

Pepin, B., Artigue, M., Gitirana, M., Miyakawa, T., Ruthven, K., & Xu, B. (this volume). Mathematics teachers as curriculum designers: An international perspective to develop a deeper understanding of the concept. In L. Trouche, G. Gueudet, & B. Pepin (Eds.), *The 'resource' approach to mathematics education*. Cham: Springer.

Pernambuco. (2012a). *Parâmetros curriculares de Matemática. Ensino fundamental e médio*. Secretaria de Educação: Recife-PE.

Pernambuco. (2012b). *Parâmetros curriculares de Matemática. Educação de jovens e adultos*. Secretaria de Educação: Recife-PE.

Perrin, D. (2007). L'expérimentation en mathématiques. *Petit x, 73,* 6–34.

Pfeiffer, C. R. (2017). *A study of the development of mathematical knowledge in a GeoGebra-focused learning environment*. Unpublished PhD dissertation. Stellenbosch: Stellenbosch University.

Pfeiffer, C. R., & Ndlovu, M. (2018). Teaching and learning of function transformations in a GeoGebra-focused learning environment. In V. Gitirana, T. Miyakawa, M. Rafalska, S. Soury-Lavergne, & L. Trouche (Eds.), *Proceedings of the re(s)sources 2018 international conference* (pp. 324–327). Lyon: ENS de Lyon. Retrieved on November 8th, 2018, at https://hal.archives-ouvertes.fr/hal-01764563.

Piaget, J. (1955). *The construction of reality in the child*. London: Routledge & Kegan Paul Limited.

Piaget, J. (1964). *Six études de psychologie*. Genève: Edition Gonthier.

Poisard, C., Bueno-Ravel, L., & Gueudet, G. (2011). Comprendre l'intégration de ressources technologiques en mathématiques par des professeurs des écoles. *Recherches en didactique des mathématiques, 31*(2), 151–189.

Polya, G. (1945/2004). How to solve it: A new aspect of mathematical method. Princeton, Princeton University Press.

Povey, H. (2014). The origins and continued life of SMILE mathematics. *Mathematics Teaching, 241,* 5–6.

Priestley, M., Biesta, G., & Robinson, S. (2017). *Teacher agency: An ecological approach*. London: Bloomsbury Academic.

Prieto, L. P., Sharma, K., Dillenbourg, P., & Jesús, M. (2016). Teaching analytics: Towards automatic extraction of orchestration graphs using wearable sensors. In *Proceedings of the sixth international conference on Learning Analytics & Knowledge (LAK '16)* (pp. 148–157). New York: ACM. https://doi.org/10.1145/2883851.2883927.

Prieur, M. (2016). *La conception codisciplinaire de méta ressources comme appui à l'évolution des connaissances des professeurs de sciences. Les connaissances qui guident un travail de préparation pour engager les élèves dans l'élaboration d'hypothèses ou de conjectures*. PhD. Lyon, France: Université de Lyon, https://hal.archives-ouvertes.fr/tel-01364778v2/document

Proust, C. (2007). *Tablettes mathématiques de Nippur (with the collaboration of Antoine Cavigneaux)*. Istanbul: Institut Français d'Etudes Anatoliennes, De Boccard.

Proust, C. (2008). *Tablettes mathématiques de la collection Hilprecht (with the collaboration of M. Krebernik and J. Oelsner)*. Leipzig: Harrassowitz.

Proust, C. (2012a). Reading colophons from Mesopotamian clay-tablets dealing with mathematics. *NTM Zeitschrift für Geschichte der Wissenschaften, Technik und Medizin, 20*(3), 123–156.

Proust, C. (2012b). Teachers' writings and students' writings: school material in Mesopotamia. In G. Gueudet, B. Pepin, & L. Trouche (Eds.), *From text to 'Lived' resources: Mathematics curriculum materials and teacher development* (pp. 161–179). New York: Springer.

Proust, C. (2014). Does a master always write for his students? Some evidence from Old Babylonian Scribal Schools. In A. Bernard & C. Proust (Eds.), *Scientific sources and teaching contexts throughout History: Problems and perspectives* (pp. 69–94). New York: Springer.

References 529

Proust, C. (2015). La chanson des mathématiques dans l'*Edubba*. In M. C. Bustamante (Ed.), *Scientific writings and orality* (pp. 19–49). Turnhout: Brepols (Archives Internationales d'Histoire des Sciences).

Proust, C. (2016). Floating calculation in Mesopotamia (translation of "Du calcul flottant en Mésopotamie", 2013). *Cuneiform Digital Library Preprints (CDLP), 05*.

Proust, C. (forthcoming). Volume, brickage and capacity in Old Babylonian mathematical texts from southern Mesopotamia. In K. Chemla, A. Keller, & C. Proust (Eds.), *Cultures of computation and quantification*. Heidelberg/New York: Springer.

Proust, C. (in press-a). Algorithms through sets of problems in Old Babylonian cuneiform texts: Steps without meaning. In C. Proust, M. Husson, & A. Keller (Eds.), *Practices of reasoning in Ancient Mathematics and astral sciences*. New York: Springer.

Proust, C. (in press-b). *A diachronic picture of mathematics in Nippur, from Sargonic to Late-Babylonian periods* (M. Rutz, & J. Steele, (Eds.). Scholarship in Nippur.

Psycharis, G., & Kalogeria, E. (2018). TPACK addressed by trainee teacher educators' documentation work. In V. Gitirana, T. Miyakawa, M. Rafalska, S. Soury-Lavergne, & L. Trouche (Eds.), *Proceedings of the re(s)source 2018 international conference* (pp. 328–331). Lyon: ENS de Lyon. Retrieved on November 8th, 2018, at https://hal.archives-ouvertes.fr/hal-01764563.

Quadling, D. (1996). A century of textbooks. *Mathematical Gazette, 80*(487), 119–126.

Quentin, I. (2012). *Fonctionnements et trajectoires des réseaux en ligne d'enseignants*. Thèse de doctorat. Paris: ENS Cachan.

Quéré, N. (2018). Collective designing of open educational resources: What effects on teachers' design capacity? In V. Gitirana, T. Miyakawa, M. Rafalska, S. Soury-Lavergne, & L. Trouche (Eds.), *Proceedings of the re(s)sources 2018 international conference* (pp. 215–218). Lyon: ENS de Lyon.

Rabardel, P. (1995a). *Les hommes et les technologies, approche cognitive des instruments contemporains*. Paris: Armand Colin.

Rabardel, P. (1995b). *Les hommes et les technologies. Une approche cognitive des instruments contemporains*. Paris: Armand Colin (English version at http://ergoserv.psy.univ-paris8.fr/Site/default.asp?Act_group=1).

Rabardel, P. (1999a). Eléments pour une approche instrumentale en didactique des mathématiques. In M. Bailleul (Ed.), *Actes de la Xe Ecole d'été de didactique des mathématiques* (pp. 202–213). Caen: IUFM.

Rabardel, P. (1999b). Le langage comme instrument ? Éléments pour une théorie instrumentale étendue. In Y. Clot (Ed.), *Avec Vygotski* (pp. 241–265). Paris: La Dispute.

Rabardel, P. (2002a). *People and technology – A cognitive approach to contemporary instruments*. Paris: Université Paris 8. https://hal-univ-paris8.archives-ouvertes.fr/file/index/docid/1020705/filename/people_and_technology.

Rabardel, P. (2002b). *People and technology: A cognitive approach to contemporary instruments*. Retrieved from https://halshs.archives-ouvertes.fr/file/index/docid/1020705/filename/people_and_technology.pdf

Rabardel, P. (2002c). *People and technology: A cognitive approach to contemporary instruments*. Paris: Université Paris 8. Retreived at https://hal.archives-ouvertes.fr/hal-01020705.

Rabardel, P., & Bourmaud, G. (2005). Instruments et systèmes d'instruments, in P. Rabardel, P. Pastré (dir.), *Modèles du sujet pour la conception. Dialectiques activités développement* (pp. 211–229). Toulouse: Octarès.

Radford, L. (2008). The ethics of being and knowing: Towards a cultural theory of learning. In L. Radford, G. Schubring, & F. Seeger (Eds.), *Semiotics in mathematics education: Epistemology, history, classroom, and culture* (pp. 215–234). Rotterdam: Sense Publishers.

Ratanayake, I., & Thomas, M. (2018). Documentational genesis during teacher collaborative development of tasks incorporating digital technology. In V. Gitirana, T. Miyakawa, M. Rafalska, S. Soury-Lavergne, & L. Trouche (Eds.), *Proceedings of the re(s)sources 2018 international conference* (pp. 219–222). Lyon: ENS de Lyon.

Ratnayake, I., & Thomas, M. (2018). Documentational genesis during teacher collaborative development of tasks incorporating digital technology. In V. Gitirana, T. Miyakawa, M. Rafalska, S. Soury-Lavergne, & L. Trouche (Eds.), *Proceedings of the re(s)source 2018 international conference* (pp. 219–222). Lyon: ENS de Lyon. Retrieved on November 8th, 2018, at https://hal.archives-ouvertes.fr/hal-01764563.

Recker, M. M., Dorward, J., & Nelson, L. M. (2004). Discovery and use of online learning resources: Case study findings. *Educational Technology & Society, 7*(2), 93–104.

Remillard, J. T. (1999). Curriculum materials in mathematics education reform: A framework for examining teachers' curriculum development. *Curriculum Inquiry, 29*(3), 315–342.

Remillard, J. T. (2000). Can curriculum materials support teachers' learning? *Elementary School Journal, 100*(4), 331–350.

Remillard, J. T. (2005). Examining key concepts in research on teachers' use of mathematics curricula. *Review of Educational Research, 75*(2), 211–246.

Remillard, J. T. (2010). Modes d'engagements: comprendre les transactions des professeurs avec les ressources curriculaires en mathématiques. In G. Gueudet & L. Trouche (Eds.), *Ressources vives. Le travail documentaire des professeurs en mathématiques* (pp. 201–216). Rennes/Lyon: Presses Universitaires de Rennes et INRP.

Remillard, J. T. (2012). Modes of engagement: Understanding teachers' transactions with mathematics curriculum resources. In G. Gueudet, B. Pepin, & L. Trouche (Eds.), *From text to 'lived' resources: Mathematics curriculum materials and teacher development* (pp. 105–122). New York: Springer.

Remillard, J. T. (2013, May). *Beyond the script: Educative features of five mathematics curricula and how teachers use them.* Paper presented at the annual meeting of the American Educational Research Association, San Francisco, CA.

Remillard, J. T. (2016). Keeping an eye on the teacher in the digital curriculum race. In M. Bates & Z. Usiskin (Eds.), *Digital curricula in school mathematics* (pp. 195–204). Greenwich: Information Age.

Remillard, J. T. (2018a). Examining teachers' interactions with curriculum resource to uncover pedagogical design capacity. In L. Fan, L. Trouche, C. Qi, S. Rezat, & J. Visnovska (Eds.), *Research on mathematics textbooks and teachers' resources: Advances and issues* (ICME-13 monograph) (pp. 69–88). Cham: Springer.

Remillard, J. T. (2018b). Mapping the relationship between written and enacted curriculum: Examining teachers' decision making. In G. Kaiser (Ed.), *Invited lectures from the 13th international congress on mathematical education.* New York: Springer.

Remillard, J. T., & Bryans, M. B. (2004). Teachers' orientations toward mathematics curriculum materials: Implications for teacher learning. *Journal of Research in Mathematics Education, 35*(5), 352–388.

Remillard, J., & Heck, D. J. (2014). Conceptualising the curriculum enactment process in mathematics education. *ZDM – Mathematics Education, 46*(5), 705–718.

Remillard, J. T., & Kim, O.-K. (2017). Knowledge of curriculum embedded mathematics: Exploring a critical domain of teaching. *Educational Studies in Mathematics, 96*(1), 65–81. (view online: http://rdcu.be/qajL).

Remillard, J. T., & Kim, O. K. (forthcoming). *Comparing elementary mathematics curriculum materials: Implications for teachers and teaching.* New York: Springer.

Remillard, J.T., & Van Steenbrugge, H., (in preparation). A multimodal analysis of the voice of six teacher's guides from the United States, Flanders, and Sweden.

Remillard, J. T., Van Steenbrugge, H., & Bergqvist, T. (2014). A cross-cultural analysis of the voice of curriculum materials. In K. Jones, C. Bokhove, G. Howson, & L. Fan (Eds.), *Proceedings of the first international conference on mathematics textbook research and development* (ICMT-2014) (pp. 395–400). Southampton: University of Southampton.

Remillard, J.T., Van Steenbrugge, H., & Bergqvist, T. (2016, April). *A cross-cultural analysis of the voice of six Teacher's guides from three cultural contexts.* Paper presented at the annual meeting of the American Educational Research Association, Washington, DC.

References 531

Remillard, J. T., Van Steenbrugge, H., & Trouche, L. (2017). Teacher-resource use around the world. In G. Schubring, L. Fan, & V. Giraldo (Eds.), *Proceeding of the second international conference on mathematics textbooks, research and development* (pp. 129–132). Rio de Janeiro: Instituto de Matemática, Universidade Federal do Rio de Janeiro. http://www.sbembrasil.org. br/files/ICMT2017.pdf.

Remillard, J. T., Reinke, L. R., & Kapoor, R. (2019). What is the point? Examining how curriculum materials articulate mathematical goals and how teachers steer instruction. *International Journal of Educational Research, 93*, 101–117.

Rezat, S. (2009). *Das Mathematikbuch als Instrument des Schülers. Eine Studie zur Schulbuchnutzung in den Sekundarstufen*. Wiesbaden: Vieweg+Teubner.

Rezat, S. (2011). Interactions of teachers' and students' use of mathematics textbooks. In G. Gueudet, B. Pepin, & L. Trouche (Eds.), *From text to 'lived' resources. Mathematics curriculum materials and teacher development* (pp. 231–246). New York: Springer.

Rezat, S., & Sträßer, R. (2012). From the didactical triangle to the socio-didactical tetrahedron: artifacts as fundamental constituents of the didactical situation. *ZDM – Mathematics Education, 44*(5), 641–651.

Rezat, S., Visnovska, J., Trouche, L., Qi, C., & Fan, L. (2018). Present research on mathematics textbooks and teachers' resources in ICME-13: Conclusions and perspectives. In L. Fan, L. Trouche, C. Qi, S. Rezat, & J. Visnovska (Eds.), *Research on mathematics textbooks and teachers' resources. Advances and issues* (pp. 343–358). Cham: Springer.

Richey, R. C., Fields, D. C., & Foxon, M. (2001). *Instructional design competencies: The standards*. ERIC Clearinghouse on Information & Technology, Syracuse University, 621 Skytop Rd., Suite 160, Syracuse, NY 13244–5290.

Robert, A., & Rogalski, J. (2002). Le système complexe et cohérent des pratiques des enseignants de mathématiques: une double approche. *Revue Canadienne de l'Enseignement des Sciences, des Mathématiques et des Technologies, 2*(4), 505–528.

Robert, C., & Treiner, J. (2004). Une double émergence. *Bulletin de l'Union des Physiciens, 98*(867), 1385–1397.

Robson, E. (2001). The tablet house: A scribal school in Old Babylonian Nippur. *Revue d'Assyriologie, 95*, 39–66.

Robson, E. (2008). *Mathematics in Ancient Iraq: A social history*. Princeton: Princeton University Press.

Robutti, O. (2018). Meta-didactical transposition. In S. Lerman (Ed.), *Encyclopedia of mathematics education*. Heidelberg: Springer.

Robutti, O., Cusi, A., Clark-Wilson, A., Jaworski, B., Chapman, O., Esteley, C., & Joubert, M. (2016). ICME international survey on teachers working and learning through collaboration: June 2016. *ZDM – Mathematics Education, 48*(5), 651–690.

Rocha, K. (2018a). Uses of online resources and documentational trajectories: The case of Sésamath. In L. Fan, L. Trouche, S. Rezat, C. Qi, & J. Visnovska (Eds.), *Research on mathematics textbooks and teachers' resources: Advances and issues* (ICME 13 Monograph) (pp. 235–258). Cham: Springer.

Rocha, K. (2018b). Les trajectoires documentaires, une proposition de modèle pour analyser les interactions des enseignants avec les ressources au fil du temps: la plateforme AnA.doc, un outil d'instrumentation de cette analyse. In *Objets, supports, instruments : regards croisés sur la diversité des ressources mobilisées en interaction. SHS Web of Conferences, 52, 02004*. Retreived at https://doi.org/10.1051/shsconf/20185202004.

Rocha, K., & Trouche, L. (2017). Documentational trajectory: A tool for analyzing the genesis of a teacher's resource system across her collective work. In T. Dooley & G. Gueudet (Eds.), *Proceedings of the tenth congress of the European society for research in mathematics education (CERME10)* (pp. 3732–3739). Dublin: DCU Institute of Education and ERME.

Rocha, K., Trouche, L., & Gueudet, G. (2017). Documentational trajectories as a means for understanding teachers' engagement with resources: The case of French teachers facing a new curriculum. In G. Schubring, L. Fan, & V. Geraldo (Eds.), *Proceedings of the second international* conference on mathematics textbook research and development (pp. 400–409). Rio de Janeiro: Instituto de Matemática, Universidade Federal do Rio de Janeiro, consulté à l'adresse. http://www.sbembrasil.org.br/files/ICMT2017_.pdf.

Rodrigues, A., Baltar, P., & Bellemain, F. (2018). Analysis of a task in three Environments: Paper and pencils, manipulative materials and Apprenti Géomètre 2∗. In V. Gitirana, T. Miyakawa, M. Rafalska, S. Soury-Lavergne, & L. Trouche (Eds.), *Proceedings of the Re(s)source 2018 International Conference* (pp. 223–226). Lyon, ENS de Lyon: . Retrieved on November 8th, 2018, at https://hal.archives-ouvertes.fr/hal-01764563.

Rouse Ball, W. W. (1908). *A short account of the history of mathematics* (4th ed.). London: Macmillan.

Rousseau, D., & Morvan, M. (2000). *La dénomination*. Paris: Odile Jacob.

Rowland, T. (2013). The knowledge quartet: The genesis and application of a framework for analyzing mathematics teaching and deepening teachers' mathematics knowledge. *Journal of Education, 1*(3), 15–43.

Rowland, T., Huckstep, P., & Thwaites, A. (2005). Elementary teachers' mathematics subject knowledge: The knowledge quartet and the case of Naomi. *Journal of Mathematics Teacher Education, 8*, 255–281.

Rubio, G. (2007). Writing in another tongue: Alloglottography and scribal antiquarianism in the Ancient Near East. In S. L. Sanders (Ed.), *Margins of writing, origins of cultures: Unofficial writing in the ancient Near East and beyond* (pp. 33–70). Chicago: The Oriental Institute.

Rudd, T. (2007). *Interactive whiteboards in the classroom*. Bristol: Futurelab Report – IWBs.

Ruthven, K. (2007). Teachers, technologies and the structures of schooling. In D. Pitta-Pantazi & G. Philippou (Eds.), *Proceedings of the fifth congress of the European society for research in mathematics education* (pp. 52–67). Larnaca: Department of Education – University of Cyprus and ERME.

Ruthven, K. (2008). Teachers, technologies and the structures of schooling. In D. Pitta-Pantazi & G. Philippou (Eds.), *Proceedings of the fifth congress of the European society for research in mathematics education (CERME 5)* (pp. 52–67). Larnaca: Cyprus.

Ruthven, K. (2009). Towards a naturalistic conceptualisation of technology integration in classroom practice: The example of school mathematics. *Education & Didactique, 3*(1), 131–149.

Ruthven, K. (2010). Constituer les outils et les supports numériques en ressources pour la classe. In G. Gueudet & L. Trouche (Eds.), *Ressources vives. Le travail documentaire des professeurs en mathématiques* (pp. 183–200). Rennes/Lyon: Presses Universitaires de Rennes et INRP.

Ruthven, K. (2014). Frameworks for analysing the expertise that underpins successful integration of digital technologies into everyday teaching practice. In A. Clark-Wilson, O. Robutti, & N. Sinclair (Eds.), *The mathematics teacher in the digital era* (pp. 373–393). Dordrecht: Springer.

Ruthven, K. (2018). Instructional activity and student interaction with digital resources. In L. Fan, L. Trouche, C. Qi, S. Rezat, & J. Visnovska (Eds.), *Research on mathematics textbooks and teachers' resources: Advances and issues. ICME 13 monograph* (pp. 261–275). Cham: Springer.

Ruthven, K., Hennessy, S., & Deaney, R. (2008). Constructions of dynamic geometry: A study of the interpretative flexibility of educational software in classroom practice. *Computers & Education, 51*(1), 297–317.

Sabra, H. (2011). *Contribution à l'étude du travail documentaire des enseignants de mathématiques: les incidents comme révélateurs des rapports entre documentations individuelle et communautaire*. PhD. Lyon, France: Université Lyon 1, https://tel.archives-ouvertes.fr/tel-00768508/document

Sabra, H. (2016a). L'étude des rapports entre documentation individuelle et collective: Incidents, connaissances et ressources mathématiques. *Recherches en Didactique des Mathématiques, 36*(1), 49–96.

Sabra, H. (2016b). L'étude des rapports entre documentations individuelle et collective: Incidents, connaissances et ressources mathématiques. *Recherches en Didactique des Mathématiques, 36*(1), 49–95.

References

Salaün, J.-M. (2012). *Vu, lu, su. Les architectes de l'information face à l'oligopole du Web*. Paris: La Découverte.

Salaün, J.-M. (2016). Quelques leçons du MOOC Archinfo sur la collaboration et l'évaluation par les pairs. Séminaire du projet MORCEF. ENS de Lyon.

Salinas, U., & Trouche, L. (2018). Uso de gestos –como recurso-mediador– por un profesor de bachillerato para enfrentar un desafío didáctico no previsto por él. *Unión. Revista iberoamericana de educación matemática, 54*, 6–24. http://asenmacformacion.com/ojs/index.php/union/article/view/369.

Salinas-Hernandez, U., Sacristan, A. I., & Trouche, L. (2018). Technology integration into mathematics classrooms: case study of a high-school teacher's use of GeoGebra. In V. Gitirana et al. (Eds.), *Proceedings of the re(s)sources 2018 international conference* (pp. 88–91). Lyon: ENS de Lyon.

Sánchez, M. (2010). Orquestación documentacional: herramienta para la estructuración y el análisis del trabajo documentacional colectivo en linea. *Recherches en didactique des mathématiques, 30*(3), 367–397.

Santacruz, M., & Sacristan, A.-I. (2018). Reflecting on the paths for selecting digital resources for (geometry) teaching: The case of a first grade teacher. In V. Gitirana, T. Miyakawa, M. Rafalska, S. Soury-Lavergne, & L. Trouche (Eds.), *Proceedings of the re(s)sources conference* (pp. 92–95). Lyon: ENS de Lyon. Retrieved November 8, 2018, at https://hal.archives-ouvertes.fr/hal-01764563.

Sayac, N. (2018). What resources and assessment logic to design tests in mathematics at primary school in France? In V. Gitirana et al. (Eds.), *Proceedings of the re(s)sources 2018 international conference* (pp. 96–99). Lyon: ENS de Lyon.

Sayah, K. (2018). *L'intégration des ressources de Sésamath au collège: un moteur pour le développement du travail collectif des enseignants de mathématiques en Algérie. PhD, Université Lyon, 1*.

Sayah, K. (2018a). Analyse de la structure d'un système de ressources, articulation entre aspect dynamique et aspect statique: cas d'une enseignante des mathématiques. In V. Gitirana et al. (Eds.), *Proceedings of the re(s)sources 2018 international conference* (pp. 100–103). Lyon: ENS de Lyon.

Sayah, K. (2018b). *L'intégration des ressources de Sésamath au collège : un moteur pour le développement du travail collectif des enseignants de mathématiques en Algérie*. Thèse de doctorat. Lyon: Université Claude Bernard Lyon 1.

Scardamalia, M. (2002). Collective cognitive responsibility for the advancement of knowledge. In B. Smith (Ed.), *Liberal education in a knowledge society* (pp. 67–98). Chicago: Open Court.

Scherrer, J., & Stein, M. K. (2013). Effects of a coding intervention on what teachers learn to notice during whole–group discussion. *Journal of Mathematics Teacher Education, 16*(2), 105–124.

Schmidt, W.-H., Hsing, C. W., & McKnight, C. C. (2005). Curriculum coherence: An examination of US mathematics and science content standards from an international perspective. *Journal of Curriculum Studies, 37*(5), 525–559.

Schneuwly, B. (1994). Contradiction and development: Vygotsky and paedology. *European Journal of Psychology of Education, 9*(4), special issue. Learning and development: Contributions from Vygotsky, 281–291.

Schoenfeld, A. H. (1985). *Mathematical problem solving*. Orlando: Academic.

Schoenfeld, A. H. (2010). *How we think: A theory of goal–oriented decision making and its educational applications*. New York: Routledge.

Schoenfeld, A. H. (2011a). *How we think: A theory of goal-oriented decision making and its educational applications*. New York: Routledge.

Schoenfeld, A. H. (2011b). Reflections on teacher expertise. In Y. Li & G. Kaiser (Eds.), *Expertise in mathematics instruction*. Boston: Springer.

Schön, D. (1983). *The reflective practitioner*. New York: Basic Books.

Sensevy, G. (2010a). Formes de l'intention didactique, collectifs et travail documentaire. In G. Gueudet & L. Trouche (Eds.), *Ressources vives. Le travail documentaire des professeurs en mathématiques* (pp. 147–163). Rennes/Lyon: Presses Universitaires de Rennes et INRP.

Sensevy, G. (2010b). Formes de l'intention didactique, collectifs, et travail documentaire. In G. Gueudet & L. Trouche (Eds.), *Ressources vives. Le travail documentaire des professeurs en mathématiques* (pp. 147–161). Rennes/Lyon: Presses Universitaires de Rennes et INRP.

Sensevy, G. (2011). *Le sens du savoir. Éléments pour une théorie de l'action conjointe en didactique.* Bruxelles: De Boeck.

Sensevy, G. (2012). Patterns of didactic intentions, thought collective and documentation work. In G. Gueudet, B. Pepin, & L. Trouche (Eds.), *From textbooks to 'Lived' resources: Mathematics curriculum materials and teacher documentation* (pp. 43–57). New York: Springer.

Sésamath. (2009). *Le manuel Sésamath 6e* (Génération 5 ed.). Chambéry: Sésamath.

Shaaban, E., Khalil, I., & Trouche, L. (2015). Interactions between digital resources and biology teachers' conceptions about genetic determinism: A case study of two Lebanese teachers. *International Journal of Science and Research, 4*(10), 1190–1200.

Sherin, M. G., & Drake, C. (2009). Curriculum strategy framework: Investigating patterns in teachers' use of a reform-based elementary mathematics curriculum. *Journal of Curriculum Studies, 41*(4), 467–500.

Sherman, M. F., & Cayton, C. (2015). Using appropriate tools strategically for instruction. *Mathematics Teacher, 109*(4), 306–310.

Sherman, M. F., Cayton, C., & Chandler, K. (2017). Supporting PSTs in using appropriate tools strategically: A learning sequence for developing technology tasks that support students' mathematical thinking. *Mathematics Teacher Educator, 5*(2), 122–157.

Shulman, L. S. (1986). Those who understand: Knowledge growth in teaching. *Educational Researcher, 15*(2), 4–14.

Shulman, L. S. (1987a). Knowledge and teaching: Foundations of the new reform. *Harvard Educational Review, 57*(1), 1–21.

Shulman, L. S. (1987b). Knowledge and teaching: Foundations of the new reform. *Harvard Educational Review, 57*(1), 1–22.

Siedel, H., & Stylianides, A. J. (2018). Teachers' selection of resources in an era of plenty: An interview study with secondary mathematics teachers in England. In L. Fan, L. Trouche, C. Qi, S. Rezat, & J. Visnovska (Eds.), *Research on mathematics textbooks and teachers' resources. Advances and issues* (pp. 119–144). Cham: Springer.

Siemens, G. (2005a). *Connectivism: a learning theory for the digital age.* Retrieved July 2016 from http://www.elearnspace.org/Articles/connectivism.htm

Siemens, G. (2005b). Connectivism: A learning theory for the digital age. *International Journal of Instructional Technology and Distance Learning, 2*(1), 3–10. http://www.itdl.org/Journal/Jan_05/article01.htm. Accessed 28 Sept 2017.

Silva, A. (2018). *Concepção de um suporte para a elaboração de webdocumentos destinados ao ensino da geometria: o caso das curvas cônicas.* Dissertação do mestrado. Programa de Pós-graduação em Educação Matemática e Tecnológica. UFPE, Recife.

Silva, J. P., & Lima, I. M. S. (2017). Atividades Matemáticas propostas por Professores que ensinam na EJA Campo ? Ensino Médio. *Revista Paranaense de Educação Matemática, 6,* 246–268.

Simon, M. A. (1995). Reconstructing mathematics pedagogy from a constructivist perspective. *Journal for Research in Mathematics Education, 26*(2), 114–145.

Simon, M. A., & Tzur, R. (2004). Explicating the role of mathematical tasks in conceptual learning: An elaboration of the hypothetical learning trajectory. *Mathematical Thinking and Learning, 6*(2), 91–104.

Simon, M. A., Tzur, R., Heinz, K., Kinzel, M., & Smith, M. S. (2000). Characterizing a perspective underlying the practice of mathematics teachers in transition. *Journal for Research in Mathematics Education, 31*(5), 579–601.

Siqueira, J. E. M., & Bellemain, F. (2018). A dynamic multirepresentational resource for conics. In V. Gitirana, T. Miyakawa, M. Rafalska, S. Soury-Lavergne, & L. Trouche (Eds.), *Proceedings of the re(s)source 2018 international conference* (pp. 359–361). Lyon: ENS de Lyon. Retrieved on November 8th, 2018, at https://hal.archives-ouvertes.fr/hal-01764563.

References

Sleep, L. (2009). *Teaching to the mathematical point: Knowing and using mathematics in teaching*. Unpublished PhD. University of Michigan, USA.

Sleep, L. (2012). The work of steering instruction toward the mathematical point: A decomposition of teaching practice. *American Education Research Journal, 49*(5), 935–970.

Smith, D. E. (1904). *The teaching of elementary mathematics*. New York: The MacMillan Company.

Smith, M. S., Bill, B., & Hughes, E. K. (2008). Thinking through a lesson: Successfully implementing high-level tasks. *Mathematics Teaching in the Middle School, 14*(3), 132–138.

Sokhna, M. (2006a). *Formation continue à distance des professeurs de mathématiques du Sénégal: genèse instrumentale de ressources pédagogiques*. Thèse de doctorat. Montpellier: Université Montpellier II.

Sokhna, M. (2006b). *Formation à distance des professeurs de mathématiques au Sénégal, genèse instrumentale de ressources pédagogiques*. PhD, Université Lyon 1. Retreived at https://tel. archives-ouvertes.fr/tel-00917620

Sokhna, M. (2018a). Systèmes de ressources et intégration des TICE : quels critères de sélection ? In V. Gitirana et al. (Eds.), *Proceedings of the re(s)sources 2018 international conference* (pp. 109–112). Lyon: ENS de Lyon.

Sokhna, M. (2018b). Systèmes de ressources et intégration des TICE: quels critères de sélection ? In V. Gitirana, T. Miyakawa, M. Rafalska, S. Soury-Lavergne, & L. Trouche (Eds.), *Proceedings of the re(s)sources conference* (pp. 109–112). Lyon: ENS de Lyon. Retrieved November 8, 2018, at https://hal.archives-ouvertes.fr/hal-01764563.

Sokhna, M., & Trouche, L. (2015). Formation mathématique des enseignants: quelles médiations documentaires? In L. Theis (Ed.), *Pluralités culturelles et universalité des mathématiques : enjeux et perspectives pour leur enseignement et leur apprentissage. Actes Espace mathématique francophone* (EMF 2015) (pp. 624–639). Alger: Université des Sciences et de la Technologie Houari Boumediene.

Sokhna, M., & Trouche, L. (2016). Repenser la formation des enseignants en France et au Sénégal: une source d'interactions fécondes. In M. Artigue (coord.), La tradition didactique française au delà des frontières. Exemples de collaborations avec l'Afrique, l'Amérique latine et l'Asie (pp. 27–38). *Présentation de la communauté didactique française à ICME 13*, Hambourg. http://www.cfem.asso.fr/cfem/Collaborationsdidactiquesfrancaises.pdf

Stein, M. K., & Kim, G. (2009). The role of mathematics curriculum materials in large-scale urban reform: An analysis of demands and opportunities for teacher learning. In J. T. Remillard, B. A. Herbel-Eisenmann, & G. M. Lloyd (Eds.), *Mathematics teachers at work: Connecting curriculum materials and classroom instruction* (pp. 37–55). New York: Routledge.

Stein, M. K., & Smith, M. S. (1998). Mathematical tasks as a framework for reflection: From research to practice. *Mathematics Teaching in the Middle School, 3*(4), 268–275.

Stigler, J., & Hiebert, J. (1999). *The teaching gap: Best ideas from the world's teachers for improving education in the classroom*. New York: The Free Press.

Stockero, S. L., & Van Zoest, L. R. (2013). Characterizing pivotal teaching moments in beginning mathematics teachers' practice. *Journal of Mathematics Teacher Education, 16*(2), 125–147.

Sun, X. (2013). Trends in mathematics education in contemporary China. In J. Wang (Ed.), *Mathematics education in China: Tradition and reality* (pp. 303–322). Singapore: Gale Asia.

Swan, M. (2014). *Design based research, encyclopedia of mathematics education*. New York: Springer.

Swidan, O., Arzarello, F., & Sabena, C. (2018). Teachers' interventions to foster inquiry-based learning in a dynamic technological environment. In V. Gitirana, T. Miyakawa, M. Rafalska, S. Soury-Lavergne, & L. Trouche (Eds.), *Proceedings of the re(s)source 2018 international conference* (pp. 332–335). Lyon: ENS de Lyon. Retrieved on November 8th, 2018, at https:// hal.archives-ouvertes.fr/hal-01764563.

Tabach, M. (2011). A mathematics teacher's practice in a technological environment: A case study analysis using two complementary theories. *Technology, Knowledge and Learning, 16*(3), 247–265.

Tabach, M. (2013). Developing a general framework for instrumental orchestration. In B. Ubuz, Ç. Haser, & M. A. Mariotti (Eds.), *Proceedings of the eighth congress of the European society for research in mathematics education* (pp. 2744–2753). Ankara: Middle East Technical University and ERME.

Tabchi, T. (2018). University teachers-researchers' practices: The case of teaching discrete mathematics. In V. Durand-Guerrier, R. Hochmuth, S. Goodchild, & N. M. Hogstad (Eds.), *Proceedings of the second conference of the International Network for Didactic Research in University Mathematics (INDRUM 2018, 5 April–7 April 2018)* (pp. 432–441). Kristiansand: University of Agder and INDRUM.

Takahashi, A. (2005). Tool for lesson study: Template for a lesson plan. In P. Wang-Iverson & M. Yoshida (Eds.), *Building our understanding of lesson study* (pp. 63–64). Philadelphia: Research for Better Schools.

Tan, S., Fukaya, K., & Nozaki, S. (2018). Development of bansho (Board Writing) analysis as a research method to improve observation and analysis of instruction in Lesson Study. *International Journal for Lesson and Learning Studies, 7*(3), 230–247.

Tanaka, Y. (2013). *Jidō ga iyoku-teki ni tsuikyū suru sansū-teki katsudō no kufū: dai 6 gakunen "kakudai-zu to shuku-zu" no jissen wo tōshite* [Mathematical activities in which children are motivated to participate: The teaching practices of a grade 6 lesson "enlarged and reduced figures"]. Document distributed at the monthly meeting of research Association for Mathematics Teaching in Jōetsu on 31st July, 2013.

Taranto, E. (2018). *MOOC's Zone Theory: creating a MOOC environment for professional learning in mathematics teaching education*. PhD dissertation. Turin University.

Taranto, E., Arzarello, F., & Robutti, O. (2017a). *MOOC: repository di strategie e metodologie didattiche in matematica, Annali online della Didattica e della Formazione Docente 14* (pp. 257–279).

Taranto, E., Arzarello, F., Robutti, O., Alberti, V., Labasin, S., & Gaido, S. (2017b). Analyzing MOOCs in terms of their potential for teacher collaboration: The Italian experience. In T. Dooley & G. Gueudet (Eds.), *Proceedings of the tenth congress of European society for research in mathematics education (CERME10)* (pp. 2478–2485). Dublin: DCU Institute of Education and ERME.

Taranto, E., Arzarello, F., & Robutti, O. (2018). MOOC as a resource for teachers' collaboration in educational program. In V. Gitirana, T. Miyakawa, M. Rafalska, S. Soury-Lavergne, & L. Trouche (Eds.), *Proceedings of the re(s)source 2018 international conference* (pp. 167–170). Lyon: ENS de Lyon. Retrieved on November 8th, 2018, at https://hal.archives-ouvertes.fr/hal-01764563.

Tchounikine, P. (2011). *Computer science and educational software design—A resource for multidisciplinary work in technology enhanced learning*. New York: Springer.

Thijs, A., & Van den Akker, J. (2009). Curriculum in development. In *Enschede*. Dordrecht: SLO.

Thomas, A., & Edson, A. J. (2018). An examination of teacher-generated definitions of digital instructional materials in mathematics. In V. Gitirana, T. Miyakawa, M. Rafalska, S. Soury-Lavergne, & L. Trouche (Eds.), *Proceedings of the re(s)source 2018 international conference* (pp. 340–343, Lyon). ENS de Lyon. Retrieved on November 8th, 2018, at https://hal.archives-ouvertes.fr/hal-01764563.

Thomas, M. O. J., & Hong, Y. Y. (2005). Teacher factors in integration of graphic calculators into mathematics learning. In H. L. Chick & J. L. Vincent (Eds.), *Proceedings of the 29th conference of the international group for the psychology of mathematics education* (Vol. 4, pp. 257–264). Melbourne: University of Melbourne.

Tiberghien, A. (2000). Designing teaching situations in the secondary school. In R. Millar, J. Leach, & J. Osborne (Eds.), *Improving science education: The contribution of research* (pp. 27–47). Buckingham: Open University Press.

Tiburcio, R., & Bellemain, F. (2018). Computational engineering, didactical, educational software, software engineering. In V. Gitirana, T. Miyakawa, M. Rafalska, S. Soury-Lavergne, & L. Trouche (Eds.), *Proceedings of the re(s)source 2018 international conference* (pp. 262–264). Lyon: ENS de Lyon. Retrieved on November 8th, 2018, at https://hal.archives-ouvertes.fr/hal-01764563.

References 537

Tinney, S. (1999). On the curricular setting of Sumerian literature. *Iraq, 61*, 159–172.

Trgalová, J. (2010). Documentation et décisions didactiques des professeurs. In G. Gueudet & L. Trouche (Eds.), *Ressources vives. Le travail documentaire des professeurs en mathématiques* (pp. 271–291). Rennes/Lyon: Presses Universitaires de Rennes et INRP.

Trocki, A., & Hollebrands, K. (2018). The development of a framework for assessing dynamic geometry task quality. *Digital Experiences in Mathematics Education, 4*(2–3), 110–138.

Trouche, L. (2003). *Construction et conduite des instruments dans les apprentissages mathématiques: nécessité des orchestrations.* HDR. Paris: Université Paris Diderot-Paris 7. https://telearn.archives-ouvertes.fr/file/index/docid/190091/filename/Trouche_2003.pdf

Trouche, L. (2004). Managing the complexity of human/machine interactions in computerized learning environment: Guiding students' command process through instrumental orchestrations. *International Journal of Computers for Mathematics Learning, 9*(3), 281–307.

Trouche, L. (2005). Construction et conduite des instruments dans les apprentissages mathématiques : Nécessité des orchestrations. *Recherches en Didactique des Mathématiques, 25*, 91–138.

Trouche, L. (2005a). Les IREM: des raisons des réseaux. *Plot 11*, 2–7, consulté le 17 mai 2016 à. http://www.apmep.fr/IMG/pdf/IREM.pdf

Trouche, L. (2005b). An instrumental approach to mathematics learning in symbolic calculators environments. In D. Guin, K. Ruthven, & L. Trouche (Eds.), *The didactical challenge of symbolic calculators: Turning a computational device into a mathematical instrument* (pp. 137–162). New York: Springer.

Trouche, L. (2009). Penser la gestion didactique des artefacts pour faire et faire faire des mathématiques: histoire d'un cheminement intellectuel. *L'Educateur, 3*, 35–38.

Trouche, L. (dir.) (2014). *EducMap, pour une cartographie dynamique des recherches en éducation.* Research report CNRS-Université de Lyon. https://hal.archives-ouvertes.fr/hal-01546661

Trouche, L. (2016a). The development of mathematics practices in the Mesopotamian Scribal Schools. In J. Monaghan, L. Trouche, & J. M. Borwein (Eds.), *Tools and mathematics: Instruments for learning* (pp. 117–138). New York: Springer.

Trouche, L. (2016b). Didactics of mathematics: Concepts, roots, interactions and dynamics from France. In J. Monaghan, L. Trouche, & J. Borwein (Eds.), *Tools and mathematics: Instruments for learning* (pp. 219–256). New York: Springer.

Trouche, L. (2016c). Prendre en compte les métamorphoses du Numérique. *Union, 45*, 7–23.

Trouche, L. (2017). L'enseignement des mathématiques, un point de vue international centré sur les ressources des professeurs. *La lettre de Grema, 17*, 2–6.

Trouche, L. (this volume). Evidencing the missing resources of the documentational approach to didactics, towards new programs of research. In L. Trouche, G. Gueudet, & B. Pepin (Eds.), *The 'resource' approach to mathematics education.* Cham: Springer.

Trouche, L., & Drijvers, P. (2010). Handheld technology: Flashback into the future. *ZDM – Mathematics Education, 42*(7), 667–681.

Trouche, L., & Drijvers, P. (2014). Webbing and orchestration; two interrelated views on digital tools in mathematics education. *Teaching Mathematics and its Applications, 33*(3), 193–209.

Trouche, L., & Pepin, B. (2014). From instrumental to documentational approach: Towards a holistic perspective of teachers' resource systems in higher education. *Research in Mathematics Education, 16*(2), 156–160.

Trouche, L., et al. (1998). *Expérimenter et prouver. Faire des mathématiques au lycée avec des calculatrices symboliques. 38 variations sur un thème imposé.* Montpellier: IREM, Université Montpellier 2.

Trouche, L., Drijvers, P., Gueudet, G., & Sacristan, A. I. (2013). Technology-driven developments and policy implications for mathematics education. In A. J. Bishop, M. A. Clements, C. Keitel, J. Kilpatrick, & F. K. S. Leung (Eds.), *Third international handbook of mathematics education* (pp. 753–790). New York: Springer.

Trouche, L., Trgalová, J., Loisy, C., & Alturkmani, M. (2018a). *Ressources vivantes pour l'enseignement et l'apprentissage* (Rapport scientifique des composantes IFE et S2HEP). Lyon: Ens de Lyon. https://hal.archives-ouvertes.fr/hal-01743212v2

538 References

Trouche, L., Gueudet, G., & Pepin, B. (2018b, Online First). Documentational approach to didactics. In S. Lerman (Ed.), *Encyclopedia of mathematics education*. New York: Springer. https://doi.org/10.1007/978-3-319-77487-9_100011-1.

Trouche, L., Trgalová, J., Loisy, C., & Alturkmani, M. (2018c). *Ressources vivantes pour l'enseignement et l'apprentissage. Rapport scientifique des composantes IFE et S2HEP.* https://hal.archives-ouvertes.fr/hal-01743212v2

Trouche, L., Trgalová, J., Loisy, C., & Alturkmani, M. (2018d). *Ressources vivantes pour l'enseignement et l'apprentissage. Contribution des composantes IFÉ et S2HEP de l'ANR ReVEA.* ENS de Lyon. https://hal.archives-ouvertes.fr/hal-01743212

Trouche, L., Gitirana, V., Miyakawa, T., Pepin, B., & Wang, C. (2019). Studying mathematics teachers interactions with curriculum materials through different lenses: towards a deeper understanding of the processes at stake. *International Journal of Educational Research, 93*, 53–67. Retrieved on February 21st at https://doi.org/10.1016/j.ijer.2018.09.002.

Tuffery-Rochdi, C. (2016). *Les ressources au cœur des pratiques des enseignants de mathématiques. Le cas de l'enseignement d'exploration MPS en seconde.* PhD. St Denis, France: Université de La Réunion, https://tel.archives-ouvertes.fr/tel-01391464/document.

Ulrich, C. (2015). Stages in constructing and coordinating units additively and multiplicatively (Part 1). *For the Learning of Mathematics, 35*(3), 2–7.

Umameh, M. A. (2018). A mathematics teacher's use of digital resources for formative assessment. In V. Gitirana, T. Miyakawa, M. Rafalska, S. Soury-Lavergne, & L. Trouche (Eds.), *Proceedings of the re(s)source 2018 international conference* (pp. 171–174). Lyon: ENS de Lyon.

Valverde, G. A., Bianchi, L. J., Wolfe, R. G., Schmidt, W. H., & Houang, R. T. (2002). *According to the book: Using TIMSS to investigate the translation of policy into practice through the world of textbooks.* Dordrecht: Kluwer academic publisher.

Van den Akker, J. (2003). Curriculum perspectives: An introduction. In J. van den Akker, W. Kuiper, & U. Hameyer (Eds.), *Curriculum landscapes and trends* (pp. 1–10). Dordrecht: Kluwer Academic Publishers.

van Dijke-Droogers, M., Drijvers, P., & Bakker, A. (2018). From sample to population: A hypothetical learning trajectory for informal statistical inference. In V. Gitirana, T. Miyakawa, M. Rafalska, S. Soury-Lavergne, & L. Trouche (Eds.), *Proceedings of the re(s)source 2018 international conference* (pp. 348–351). Lyon: ENS de Lyon. Retrieved on November 8th, 2018, at https://hal.archives-ouvertes.fr/hal-01764563.

Van Steenbrugge, H., Remillard, J., Krzywacki, H., Hemmi, K., Koljonen, T., & Machalow, R. (2018). Understanding teachers' use of instructional resources from a cross-cultural perspective: the cases of Sweden and Flanders. In V. Gitirana et al. (Eds.), *Proceedings of the re(s) sources 2018 international conference* (pp. 117–121). Lyon: ENS de Lyon.

Vandebrouck, F. (2010). Ressources et documents, le cas de la démarche expérimentale en mathématiques. In G. Gueudet & L. Trouche (Eds.), *Ressources vives. Le travail documentaire des professeurs en mathématiques* (pp. 253–269). Rennes/Lyon: Presses Universitaires de Rennes et INRP.

Vandebrouck, F. (Ed.). (2013). *Mathematics classrooms: Students' activities and Teachers' practices.* Rotterdam: Sense Publishers.

Veldhuis, N. (1997). *Elementary education at Nippur, the lists of trees and wooden objects* (Ph. D. dissertation), University of Groningen, Groningen.

Vergnaud, G. (1990). La théorie des champs conceptuels. *Recherches en Didactique des Mathématiques, 10*(2-3), 133–170.

Vergnaud, G. (1991). La théorie des champs conceptuels. *Recherches en Didactique des Mathématiques, 10*(2), 133–170.

Vergnaud, G. (1993). Teoria dos campos conceituais. In L. Nasser (Ed.), *Anais do 1° Seminario Internacional de Educaçao Matemática do Rio de Janeiro* (pp. 1–26). Rio de Janeiro: UFRJ Projeto Fundão, Instituto de Matemática.

References   539

Vergnaud, G. (1996). The theory of conceptual fields. In L. P. Steffe, P. Nesher, P. Cobb, G. A. Goldin, & B. Greer (Eds.), *Theories of mathematical learning* (pp. 210–239). Mahwah: Laurence Erilbaum.

Vergnaud, G. (1998). Towards a cognitive theory of practice. In A. Sierpinska & J. Kilpatrick (Eds.), *Mathematics education as a research domain: A search for identity* (pp. 227–241). Dordrecht: Kluwer Academic Publisher.

Vergnaud, G. (2009a). The theory of conceptual fields. *Human Development, 52*(2), 83–94. https://doi.org/10.1159/000202727.

Vergnaud, G. (2009b). Le concept d'algorithme en psychologie: *entretien réalisé par Nicolas Paratore.* http://paratore-nicolas.com/articles/concept_algo-3.pdf

Vergnaud, G. (2011). Au fond de l'action, la conceptualisation. In J. M. Barbier (Ed.), *Savoirs théoriques et savoirs d'action* (pp. 275–292). Paris: Presses Universitaires de France.

Verillon, P., & Rabardel, P. (1995). Cognition and artifacts: A contribution to the study of thought in relation to instrumented activity. *European Journal of Psychology of Education, 10*(1), 77–101.

Vermersch, P. (1994a). *L'entretien d'explicitation.* Issy-les-Moulineaux: ESF éditeur.

Vermersch, P. (1994b). *L'entretien d'explicitation en formation continue et initiale.* Paris: ESF.

Vermersch, P. (2012). *Explicitation et phénoménologie.* Paris: PUF.

Villamizar, F., Cuevas, C., & Martinez, M. (2018). A proposal of instrumental orchestration to integrate the teaching of physics and mathematics. In V. Gitirana, T. Miyakawa, M. Rafalska, S. Soury-Lavergne, & L. Trouche (Eds.), *Proceedings of the re(s)source 2018 international conference* (pp. 352–355). Lyon: ENS de Lyon. Retrieved on November 8th, 2018, at https://hal.archives-ouvertes.fr/hal-01764563.

Visnovska, J., & Cobb, P. (2019). Supporting shifts in teachers' views of a classroom statistical activity: Problem context in teaching statistics. *Mathematical Thinking and Learning.* https://doi.org/10.1080/10986065.2019.1576003.

Voltolini, A. (2018). Duo of digital and material artefacts dedicated to the learning of geometry at primary school. In L. Ball, P. Drijvers, S. Ladel, H. Siller, M. Tabach, & C. Vale (Eds.), *Uses of technology in primary and secondary mathematics education* (pp. 83–99). Cham: Springer.

Voogt, J., Laferrie're, T., Breuleux, A., Itow, R., Hickey, D., & McKenney, S. (2015). Collaborative design as a form of professional development. *Instructional Science, 43*(2), 259–282. https://doi.org/10.1007/s11251-014-9340-7.

Vygotski, L.S. (1931/2014). *Histoire du développement des fonctions psychiques supérieures* (Trad. F. Sève). Paris: La Dispute [1st ed. 1931].

Vygotski, L.S. (1931–1934/2018) *La science du développement de l'enfant. Textes pédologiques 1931–1934* (Trad. I. Leopoldoff). Berne: Peter Lang.

Vygotski, L. (1978). *Mind in society.* Cambridge, MA: Harvard University Press.

Vygotsky, L.S. (1931/1997). The history of the development of the higher mental functions. In R.W. Rieber (Ed.), *The collected works of Vygotsky, 4* (pp. 1–251). New York: Plenum Press [1st ed. 1931].

Vygotsky, L. S. (1978a). *Thought and language.* Cambridge: MIT Press. (Original work published 1934).

Vygotsky, L. (1978b). *Mind in society: The development of higher psychological processes.* Cambridge: Harvard University Press.

Vygotsky, L. S. (1978c). *Mind in society.* Cambridge, MA: Harvard University Press.

Wang, J. P. (2012). *Mathematics education in China: Tradition and reality.* Singapore: Cengage Learning Asia Pte Ltd.

Wang, C. (2018a). Mathematics teachers' expertise in resources work and its development in collectives. A French and a Chinese cases. In L. Fan, L. Trouche, S. Rezat, C. Qi, & J. Visnovska (Eds.), *Research on mathematics textbooks and teachers' resources: Advances and issues (ICME-13 monograph)* (pp. 193–213). Cham: Springer.

Wang, C. (2018b). Mathematics teachers' expertise in resources work and its development in collectives. A French and a Chinese cases. In L. Fan, L. Trouche, S. Rezat, C. Qi, & J. Visnovska (Eds.), *Research on mathematics textbooks and teachers' resources: Advances and issues* (pp. 193–214). Cham: Springer.

Wang, C., Trouche, L., & Pepin, B. (2018). An investigation of Chinese mathematics teachers' resources work and their professional development in collectives. In G. Schubring, L. Fan, & V. Giraldo (Eds.), *Proceeding of the second international conference on mathematics textbooks, research and development* (pp. 144–157). Rio de Janeiro: Instituto de Matemática, Universidade Federal do Rio de Janeiro. http://www.sbembrasil.org.br/files/ICMT2017.pdf.

Wang, C., Salinas, U., & Trouche, L. (2019). From teachers' naming systems of resources to teachers' resource systems: Contrasting a Chinese and a Mexican case. In U. T. Jankvist, M. van den Heuvel-Panhuizen, & M. Veldhuis (Eds.), *Proceedings of the eleventh congress of the European society for research in mathematics education* (pp. xxxx–yyyy). Utrecht: Freudenthal Group & Freudenthal Institute, Utrecht University and ERME.

Wang, C., Salinas, U., & Trouche, L. (2020 To be published). From teachers' naming systems of resources to teachers' resource systems: Contrasting a Chinese and a Mexican case. In U. T. Jankvist, M. van den Heuvel-Panhuizen, & M. Veldhuis (Eds.), *Proceedings of the eleventh congress of the European society for research in mathematics education*. Utrecht: Freudenthal Group & Freudenthal Institute, Utrecht University and ERME.

Warwick, D., & Osherson, S. (Eds.). (1973). *Comparative research methods: An overview*. Englewood Cliffs: Prentice Hall.

Watanabe, T., Takahashi, A., & Yoshida, M. (2008). Kyozaikenkyu: A critical step for conducting effective lesson study and beyond. In F. Arbaugh & P. M. Taylor (Eds.), *Inquiry into mathematics teacher education* (AMTE monograph series) (Vol. 5, pp. 131–142). San Diego: Association of Mathematics Teacher Educators.

Webb, M. E. (2008). Impact of IT on science education. In J. Voogt & G. Knezek (Eds.), *International handbook of information technology in primary and secondary education* (pp. 133–148). London: King's College London.

Wenger, E. (1998a). *Communities of practice. Learning, meaning, identity*. New York: Cambridge University Press.

Wenger, E. (1998b). *Communities of practice: Learning, meaning, and identity*. Cambridge, MA: Cambridge University Press.

Wertsch, J. V. (1991). *Voices of the mind: A sociocultural approach to mediated action*. Cambridge, MA: Harvard University Press.

Wertsch, J. V. (1998). *Mind as action*. New York: Oxford University Press.

Wertsch, J. V., & Toma, C. (1995). Discourse and learning in the classroom: A sociocultural approach. In L. Steffe & J. Gale (Eds.), *Constructivism in education* (pp. 159–174). Hillsdale: Lawrence Erlbaum Associates, Inc..

Wohlleben, P. (2017). *La vie secrete des arbres. Ce qu'ils ressentent. Comment ils communiquent. Un monde inconnu s'ouvre à nous*. Paris: Editions des Arènes.

Xu, B., & Recker, M. (2012). Teaching analytics: A clustering and triangulation study of digital library user data. *Educational Technology & Society, 15*(3), 103–115.

Yang, Y. (2009). How a Chinese teacher improved classroom teaching in teaching research group: A case study on Pythagoras theorem teaching in Shanghai. *ZDM - Mathematics Education, 41*(3), 279–296.

Yang, X., & Leung, F. K. S. (2015). The relationships among pre-service mathematics teachers' beliefs about mathematics, mathematics teaching, and use of technology in China. *EURASIA Journal of Mathematics, Science and Technology Education, 11*(6), 1363–1378.

Yang, Y., Li, J., Gao, H., & Xu, Q. (2013). Teacher education and the professional development of mathematics teachers. In J. Wang (Ed.), *Mathematics education in China. Tradition and reality* (pp. 205–238). Singapore: Cengage Learning Asia Pte Ltd..

Ye, L., & Si, H. (2017). *Study and practice of "PET" collaboration model based on teacher professional development. The Inservice Education and Training of School Teachers* (Vol. 2, pp. 9–12).

Yoshida, M. (2005). Using lesson study to develop effective blackboard practice. In P. Wang-Iverson & M. Yoshida (Eds.), *Building our understanding of lesson study* (pp. 93–100). Philadelphia: Research for Better Schools.

References

Yuan, Z., & Li, X. (2015). "Same content different designs" activities and their impact on prospective mathematics teachers' professional development: The case of Nadine. In L. Fan, N.-Y. Wong, J. Cai, & S. Li (Eds.), *How Chinese teach mathematics. Perspectives from insiders* (pp. 567–589). Singapore: World Scientific Publishing.

Yvon, F. (2012). Penser la formation professionnelle avec Vygotski. In F. Yvon & Y. Zinchenko (Eds.), *Vygotski, une théorie du développement et de l'éducation* (pp. 381–398). Moscou et Montréal: Université d'État de Moscou Lomonossov et Université de Montréal.

Zbiek, R. M., & Hollebrands, K. (2008). A research-informed view of the process of incorporating mathematics technology into classroom practice by inservice and prospective teachers. In M. K. Heid & G. Blume (Eds.), *Research on technology in the learning and teaching of mathematics: Syntheses and perspectives*. Charlotte: Information Age Publishers.

Zbiek, R. M., Heid, M. K., Blume, G. W., & Dick, T. P. (2007). Research on technology in mathematics education: A perspective of constructs. In F. K. Lester (Ed.), *Second handbook of research on mathematics teaching and learning* (Vol. 2, pp. 1169–1207). Charlotte: Information Age.

Zhao, Z., Cook, J., & Higgen, N. (1996). Online learning for design students. *ALT-J, 4*(1), 69–76.

Zheng, B., Warschauer, M., Lin, C. H., & Chang, C. (2016). Learning in one-to-one laptop environments: A meta-analysis and research synthesis. *Review of Educational Research, 86*(4), 1052–1084.

Index

A

Activity structure, 52, 402
Activity theory, 4, 36, 38, 100, 102, 106, 107, 110, 111, 203, 219, 329, 330, 374, 378, 380, 382, 394, 410, 412, 461, 462, 474, 496
Anthropological Theory of the Didactic (ATD), 4, 24, 38, 92, 93, 98, 226, 227, 248, 461, 476
Artifact/artefact, 3, 20, 54, 85, 94, 128, 146, 175, 202, 293, 326, 394, 450, 492
  affordance, 304, 309, 372, 395, 399, 408, 430
  constraint, 372, 395, 399, 408, 430
  tool, 175, 176, 178, 191, 203, 303, 304, 306, 395, 397, 399, 401, 419

C

Collective, 3, 19, 51, 96, 124, 146, 188, 198, 258, 327, 392, 449, 492
  community of practice, 21, 36, 98, 463
  institution, 4, 148, 216, 377
  institutional context, 259
  work, 3, 21, 99, 134, 156, 239, 258, 327, 392, 450, 452
Comparative study, 11, 53–54, 107, 112, 146, 147, 343, 477, 478
  cross-cultural, 188–190
  international perspective, 8, 146–148
Continuous process (of development), 18, 242, 361
Cultural-historical activity theory (CHAT), 4, 36, 106, 110, 111, 410, 496

Curriculum, 2, 21, 44, 63, 96, 122, 147, 174, 201, 259, 324, 392, 454, 492
  ergonomics, 4, 38, 476, 491, 492, 499–501
  level(s), 129–131, 136
  materials, 2, 21, 51, 96, 126, 134, 174, 260, 324, 415, 498
  programme/scheme, 44, 49–51, 133, 355
  representations, 129, 130
  resource(s), 2, 29, 49, 97, 122, 175, 210, 259, 355, 410, 457, 491
  script, 21, 52, 492
  spider web, 129–132
  support, 180

D

Design, 2, 19, 44, 64, 98, 122, 149, 174, 200, 258, 324, 391, 449, 492
  d-esign, 128, 138
  D-esign, 128, 136, 138
  dimensions of teacher design, 128, 141
  of learning environments, 10, 394, 424–434
  mode(s) of teacher design, 8, 122, 123, 125–129, 132, 136, 140
  for use, 20, 424, 425, 427–429, 433, 434
  in use, 20, 126, 138, 332, 355, 410, 424–426, 430, 433, 434, 492
Didactical structures, 7, 62, 81–84
Documentational approach to didactics (DAD), 2, 17, 54, 90, 146, 174, 199, 261, 325, 393, 448, 492

© Springer Nature Switzerland AG 2019
L. Trouche et al. (eds.), *The 'Resource' Approach to Mathematics Education*,
Advances in Mathematics Education,
https://doi.org/10.1007/978-3-030-20393-1

Documentational approach to
didactics (DAD) (*cont.*)
document, 18, 54, 202, 261, 326, 409, 458, 492
documentational expertise, 327, 331, 376, 416, 453
documentational genesis, 22, 99, 261, 327, 394, 492, 494
documentational mediation, 203, 205, 474
documentational trajectory/trajectories, 104, 174, 177, 266, 269, 270, 327, 394, 408, 414, 416
documentation valise, 471, 472
documentation work, 4, 9, 17–18, 94, 262, 325, 408, 459
documentation-working mate, 327, 358, 463, 468
document system, 20, 23
Durell's *A New Geometry*, 7, 47, 48

E
Educational technologies, 3, 19, 21
Embodiment, 406, 407
embodied perspective, 394, 406
gesture, 406, 407
Euclid's *Elements*, 7, 45, 46
Exercises, 19, 29, 34, 35, 46–48, 55, 62, 64, 70, 71, 73, 74, 84, 85, 111, 124, 179, 211, 213, 226–228, 234–236, 246, 250, 275, 277, 283, 289, 410, 434, 495, 500

I
Inquiry-based learning, 392, 410, 421
Instrumental approach to didactics (IAD), 449, 451, 452, 459
instrument, 460
instrumental genesis (IG), 10, 20, 94, 176, 302, 391
instrumentalization, 20, 94, 202, 302, 341, 395, 455
instrumental orchestration(s) (IO)
chaining orchestrations, 393, 402, 404, 405, 434
didactical configuration, 393, 401, 405, 426
didactical performance, 393, 400–402, 405–407, 426, 434
exploitation mode, 393, 401, 405, 426
instrumental meta-orchestration, 409, 416, 422

student-centered orchestration, 400, 402, 403, 434
teacher-centered orchestration, 403, 405, 420
instrumentation, 460
Intention, 8, 20, 25, 32, 47, 49, 52, 57, 98, 101, 125, 127, 130, 160, 187, 241, 262, 282, 288, 291, 295–299, 305, 311, 337, 341, 374, 376–378, 380, 399, 401, 450, 493, 500, 501

J
Joint Action Theory in Didactics (JATD), 24, 99, 106, 394, 411

L
Learning support, 331–338, 340, 342, 353
Lesson plan(ning), 134, 137, 146, 154, 157, 159–162, 164–169, 214, 215, 220, 223–227, 245, 246, 263, 265, 281–291, 337, 338, 396, 417–418, 461
progression, 134, 160, 461
Lexicon project, 90, 112–114, 478, 480
naming systems, 478, 480
Long-term (studies), 267, 310, 314, 353

M
Mathematical Pedagogical Technology Knowledge (MPTK), 411

N
Networking (of theories, enterprise), 2, 7, 10, 39, 90–114, 260, 262, 301, 310, 311, 390, 393, 394, 408, 410–412, 416, 434, 451
combining, coordinating theories, 99, 100
locally integrating theories, 91, 99
scale of networking, 93, 97
theoretical connections, 97–101

P
Participatory perspective, 9, 176, 177
Practice-based activity/professional development, 8, 168
Practice report, 159, 165, 168
Procedures, 69, 80–83, 85, 86, 175, 224, 329, 368, 369, 372, 405, 409, 423, 428, 460

Index

R

Reflective investigation (methodology), 23, 25–26, 30–32, 34, 96, 104, 205, 211, 215, 225, 231, 266, 269, 271, 272, 280, 313, 314, 341, 414, 466, 468, 498
  methodological contract, 263, 453, 468, 473
Research-oriented activity/professional development, 168
Research praxeology, 7, 8, 90–95, 97, 99, 100, 103, 105, 107, 109, 112–114, 476, 477
'Resource' approach to mathematics education (RAME), 1–4, 8–12, 17–39, 44–57, 62–87, 90–114, 122–141, 146–170, 174–191, 198–251, 258–315, 324–383, 391–434, 477, 492–501
  coherence (of a resource), 262, 291–300, 311
  daughter resource(s), 201, 213, 230, 231, 234–237, 340, 343, 350, 453, 458
  digital resource(s), 4, 96
  instructional resources, 179, 185, 186, 210, 212, 355, 381, 382, 415
  mother resource(s), 199, 201, 212, 214, 230–240, 244, 250, 251, 453, 458
  pivotal resource(s), 27, 33, 38, 201, 211, 213–214, 232, 234–239, 250, 251, 345, 347–349, 351, 352, 377, 453
  resource, 2–12, 477, 491
  structuring mother resource(s), 199, 201, 213, 230–232, 234–235, 237, 239, 250, 251, 453, 458
  transitional resource(s), 218, 220–223, 250
Resource system(s), 3, 21, 44, 84, 96, 150, 198, 258, 328, 391, 453, 494
  constitution of a resource system, 200, 208, 209, 215, 220, 222–224, 229, 249, 250
  digital resource system(s), 416
  evolution of a resource system, 199, 202–206, 240–248, 250
  metamorphosis of a resource system, 218–222, 394, 414, 416
  resource system(s) for studying (RSS), 218, 220–228
  resource system(s) for teaching (RST), 208, 218–228, 237, 344
  Schematic Representation of Resource System (SRRS), 26, 38, 96, 104, 231, 232, 235–238, 272, 357, 498

structure of a resource system, 200, 201, 211, 240, 241, 251

S

Scheme, 4, 20, 44, 94, 125, 146, 177, 199, 261, 326, 394, 456, 492
  class of situations, 55, 146, 242, 270, 326, 344, 356, 460, 461
  operational invariants, 20, 55, 95, 146, 224, 261, 326, 395, 460, 492
  utilization scheme, 55, 56, 146, 170, 302, 304, 326, 327, 333, 394, 395, 398, 400, 415, 426, 430, 433, 459
School-based teaching research, 134, 148, 152
Sexagesimal place-value notation
  metrological table, 67–70, 72, 85
  reciprocal, 70, 85
Socio-didactical tetrahedron (SDT), 5, 324, 325, 329, 330, 375, 376, 379
Spiral, 82, 83
Structuring features of classroom practice (SFCP)
  time economy, 21, 52
Students, 3, 18, 46, 62, 94, 123, 148, 175, 200, 261, 324, 391, 448, 494

T

Teacher, 2, 17, 44, 62, 94, 122, 146, 174, 198, 258, 324, 391, 448, 491
  association, 146, 157–159, 163, 166, 168, 410
  capacity, 177, 178, 180, 331, 363, 364
  customization, 126
  design, 8, 29, 122, 296, 341, 410, 417
  design capacity, 38, 122–125, 327, 354, 374, 410
  education, 4, 28, 108, 133, 201, 300, 331, 392, 452, 470
  expertise, 124, 356, 357, 362
  guide, 175, 179–183, 185, 186, 188, 190, 209, 212, 213, 245, 365, 367, 371
  as participatory designers, 125–127
  pedagogical design capacity (PDC), 180–185, 327–329, 331, 354, 363, 364, 370, 374, 376, 380, 428, 431–433, 465
  professional development, 4, 8, 98, 134, 140, 151, 153, 170, 305, 342, 359, 381, 464–466

Teacher (*cont.*)
resource interactions, 178, 185, 381
Teaching Research Group (TRG), 8, 104, 105, 127, 137, 138, 146, 150, 152, 153, 168, 357
Teaching Research Office (TRO), 134, 137, 148–150, 152, 153, 157, 168
Techniques, 7, 52, 53, 92, 96, 98, 226, 228, 302, 304, 338, 395, 396, 401, 406, 431, 469, 470, 476
Technological, pedagogical and content knowledge (TPACK), 393, 401, 411, 417, 432, 474
Textbooks, 2, 27, 44, 97, 125, 146, 179, 201, 261, 333, 392, 450
Tools, 3, 19, 48, 64, 90, 125, 175, 203, 261, 325, 392, 449, 492

V
Variation, 57, 70, 72, 73, 84, 85, 103, 182, 185, 187, 189, 270, 282, 287, 315, 403, 429, 448, 474
Vygotsky
Vygotsky's historical-cultural theory, 312, 314

W
Webdocument (webdoc), 6, 239, 449, 468, 472, 473, 482
Wholeness, 265, 266, 312–314
Working environment, 21, 51, 341

CPSIA information can be obtained
at www.ICGtesting.com
Printed in the USA
LVHW052259281220
675134LV00006B/41